Is There an Author in This Text?

Is There an Author in This Text?

Discovering the Otherness of the Text

Peter A. Sutcliffe

WIPF & STOCK · Eugene, Oregon

IS THERE AN AUTHOR IN THIS TEXT?
Discovering the Otherness of the Text

Copyright © 2014 Peter A. Sutcliffe. All rights reserved. Except for brief quotations in critical publications or reviews, no part of this book may be reproduced in any manner without prior written permission from the publisher. Write: Permissions, Wipf and Stock Publishers, 199 W. 8th Ave., Suite 3, Eugene, OR 97401.

Wipf & Stock
An Imprint of Wipf and Stock Publishers
199 W. 8th Ave., Suite 3
Eugene, OR 97401

www.wipfandstock.com

ISBN 13: 978-1-62032-823-1

Manufactured in the U.S.A.

All Scripture quotations, unless otherwise indicated, are taken from the New King James Version®. Copyright © 1982 by Thomas Nelson, Inc. Used by permission. All rights reserved.

Scripture quotations from *THE MESSAGE*. Copyright © by Eugene H. Peterson 1993, 1994, 1995, 1996, 2000, 2001, 2002. Used by permission of NavPress Publishing Group.

Contents

Preface   vii

Acknowledgments   x

1   Scripture in the Hermeneutical Marketplace   1

2   The Conundrum and Paradox: A Way Forward Part 1: The Issues of Audience, Text, and Language   16

3   The Conundrum and Paradox: A Way Forward Part 2: The Issue of Authorial Intent   46

4   The Conundrum and Paradox: A Way Forward Part 3: Current Philosophical Opinion   71

5   "The Reports of the Author's Death Have Been Greatly Exaggerated"   111

6   The Presupposition of Authorial Intent   140

7   Metaphysics: Unrealistic Constraint or Realistic Context   158

8   Authorial Intent as the Metaphysical Subject and Presence   186

9   The "Who?" Question: Is There a Speaking Voice of the Text?   208

10   Intentionality and Authorial Intention: The "Speaking" Voice   236

11   Disclosing the Being of the Text: Reanimation of the Objectified Text   265

Contents

12	Interpretation Theory: Discovering the *Otherness* of the Text, The Issue of Understanding	301
13	Interpretation Theory: Discovering the *Otherness* of the Text, The Issue of Meaning: The Instantaneous Differential Perception of Understanding	351

Bibliography   419

Name Index   425

Subject Index   427

Preface

THE COMMON CHRISTIAN BELIEF is that God inspired human authors to write the biblical text with a view to speaking through these authors, both locally in their own time and universally beyond it. Subsequently, this common belief also usually involves a view that God continues to speak to any present reader by means of the text those authors had written. If the assertion that God speaks in and through the text is to have any validity within hermeneutics, that is, the task of interpretation, it raises three primary questions. First, can an interpreter understand and deal with an author's intention related to written text? Second, what is the nature of the literary text that presents itself to the interpreter? Third, what happens to a person, and what do they do, that results in *understanding* and *meaning* in the task of interpretation?

The following challenges, however, have been raised in general hermeneutics, and have led to concerns within each of these questions themselves. First, any assertion of an author's psyche, hence the author's *intention-to*, directly communicating and impacting meaning in the interpretive process, is held to be untenable. Therefore, in the formation of discourse, called the act of *parole*, the focus in considering an author's intention shifts from the subjective form of *intention-to*, which logically precedes the act of *parole*, to the adverbial form of *intentionality*. The latter is subsequent to *parole* but, as a qualifier of a verb, describes the action of the author, therefore shifting emphasis from the person of the author to the impersonal ontology of the event. Consequently, to speak of *intention-to*, which relates to the consciousness of a person, becomes problematic for both demonstration and evaluation of authorial *intention-to* in the hermeneutical task since the text, in having an impersonal ontology, doesn't possess a consciousness.

Second, the categorization of all *being* as either personal or impersonal consigns and limits the author's work to an impersonal ontology. This has the effect of denuding the text of any concept of authorial intention and, as a result, also the *being* of the composition, since the composition is the "work of art" *intentioned* by the author. Recognition and analysis of the entity of the composition reveals aspects of impersonal being but also aspects of personal being, which impersonal ontology cannot accommodate, thus exposing the deficiency of such categorization of the composition. The written text becomes an impersonal stretch of language, with the author's discourse lost as discourse of a person.

Third, *meaning* is recognized as a reflective task unique to each individual, disclosing a relativization that excludes an assertion of singularity of meaning, that is, sameness of meaning for both author and interpreter is not precisely possible. Hence the concept of an *absolute meaning* independent of the observer, from the human perspective where the task of hermeneutics occurs, appears *meaningless*. Furthermore, *meaning*, belonging to a personal ontology, is an act of a consciousness, hence of a person not a text. The consequence of the above is that the meaning of a text, as assigned by the interpreter, is presumed unaffected by any actual presence of authorial *otherness*; hence any imputation and impact of *otherness* exists only in an interpreter's imagination. Therefore, sameness of meaning as a criterion for interpretation is also untenable.

Are these arguments and conclusions debatable? Certainly, an author's understanding in his or her discourse must be considered as an absolute, being the point of origin. However, is there a constant in the process that, despite sameness of meaning not being possible, assists in affecting a relativity that allows equivalence of meaning between author and interpreter in the disclosure of understanding? Are there assumptions, assertions, and inferences not properly investigated that bear closer scrutiny? Does the author's intention undergo transformation as an attribute of psyche to become an attribute of the discourse in the composing of the text? Is the current perception of the nature of the text invalid and artificially narrow with its subsequent loss of the ability of the composition to communicate? If the answer to the above questions for human authors and their written text is *no*, then the only answer for an individual seeking to retain the belief that God speaks in and through the text in communicating his intention, lies in a special hermeneutic. This would require a different task of hermeneutics for either dealing with the sacred text in separation from the secular or for dealing with the sacred nature of such texts. Alternately, if an examination of the reasoning of general hermeneutics leads to the conclusion that the answer to these questions is *yes*, for all authors, then there is no need of a special hermeneutic, as it is misconception and misdirection that has confused the issues.

The postmodern position has determined much of the agenda in current hermeneutical practice in both secular and sacred thought on interpretation. It has developed under the powerful influence of Heidegger, Gadamer, and Ricoeur. Philosophers such as Derrida and Barthes have also impacted this development. Despite many positive and powerful contributions, there are assumptions, assertions, and inferences that have misinterpreted the hermeneutical task and have subsequently led to wrong conclusions that, in turn, have misdirected the understanding of the hermeneutical task. The impact on the task of hermeneutics must be explored. We must consider the positive contributions that have been made and also examine the validity of the presuppositions and inferences that precede these contributions. Further, this investigation must be conducted in the light of the equally powerful insights of evangelical theorists in examining the hermeneutical task. Throughout, the aim must be disclosure of the hermeneutical task, not the justification of a point of view.

There is a way forward for the individual who desires to retain the value of Scripture. This can occur without having to opt out of hermeneutical debate to take refuge in a special hermeneutic, which circumvents the argument and leaves the individual marginalized in general debate. The answer lies in reevaluation and review of these arguments and the philosophical hermeneutics that underlie these issues. This is the subject matter of this book. These issues and their impact on the interpretive process are explored, and what is uncovered herein leads to new and transformed approaches to hermeneutics.

Acknowledgments

WITH SPECIAL THANKS AND appreciation to my wife, Ann; my daughters Ruth, Sarah, and Elizabeth, and their families; Dr. Roli DelaCruz, a thoughtful encouraging mentor and supervisor; and Dr. Mark and Jenny Harwood, without whose support and encouragement this work would not exist.

1 Scripture in the Hermeneutical Marketplace

Introduction:
The Conundrum and Paradox of Scripture

THE GENERAL VIEWPOINT OF Christianity concerning scriptural text presents a reader with a conundrum and resultant paradox that offers both a hermeneutical problem and an opportunity for hermeneutical development. It is generally believed within a worldview impacted by Christianity that in some way, via the scriptural text, God both reveals himself and speaks in the contemporary setting. However, the authorship of the actual physical text of Scripture is that of a human hand and not a divine hand, and this poses the conundrum: "How has God spoken in the biblical text?" Subsequently, the message of Scripture in that text is, at the same time, paradoxically, both a human message and a divine message.

Usually the idea of a conundrum is lighthearted and for amusement. Nevertheless, the basic idea of the conundrum is that of a confusing and difficult problem or question. Certainly the concept of Scripture as a vehicle for both a human and a divine voice at the same time qualifies as a true conundrum. This same Scripture is a message by an historical author to people who lived in history, yet its message is conceived of as being divine and is addressed to a universal audience of those who believe. As a proposition, this seems to combine contradictory features that carry the implication of a paradox regarding the message of Scripture.

The conundrum and paradox are the direct result of belief about the literary text of Scripture, hence conferring the status of sacred text on what would otherwise be treated as literary text. This is true of all sacred text, regardless of the faith under consideration. This concept of belief therefore has significant impact on meaning, hence interpretation. This is easily demonstrated by simply considering an issue such as morality. Belief will have a determinative impact on perception of what is moral, amoral, or immoral. This distinction, due to the impact of belief on meaning, is the primary trigger in many contemporary debates on a wide range of issues. However, does this impact on interpretation occur due to special usage of meaning within the task of hermeneutics? Alternatively, is this impact due to the existence of a special hermeneutics of belief, which therefore result in a different task of hermeneutics?

The answer to the latter scenario is the proposal of special hermeneutics. Whilst allowing an approach to faith that doesn't have to answer questioning as to validity within the practice of hermeneutics applied to texts outside the faith, it does place the person isolated in a different world hermeneutically. To use a popular imagery and give it a twist, it would create a situation where Christians are from Mars and non-Christians from Venus, with the result that communication between Martians and Venusians is perceived to be difficult if not impossible![1] Do Christians and non-Christians not only speak a different language but also live in a different world? Even if one solved the communication issues, the interpretations would only be applicable within the world in which they were interpreted. This gives license to each world to ignore the other, but it more importantly mandates two realities, not one reality with two views.

This is a quick fix answer to a complex problem and is an unsound way to proceed; further, it seems more of an attempt to defray an argument that is perceived to be unanswerable on hermeneutical grounds other than with special hermeneutics. Yet, to not go down this road does open this belief up to inspection and interrogation within the practice and task of hermeneutics. Nevertheless, the direction taken in this book is to not go down this road of special hermeneutics, but rather to seek answers by addressing the resultant issues and questions from the perspective of the former scenario, which is that understanding of belief makes special use of principles in the task of hermeneutics. Unfortunately, what often occurs is to divide the impact of faith from the associated text with the subsequent relegation of the impact of faith to a special or faith-based hermeneutics, for example, theological hermeneutics in the case of Christianity. This is often commonly called regional hermeneutics because of its special interest, which supposedly distinguishes it from general hermeneutics that deals with texts without such presuppositions underpinning the task. However, can any hermeneut conduct hermeneutics without the task being impacted by what he or she believes about what is being interpreted? Also do presuppositons, which include belief, impact all interpretation?

The contemporary hermeneutical trend is toward a tendency to give no credence to the concept of an authorial intention that impacts meaning on the reader's side of the communication. This trend seemingly occurs for two main reasons: first, intention, as a substantive, relates to the psyche of the author who is no longer present; and second, epistemological methodology in the modern period failed to establish the validity of the idea of an absolute meaning in dealing with texts. Since meaning

---

1. This is a play on, or suggestion of a humorous twist on, the title and content of the popular book *Men are from Mars and Women are from Venus* by the relationship counselor John Gray.

is directly related to intention, the fluidity and lack of absolute meaning in the interpretive side of the hermeneutical equation tended to imply that, although an author had an intended meaning, this meaning is lost to the interpreter. Hence, meaning has become viewed as a function of texts in their attachment to readers. Therefore, though it is not immediately apparent, a further issue that is important and in need of exploration is the nature of the entity that is the author's text. The text is what the author writes and is the vehicle of the author's message. It is also the only avenue presented to the reader to receive the author's message. Its very nature is at the heart of this issue of a reader's meaning in dealing with an author's text.

Consequently, in the current environment, if God is proposed to be able to speak through the author, this voice becomes seemingly lost to the reader unless a special hermeneutic is devised. The result of this line of thinking is that the person pursuing an understanding of the divine author is seen to be operating outside the mandate of general hermeneutics. When this becomes the presupposition, what occurs is the marginalization of authors and readers working on the basis of belief and hence their exclusion from debate on issues in the "real world." It can and must be conceded that an interpreter cannot know with absolute certainty the authorial meaning from the perspective of the author, either human or divine, and further that meaning in relation to texts is not uniform across the spectrum of readers or their communities. Hence, epistemology has led further away from the idea of authorial discourse, despite valiant attempts to find correspondence between what is observed in terms of meaning and the seemingly logical concept that an author intentionally discloses an understanding in his or her composition.

However, does this line of reasoning in and of itself imply that an interpreter cannot know a relative value of that authorial voice in the interpreter's own setting within time? Further, can interpreters on the one hand realize that they cannot know the absolute value (i.e., the God's eye view of reality), yet have a degree of confidence that they can know a relative value of the absolute in their setting, that is, the God's eye view of reality from their perspective? If epistemology has led away from the voice of the author, which would be the only access to the absolute meaning that is the authorial intent, is this the direction that must be taken or is there another way of approaching the task of hermeneutics that can value an interpreter's relative meaning yet know that the process has involved listening to an authorial voice? The presence of an authorial voice will have the effect of rendering the interpreter's meaning as being relative to that of the author. Finally it must be asked, is the postmodern concept put forward a valid one; that is, is general hermeneutics a separate category that avoids the presuppositions involved in hermeneutics that are perceived as having a specialized agenda, such as biblical or theological hermeneutics?

The purpose of this book is to look at these areas and examine the hermeneutical process to seek an answer to this seeming impasse so that both the author and interpreter can approach a text with confidence in their ability to communicate in the writing and the reading. As a result, this book is also an examination of the legitimacy of the marginalization of an author or reader because of a presupposition of belief. These issues are important to the Christian who seeks to encounter and deal with the voice and message of God, believed to be associated with the biblical text. However, these issues are also important to any interpreter if there is in fact an authorial voice that should be listened to.

Further, this book endeavors to show that the concept of general hermeneutics is an abstraction, meaning that hermeneutics actually must be conducted from within a set of presuppositions that of necessity involve a dimension of belief. If so, then no interpreter engages in the ideal of general hermeneutics, but all make use of the basic principles and methodologies in the pursuit of hermeneutics, which is conducted within the interpreter's presuppositional understanding, hence beliefs, about the subject matter.

Separating Sacred and Text: A Fallacious Argument

A solution to the conundrum previously noted is the concept that the nature of text as sacred is of a different category than text as literature. That is, God speaking through the biblical text is an issue of theological hermeneutics not an issue of general hermeneutics. Such a solution has the attraction of making possible a separation of the message of God and the human message. A special theological hermeneutic would enable a reader to deal with the message of God and general hermeneutics the message of the human author. However, this has the disadvantage of fracturing understanding and interpretation of the life-world of a person. An alternative solution is to look at what a text is and does, how it relates to any intention of an author, and subsequently how, in dealing with the written communication, an interpreter arrives at meaning.

The words of the biblical text are generally accepted as having been authored by fully human people who lived in history; yet at the same time, the text is considered to be the word of God. The basis of resolving the paradox will be found in answering the conundrum above, that is, how God has spoken in relation to the text. If this is not to be regarded as developed in a special theological hermeneutic, designed for sacred texts in general and the biblical text in particular, then the answer must be developed from the basis of how any author can be seen to speak in his or her literary communication.

The orthodox view, as the starting basis, of the Protestant and hence evangelical position is that this word of God has occurred because God inspired the authors to write their text.[2] Innovations by academic scholarship in hermeneutics during the

---

2. Erickson, *Christian Theology*, 199. Erickson's statement of *inspiration* presents a good understanding of this concept within Christianity: "By inspiration of the scripture we mean that supernatural influence of the Holy Spirit upon the scripture writers which rendered their writings an accurate record of the revelation or which resulted in what they wrote actually being the Word of God."

Renaissance led to the pursuit of a literal sense of Scripture that was seen as being precise. The critical methodology that developed in the Enlightenment focused on the historical context and led to the meaning of Scripture being sought in the reality of persons and events in history. This inscriptive revelation was proposed not to have come to humanity immediately but mediately through historical events.[3] Ladd says of Scripture that it is "God's word spoken to men, and then expressed in the words of men."[4] As a result, though held in the domain of belief as divine in origin, it is received as a text written by people and about people who lived in historical contexts.

Gordon Fee stated that because of this view of the biblical text "as human words in history the eternal word has historical particularity."[5] The word of God was addressed to, and conditioned by, a specific historical context.[6] The language used in this communication is not a specialized religious language but can involve a specialized use of ordinary language.[7] The example given by Anthony Thiselton is that "hearing God" is not a special word for hearing but a special meaning of the word "hearing." This is consistent with the view that a special theological hermeneutic need not be seen as demanded by the nature of the text. It is not necessary to develop a special theological hermeneutic but rather recognize that a specialized use of hermeneutics can be employed.

Thiselton takes up the point of other authors that faith should not be seen to constitute another avenue of knowledge outside the processes of human understanding.[8] He notes that the Holy Spirit, as the divine agent of the text, works through these processes of human understanding, if not entirely, certainly in the majority of situations.[9] If not, then the strange situation would exist where, for understanding of the text to occur, the Scripture would call for a presupposition of the faith it seeks to create.[10]

Any proposed answer involving separation of sacredness and text as a solution to the conundrum assumes, at the very least, a "super" human understanding of that which is sacred. It would also assume that texts not directly designated as being "sacred" texts possess no "belief" dimension in their nature nor involve a "belief" category of knowledge. However, Thomas Kuhn observed that within scientific communities, people "whose research is based on shared paradigms are committed to the same rules and standards for scientific practice."[11] He takes this further and notes that this commitment "and the apparent consensus it produces *are prerequisites for normal*

---

3. Pannenberg, *Jesus—God and Man*, 178.
4. Ladd, *New Testament and Criticism*, 84.
5. Fee, *Gospel and Spirit*, 30.
6. Ibid.
7. Thiselton, *Thiselton On Hermeneutics*, 531.
8. Ibid., 93.
9. Ibid., 92.
10. Ibid., 93.
11. Kuhn, *Structure of Scientific Revolutions*, 11.

science"[12] Therefore, they are committed to a "body of belief" that is not determined alone by observation and experience.[13] The conduct of researching "normal science" is based upon acceptance by the researcher of "*past* scientific achievements."[14] This acceptance is essentially a foundational belief system on which the research can proceed.[15] Consequently, the dimension of belief is integral to science.

Thus, the researcher begins with a belief, and the research results are examined in the light of these beliefs. As a result, this "belief" impacts the process of investigation and is subsequently also impacting how the results are interpreted. How that "body of belief" in the scientific community is developed may not be either apparently or overtly metaphysical in a sense that would be understood in the domain of ontotheology. However, the process does involve belief, which implies a metaphysical dimension that is operational within those who conduct the scientific research. This involvement of belief in this process is simply just not acknowledged. Consequently, it would seem reasonable to suggest that any texts generated by a scientific community involve a belief dimension, which, if "belief" and text are always to be regarded as separate categories, should be subject to special hermeneutics in respect to the domain of belief. Similarly, any historian holds beliefs about the recorded history and these beliefs will impact the selection and presentation of material set out as history, which by the same reasoning would require separation from the text. Yet no one would propose such distinctions be made with either of these types of texts.

Furthermore, an inherent assumption in any separation of sacredness and text, for hermeneutical purposes, is that, in dealing with a text, an interpreter is capable of conducting hermeneutical inquiry *a-belief*, that is, without belief. However, belief is a part of the presuppositions of every person, therefore consequently of any interpreter. It is well recognized that no interpreter approaches the task of hermeneutics presupposition-less.[16] It would seem illogical then to suppose that the presuppositions of an interpreter included no presuppositions about belief. The assertion that belief should be, or even can be, removed from the text for hermeneutical purposes is therefore proposed as a fallacy. The conundrum of Scripture is not solved by such a proposed solution.

An interpreter cannot have imposed on them Christian belief as a prerequisite for hermeneutics, but they also cannot ignore or avoid the belief dimension of the presuppositions of the author and intended audience of the text. Especially if, as in the case of the biblical text, authors understood and believed themselves to be directly under a divine influence in what they had written, which by the aforementioned reasoning

12. Ibid.
13. Ibid., 4.
14. Ibid., 10.
15. Ibid.
16. Thiselton, *Two Horizons*, 114. See also Vanhoozer, *First Theology*, 19. Vanhoozer notes that postmodern critics and philosophers have exploded the myth of the neutral observer.

directly impacts the text.[17] Due to the belief domain of the author, this divine influence would constitute an integral part of the text, which cannot be separated from the text in respect to meaning. It is therefore important to examine how such an influence would operate upon an author and how it is to be hermeneutically evaluated.

These original human authors of the biblical text spoke to their own time. They were not focused on future audiences, or readers, even when they saw themselves as writing Scripture.[18] However, it could not be argued successfully that they had no idea or thought of future audiences. Nevertheless, even if the primary focus of an author were that of a future audience, it would also seem logical that the presuppositions of the author about the future audience would be in terms of an audience known to the author. Consequently, considering a text from within its *Sitz im Leben*, or "in life setting," is an essential element of the hermeneutical process.[19] The writers belonged to their own time, their texts are addressed to specific people, and their intent is understood in that context. Consequently, if any impact of authorial intent is to be associated with the text, then any understanding of a divine communication must develop from this position; that is, interpretation must involve the situation in which the author spoke, and it also must involve a domain of belief knowledge that was understood by the author.

The Paradox: An Issue of Authorial Intent

The paradox occurs because the humanly authored Scripture is proposed to be at the same time both a human communication, due to authorship in the inscriptive process, and a divine communication, due to a guiding inspiration of the human author in the inscriptive process. Any assertion that a divine author, through inspiration of the human author, had an intention either other than that of the human author or beyond that of the human author, would suggest a special hermeneutic is required (e.g., concepts such as *sensus plenior*, or fuller meaning). This could be seen to be a way of resolving issues such as Paul's use of Hosea in Romans 9:25–26, which is a prophetic text he uses to legitimize the calling of the Gentiles into a covenant relationship. It would be difficult to place this intent within the scope of Hosea's intent, whose address concerns the northern kingdom, or Israel, in the days of the divided kingdom.[20]

---

17. Erickson, *Christian Theology*, 199. This is integral in the concept of inspiration, in orthodox Christianity, so rendering Scriptures as sacred text. Scriptural texts that can be seen to support this view are Heb 1:1–2 and 2 Pet 1:19–21.

18. Marshall, *Beyond The Bible*, 15.

19. Stendhal, "Biblical Theology, Contemporary," 419. The importance and critical nature of the historical setting as the beginning of hermeneutics is the theme of his article. He notes that all branches of theology should depend on this historical underpinning, 421.

20. The address concerns Israel (e.g., see Hos 1:4 and 3:1; yet 1:11 shows that this is not the united Israel but the divided kingdom that became known as Israel and Judah).

Alternatively, an assertion that could be proposed is that the meanings are coincident, and therefore what the human author intended, is the divine intention. Whilst providing a means for resolving the paradox, this assertion would result in the equation that, in regard to Scripture, "what it meant" for the past audience equals "what it means" for the contemporary audience. This approach would require the world to be monocultural or that the established kingdom of God in this world is to be monocultural and hence would require a special hermeneutic to overcome problems such as those associated with the historical particularity of the Scripture. This assertion also fails to address the horizon of interpreters and their historical particularity. Therefore, it is suggested that it is more profitable to seek an alternative understanding to either of these options.

The very concept of intentionality concerning the text, be it the message of either the divine or human author, raises the issue of authorial-discourse interpretation; and at the other end of the scale, reader-response interpretation. If the authorial intent is either undetectable or absent, then a special hermeneutic will be required in the reader-response situation in order to understand the message of God, which cannot be detected as part of an authorial discourse and must now be directly communicated to the reader. The paradox would exist in the reading, regardless of any paradox involved in the writing.

Consequently, avoidance of resorting to an appeal for a special theological hermeneutic requires an understanding of how, firstly, any author communicates in his or her literary communication. However, this is problematic for it has the apparent implication of involving a knowing of the mind of the author. Secondly, if, in answering the conundrum of Scripture, a voice other than the literary author's is detectable as impacting the author of a text, then how does this other voice speak through the author's text? In the case of the conundrum of Scripture, the special use of hermeneutics would involve identifying the voice other than the author's with the person of the Holy Spirit. In the case of the paradox of Scripture, the special use of hermeneutics would be recognition of the "mind of Spirit" or the "mind of Christ" conveyed in the text.

All of this raises the question of intentionality, because the paradox is caused by the inherent assumption that a literary text involves an authorial intent, which in the case of Scripture in the first instance, in terms of approaching the scriptural text, is the product of a human author. If the divine author is speaking through the human author and not just to the human author, then the divine and human authorial intent are intertwined. If meaning is a function of the reader without respect to any authorial intent there is no paradox in regard to the text. Any paradox is resident within the reader and is a function of the reader's interpretation of the text.

(a) The Issue of the "Intentional Fallacy"

If authorial intent is seen to be a factor in the creation of authors' texts, then such texts cannot be understood in the present if they are not first understood in their own time and context.[21] Philip Esler discusses the "intentional fallacy" argument raised by W. K. Wimsatt Jr. and Monroe Beardsley that has been used to undermine the hermeneutical importance of authorial intent.[22] Esler correctly observes that Wimsatt and Beardsley themselves pointed out that their concept applied to poetry specifically, and works of art generally. They also noted that, in what they called practical texts, authorial intent was vital.[23] Nevertheless, this admission has been largely overlooked in the desire to use the concept of the intentional fallacy to diminish the emphasis on authorial intent in dealing with texts.

The observation of Wimsatt and Beardsley was that authorial intent was neither available nor desirable as a standard for judging the *success of a work of literary art*.[24] However, there are some observations that can be made that are important. First, a work of art generally interacts with the subjective dimension of a person. This dimension is both personal and individual, and informs a person's response to a work. This response is a subjective personal evaluation of the work of the author. The author offers a work to generate this response, and, as such, the eliciting of a subjective response could be argued to fall within the domain of authorial intent. It would seem that an inherent assumption in Wimsatt and Beardsley's argument is that authorial intent, as it relates to the work of art, does not include eliciting the response of the subjective domain of the interpreter. Yet they do note that the meaning of a poem attaches to a person in regard to the interpreter's personality or state of soul.[25] This is clearly the readers' subjective domain. Consequently, it would also seem to be logical to assume that this is part of the authorial intent, because this would also form a dimension of the thinking of the author.

Further, it should be noted that, like Paul Ricoeur,[26] Wimsatt and Beardsley focus on the detached nature of the text from the author who created it.[27] Although they do not state it, their assumption and reasoning is similar to that of Ricoeur;[28]

21. Thiselton, *Thiselton On Hermeneutics*: 55.

22. Esler, *New Testament Theology*, 92. See footnote 29 for the text to which Esler refers.

23. Ibid., 93.

24. Wimsatt, *Verbal Icon*, 3. (Italics added for emphasis.) Wimsatt notes at the beginning of the book that the first two preliminary essays were written in collaboration with Monroe C. Beardsley. This essay on "Intentional Fallacy" is the first of those essays.

25. Ibid., 4.

26. Ricoeur, *Interpretation Theory*, 43. Ricoeur discusses his concept of text detaching from the author and attaching to the reader.

27. Wimsatt, *Verbal Icon*, 5. They do not mention Ricoeur, so the assumption must be that they arrived at the same conclusion.

28. Ricoeur, *Interpretation Theory*, 29. Ricoeur specifically discusses the issue, that for him writing, and hence detachment from the author, leads to semantic autonomy of the text.

consequently, Wimsatt and Beardsley therefore consider the text autonomous with respect to the author. This concept is discussed later in this book relating to the assertion of Ricoeur. For now it is sufficient to point out that there is a high degree of difference between the concepts of being detached and autonomous. Detachment is temporal, whereas autonomy is not only temporal but also authoritative. On this score Wimsatt and Beardsley do not establish autonomy. This is not established in the work of Ricoeur either, as is shown later in this book, with the result that the authorial intent is not easily dismissed. Detachment alone cannot be used as a reason for dismissing authorial intent, but autonomy could be used in this way.

In regard to a poem, Wimsatt and Beardsley also point out that if the poet succeeds in his or her intention, then the poem itself shows this and so there is no need to ask a question concerning the author's intention. If the poet did not succeed, then the poem itself is not adequate evidence of authorial intent and a prospective interpreter must go outside the poem to discover an intention that was not effectively delivered in the poem.[29] This would seem to be the crux of the argument employed by those who seek to use intentional fallacy against authorial intent. There is an inherent fallacy in the argument of intentional fallacy itself. The only possibility of an interpreter knowing that an author didn't succeed in his or her intent would be to have that pointed out by the author. In the absence of the author an interpreter can conjecture that an author did or did not succeed and even compare this with the findings of other interpreters, but such conjecture must still be conjecture.

If the person evaluating the "work of art" wishes to go beyond the subjective, that person must consider the intention of the author concerning the author's message in the work of art. There is no need to argue, as Esler does, that in order to circumvent this argument an appeal is made to categorize Scripture as nonliterary text.[30] Esler argues, from the work of others, that to distinguish between literary and nonliterary texts is viable and clear.[31] The examples used are not convincing of themselves, for example, between a novel (literary) and a bus ticket (nonliterary). The intent of the designer of the bus ticket is that the ticket can be used to obtain bus travel, and success in doing that fulfills authorial intent. Although a novelist, by way of a fictional work, may ask readers to suspend their own belief regarding the relationship to their own reality. Novelists do fulfill their intentions by asking the readers to adopt the reality presented by the author in a desire to entertain by drawing the reader into the belief domain of the story. In other words, the intent of the author, in a fictional work, would not seem to require that readers undertake integration of the belief domain of the text into their

---

29. Wimsatt, *Verbal Icon*, 2.

30. Esler, *New Testament Theology*, 88–118. The concept developed in this chapter of his book and his proposal is that the texts of Scripture qualify as "practical texts," as per Wimsatt and Beardsley, and, as a result, authorial intent can and should be considered, even in the light of the work of Wimsatt and Beardsley.

31. Ibid., 91.

own reality. Conversely, the author of a nonfiction novel, for example, a biography, is most concerned that readers do not suspend their own reality in understanding the author's message. The intent of the author is specifically that the readers interact with the text within the sphere of the reader's belief domain.

Esler's use of Hans-Georg Gadamer's work, in understanding "play" and art, to suggest that the removal from reality in novels, as literary works, distinguish them from nonliterary works—and that this distinction is not related to authorial intent—involves inherent presuppositions about authorial intent.[32] This proposal, as noted, presupposes that the authorial intent is not just such intent, that is, the suspension one's own belief world in order to enter that of the world of the text. If the authorial intent is that the reader "escapes" the mundane, and the reader does precisely that, then the authorial intent is fulfilled in that very aspect. It also presupposes that authorial intent and authorial meaning in the text are identical.[33] In Esler's work the distinction between literary works and nonliterary works, and the subsequent movement of Scripture to the nonliterary category, is not convincing.

Esler raises the concept that nonliterary texts point to issues outside the text and seeks to move readers into these issues.[34] However, it is not outside the realm of possibility to assume that the author of a novel may intend to direct readers to issues outside the text. A novelist may use a work of fiction to espouse virtue or portray metaphysical issues, for example, allegory and myth. This would fall within the domain of authorial intent that the author would not like to see lost.

In discussing the role of the author and authorial intention in literary and nonliterary texts, Esler mentions Kevin J. Vanhoozer's claim that in dealing with the biblical text, literary knowledge is possible.[35] Esler then takes note that Vanhoozer mentions a quote from C. S. Lewis that is seen as warning "against reading the bible as 'literature.'"[36] Esler seems to be implying that Vanhoozer's mention of Lewis contradicts Vanhoozer's own concept that literary knowledge is possible. Vanhoozer notes that the very concept of literary knowledge is ambiguous as it can refer to knowledge about or gained from a text.[37] The quote from C. S. Lewis refers to the issue that to read the Bible as literature may ignore the subject matter as an inherent context.[38] This potentiality should not be ignored in methodology. Given Vanhoozer's concept

32. Ibid., 96.

33. It is proposed in this book that a distinction should be made between authorial intent and authorial meaning. This distinction is considered later in this work. Authorial meaning does indeed relate to the text and has as its referent the authorial intent. For example, in the case of a novel, the authorial intent is to capture the reader and entertain; consequently, the text is designed to fulfill that intent.

34. Esler, *New Testament Theology*, 97.

35. Ibid., 90.

36. Ibid., 91.

37. Vanhoozer, *Is There a Meaning in this Text?* 24.

38. Ibid., 157.

of literary knowledge, this use of C. S. Lewis is within his concept and is not a contradiction. Vanhoozer's usage of C. S. Lewis should rather be seen as supporting literary knowledge in dealing with Scripture; the admonition is not to rely on methodology alone in dealing with the text, that is, the Scriptures theological nature cannot be ignored.

It seems arbitrary to make the distinction of Scripture as nonliterary text. It also seems unnecessary to undertake such a distinction on the basis of an argument aimed at restoring authorial intent, because there is no real reason to see intent as lost in literary text or in literary knowledge. Rather, the issue is how the text is handled in regard to authorial intent. However, consideration of the intentional fallacy argument, although used in an attempt to trivialize the issue of authorial intent, does highlight two important issues concerning authorial intent. First, the argument shows that the real area of contention is knowability and not existence, and that this issue of the disclosure of authorial intent is important and must be investigated. Second, it also highlights that the only place this can be dealt with is the text; hence, the nature of the text is critical and must also be investigated.

Ricoeur highlights that a text, as discourse, is something said by someone to someone, and as such cannot be considered authorless.[39] In his thinking to consider the text as authorless would be a fallacy of the order of that proposed by Wimsatt and Beardsley.[40] Ricoeur states, "If the intentional fallacy overlooks the semantic autonomy of the text, the opposite fallacy forgets that a text remains a discourse told by somebody."[41] A text comes into existence—or has being as a composition—because an author *intends* its existence, and this cannot be ignored in interpretation of that text. However, the argument of the intentional fallacy correctly highlights that this *authorial intention* cannot be considered to be an aspect of the author's psyche that controls meaning in interpretation. Nevertheless, the text exists because of an *intention* that cannot be disregarded in the interpretation of that text, which has been the application of this concept of the *intentional fallacy* as proposed by Wimsatt and Beardsley.

(b) The Human Authorial Intent as Primary Task

I. Howard Marshall, representing an evangelical position, agrees that any approach to a contemporary understanding of a text must have as its origin the attempt to understand that text in its original setting and therefore deal with the meaning of the original human author.[42] However, the focus of contemporary interpreters, in any era, is a relevant understanding of the message of the biblical text for their own contemporary

---

39. Ricoeur, *Interpretation Theory*, 30.
40. Ibid.
41. Ibid.
42. Marshall, *Beyond the Bible*, 25.

setting.[43] Therefore, the contemporary interpreter, in order to address the issue of what the Scripture *does* mean, must first address the issue of what it *did* mean.

If the biblical text is not subject to a special hermeneutic, then the pursuit of what it did mean is the same as for any historic text. This is the basis of Krister Stendhal's contention that shapes the issues of "what did it mean?" and "what does it mean?" when dealing with Scripture.[44] It was previously noted that there is a presupposition of divine influence upon the author. An author's presupposition of divine influence upon the intended audience must also be considered. This means that a special use of hermeneutics is required in dealing with the impact of this influence on the authors and their texts by any interpreters. An understanding of the divine communication by means of a biblical text requires first considering the hermeneutical approach to a human author's communication by means of their text. The answer to the conundrum and resolution of the paradox will operate from the same base in the hermeneutical task; that is, although requiring a specialized use of hermeneutics, it is not a specialized hermeneutic.

The Approach to Highlighting the Hermeneutical Problem

This book is approached from the perspective of Protestant evangelical thought, and within that thought as a part of the Pentecostal community. However, no interpreter is neutral either in belief or in approach to the task of interpretation, which would allow any one interpreter to develop a normative position from which others should work.[45] All interpreters begin from a starting point of where they are when engaging the text.[46] Having presuppositions doesn't exclude different ways of seeing the world.[47] Consequently, having a particular set of presuppositions doesn't disqualify an interpreter, or require explanation and apologetic, because the path to understanding starts from where the interpreter is situated.[48]

The presuppositions of all interpreters impact their approach to the text, but the issue of authorial intentionality relates to the message of the text to be interpreted not the interpreter. In consideration of both the conundrum and paradox, created by viewing the Scripture as the word of God, the nature of the text is vital. Thiselton proposes that the nature of texts is the most radical question in hermeneutics. This is

---

43. Ibid., 12.

44. Stendhal, "Biblical Theology, Contemporary," 419. This is the subject matter of the article. Stendhal separates these as different tasks to be undertaken, essentially in isolation from one another. They are dealt with as two distinct questions.

45. Jeanrond, *Theological Hermeneutics*, 5.

46. Thiselton, *Thiselton On Hermeneutics*, 706.

47. Ibid., 76. Thiselton goes on to observe that the presuppositions held can encourage different ways of seeing the world.

48. Ibid., 627.

because interpretation doesn't rest just in the needs of the reader but more particularly on the very nature of the text considered.[49] Consequently, how the text is viewed and how it is operative in its function is highly significant.

The conundrum of Scripture carries an inbuilt assumption as its primary assertion, which is that an author can in some way intentionally communicate through a text. This assertion immediately brings to the fore the issue of authorial intentionality. The related issue of the impact of belief and its subsequent communication draws attention to the nature of the text. The paradox, associated with the scriptural text, is created by the view that the Scripture is at the same time both a human and a divine communication. Therefore, the first question is how does the human author communicate in relationship to the text? Consequently, any projection of divine communication relates in the first instance to answering this question of human communication. This question also raises the issue of the nature of authorial intent's relationship to the author's text. If the authorial intent is located within the text, this implies that the solution of the paradox would require an explanation of how two authorial intents can be resident in the same text, without recourse to a special hermeneutic. Conversely, if the authorial intent is not located within the text, then how is it related to the text? How can two authorial intents speak through the same text without one voice being subsumed by the other? Consequently, is theological hermeneutics a specialized hermeneutic developed to deal with adding a voice to a text? Alternately, is theological hermeneutics a specialized use of hermeneutics to deal with an operational voice other than that of the author? Thus, consideration of the conundrum and paradox of Scripture can only be addressed by an examination of both the authorial intent and the nature of the text.

These primary issues of authorial intentionality and the nature of the text are those that will be pursued in this book. An important purpose of this book is to show that these two issues are vital in all texts, not just sacred text and, consequently, do not imply a special hermeneutic. In the course of our journey the mode of the impact of belief on the author, and hence the text, are examined. This examination will offer directions to explore the special use that can be made of its results in theological hermeneutics.

The apostle Paul uses a text from Genesis (vs. 15:6) as the basis for the imputation of righteousness by faith, quoted in Rom 4:3. He did not discover a text he did not know.[50] What appears to have occurred is that his perception changed of the text he already knew. This is what is proposed in this book, that is, a new perception of written text that leads to new understanding of authorial intent.

---

49. Thiselton, *New Horizons*, 49. This is a broad statement embracing all hermeneutics, not just biblical hermeneutics.

50. Though Paul was born in Tarsus, he declares that he was raised from his youth in Jerusalem and studied under the rabbi Gamaliel, Acts 22:3. He declares that he was thoroughly trained, and so it would defy credulity to suggest he had never read the text of Genesis before.

In order to establish a basis for our examination of authorial intention and the text, an analysis of five issues is pursued from within current hermeneutical debate. This process will take a more in-depth view of both authorial intent and the nature of a text as they are currently understood. The purpose is to establish a *prima facie* case for a reexamination of these issues due to the inadequacy of what is accepted in current hermeneutical inquiry. Following the discussion of these issues and an examination of related proposals, there will be developed a working hypothesis, or proposal, concerning the issue of authorial intent and how written text should be viewed. Subsequent chapters of this book examine the validity, impact, and implications of this proposed hypothesis.

2 The Conundrum and Paradox

A Way Forward

Part 1: The Issues of Audience, Text, and Language

Introduction

THE CONUNDRUM OF SCRIPTURE, since it relates to the extension of the author's speaking to that of the speaking of God, immediately raises the issue of the concept of authorial intent in relationship to a text as an author's communication. This occurs because the issue of authorial intent is foundational to any assertion of the speaking of the author and therefore is an inherent assumption of the conundrum of Scripture. The paradox, which is that the text is at the same time both a human and divine communication, raises the issue of the nature of the text in this communication. It also raises the subsequent issue of the interpreter's meaning in engaging the text and its relationship, if any, to the author's meaning. This overall debate has traditionally related primarily to the two ends of the issue—that is, the author's meaning and the interpreter's meaning.

The very words *intention* and *meaning* appear to be so closely associated that they seem to be almost capable of being used interchangeably. The concept of an author's intention, in Romanticist hermeneutics, therefore became closely associated with the concept of the author's meaning and subsequently to the issue of "knowing" the author's meaning, and hence an issue of epistemology. The issue of authorial intent pursued in this way becomes that which is related to the psyche of the author. However, what was not considered is that in the act of *parole*[1] there is a transforma-

---

1. Saussure, *Course in General Linguistics*, 13–14. Saussure's conception of *parole* in linguistics is

tion of authorial intention, as related to the psyche—hence, *being*—of the author, into authorial intent, as related to the *being* of the composition.

The authorial intent is associated with the psyche of the author at inception, but is operational within the composition due to association with the text. The use of the term *authorial intent* in hermeneutics should be concerned with its operational effects in the composition, not its association with the psyche of the author, from which it is detached. As a result, the debate within modernism subsequently focused incorrectly on establishing the validity of sameness of meaning. The true focus should be that of sameness of *understanding* of author and interpreter, not that of *meaning*. This approach focuses on the issue of the disclosure of the text not that of the *knowing* of the interpreter.

There are five issues that have bearing on these concepts of the author's intention, the nature of the text, and the issue of interpretive meaning. (Three of these issues are covered in this chapter and two are covered in chapter 3.) The basic format of discourse is that *someone* said *something* to *someone*. However, in interpretation of texts the interpreter begins, not with *the someone* who said something but instead with *the something* that is said. Consequently, the entrance to the discourse regarding the written text is as an audience in an encounter with what was said. In this chapter the first three of these issues are dealt with, starting with the audience and then the text of what was said.

A Changing Audience

Marshall has suggested that authoritative meaning can undergo change and is consequently a relative value to some degree. He states that the "closing of the canon is not incompatible with the non-closing of the interpretation of that canon."[2] Stanley Grenz notes that the intent of a biblical text begins in the original human author's intention but "is not exhausted by it."[3] The efforts of any interpreter cannot "exhaust the Spirit's speaking to us through the text."[4] An authoritative meaning in one setting may have a different authoritative meaning in a different setting.[5] This raises the question of what is changing and to what it is relative. The author, the historical context of the work, and the historical particularity of the intended audience do not undergo change in the case of historic texts.[6]

---

that of the executing of speech by a person. This concept in Saussure's work will be considered in later chapters.

2. Marshall, *Beyond the Bible*, 54. Italics are original.

3. Grenz and Franke, *Beyond Foundationalism*, 73.

4. Ibid.

5. Marshall, *Beyond the Bible*: 56. The context of Marshall's comments is the uses of the Old Testament in the New Testament.

6. Stein, "Benefits of an Author-Oriented Approach," 458.

It has become generally recognized and accepted that interpreters are also conditioned by their historical context; subsequently each brings his or her resultant presuppositions to the task of hermeneutics, which impacts the hermeneutical task.[7] Though interpreters may seek to accommodate their prejudices with respect to the text, they must recognize that a "completely detached unbiased stance is impossible."[8] The contemporary interpreters, in any era, contribute something of themselves in pursuit of a hermeneutical task.[9] Marshall observes that this problem should not be overemphasized and that, although absolute objectivity is not possible, a significant relative objectivity is possible.[10]

The presuppositions of both the author and the intended audience are not undergoing change with respect to historic texts. In Ricoeur's thought the act of composition of a written text fixes the temporal instance of discourse, and the event of an author communicating by creation of a text appears and then disappears.[11] However, the values of the presuppositions of the author and intended audience are fixed in the creation of the text at that time of its creation.

The presuppositions of any unintended audience, which includes a contemporary interpreter with historic texts, will involve differences, especially since they are historically distanced from the text. The unintended audience is changing and this is what results in interpreted meaning undergoing change. In such a scenario, the concept of authorial meaning can appear to undergo change due to the impact of the contemporary context and yet still be authoritative in its setting, as Marshall observed (e.g., morality may be the aim of the author but what acts are moral or immoral may vary with, and even within, a culture).

Consequently, in the hermeneutical task, an interpreter, who is not part of the intended audience, will impact meaning, which results in some degree of change of what the interpreter observes by the very process of observing it. Hermeneutics is generally understood to be the science and art of interpretation. The Heisenberg uncertainty principle, as one of science in general, thus appears to be paralleled in hermeneutics as science.[12] If this principle (the impact of the observer results in some change, no mat-

---

7. Thiselton, *Two Horizons*, 11. See also, Fee, *Gospel and Spirit*, 26. Fee notes that every interpreter "brings to a text a considerable amount of cultural baggage and personal bias" and so possesses a relative objectivity in the task of interpretation. It was also previously noted that Vanhoozer observes that postmodern critics and philosophers have exploded the myth of neutrality.

8. Stanton, "Presuppositions," 62.

9. Marshall, "Historical Criticism," 16.

10. Marshall, *Beyond the Bible*, 25. Consequently, a pragmatic, or relative, value is within the province of the interpreter.

11. Ricoeur, *Interpretation Theory*, 26.

12. Thiselton, *Two Horizons*, 159, 88. Thiselton notes that in the world of post-Newtonian physics, due to work like Heisenberg's Principle of Uncertainty, many scientists adopt a different approach to knowledge. The impact of this on hermeneutics in the area of objectivity and perception of reality should be considered. See also, Vanhoozer, *Is There a Meaning*, 128. Vanhoozer takes note of the

ter how minimal) is accepted, then the equation *what it meant equals what it means* is not valid for the interpretation of meaning beyond the intended audience.

Furthermore, if recovery of the human authorial meaning as a pure absolute value is impossible, as Marshall has contended,[13] then it follows that the value *what it meant* concerning individual texts within the composition, as an absolute value, is also unrecoverable. The only authoritative voice that could eliminate uncertainty on the relationship of an interpreter's observed value of *what it meant* to the absolute value would be that of the author.[14]

The interpreter, from within the community of faith, may desire to raise the assertion that, since the text is the word of God and the Spirit remains attached to the text, the divine author can be authoritative. This is a reasonable assertion within the context of faith. However, the interpreter would have to postulate one of two possible scenarios. The first course could be to appeal to a special hermeneutic. The speaking of the Spirit will still involve dealing with words because this is the medium of the Spirit in being able to communicate with the interpreter.[15] Consequently, this postulates that the Spirit somehow speaks through the text other than through its existence as a literary text, that is, suggesting the need for a special hermeneutic. This is what leads to a solution of the conundrum that has been adopted of the separation of sacred from text, in the case of sacred texts.

The second appeal could be made to phenomenology. In the phenomenological method the essential reality of a thing is intuited; that is, it is "apprehended by an immediate presentation of itself to the understanding."[16] Gordon Anderson sees that the major problem with phenomology is that phenomenologists are not able to describe a method in a way that discloses how intuition works.[17] Hence, a phenomological exercise would not be exactly repeatable for other interpreters. However, this sort of approach does accommodate the speaking of the Spirit to an individual.

The Pentecostal concept of revelation appears similar to the phenomenological method.[18] Raymond Brown's concept of *sensus plenior* (fuller meaning) also appears

---

Heisenberg's "uncertainty principle" in physical sciences and is concerned about the extension of this principle of physics into hermeneutical science.

13. Marshall, "Historical Criticism," 16.

14. Gadamer, *Dialogue and Dialectic*, 126. The observation about a text being subject to possible changes by the reader, in the author's absence, that only the author can correct, is Gadamer's. His thought is that Plato must have understood this because of the inherent structure of his work. He discovers in Plato's work an unwritten dialectic that will continuously refer the reader from the "one, " or whole, to the many parts. But these refer back to the one, so there is opportunity to correct the reader. However, it follows that if the author is the only one who can correct, then the author is similarly the only one who can endorse a meaning.

15. Beardsley, *Thinking Straight*, 5. Beardsley asserts that all thinking is done in words and relies on articulation in a sentence for clarity and existence.

16. Anderson, "Pentecostal Scholarship," 118.

17. Ibid.

18. Ibid.

to be similar, in that it concerns revelation of a deeper meaning in the text not intended by the original author but is seen by the contemporary interpreter. William Sanford LaSor discusses Raymond Brown's concept of *sensus plenior*, which has been used to describe this concept of extending the meaning of the original human author. The *sensus plenior* is the additional meaning intended by God but not clearly intended by the human author.[19] The human author does not intentionally pass on the *sensus plenior* even if aware of it.[20] Gordon Fee does admit the possibility as "revelation" of *sensus plenior* but limits the occurrence to the inspired writers of the scriptural text.[21] His reasoning is "Who speaks for God as an authoritative voice?"[22]

This simply brings the argument back to the problematic of discerning the authoritative voice of the author in confirming that an interpretation is relative to the absolute of the author's meaning. This same caution and reasoning would apply to the interpreter who appeals to phenomenology to speak for the divine author. Without the ability to establish an impact of authorial voice, meaning cannot be regarded as relative to the absolute of the author's meaning but is purely relativism in relationship to meaning. The nature of the biblical text does allow for phenomenological interaction, as Anderson noted, that impacts the individual, but clearly this cannot be generally applied beyond the individual as authoritative.

Appeal to a special hermeneutic sets up theological hermeneutics as a separate branch, or discipline, of hermeneutics. However, if the Bible is indeed the words of men in history, as contended by Geore Eldon Ladd, and God's intention is to communicate with humanity, it would seem that God would work within human capabilities.[23] Hence, rather than appeal to a special hermeneutic, or appeal to phenomenology theologically applied, it is preferable to identify how any author "speaks" through their text in the hermeneutical process.

If the contemporary value of the "what it means" of a text is tied to the historical value "what it meant," then an insoluble degree of uncertainty is introduced into the value "what it means." Thiselton observes that Gadamer devotes one third of *Truth and Method* to the issue of the "pastness" of the past.[24] Thiselton also agrees with Gadamer that this pastness of the past cannot be dismissed or "exaggerated"; it is a significant issue.[25] Gadamer contends that the writer of history "distant from the events" never gives a description of the world that was, but, rather it is the writer's interpretation, from within his or her own context, of the world that was.[26]

---

19. LaSor, "Interpretation of Prophecy," 106.
20. Ibid., 108.
21. Fee, *Gospel and Spirit*, 19.
22. Ibid.
23. Thiselton, *Thiselton On Hermeneutics*, 93.
24. Thiselton, *Two Horizons*, 53.
25. Ibid., 63.
26. Gadamer, "Universality of the Hermeneutical Problem," 181.

A contemporary interpreter can voice an authoritative view on "what it meant" as a prelude to "what it means." Marshall's observation that a significant relative objectivity is possible is valid. However, despite this assertion, a contemporary interpreter cannot be *the* authoritative voice on "what it meant" due to recognition of his or her own prejudices that form part of his or her presuppositions. The authoritative voice is no longer present. Hence, there is uncertainty concerning "what it means" if "what it meant" is understood to equal "what it means." The degree of uncertainty in the determination of "what it meant" is irrelevant, because in the absence of the author there is no clear authoritative voice regarding the degree of uncertainty, or where that uncertainty lies. A slight degree of uncertainty may not be significant over a short period of time but can become a much larger degree of uncertainty over a long period of time.

If Marshall is correct, then the degree of uncertainty need not be regarded as hindering a viable value of "what it meant" on each occasion of interpretation. Nevertheless, the central point remains that no contemporary interpreter can make the assertion "what it meant equals what it means." An absolute value of "what it meant," though admitted to exist, is inaccessible to the contemporary interpreter as an absolute value in the absence of the author. Consequently, any systematic search for certitude begins with uncertainty.

There is no unambiguous direct access to the authoritative voice, neither the divine nor the human, to either eliminate the degree of uncertainty or to specify its nature. Since the answer to the conundrum of Scripture points the way to the solution of the paradox of Scripture, a reevaluation of what is taking place in the process of hermeneutics, and the special use of this in theological hermeneutics, is necessary. The assertion "what it meant equals what it means" should be avoided as a dictum. There are dynamics of why meaning changes in the case of an unintended audience, and how those changes impact contemporary understanding needs to be considered.

The Nature of the Text: Preliminary Considerations

The classical humanist model of a text is that of a unit of language used to express the thoughts and ideas of an author. The text is seen to point to a world outside the text.[27] The text is essentially the written verbal description of something that exists in the mind of the author, which the author desires to communicate. The Romanticist hermeneutic began to take account of the impact of the world of the reader.[28] However, texts were still seen as "linguistically mediating interpersonal communication;" consequently, authors could be conceived of as directly addressing the reader.[29] This led to the development of the idea, which fitted well with the concept of the biblical

---

27. Thiselton, *New Horizons*, 55.
28. Ibid., 56.
29. Ibid.

text, that authors and their context formed part of the text itself.[30] The focus in this situation is the world behind the text.

The world behind the text can seem remote and lead to a possible disconnection.[31] An over-preoccupation with the historical paradigm tended to create a gulf between critical scholarship and the practice of faith.[32] Reassessment and reevaluation became necessary in the light of developments in literary theory.[33] This moved the emphasis to the world of the text.

Vanhoozer, in a tribute to Paul Ricoeur, declares that Ricoeur's central insight is that the interpreters situate themselves in front of the text. In this case, symbol gives rise to thought and the text opens up a new world in front of the reader.[34] The appeal of this for biblical studies has been the consideration of standing in front of the text and experiencing its operative effects.[35] A focus on the world in front of the text, however, can lead to a disjoint of "community knowledge," which is part of the world behind the text.[36]

A Pentecostal writer on this subject is Randolph Tate, whose ideas concern the three worlds involved in interpretation.[37] These are the worlds of the author, text, and reader. They cause three primary concepts when developing theories of the locus of meaning, which are "author centered," "text centered," and "reader centered."[38] His own proposal is that these three approaches are not mutually exclusive, nor is one approach more important or determinative.[39] It is the integrated approach of the "interplay" involving all three worlds that results in meaning.[40] Recognition in hermeneutics of these three worlds associated with an author's text leads to the conclusion that none should be ignored in the pursuit of understanding.

The work of Walter J. Ong on literacy and orality has highlighted that the composition is a direct creation in written form, as distinct from transcription. Even where the author of a composition is transcribing material, they supply a context in composition that prejudices the impact of any transcription on the reader. This prejudice is the author's view of reality or the reality he or she wishes to create for the reader. It is the creation of the composition that has led to the focus on the text.[41] Also, as noted previ-

30. Ibid.
31. Ibid., 57.
32. Ibid.
33. Ibid., 56.
34. Vanhoozer, "The Joy of Yes," 27–28.
35. Thiselton, *New Horizons*, 57.
36. Ibid.
37. Tate, *Biblical Interpretation*, xv–xxi.
38. Ibid., xvi.
39. Ibid., xx.
40. Ibid., 255.
41. Ong, *Orality and Literacy*, 10.

ously, it is a false assumption to equate oral verbalization with written verbalization. The text becomes emancipated from the oral situation in the composition.[42]

The hermeneutical problem originally developed within the pursuit of exegesis in seeking to understand texts.[43] Discovery of a hermeneutical problem was due to interpretation of a text occurring within a community and its traditions, hence its presuppositions.[44] Ricoeur states that the "connection between interpretation and comprehension, the former taken in the sense of textual exegesis and the latter in the broad sense of the clear understanding of signs, is manifested in one of the traditional senses of the word 'hermeneutics.'"[45] Hermeneutics establishes a relationship between exegesis as a technical pursuit and the issues of meaning and language.[46] In the development of the study of languages and with the work of Friedrich Schleiermacher and Wilhelm Dilthey the hermeneutic problem becomes a philosophical problem.[47]

It is here, and because of this, that Ricoeur sees that the place of attachment of the hermeneutic problem in philosophical endeavor is within the "domain of *phenomenology*."[48] The assigning of understanding to method leaves it entrapped within methodology and the "presuppositions of objective knowledge and the presuppositions of the Kantian theory of knowledge."[49] In the Kantian philosophical perspective, all knowledge begins with experience and reasoning is the assimilation of knowledge into our existence.[50] Methodology pursues this knowledge and, consequently, what is known and how it is known is restricted to methodology.

It would seem that, in part, Ricoeur's objection to this view is that the knowledge is acquired by experience rather than just experienced. The reader, in order to understand, experiences understanding rather than acquires it. Essentially in the Heideggerian concept of *Dasein*, Ricoeur sees a mindset that doesn't drive a wedge between the ontology of understanding and that of the epistemology of interpretation.[51] Mar-

---

42. Thiselton, *New Horizons*, 56.
43. Ricoeur, *Conflict of Interpretations*, 3.
44. Ibid.
45. Ibid., 4.
46. Ibid.
47. Ibid., 5.
48. Ibid., 6.
49. Ibid., 7.

50. Kant, *Immanuel Kant's Critique*, 41. All knowledge that is understood, or acquired, is empirical, since it comes through experience. In modernity this places the issue of understanding in the domain methodology.

51. Ricoeur, *Conflict of Interpretations*, 6–7. (Italics added). In Kant's understanding there is knowledge that does not arise from experience. He reasons when all that belongs to the senses is eliminated from experience, then the remainder is *a priori* knowledge, and this is the field of universals that empirical knowledge cannot supply, Kant, 42. The science by which this knowledge is known is metaphysics, Kant, 46. The two forms of knowledge have no knowledge of one another; one is methodologically established, hence, methodologically known; and the other, as *a priori*, is an aspect of human beings forming part of understanding, and it would seem that this is what Ricoeur

tin Heidegger's concept of *Dasein*'s temporality is a continuum between birth (Being toward the beginning) and death (Being toward the end).[52] What takes place in this in-between is a sequence of experiences in time.[53]

However, *Dasein* does not exist as the sum of these experiences, which are transient, but always exists in the now, or present experience.[54] History as a science treats these historical events, or experiences, as "Object," and the event is discarded.[55] The Kantian perspective treats experience as the acquisition of knowledge;[56] therefore, when this occurs the event of understanding is lost in the treatment of knowledge as object. This would seem to be Ricoeur's reasoning in finding in *Dasein*, what is for him, a better model for interpretation that involves the being-there of the person interpreting. In Ricoeur's thought understanding is no longer a method of acquiring knowledge but a style of being itself.[57] A person works out from the place of being to objective assessment and does not discover being through methodological objectivity.

Hermeneutics is not just a matter of methodology and objective knowledge. In the work of Ricoeur there is recognition that a description of the process, a philosophy, must be developed that doesn't limit knowing to the limitations in modernism. Walter Brueggemann has observed that the rise of science and its resultant epistemology of the Enlightenment produced interpretation informed by historical criticism.[58] This connection with modernism held sway for over two hundred years so that the culture-bound nature of the process was not perceived.[59] This is what Ricoeur noted about interpretation; it always occurs within a tradition and hence a set of presuppositions need to be recognized for their impact on the process of interpretation. Methodology is a means of analysis and therefore is a tool, but the meaning of the analysis, the fruit of the analysis, is not determined by the methodology but by the interpreter as the user. Methodology is analysis. Methodolgy is not the means of the creation of texts, or of their understanding.

Brueggemann postulates, on the basis of his research, that the rise of modernity happened in the midst of a chaos that sought verifiable stability. Theological interpretation followed this trend and a methodology was created of a tight system of certitude wherein the absolute is achievable via methodology.[60] Ricoeur's work has

---

is referring to in the driving of a wedge between an ontology of understanding and an epistemology of interpretation.

52. Heidegger, *Being and Time*, 426–27.
53. Ibid., 425.
54. Ibid., 426.
55. Ibid., 427. (Italics and capitalization original.)
56. Kant, *Immanuel Kant's Critique*, 41.
57. Ricoeur, *Conflict of Interpretations*, 7.
58. Brueggemann, *Bible and Postmodern Imaginations*, 1.
59. Ibid.
60. Ibid., 4–5.

highlighted that this description of the hermeneutical process is inadequate and that a new evaluation of the process is needed.

In dealing with a text Ricoeur has rightly observed that there is a need to go beyond semiotics to semantics, which will be discussed further in chapter four of this book. It is the sentence as a unit that allows an evaluation of what is occurring in the discourse.[61] In the sentence, language becomes related to world and this world is what is communicated.[62] The sentence is therefore the basic unit of the text of a composition. It is the smallest individual unit of the author's creation. The sentence is composed of words, but the text is composed of sentences, the context of which is the composition.

It was noted previously that composition includes elements that convey aspects of an oral situation that set a context for discourse. The composition is not simply transcription but the assertion of a will to construct and convey the viewpoint of its author. The composition will include subjective elements that describe the effect on characters within the composition in a way the reader can be both empathetic and sympathetic with, and it will also contain elements that show how authors themselves feel about aspects of what is narrated. The composition will also need to include elements that can engender perlocutionary acts, if there is an authorial intent to produce them.[63] The composition will also need to impart knowledge that belongs to the tradition in which it and the author stand, as this has a shaping effect on the composition and its interpretation. However, all of these aspects of the composition will need to be achieved in a way that the reader can possess or identify with this knowledge, and not just be informed about it. This requires the author to engage the presuppositions of the reader to seek an interaction with the authorial intent to "see" what the author "saw."

The issue of the nature of the text raises the question of its identity as an entity. This necessarily draws into consideration the question of ontological issues. The concern of this book is the issue of hermeneutics, which of necessity examines a number of philosophical issues, and hence involves topics such as ontology. Hermeneutics, as the art and science of interpretation, deals with the process that someone (i.e., a person who is the author or writer) said something (i.e., the text) that someone (i.e., a person who is the reader/interpreter) will seek to understand and appropriate into his or her world as having meaning. Ontology can broadly be seen to deal with, first, whether entities exist and, second, the nature and relationship of those entities that exist.[64] However, the object in this book is not to deal with whether or not these enti-

---

61. Ricoeur, *Interpretation Theory*, 20.

62. Ibid. This helps illuminate Ricoeur's stance to move the hermeneutic problem to *phenomenology*, which he perceives relates to being and life.

63. In the case of the text of the Epistle of James, the text of the author clearly intends the perlocutionary act to be a motivation to change.

64. Hofweber, "Logic and Ontology," section 3.

ties—that is, *someone* as author, *something* as text, and *someone* as interpreter—exist, but instead to deal with them as existent entities. Therefore, the object in any discussion of ontological issues here is the more general sense of ontology as consideration of these existent entities in their general features and interrelationships.

Forms of Knowledge Operational in Language

There are forms of knowing other than rational objective knowledge that are important in understanding, which an author may wish to present to a reader.[65] This seems to be what Ricoeur has recognized, and sought to allow a place for, in pursuit of understanding, as outlined previously. Yet the unit, or basic element, available to the author to use for creating and achieving this is words used in a sentence; thus, the sentence is the basic unit of language.[66] The grammatical-historical methodology will serve as a means of analysis, for an interpreter, of the objective knowledge of the composition; but it is inadequate, on its own, to deal with the composition to achieve understanding and solve the hermeneutical problem.[67]

If, as N. T. Wright has recognized, aesthetics and belief, though subjective, are part of knowing, then an author and interpreter must connect with this knowledge, which cannot occur through current methodology. Yet if this is part of the authorial communication, then it occurs in and through the text, or more accurately the composition. Authors use sentences in a composition as their basic unit but seek to convey more than objective knowledge. Similarly, if, as recognized by Thiselton, the knowledge of belief is transmitted in community, then the communication of authors must engage this belief in readers. Again, the only means of this is the composition they create. This concept, that there is knowledge that presents itself to the reader but that is not acquired methodologically, is an important insight gained from Ricoeur's thought.

In recognizing Heidegger's observation that language is not grounded in words themselves, or in abstract considerations about propositional logic, but in sharing communication between people, Thiselton makes his own observation of the importance of this for New Testament hermeneutics. Understanding is not simply research

---

65. Wright, *New Testament*, 32–33. Wright argues that it is obvious that not all knowledge possessed by a person is of the form of rational knowledge. Further, the downgrading of other forms of knowing such as metaphysics and theology is stance of modernity rather than a fact of either their knowability or value.

66. Vanhoozer, *First Theology*, 166. Vanhoozer also states that the knowledge we have as human beings is indirect not direct. It comes to us mediated by language, 327.

67. Ibid. See also, Thiselton, *Two Horizons*, 188. Thiselton notes that the work of Born and Heisenberg in post-Newtonian physics brought changed conceptions of reality. As a result, methodology must be appropriate to the object of the inquiry. It is not a "one size fits all" situation.

of words but "communication between two sets of horizons."[68] In Thiselton this is the fusion of the horizons.[69]

G. B. Caird notes that a translator, who is therefore an interpreter, cannot succeed in translation unless he or she recognizes that the translation cannot be merely transference from one language to another. Translators must also transfer thought forms.[70] Stendhal similarly notes this in the search for the "what it means" of the biblical text, that is, contemporary understanding.[71] Caird also notes that in one sense the Bible is written in *languages* but the *language* of the Bible is the fact that it was written in words.[72] Consequently, communication occurs between an author and interpreter beyond the level of words and their meanings, but the vehicle that must convey all of the communication, the composition, is written in words.[73] Schleiermacher saw language as the "only presupposition in hermeneutics and everything that is to be found, including the other objective and subjective presuppositions must be discovered in language."[74]

Consequently, with text as composition, as opposed to text as transcription, understanding an author's communication involves objective knowledge, subjective knowledge, and, third, what can be categorized as pistology,[75] dealing with belief knowledge. The reader/interpreter acquires the knowledge of, and interacts with, these forms of knowledge in the process of understanding an author's work. It is further proposed that these categories apply to all texts and not just sacred texts; sacred texts require specialized use of hermeneutics in dealing with the pistology, not a specialized hermeneutic.[76] All three categories of knowledge are capable of being verbally described; the issue is their acquisition as knowledge, or presence in the text, for an interpreter's understanding of the author's composition.

68. Thiselton, *Two Horizons*, 168.

69. Ibid., 16. This is the theme of Thiselton's book. He makes reference to Gadamer's concept of fusion of horizons, which he indicates he has used. His distinction is nominating the horizons of the interpreter and text.

70. Caird, *Language and Imagery*, 2. (Italics are added for emphasis.)

71. Stendhal, "Biblical Theology, Contemporary," 427.

72. Caird, *Language and Imagery*, 2. Caird is highlighting that the cultural gap, created by languages, should be neither ignored nor over emphasized. Though written in languages, the Bible exists as a single book written in words through the languages.

73. Vanhoozer, *First Theology*, 327.

74. Schleiermacher, *Hermeneutics*, 50.

75. The term *pistology* (given the meaning of the study of faith as knowledge) has been created by the author as a way of handling belief knowledge as a category. This word is simply a combining of the Greek words *pistis* (faith) and *logos* (the word or discourse about). Hence, *pistology* is used to designate a study of human belief. Use of the word *theology* as a general word for belief was not adopted, as this has particularity and distinct connotations of Judeo-Christian belief, but the concept of belief itself is universal. Therefore, *pistology* is a preferred term for studying belief in a universal sense.

76. Thiselton, *Thiselton On Hermeneutics*, 531. The example he uses is that hearing God is not a special word for hearing but a special meaning of the word hearing. Therefore, hermeneutics is the same for both.

The word *knowledge* is appropriate, since it would seem almost axiomatic that what can be verbally described must also itself be known in order to be verbally described. The problem is that concepts such as the subjective and belief categories of knowledge have tended to be regarded as irrational, and consequently opposed to reason.[77] Hence, whilst their existence is acknowledged they are considered unreasonable, and therefore not knowledge as such. Nevertheless, just because these concepts of the subjective and belief are not acquired via a process of rational reason doesn't change their value in reasoning or knowability. They are capable of verbal description since a person can describe that he or she loves and *that* he or she believes; also *what* he or she believes is verbally describable. As such they are knowledge. Wright noted that these other forms of knowledge are acknowledged but downgraded because they don't fulfill the criteria of the modern era's positivism that has held sway.[78] Since the subjective and pistological forms of knowledge are knowable they can be subjected to a process of reasoning once held as knowledge, and as such constitute genuine forms of knowledge.[79]

There is knowledge that is rationally acquired (i.e., the category of *rational* objective knowledge), which is the usual concept of knowledge.[80] However, there is also knowledge acquired that is *arational* (i.e., knowledge not based on or governed by reason).[81] James Martin suggests that, hermeneutically, objectivity and subjectivity work dialectically.[82] This would imply that a dynamic interaction is occurring in interpretation that facilitates understanding. In the Pentecostal tradition the hermeneutic must function to both explain a text and activate it in the life of the person.[83]

Finally, there is knowledge that is acquired from *nonrational*[84] sources, and this is the domain of belief, which is also part of the community knowledge.[85] Whilst arational knowledge arises within a person immediately in response to stimuli in relationship to someone or something, nonrational knowledge is imparted as knowledge,

77. Wright, *New Testament*, 33.

78. Ibid.

79. Thiselton, *Thiselton On Hermeneutics*, 39. In engaging in Theological Hermeneutics, Thiselton notes that "actualization" in hermeneutics strikes an accord with the account of belief in theology. A network of belief is seen in a person's disposition to respond and manifest their belief in attitudes and actions. This is dealing with the "cash-currency" of belief. Therefore, belief has been acquired as knowledge in this process.

80. Kant, *Immanuel Kant's Critique*, 41. This is the basic concept of Kant that is widely accepted in modern methodology. All knowledge begins with experience and that which is knowable presents itself, and experience makes it known by reasoning.

81. Wright, *New Testament*, 33.

82. Martin, "Toward a Post-Critical Paradigm," 380.

83. Dempster, "Paradigm Shifts," 132. This concept is similar to Thiselton's comment on Theological Hermeneutics and the actualization of belief as part of the package of understanding.

84. The creation of the term *nonrational* and the rationale for its use is discussed in a following section entitled; (B) *Nonrational* Knowledge, 33.

85. Thiselton, *Thiselton On Hermeneutics*, 702.

and is therefore acquired in a community relationship.[86] This community knowledge can be challenged, shaped, and reshaped in reasoning processes. The issue becomes how this occurs in relationship to an author's text. It is also important to recognize that this knowledge can be both explicit (by assertion or reference by the author), and implicit (by reference to the tradition[s] in which the author and intended audience stand), in the author's text. Thiselton suggests that the inherited knowledge of the community (i.e., tradition) makes it easier or more difficult for an individual to raise questions about knowledge.[87] This implies that belief as knowledge impacts, by facilitating or hindering, the acquisition of rational knowledge. In this situation belief becomes essentially a context for rationally acquired knowledge.

Therefore, it would seem to be within the bounds of reason to assume that a concern for any author in creating a composition is to seek to establish an intimate relationship with the reader. Failure to create this relationship means that neither arational nor nonrational knowledge can be imparted.[88] It also would seem to be within the bounds of reason to suggest that a new approach, other than that developed in the grammatico-historical approach, which can detect and evaluate the categories of knowledge other than the rational, is needed for achieving the hermeneutical aim of understanding. The reader has presuppositions in these areas of knowledge that orient him or her in the task of reading the text; and the author, to establish a world with the reader, must engage these presuppositions in dialogue to establish relationship.

An Introduction to Arational and Nonrational Knowledge

The preceding discussion set out to establish that these forms of knowledge exist and are knowable. The concepts of forms of knowledge other than rational objective knowledge are not new. Prior to the modernist era and current methodologies, the German philosopher Georg Hegel differentiated between what he titled Objective and Subjective Religion.[89] Objective Religion was identified as "the faith that is believed," whereas Subjective Religion is expressed in feelings and actions.[90] Subjective Religion is living and individual, whereas Objective Religion "is a matter of abstraction."[91] Although Hegel was discussing religion, not the interpretation of texts, his discussion recognizes that there is within people's understanding of themselves both objective

---

86. Israel, Albrecht, and McNally, "Pentecostals and Hermeneutics," 151. The authors assert that spirituality is communicated by rituals, which are communal acts.

87. Thiselton, *Thiselton On Hermeneutics*, 706.

88. Ahn, "Various Debates," 28. Ahn notes as a pastor trained in evangelical methodology, he found that methodology alone did not develop an interaction between the interpreter and text. The methodological approach cannot allow the objective and subjective to coexist, as the subjective is seen to subvert meaning. This leaves a lot to be desired in his opinion.

89. Georg W. F. Hegel, "Early Theological Writings," 43.

90. Ibid.

91. Ibid.

and subjective aspects, which are both vital. His observation that Objective Religion is "the faith that is believed" points to another avenue of the incorporation of belief or nonrational knowledge into an authors' text. Hegel's analogy for Objective Religion is the "cabinet of the naturalist" full of specimens, which shows that his use of "faith" in the expression is related to propositional truth.[92]

Newman also showed in his work *A Grammar of Assent* that propositions are used in making assertions.[93] The mental act of assent in relation to an assertion displays unconditional acceptance of the assertion.[94] This would constitute statements of faith. Hence, the concept of the proposition equips language with a vehicle for setting out belief knowledge, which can be accepted (indicating belief and hence describable as faith) or rejected (indicating unbelief and hence an absence of faith).

The preceding section has also sought to establish that although current methodologies are knowable, in dealing with texts employed in hermeneutics methodologies are inadequate to evaluate and detect these other forms of arational and nonrational knowledge, apart from their verbal description. Their application in the process of understanding will require more than acknowledging their existence by their description. The application and usage of arational and nonrational knowledge will require some form of understanding of how they form part of the text and are detected by the interpreter in the process of understanding.

The development of the terms *arational*, to categorize the aesthetic and subjective, and *nonrational*, to categorize belief knowledge, are original in the understanding of this author. Consequently, the following discussion of these categories as inherent within texts requires a descriptive approach that is original. However, as a way of progressing from supposition and conjecture toward a healthy debate that recognizes and seeks to evaluate these areas, this author will endeavor to find possible attachments to current debates and describe what is known about key aspects of these categories.

Thiselton noted that, in order to go beyond the accumulation of linguistic and historical data, philosophical concepts must be included in the task of hermeneutics.[95] As noted previously, categories that come from outside the Bible are not necessarily wrong, and the conceptual tools of the philosopher can greatly assist with understanding.[96] Gadamer, as a philosopher, saw himself as describing the way things are; he was not proposing a methodology.[97] Hence, philosophy can be seen as providing descriptive tools that can be helpful, but it is not necessary to either adopt a philosophy of, or uncritically accept concepts of, a philosopher. Philosophical discussions are useful

---

92. Ibid.
93. Newman, *Grammar of Assent*, 2.
94. Ibid., 8.
95. Thiselton, *Two Horizons*, 5–6.
96. Ibid., 9.
97. Gadamer, *Truth and Method*, 465.

(a) Arational Knowledge

The *arational* category of knowledge includes the range of aesthetics, the concept of intuition and emotions that an author may seek to illicit and/or convey. This category also includes the "givens" or "being-there" of humanity in the biblical text.[98] An author can state, and thereby describe these aspects, but not convey them so that the reader will possess that knowledge within his or her own being to move to understanding. Thiselton discusses what can be seen as an example of what is being considered. He notes that mood can be used to direct a person's attention to what is inevitable in life. It can be used to turn attention away from the possibilities to the actual, and therefore mood possesses hermeneutic value.[99] In this situation an author would not be looking for either psychological understanding or empathy but actual emotional impact.[100] As feelings they would be considered subjective and not subject to reason and hence acceptable knowledge.

The following illustrations from Scripture assist in an understanding of this concept. First, in John 16:19–22, Jesus pointed out to the disciples that in saying he was going away he was speaking about his death at Calvary. He noted that this event would make them sorrowful and sad, but he then spoke of his resurrection (see verse 22, where he predicted he would see them again beyond that time). He told them that once they understood that this event had occurred (i.e., death and resurrection), they would have great joy. This joy would open up and direct them into an entirely new dimension of relationship with God. Essentially, Jesus set a context for understanding what their mood should be so that they would understand the possibilities before them. In post-resurrection appearances recorded in Luke 24:44–52, Jesus conducted a study where he expounded texts in the law of Moses, Psalms, and the Prophets that gave them an understanding that what he predicted of his death had come to pass. The result of this understanding was great joy, (see verse 52), which is what he had prepared them for as noted in the text of the Gospel of John. The written text shows that, in understanding a text, the effect was a communication of a mood of joy that in turn directed the attention of the disciples to new possibilities.

A second example illustrates that mood can cause misunderstanding. In Neh 8:1–12 there is recorded a public meeting conducted by Ezra the priest. He read the

---

98. Kant, *Immanuel Kant's Critique*, 42. Kant saw that there is a knowledge that is somehow inherent in the being of a person. It is this knowledge that empowers the ability to know. These are universals and are conceived of as independent of our experience, 43. This would infer that they could be seen as "givens" of humanity, which accords with the biblical view.

99. Thiselton, *Two Horizons*, 162.

100. Ibid.

law to the people and was assisted by others to help the people understand the text. When people heard and understood the text they all began to weep, indicating a melancholy attitude of remorse, thereby suggesting that they experienced degrees of guilt. However, upon seeing this, Ezra and those helping him told the people that their mood was incorrectly directing their understanding of the text, see verses 8–9. The purpose of the meeting was that they should understand it to be a special day, and one of joy and blessing. It does not seem too speculative to say in this case that the mood adopted in encounter with the text directed the audience away from its possibilities. The mood the interpreter Ezra sought was one that would direct the people to its possibilities.

Both the author and reader already each possess the "givens" so that each has immediacy of affinity with these in the other. The object of the author is to elicit response. This aspect of the communicative process of the text lends itself to the *phenomenological* description of intuited knowledge, and as Ricoeur has observed, current methodology is no use here. This is also the observation of Anderson, noted previously, that phenomenology cannot supply a methodological process. This is subjective knowledge, which accords with the scriptural text and can be described but not acquired through grammatico-historical methodology. It is individual and subject to description but cannot be obtained through an objective process of reasoning

The written text of Scripture asserts that the gospel, the understood then communicated text, has both a subjective and an objective category. Paul noted that the gospel came in "word," establishing that there is an objective element communicated. However, he also states that the gospel came in "power, and in the Holy Spirit and in much assurance. . ." thereby involving subjective and experiential elements (1 Thess 1:5). The phrase "much assurance" or alternately "great conviction" as a concept is not quantifiable but is evidently knowable. Furthermore, it came with the word; that is, it was imparted concurrently with the objective knowledge. It is noted in 1 Thess 1:6 that the word was received "in much affliction (which is objectively knowable) and with joy of the Holy Spirit (which is subjective but still knowable)." If the genitive "with joy of the Holy Spirit" is taken in the ablative sense of the genitive, then the Holy Spirit imparted the joy in the process of communication.

If it is assumed that Jesus did not communicate in Koiné Greek but, as is more likely, in Aramaic,[101] then the words attributed to Jesus in John 15:11 are an interpretation within a composition by the author of the gospel, which show that the author perceived Jesus' desire to impart subjective knowledge in his discourse: "These things I have spoken to you, that My joy may remain in you, and *that* your joy may be full." Joy as arational knowledge is acquired with the objective knowledge and can be described but not conveyed in a methodological analysis of the text. Further, there is no quantitative assessment of when the reader/interpreter's joy is full.

---

101. Stendhal, "Biblical Theology, Contemporary," 427. Stendhal notes that the student of the Greek gospel is already once removed from the Aramaic vernacular of Jesus' teachings.

(b) Nonrational Knowledge

In the domain of knowledge, *nonrational* knowledge is neither objective nor subjective. The term *nonrational* is suggested because objective rational knowledge is neutral, concerning the knowledge related to belief. Nonrational knowledge is not related to rational reason, but it is not subjective; that is, it is not dependent upon and related to feelings or simply personal opinion. The fact that anecdotal evidence suggests that nonrational knowledge has an intuitive aspect and that belief can occur immediately does not move its classification to the subjective. It has already been noted that Hegel recognized that resident faith could be considered from both an objective and subjective point of view. Yet the faith is already resident in order to be discussed; therefore, it is not the result of either, but the objective and subjective points of view are a means of its description.

The facility of "belief" is also a "given" in the biblical text of human existence, and "faith" is the knowledge of belief or its content. There is an inherent aspect of human consciousness that is able to perceive and reason with this knowledge that is "belief." It has been previously noted that this knowledge is transmitted in relationship, and hence in community. Belief can have subjective input in that a person can know how he or she feels about it; and that person can communicate a verbal description both of the nonrational knowledge and how he or she feels about it. However, though capable of being verbally described as knowledge, a process of rational reason does not acquire belief, hence faith.

The philosopher Blaise Pascal in the *Pensées*, published in 1656, said concerning God (and therefore by extension the domain of faith): "God is, or He is not." But to which side shall we incline? Reason can decide nothing here. According to reason, you can do neither the one thing nor the other; according to reason, you can defend neither of the propositions."[102] Pascal noted that a person *must* wager on one or the other of these propositions, and therefore decide on one or the other, since they are already embarked on life.[103] Essentially the implication is that a person must bet their life on this decision. Reason as a rational objective process is not impacted by either choice,[104] which implies that rational objective reason is not involved in the process of choice. Therefore, this involves nonrational knowledge in terms of its acquisition. As describable knowledge it can be handled with a process of reason, but it is not acquired by objective rational reason.

Immanuel Kant follows a similar line of reasoning. He notes that if it is admitted that something exists, then there must be that which exists *necessarily*.[105] In his discussion of *a priori* knowledge he noted that there are universals that empower the

---

102. Pascal, "Pensées," sect. 233.
103. Ibid. (Italics added.)
104. Ibid.
105. Kant, *Immanuel Kant's Critique*, 496. (Italics original.)

ability to know.[106] It would seem that this is a basis of his reasoning. The thing that is contingent exists on the basis of another contingency. Thus, if a person works backward through each cause and its subsequent cause, that person must come to a cause that is not itself contingent.[107] This is the reasoning by which a person can "advance to the primordial being," which is an absolute beginning point.[108] Kant sees that the natural progress of human reason is to start by persuading itself of the absolute.[109] However, when Kant seeks to deal with the question of identity of this absolute primordial being, his conclusion is that "the argument has failed to give us the least concept of the properties of a necessary being, and indeed is utterly ineffective."[110] Kant concludes that in all eras of human existence, the postulation of the existence of this being has existed.[111]

His conclusion is similar to that of Pascal for whom the existence of God is apprehended as knowledge by the operation of faith, that is, the assertion of nonrational knowledge.[112] In the thinking of Pascal, humanity through the process of reason is not capable of knowing either that God is or what God is.[113] However, in the thinking of Kant the existence of God is knowable in terms of detection, but an identity of that being is unfathomable from the perspective of rational objective reason. Kant acknowledges that the realm of nonrational knowledge exists, but human reason is not capable of arriving at its disclosure; that is, human reason can arrive at a revelation that it exists but not of its content. This seems to accord with Paul's reasoning in Rom 1:19–20 that the unseen God (hence, unknowable in terms of identity) is inferred by the creation itself. The difference between the two positions is that Pascal exhorts leaving rational reasoning as a way of knowing so that a person can indeed come to knowledge of the Supreme Being. Kant is content to not know and evidently sees it as unknowable.

In the philosophy of Pascal, objective rational reason is abandoned and the inquirer starts with the proposition of the divine. This carries the implication that understanding starts with acceptance, or believing, and once engaged there is interpretation into the life of a person. Conversely, in the philosophy of Kant objective rational reason arrives at acknowledgment of the divine, but then ceases and abandons the search as unsolvable. The divine identity is not identifiable through reason, thus leaving the "essential being" as unknowable. Anything further than this is the realm

---

106. Ibid., 42.
107. Ibid., 496.
108. Ibid.
109. Ibid., 497.
110. Ibid., 498.
111. Ibid., 501.
112. Pascal, "Pensées," sect. 233.
113. Ibid.

of metaphysics.[114] In Acts 17:23 Paul used an altar, dedicated "To the Unknown God," as a starting point to proclaim a knowledge of the identity he had discovered, of this unknown God, to the religious leaders in Athens. Although reference to this text cannot be claimed to represent the Kantian perspective and that of Pascal, the story does have illustrative value.

Consequently, pursuit of the divine based on rational objective reason can only proceed to an agnostic state at best. Both philosophers agree that rational objective reason concludes that it can't conclude and doesn't know the answer, which is the definition of agnostic. An analysis based in rational reason can only be certain that it is uncertain and does not know. In current methodological investigation of a text the description of belief can be detected where it is explicit. However, via rational objective reason the interpreter can neither acquire the description of belief for the purposes of understanding nor can the degree of its impact on the author, the text, or the audience be successfully evaluated. Consequently, there is no presentation of objective rational knowledge an author could use that will result in the interpreter reasoning belief and hence the impact of faith (i.e., belief knowledge) in understanding the author's communication. What is required is nonrational objective and subjective reasoning.

It was noted previously that belief, and hence faith, is knowledge that is imparted in relationship and hence community. Fee has noted that not every biblical text is the word of God in the same way.[115] He believes it should be axiomatic that the genre of the text is considered.[116] The different genres are a means of communicating and can be helpful in these areas of arational and nonrational; for example, poetry can convey emotive information that connects with the imagination.[117]

Narrative is an example of one means of transmission of nonrational knowledge in developing a composition. The biblical narrative is interpreting God into the lives of people as it unfolds. In looking at the story in the text of Deut 26:5–10, author James Limburg notes that the reading of the story moves from "they" (being the ancestors of the reader), to "us" (the reader becomes included in the story even though never in Egypt), and then to "I" (the story becomes personalized and the reader is now at the front of the story).[118] The affinity of Limburg's assessment with the development of the philosophical description of hermeneutics and the world behind the text, the world of the text, and the world in front of the text as moving the interpreter in the direction of understanding is unmissable. Limburg identifies within the biblical text "three major historical works which tell the story of God and God's people."[119] This total narrative

---

114. Kant, *Immanuel Kant's Critique*, 46.

115. Fee, *Gospel and Spirit*, 89.

116. Ibid.

117. Wimsatt, *Verbal Icon*, 5. Wimsatt and Beardsley suggest that the meaning of a poem attaches to a person as expression of personality or state of soul rather than meaning as an ideal object.

118. Limburg, *Old Stories*, 5.

119. Ibid., 6.

is the thread that unites the Hebrew Bible. In the same fashion the New Testament develops where the core of the Christian faith is a story.[120]

Storytelling is a "hot," or dynamic, medium because it engages the imagination of the hearer.[121] This occurs when the hearer becomes actively "involved with" the story and thereby becomes "part of" the story.[122] The person hearing is interpreting the story into their own understanding, thereby placing themselves within the story.[123] This could be seen to be the thrust of 1 Cor 10:6–11 where it seems that Paul is exhorting the Corinthian believers to put themselves in the story and learn from what happened in the wilderness wanderings. They are to interpret it into their own lives. A further example of this appeal to narrative is found in Heb 3:7–4:13.

The imagination in concert with the presuppositional world of the person is able to cause the reader to interpret the text into his or her world. Dealing with the text in the present, and consequently in relationship to the question "what it means," requires engagement of the reader's imagination (i.e., the human capacity to picture, portray, receive, and practice).[124] Hence, narrative is an important genre of the biblical text because it opens the way for bringing the interpreter to a place of understanding and therefore revelation. In this process the tradition of faith as knowledge is acquired.

Vanhoozer notes that culture presents an outworking of a person's "ultimate beliefs and values," which is where the belief system is lived out.[125] It is what gives individuals their historical particularity.[126] It is a means of sharing the mindset of these values and beliefs.[127] Consequently, a tradition "is a kind of ongoing cultural interpretation of certain foundational works."[128] As noted previously, the subculture of Pentecostalism ritual, hence tradition, has interpretive value.[129] Culture is transmitting a mindset through its tradition that becomes part of the individual members of that community. Thiselton notes that even things such as the appeal to "common sense" within a community are essentially an almost subconscious recognition of the value of community knowledge in the life of the individual.[130] This transmission happens not only geographically but also in time to successive generations.[131] Fee sees hermeneutics as a community affair, the impact of which extends back to the first

---

120. Ibid.
121. Ibid., 12.
122. Ibid.
123. Ibid., 14.
124. Brueggemann, *Bible and Postmodern Imaginations*, 13.
125. Vanhoozer, *First Theology*, 310.
126. Ibid.
127. Ibid., 316.
128. Ibid.
129. Israel, Albrecht, and McNally, "Pentecostal's and Hermeneutics," 152–53.
130. Thiselton, *Thiselton on Hermeneutics*, 705.
131. Ibid., 706.

Christian community of apostolic times.[132] Tradition has a significant impact on interpretation because of the values and beliefs that are transmitted by the community as nonrational knowledge through the individual's relationship to the community.

An extended quote from the work of Ricoeur shows that this concept should not be regarded as simply a special feature of sacred text:

> We feel that interpretation has a history and that this history is a segment of tradition itself. Interpretation does not spring from nowhere; rather, one interprets in order to make explicit, to extend, and so to keep alive the tradition itself, inside which one always remains. It is in this sense that the time of interpretation belongs in some way to the time of tradition. But tradition in return, even understood as the transmission of a *depositum*, remains a dead tradition if it is not the continual interpretation of this deposit: our "heritage" is not a sealed package we pass from hand to hand, without ever opening, but rather a treasure from which we draw by the handful and which by this very act is replenished. Every tradition lives by grace of interpretation, and it is at this price that it continues, that is, remains living.[133]

Authors stand in a tradition and have a belief about their subject matter that, at the very least, impacts the authorial intent. Ricoeur's view is of tradition in relationship to the text and its system hence his focus is linguistics not history. Nevertheless, the principle he outlines holds for historicity as well. Tradition is the transmission of beliefs and opinions that have reached and impacted the author, and these beliefs then extend from the author to the interpreter. The verbal description of belief supplies the content of the tradition. In the case of sacred text it not only influences but also shapes the authorial intent and, consequently, directly shapes the author's composition. This belief is received and transmitted by both the author and the interpreter. If the interpreters do not place themselves within that community tradition, for the purposes of interpretation, then they do not receive the transmitted "community knowledge." Therefore, if interpreters do not receive the "community knowledge," they cannot interpret the text's message.

Fee's observation concerning the biblical text (i.e., that interpretation happens within the Christian community, the heritage of which goes back to the apostolic times) agrees in principle with Ricoeur's philosophical observation.[134] The opening line of Matthew's Gospel shows that this tradition itself builds on a tradition that stretches back to the times of Abraham and, hence, the end of the primal history (Matt 1:1). The tradition in which it stands is the Judeo-Christian heritage. The beginning of John's Gospel has echoes of the primal history, with its similarities to the beginnings

---

132. Fee, *Gospel and Spirit*, 69.
133. Ricoeur, *Conflict of Interpretations*, 27. (Italics original.)
134. Fee, *Gospel and Spirit*, 69.

of Genesis in the LXX.[135] It is in the process of interpretation within the tradition that this tradition itself remains living within the community. The writer of the biblical text stands in a tradition that represents itself as going back to the creation of humanity. The writers and readers of the text understand themselves to stand in this tradition as they write and read respectively, and, as Ricoeur has observed, their respective tasks remain in that tradition. They work from it and they work to it. This cannot be ignored in the hermeneutical process.

The interpreter within the community of faith and the interpreter outside the community are dealing with the same text. As was suggested previously, the authoritative meaning of a text can undergo degrees of change in differing interpreters' contexts and these two situations clearly represent differing interpreters' contexts. Interpreters who place themselves outside the community of faith can, with the qualification of consideration of the faith of the author, deal with the pursuit of "what did it mean" but not with the pursuit of the issue of "what does it mean." The determinative factor is the approach to the nonrational aspect of the text, not the rational aspect of the text.

Fee points out that the exegetes from outside the community of faith who do not hold the belief themselves cannot deny or ignore the belief of the authors of the text.[136] The exegete can obtain and know the information; but, as was observed previously, understanding is assimilation into a person's presuppositional world, and in the biblical text this is the presuppositional world of the believing community.[137] In the case of belief, to understand is to hold the belief. Unbelief is an absence of belief due to a decision not to acquire belief, that is, a decision not to give assent to the propostion of belief. The only other option, which is to be agnostic, is by definition "to not know," hence, on the one hand, to not have acquired the nonrational knowledge of belief, yet on the other to not have rejected the proposition and acquired the nonrational knowledge of unbelief. The issue of hermeneutics is not the validity or otherwise of the position taken by the interpreter or author, as validity is a matter of perspective.

The preceding discussion of the category of nonrational knowledge shows that nonrational knowledge is not communicated through rational means, that is, rational methodologies. Its very nature places it in a different category of knowledge to rational knowledge. However, as has been noted, all authorial communication through written text happens through language and is expressed in words. Hence, all knowledge is subject to verbal description. The verbal description of nonrational knowledge is found in the tradition of the community. In the area of belief knowledge (i.e., faith), a person standing in the flow of tradition acquires the community impartation of nonrational knowledge. This verbal description is available to interpreters, as a context and understanding of belief, in the life of the community and individual, and in

---

135. Carson, *Gospel According to John*, 113. Carson highlights the clear identification with the creation.

136. Fee, *Gospel and Spirit*, 27.

137. Fee, *Listening to the Spirit*, 15.

the interpretation of texts standing in that tradition. In the orthodox Christian community this mentoring tradition is seen as personified in the Holy Spirit. However, as noted by Stendhal, for an interpreter to deal with the "meant" of the author, it is not necessary that the interpreter take any belief position on this personification.[138] The impact and effect is detectable and can be evaluated in the tradition of the community. If the interpreter wishes to address the contemporary meaning of the biblical text, such efforts will entail dealing with belief in the person and work of the Holy Spirit.[139]

Some Scriptural Illustrations of *Nonrational* Knowledge

It has been proposed in this work that belief can be seen in the biblical account to have been an attribute of the created human being; that is, it is a "given" of human being. A brief outline of this implication in Scripture will show a basic understanding at this point. In Rom 4:3, in the midst of a discussion concerning being justified by faith, the Scriptural evidence Paul quotes is Gen 15:6 where it is recorded that Abraham believed God and this was imputed to him with a view to righteousness. Paul notes that this divine imputation of righteousness bestowed due to Abraham's belief predates circumcision, law, and covenant with the nation and so transcends them as the means of righteousness. The act of circumcision was conducted with a faith Abraham already had (Rom 4:11), which by inference stems from the declaration recorded in Gen 15:6. It is not reported that God gave Abraham belief as an endowment at that moment, what is recorded is that God responded to the operation of belief by imputing righteousness. In fact there is no record of endowing or causing belief; there is only the recording of its operation. In this passage the faculty of belief is a given. The issue is what a person does with that faculty.

The Scripture in Heb 11:3 declares that it is by faith that we can understand or discern that the ages were structured and made to function by the word of God. The echoes of Genesis certainly link "ages" with the concept of the creation of the universe. Yet the phrase, "By faith we understand that the worlds were framed by the word of God" can also be referring to the eras of human existence. The same formation of the dative case for both "faith" and "word" is unqualified, which indicates that they are functioning in a similar way in terms of impersonal agency; hence, the statement "by faith . . . by word . . . " seems sound. The verb "to know" or "to discern" is present active indicative, indicating being in a state of knowing. Therefore, either the appeal is seen to be to a form of "leap of faith" mentality, or faith that results in a knowability, hence indicating that because of belief in God a person can believe the statement in the sense of acceptance without really understanding it. Conversely, the statement can also infer that through the agency of belief, a person gains specific knowledge (i.e., faith), which

---

138. Stendhal, "Biblical Theology, Contemporary," 422.
139. Fee, *Listening to the Spirit*, 14.

results in an understanding that this universe and its eons are creations of God. In this case assent to this statement becomes the basis of nonrational objective reason.

The passage Rom 10:8–17 certainly suggests that faith is a knowledge that can be given verbal description (i.e., the word of God) and is passed on, or transmitted, in community. In Rom 10:17 the article precedes the word *faith*, and so this indicates that it is the Christian faith that is transmitted, not faith as an object in itself (i.e., it is "the faith" that comes through hearing not the concept of faith). The events recorded in Acts 3:1–16, on the healing of a lame man, portray immediate faith knowledge that results in the healing.[140] In another interesting narrative in Acts 14:8–11, on another case of a lame man being healed, the Scripture declares that Paul perceived in the man himself faith to be healed. This was an immediate knowledge the man received whilst listening to Paul communicate. It is also significant that Paul could perceive the presence of this knowledge in the man. If the knowledge is indeed nonrational and is transmitted and acquired only this way, it would follow that only a person having belief in that tradition would perceive this knowledge, yet this is not a prerequisite to describe it.

The Scripture notes that Jesus declared of himself that he was "the truth" (John 14:6). This passage does not record him as declaring he was "the information" or "the set of facts." He asserts himself to be the truth, and as such truth is living and dynamic, not conceptual and static. The worldview of people consists of their presuppositions of what is real and true.[141] Truth is the context into which information fits to make it real and living. The *nonrational* category of knowledge provides the context for understanding of the category of *rational* knowledge.

The Impact of *Nonrational* Knowledge on Understanding

Every interpreter in approaching the text comes to the material "with interpretive frameworks already in place."[142] The Christian faith, expressed in its tradition, cannot be excluded from the interpretive process in dealing with texts because other "faiths" are not excluded, (e.g., modernity, empiricism, and naturalism).[143] Therefore, interpreters, holding a faith other than that of the authors of texts, should seek to understand and make accommodation for their own prejudices.[144] Whilst they should acknowledge that an unbiased stance is not possible, Marshall has noted—referred to previously—that this need not be over exaggerated in terms of an interpreter's ability

---

140. The implication is that this knowledge is in Peter, since at no time is the lame man recorded as having had that knowledge until healed.

141. See a later section in chapter 4, (a) Connecting Presuppositional Worlds, and Charles Kraft's concepts on worldview.

142. Vanhoozer, *First Theology*, 160.

143. Ibid.

144. Stanton, "Presuppositions in New Testament Criticism," 62.

to undertake the task. The interpreter, from outside the community of faith, cannot exclude the faith of the author and its impact on what he had written in understanding his message and must, consequently, allow this faith to be the "glasses" he wears in the interpretive task.

Fee states that the aim of all true biblical exegesis is spirituality.[145] Only when exegesis is done in this way is it consistent with the intent of the text.[146] Bultmann recognized that interpretation involves a presupposition of vital interest of the interpreter for the subject matter of the text. As a result the interpreter investigates the text in a purposive manner.[147] The biblical text is addressing itself to the spirituality of the interpreter, and only when the interpreter investigates the text from the perspective of the believing community is the interpreter positioned to be consistent with the intent of the text.

(c) The Creative Facility of Speech: The "Given" of Human Being

The "givens" of the human condition, from which the authors of the scriptural text present their composition, can in part be inferred from the primal history of the book of Genesis in chapters 1 through 11. Two aspects of the biblical text in the primal history of Genesis 1–11 stand out on this subject. First, there is no record of humanity learning how to communicate; and even the facility of communication by speech is a given in the biblical text. These are seemingly divine endowments and are therefore in the biblical view "givens" of the being of humanity. Second, understanding itself appears to be an inherent ability. There is no record of either humanity being taught to understand or having difficulty with understanding either the divine or the human. Both the human-human and divine-human dialogues occur naturally and immediately. The human state appears to naturally tend to understanding. Interestingly, it is misunderstanding that is the result of divine intervention (see Gen 11:1–9); the natural human condition is apparently that of understanding. The desire for understanding will always seek the resolution of misunderstanding.

Friedrich Schleiermacher, considered by many as the father of modern hermeneutics, is credited with developing the concept of General Hermeneutics in proposing a basic set of guidelines for all texts.[148] His basis was the assumption of the occurrence of misunderstanding and a consequent seeking of understanding.[149] Schleiermacher reasoned that there must be some point of contact between the interpreter and the text. However, for hermeneutics to be necessary there must also be

---

145. Fee, *Listening to the Spirit*, 5.
146. Ibid.
147. Bultmann, "Problem of Hermeneutics," 119.
148. Klemm, "Introduction to Schleiermacher's Address," 56.
149. Ibid.

some strangeness, and with this strangeness misunderstanding becomes possible.[150] Hermeneutics begins here and is the process that removes this strangeness by eliminating the misunderstanding.

In this scenario, as in the biblical narrative, the effort toward understanding is a result of the presence of misunderstanding. The question of understanding is not raised until the situation of misunderstanding occurs. In Acts 17:26 Paul makes the observation, it must be assumed on the basis of the Genesis record, that God made all humanity from one person. This, coupled with the primal history of Genesis 1 to 11, leads to the conclusion that in the biblical mindset all subsequent languages developed from that one event in the primal history.

Ong notes that in natural languages rules of grammar are a secondary development because a language is first spoken and then is abstracted to be stated and used in literacy.[151] The biblical record, showing language to be a given of the created state as noted previously, supports this view. This implies that language as a formal system is secondary, and that speech is primary in language development. Language is learned in practice in its usage rather than in theory on the basis of its rules of grammar. A natural affinity to be able to speak to another person, and hence communicate, would be expected on the basis of the biblical record that all languages develop from the one common event.

This narrative section of the Genesis record of the primal history provides the answer to the question concerning how and why we have different cultures, or people groups, and different languages, if all humanity descends from one person.[152] Morgenstern relates ancient rabbinic tales that the original singular language was Hebrew, spoken by God, angels, and humanity.[153] Morgenstern, along with many commentators, sees the real purpose of the Genesis narrative is to recount the assertion of the fallen nature in pride. Also in common with other commentators, such as Umberto Cassuto, he takes note that this final narrative of the primal history links directly to the Abrahamic narrative.[154] God chooses one people and separates them out to retain that one language, so confounding the language of the rest of humanity.[155] If this view was taken, then all languages are developed from that one language, and language itself is the "given."

---

150. Schleiermacher, "Academy Addresses of 1829," 65. He sees no need for hermeneutics when (a) something is totally foreign, since hermeneutics is then not possible; and (b) something is devoid of strangeness, since hermeneutics in this case is not necessary because there is nothing strange to remove.
151. Ong, *Orality and Literacy*, 7.
152. Morgenstern, *Book of Genesis*, 86.
153. Ibid.
154. Cassuto, *Commentary on the Book of Genesis*, 225.
155. Morgenstern, *Book of Genesis*, 87.

Cassuto argues a strong case that what is meant in Gen 11:1 is that humanity had one language at this time, which they all spoke.[156] The account of nations in Genesis 10 suggests that humanity already possessed different languages, if the text is examined sequentially from Genesis chapter 10 to chapter 11. However, the placement of chapter 10 can be seen to be a deliberate "dischronologization" with respect to Genesis 11.[157] Hamilton also offers an alternate explanation that the one language was a "lingua franca" for the different language groups.[158] If so, there is a linguistic sequential nature to the text.[159] The confusion of languages results from the loss of the "lingua franca," and hence there is a loss of communication capability.[160] In this situation differing languages is not a development from confounding a single language, but the loss of a single language.

It would seem logical that if all humanity descended from one person, then there would exist a time when all people spoke a single language. However, the phenomenon of subculturation, with its development of unique use of language, and the development of colloquialisms, can occur fairly rapidly. This would lend credence to Hamilton's suggestion, particularly if taken over a long period of time. Although "dischronologization" would seem to be the most likely explanation of the nature of the text, the explanation of Hamilton is not without merit. The important point is that proceeding on the idea that a "given" of humanity is a single unique language is fraught with problems. For example, there is no evidence that any language tends to possess an integrity that maintains its purity for communication. In fact all languages do tend to subculturation, inflation (in words, idioms, phrases, and so on) and syncretism (even with other languages), all of which lead to change in the language, but all of which also contribute to an adapability of language to the human situation.

The Genesis narrative illustrates the fact that language can be tenuous and can undergo rapid change. The constant is the facility of speech, or an ability to use a language. Language is a medium used in speech for communication. Language is developed for the purpose of communication and is highly adaptable by a person for the purpose of communication. The same or similar symbols of a language can have radically different meanings in different people groups.[161] Consequently, language is used to communicate and is not the repository of meaning, which would have to be considered if language was a "given" of humanity. It is the facility of speech that is a "given" of humanity. The importance of the confounding of languages is the stimulus of an awareness of misunderstanding and a need for understanding.

156. Cassuto, *Commentary on the Book of Genesis*, 239.
157. Hamilton, *Book of Genesis*, 347, 350.
158. Ibid., 350.
159. Ibid.
160. Ibid., 355.
161. Nida, *Message and Mission*, 1.

This is the original "given," that is, the facility of the ability for communication through speaking a language. The reader is presented in Gen 11:1 with a record that states that the whole of humanity had at least a lingua franca, if not a single language, at that time. In Schleiermacher's view it is differences of language that directly raise the issue of misunderstanding. In the biblical view of human history the concept of hermeneutics arising due to variety of languages, leading to understanding as the resolving of misunderstanding, would not occur in the primal situation. It is the confounding of languages that makes humanity aware of misunderstanding and provides the impetus for seeking understanding.

This raises the question of what understanding would mean prior to this confounding of language leading to languages. In the silence of Scripture, as noted previously, being in a state of understanding appears to be a natural state of humanity. When there is no difference there is no need of resolution of difference. The book of Proverbs contains many exhortations concerning *understanding*; and with the exhortation to get wisdom (Prov 4:7), there is a more urgent exhortation to get *understanding*. Here the implication is not that of misunderstanding but of not knowing, of not being in possession of the knowledge of what is wisdom.

Understanding is the result of the desire to know, but requires the presentation to the individual that he or she is in a place of *not knowing*. The concept of misunderstanding also places the individual in a place of a realization of not knowing, hence in misunderstanding there is also a desire to know; otherwise, an individual would not engage in the process of interpretation in order to understand. However, understanding is not just being in possession of information but is the appropriation of information into the presuppositional world of a person. Even where the knowledge understood is not accepted as true, this itself becomes part of the presuppositional world of a person.

The author of a composition seeks to connect with the *given* of a person that he or she will naturally seek to understand. If the reader believes that he or she already knows and understands what the author is saying, then there is a tendency to stop reading or gloss over the composition with only cursory reading. Hence, the author, to stimulate the desire to know, must create within a reader a sense of not knowing, and, may even deliberately use misunderstanding as a tool. The author seeks to connect with a reader's tendency toward immediate acquisition of knowledge to stimulate the desire to know.

The composition, as a direct creation as written text, employs rules of grammar and the abstraction of language as part of the means of communication; that is, they form part of its ability to "speak." The author can employ verbal descriptions since, as noted, all three categories of knowledge can be verbally described. Understanding requires that the reader/interpreter develop direct affinity and apprehension of all these categories in interpretation. However, current methodology cannot discern or detect, in the text, the categories of *arational* or *nonrational* knowledge. The existence of these categories can be recognized but generally are not considered significant in the process of interpretation due to this problem. Restriction of meaning to methodological fruits could result in the loss of these categories of knowledge; at the very least it will result in a minimizing of the impact of these categories of knowledge.

An illustration can be seen in the love between a parent and child. Love itself is intuitive: a person can reason why he or she loves but cannot acquire love by a process of reasoning. Even before verbal communication via language can occur, a parent can "know" that he or she is loved by the child; and, conversely, the child can "know" he or she is loved by the parent. The knowledge is acquired arationally and doesn't require objective description before its acquisition; nor is it imparted through objective description. An author incorporating this into a composition can describe the love but relies on the reader's experience for immediacy of understanding of that love.

3 The Conundrum and Paradox

A Way Forward

Part 2: The Issue of Authorial Intent

Introduction

THE PREVIOUS CHAPTER BEGAN the investigation of five issues that have bearing on the concepts of the author's intention, the nature of the text, and the issue of interpretive meaning. Following the basic format of discourse as *someone* said *something* to *someone*, it was noted that in the case of written discourse the interpreter begins not with *the someone* who said something but *the something* that was said. The format of discourse in this case becomes essentially *something* was said to *someone* by *someone*. The previous chapter therefore examined the first three issues, which concerned *the something* said and *the someone* to whom it was said—the audience.

This chapter looks at the final two issues that relate to *the someone* who said *something*. The issue of authorial intention is central to this investigation. Authorial intent is implied by the very nature of the composition, and in the remaining two proposals under consideration it stands as a logical aspect, though difficult to define and evaluate. These final proposals specifically focus on the aspect authorial intent as related to the entity of the composition. The first of these examines the very nature of the authorial intent in relationship to the text, and the second examines the nature of the authorial intent in the interpretive event.

The Nature of the Authorial Intent: An Antecedent

An antecedent is that which exists before and logically precedes something. Authors have meaning they wish to communicate and intentionally form an understanding of that meaning that is then communicated. Consequently, the authorial intent stands as the antecedent and precursor of the written text.

(a) The Association with Composition

Vanhoozer's approach shows his tendency to consider authorial intent and meaning as interchangeable. He asserts that "Meaning is independent of our attempts to interpret it."[1] Thus, he separates the concept of meaning as normative, being the author's meaning, from understanding as descriptive, which is something that happens to interpreters.[2] This presents *meaning* as an ideality independent of a consciousness, although essentially it would seem that he simply wishes to separate authorial meaning from reader/interpreter meaning, due to his or her understanding. However, the issue remains as to the recoverability of authorial meaning as an absolute value and as a knowable criterion. Further, what must be examined is whether authorial meaning equates with authorial intent.

It is proposed that the term *authorial meaning* would indeed relate to an incidence of text, as part—in the concept of fragment—of a composition in both its literary context and that of its intended audience. However, the term *authorial intent* is proposed to relate to the composition, or work, as a whole. This distinction between a composition and an incidence of text is important. It is the distinction between an entity and a disconnected fragment of that entity, the context of which is the composition. The composition is a distinct entity, which is an issue that will be developed in this book, the idea of which is a development different from that of orality.

Thiselton has noted the work of Walter Ong and others in describing a difference between orality and textuality.[3] A textual hermeneutic raises different hermeneutical dynamics to that of an oral hermeneutic, and this should be considered in the treatment of texts.[4] Ricoeur has asserted that written text is a special case of discourse and, in fact, is the fulfillment of discourse.[5] In the written text the bearer of the message is now a nonhuman voice. Ricoeur asserts "material marks" now convey the message.[6] Discourse can refer to both text and conversation or dialogue. However,

---

1. Vanhoozer, *Is There a Meaning*, 11. This forms part of his preface.
2. Vanhoozer, "Discourse on Matter," 6.
3. Thiselton, *New Horizons*, 56.
4. Ibid.
5. Ricoeur, *Interpretation Theory*, 25.
6. Ibid.

if there is a hermeneutical distinction between textuality and orality, then caution is needed in using the word *dialogue* when specifying its referent.

Writing, and hence textuality, is a secondary modeling system that is dependent on a primary system of spoken language.[7] Orality exists without textuality, but the reverse is not true because textuality comes into existence out of orality.[8] However, Ong also states that "abstractly sequential, classificatory, explanatory examination of phenomena or of stated truths is impossible without writing and reading."[9] The creation of the text leads to the concept of study, because primarily oral cultures don't "study," although they do have extensive methods of learning, and learn and possess great depths of wisdom.[10] Therefore, the written occasion of discourse directly into text (i.e., the composition) should be handled differently than the situation of oral discourse.

Textuality begins as transcription of oral discourse and then moves to the idea of composition.[11] Ong states it is a false assumption that oral verbalization is essentially the same as written verbalization.[12] Consequently, it seems valid to assert that it would be wrong to hermeneutically treat a composition as though it was simply a dialogue between the author and the intended audience. The hermeneutics of textuality invite a different dynamic to those of an oral hermeneutic.[13] The composition contains more than the transcription of propositional information. Ong states that to "make yourself clear without gesture, without facial expression, without intonation, without a real hearer, you have to foresee circumspectly all possible meanings a statement may have for any possible reader in any possible situation, and you have to make your language work so as to come clear all by itself, with no existential context."[14]

Further, the composition requires that the writer fictionalize the intended audience and fictionalize a mood for the context of the text.[15] In the same way the reader must fictionalize the author.[16] The very word *composition* suggests the incorporation of the presuppositional world of the composer (author) in the creation of the text. The reader/interpreter must first imagine, and then directly deal with, this world of the text as a creation from the world of the author.

---

7. Ong, *Orality and Literacy*, 8.
8. Ibid.
9. Ibid.
10. Ibid., 9.
11. Ibid., 10.
12. Ibid.
13. Thiselton, *Two Horizons*, 56.
14. Ong, *Orality and Literacy*, 104.
15. Ibid., 102. Ong is not denying a real intended audience, but that for the purposes of writing the composition the writer creates a fictional audience in dialogue at the time of writing. This audience exists in the domain of the imagination of the writer.
16. Ibid.

Thiselton notes that Ricoeur's contention for the autonomy of the text is based on his observation that the reader is absent in the writing and the author is absent in the reading.[17] Textuality, with the concept of author and reader, replaces the situation of dialogue where the communicator connects with the ear of the listener.[18] Ricoeur also recognizes this distinction in his philosophy, observing that the relationship "writing-reading" is not a case of the relationship "speaking-hearing."[19] In the case of text the author seeks to communicate with the reader who is not present. The reader then seeks to understand the communication of an author who is not present. In the situation of oral communication, elements are present that are not present in the transcription process, as Ong noted in the difference between orality and textuality. Hence, textuality, in communicating with the reader, requires composition for revelation of the elements that are not present in transcription. This composition is related to the text that is used by an interpreter in understanding the author's communication.

Consider the following example using initially the transcription of a statement: "You are to be congratulated on your realization of the truth presented before you." The locution can be seen to perform the illocutionary act of bestowing congratulations. However, if it were noted that the situation was political debate, and the statement was made in a derisive tone, the intent would be sarcasm. Conversely, if it were noted that the situation was a courtroom and the statement was made in the dismissal of a jury after a trial, and, further, that tone was warm and respectful, then the intent would indeed be congratulations. The same locution performs differing illocutions, and only composition seeking to paint the whole picture in words can enable the reader, absent to the dialogue, to see what the author of the text is saying and doing in his or her locution. This desire to communicate an understanding is the birthing of authorial intent, and it is the composition that fulfills the authorial intent.

In this example there are three "scenarios" of potential authorship. First, the speaker can become the author to explain to another party what took place. Second, the object of the comment could become an author for the same purposes. Third, a witness or participant could become an author to describe to a third party how the witness saw the events. All three scenarios could conceivably supply differing compositions because, in each case, the writer of the composition is giving the view from his or her presuppositional world. This is simply what Gadamer is taking note of in his observations. The composition is written within the presuppositions of the author. The "pastness" of the events compounds this situation when the author is historically distant from the events. In each case the purpose of the composition is to enable the reader to see the view from the author's presuppositional world concerning the events described. Once the text becomes an historic text, the issue becomes one of historical meaning.

17. Thiselton, *Two Horizons*, 56.
18. Ibid.
19. Ricoeur, *Interpretation Theory*, 29.

(b) Authorial Intent and Authorial Meaning: A Nuance of Difference

Vanhoozer asserts that the ultimate purpose of interpretation is to "reconstruct the single correct meaning of the text,"[20] where this single correct meaning is the author's meaning.[21] He states, and thereby defines, interpretation as being "the quest for meaning, that is, the author's intended message."[22] This statement implies that, in his view, authorial meaning equates with authorial intention. Vanhoozer considers the book to be the context of the text and as such a closed unit, enclosed by the will of the author.[23] However, it often seems that each incident of text is an encapsulation of authorial intent. When discussing the individual text, his reference is also authorial intent. If this is the case, then Vanhoozer's inherent assumption is that every instance of the text in the composition is a direct "enfleshing" of the authorial intent.

However, it is proposed that there is a nuance of difference between authorial intent and authorial meaning that is significant. Authorial intention is what the reader should understand from the communication. Authorial meaning is the inscripturation of that resolve that is the entity of the text, and as such includes the explanation and development of that intention. Authorial meaning, in regard to a text as a fragment of a composition, not only relates to the authorial intent but also to the part that the text as a fragment of the composition plays in its immediate setting. Consequently, authorial meaning does relate directly to the text; and further, authorial intention lies behind the authorial meaning and acts as its antecedent. In this situation, authorial meaning does remain attached to the text, but authorial intent does not have to be viewed as attached to the text. Authorial intent is the referent of the text. Yet it is also true that, in the formation of the text, there must be associated with the text the means of interacting with the operational effects of this authorial intent.

Thiselton notes that, in his view, authorial intent "*is better understood adverbially: to write with an intention is to write in a way that is directed towards a goal.*"[24] This concept highlights intention as the modifier or qualifier of that goal, or the doing of the author. Authorial intent relates to "what" the author has intentionally done. The focus on what has been done when taking the adverbial view of authorial intent moves away from the idea of the active agent whose intention was involved, toward the idea of what was done, and hence further away from the issue of meaning, since meaning is an act of persons. An interpreter can speculate about the author's meaning, but the meaning will be the interpreter's not the author's. The direction of reference has moved away from the agent and his or her intention. An alternate view to the

---

20. Vanhoozer, *Is Tthere a Meaning*, 76.

21. Ibid., 75.

22. Ibid., 74.

23. Ibid., 104. He states concerning the book, "It is a totality, a structured whole with thematic coherence—ideological 'glue.' Books are 'closed,' or rather enclosed, by the author's will. Symbolized by a book's binding."

24. Thiselton, *New Horizons*, 560. (Italics original.)

adverbial understanding of *intention* is an important development that will be explored in later chapters of this work.

The concept of the search for authorial intent, in this adverbial view, would be irrelevant since the existence of the text would be the authorial intent. This view would lend credence to an aspect of the intentional fallacy, proposed by Wimsatt and Beardsley, since if the text is the authorial intent successfully communicated by the author, then there is no need to look for it.[25] As Wimsatt and Beardsley observe, if the author did not successfully communicate his or her intention, then there is nowhere else to go looking other than the text.[26] In Thiselton's concept an interpreter would need to speak about the authorial goal. Doing so simply shifts the search but doesn't change the dynamics or solve the problem.

If instead of being seen adverbially authorial intent is seen as a noun, then the intent of the author is seen as the subject matter (the "about" or *Sache*[27]), which is what seems to be Vanhoozer's understanding.[28] What is better considered adverbially is the authorial meaning as modifier or qualifier of the authorial intent. This meaning, associated with the text, is attached to the text and, subsequently, linguistics will be critical in perceiving it. As a modifier or qualifier of the authorial intent, the authorial meaning is a means of dealing with the authorial intent. Thiselton's own observation that a person can do the methodology and still not understand the text, thus showing the need to incorporate other areas such as philosophical description, itself points to the folly of restriction to linguistics.[29]

Vanhoozer defines the text of the composition as a *"communicative act of a communicative agent fixed by writing."*[30] The word "fixed" suggests that this essentially corresponds to Stendhal's "meant" of the author.[31] Vanhoozer does not seem to observe the clear distinction between the "what it meant," as a primary task, and "what it means," as a secondary task, that Stendhal does. Vanhoozer does note that once an author has enacted his or her communication, it is seen as *"meaning accomplished."*[32]

25. Wimsatt, *Verbal Icon*, 2.

26. Ibid.

27. The German term *Sache* is prominent in the work of Gadamer, having the lexical idea of thing, matter, or subject and thereby provides a good scope for usage as the idea of "the saying of the discourse," which is the way in which Gadamer has developed it.

28. Vanhoozer, "Discourse on Matter," 7.

29. Thiselton, *Two Horizons*, 5.

30. Vanhoozer, *Is There a Meaning*, 225. (Italics original.)

31. Stendhal, "Biblical Theology, Contemporary," 422. The historical "what it meant" is found using methodology to discover "what these words meant when uttered or written."

32. Vanhoozer, *Is There a Meaning*, 262. (Italics original.) Vanhoozer is a strong advocate of the grammatico-historical method; the issue discussed concerns a recognized distinction between the tasks, or it implies that he tends more to advocate "what it meant" equals "what it means." He does make a distinction between theological aims (perhaps hermeneutics) and the norm of the authors meaning. However, this still does not show a distinction in the two aspects. See also Vanhoozer, *First Theology*, 276–77.

Consequently, Vanhoozer's reference is primarily to the meaning of the fixed written text. If the nuance of difference is not maintained between authorial intent and authorial meaning, then authorial intent is tied to linguistics, being either attached to or contained within, the text. This is essentially a structuralist point of view.

Stendhal notes that it is widely held that there is no language into which the Bible cannot be translated.[33] Caird notes that the act of translating itself cannot be successful if the translator simply seeks transference of one language into another. The translator must also transfer thought forms and presuppositions.[34] Consequently, every act of translation must involve some interpretation, which Stendhal does recognize, because he notes that every great translation is a creative effort for this very reason.[35] Stendhal also acknowledges this important aspect (i.e., of transference of thought patterns) as one of interpretation by theologians in seeking the "what it means" of the text.[36] Therefore, also in pursuing the "meant" of a text the limitations of linguistics should be recognized.

However, what is more strongly implied is that the moment an interpreter begins to move away from "what it meant" he or she is moving into an area of the referent of the text. The authorial meaning, as the value of "what it meant," is a fixed value of the authorial intent at a particular point in time; that is, in its historical setting. Consequently, maintaining the nuance of difference is an important distinction; because when this is maintained, the authorial intent is that which can be translated into other languages and historical situations. The authorial meaning is the authorial intent for a particular audience in a particular situation. It is therefore a relative value of the authorial intent; it is relative to that audience and point in time. The authorial intent, being the antecedent of the authorial meaning, is that which is capable of transcending the situatedness.

An illustration of this need to consider a difference in authorial intent and authorial meaning can be seen in the Gospel of John. In John 20:30–31 the author seemingly sets out the broad intention of his composition. In this text the author reveals his reason the text came into being as a composition. The author composed a selective narrative of the acts that Jesus did, deliberately including some and deliberately excluding others, declaring about the ones he chose that "these are written that you may believe that Jesus is the Christ, the Son of God, and that believing you may have life in His name." This is the author's controlling thought behind the text and acts essentially as the antecedent of the text. It has influenced which narratives have been selected and clearly has shaped the handling of those narratives in the composition. The authorial meaning in the individual text is directing the reader toward this authorial intent. The authorial intent can be fulfilled without the absolute value of "what it meant" and

---

33. Stendhal, "Biblical Theology, Contemporary," 427.
34. Caird, *Language and Imagery of the Bible*, 2.
35. Stendhal, "Biblical Theology, Contemporary," 427.
36. Ibid.

even with an imprecise value of authorial meaning in some texts that are part of the composition.

Vanhoozer does discuss this aspect in John but argues that the writer's desire to elicit belief is a perlocutionary effect. As such it should not be considered as part of the communicative action of the author.[37] A lot of Vanhoozer's development of the concept of relating authorial intention to the illocutionary act is developed on the basis of John Austin and John Searle's approach to speech-act theory.[38] Yet Vanhoozer notes that Austin himself was not convinced that the perlocutionary effects are so easily separated from the illocutionary act.[39] Can it be stated that if a person reads the gospel and does not subsequently develop belief in Jesus that this person will have either fulfilled or understood the authorial intention? Furthermore, if by "understanding" what was meant simply equates to understanding that the author believes this assertion, this is not the stated intention in the text. The verb "to believe" is second person aorist subjunctive, and as such the subject addressed in the statement is the reader. The author's intention is that the reader believes.

Western thought has sought to distinguish between knowledge and belief; knowledge is apprehended and tested by individuals for themselves and belief is that which the individual has "taken over" from the community.[40] Critical thought begins when an individual distrusts this community knowledge until proven for the individual himself.[41] Consequently, in this mindset, knowledge acts as adversary to belief and belief is therefore not considered knowledge.[42] Thiselton notes that in this setting the concept of community knowledge becomes essentially an oxymoron.[43]

However, the individual begins the search for knowledge with a preexisting "shared public world" that provides not only transmitted knowledge but shapes the quest for individual knowledge.[44] Without this shared knowledge, which also includes language, there is no foundation for individual investigation. Language itself provides resources without which the process cannot even begin.[45] What can be known about the world is mediated through language and is not known apart from language.[46] Consequently, belief is a form of knowledge that, although not arrived at after a process of reasoning on the basis of rational knowledge, is nevertheless a knowledge acquired in

---

37. Vanhoozer, *First Theology*, 179.
38. Vanhoozer, *Is There a Meaning*. 208–9.
39. Vanhoozer, *First Theology*, 185.
40. Thiselton, *Thiselton On Hermeneutics*, 701.
41. Ibid., 702.
42. Ibid.
43. Ibid.
44. Ibid., 703.
45. Ibid.
46. Vanhoozer, "World Well Staged? 21.

communication, as in Rom 10:17. If not acquired, the communication has failed in its intent. Hence, to understand the communication of John in his Gospel is to believe it.

Vanhoozer argues that authorial meaning, and hence intention, relates to understanding the author's communication and not the effect that has on the reader/interpreter.[47] It would seem from John 20:30–31 that the author's own communication is an intention of belief and subsequent life, and this is the controlling thought behind the composition; for the author, understanding equals belief. Each incident narrated in the gospel is a description of the incident that is given in such a way that it will contribute to the intent of the author. Authorial meaning, in the individual texts within the composition, will not only relate to the authorial intention but will also be relative to the incident narrated.

The perlocutionary effect is the effect on the reader of belief, not the act of believing. The reader who understands believes, and, consequently, this belief will have an impact on the reader's life. It is what the reader does about his or her belief that is the resultant effect that this belief has had upon that individual. The reader can choose not to retain the belief, or even disregard it in his or her life. In the Epistle of James the author makes an observation about a person who believes but disregards that belief in his or her everyday life (see Jas 1:22–25). A person shows the effect of the perlocutionary act in what he or she does about his or her belief. If a reader does not adjust his or her life and live according to the impact of that belief, then the faith, or act of belief, dies within that individual, (see Jas 2:17–18). Ricoeur notes that if an interpreter disregards the tradition in which the text stands (i.e., the belief that is its context, as is argued in this work), then that tradition dies in that interpretation.[48] In John's Gospel belief is understanding and not a perlocutionary act. The perlocutionary act is what is done about belief; obedience to belief is operational, or living, faith.

Ricoeur proposes that the perlocutionary act, which is performed by the reader, is less than intentional (on the part of the reader) and is the least communicable aspect of the speech act.[49] This is primarily because in this act the nonlinguistic has priority over the linguistic.[50] Nevertheless, the perlocutionary act can clearly fall within the authorial intent. In the case of belief, Jesus regards the adoption of belief as intentional on the part of the hearer (Mark 1:15).

A further difference between authorial intent and meaning can be illustrated in the development of a composition in the English language. In the English language a sentence should have one single idea, and a paragraph should develop one central thought. Each sentence within the paragraph, with its one central idea, is developing that one central thought; and each sentence is purposed to contribute to that one

---

47. Vanhoozer, *First Theology*: 180.

48. Ricoeur, *Conflict of Interpretations*, 27. In the case of the biblical text, if not all sacred text, the belief tradition is the history in which it stands.

49. Ricoeur, *Interpretation Theory*, 18.

50. Ibid.

central thought. The central thought is the intent, and the development of the sentences is the explanation of that thought. An author can employ different approaches to the central thought to help position the reader to "see" that central point. These approaches can work in unison, but they can also work individually. Consequently, there can be a degree of redundancy within the paragraph, so that the central thought is recoverable even if all the individual ideas in each of the sentences are not completely interpreted. In this example the intent of the author is to deliver an understanding of the central thought and not the precise meaning of each and every sentence.

Even in the case of a novel there is an observable difference between authorial intent and authorial meaning. The aim of the author of a novel is to entertain, and the author develops a story he or she believes will capture the attention of the reader and draw that reader into the story. This intent controls an authorial meaning in the text, but the authorial intent is to entertain and the authorial meaning is the act of entertaining. Similarly in advertising a product, the intent is that a person purchases the product. The intent is to purchase and the authorial meaning in the copy (i.e., the text) of the advertising is an act of persuasion to that end. In all probability, if the product is purchased, the author considers his or her intent fulfilled whether or not the purchaser correctly assigned meaning to every sentence of the text.

Therefore, it is proposed that the authorial intent concerns the "big picture" of the composition and guides the development of the texts that form the composition, and thereby acts as the antecedent of the individual text. Authorial intent is the influencing agent of the authorial meaning in the individual texts, but it is not identical to authorial meaning. The authorial meaning refers to the authorial intent and is the means by which the latter is made known. The authorial intent, rather than being discussed from the point of view of either attachment or detachment in relation to the text, should instead be viewed as the context of the text that allows the text as composition to address the *Sache*. Therefore, it is important to consider the individual text and its function within authorial meaning in revealing the authorial intent, which is the understood message.

THE NATURE OF AUTHORIAL INTENT IN THE INTERPRETATIVE EVENT

Thiselton proposes that in dealing with historic texts such as the Bible, two sets of variables must be brought into close proximity. These are the horizons of the interpreter and the text, which for Thiselton means working toward a fusion of these horizons. Indeed, this is the subject matter of his book *The Two Horizons*.[51] The fusion of horizons involves philosophical descriptions and categories. Thiselton agrees with the thought of Ludwig Wittgenstein that philosophy doesn't lead to propositions but

---

51. Thiselton, *Two Horizons*, 17.

functions at the level of clarifying propositions.[52] Thiselton also sees grammatico-historical methodology as indispensible in the horizon of the text.[53] Another important component in this fusion is the study of language itself, which is seen as central to hermeneutics and, by implication, to solving the hermeneutic problem.[54]

Ricoeur also considers these two horizons, which he titles as the "time of transmission" and the "time of interpretation."[55] Ricoeur's object is to seek a means of relating these two times and bringing them together, which is the same form of reasoning as Thiselton's fusion of horizons. He observes that there is no apparent connection between these two times that performs the task of allowing interpretation to enter "the time of tradition."[56] The time of tradition is the history of the text and hence its time of transmission. His proposition is to postulate the existence of a third time in the process of understanding, which he calls the "time of meaning itself."[57] He designates this as a "temporal charge, initially carried by the advent of meaning."[58] Evidently this is a transient appearance within the process that facilitates the intersection of the times of transmission and interpretation. The pattern for such a "charge" is found in the concept of the symbol, which Ricoeur has developed in other works.[59]

The symbol has the structure of double meaning, not only semantically but also nonsemantically; the nonsemantic aspect is a later development in Ricoeur's thinking.[60] The nonsemantic aspect develops because the symbol lacks autonomy and is bound by the differing disciplines that draw various lines of approach to the symbol (e.g., in religion, psychoanalysis, and so forth).[61] The issue is not the use of a particular symbol. Rather the very principle of the symbol itself is the issue. The nature of the symbol is that of double meaning, hence, its suitablility to conceptualize the temporal charge of meaning. The temporal charge of meaning operates with symbolic function.[62]

So as to allow this function to operate, Ricoeur establishes his view that there is an aspect of the total picture that is independent of the observer, or interpreter. He views linguistic studies as having established a reversal between system and historicism.[63] Historicism had been the primary approach to the task of interpretation. In

---

52. Ibid., 29. Thiselton sees that Wittgenstein's concept of philosophy was to open the eyes of the reader to see what was always there, 371.

53. Thiselton, *New Horizons*: 559.

54. Thiselton, *Two Horizons*: 369.

55. Ricoeur, *Conflict of Interpretations*, 27.

56. Ibid.

57. Ibid., 28.

58. Ibid.

59. Ibid.

60. Ricoeur, *Interpretation Theory*, 45.

61. Ibid., 58.

62. Ricoeur, *Conflict of Interpretations*, 36.

63. Ibid., 31.

historicism what comes first is the study of the past, which is now regarded as being established and so is not independent of the observer. However, in the system of linguistics, the author uses the system itself to communicate.[64] The system is evaluated synchronically not diachronically; it is the meaning of the usage of the semiotic tools at the time of usage that is important not their development diachronically.[65] The diachronic analysis is descriptive and philosophical. Further, this system is operating in the author at an unconscious level and hence is nonreflective and nonhistorical.[66] This is important, as what is established is a relationship of the observer and the system that is independent of the observer.[67]

The symbol has nonsemantic double meaning and, similarly, there is not only the linguistic but the nonlinguistic aspects that provide context to language, such as social systems that communicate (e.g., language, kinship, and so on).[68] Since these aspects operate independent of the observer, they are capable of functioning between the times of transmission and interpretation.[69] In symbolic function it would seem that Ricoeur proposes that this concept develops the temporal charge that allows intersection and hence understanding.

One important inherent assumption in this line of thought is that the author has unconsciously used the linguistic system. In fact, as previously noted, in the case of composition this may be at least incomplete if not incorrect. In the work of Ong it was observed that a composition is created directly into written form. Therefore, it would seem logical to assume that the author will have consciously thought through the use of the linguistic system to some degree. In the case of the oral situation, or spoken dialogue, it may seem reasonable to assume that the speaker, as an oral author, does unconsciously use the linguistic system. Conversely, in the case of composition it is reasonable to assume a conscious usage of the linguistic system. The author may even use that system itself to convey meaning. There is every reason to assume that to some degree the author, prior to writing, has indeed been reflective in considering the system of linguistics he or she will employ. Certainly, during the process of writing, this reflection will form a conscious part of the author's thinking. In this case the linguistic system is not a neutral medium of conveyance of communication but an active integral part of the author's message.

The concept that the linguistic system is independent of both author and interpreter is an innovative approach. On the surface this would indeed seem to be the

64. Ibid.

65. Ibid., 32.

66. Ibid., 33. It can only be assumed that his thought is that this aspect is independent of the author since it is nonreflective and nonhistorical.

67. Ibid., 34.

68. Ibid., 36. Ricoeur is highlighting the fact that language is not just word meanings but carries cultural factors that communicate in the verbalization of a language.

69. Ibid.

case, since the observer cannot change the system that the author used. However, the observer observes from within a linguistic system, and it also would seem simplistic to assume that the system from within which the observer observes is not to some degree impinging on the system they observe. It is also reasonable to assume that the observer's observation will be undertaken with a consciousness of his or her own system.

Ricoeur's viewpoint, taken overall, seems to propose another way of stating the grammatico-historical approach. The semantic moment of the system (the "grammatico" component) is examined first synchronically, and then the nonsemantic moment (the "historical" component) is examined diachronically. The synchronic is science and the diachronic is description. This analysis may seem overly simplistic but does broadly show the issues identified by Ricoeur. The difference between Ricoeur and the evangelical approach is the method of approach. In Ricoeur it is through the text and its properties as text but not as composition, since no value is given to the authorial intent. The evangelical approach is the text as created by an authorial intent, therefore having historical particularity that is part of the science.

In the work of Ricoeur the written text escapes the horizon of the author.[70] In his thought, authorial intention may be impossible to attain; and even if attainable it may be useless, or even a hindrance, to interpretation.[71] The text carves out its own niche by severing itself from the authorial intent.[72] The text consequently, in this reasoning, becomes autonomous with respect to its creator: the author.

Even the view that the reader is absent in the writing and the author absent in the reading, as noted by Ricoeur, should be qualified. The statement is on the surface temporally true and really just a logical observation. However, it is not philosophically true. The author of a text has an intent he or she wishes to convey to an intended audience, and the concept of that audience shapes the composition. It is not the intent that is shaped by the audience but the communication of that intent, that is, the composition. The author is not just communicating, he or she is communicating to someone. Furthermore, the author is communicating a specific something not just anything.[73] The occasional nature of epistles is beyond dispute.[74] The occasion is the reason the author wrote the text, and by extension it can be said that there is a reason in all texts that occasions the author to write. The authorial intent is what he or she intended to do in response to the occasion. This leads to the creation of the text.

Ong noted that reading a text results in the reader converting it to sound, either literally or figuratively, in the imagination.[75] This means that the reader carries on a dialogue even if in the imagination. This dialogue may not consciously be with the

---

70. Ricoeur, *Interpretation Theory*, 30.
71. Ibid., 76.
72. Ibid.
73. Vanhoozer, "Discourse on Matter," 25.
74. Fee, *Gospel and Spirit*, 23.
75. Ong, *Orality and Literacy*, 8.

author as such, but it is a dialogue with the authorial intent by virtue of the fact of dealing with the composition.[76] Therefore, the author is at least unconsciously, if not many times consciously, present in the reading. Philosophically this would mean that an imagined reader is present in the writing and an imagined author present in the reading. In such a situation the text is not autonomous and independent of the author; nor is the reader able to ignore the author in the reading. These detachments are temporal, not philosophical.

The basis of Ricoeur's interpretive dialogue is a dialogue with the autonomous text, hence his seeking of an answer, in the text, to the hermeneutic problem of relating time of transmission to the time of interpretation. His answer is to search for an element that fulfills that of symbol but is independent of the observer. The critical hinge to his argument, and perhaps his philosophy, is the autonomy of the text with respect to any authorial intent. Therefore, the text can be examined on its own merit as independent of the author. As noted previously, if the observations on the author and reader and their involvement in the writing and the reading are valid, this will undo the hinge of the concept. Nevertheless, the philosophical description of what answers the criteria for relating transmission and interpretation, as being found in the symbol, is illuminating.

(a) The Symbolic Function of the Authorial Intent

In consideration of the issue of a biblical text's relevance for the contemporary situation Fee declares, "nearly everything depends on the presuppositions of the interpreter."[77] In this contemporary postmodern concept, the emphasis has moved to the text and reader. The contemporary situation implicitly recognizes that the interpreter is indeed independent of the text and original audience, both linguistically and historically. They are therefore an unintended audience. Consequently, following the suggestion of Ricoeur, what is needed is a "particle" that is independent of the text (not "from" the text) and independent of the interpreter (again not "from" the interpreter; for if there is no connection, there is no possibility of hermeneutics). Accordingly, what is required of any proposed "particle" is that it itself is unchanged by the text and the interpreter. What is proposed is that the authorial intent fulfills the criterion of a "particle" that will allow the time of transmission to enter the time of interpretation.

---

76. Barthes, "Death of the Author." Barthes notes the occurrence of a speaking voice. However, his argument is against this being the author, 2. This is the basis of the title of this article, and this issue of the supposed "Death of the Author" will be addressed later in this book. It is sufficient to note at this time the concept of the speaking voice addressing the reader. It will be argued that this narrator, although not the person of the author, is the recognition of what will be identified as the *intentionedness* of the composition, which is due to the authorial intent, and that, as with all works of art, this "voice" speaking for the author has the ability to address and confront.

77. Fee, *Gospel and Spirit*, 27.

An important provision is that the authorial intent is seen as the antecedent of the text and not contained in the text.

Perception of the authorial intent as the antecedent of the text results in the following format of their relationship: *if the authorial intent (concerning the sache or matter) is, then the textual communication (resultant written text) is*. However, reversal of the situation is not possible. That is, their relationship cannot be formatted the following way "if the textual communication (resultant written text) is, then the authorial intent (concerning the *sache* or matter) is." This situation occurs because the result cannot be the condition, or cause, of the decision to act. The existence of the written text points to, or refers to, the existence of an authorial intent, but as its antecedent. Further, Vanhoozer notes that the author is the controlling presence that gives unity to the composition.[78] The author is not only the cause of the text, the "that it is," but also determines what it counts as, the "what it is."[79] Consequently, the authorial intent is the condition (protasis) under which the written text exists (apodosis). The text cannot be the condition under which the authorial intent exists.

The authorial intent is the precursor of the existence of the text and therefore represents the view of the author concerning the matter to be communicated. If the purpose of the communication is to see what the author saw concerning a matter, then the intent within authorial intent is disclosure of the matter to the reader/interpreter. The authorial intent as antecedent is not itself the matter to be disclosed but the means of disclosure. Therefore, it concerns an understanding from the author's perspective.

The ultimate purpose in hermeneutics concerns understanding a discourse that Vanhoozer also sets forth as "what someone says to someone about something."[80] In the postmodern situation advanced by Ricoeur, where both the author and intended audience are excluded, the form of this statement effectively becomes, "something is said." Yet the "someone" who communicates is the author and the "something," the communication, is in its saying determined by the authorial intention. The relationship between these two things is the "someone" to whom it was said. Consequently, the authorial intention is a set of presuppositions an author possesses that shapes his or her view on a matter, which the author has decided to communicate on a subject. Hence, using the term Vanhoozer borrows from Gadamer, it is the context of the *Sache*, or matter, to be communicated in which it must be viewed.[81]

The communication is not the mind of the author on everything; it is specifically the mind of the author on the *Sache*. The authorial intent exists before the text and is that to which the text refers. It is also the condition under which the text comes into existence and, as such, the authorial intent is the antecedent of the text. As the antecedent of the text, authorial intent itself is unchanged by the text because the flow of

78. Vanhoozer, *Is There a Meaning*, 104.
79. Ibid., 228.
80. Vanhoozer, "Discourse on Matter," 25.
81. Ibid., 31.

authority is from the protasis to the apodosis, not the reverse. Authorial intent is also unchanged by the interpreter, as any interpreter's meaning, or intent, different to the author's is not the author's. The authorial intent qualifies, to use Ricoeur's terminology, as that which can fuse the relationship of the time of transmission and the time of interpretation.

The convergence in the works of Thiselton, Vanhoozer, and Ricoeur is on the text as the point of dialogue. However, Thiselton and Vanhoozer investigate the text to illuminate the authorial intent that led to the creation of the text. This is consistent with the relationship that exists between the author and the text. In the case of Ricoeur the text, as "detached" and therefore "autonomous," discloses its own intended meaning to the reader and the relationship is now reversed, since the text becomes the cause of an intended meaning for the reader; that is, the text is now the antecedent of the reader's meaning without reference to authorial intent. In fairness to the work of Ricoeur it should be noted that his observations about tradition can be seen to give the author a voice in the process, but it is not a decisive voice. It is important to acknowledge that "detached" is a valid description of the temporal relationship between the author and text. Autonomy, however, authorizes the text to act decisively, independent of the author, which is what Ricoeur proposes. Autonomy is not acknowledged as a fait accompli and, in fact, as this book unfolds the opposite is demonstrated as more consistent with what is observed; that is, the *Sache* is disclosed in the composition in its relationship to the antecedent of the authorial intent.

The philosophy of Thiselton and Vanhoozer appears to make the assumption that the authorial intent is either located in the text or attached to the text. If the view is that of location within the text, this could be seen to lead to an almost philosophically pantheistic idea that the text and the authorial intent are identical, or, alternately, that which is created, the text, contains its creator, the author. These inferences would not be philosophically those of the biblical perspective, yet they would be difficult to refute from a hermeneutical viewpoint if the locus of the authorial intent is the text. On the one hand it would seem illogical to state that an infinite God is identical with a finite revelation of himself. Also on the other hand it would seem equally illogical to state that all that can be known of God, the creator, is contained within the text, or creation.[82]

However, if the view is that of attachment, the issue becomes how the authorial intent is attached to the text. If the concept of attachment is taken literally, the issue is then primarily linguistic in nature. When this literal view is taken, in order to avoid the idea of the authorial intent being contained within the text, also needed is a corresponding proposal on how the investigation of the authorial intent is to move from a linguistic to a nonlinguistic approach. Conversely, if the concept of the attachment is figurative, then the nature of the attachment is referential.

---

82. Cranfield, *Romans*, 32. Cranfield notes that although God has truly revealed himself in his creation, it is obviously only to a limited extent.

This referential concept would seem paralleled in the text of Rom 1:19–20. The created world is a source of direct knowledge about the creator.[83] Consequently, as a source of knowledge, the creation functions like a text that refers to the creator in its knowledge. The paradox of "invisible" and "clearly seen" in the text appears to be a deliberate paradox.[84] The use of such a deliberate paradox of "invisible" and "clearly seen" points to the referential nature of the text as knowledge of God. The referential nature is inherent and primary; there is no need for another proposal on how it is referential.

The classic view of texts was that of their ability for reference to worlds outside the text.[85] This fell into disfavor in modern times seemingly due to "ontological conundrums centering on the nature of reality and the nature of referents."[86] This disfavor of reference was related to a "desire to avoid the metaphysical problems that focus on the relationship of language to reality."[87] Clarence Walhout suggests the term "*descriptive reference*" as a way of overcoming the problem.[88] In this way language can be allowed to point, or refer, to "objects or states of affairs" that are extra-linguistic without the concept of reference becoming embroiled in ontological arguments.[89] The basis of this argument against reference is in reality not metaphysics *per se*, rather it is primarily and specifically about Western metaphysics and specifically its development in ontotheology. The result of this debate was the concealment of the ontological issues that are involved and critical in the interpretive event, such as the ontological nature of the authorial intent itself.

If the text is detached from the author, as Ricoeur has pointed out, then unless the authorial intent is seen as inherent in the text, or directly attached to the text, it can be argued that the text is detached from the authorial intent that caused it, rendering authorial intent ineffective. When the authorial intent is seen as the antecedent of the text, this temporal detachment is not significant because the text inherently refers back to authorial intent as the referent of the text, but authorial intent itself is not a part of the text. The "meant" of the author is available in the written text and can be methodologically pursued by an interpreter.[90] It is the "meant" of the author that refers back to the authorial intent. The authorial intent then assumes the potential double meaning of the symbol; it is able to relate both to the "what it meant" of the author and the "what it means" of the interpreter, being able to be expressed in other languages and thought patterns.

83. Erickson, *Christian Theology*, 154.
84. Cranfield, *Romans*, 32.
85. Thiselton, *New Horizons*, 55.
86. Walhout, "Narrative Hermeneutics," 72.
87. Ibid., 73.
88. Ibid. (Italics original.)
89. Ibid.
90. Stendhal, "Biblical Theology, Contemporary," 422.

If instead the authorial intent is viewed as inherently contained in the text (i.e., textual meaning equals authorial intent), then the detachment from the author is also not significant. In this case it would be assumed that the authorial intent detached with the text and meaning, as authorial intent, would be a linguistic property of the text. Yet Vanhoozer himself suggests that meaning should not be seen as a property of texts.[91] Meaning is a function of persons; it is something they do and a text is a site for a work of meaning.[92] The person, either the author or interpreter, imputes the meaning itself.[93] It would seem that it would be unwise to proceed on the basis that authorial intent, which directly relates to the issue of meaning, is inherent within the text because meaning would then be a property of the text.

Nevertheless, this seems largely the position of Vanhoozer, although he does not state that the authorial intent equals meaning of the text. It is nonetheless the implication of his position. If Ricoeur's contention of detachment is valid, then unless the authorial intent can be reattached, or the authorial intent does indeed somehow reside in the text, or the authorial intent is directly attached to the text, this does present a hermeneutic problem for the interpreter who desires to use the authorial intent as a reference in meaning. Authorial meaning is the "what it meant" of an author for a particular audience at a particular time. Reader meaning is the "what it means" of an author to a particular audience in the contemporary setting. The relationship between the two, the antecedent of both, should be the authorial intent. It is proposed that recognition of the difference between authorial intent and authorial meaning circumvents the problems.

(b) Authorial Intent in Communication Modeling

If interpretation is a communicative event in encounter with the text,[94] as advocated by the preceding convergence on the text, then the basic concept of how the authorial intent is to be viewed in this communication should be examined. The modeling of communication that occurs makes the "text" the default source of communication and the interpreter the receptor of that communication. In *Christian Communication Reconsidered*, John Bluck suggests that the basic circular model is a good place to start.[95] Whilst it must be noted, Bluck is speaking about communication of the gospel and not hermeneutics; if the interpretive event is a communicative one, then this communication model should still hold. The basic diagram is as follows:

---

91. Vanhoozer, *Is There a Meaning*, 202.
92. Vanhoozer, "Discourse on Matter," 26.
93. Ibid.
94. Ibid., 27. Vanhoozer states he believes in authorial discourse and the possibility of understanding it. He notes in a footnote that this is not an "ideal object" but a "communicative act."
95. Bluck, *Christian Communication Reconsidered*, 9.

Figure 1. The Circle Model of Communication

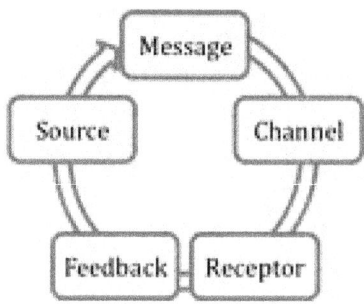

In this modeling the Text = Source (i.e., that which is communicating with the interpreter); the Interpreter = Receptor (i.e., that with which the Source is in communication); and in this case the Authorial Intent = Message (i.e., the *Sache*, or matter, communicated); the act of Reading = Channel.

Vanhoozer agrees with Gadamer and Ricoeur that hermeneutics is ultimately a matter of discerning the discourse: "what someone says to someone about something."[96] The interpreter employs methodologies and academic approaches, but the aim is what the author, or in Ricoeur's view the text, said and did with regard to a matter.[97] The *Sache* (or matter) of the text is the master that both the author and interpreter must serve.[98] It is the substance of the communication. However, the obvious question is, "Can the creation be master of the creator?"

In fairness to Vanhoozer's work, it should be observed that his view is that the *Sache* is presented in a language, and that he is proposing the concept in which both the author and the reader are citizens of language.[99] Consequently, both author and reader must be responsible members of language in the communication, hence the concept of *Sache* as master. Vanhoozer's view of language is that it "is a kind of sacrament, a means of communicating meaning through verbal signs."[100] It seems reasonable to state that what the author wishes to convey must be conveyed with regard to the means of conveyance, that is, language. However, language is the means used by the author in communication. The means of anything is used at the discretion of the user, as master. An author can use language incorrectly and can even employ incorrect usage as a communicative device.[101] It is the desire to communicate that is the master for the author, not the matter to be communicated. Observance of the rules of

---

96. Vanhoozer, "Discourse on Matter," 25.
97. Ibid.
98. Ibid., 7.
99. Vanhoozer, *Is There a Meaning*, 204.
100. Ibid., 39.
101. Thiselton, *New Horizons*, 80. Thiselton alludes to this in the Apocalypse of John.

The Conundrum and Paradox

language is dictated by this desire to communicate. Consequently, the mechanism of communication is the prime issue for the author.

Vanhoozer's position is that the source of the text is the author, who is not only the cause of the text and responsible for its creation, the "that it is," but also what it counts as, the "what it is."[102] His interest is in what the author has said, but considering these observations on communication, in his scenario, the author should become the source and the authorial intent the message with the text as channel. The author is indeed the source of the creation of the text, as Vanhoozer has observed, but for interpretation to be possible as a communicative act in the contemporary setting, the author must be replaced by the text as the source. The problem of an author as source is that all agree the author is no longer present.

In theological hermeneutics, in the case of the biblical text, an answer may be sought by proposing dialogue with the Holy Spirit who, as the divine author, remains attached to the text. However, as observed in the introduction of the first chapter of this book that discusses the issue of the conundrum of Scripture, this does not solve the hermeneutical problem of dealing within the human realm. Even in adopting an orthodox view of Scripture as the word of God, it is still a communication to humanity, though of divine origin in this view, and must be understood first begin from the human realm in order to operate out into the divine realm in disclosing the divine mind.[103]

Fee, a scholar within the Pentecostal community, who has an absolute conviction of the Spirit's involvement with the interpreter and text,[104] acknowledges that exegesis using the tools of grammatico-historical methodology is essential in dealing with the "meant" of the author.[105] The recognition of the involvement and attachment of the Holy Spirit to the text in orthodox evangelical understanding doesn't circumvent the hermeneutical issues.[106] Any suggested special hermeneutic would have to remove the text from normal processes and considerations. This would result in the conundrum of Scripture being answered by a separation of the sacred and text. If this is to be avoided, then the text remains the source because there is no way of establishing an authoritative voice of the divine author within the normal process of human investigation.

When the text is the source, then the argument regarding meaning becomes one of linguistics,[107] which is the direction for both Vanhoozer and Thiselton. This is also

---

102. Vanhoozer, *Is There a Meaning*, 228.

103. Thiselton, *Two Horizons*, 90. Thiselton notes that the Spirit works through normal human processes. This is consistent with the recognition that the purpose is communication with humanity and occurs within the human realm.

104. Fee, *Listening to the Spirit*, 14.

105. Ibid., 9.

106. Thiselton, *Two Horizons*, 90–91.

107. Vanhoozer, *Is There a Meaning*, 202.

the ground Ricoeur stands upon, without the constraint of authorial intent. Whilst there may be reference to what the author meant, the only meaning in the process is that of the interpreter. The only true judge of what the author meant is no longer available.

Vanhoozer defines a text as "*a communicative act of a communicative agent fixed by writing.*"[108] He later gives a more expanded version: "A text is a complex communicative act with *matter* (propositional content), *energy* (illocutionary force), and *purpose* (perlocutionary effect)."[109] The first quote shows the preeminence of the author and the second is an expansion of the comment "fixed by writing" in the first. Essentially, Vanhoozer focuses on the illocutionary act, what the author does in the writing, as the access to the authorial intent. He states that the literal sense of a text "is the sum total of those illocutionary acts performed by the author and with self-awareness."[110] In the language used in the text and by the interpreter's observation of grammar, using a methodology of speech-act theory, the authorial intent can be identified and known. This does not place the authorial intent within the text as containing meaning, but it does indicate and imply an attachment of the authorial intent to the text, which in itself would satisfy the criteria of communication for interpretation to be possible.

The advantage of this approach is that the source now becomes the authorial intent for the purposes of the communicative act. The text takes the place of the message. Reading, or hearing, takes the place of the channel in the communicative act. In this situation either the text is a form of referent to the authorial intent, for example, as in the Ricoeurian concept of symbolic function of text, or it is an equivalent of the authorial intent in written language. However, in a discussion concerning the use of the concept of metaphor to describe texts found in Ricoeur, Vanhoozer is disparaging of this concept.[111] His primary concern is indeterminacy, which is a feature of the metaphor having the facility of double meaning. Ricoeur uses metaphor as the "touchstone" because of this feature, but he uses it as an entrance to the concept of the symbol—having the same tendency but the extra dimension of nonlinguistic double meaning.[112] Whether or not it is Vanhoozer's intention, his reasoning leaves the authorial intent essentially hermeneutically equivalent to the written text. The text becomes a means of enfleshing the authorial intent. In Christian theology the divine authorial intent was enfleshed in Jesus; however this was not an enfleshing within the text. Even in this case, Jesus is the antecedent of the text.

---

108. Ibid., 225. (Italics original.)

109. Ibid., 228. (Italics and parentheses original.)

110. Vanhoozer, *First Theology*, 178. In this section Vanhoozer develops this concept of dealing with the text in speech-act theory, especially the illocutionary act as the means of understanding the authorial intent.

111. Vanhoozer, *Is There a Meaning*. See pages 131–35.

112. Ricoeur, *Interpretation Theory*, 45. This is the subject matter of the chapter. Ricoeur's use of symbolic function as a description of the interpretive process is noted previously.

Bluck's consideration of Christian communication highlights an immediate problem for this situation. Bluck notes that the message can never be acquainted with meaning, since meaning is receptor dependent.[113] If the text is the equivalent of the authorial intent, as the "meant" of the author, then it is not just a means of meaning but also actually a vehicle of meaning. This would suggest a transfer of meaning to the receptor via the vehicle of the text. Vanhoozer does not consider meaning as a property of texts. Rather, meaning is a function of persons, something they do.[114] His view is that a text only has meaning (as a noun) when someone means (as a verb) something in its use.[115]

Certainly Vanhoozer's suggestion and observations agree with Bluck that meaning as a function of persons belongs properly to the receptor, in this case the interpreter. Yet here is the conundrum of his concept; how can that which does not have meaning be the meaning of the author? For there to be any approach to accepting this model of interpretation as a communicative act, the "meant" of the author would need to be demonstrated as enfleshed in the text; that is, meaning would indeed have to reside in the text. Therefore, every individual text of the composition is a piece of the authorial intent and failure to interpret any part, or indeed loss of an individual text, would result in an incomplete authorial intent.

(c) The Referential Nature of the Authorial Intent

It would seem more productive to proceed with the concept of the text as having descriptive reference to the authorial intent (i.e. as has been proposed the authorial intent is the referent of the text and acts as its antecedent). Ricoeur's model has demonstrated how this can happen. Following the advice of Thiselton, there can be a use of philosophical description without adoption of its mindset. The very concept of interpretation for the contemporary situation is the idea that what was said can be restated in other words and other languages.[116] The contemporary meaning is effectively sought as that which the author would have meant if they had stated it in the contemporary situation. It can also be adapted to differing disciplines; the interpretation of the biblical text into the contemporary situation assumes the biblical text can address the totality of life. This suggests that authorial intent possesses the symbolic function of double meaning both linguistically and nonlinguistically when authorial intent is considered as the antecedent of the text.

If, as proposed previously, the authorial intent is seen not as enfleshed in the text but acting as the antecedent of the text, this automatically includes the idea of the text as inherently referential to the authorial intent. At issue is how this referent

113. Bluck, *Christian Communication Reconsidered*, 10.
114. Vanhoozer, *Is There a Meaning*, 202.
115. Ibid.
116. Stendhal, "Biblical Theology, Contemporary," 427.

function operates. How does authorial intent relate to the "meant" of the author and hence result in understanding of the "meant" of the author as "meaning" in the interpreter? Thiselton asserts that understanding remains "a single, complex, interactive, process in which the interpreter's own developing understanding undergoes constant revision, modification, and correction."[117] Assigning meaning is therefore a dynamic process rather than a static fixed process. Thiselton sees that the formation of a comprehensive theory of meaning is unrealistic. This is not an observation of skepticism about meaning but a realization that an abstract idealized concept of meaning is unrealistic.[118] There is a need to consider the particular cases, that is, the situational context.[119] Meaning is not only dynamic, and undergoes adaptation, but it is also not "one size fits all."

Certainly Vanhoozer is not suggesting a static process. He asserts a process of questioning to determine which inferences the interpreter makes are valid and do justice to the authorial intent.[120] Whilst he does not use the word dialectic, it nevertheless fits the model he suggests. The model of a dialectic, where the other pole of the dialectic is the text, will bring the interpreter full circle back to the hermeneutics of Ricoeur.

Vanhoozer, as with most theologians, recognizes that no theologian sees from the divine perspective.[121] Yet theologians have to deal with the existence of absolute truths.[122] So it would seem that in the model of Vanhoozer the interpreter moves in the direction of absolute truth. If this was the case, then the passage of time should result in clear perception and less dissention, which does not occur. Also, this movement should result in less commentaries and commentaries that gradually approach the definitive meaning of the word of God, which is also not occurring. As an ultimate destination such movement should also result in a monocultural world, as that is the only way there will be even a possibility of attaining the divine perception of absolute truth. Even then there is an inherent assumption that this is, or would be, the divine culture. There can even be an assumed allusion to this assumption in texts such as Eph 4:11–16, which apparently lend credence to this concept.

Yet this movement ignores the fact that the multicultural world is not a human but a divine creation (Gen 11:1–9; Acts 17:24–27). Further, Acts 17:27 puts a positive spin on this multiculturalism, for it facilitates communication of the gospel. It was noted, in mentioning these texts previously, that the creation of misunderstanding places the focus on understanding in communication and thereby activates the presuppositional world of a person. It would seem that the presupposed divine influence

---

117. Thiselton, *New Horizons*, 559.
118. Thiselton, *Thiselton On Hermeneutics*, 530.
119. Ibid.
120. Vanhoozer, *First Theology*, 183.
121. Ibid., 309.
122. Ibid., 153.

does not desire humanity to resume a monocultural situation. The search of the absolute as a pure value is not realistic and is not consistent with Scripture. What would be consistent with Scripture is a maturation process that sought a relative value and expression of the absolute within the interpreter's historical particularity.

Marshall's observation that an authoritative meaning in one context may have a different authoritative meaning in another context was discussed previously. It was noted that changing meaning implies that some aspect of the communicative process changes with a change of context. The presuppositional world, and hence worldview, of the interpreter changes from one cultural situation to another. Further, the tendency to subculture within a culture shows that at least nuances of differences exist within a given culture. What is sought is not a watering down or diminishing of the absolute, but rather an understanding of the absolute in the relative situation.

Postmodernism has rejected the concept of the absolute because modernism failed to produce it. This occurred because modernism sought the absolute as a pure ideal value; but modernism did not recognize that within culture the absolute is not producible as an abstract value but only as a value relative to the context of the interpreter. Meaning as an act of persons is always contemporary and situational. Assigning meaning and yet avoiding relativism as a defining ideology for the person in the comtemporary situation is acheivable by maintaining a relationship between the relative value and the absolute, where the absolute is always the antecedent of the relative value.

The problem for any person is awareness that the absolute has been engaged in the process of assigning meaning. One indicator on tackling this problem is given in considering Paul's approach to life, as outlined in Scripture. In Acts 23:1 he declares that he has lived in all good conscience before God, as an explanation and apologetic for his interpretation of the divine will into his life. In 2 Cor 1:12 he shows that he measured life by acting referentially with his conscience. Hence, acting in accordance with belief and monitoring the relationship between belief and interpretation brings about the relationship between relative and perceived absolute. Belief, hence nonrational knowledge, supplies the context and allows engagement of what is believed absolute by a person. The issue of the correctness of a perception of that which is absolute is not a hermeneutical issue. The example used is a particular belief (that of Christianity) and is based upon the biblical text; however, the principle is the same whatever the belief, that is, the context in which life is conducted. What is believed about reality will provide the context for interpretation that allows a relative value situationally without moving to relativism.

Fee has noted that the need to arrive at an absolute value seeks elimination of ambiguity by imposition of legalities.[123] Cultural diversity is a creation of God, and God speaks through an eternal word historically conditioned in this diversity by his own choice.[124] The interaction of the divine and human leads to a concept of diversity within an essential unity. There is diversity due to historical particularity and unity due to the divine origin.[125] Parker notes that the belief that textual criticism seeks the recovery of the original unified text of Scripture is mistaken.[126] There is no one original text and there are differences in the texts that are extant because of situational adaptation.[127] The indeterminacy of the text is not a hindrance to interpretation but allows for a process of adaptation.

Both the text and the interpreter live in indeterminacies. This should not be seen as a problem but as an opportunity for understanding. As Fee noted, the tendency to pursue the absolute as absolute leads to settling the uncertainties by a legalistic approach that has the effect of regimenting society. If this was successful, the question must be asked whether God might not feel he must act again as he did in Gen 11:1–9.

Vanhoozer observed that in the hermeneutics proposed by Schleiermacher, the object was to know and understand an author better than he or she understood him or herself.[128] This would indicate that what would be required is for the interpreter to adopt the mindset of the author. This is also not realistic as a total objective. The authorial intent *is* the view of the author due to the presuppositional world of the author, but not on everything. The authorial intent *is* the view concerning the *Sache* or matter of the text. The desire of the author is for the intended audience to see what the author saw about the *Sache*. The authorial intent, in acting as the antecedent of the text (i.e., it is what the text refers back to), is what has preceded the text and acted as the cause of its being as text.

---

123. Fee, *Listening to the Spirit*, 33.
124. Ibid.
125. Ibid., 34.
126. Parker, *Living Text of the Gospels*, 3.
127. Ibid., 4.
128. Vanhoozer, *Is There a Meaning*, 231.

4 The Conundrum and Paradox

A Way Forward

Part 3: Current Philosophical Opinion

Introduction

THE FOLLOWING IS A summary of the implications of the five issues considered in the previous two chapters. These issues concern current hermeneutical practice and thought, especially the relationship of current Evangelical thought to current hermeneutical practice. In this chapter, proposals will be put forward relating to these issues that open the way for a reevaluation and redevelopment, leading to new perception of the issues of authorial intent, the nature of the literary text, and the critical issue of understanding in relation to resultant meaning in the hermeneutical task.

Bultmann and others have recognized that reading, hence research, is done in a purposive manner that is directed by presuppositions. The presuppositions that bring us to these issues are that God has spoken and that God speaks in relationship to the biblical text. However, the continued retention of such presuppositions requires an examination of these issues in the hermeneutical task. This is due to the strong case and well-argued perception in postmodern thought, which questions the central critical concept that authorial intention can be communicated in written discourse. The belief that it is God who does the speaking is a matter of belief. The act of God speaking and an interpreter understanding is the task of hermeneutics. Therefore, this case and its argumentation must be investigated to see if the continued holding that God intentionally spoke and can intentionally speak is viable as a belief within the task of hermeneutics. This is the subject matter of the succeeding chapters in this work.

The recognition of the presuppositions bringing us to the task also requires an overview of key voices inside the Evangelical perspective. Also under examination are the key voices within the development of postmodern thought that have questioned the communicability of intention within written text. If authorial intent is communicable, then an interpreter can understand an author's intentional discourse. If authorial intent is not communicable, then the presuppositions of God both having spoken and speaking to an interpreter is no longer a matter of the hermeneutical task, but rather it is a matter of special hermeneutics (i.e. a different hermeneutical task) or, alternately, mysticism. By projecting from these proposals and also an overview of some current voices on the matter, this work seeks to provide insight on current philosophical opinion. The resultant discussion in the succeeding chapters of this book will bring into focus that these issues, although addressed because of presuppositions concerning the speaking of God, are central to all literary texts; Christianity simply makes special use of the principles operational in the task of hermeneutics related to all literary texts.

Observations Concerning the Five Proposals

The prima facie case for the five issues previously outlined provides a sufficient basis for these issues to be functioning propositions rather than contingent assumptions. Although they do interact, each issue stands on its own merit, and each is within an understanding of the current state of hermeneutics. The following statements of them here are not necessarily the headings that designate them in the text, but they are statements of their essential content based on the flow of the text.

Proposition 1. The Impact of a Changing Audience Is Relativity in Meaning

This concept seems a logical position that is based on an analysis of the works of Marshall and Thiselton, especially in recognition of this impact in biblical texts. Vanhoozer, although not acknowledging impact on changing meaning, also acknowledges that the presuppositions of the interpreter are indisputably impacting the task. Fee also grants this as essentially a given in hermeneutics. If the extension of this concept to a general rule is valid, which seems to be a position widely held, then the fact that uncertainty is part of the process must be considered. The objective is to outline a descriptive method that takes account of that degree of uncertainty and as a method operates in its presence. Further, it is desirable to outline a descriptive method that not only operates effectively in the presence of uncertainty but also avails the use of it in the process.

Proposition 2. Texts Engage Interpreters in an Event of Understanding

An author creates a textual composition as a means of communication due to his or her authorial intent concerning a subject matter. The authorial intent develops initially within the horizon, and hence world, of the author. However, the commitment to communicate causes the author to frame the text in the light of the horizon, hence world, of an intended audience, which represents a fusion of horizons of author and intended audience that essentially functions as though there is a world of the text. Factors such as the operative effects of the text cause the text to begin to open up a world for the reader that is a world opening in front of the text.

The advent of the unintended reader, which includes readers from differing cultures or even subcultures to those anticipated by the author, introduces a new horizon in the interpretive process. The text now is opened into a new world in front of the text, rather than itself opening up a new world in front of the text. This raises issues such as historicity and hence, for understanding, the examination of what a text meant and subsequently what it means in the world of the reader.

The event of understanding must consider all three worlds. If the impact of the world of the author is not evaluated, then elements such as the tradition in which the author and his or her work stand will be lost. As Ricoeur has noted, if this element is lost the text becomes a dead text. If the world of the text is not evaluated there is no basis for knowing the "meant" of the author. If the only world considered is the world in front of the text, then the only meaning possible is the reader's, with no basis for meaning that is relative to that of the author.

However, in this event of understanding the text is not just conveying information as a passive vehicle for meaning. Knowledge is not only acquired due to the efforts of the reader but is imparted and experienced in the process of understanding. Because the textual composition is a direct creation into literary form, it must supply not only information but also context and explanation. The only vehicle available to the author is the sentence as the basic unit of meaning and the presupposition of language.

The problem is that methodologies developed for undertaking the analysis of a text have all been developed in modernism and consequently assume that knowledge is acquired. Hence, such methodologies are not able to accommodate knowledge that is inspired intuitively or knowledge that is imparted. Further, such methodologies, seen as a means of acquiring knowledge, also assume that knowledge itself is of the form of rational objective knowledge. Modern methodology is therefore inadequate for dealing with forms of knowledge other than rational, for example, subjective elements and belief. The subjective elements are what engage the reader in dealing with a text to draw the text into the reader's own world. Belief, or *pistological* elements, create the context or relation to reality in which informational elements such as objective knowledge are held. It is important to reexamine the text and its function in all aspects in the event of understanding.

Proposition 3. Understanding Involves Rational, Arational, and Nonrational Categories of Knowledge

Studiers of theology, along with those who study any field impacted by belief, have long recognized that there is a dimension beyond the rational human mind and that the human constitution involves what is often referred to as a metaphysical aspect. Generally speaking this aspect is usually separated from the concept of knowledge and not discussed as knowledge. The avoidance of discussing this metaphysical aspect as knowledge has developed in modernism, under the influence of philosophers who have separated faith from knowledge. In more recent times this assessment has begun to be strongly challenged in theological circles, although it has already been widely challenged and accepted in philosophical works. An example of this challenge to this status quo in thinking is the work of N. T. Wright.

The concept of knowledge beyond the scope of rational knowledge can also be inferred in other works, such as those of Vanhoozer, Thiselton, and Fee, in discussions concerning the believing community and tradition. The designation of the subjective element as arational is merely a recognition of a lack of relationship to reasoning from a rational objective perspective. The designation of the concept of faith knowledge is nonrational. The broad concept that faith and belief are different categories to human reasoning is not new but is widely accepted.

The term *pistology* is created in part to help avoid the baggage and preconceptions involved in using the term *theology*. Pistology was created to be a universal term that recognizes that belief is a "given" of humanity, which is supported in the biblical text, and does not just belong to the community of the Christian faith. Belief is an aspect of the being of humanity. The biblical text of 2 Thess 3:2 has been used to indicate that some people do not have faith, that is, not all people are people who hold beliefs. However, the definite article is present, and so a sounder reading would be "not all have the faith," which, in the context of the passage, would indicate the Christian faith. Christian faith is not only an act of belief, it is belief in something, that is, there is also content (see Rom 10:8–10). Belief is a faculty of all people, or the Divine could not command belief in Christ for salvation. The belief of a person sets the context for that person's approach to the task of hermeneutics (i.e., the recognition that an interpreter is never without presuppositions in approaching the task), which includes the belief dimension.

When it is recognized that there are other categories of knowledge, even just to the recognition that subjective elements are normal, acceptable, and not only are part of, but also integral to, existence and hence interpretation, this becomes a methodological problem in dealing with texts. Current philosophical descriptions thus become inadequate, and this indicates a new way of looking at accepted concepts is needed.

Proposition 4. Authorial Intent Functions as Antecedent of a Composition

There is a difference between orality and literacy, which is important. Written text is a direct creation. This assertion challenges the inherent assumption, traditionally made hermeneutically, that written texts are similar to oral discourse. Whilst some commentators have noted that there is an important distinction to be made between orality and literacy, these commentators have not clarified that this distinction is because composition is a directly literary act. The composition as a conceptual creation is the means by which an author communicates to an intended audience. The written composition is the creation of a text that has the authorial intent as its antecedent.

The composition involves creation of a text that must convey not only information but also elements that are part of a dialogical situation, but not directly transmitted as information. The only vehicle for this as a semantic unit is the sentence, and so an authorial meaning is associated with the text that is designed to allow the authorial intent to disclose the *Sache*. The goal is that the interpreter understands a matter from the perspective of the authorial intent. The authorial intent is the direct cause of authorial meaning and so is related referentially to this meaning, but the authorial meaning is also situational in context within the text. Consequently, the authorial meaning refers to the authorial intent but does not contain it.

It is possible to give simple illustrations, for example, advertising copy, that show authorial intent can be seen as achieved without the reader fully achieving understanding of the authorial meaning in every instance of text. Consequently, it is not an unrealistic suggestion that while authorial meaning has linguistic attachment to the text, authorial intent is directly related to the text but not directly attached to it in a way that would allow current epistemological methodology to access it. Ricoeur has noted that the author becomes detached from the text the moment the text is released into the world of readers. If the authorial intent is seen as attached to the text, an argument must be developed to illustrate that it remains attached, as in Vanhoozer and Thiselton (since Thiselton sees hermeneutics as involving a dialogical event with the text in a similar concept to Vanhoozer). If the argument for authorial intent remaining attached to the text is not convincing, then an argument will need to be developed that shows how authorial intent becomes reattached to the text. It seems more fruitful to accept authorial intent's relationship to the text as previously described as antecedent, and then seek to describe how this comes within the hermeneutical process. Linguistic and historical analysis is critical in approaching authorial meaning, but understanding of the authorial intent is arguably seen as being beyond this step.

If the authorial intent is the antecedent of the text that guides the development of the text, then this intent is both consciously and subconsciously part of the authorial mindset during the development of all the text in the composition. In Vanhoozer, Thiselton, and Fee there is common agreement that the authorial intent is driving the production of the text. However, authorial intent guides the composition, and it is not something seen as contained within every text in a composition. Nevertheless, the authorial intent is that which gives rise to every text in the composition, and that which gives every text cohesion as an integral part of the composition.

Proposition 5. Authorial Intent Acts Referentially in the Interpretive Event

This proposition picks up on a concept suggested by Ricoeur in the hermeneutical process. Ricoeur noted that the potential for double meaning in the symbol lends itself to being a model for the process of dealing with texts by interpreters. Vanhoozer looks at but rejects this concept, due to "indeterminacy." However, part of the problem is the concept of the "determinate" or "absolute." Vanhoozer admits no theologian enjoys a "God's eye view" (as do most theologians), yet he ignores the relative nature implied in recognition of this.

When this concept of relative value of the absolute in the human situation is accepted, then acknowledging the referential nature of the authorial intent as able to relate to both text and interpreter is a more positive view. It has long been recognized that a text can be restated in another language and culture. The very concept of dynamic equivalence, widely accepted in theological circles in interpretation and translation, shows the ability of the authorial intent to relate to a time other than the time of its expression into written text.

AUTHORIAL INTENT AND THE COMPOSITION

As indicated in the preceding proposals, this examination reveals that the authorial intent is not easily disposed of, and yet engaging and identifying it presents an impasse to the hermeneut who seeks to retain its value. The attempts to accommodate authorial intent within current epistemological methodology in Vanhoozer and Thiselton are not convincing, although their argument for its existence are. Vanhoozer's book *Is There a Meaning in This Text?* is essentially devoted to the topic of defending the impact of the author on the meaning of a text. The first half of his book is an insightful and extensive examination of the inherent dangers in the postmodern movement in the interpretation of texts, and especially its extreme understanding in deconstruction. Thiselton has addressed the positives and negatives in his numerous volumes, examining the philosophical disciplines and their implication for Christian interpreters. Yet on the subject of authorial intent, Thiselton's primary emphasis is upon the adverbial understanding, which as previously discussed, really achieves no more than the acknowledgement that the text is evidence that an authorial intent existed. The adverbial view however offers no real indications on the evaluation of authorial intent as the *intention-to* of the author. The focus is on the action done not the one doing it, thus not the *intention-to*.

Even within Pentecostalism diverging views exist concerning the postmodern turn, from people such as Timothy Cargal,[1] who advocates embracing the postmodern turn, and, alternately, people such as Robert Menzies,[2] who advocates strongly for cautious dialogue rather than embracing the postmodern turn. What is generally recognized is that in this area of authorial intent, certain problems with the Romanticist viewpoint have been elucidated, and hermeneutics has been changed with the result that authorial intent has become passé as a subject, and its advocates viewed as traditionalists at best. Hence the impasse: authorial intent holds solid reasoning for its existence but no clear way forward in current methodology to evaluate its impact on interpretation.

Primarily Vanhoozer, and to some degree Thiselton, seek the answer to the impasse in speech-act theory by way of the concept of the illocutionary acts performed by the author in the text. What will be covered in the development of this book is that (1) the speech acts (i.e., the locutionary, illocutionary, and perlocutionary acts) remain locked into an epistemological evaluation of the ontology of the impersonal event and (2) Ricoeur's work in *Oneself as Another* has underscored the terminal nature of this ontology in dealing with the question of the agent.

The entity of the composition, with its implication of intentionality, which is essentially lost in not only detaching the entity of the text but declaring it autonomous with respect to meaning, highlights the need to examine the entities of the text and composition and also their relationship. The realization that a literary text is not only to be engaged within terms of rational knowledge but also arational and nonrational knowledge further exemplifies the need to reevaluate the entity of the text. These engagements act essentially as dimensions of the text, which therefore goes from a one-dimensional entity, in the approach adopted in current epistemological methodology, to a three-dimensional entity.

Whilst epistemology can recognize the existence of language associated with these other forms of knowledge, it is inadequate to deal with them. Furthermore, the

---

1. Cargal, "Beyond the Fundamentalist-Modernist Controversy," 170. He contends that pastors in the Pentecostal pastorates already operate a form of precritical hermeneutics. The general argument he presents in his article is that Pentecostal pastors should seek their hermeneutics in the postmodern approach.

2. Menzies, "Jumping off the Postmodern Bandwagon," 115–20. In this article Menzies recognizes what Cargal points out, i.e., that the Pentecostal pastorate could be susceptible to postmodern thinking; however, he advocates caution in acceptance of its primary tenets. Menzies especially recognizes the potential loss of the implications of authorial impact, 116.

realization that the concept of *intention-to* directly relates to the agent points to the idea that authorial intent has at least an ontological nature that has not been considered in the task of hermeneutics. The need to rescue this aspect of the entity of the composition, which is associated with the authorial intent, is not just a matter of safeguarding the idea that God can speak in and through the text; it is a matter of rescuing the entity of the composition itself, which is a literary criterion. As Vanhoozer has observed, the "fates of the author of traditional literary criticism and of the God of traditional theism stand or fall together."[3]

In the light of the discussion so far, the text acts as a stimulus to meaning in the interpreter. Hence, the text stimulates engagement with the authorial intent in a dialectical, or self-dialogical, fashion about the subject matter of the text; but not only does the text stimulate self-dialogue, the text also shapes it. Consequently, the text of an author is not an enfleshing of the authorial intent but a vehicle to allow interaction with the authorial intent. Authorial intent is not in the text, as is inferred in Vanhoozer,[4] but is better viewed as a referent of the text. Missiologist and anthropologist Charles Kraft defines meaning as "the structuring of information in the minds of persons."[5] If meaning exists for persons, as noted previously, and occurs in the minds of persons, then the strict concept of authorial meaning, as opposed to the interpreter's reconstruction of it, exists in the living author not in the text.

In literacy, as opposed to orality, words appear similar to things. Ong states people think of words as the "visible marks signaling words to decoders, i.e. we can see and touch words in texts and books."[6] Consequently, meaning can appear to be in the words. Vanhoozer indicates his agreement with Ricoeur's assertion that the sentence is a new entity with a meaning that is not just based on the sum of its parts, for example, words and phrases.[7] This is the field of semantics.

Written words are a residue of discourse, and oral tradition has no such residue.[8] In a very real sense interpretation can be seen as the reanimation of the residue. Meaning is associated with the living text, that is, occurring within a person not in a written text. In Heb 1:1–3 the definitive statement of the communicating God is stated as being the person of his Son, Jesus. This definitive statement is in a person, not a text, and so John 1:14 declares that the word, or discourse of God, became flesh. The referent, the person of Jesus, exists before the text and the text has a referential link to the person. The living word and its meaning exist in a person. In all instances of

---

3. Vanhoozer, *Is There a Meaning*, 71.

4. Ibid., 29. He discusses his view of the implications for the church if no meaning is seen "in texts." There is some ambivalence in his view, as in "Discourse on Matter," 25, where he designates texts as "the site for a work of meaning" and notes words have meaning for people not as inanimate objects.

5. Kraft, *Christianity in Culture*, 135, 148.

6. Ong, *Orality and Literacy*, 11.

7. Vanhoozer, *IsTthere a Meaning*, 204.

8. Ong, *Orality and Literacy*, 11.

composition in texts, the living word and its meaning exist in the authors. The text is designed to associate readers with this living word and its meaning.

In the hermeneutics of Ricoeur, symbol is used as a description of the process of dealing with a text due to the symbol's ability of double meaning. If the text is a vehicle for interaction with the authorial intent, and not a vehicle of the authorial intent, then the authorial intent shares qualities with the symbol. The authorial intent relates to the meaning associated with the author's text but is not attached to the text. Authorial intent exists, whatever the state of the text. Also, a text can be restated in another time and in another language. The very concept of dynamic equivalence in translation acts as essentially anecdotal evidence that the authorial intent stays related to the text but not attached to it. Hence, the authorial intent is capable of double meaning; that is, it can relate to the time of transmission and to the time of interpretation.

Authorial intent shapes what an author has decided to communicate and inherently involves his or her presuppositions concerning a matter. The authorial intent in this process is acting as the antecedent of the text; hence, the preceding proposal of this description that concerns the relationship between text and authorial intent. The text makes reference to the authorial intent. The object of Vanhoozer's emphasis on speech-act philosophy is to "break free of the tendency either to reduce meaning to reference or to attend only to the propositional content of Scripture."[9] However, it has been observed that the author, in a composition, must use reference to communicate what is not communicated in transcription. The categories of knowledge involving arational and nonrational aspects don't communicate without reference. These elements are suggested as vital in interpretation, where the arational attaches the interpreter to the text, engaging an interpreter in the task; and the nonrational sets the view of reality that will be the context for understanding. Interpretation of this referential aspect of the text is indispensible in interpretation of the *Sache* of the author. The presuppositions of the reader must be engaged so as to deal with these issues, and this involves reference.

(a) Connecting Presuppositional Worlds

The facility of speech as using a language, in the biblical record, is a given of humanity; to use Heidegger's concept, it is an attribute of *Dasein*, the being-there, of a person. Ong notes that, in his view, human society essentially always has a language that is usually spoken.[10] Language is the means by which a person can express his or her view to another person. Language therefore functions between the presuppositions of a person and the world. Consequently, language is an important means of gaining

---

9. Vanhoozer, *First Theology*, 163.

10. Ong, *Orality and Literacy*, 7. He notes that sign languages are a substitute for speech and are therefore secondary not primary.

insight into the worldview of another person, and subsequently of communicating with that person.

Kraft states that people groups organize their perception of reality to determine what "can or should be, what is to be regarded as actual, probable, possible and impossible."[11] These perceptions are therefore the presuppositions through which life is viewed, evaluated, and lived. It is from these presuppositions that the makeup of what constitutes their worldview will be developed.[12] Their worldview determines the values system of the people group, and from this basis interacts with and impacts every other aspect of their existence as a people group.[13] The concept of understanding includes the ideas of perception of meaning, significance, and explanation of something; it also includes the idea of being knowledgeable about the nature and character of things (i.e., it is to understand something). Clearly, understanding happens within the presuppositional world of a person and is expressed in that person's view of reality, that is, in his or her view of the world or worldview.

These presuppositions can be converted into verbal descriptions for the purpose of communication, that is, converted into language. In actual dialogue with another person, both verbal communication and nonverbal communication are present. Nonverbal communication can be rich in significance.[14] Also, it has been noted that categories of knowledge are known that are not available in the text through rational objective processes, and hence methodology, but rely on the experience of the reader (in the case of arational knowledge) and the pistology of the reader (in the case of nonrational knowledge). The presuppositions of a person include all forms of knowledge. In dialogue, via the means of language and interpersonal interaction, these presuppositions are communicable.

The rational aspect of a text lacks some of these dimensions. The author must use verbal description to create an opportunity for understanding in these other areas; that is, the author must create a composition. Hence, the text facilitates the understanding of the presuppositional world of a reader/interpreter by acting in a way that can associate authorial meaning with interpretive meaning. It acts between the presuppositional worlds of the author and interpreter. Since presuppositions constitute the view of reality, they are capable of being approached from differing perspectives, giving them the same flexibility of double meaning in the symbol. When the text is seen as a vehicle for the composition, disclosed by the authorial intent, which includes the presuppositions of an author on a matter, the text can function for a multidisciplinary approach to the symbolic nature of the authorial intent.

It was previously noted that in the historic text the historical particularity of both author and audience, and the authorial intent, are fixed. Due to the nature of

11. Kraft, *Culture*, 53.
12. Ibid.
13. Ibid.
14. Ong, *Orality and Literacy*, 7.

transmission, recovery of a single original text or complete knowledge of the historical particularity may present difficulties. Critical disciplines can address these issues so that any uncertainty can be evaluated in the process of interpretation. However, when the view is taken that the text is a vehicle of the composition as opposed to its identification with the composition, since the authorial intent as antecedent becomes a referent of the text, any indeterminacy in these areas need not be seen as critical to understanding the authorial intent or impeding access to it. This accessibility of the authorial intent allows the text to function in both the time of transmission and interpretation.

This view of a text positions the reader at a distance from the time of transmission, and not part of the intended audience, to deal with the "meant" of the author. The interpreter from outside the community of faith must give due regard to the tradition both of the author and the intended audience up to and including the time of transmission. Further, this view of the functioning of a text positions the interpreter within the community of faith. Thus, standing in the same tradition as the text, the reader is able to arrive at a concept of the authorial intent in a contemporary situation, that is, the contemporary "meaning" of the historical "meant" of the author. In order to achieve this, the interpreter must observe the same constraints as the interpreter from outside the community of faith in order to arrive at the concept of the "meant" of the author. The interpreter must regard the tradition of the text and its transmission as well as the tradition of the community, of which they are part, in regard to the text. It is a relative value of what authors would mean if they were placed in the contemporary situation of interpreters.

(b) Implications for Biblical Hermeneutics

Certain implications for biblical interpretation are significant in theological hermeneutics. When this concept of the text outlined above is adopted there is no need to suggest a special hermeneutics. The assertion that God has spoken in the text is a belief about the text. Even where a writer asserts that they speak for God or from God, there is nothing about the language that inherently makes this claim different from any other claim. The difference is the pistology[15] (or theology, in the case of the biblical text) of the author. The recognition of the text as a vehicle of the composition, which is available for the interpreter in understanding the composition, positions the interpreter to access the knowledge involved in understanding so that he or she can incorporate the *rational, arational,* and *nonrational* categories. All these categories are part of the presuppositional world of a person, and so all must be engaged in the interpretive process.

---

15. See previously in ch. 2 "Forms of Knowledge Operational in Language" for the suggestion of this word as a way of studying and dealing with the understanding of belief knowledge.

Fee suggests spirituality is the aim of exegesis of the biblical text, and only when exegesis is done with this aim is it done in accordance with the intent of the text.[16] In the biblical text spirituality relates to involvement with the Holy Spirit.[17] Vanhoozer asserts that God is present in Scripture "as a communicative agent" as the ultimate author.[18] In this situation an interpreter, with a pistology that is consistent with Christianity, can employ a special use of hermeneutics in direct communication with God as the ultimate author of the text. In dealing with the Scripture the reader is not just being informed about God but is actually interacting with him.[19] Communicating with the supernatural requires a corresponding set of beliefs.[20] It requires a relevant pistology, or in the case of biblical text, a theology, or set of presuppositions concerning belief.

It was previously noted that the interpreter from outside the community of faith is able to deal objectively with the "meant" of the author for the intended audience. Due to a different pistology to both author and audience, such an interpreter cannot deal comprehensively with the authorial intent in relationship to contemporary meaning. This interpreter can evaluate a verbal description of both the arational and nonrational aspects by the author and audience; like all knowledge these categories are subject to verbal description. Such an interpreter is able also to investigate the tradition of the text and community because of the time of transmission of the text, where there is an accessible historicity of that time of transmission. Further, in order to gain some objective understanding of the meaning of the text developed over time, it is possible to involve "reception history," which deals with the impact of a text not only for the intended audience but also for subsequent audiences.

However, special use of hermeneutics is required for understanding what the text means in the contemporary situation. As Ricoeur has noted, regarding all texts, each text stands in a tradition and that tradition only lives when understanding occurs within the tradition. Fee asserts that for exegetes to come to full understanding of the biblical text, they must approach the text with an absolute conviction concerning their own *pistology* that they are dealing with God's word.[21] In Fee's estimation spirituality must precede exegesis as well as follow it.[22] Hence, the requirement of a special use of hermeneutics is simply sound hermeneutics that deals with the text within its own tradition.

---

16. Fee, *Listening to the Spirit*, 5.
17. Ibid.
18. Vanhoozer, *First Theology*, 34.
19. Ibid., 35.
20. Nida, *Message and Mission*, 18.
21. Fee, *Listening to the Spirit*, 14. The term *pistology* is not used by Fee. It is used as a descriptive term whose derivation has been alluded to previously.
22. Ibid., 6.

The Conundrum and Paradox

Fee has noted that not only did the Spirit inspire the authors of Scripture but that they also brought their own spirituality to their task.[23] True exegesis should engage the authors' spirituality and not just their words.[24] This engagement should happen in such a way as to become part of that spirituality.[25] As in the issue of narrative discussed previously, this approach allows the readers to orient themselves so that they are able to communicate with the *pistological* knowledge of the authorial intent and be impacted by it.

In engaging the presuppositional world of the authors, the readers are engaging a presuppositional world that gave rise to the authorial intent, which intent purposed the creation of the text. In this setting, readers are positioned by direct engagement with the presuppositions of the divine and human authors to find, in their own presuppositional world, a contemporary meaning.

It is important to realize that both the interpreter and the text stand in traditions that form the context of the task of interpretation. Thiselton discusses the issue of reception history and retrospectively considers it to be something he should have included from the beginning.[26] This discipline involves studying the history of texts and how they are perceived and received by the community of faith, which shape theology and are in turn impacted by theology.[27] This draws the tradition of the community, in dealing with texts, into consideration when approaching the concept of contemporary meaning. In this way reception history represents a thread of the interaction with the divine mind by the community of faith, of which the interpreter is part. This is not to advocate traditionalism, which controls the process, but tradition as mentor, which informs the process. Due to the nature of nonrational knowledge, as belonging to the community, and passed on in community, these issues will be important in the hermeneutical pursuit of understanding.

Consideration of the proposals discussed previously suggests that a new philosophical description of how texts function and are interpreted should be developed. The proposed philosophical description of the interpretive event is that a text acts as a vehicle of the composition that, in turn, provides a vehicle for the interpreter allowing interaction with the authorial intent as the *intentioned-ness* of the text. This interaction results in disclosure of the author's composition in the contemporary setting of the interpreter. This disclosure positions the interpreter to assign meaning in relationship to the author's composition, that is, to interpret the author's composition in the comtemporary situation. There are implications for hermeneutics that are significant if, upon investigation, this philosophical description is accepted as valid. The concept of "special hermeneutics" becomes legitimately a "special use" of the hermeneutics

23. Ibid., 11.
24. Ibid.
25. Ibid.
26. Thiselton, *Thiselton On Hermeneutics*, 36, 39.
27. Ibid., 39.

that applies to all texts. The belief aspect of sacred text cannot be separated from the text, since the belief of authors and intended audiences form an integral part of any text. The nature of the biblical text as sacred text, where that belief is seen to directly control the authorial intent, and thus the text, requires a special use of hermeneutics rather than a special hermeneutic. Furthermore, the belief of the interpreter and the interpreter's treatment of the belief of the author and intended audience are critical. The following hypothesis is the basis of the unfolding discourse of this book.

Proposed Hypothesis to be Examined

Authorial intent is that which gives being to the entity of the composition in relationship to a text, so that an observer is positioned to understand what the author understood, that is, see what the author saw.

Philosophical Perspectives: Authorial Voices in the Debate

In considering the aforementioned five issues in current debate, it has been noted that the author as the creator of the text gives being to the composition that is the text. The subsequent chapters of this book will reveal an important disclosure regarding the ontological nature of the authorial intent. The recognition of the ontological nature of the authorial intent subsequently raises the issue of the *being* of the entity of the composition, an entity to which the authorial intent *gives being*, and therefore which, as an entity, is related to that of the author's text. Thiselton has labeled this issue of the nature of the text as the "most radical question of all in hermeneutics," in the light of current debate and theories.[28] Any assertion concerning an impact of authorial intent itself raises the need to deal with the very notion of intention and the resultant issue of meaning and the composition. Authorial intent, the nature of the text and the concepts of understanding and meaning in relationship to the text must be examined in the twin approach of philosophical issues and practical issues. The philosophical issues are theoretical and descriptive, and the practical issues are those of detection and understanding of both the epistemological and ontological aspects.

The consideration and evaluation of the philosophical perspective concerning these issues occurs in dealing with those individuals who are doing the describing. The following are important figures standing directly in the line of the development of the philosophical perspective. The contemporary thought on authorial intent and the being of the text, together with the subsequent issue of understanding and meaning, has been greatly impacted by the work of the following authors both inside and outside the Christian sphere.

---

28. Thiselton, *New Horizons*, 49.

Three Primary Authors Encountered in the Hermeneutical Debate

A central issue pursued throughout this book is that of the authorial intent and its function in the ontological interpretation of the entity of texts (i.e., *in disclosure of the being of the text*), and as a result is a descriptive task that occurs prior to epistemological interpretation (i.e., *in dealing with the content of texts*). These two tasks function together in disclosing the matter of the composition. The approach taken in this investigation follows a consideration of authorial intent and the "being" of the composition and the text with which it is identified.

This book is written from within the Christian community and each of the primary writers in the ensuing literary dialogue place themselves within this community, regardless of individual persuasion within the broad community. Since the issue is first of all theoretical, and therefore philosophical, the work of Anthony Thiselton is considered. Thiselton has dealt extensively with the work of various philosophers and their relationship to the task of hermeneutics. Thiselton has recognized that beginning with Friedrich Schleiermacher, then Wilhelm Dilthey, and the subsequent direction of the development of hermeneutics, philosophical concepts have become important because a person could be methodologically equipped but still not understand a text.[29] Thiselton, though holding the view of authorial-discourse interpretation, does not address the issue of authorial intent at length in his works, but he does consider each of the other authors that will be considered and their philosophical concepts involved.

Kevin Vanhoozer is an evangelical theologian who has been a passionate advocate for the retention of authorial intent in the task of hermeneutics. Vanhoozer contends that in dealing with meaning in relation to texts the author is not only the primary cause of its existence but also the authoritative voice in determining what it counts as.[30] An objective of his work *Is There a Meaning in This Text?* is to establish a methodology whereby the goal of interpretation is viable and meaning is in fact demonstrably and uniquely that of the author.[31]

Vanhoozer does not ignore the philosophical issues that impact this concept of authorial intent, acknowledging that in the background of this hermeneutical task "lurk philosophical and theological issues that are all too often overlooked."[32] However, he views his work in *Is There a Meaning in This Text?* as a normative treatment of this issue, therefore concerning methodology, but admits that there is a need to consider the descriptive (hence philosophical) issue, which concerns "what actually

---

29. Thiselton, *Two Horizons*, 5. Thiselton also notes that the issue is that methodologies do not complete the hermeneutical process, 22.

30. Vanhoozer, *Is There a Meaning*, 228. In essence this concept of meaning related to authors is the theme of the book.

31. Ibid., 76.

32. Ibid., 29.

happens in understanding."[33] In what he admits is a rough generalization, he proposes that the normative task is epistemological and that the descriptive task is ontological.[34] Thus, Vanhoozer relegates the ontological discussion to a secondary role, which is proposed in this book to be the exact opposite of what should happen. Hence, Vanhoozer, although recognizing the philosophical impact in relationship to interpretation of texts, is a proponent of the epistemological consideration of the concept of authorial intent as determinate in the discussion of meaning of the text, independent of any particular interpreter. He notes "meaning is independent of our attempts to interpret it."[35] Therefore, he proposes meaning as an ideal that exists as *other* with respect to persons.

The third primary author is the philosopher Paul Ricoeur, who together with Gadamer, stands as a significant philosopher in the development of hermeneutics in the postmodern era. Thiselton regards Ricoeur important as a philosopher in the discussion of hermeneutics as, although holding Christian presuppositions[36] as a believer, he nevertheless comes to the task without a "theological axe to grind."[37] Thiselton notes that in Schleiermacher and Dilthey, hermeneutics moved to include "interpretation and understanding of human persons, or that which is 'Other' in human life."[38] As a result hermeneutics has flowed on to "a hermeneutics of lived experience," and in the recent works of Ricoeur, within the postmodern paradigm, "we reach a hermeneutic of selfhood and of human action."[39] However, the problem is that this postmodern focus on personhood has focused on the interpreter and specifically excluded the author.

Consequently, authorial intention, as impacting hermeneutically in the issue of interpretation, is specifically rejected. In this Ricoeur is one of the strongest voices. In the written text "the author's intention and the meaning of the text cease to coincide."[40] Ricoeur regards that in the appearance of the written text the mental intention of the author and the verbal meaning of the text become separated.[41] As an important figure

---

33. Vanhoozer, "Discourse on Matter," 6.

34. Ibid., 7.

35. Vanhoozer, *Is There a Meaning*, 11. In the preface to the book, he shows his commitment to this issue in the hermeneutical task despite current postmodern theory, which he discusses at length in his work.

36. Ricoeur, *Oneself as Another*, 24. Ricoeur observes that the book *Oneself as Another* is written with an understanding of his own Christian faith and convictions, but not written from them. See also, Ricoeur, *Conflict of Interpretations*, 270. Ricoeur notes that he doesn't regard himself as dogmatic when it comes to theology.

37. Thiselton, *Two Horizons*, 109.

38. Thiselton, *Interpreting God and the Postmodern Self*, 47.

39. Ibid., 47, 48.

40. Ricoeur, *Interpretation Theory*, 29.

41. Ibid.

in the development of postmodernism's impact on hermeneutics, his work on this issue must be considered.

(a) Anthony C. Thiselton

Thiselton has been a detailed and thorough exponent of the discussion of philosophers and their works in relationship to the processes of hermeneutics. He suggests that the work of philosophers provides tools that can prove useful, but such tools should not overrun the process.[42] As a result his work interacts at some point with most, if not all, of the other authors noted in this work. Thiselton advocates a willingness to consider the works of philosophers, noting that concepts that come from outside the biblical domain are, of necessity, neither wrong or inappropriate.[43]

Thiselton's basic concept develops from the recognition that interpretation involves two sets of horizons that interact, those of the text and the interpreter.[44] The concept of the fusion of these two horizons, drawing on the work of Gadamer, is important in the development of his work.[45] In the work of both Thiselton and Vanhoozer, as evangelical authors dealing with this subject, the focus is the written text. Certainly this is what is presented to the reader/interpreter and so must be the point of origin of the task. However, this approach leads to a problem within hermeneutics in dealing with intention. The concept of intention either relates directly to the agent or what that agent has intentionally done. Relating intention directly to the agent carries the implication of engagement of the consciousness, or psyche, of the author. The primary and any subsidiary authors considered in this work view this concept, prevalent in Romanticist hermeneutics, to be unsustainable in hermeneutical theory. Nevertheless, the text can reasonably be seen to be what the author has intentionally done (i.e., it represents an authorial intention), which both Thiselton and Vanhoozer focus upon.

In this vein of thought Thiselton suggests that the issue of authorial intention is best understood adverbially, as a qualifier of the action of the author.[46] However, the work of Ricoeur has taken note that when consideration is taken from the concept of an action, the ontology is not personal as relating to the agent but impersonal as relating to the "what" of the action.[47] This is the logical consequence of the very idea of the consideration of an action; that is, it concerns what is done. Hence, consideration

---

42. Thiselton, *Two Horizons*, 9.
43. Ibid.
44. Ibid., 15, 439.
45. Ibid., xix.
46. Thiselton, *New Horizons*, 560.
47. Ricoeur, *Oneself*, 60–61. This is the theme of the chapter.

of authorial intent primarily from its adverbial sense in hermeneutics presents only a weak attestation to the author as agent.[48] The focus is the "what" not the "who."

The encounter with otherness in this situation becomes the encounter of an object, that is, a "what" rather than a person. In Heidegger's ontological concepts every entity is either a "who," as existence, or a "what," which he termed present-at-hand.[49] The text would therefore be considered as a present-at-hand entity. However, in Heidegger all such entities are worldless,[50] and are unmeaning;[51] that is, they neither mean, as intention, nor possess meaning. The text therefore is both worldless and unmeaning as an entity in this conceptualization. Consequently, meaning is either a function of the author or interpreter. These are the only entities who are personal, hence capable of meaning. The issue of authorial meaning therefore becomes problematic, because interpreted meaning cannot be viewed as that of the person of the author. The direction taken in postmodern thought, under the influence of philosophers such as Gadamer and Ricoeur, is that meaning is an issue of the interpreter, with the exclusion of any impact of the authorial intent. Therefore, any reference to authorial meaning becomes essentially invalid in their philosophical paradigm.

Thiselton does not specifically seem to endorse Heidegger's concept of twofold categorization of *being*, having considered Heidegger's work to some depth in a complete section of *The Two Horizons*; however, nor does Thiselton directly address or present an alternative proposal. Thiselton does raise the issue of the entity of the text in his observation noted previously that "The most radical question of all in hermeneutics concerns the nature of texts, because the decision to adopt given interpretive goals depends not simply on the needs of the modern reading community but also more fundamentally, on the nature of the particular text which is to be understood."[52] His discussion, however, considers the philosophical development of the usage of texts and doesn't consider the being of the text as an entity. The problem is that if the Heideggerian concept is viewed as correct and adopted, either directly or by default, then the text has neither meaning nor a world, and to speak of either is misleading.

Thiselton has noted that the concept of the formation of a comprehensive theory of meaning is unrealistic.[53] He is not expressing skepticism about the concept of meaning, rather he is simply noting that meaning cannot be developed as an idealized concept; instead there is a need to look at particular cases.[54] Thiselton expressed similar thoughts on the issue of understanding, noting that understanding remains "a single, complex, interactive process in which the interpreter's own developing under-

---

48. Ibid., 68.
49. Heidegger, *Being and Time*, 71.
50. Ibid., 81.
51. Ibid., 193.
52. Thiselton, *New Horizons*, 49.
53. Thiselton, *Thiselton On Hermeneutics*, 530.
54. Ibid.

standing undergoes constant revision, modification and correction."[55] Therefore, it seems reasonable to suggest that the idea of a single universal meaning is not in fact possible; consequently it also is not the endpoint to which hermeneutics should be aimed. Therefore, it is important to consider the issue of understanding and meaning if there is to be any relationship of this issue to the concept of authorial intention in interpretation.

Whilst recognizing the concept of directedness related to intention in the speech-act theory, Thiselton does query the restricting of this understanding of intention to the paradigm of speech-act.[56] Thiselton suggests four considerations in the modeling used in hermeneutical traditions.[57] First, he supports the value of historical reconstruction as a valid context in many cases in relationship to meaning. He does recognize the importance of historical aspects in the hermeneutical task, and his work deals with a range of authors on issues related to historical concerns. Second, he suggests recognizing that the concept of historical criticism does not imply only modernistic methodology. Third, he notes that many biblical texts address a directed goal, which is identifiable as authorial intention, provided in his view an adverbial understanding of intention is taken. Fourth, he considers it a mistake to assume that Schleiermacher gave priority to authors over texts. Thiselton, however, believes Schleiermacher to be ahead of his time in recognizing that interpretation revolves around the two axes of the author and the linguistic.[58] Authorial intention relates to directedness in texts, but it is not resolvable in the impersonal ontology of the event.

Thus, the issue of the entity of the composition in relation to the text must be taken further, when authorial intent is recognized as integral to the task of hermeneutics. The primary reasons for ambivalence and misunderstanding concerning authorial intent relate to its capture by epistemology when its primary locus should be ontology. When the ontological nature of the authorial intent is followed, the being of the composition in its relation to the text is disclosed.

As noted previously, Thiselton recognizes the importance of philosophical aspects due to their impact on the concept of horizons. He indicates that in discussion of pre-understanding he prefers the concept of "horizon" to that of "presupposition."[59] The concept of horizon implies an understanding in life, whereas that of presupposition expresses an idea of rootedness in beliefs and doctrines.[60] Thiselton states, "The horizon or pre-intentional background is thus a network of revisable expectations and assumptions which a reader brings to the text, *together with* the shared patterns of behavior and belief with reference to which processes of interpretation and under-

---

55. Thiselton, *New Horizons*, 559.
56. Ibid., 560.
57. Ibid.
58. Ibid.
59. Ibid., 45.
60. Ibid.

standing become oriented."⁶¹ However, at the point of involvement in the act of *parole* by the author the effect is that a horizon functions as a presupposition for the author. Therefore, the use of the word presupposition, though having philosophical baggage, does imply that the application of cognitive processes is involved as well, which it is also important to recognize.

(b) Kevin J. Vanhoozer

Vanhoozer represents a strong contemporary voice within Evangelicalism, if not in general, advocating the philosophical and practical importance of the author and his or her intention in hermeneutically dealing with a text. Whilst Vanhoozer's discussion occurs within the Christian community, his consideration is of the concept of texts and textuality in general; that is, what he proposes is not a special hermeneutic. As was noted in discussion of the work of Thiselton, this whole argument highlights the nature and concept of the text. Vanhoozer agrees that any theory on interpretation concerns this vital issue of the nature of the text.⁶² Vanhoozer defines a text as "*a communicative act of a communicative agent fixed by writing.*"⁶³ In another, later work he noted of a text that it "is a set of marks (words) that fixes the meaning of the author."⁶⁴ The result of this, concerning meaning, is that "meaning is located in the author's intention to convey a particular message through signs."⁶⁵ This line of thinking effectively places authorial intention as located within the text.

Vanhoozer sees within his thought a distinction from that of E. D. Hirsch's consciousness. First, he sees that his own proposed view of authorial intention and meaning is accessible publicly, whereas the author's consciousness is not accessible in the absence of the author and, second, that past acts are not only fixed by writing but also in history.⁶⁶ In an attempt to avoid the question of consciousness, Vanhoozer seeks to move the issue to the "communicative act." However, the attempt to engage the text through the concept of an act, though seemingly logical as the point of contact for the interpreter, brings the issue of hermeneutics into the realm of the ontology of the impersonal event, which is highlighted by Ricoeur.

The problematic for addressing the issue of authorial intention directly in the situation of the event is that the concept of *intention to* cannot relate to an impersonal ontology, which is the *being* of the text in current perspectives. At its inception authorial intent is related to a personal ontology, that of the author. That which is

---

61. Ibid., 46.

62. Vanhoozer, *Is There a Meaning*, 103. It is interesting that to discuss the nature of the text he specifically opts to not talk about meaning but the idea of the text.

63. Ibid., 225. (Italics original.)

64. Vanhoozer, *First Theology*, 314.

65. Vanhoozer, *Is There a Meaning*, 43.

66. Ibid., 225.

impersonal cannot form an *intention to*, hence although an act can be intentionally done the act itself does not act intentionally. As a result, in this view of textual interpretation, any search for authorial intent as that of the person of the author must end with an inability to discover it. It is simply not available in the current view of the impersonal ontology of the text. Thus, an ontological impasse occurs if the idea of authorial intention is to be pursued in current understanding. The text does not possess a consciousness and cannot be viewed as having a personal ontology. Therefore, if the ontology of the text is that of the impersonal, then Ricoeur is correct and the authorial intention disappears.

As well as the issue of the nature of the text, the issue of fixity of meaning is also problematical with the recognition that a changing audience results in "apparent" changing meaning. The real issue is that meaning is a cognitive reflective activity (it involves a knowing) that is unique to each person, with the result that the only "person" who can know meaning in an absolute sense is the "person" who is able to be somebody and yet everybody at the same time. Within the domain of belief systems, this can only be God (where God is perceived as personal, or no such person who knows in this sense exists and all is indeed relative), and Vanhoozer admits that no one person enjoys the divine viewpoint in an absolute sense.[67] It would seem prudent to seek an alternative concept of sameness to that of meaning for expression of the nature of intention. This is a feature of this work, that is, a shift in emphasis from meaning to understanding as the criterion for discussion of sameness in relating communicator and receptor.

Whilst it can be agreed that there is a "meant" of an author that is the antecedent of the text (i.e., the reason for the being of the text in the first place), to speak of fixity can only apply to the "meant" as a past situation. An author can have moved on and even revised his or her thinking, and can even have a differing meant in a later text; but none of this alters the "meant" that gave birth to the original text. Hermeneutics cannot interest itself in speculation or revision, since to do so is to not deal with the author's composition; it is indeed an attempt to deal with the author's consciousness. Stendhal placed the first task of hermeneutics, in relationship to meaning, to be that of the "meant" of the author.[68] This would seem to be the actual quarry of Vanhoozer, who states, concerning the goal of interpretation, that it is "to reconstruct the single correct meaning of the text."[69]

Yet, as was previously discussed, Thiselton has noted that the idea of a single correct meaning is quixotic. Heidegger has helped to bring light onto this issue that brings into focus why such an aim is quixotic. Heidegger points out that interpretation

---

67. Vanhoozer, *First Theology*, 309. He notes that this results in the Word of God needing to be interpreted. Yet in this admission is the implication that meaning will therefore be unique to the interpreter.

68. Stendhal, "Biblical Theology, Contemporary," 419.

69. Vanhoozer, *Is There a Meaning*, 76.

arises in the desire to bring within the domain of one's own horizon (in the sense that Thiselton uses this word, as noted previously) that which has been understood, for example, in a communication. Heidegger states this in the following way: he asserts that in interpretation "understanding appropriates understandingly that which is understood by it."[70] Gadamer saw that the higher truth of hermeneutics is that of translation, in that it makes what is foreign (the issue of understanding therefore is prior in the very concept of perception of something as foreign) one's own.[71] Interpretation doesn't destroy or simply reproduce but, instead, explicates the matter of the text within a person's own horizons, thereby "giving it new validity."[72] Meaning relates to what Gadamer calls this "new validity." To express this in the thought of Heidegger, it is the disclosure to one's self so that what was foreign now is one's own and intelligible to oneself.[73]

Consequently, meaning is a personalization and therefore unique to each person; hence, any attempt at universalization is indeed quixotic. Vanhoozer seems to essentially acknowledge this in his recognition that meaning is related to persons, not inanimate objects.[74] The text is not a person, and unless a new conceptualization of the nature of the text and the composition is developed, as it is in this book, Vanhoozer is faced with seeking meaning in what is unmeaning. This occurs because meaning, which belongs to a personal ontology, is sought in the ontology of the impersonal event, as noted by Ricoeur. Vanhoozer's attempt to traverse this impasse, and avoid being caught in this quixotic state, is shown in his attempts to connect meaning and the text.

In Vanhoozer's thinking a text is "the site for a work of meaning."[75] This results in a situation where his desire is to access the meaning that existed in the author, and the text is the means to this end, which is a similar contention to Stendhal. Yet, he recognizes that "To believe that there is a meaning in texts is, as we shall see, an act of faith."[76] The faith is communicated in language, which is "a kind of sacrament, a means of communicating meaning through verbal signs."[77] If Vanhoozer is not proposing a special hermeneutic in using the word *sacrament*, then his idea must relate to the concept of connection of the outward and visible, the text, and the inward and spiritual or existential, as the author's meaning. It is in essence a model of referencing

---

70. Heidegger, *Being and Time*, 188.

71. Gadamer, *Philosophical Hermeneutics*, 94. The parenthetical comment is an observation, which seems to be the thrust of his comment on hermeneutical consciousness, in his observation that its power is the ability to *see* what *is* questionable, 13.

72. Ibid.

73. Heidegger, *Being and Time*, 193.

74. Vanhoozer, "Discourse on Matter," 26. This is similar to Heidegger's conception of being as related to either a "who" or a "what."

75. Ibid.

76. Vanhoozer, *Is There a Meaning*, 30.

77. Ibid., 31.

that purports to make available the anterior meaning of the author so as to be directly accessible to the interpreter.

Vanhoozer's concern is that in postmodernism, especially in deconstruction, absolute values are unobtainable, and so there is a loss of transcendence in the loss of the author and their meaning. In a desire to illustrate this sort of thinking, Vanhoozer uses as an analogy that of moving from Newtonian mechanics to that of Einsteinian relativity.[78] The direction of flow he is suggesting is this: Newton represented the book as the unity and stable meaning, and Einstein represented the autonomous text, which is a "field of shifting forces."[79] Vanhoozer's decrying of a "special relativity" theory of hermeneutics strengthens his view of seeing this shift as a negative development.[80] However, the usage of this analogy actually misunderstands the nature of the work of Einstein. The work of Einstein showed that the basic premise of Newtonian mechanics was wrong.[81] Newton based his work on the assumption of a point of absolute rest, and his theories were based on this. Einstein, however, was able to show that this observation and theory was actually a relative situation.[82] As such Newton's concepts worked within a frame of reference but not outside it; hence, it was a limited view. The key to Einstein's theory was his critical insight that the speed of light in a vacuum was constant, independent of the frame of reference of the observer.[83]

Therefore, to find the relative situation at any point requires access to an absolute constant reference point, which by nature transcends, as it is independent of an observer. This constant in Einstein's work was the speed of light. Placing the Bible in the Newtonian reference locks it into a view that has a flaw. The absolute is placed in the wrong system. Newton placed the absolute in space, but Einstein realized that anything in space was relative, and the absolute was independent of space. Texts can in fact be a "field of shifting forces" that can provide relevant relative value, provided there is an absolute point of reference. In the work of Vanhoozer the absolute point of reference for meaning in the biblical text is the meaning of the human author; to reiterate his dictum on the goal of interpretation, it is "to reconstruct the single correct meaning of the text."[84]

However, this places the absolute in the wrong frame of reference. The shifting field is in fact the concept of meaning; that is, meaning is always relative, being unique to each person. The issue becomes: to what is it relative? It is quite logical to believe

---

78. Ibid., 105.

79. Ibid.

80. Ibid., 106.

81. Polanyi, *Personal Knowledge*, 12.

82. Ibid.

83. Ibid., 10. Polanyi states that he personally spoke to Einstein who confirmed that his theory was not the result of investigating empirical data but developed from theory alone; although since its inception it has proven a reliable reference point in science.

84. Vanhoozer, *Is There a Meaning*, 76.

that authors have a meaning when they wrote their text; and having existed, meaning exists as an absolute, being itself the antecedent of the text. However, in reality the authors' meaning is also relative to their own situatedness and horizons. Meaning is a temporal entity and exists only within those horizons. As noted previously, it is quite conceivable that authors will review and revise their text, hence indicating a change of meaning. This can continue, as Vanhoozer has noted, as a shifting field of forces. The problem occurs because of the perceived domain of the absolute as that of meaning.

Vanhoozer declared the text a site of meaning; however, the site of something is where that something is, and is not the sign that points to it, or references it. The site of a house is where the house actually exists as an entity. Therefore, to proclaim a text as a site for a work of meaning places meaning at the site; that is, it places meaning actually in the text, not just referenced by it. This situation cannot occur unless the consciousness of the author, in the person of the author, exists at the site. This is not the case. Clearly this implication is not what Vanhoozer himself intends, since he acknowledges the author's meaning as anterior to the text. The very idea of authorial-discourse interpretation assumes a representative nature of the text in relationship to intention. Furthermore, this modeling has not overcome the problematic of the individual and the unique nature of meaning. Whilst, if absolute meaning exists, it is then possible that two individuals can have the same meaning, this must however be considered as improbable. Also, since to each the meaning appears unique, who or what can mediate showing sameness? The question therefore is: what can exist as an entity at the site whose whole raison d'être is to reference or disclose that which is other than itself, and that is itself related to the cognitive issue of meaning, in such a way as therefore having itself the appearance of meaning?

The analogy that suggests itself for such an entity is the picture, especially the photograph. A painting, as a work of art, like all works of art, is not directing the observer to its referent, for example, scenery (as in a landscape) or person (as in the case of a portrait or statue). Rather the object is, knowing the referent, to then observe that which references, that is, the work of art itself is the object to be viewed. However, the photograph, though it can be raised to the level of work of art, generally has the purpose of directing attention to what is disclosed in the photograph. The object is to see what the photographer saw. In the case of an event, if the photographs are close together in timing, the observer can, in the domain of their imagination, even "see" the event. This is neither a re-creation of the event as an event nor a reliving of the actual event; it is itself a new event, or a performance of the original event. This indicates that within human being is an aspect of consciousness that is ontic in nature, in that it discloses the entities viewed to the interpreter as having being so that they are "seen" as entities within a world.

In Heidegger's development, understanding is existential being that functions in disclosing.[85] The realm of the absolute may be more properly pursued in under-

---

85. Heidegger, *Being and Time*, 184–85. It will be suggested in the work following that this

standing rather than meaning, or to put it another way, in the idea of ontology rather than epistemology; hence the importance of the disclosure of the ontological nature of authorial intent and its relationship to understanding, as the disclosure of what the author saw. Heidegger saw also that in understanding, there is a tendency to relate what is understood as meaning.[86] However, this in reality was the disclosure of entities in their being; the concept of meaning was the result of the process of personalization.[87] Consequently, understanding presents as meaning to the interpreter (it relates to meaning), but it can stand as distinct from it. Understanding is to see what the author saw, and as a result the text can involve an entity that references in itself to disclose what the author saw.

It seems that in his later work, Vanhoozer may even have moved more in this direction in his own thinking. Vanhoozer views Gadamer's central insight, which is important to hermeneutics, to be that understanding is not due to methodology, but is an act of "the matter of the text," which happens to the interpreter.[88] This is primarily the development within hermeneutics of what Heidegger observed. Vanhoozer further notes that the miracle of understanding is undergirded by ontology.[89] However, despite this acknowledgment, it is in the same article that he notes that the normative task will relate to meaning.[90] The importance of Vanhoozer's work is the powerful and articulate argument for the author and his intention. The problem for Vanhoozer's work is that he searches for the absolute where it doesn't exist, searching within human temporality for meaning. In particular, Vanhoozer's ontology is, in the end, locked into the ontology of the impersonal event. Consequently, the issue of the nature of the text is paramount in the discussion.

(c) Paul Ricoeur

Ricoeur is one of the prime philosophers to argue against authorial intent in the hermeneutical task. His understanding of the text as having the impersonal ontology of an action, being a presupposition in his work, is an important basis of his argument. Ricoeur in his works discloses the tradition and presuppositions that he places himself within, in the task of hermeneutics. In this consideration he notes that he presuppositionally "remains within the sphere of Husserlian *phenomenology*."[91] The revival in hermeneutics that occurred under Schleiermacher considered "*what it is to understand*"

---

concept in phenomenology, if taken in the view of spirit as substance in being, becomes in essence an attribute of spirit.

86. Ibid., 192.
87. Ibid., 193.
88. Vanhoozer, "Discourse on Matter," 28.
89. Ibid.
90. Ibid., 6.
91. Ricoeur, *From Text to Action*, 12. (Italics original.)

as the central issue of hermeneutics.[92] It is in the exploration of understanding itself that led to hermeneutics being able "to graft itself onto phenomenology."[93] This pursuit of understanding is an important theme in this work, and the ontological setting that comes through Heidegger, Gadamer, and Ricoeur is a central factor in this effort. In Ricoeur's view interpretation of texts is "the making explicit of this ontological understanding."[94] The implications of phenomenology, its view on being, especially in Heidegger, together with its limitations, will be considered.

It is in moving into self-understanding (the making of one's own that which is foreign in the interpretive task) that there is also a movement into epistemology.[95] This is more pronounced in Ricoeur than either Heidegger or Gadamer. This occurs as all self-understanding is "*mediated* by signs, symbols and texts" and "in the last resort understanding coincides with the interpretation given to these mediating terms."[96]

Ricoeur proposes that it is in the written text that there is a "threefold semantic autonomy" that the text as representing discourse acquires, which are those regarding authorial intention, the reception by the original recipients, and the historical setting of its production.[97] These are central and critical elements of Ricoeur's theory. For Ricoeur the task of hermeneutics is twofold: "to reconstruct the internal dynamic of the text, and to restore to the work its ability to project itself outside itself in the representation of a world that I could inhabit."[98] Both of these aspects of hermeneutics are consistent with Christianity; certainly there is also a vital interest in understanding as critical in Christian life.

The problem is not with the task Ricoeur undertakes, but what he forsakes in pursuing the threefold semantic autonomy as a presupposition of the task, which is the central issue. The forsaking of these is on the basis of phenomenology as developed in Heidegger and Gadamer, which is itself questionable. As noted previously, in considering both Thiselton and Vanhoozer, the phenomenological concept of being leaves the nature of the text as entity relegated to the impersonal. Consequently, all of these authors considered the nature of the text to be pivotal, and yet this nature remains largely unexplored in their works. This exploration of the nature of the text is an important task in this book.

92. Ibid., 14. (Italics original.)
93. Ibid.
94. Ibid.
95. Ibid., 15.
96. Ibid.
97. Ibid., 17.
98. Ibid., 18.

Subsidiary Authors Encountered in the Hermeneutical Debate

The following authors do not necessarily hold Christian presuppositions themselves. In their work their proposals and concepts would indicate that, if they are in possession of Christian presuppositions, it has not directly impacted their understanding of texts. Conversely, their understanding on the issues pursued in this work would seem opposed to such presuppositions in regard to the issues of the being and functioning of texts. Therefore, their voices present a balance on the questions and issues under consideration in this book.

(a) Hans-Georg Gadamer

Thiselton regards Hans-Georg Gadamer as an important philosophical figure in the transition from the modern to the postmodern era, crediting him with facilitating the movement to a new paradigm in hermeneutics.[99] Gadamer's opinion is that in Romanticist hermeneutics there was an over preoccupation with historical criticism and authorial intention, which to him was the wrong direction.[100] Once the text is released, the author becomes a reader who has no more authority than any other reader in interpretation.[101] As an author standing in the phenomenological persuasion that has impacted postmodernism, along with Ricoeur, Gadamer's work has itself had a significant impact on the movement away from the author's intention in the hermeneutical task.

(b) Jacques Derrida

Whilst in Gadamer and Ricoeur there is a denial of impact of authorial intent, in Derrida and deconstruction there is a denial of the author; hence, authorial intent is a meaningless term. This is not a denial that there is a writer, but a denial of the concept of authorship. This has an obvious relationship to those of authorization and creation of the text, as related to any meaning. Meaning, as a word, is closely related to the word intention, and they can in many instances be used interchangeably. Therefore, to talk about authorial intent is to speak of the author's meaning, and for Derrida anterior meaning can't exist in any way associated with a text.[102] The idea of anterior meaning that is related to the text is an issue of referencing, and for Derrida *"there is nothing outside the text."*[103]

---

99. Thiselton, *New Horizons*, 314.
100. Gadamer, *Truth and Method*, 153.
101. Ibid., 170.
102. Derrida, *Writing and Difference*, 10.
103. Derrida, *Of Grammatology*, 158. (Italics original.)

This referencing is simply what Derrida calls an "auto-affection," which is something generated in the imagination of the writer and reader; it is the giving of oneself the pleasure of imagining a presence or anterior meaning, and as such is imaginary and not related to reality.[104] In the thought of Derrida, writing is "inaugural" and doesn't know where it is going; meaning is its future, not its past.[105] In the deconstruction of the husk of metaphysics, which envelops the text, the author is deconstructed as part of this husk, with the consequence that authorial intent is rendered a phantasm.

However, the importance of Derrida's work is for what his argument in fact highlights and brings into focus. Thiselton noted that the path Derrida takes in developing his view of textuality is a philosophical one.[106] Derrida's philosophical argument constitutes a virtual tirade against Western metaphysics.[107] Hence, Derrida's argument against the concept of the author and authorial intent is an ontological argument. In so doing he exposes the ontological nature of authorial intent as it should be, and shows the link between author and the idea of the divine. Vanhoozer makes the incredible and ironic statement that "Deconstruction wholly inadvertently and with some irony, proves that God is the condition of the possibility of meaning and interpretation."[108]

(c) Martin Heidegger

The work of Derrida brings to the fore the ontological nature of authorial intent. As a result any investigation of ontology must interact with the work of Martin Heidegger in *Being and Time*. Heidegger stands in the direct line to Gadamer and thence to Ricoeur and Derrida, all of who espouse phenomenology as their presuppositional framework for developing their theories. Any investigation of the being of the composition and text must examine Heidegger's views on these issues. Furthermore, Heidegger's ontology considers not just the act of understanding but also the relationship of understanding to being.

(d) Roland Barthes

Roland Barthes, together with his contemporary Paul Ricoeur and their younger contemporary Jacques Derrida all figured strongly in twentieth century French philosophy and especially in philosophical hermeneutics, including the postmodern turn away from the author to the reader. Barthes' thoughts on the author are essentially

---

104. Ibid., 97–98.
105. Derrida, *Writing and Difference*, 11.
106. Thiselton, *New Horizons*, 104.
107. Derrida, *Of Grammatology*, 3.
108. Vanhoozer, *Is There a Meaning*: 198.

The Conundrum and Paradox

summed up in his famous 1967 essay "The Death of the Author."[109] The thought of Barthes stands closer to Derrida on the concept of the author as a theoretical concept. Like Ricoeur, Barthes essentially focuses on the autonomy of the text as the primary reasoning, though argued as a disjunction rather than a detachment as in Ricoeur. However, Barthes moved in a similar direction to Gadamer in his views on language; language exists as the horizon of expression.[110] There is nothing but language.[111] Although Gadamer raised the idea of language to that of a universal with metaphysical impact, he retained the idea of the impact of the author through an inbuilt dialectic, so that the reader could not just make what they will of the text.[112] Barthes, however, like Derrida, casts of all restraint of the author, declaring that as "institution, the author is dead."[113]

However, Barthes does seem to recognize, as do Ricoeur and Gadamer, a seeming presence of the author within the text when, in discussing the concept that a text chooses the reader, Barthes states "lost in the midst of a text (not behind it, like a *deus ex machina*) there is always the other, the author."[114] Here, it seems Barthes reflects on the person who writes, as opposed to the institutional concept of the author, which he specifically rejects. Whatever his allusions, the author, though other, does not operate as an authoritative voice (operating out of the machine) on meaning because "a text does not consist of a line of words, releasing a single 'theological' meaning (the 'message' of the Author-God), but is a space of many dimensions."[115] The author seemingly has presence but no interpretive impact. Yet, like both Gadamer and Ricoeur, Barthes in the midst of his argument against authorship makes reference to particular authors—not just their texts—attributing to them as authors the reasoning against authorship.[116] His phrasing directly attributes ideas to the authors, neither to the text used by the reader nor to himself as the reader handling the text. In Barthes view the reader is where the text, with its multiplicity of possibilities, finds a unified *voice* and hence speaks).[117]

His view of the author as a writer is similar to the thinking of Derrida in that the writer combines words to express and imitate reality. But in the desire to "express himself," he can only use words that in turn are defined by other words, and these interact "ad infinitum."[118] Also, in Barthes' thinking not only is the author neuter

---

109. Barthes, "Death of the Author," 1.
110. Barthes, *Writing Degree Zero*, 13.
111. Barthes, *Pleasure*, 9.
112. This concept in Gadamer's work is considered in later chapters of this book.
113. Barthes, *Pleasure*, 27.
114. Ibid. (Italics original.)
115. Barthes, "Death of the Author," 4.
116. Ibid., 3–4. There are a number of examples in these pages.
117. Ibid., 5.
118. Ibid., 4–5.

but the reader also loses the concept of a personal ontology.[119] In this way the whole process effectively has an impersonal ontology,[120] which, as Ricoeur showed, assumes an incorrect ontological basis from which to speak of understanding and meaning in relation to a text, if the object is to make what is foreign one's own, as personal.[121] Essentially, the paradigm of discourse in Barthes' position is reduced from *someone said something to someone*, to that of *something is written*; there is no longer a saying in the doing and no longer a *someone* who said it or a *someone* to whom it was said. It is admitted that Barthes doesn't use this terminology of ontology, but it is his effective position.[122]

Consequently, from an ontological viewpoint, in Barthes' paradigm, to speak of meaning in relation to a text, in the sense of formation of meaning, is meaningless because meaning relates to a personal ontology. General thought in hermeneutics is in agreement that meaning is an act of persons. In Heideggerian thought, meaning is something that only a being whose being is that of *Dasein* has the capability for; the impersonal present-at-hand, such as a text, does not have this capability.[123] If entities are either personal or impersonal, then to speak of a text as having or projecting meaning presents a complete ontological impasse. Consequently, if meaning is to exist in Barthes' line of reasoning, then it must be exclusively anterior even to the act of reading itself.

Therefore, in this reasoning, meaning has become solely the province of the person of the reader who is unimpacted by any anterior meaning, let alone any authorial meaning. Yet, as noted previously, almost perversely in the light of his own theories, Barthes himself acknowledges the impact of other authors' thinking on his own thinking, treating what they say as having meaning in the saying. He also seems to treat his own essay of "The Death of the Author" as having self-evident meaning, so that the reader should understand that the idea of the author exists no more. Meaning has been snatched out of the hands of the author, in theory but not in practice, to then be placed in the hands of the reader. As Barthes himself notes at the conclusion of his essay, for the release of the birth of the reader, the death of the author is offered as a ransom.[124]

---

119. Ibid., 5.

120. Ibid., 2. Literature, and therefore the text, is also neuter.

121. In Ricoeur's work *Oneself as Another*, Ricoeur deals at length with this issue, which together with its implications, are discussed in later chapters of this book.

122. Barthes, "Death of the Author," 4. Although Barthes is not as vocal as Derrida on ontotheology, his work nevertheless shows this problem is not far from his thoughts in linking God and the author, and also linking any emphasis on authorial impact on meaning to a theological concept.

123. Heidegger, *Being and Time*, 193.

124. Barthes, "Death of the Author," 6.

A Philosophical Basis for Hermeneutics

Barthes' ransoming of the author seems to have developed as a result of his understanding of the nature of the text. Note was taken previously of Barthes' emphasis on language. For Barthes, linguistics has exposed utterance as a "void process" that itself functions without the requirement of a person.[125] He asserts his agreement with the thought of Stéphane Mallarmé—who substituted language itself for man—that language speaks, not the man; and it is language that performs, not the self.[126] Writing, for Barthes, is the site where both the writer and reader seek pleasure,[127] and writing is "the science of the various blisses of language."[128] His thinking thus seems to stand close to Derrida's development of auto-affection as the place of presence and meaning.[129] Language is the pervading ambience in which the writer works "yet without endowing it with form or content."[130] In the end the writer simply produces language.

Therefore, language becomes the neutral place from which both writer and reader can make what they will of meaning, which will move in the direction of what gives them pleasure. In Barthes, as in Derrida, one neither traverses nor transcends the text on the issue of understanding and meaning, one invents; that is, the reader becomes the author of meaning, as there is no anterior meaning. In effect therefore there is no interpretation, as it is not the discourse of another that is explicated and explained.[131] The text is simply a stretch of language, and interpretation undergoes reduction to translation. Consequently, there is not relativity of meaning, as relative to someone, but relativism in meaning.

Barthes' emphasis is on a linguistics of semiotics in dealing with a written text.[132] In writing, everything is handed over to the symbol.[133] This symbolism effectively becomes an approach to language that treats the text primarily as code. Ricoeur realized that semiotics was inadequate in dealing with discourse, and so moved his emphasis in relation to discourse meaning to the field of semantics, the meaning of sentences.[134]

125. Ibid., 3.

126. Ibid.

127. Barthes, *Pleasure*, 4.

128. Ibid., 6.

129. Ibid., 57. Barthes extols the hedonistic search in dealing with texts, which would seem to confirm the observation. Derrida's conception of auto-affection as a pleasure one gives oneself in interpretation is previously mentioned and is discussed at length in later chapters of this book.

130. Barthes, *Writing*, 9.

131. Reynolds, "Jacques Derrida." In his introduction Reynolds notes that in deconstruction invention of meaning is its aim. Consequently, deconstruction is an authoring of a reader's meaning, not an interpretation of another's discourse.

132. Barthes, *Elements of Semiology*, 14, 35. This is the book's theme, and these pages highlight this.

133. Barthes, "Death of the Author," 2.

134. Ricoeur, *Interpretation Theory*, 11. Ricoeur defines semantics as the linguistics of discourse, 13.

The sentence is that of which discourse is composed, and is also that which is the smallest unit of discourse—not the word as in the semiotic approach. In the concept of *langue*, words have meanings assigned to them within the concept of *signifier* and *signified*. Such concepts are based on the work of Ferdinand de Saussure. Semiology, developed from the work of Saussure, as the study of signs and symbols, thus becomes involved with the idea of a code and investigates linguistics from this perspective of the code. Alternatively, Ricoeur proposes that language has two irreducible entities, those of the sign and sentence.[135] It is this reduction of language to the sign, which is so important in *langue*, that Ricoeur moved away from in his interpretation theory.[136]

Barthes proposes that *langue* is language minus speech, with *parole* being the individual act of selection and hence actualization of language.[137] Barthes' assertions about language are noted previously, that is, that speech is impersonal; it is language that speaks, not the person, and that language is essentially the atmosphere in which the writer draws breath. All of which leads to the conclusion that for Barthes the act of *parole* simply causes *langue* to be expressed as language. The person expressing *langue* as language is purely expressing a means of language and is not the author of a composition. Barthes ignores the very thing he himself alludes to; that is, he ignores the implication of intentionality in his own defining of *parole* as an individual selection and actualization. By avoiding a personal ontology, he is able to avoid discussing the issue of this intentionality, because for Barthes intentionality doesn't exist in regard to language as written text.

There are two related yet distinct issues of concern previously raised that present themselves in Barthes' formulation. Though raised in the consideration of Barthes' work, these concerns also represent the heart of the hermeneutical problem. As a result they also present a basis from which to launch a more in-depth discussion of the hermeneutical problem and also suggestions for its solution.

Hermeneutics concerns the art and science of interpretation. Interpretation of written text concerns elucidation of significance, hence meaning, and consequently involves an explanation to oneself by the reader. This explanation is a basis for subsequent proposing of significance, hence meaning for the reader, of that which has been communicated by another person. Understanding, which brings within a person's perception that which is other than self, is therefore the beginnings of the interpretive event. Subsequently, what is understood becomes explained to self, and therefore becomes *known* in an epistemological investigation. The signification of what is *known* is then given meaning, hence significance, in the life of a person, that is, the interpreter. What has not been considered in the postmodern situation is the ontological interpretation inherent in *understanding* itself when dealing with the entity of the text as the composition of another person. Is the disclosure in the understanding

---

135. Ibid., 6.
136. Ibid., 11.
137. Barthes, *Elements*, 14–15.

a self-disclosure of the reader or a self-disclosure to the reader by the entity of the text-composition? Postmodernism's consideration of ontological issues has almost exclusively concerned the reader.

The essential pathway suggested in the concept of discourse is *someone* said *something* to *someone*. The issue becomes: is that interpreted meaning developed in an isolation of the interpreter from the author who communicated, or, should this meaning be developed in an understanding of the meaning the *knowing* had to the one communicating? This question could be rephrased: is meaning a result of dealing with a text, or, is meaning the result of dealing with an intentionally impacted text? If a text is a communication (i.e., a message transmitted from a person to another person), then interpretation must involve not only a *knowing* of *what* is communicated but also an understanding of this *what* of the communication within the context and being given to it by the one communicating. The problem is that if there is no *communing* of persons, then how is there *communication* between persons? In the case of written text, communication occurs in the absence of the one communicating. This is where solving this problematic becomes significant.

These issues of concern, raised in examining Barthes' concepts, can be stated as, first, problems of inconsistency in understanding the ontological process occurring in interpretation, which itself leads to the disclosure of a problematic ontology of the being of the text. Second, there exists a problematic in extension of the linguistics of semiotics to written text. This extension becomes reformulated as an issue of code and message.

(a) A Problematic Ontology

The problematic ontology previously outlined means that to speak of *meaning* in regard to the text as discourse of another, in postmodern thought, is *meaningless*. Speech logically belongs to *someone* and yet in Barthes' understanding, in the actualization of the system of *langue* in writing, the result is language, which then *speaks*, not the *someone*. Consequently, any vestige of personal ontology is stripped from speech in relation to writing. Therefore, there is not communication between persons, just the perception of one communicating and one being communicated with, without any connection between these two events other than an impersonal event of writing and the resultant appearance of the impersonal text. Because in Barthes' treatment language consists of *langue*, which is impersonal as the system, speech becomes an impersonal expression of *langue*. There is no anterior meaning and hence nothing communicated; there is only invention of a message, hence meaning and application, by a reader. Any similarity between the meaning of the one communicating—should he or she be asked—and that of the one reading is pure coincidence. What is created is a text and what is interpreted is a text, but there is no relationship between *create* and *interpret*, just a *disjunction*—to use Barthes' term—between them that is the text.

In the thought of Derrida, writing is inaugural and is distinct from speaking; it is a supplement to speech, or an addition, which itself can be dispensed with because it is a supplement.[138] However, Thiselton notes that Julia Kristeva, though postmodern and close to the thought of Derrida, has reinstituted the concept of a speaking voice related to the text.[139] Therefore, speech in relationship to the verbal situation (i.e., related to a personal ontology) is not the same as speech in the written text, which is related to an impersonal ontology. If therefore speech is presumed to become impersonal in the writing, then the situation is created where a personal ontology (i.e., speech in relationship to the author) moves to an impersonal ontology (i.e., speech in relationship to the written text). This ontological shift is hermeneutically significant.

Ricoeur has recognized, and clearly outlined, an aporia, or impasse, inherent in the interpretive event of a text in moving from epistemology to ontology, that is, in the process of reestablishing discourse in a personal ontology from the impersonal of the text.[140] In the descriptive process a person moves from being, hence subject, to a third person status, hence object, and now becomes only the concept of a person. A loss of personal ontology that is inherent in the creation of the text must be overcome if the discourse is to be an interpretation of what someone said. Essentially, Ricoeur is noting that in interpretation of texts one begins with the something said, not the someone saying; hence, pursuit of the question *who*, as related to a personal ontology, is captured by the question *what* and the impersonal ontology of the text.

The result of this capture is the treatment of understanding as an aspect of knowing, hence epistemological, rather than as experiential, hence ontological, and therefore happening to a person (i.e., the acquisition of knowledge by a person), rather than disclosure of being to a person.[141] In Heidegger's ontological analysis *understanding* is an *existentiale* of a person's being, that is, a given of being not an acquisition by a being.[142] Epistemology involves the methodology employed in the descriptive task of interpretation, without which there is no knowing, and without which therefore there can be no meaning of the text for the reader that is relative to the text. Nevertheless, meaning is the result of a personal ontology and not a property of the text as an entity

---

138. Derrida, *Of Grammatology*, 144. See also *Writing*, 11. Derrida views writing as a distinct form that is a supplement to speech. Writing is the beginning of something itself not just the continuation of discourse by means other than verbalization. Ricoeur notes this aspect in Derrida's work and points out that, in doing this, what Derrida has sought to do is to give it a different root to speech. However, for Ricoeur they are both modes of discourse, and they are similarly constituted as discourse: Ricoeur, *Interpretation Theory*, 26. It can be agreed that verbalization and writing are both modes of discourse, but, as Barthes has noted contra Ricoeur, written discourse can speak.

139. Thiselton, *New Horizons*, 128.

140. Ricoeur, *From Text to Action*, 51. This concept of the aporia is discussed at length in chapter 11 of this book.

141. Ricoeur, *Conflict of Interpretations*, 6–7. This basic distinction in Ricoeur's thought has been dealt with previously in this book.

142. Heidegger, *Being and Time*, 385.

The Conundrum and Paradox

in the world.[143] Thus, an impasse exists in proceeding with the task of interpretation of discourse. Ricoeur proposes a hermeneutics of the self to traverse this aporia in moving from the impersonal ontology of the text to a personal ontology of the interpreter in hermeneutics, which will be examined in later chapters of this book. However, if the discourse is firstly the discourse of a person, then for the text still to be related to the discourse of a person (i.e., the author or writer) interpretation begins with the same impasse and does not just conclude with it. Thus, the very concept of interpretation that employs the descriptive task would have to be considered to be a mystical approach. This would occur since what is proposed is transcendence in both the creating of the text and the use of epistemology in interpreting the text, which raises the issue to one of pistology, that is, an issue of belief about the text.

It is no wonder that this approach has had to focus itself exclusively on the concept of the text being an impersonal code, as representing a message, rather than text being a message. In this way the issue of ontology is avoided by not being addressed in the reduction of the entire process to an impersonal ontology. If the text has being as a message, an insurmountable ontological problem occurs in interpreting the text in current thought. Whilst Ricoeur does deal with the issue of moving from the impersonal ontology of the text to meaning as belonging to the ontology of a person, what he does not deal with is how the text became impersonal; he just accepts that it is, possibly based on Heideggerian thought. Barthes makes the following observation, which reveals his own ontological presuppositions, and as such it is important:

> Once an action is recounted for intransitive ends, and no longer in order to act directly upon reality—that is, finally external to any function but the very exercise of the symbol—this disjunction occurs, the voice loses its origin, the author enters his own death, writing begins.[144]

The act of writing itself directly, for Barthes, frees the process from ontological considerations. In Ricoeur's thought the act of writing is personal, and it is in the detachment that there is a movement to an impersonal ontology. This movement remains uninvestigated in Ricoeur. But for Barthes there is no movement from a personal to an impersonal ontology. The act of writing in Barthes' thought, as having "intransitive ends," places the text in the situation of not acting as a referent to a subject, that is, an author. Action to reality no longer relates; that is, explanations and ontological implications are no longer needed or considered. All further engagement of the text is handed over to the symbol. The act of writing *is a disjunction* resulting in an autonomous text. This autonomy, in Barthes work, is inherent in its creation and is not simply due to a detachment of the authored written text from the author.

Ricoeur, as a postmodern philosopher, also recognizes that the nature of the text is that of an impersonal ontology, since it is the *something* said. However, he also

---

143. Ibid., 193.
144. Barthes, "Death of the Author," 2.

recognizes that at its inception the text is related to a personal ontology, and hence for Ricoeur the text has an author but not a speaker.[145] As Ricoeur asserts, to ignore this is to ignore the most basic nature of a discourse as *something* (impersonal for Ricoeur) told by *someone* (having a personal ontology).[146] In Ricoeur's theory it is detachment from the personal that results in the autonomous text, which then assumes the ontology of an impersonal event. However, meaning for the reader in Ricoeur's theory is the result of traversing the ontological impasse from the impersonal to the personal, so as to become meaning as interpretation of the text, in the ontology of a person. This interpretation, in the ontological movement, is impacted by a self-projection of the *otherness* of the author—i.e., a dynamic within the hermeneutics-of-the-self of the reader—it is not recognition of an actual impact due to that which is other than the self and that is in any way related to the author.

Barthes is the author who importantly and significantly highlights the appearance of a *speaking voice* (thus *speech*) that addresses the reader when the reader deals with written text (so that the reader has the sense of being *spoken-to*).[147] This *speaking voice* does not just appear as an impersonal presence but actually is impersonal and neuter at conception.[148] Barthes recognizes the appearance of a *speaking voice* related to a text, but he rejects relating this *voice* to a person and thereby also voids the idea of anterior meaning. For Barthes this *voice* is writing, hence having an impersonal ontology.[149] Meaning is the result of what a reader does with a code he or she encounters and decodes in the atmosphere of language.

In contrast to Barthes, Ricoeur states that what occurs in the act of *parole* is that "a particular speaker [hence person] produces *parole* as a particular message."[150] The contrast suggested is that in Barthes' theories it seems *parole* is a means for *langue* to express itself as language;[151] whereas for Ricoeur *parole* is the event that is the production of language; it is the genesis of discourse.[152] Ricoeur's view thus indicates that there is an unexamined traversing from the personal ontology of the author to the impersonal ontology of the message in the act of *parole*, resulting in opaqueness to this traversing due to the impersonal ontology of the text. This text is the entity presented to the reader. There is uniqueness of the person that results in a unique message. This particularity evidently remains with the text and itself should indicate the impact of intentionality; hence, this traversing should therefore have been evaluated and con-

---

145. Ricoeur, *Interpretation Theory*, 30.
146. Ibid.
147. Barthes, "Death of the Author," 2.
148. Ibid., 2, 5.
149. Ibid., 2.
150. Ricoeur, *Interpretation Theory*, 3. (Bracket comment added for emphasis; italics original.)
151. It seems reasonable to remain within the impersonal nature assumed by Barthes; hence, *langue* must express *itself* to exist as language apart from any personal ontology.
152. Ricoeur, *Interpretation Theory*, 7.

sidered in the interpretation of texts. Ricoeur himself either does not see this concealment in the act of *parole* or simply ignores the movement from a personal ontology of the author at inception to an impersonal ontology of the text. Ricoeur instead focuses on the movement from the impersonal ontology of the text to the personal ontology of the reader. This occurs because the reader encounters not a person but a text, the *something* that was said. Is the opaqueness due to an inadequate understanding of the ontology of the text? In this Ricoeur has ignored an impasse that is the equivalent of the one he does consider. It is important to investigate and consider what Ricoeur has seemingly ignored.

Consequently, for Ricoeur, authorial intent exists at inception of the text, that is, a particular person creates a particular message. This text would not subsequently exist as an expression of language without the intention of the author. Accordingly, at least in the adverbial sense of intentionality,[153] and as Ricoeur agrees, the text has an author. The concept of meaning of the text in the event of writing is that of the person of the author. However, for Ricoeur, it is the detachment from the author occurring in the release of the written text into the world of readers that results in the autonomous text. This autonomy means for Ricoeur that the author, whose intention gave rise to the text, has no direct avenue of impact of authorial intentionality in interpretation.

Therefore, for Ricoeur, the text does have an author but doesn't have a speaking voice, contra Barthes, for whom the text doesn't have an author but does have a speaking voice. For Barthes, language speaks, not people; but for Ricoeur language doesn't speak, people do.[154] For Barthes it is obvious that the text has a *speaking voice* in that he noted himself to be directly addressed by the text; but for Ricoeur it is obvious that texts do not discourse (i.e., undertake an act of *parole*), people do. Hence, the text as impersonal cannot have a *speaking voice*. And, as such, a dilemma of a problematic ontology of the text in postmodern thought occurs, which indicates an understanding of the nature and being of the text that is inadequate, not only in postmodernism but in philosophical hermeneutical thought.

(b) A Problematic Linguistics

The first of these problems, considered in an examination of Barthes' proposals, indicate a faulty approach to methodology in a failure to consider the ontological interpretation involved in hermeneutics. However, the examination has also highlighted the need to reevaluate not just the ontological process in interpretation but also the ontology of the text itself (i.e., the nature and being of the text), due to an inadequate ontology of the text not only in postmodern hermeneutics but also in philosophical

---

153. The word *intentionally* is the adverb of *intent*. As an adverb it modifies a verb and consequently relates to the doing of the writing (i.e., it can be stated that the text exists *by intention* without any hermeneutical conclusions being drawn at this point).

154. Ricoeur, *Interpretation Theory*, 13.

hermeneutics generally. The second of these problems indicates a potentially faulty presupposition for Barthes' position, and this presupposition is foundational in his thought: the reduction of language to the sign, especially in dealing with the written text.

In his impacting essay "The Death of the Author," Barthes confirmed what he had asserted in other texts, as noted previously, that linguistics of semiotics presents the paradigm for dealing with the written text. Ricoeur styled this a "unidimensional approach to language," which for him is an incorrect direction.[155] Ricoeur proposes that although the sentence is composed of signs, it is not itself a sign; and as such, semiotics is inadequate to handle the entity of the sentence.[156] For Ricoeur "there is no way of passing from the word as a lexical sign to the sentence by mere extension of the same methodology to a more complex entity."[157] The problem is that the sentence is not a species of a more complex word, "it is a new entity."[158]

The sign, consisting of *signifier* and *signified*, as developed in the work of Saussure, is the basis of the understanding of *langue* and presents the basis of the linguistics of semiotics. The sentence cannot be treated in this fashion, in which the signifier becomes essentially code for the signified, and the sentence therefore a code for discrete units of a message. Ricoeur gives a detailed and in-depth argument for his own reasoning against this, which is very insightful.[159] The lexical nature of *langue* is such that one captures the signifier and is able to "look up" the signified in a dictionary, lexicon, or even a book on idiomatic use of language in culture or subculture. Therefore, within the system of language (i.e., *langue*), signs point to other signs within the system.[160] In the usual sense of usage of language one looks up the meaning of a word, or even term, and encounters an agreed set answer to the inquiry. Ricoeur, in his discussion, emphasizes this sense of discrete entities in *langue* does not apply in *parole*. There is no corresponding lexical source for a discrete meaning of the sentence; hence, though composed of signs, the sentence itself is not a sign. Yet, the hermeneutical concern is meaning of a sentence; hence, for Ricoeur the issue is the linguistics of semantics and not the linguistics of semiotics.

If one looks up the *meaning* of a word in a lexicon, one encounters a series of words, and quite often sentences, of explanation of that meaning. If, conversely, one looks up the meaning of a word originally found in the first sign, one does not find a unique reference to the first sign but a series of words and sentences again, of which the original word may be given as one such meaning. If the domain of interpretive endeavor is semiotics, then one could say here that a sign simply directs attention to

155. Ibid., 6.
156. Ibid., 7.
157. Ibid.
158. Ibid.
159. Ibid., 1–23. This is an important concept articulated in this first essay.
160. Ibid., 20.

The Conundrum and Paradox

other signs. Derrida placed the concept of structuralism in linguistics as belonging "to the domains of imagination" and that writers "take nourishment from the fecundity of structuralism."[161] Whilst Derrida's agenda was to highlight the impact of history in structuralist practice, as is done in post-structuralist thought, his observation does highlight that semiotics applied to the sentence makes meaning a creative event of a reader, not the interpretation of a received discourse.

Barthes observes that surrealism, in attempting the subversion of codes, exposed the reality that codes cannot be destroyed. But for Barthes codes are simply played with "by abruptly violating expected meanings," and in this way, in the move to modernity, surrealism helped secularize the image of the author.[162] The use of the idea of codes creates a situation where the language of the code points to other language in an attempt to disclose a message not disclosed in the code as code. In the thought of Ong, text is a visual design "made into utterance by a code that is existing and functioning in a living person's mind."[163] The code doesn't reside in the text; it is a function of the one decoding. The success or failure of such a process could only be determined by the existence of an absolute (i.e., codebook) with which comparison could be made. Without such a reference, to speak of discourse meaning in the decoding is merely a matter of reader preference. Again, there is no real interpretation but, rather, imputation. As Barthes noted, this process can proceed ad infinitum, and many messages, hence meaning or significance, become possible due to meaning being a creation of the reader.

The emphasis of the postmodern shift to the reader places disclosure of understanding, from which meaning is determined, as a function of a reader initiative. If, however, alternatively understanding is perception by the reader of the self-disclosure of the text, therefore a function of intentionality of the author, the concept of code is inadequate. In this case the text is not just a code for the message; it is the message. The paints on a canvas are not code for the picture portrayed but are that which disclose the picture to the observer, that is, they are the picture. They function together in a disclosive manner. Similarly words, in the text as composition, are used intentionally by the author in the creation of sentences with the purpose of disclosing the message of the composition to the reader.

Ricoeur recognized polysemy, especially in word meaning, that confers potential upon sentence meaning. But he also recognized that in the case of verbal discourse this is shut down by the concurrence of speakers meaning and sentence meaning. In Ricoeur's thought, sentence meaning is an ideality that, though a creation of the author, is a function of neither the author nor the reader in the detachment, and this ideality is what mediates in the interpretive process in a fusion of the horizons of the

---

161. Derrida, *Writing*, 4.
162. Barthes, "The Death of the Author," 3.
163. Ong, "Text as Interpretation," 9.

author and interpreter.[164] It is the detachment that releases this polysemy to impact sentence meaning in a way not possible in the speaking situation. However, this polysemy can be simply seen to be a function of what is noted previously. The lexical value of a word points to other words, which themselves can point to other different words. Consequently, there are many nuances of differences possible that impact meaning in this process. One can imagine that over a period of time the differences can be significant. If in the same way, as in the thought of Derrida, the sentence as a sign simply points to other signs. Taken as a code functioning in the reader's imagination the multiplicity of meanings becomes explosive, since it becomes a function not only of potentiality intra-sentence but extends this fecundity of meaning to an impact inter-sentence.

It is perhaps Gadamer who raises the most serious objection to the analysis that treats language as code and symbols. Gadamer notes that a philosophy of language that treats language idealistically raises a critical question that strikes at the heart of the more structural approaches to language. He states, "by directing attention to the "form" of language, does it not isolate language from what is spoken in and mediated through it?"[165] If language becomes isolated from what it says, then how does it say it if not in language? This simply projects the idea of some form of metalanguage. Language is the message, not the symbol of a message.

(c) The Journey Ahead

The ontology of the text is philosophically inadequate to the processes so far described in the practice of hermeneutics. This is a major issue that must be explored. The pronouncement of the death of the author has ignored the impact of authorial intentionality that continues to surface, even if only by implication, despite every attempt to ignore and erase it. Whilst it can be agreed that the impact of authorial intent cannot be viewed in the concept of direct impact of the psyche of the author that determines meaning, it must also be investigated as to why and how intentionality of the author does have impact, yet not as psyche of the author. What must also be explored is that it is the concept of *understanding* that allows the traversing from the idea of meaning of the person of the author to that of the person of the reader through the ontology of the text. The concept of understanding is able to relate these two aspects without reducing them to the level of *sameness of meaning* as either a goal of interpretation or a criterion of an interpertation's success in disclosing the composition.

---

164. Ricoeur, *Interpretation Theory*, 93.
165. Gadamer, *Philosophical Hermeneutics*, 76.

5 "The Reports of the Author's Death Have Been Greatly Exaggerated"*

Introduction

THE CONCEPT OF THE conundrum and paradox of Scripture has acted as a broad basis for the discussion concerning the issues in the previous three chapters. The concept of the conundrum of Scripture raised issues related to authorial intention and the presence of voices associated with the text. The paradox of Scripture raised issues surrounding the nature of the text and how it is a vehicle for a message, therefore how the voice "speaks" to the reader. This concept of the conundrum and paradox of Scripture initially arises because of a belief about the scriptural text by an interpreter.

However, the issues that have been raised by this assent to the belief causing the conundrum and paradox are hermeneutical ones. These issues relate initially to human communication and precede any consideration of divine communication. At the conclusion of chapter four, the consideration of the philosophical basis of our discussion showed the path ahead. This indicated that the issues of authorship, hence authorial intent, and the nature of the text, with its relationship to the composition, require revision. Indeed, a review of thinking regarding the nature and operation of these issues is in order. There is the third issue of *understanding* in relationship to the text that must also be pursued in considering an author's communication and the interpretation of that communication.

The issue of authorial intent raised by the conundrum is primary as it touches on the very possibility of the idea of authorial discourse in interpreting the message associated with a text. If the author has no voice, then there is no authorial message and the only possible message is that from the voice of the reader. In this situation there is no conundrum, since the reader has become both the creator and the vehicle

---

* This is an adaptation of a Mark Twain quote, see 112.

of the message. The paradox, hence the nature of the text, becomes important once it is established that the author has a voice and there is a message that has been communicated. The reader is the means of the continuation of discourse of the author's communicated message.

The postmodern declaration of the autonomy of the text has rendered the concept of authorial intent as *passé*, and so any impact of the author on interpretative meaning as irrelevant. There is no authorial voice, and any voice is simply an interpreter giving voice to the autonomous text. The adaptation of a Mark Twain quote for the title of this chapter exemplifies the situation. Mark Twain's death was reported in the presence of his life. The postmodern reports of the death of the author are exaggerated, and what has occurred in treating the text as autonomous is a failure to recognize the author's continuing impact.

Roland Barthes famously pronounced the passing of the author in his essay "The Death of the Author," which was considered in the last chapter. However, his pronouncement of the death of the author is not only premature but ill advised and misguided. It was noted that his assertion was based on both an inadequate ontology and suspect presupposition of a semiotic approach to language as discourse. Ricoeur has highlighted that linguistics of semiotics is not suitable for discourse, and so linguistics of semantics is needed. However, although not pronouncing the death of the author, Ricoeur's view of autonomy renders authorial intent ineffective in interpretation, with no direct avenue to *speak* to an interpreter's meaning. Thus, for Ricoeur the text has an author and not a speaker. Conversely, Barthes asserted the text has a speaker—albeit an impersonal voice—but not an author. Barthes' argument for the concept of a speaking voice of the text is sound, and it is a concept now widely accepted, even in postmodern thought. Is it possible that the postmodern assertion of either detachment or disjunction of the text, thereby granting the text autonomy, has simply caused the impact of authorial intention to be concealed and imprisoned in a philosophical guise with no hope of *parole*?

Authorial Intent and the Speaking Voice of the Text

Whilst not addressing the issue of authorial intent in relationship to the matter of the text, Ong suggests that writing is the interruption, or suspension, of discourse and that the reader is the vehicle of resuming the discourse.[1] Only with the advent of the reader, through whom the discourse is resumed, does verbalized meaning continue.[2] The text, as written text prior to being engaged by the reader, is "but a visual design."[3] When the reader is engaged with the text, the text is part of the discourse, but "the utterance making the discourse is *not in* the physical text but *only in* the reader or

---

1. Ong, "Interpretation," 9.
2. Ibid.
3. Ibid.

readers (or, originally, in the writer)."⁴ The text is only expressed through the reader and only through interpretation are written marks changed back into meaning.⁵

Nevertheless, if there is an authorial voice associated with the creation of the written text, which in Ong, as in Gadamer and Ricoeur, is noted as originally existing in the event of writing of the text, it is, by logical extension, the authorial discourse that is resumed by the reader. If it is the logical extension to consider that it is the author's discourse that is resumed the question that must be asked concerns the possibility of the nature of any impact of an author in the interpretation of his or her discourse? Ricoeur has noted that, in his view, the concept of the intentional fallacy of Wimsatt and Beardsley is matched by an equal fallacy of the authorless text. In Ricoeur's thought the text "has an author and no longer a speaker."⁶ Yet in Ricoeur's thought, the author has no avenue of direct *voice* in the interpretation, and therefore meaning, of what is by agreement initially an authorial discourse. Ricoeur has recognized that if there is a *voice* associated with a discourse, as in dialogue, meaning relates to the *speaker's* voice.⁷ Consequently, for Ricoeur and Ong, by extension any *voice* of the resumed discourse must be the reader and meaning becomes the reader's. The reader develops this authorial discourse meaning in the absence of any direct impact of authorial intention. In this situation, although logically meaning is of an author's discourse, in what is almost a perverse turn of events, it is not the author's meaning nor is the interpreted discourse impacted by the author's meaning.

Ong has clearly highlighted the personal nature of discourse, and the text is not the discourser, the reader is; the text is the matter that is the basis and substance of the discourse. Consequently, the written text, prior to its attachment to, and engagement by, a reader has as its referent an authorial discourse of which it itself is evidently purely representative. Hence, in Ong's thought the text is not the discourse but refers to the discourse. The voice of the resumption of discourse is the reader's voice but it is the author's discourse, as the referent of the reader's discourse, which is resumed by the reader's voice. Accordingly, it can be asserted, on this basis, that the written text has as its referent an authorial discourse. Therefore, it is an authorial discourse, and hence an authorial intent, that is the antecedent of the written text. Thus, if, as the reasoning of Ricoeur and Ong suggests as noted previously, meaning is the reader's not

---

4. Ibid. (Italics added; bracket comment original.)

5. Gadamer, *Truth and Method*, 349.

6. Ricoeur, *Interpretation Theory*, 30. Ricoeur recognizes that if it is a fallacy to assert the operation of authorial intent as an aspect of the psyche of the author in written discourse meaning, it is an equal fallacy to assert an "authorless text" that disregards the author in meaning. The text exists because it is authored and this cannot be ignored, despite any argument over how meaning is impacted. It is this that has seemingly prevented Ricoeur from traveling the road of the more radical postmodern French thinkers such as Barthes and Derrida, who have essentially asserted the concept of the *authorless text*, and on this basis have abolished any impact by the author on meaning.

7. Ibid., 29.

the author's (although this meaning is of the author's discourse), then this meaning has been developed without any direct reference to that which is its referent.

Gadamer proposes the same concept theoretically. He proposes an internal dialectic that is the creation of the author as having an impact on meaning for the reader.[8] This results in an indirect authorial impact on meaning by the reader. Ricoeur develops a linguistic approach in his theory that can on the one hand deny direct impact of the author and yet on the other hand allow for an authorial influence on meaning, thus restraining the reader from making what he or she will of meaning. In his theory meaning is a function of both the speaker and the sentence,[9] and it is only in the case of dialogue, when the speaker is there, that these meanings coincide.[10] The author intentionally constructs the sentence, but in the absence of the author the ideality of sentence meaning is released due to the autonomy of the text. It is this autonomous sentence meaning that the reader engages. Hence, Ricoeur makes what is for him an important distinction of the author as a writer and not a speaker.

However, Barthes makes the startling observation that the reader of a text finds self being addressed by a *speaking voice* that appears to be *other* than self.[11] In the novella *Sarrasine* by Balzac, published in 1830 as part of Balzac's *La Comédie humaine*, Barthes finds himself confronted with a narrating voice and asks the question, who is speaking?[12] After considering the possibilities for the source of this voice, including Balzac as either man or author, Barthes' conclusion is that writing itself is the *voice*.[13] Because the *speaking voice* of texts addresses readers in their own present, the *voice* cannot be that of the person of the author, since the author is not present in the reading. The text does not have the ontology of a person and, as a result, the *speaking voice* cannot be identified with a person, which Barthes also notes for different reasons.[14] Yet the *voice* has an appearance of *otherness* for the reader. This appearance of *otherness* indicates powerful and yet unexplored aspects about the being and nature of the composition in relationship to the written text, which will become the subject of later chapters of this book.

The important aspect brought into focus is that the written text, which has an author and not a speaker in Ricoeur's treatment, does indeed have a discernible *speaking voice*. Both Ricoeur and Barthes propose that the text has a writer, that is, a person who wrote. Hence, this *speaking voice* is a voice distinct from the person who wrote.

8. Gadamer, *Dialogue and Dialectic*, 126.
9. Ricoeur, *Interpretation Theory*, 19.
10. Ibid., 29.
11. Barthes, "Death of the Author," 2.
12. Asking *self* this question itself shows the sense of *otherness* in the *speaking voice*.
13. Barthes, "Death of the Author," 2.
14. Ibid., 2, 5. Barthes notes that the *voice* is marked by its neutrality, and in his conclusions he specifically notes therefore that no person makes the utterance.

"The Reports of the Author's Death Have Been Greatly Exaggerated"*

This issue and its implications suggest the issue of the nature of the text is an important if not explosive issue that must be investigated.

(a) Relationship of the Voice to the Author

In the "Death of the Author," the "author" to which Barthes refers is primarily the institution of the concept of an author that, for him, developed in modern times.[15] It is the institution of the author that is dead, the concept of the person created in the idea of authorship and its controlling influence on interpretation.[16] This is not the actual person who wrote the text but what has been made of the idea of the author of the text, in order to control interpretation and meaning. Barthes' attack is on the concept of authorship. For Barthes language is the horizon within which writing and reading occurs.

In the preceding chapters of this book, a case was presented proposing that authorial intent is best viewed as different to authorial meaning, which meaning is related to the incidence of the text. This concept of authorial meaning would be coincident in part with what Ricoeur calls the verbal meaning of the text. However, the authorial intent is best understood as the antecedent of the text. This is not inconsistent with the current discussion of written texts. The authorial discourse resumed by the reader is the resultant communication, as a written text, which is composed in the act of *parole*, itself due to the formation of an authorial intention.

The central issue is whether or not the author has a referential *voice* in this disclosure to which the reader should *listen* in the formation of understanding. Subsequently, if operational, it must be examined as to how this *voice*, to be effective, can operate in a non-oral situation. If the reader's discourse *is* the continuation of the authorial discourse, although the text may *appear* to be autonomous due to its temporal detachment, this autonomy is illusory. The author possessed an authorial intent, which is then expressed as an authorial discourse in the form of a communication, which is the resultant written text. The reader is subsequently continuing this discourse. This continuity is suggested by the concept of the sequence of the communication, that is, someone (an author) said something (the composition in relationship to the text) to someone (either as an intended or unintended reader). This would seem to preclude autonomy, because the moment a reader engages the text the continuity is reestablished.

The recognition that the reader's engagement with the text is resumption of the authorial discourse raises the following question. If the reader is resuming the discourse of the author, does this imply that the reader should operate simply as an agent of the author? In one sense this would seem, on the surface of things, to be a logical

---

15. Ibid., 2. The tone and scope of the essay leads to the assumption that Barthes means the era of modernity rather than just the concept of the early to mid-twentieth century.

16. Barthes, *Pleasure*, 27.

inference. Further, if this situation is the case, is the proposal therefore essentially that the reader should become some form of neutral voice either of, or for, the author? Yet, adoption of this concept would coincide with what Ricoeur identifies as "the Romanticist ideal of coinciding with a foreign psyche," which he, along with all the authors considered, specifically rejects.[17]

Gadamer, in dealing with the issues involved with historical written text, gives an effective illustration that highlights the folly of assuming that the reader can become the de facto voice of the author. In a discussion of literary tradition he observes: "in order to be able to express the meaning of a text in its objective content we must translate it into our own language."[18] It has been noted previously that translation involves not only transference of one language to another but also the transference of thought forms and presuppositions.[19] Therefore, even if the reader is using the same language as that of the author of the text, interpretation moves beyond language. Gadamer's observations thus provide some illustrative value.

The process Gadamer discusses involves the assimilation of what is different into what is familiar, and, despite any objectivity that may be employed by the reader, the "alien being of the object" has already been subordinated into the reader's own conceptual frame of reference.[20] Therefore, at best the interpreter represents a relative understanding of the authorial intent from the perspective of the interpreter. As Gadamer states, "To try to eliminate one's own concepts in interpretation is not only impossible, but manifestly absurd."

The reader is indeed a voice of continuation of the authorial discourse, yet not from the viewpoint of the author but that of the reader. The issue is not that of the reader getting inside the author's mindset, which as Gadamer has observed is an absurdity, but rather of seeking to understand what the author would understand from the reader's perspective concerning the *Sache*, or matter of the text (i.e., an understanding that is within the reader's perspective). This is in effect the impact, as noted previously, of a changing audience, or reader, on meaning (i.e., what occurs is an understanding of the author's communication relative to the interpreter).

It is well known that authors can adapt and change what they say in the light of changed circumstances, such as feedback and input from a differing readership than who was originally anticipated. Authors can rework, redevelop, and resubmit they written texts; this is called revision. The revision supersedes the original and respresents a more contemporary understanding of the author. Revision is simply the intentional disclosure by the author of a new understanding. Hence, it could be seen

---

17. Ricoeur, *Interpretation Theory*, 92.

18. Gadamer, *Truth and Method*, 357. Later in the discussion he shows that his discussion concerns interpreting texts: "This is now confirmed by the linguistic aspect of interpretation. The text is made to speak through interpretation," 358.

19. Caird, *Language and Imagery of the Bible*, 2.

20. Gadamer, *Truth and Method*, 357.

that the unintended reader's resultant meaning, especially historically distanced from the author's original discourse, represents a form of revision in the light of changed circumstances and differing presuppositions of the reader.

In the thinking of Ong the utterance and utterer are totally separated once the text comes into existence. This is similar to the view of Ricoeur.[21] The utterer "once he has written down his text, may as well be dead" in the act of interpretation of the utterance, and it is in this sense that, for Ong, writing creates autonomous discourse.[22] The reader is therefore resuming not a dialogue, as with the author, but a monologue concerning the author's text. In Ong's view, this situation he has outlined "is, or should be, utterly commonplace in reader-oriented criticism and related criticism."[23]

In the case of a written text the authorial discourse is itself transmitted immediately as a monologue. Ricoeur's understanding is grounded in the concept that he is contrasting oral discourse as dialogue with the event of writing, a relationship that is then "shattered by writing."[24] It is an inescapable conclusion that there are no partners in dialogue either in the writing or in the discourse resumed by the reader. The creation of text is originary as monologue and it remains monologue in the continuation of discourse. There is no shattering of a dialogical situation since no dialogical situation exists in the origination of written text. Monologue is structured differently than dialogue in that monologue must intentionally include aspects that are inherent in the dialogical situation; and this distinction must be evaluated in the pursuit of understanding. Consequently, if monologue is intentionally structured differently than dialogue, this implies that monologue must be approached differently than dialogue in the event of interpretation.

The notion of the text as autonomous is the prevalent postmodern position on the concept of authorial voice. This means essentially that the text, in being released from the restraint of the author, has been removed from the impact of any authorial presence, and therefore authorial voice, in the task of interpretation by the reader.[25] As a result postmodern interpretation has moved away from an emphasis on what texts say to an emphasis of what readers do with texts.[26] Yet the logical conclusion is that the interpreter initiates the continuance of authorial discourse. This concept of an autonomous text must be addressed and examined in the discussion of any presupposition of authorial intent.

---

21. Ong, "Interpretation," 9.
22. Ibid.
23. Ibid., 10.
24. Ricoeur, *Interpretation Theory*, 35.
25. Gadamer, *Truth and Method*. Gadamer's thinking on this issue is particularly set out in 352–57. The reference by Ricoeur to the detached autonomous text has been considered previously.
26. Vanhoozer, *Is There a Meaning*, 149.

Autonomous Text: Extinguishing the Voice of the Author?

If a text is to be considered autonomous, then the voice of the author is presumed extinguished, with the subsequent loss of authorial discourse. When this is the presupposition, the author's impact is lost and the writer appears.[27] Gadamer and Ricoeur have established sound and valid arguments that highlight the effect of concepts such as detachment of the text from the author and the impact of aesthetic and historical alienations, which are issues that constitute a significant consideration in both understanding and interpretation of texts.[28] However, detachment is a temporal condition, but autonomy is an authoritative state. Further, autonomy is neither the necessary nor inherently valid consequence of detachment.

The shift from the concept of an author to a writer, as in the work of Barthes and Derrida, shifts the focus from the idea of creativity and intentionality in the formation of the composition. Ricoeur, whilst asserting the autonomy of the text, nevertheless maintains the concept of *intentioned-ness* by noting that it is a fallacy to consider that a text is authorless, as has been noted earlier in this chapter. Ricoeur, so as to not give opportunity for any impact of the author who he himself recognizes in the creation of the text, denies the author *voice*; and so for Ricoeur the text has an author and not a speaker.[29] It is interesting that Barthes' opening line of his essay "The Death of the Author" notes the *intentioned-ness* of another author, Balzac. Barthes' essay cannot be disclosed without noting that Balzac intentionally wrote the text that captured Barthes' imagination.[30] The problematic of the issue of detection and evaluation of this *intentioned-ness* doesn't disguise or obliterate its existence; detachment does not equal, nor of necessity imply, autonomy.

The abolition of the author is connected with the loss of the absolute in postmodern thought. The recognition of alienations and distanciation, within the interpretive process, impact the accessibility and perception of that which is absolute. But this does not itself demonstrate nonexistence. The loss of a consideration of the hermeneutical impact of authorial intention, taken together with the loss of reference to that which is absolute, are critical contributing factors to the view of the autonomous text.

The word *voice* is used extensively, as in this book, to refer not only to the idea of vocalization of sound, as in dialogue (i.e., the saying) but also to refer directly to perception of what is communicated (i.e., the said of the saying). This usage of the word *voice* occurs since generally the focus of attention is the message and not the sound of the voice. Even where a listener takes verbal clues, such as by emphasis and mood

---

27. Barthes, "Death of the Author," 2.

28. Thiselton, "Communicative Action and Promise," 134. Thiselton views Gadamer and Ricoeur as the "two exponents of hermeneutics who have achieved the greatest weight in the twentieth century . . ."

29. Ricoeur, *Interpretation Theory*, 30.

30. Barthes, "Death of the Author," 2.

thereby using the sound of the speaking voice, both the *voicing* and the *listening* are related to an understanding of the message communicated, not to a focus on the *voice* of the communicator. Hence, to *listen* relates not only to the hearing of the speaking voice but also to reception and perception of the message spoken.

The author's monologue as a literary work presents a unique situation wherein the act of vocalization is bypassed in the appearance of the written text and the "said" appears directly apart from vocalization. Yet monologue is still the *voicing* of a communication within the use of the word *voice*. Although a reader, including the author, can indeed subsequently vocalize the text in reading the text, this is verbalization of an extant text already *spoken* and not the emergence, or *voicing*, of the text. The text, in giving *voice* to the communication of a message, thereby has a *voice*. The issue then becomes the identity and nature of the *voice* being encountered in relationship to the text.

Barthes noted this implication of a disclosive *voice* in dealing with a text, and, as was previously noted, in his view this cannot be directly and uniquely identified as that of the person of the author.[31] However, if what is occurring is the resumption of an authorial discourse, then the *voice* that addresses the reader acts as a representative of the author. Previously, the problems were discussed concerning the assumption that the reader becomes some form of neutral agent for the author and, it was concluded, that this is not a sound direction of reasoning in the analysis of the hermeneutical situation. A reader cannot distance him or herself from his or her own presuppositions to form some form of neutral blank board on which the author can inscribe a message. Yet, here is a seeming paradox: the reader is at the same time on the one hand able to be a representative of the author and on the other hand be the *other* who listens to the *voice*, and whose presuppositions are not the author's. The work of Ricoeur on the hermeneutics of the self in *Oneself as Another*—which will be considered at length in later chapters of this book—presents a way forward in analyzing this situation and solving the paradox. The *voice* encountered has its locus for *speaking* in the *self* of the reader. This *voice* of the text is due to the ability of self to be at the same time consciously self and other than self. Consequently, the person is able to experience a disclosure to the self of this *otherness* and experience the encounter of this *otherness* in listening to the *voice* of the text. All of which is occurring within the domain of self. In this way the *voice* of the text has the appearance of being other than self. This critical observation and resultant paradox are pursued at length in the unfolding of this book.

The very concept of voices associated with a text raises philosophical issues, since this concept infers a presupposition of the ability of a text to refer to that which is outside the text. In the postmodern philosophical hermeneutics of Gadamer and Ricoeur, there is not a denial of the presence of the author as creator of a text and its subject matter in the act of writing; rather it is a denial of effective voice for the

31. Ibid.

author in interpretation once the text is written and thereby escapes the horizon of the author.[32] In the thinking of Ricoeur the authorial-discourse is fixed in the act of writing so that the "human fact disappears" and "material marks" now act in conveyance of the message.[33] Philosophically for Ricoeur the result is that the authorial *voice* is effectively extinguished in the subsequent understanding of the written text. Ricoeur's implication is that detachment from the author, being detachment from the author's personality, and hence psyche, is also equivalent to the extinguishing of any direct impact of an imposition of the will of the author on the text in interpretation of that text. Gadamer, for his part, states, "What is fixed in writing has detached itself from the contingency of its origin and its author and made itself free for new relationships. Normative concepts such as the author's meaning or the original reader's understanding represent in fact only an empty space that is filled from time to time in understanding."[34]

Gadamer describes a means that he believes assists the integrity of the authorial-discourse in written text in the absence of effective authorial voice. Based on an analysis of Plato's dialogues, Gadamer noted Plato's own observation on the weakness of writing, which is that it is exposed to both intentional and unintentional misunderstanding.[35] The text is now on its own in the absence of the author, who, in the situation of direct discussion, is able to provide insight and clarification.[36] Gadamer's observation is that Plato's expressed answer was to create within the text a dialectic that would direct the reader.[37] However, in studying the dialogues, Gadamer also believed he uncovered an inherent pattern in the dialogues, which was based on the concept that all real knowing lies in the solution of the problem of the *One* and the *Many* (emphasis added); for example, Gadamer observes that letters have meaning, but when brought together in a word meaning relates to the whole, not the individual letters.[38] A process of internal referencing between these positions (i.e., what essentially amounts to a hidden dialectic) directs the process. Ricoeur takes a similar view, which is that a "dialectic of event and meaning" is set up that governs the semantic autonomy of the text, maintaining discursive integrity.[39]

However, Ong, whilst also declaring the autonomy of the text in regard to authorial-discourse, asserts that the concept of "fixity" in regard to a written text, so

---

32. Wolterstorff, *Divine Discourse*, 153. Wolterstorff observes that Ricoeur's concept is not based on a rejection of authorial-discourse interpretation. The authorial-discourse is integral within the linguistics of the text. As such Ricoeur's is an "argument against the autonomy of authorial-discourse." The text is now that which is autonomous with respect to the hermeneutical event with the reader.

33. Ricoeur, *Interpretation Theory*, 26.

34. Gadamer, *Truth and Method*, 357.

35. Gadamer, *Dialogue and Dialectic*, 126. See also *Truth and Method*, 354.

36. Ibid.

37. Gadamer, *Truth and Method*, 354.

38. Gadamer, *Dialogue and Dialectic*, 148.

39. Ricoeur, *Interpretation Theory*, 23, 25.

important in Ricoeur and Gadamer, is not valid. The removal of the utterance from the author doesn't remove the text from discourse, as no utterance can exist outside the sphere of discourse, that is, outside a transactional setting.[40] Putting the discourse into written text can only "interrupt discourse, string it out indefinitely in time and space," but this act does not "fix" the discourse.[41]

Ong's reasoning is that a text is not essentially an utterance, as it doesn't "say" something; it is "but a visual design."[42] The utterance, the saying of something, occurs through "a code that is existing and functioning in a living person's mind."[43] When a reader takes this visual structure and "converts it into a temporal sequence of sound, aloud or in the imagination, directly or indirectly—that is, when someone reads the text . . ." the discourse is resumed.[44] Ong's observations do not cancel or contravene what Ricoeur and Gadamer have declared on the autonomy of the text—Ong is still a proponent of the text as an autonomous linguistic unit. Gadamer suggests that interpretation itself, which incorporates the reader's interaction with the text, is a mediating aspect that disappears as a linguistic endeavor bringing the *Sache* into speech.[45] Ong is simply highlighting that discourse is something a person does, not something a text does.

Ong's observation does highlight that what is fixed is the linguistic unit that is the text, not the meaning. Discourse, and hence meaning, is something a person does, not the text; the text is the subject matter of the discourse. As "visual marks" the written text has no meaning until someone reads it, and the resultant meaning is a function of a person not a text.[46] The discourse about the matter of the text does not resume without the introduction of someone meaning something in the saying. The written text is the "residue" of discourse, which by implication needs reanimation for resumption of discourse.[47] This reanimation happens with the advent of the reader. In Gadamer's words, "Writing is the abstract ideality of language."[48]

This observation, that the reader in encounter with the text supplies the voice of meaning, is not one either Gadamer or Ricoeur would disagree with; it is their position also. It is also a position that, in all probability, neither Vanhoozer nor Thiselton, in their work considered so far representing the evangelical position, would disagree with in principle, for both see meaning as a function of persons not texts. Yet, it does

---

40. Ong, "Interpretation," 9. In the philosophy of Gadamer and Ricoeur already considered, it is clear that they hold a similar, if not the same, concept.
41. Ibid.
42. Ibid.
43. Ibid.
44. Ibid.
45. Gadamer, *Truth and Method*, 359.
46. Vanhoozer, *Is There a Meaning*, 202.
47. Ong, *Orality and Literacy*, 11.
48. Gadamer, *Truth and Method*, 354.

imply that the concept of verbal meaning of the text, so important in the work of Ricoeur and Gadamer, must be a referential world that is not seen as resident within the text, since the text does not have meaning until someone means something in engaging the text. This referential world must be capable of communication with the reader that is, it must have a "voice." In whatever manner, that "voice" is heard. Consequently, any argument against authorial presence, based upon a perceived inability of a "voice" exterior to the text impacting the reader, does not in itself hold in this reasoning.

The concern for both Vanhoozer and Thiselton, and indeed the concern of Christianity, is the relationship of the reader's meaning to that of the author's. This meaning is what led to the intention-to of the author, and thus caused the author to communicate in the first place. The position of both Ricoeur and Gadamer is that the text at the time of writing was the result of a meaning the author had. But in the subsequent detachment from the author, the situation is such that the text contains internal linguistic structures that now direct the reader on the matter, or *Sache*, of the text. The author's meaning is now in the hands of the text and reader. However, if there is a *voice* of this authorial discourse that acts as *other* and brings disclosure of the *Sache* to the reader, the concept of autonomy comes into question. Barthes notes the voice exists, which he has related to writing and semiotics, resulting in a language and code that acts autonomously. However, even Barthes had to note that the writing exists intentionally. And this intentionality, as antecedent, at the very least challenges the consideration of that which is designated as autonomous, though detached.

The view of textual autonomy also involves a presupposition that the matter is directly available in the text. If what Ong has highlighted is correct, the result is that the written text is only form, not content, and hence does not, as written text, contain the matter of the text, which is content not form. The matter of the text is supposedly that which can be translated into other languages and cultural situations; that is, hermeneutics concerns the matter of the text. Evidently, this content can only become available in the reanimation, that is, on the resumption of the discourse. Therefore, the only way that the linguistic marks can deal with the content, or the matter, is by reference, since the matter is not within the text. Consequently, although the text is detached, the assertion of autonomy is not established. This situation therefore impacts interpretation of all texts, not simply sacred texts.

Ricoeur explains how, for him, the verbal meaning, or sense, of the text remains within the text. He takes as his lead the work of Edmund Husserl and Gottlob Frege; proposing the concept that meaning is not an idea in the mind, but "an ideal object" that can not only be identified but can also be continuously reidentified and restated.[49] This ideality is neither a physical nor a psychic reality, and, in the thinking of Husserl as understood by Ricoeur, these noematic objects are irreducible to the psychic side

---

49. Ricoeur, *Interpretation Theory*, 90.

of the acts themselves.[50] Consequently, the understanding of the author, which the author intended to communicate, expressed and set out in the text, is irreducible back to the consciousness that gave rise to the statements in the text.

Therefore, Ricoeur's implication is that irreducibility to the consciousness of the author is equivalent to, or includes, irreducibility to an authorial intention. Yet if meaning exists in people not texts, then this ideality now exists in an extratextual situation that is neither physical (i.e., in the text) nor psychic (in the thought world of the author because in the event of writingthe psyche involved is that of the author). Ricoeur's aim is not to deny referential meaning external to the text; he has merely developed an approach to remove referential meaning from what he views as the Romanticist's concept of authorial intent. The referential world of the author and that of the intended audience, and any ability to direct the reader back into them, are lost in the temporal detachment that results in the creation of the autonomy of the text. Ricoeur's concept of a referential world is one that opens up in front of the reader, and the psyche of the reader supplies meaning.[51]

(a) Authorial Intent in the Detachment: The Transforming Act of Parole

This hidden assumption that either the authorial intent is equivalent to the consciousness of the author or that an integral nondetachable union exists between them is important and must be examined. Ricoeur's reference to the detachment of the intention of the text from the verbal meaning of the text suggests his own view is presumably the latter.[52] Gadamer has raised the issue of the consciousness of the reader in interpretation, referred to previously. Clearly, if consciousness of the reader is significant in the interpretation of the text, then the consciousness of the author is significant in the creation of the text. It is illogical to assert that the consciousness of one is highly significant and that of the other is insignificant. The consciousness of the author forms the background, the crucible and resource of the authorial intent; that is, consciousness of the author is essentially itself the antecedent of the authorial intent, which intent has been argued previously is the antecedent of the text. The authorial intent is not the consciousness of the author but a product of that consciousness on a particular matter, the *Sache* of the text. Ricoeur offers, in a discussion concerning the relationship between *event* and *meaning*, a model for understanding both the union and the possibility of detachment of authorial intent from the consciousness of the author.

---

50. Ibid.
51. Ibid., 36.
52. Ibid., 29.

Ricoeur's concept of *event* is not only that of the physical situation of dialogue where people are communicating.[53] An important part of his concept of this *event* concerns an act of *parole*, communicated in the discourse; that is, it is the message of the communicator not just the act of speaking.[54] This act of *parole* gives rise to the said of speaking, and this is what is exteriorized and retained as *event* in written text.[55] Saussure noted that whilst *langue* is not a function of the speaker, the act of *parole* is an individual act that is willful and intellectual.[56]

Consequently, the act of *parole* is an act of intentionality;[57] as such it results in a transformation of the authorial intent from the consciousness of the author into a communicable form that is suitable for being understood. In the act of *parole* the authorial intent is detached from the psyche of the author, undergoing transformation into a communicated message. The authorial intent therefore remains an integral part of Ricoeur's *event* and cannot be dismissed on the basis of an inference without analysis, since the *event* is so important in his interpretation theory. This is mirrored in the act of understanding that takes place in the consciousness of an intended reader; that is, it is the act of *parole* that is understood. It is this act of *parole* communicated in the discourse that is subsequently available to the unintended interpreter/reader.

In Ricoeur's understanding of discourse, a basic dictum is that "*If all discourse is actualized as event, all discourse is understood as meaning.*"[58] In the case of dialogue, the event of speaking itself (which is the result of an act of *parole* resulting in a message for communication) undergoes *Aufhebung*, resulting in the situation where "the event is cancelled as something merely transient and retained as the *same* meaning."[59] Alan Bass, the translator for Derrida's *Writing and Difference*, suggests that Hegel's term *Aufhebung* is basically untranslatable due to its double meaning of conservation and negation.[60] The term suggests on the one hand a form of *sublation*; yet the term "sublation" suggests a degree of identifiable retention, which does not do justice to the idea of *Aufhebung* as it suggests retention yet without being identifiable. On the other

---

53. Ibid., 12. The physical event of someone speaking is an aspect of the total event, but not its entirety.

54. Ibid., 3. Ricoeur uses as his basis Saussure's concept of *langue* and *parole*, with *parole* being a temporal event of language and *langue* as the set of codes from which it is developed. (Discourse is "the event of language," 9, and Ricoeur explicitly identifies his concept of discourse with that of *parole*, 7.)

55. Ibid., 12. (Italics added.)

56. Saussure, *Course in General Linguistics*, 14.

57. Ricoeur, *Interpretation Theory*, 3. Ricoeur notes, "a particular speaker produces *parole* as a particular message." He further notes that a "message is intentional; it is meant by someone."

58. Ibid., 20. (Italics original.)

59. Ibid., 12. (Italics original.)

60. Derrida, *Writing*, xix. In his "Translator's Introduction," Bass states that the "various attempts to translate *aufhebung* into English seem inadequate." He therefore retains the German word in his translation.

hand *Aufhebung* suggests the idea of *subsumption*, suggesting absorption, which also is inadequate because the concept of retention is lost.

What Ricoeur has seemingly ignored is that in the act of *parole* an *Aufhebung* occurs wherein the authorial intent is negated, as consciousness of the author, and then conserved, as message, in the event of speaking. Therefore, in this *Aufhebung* the authorial intent has undergone a transformation in that it is negated in one state of being as an aspect of the consciousness of the author, to being conserved in another state of being as an integral aspect in the written communication of the author. In this transformation the authorial intent becomes an attribute of the being of the text. It is in this state that the authorial intent is therefore retained in the detachment of the written text from the author; as a result of this *Aufhebung* in the act of *parole* autonomy cannot be assumed as inherent in the detachment. Whilst the authorial intent's identification and evaluation may be problematical, this does not negate its presence; detection and recognition are separate issues to that of existence.

There are some interesting observations that arise from the positions of both Ricoeur and Gadamer that suggest the impact of this presence in the author's act of *parole*. Both Ricoeur and Gadamer make reference to the authors of the texts of which they themselves are speaking, and that the idea of the dialectic is a device to protect and assist the matter these authors are communicating. In this aspect itself they show that the text is not autonomous, since they have just described restrictions inherent in the text that have been expressly designed by the author; that is, the text cannot say whatever it would like. The text exists to address the matter the author communicated. This observation in both Gadamer and Ricoeur would also indicate that the jump to autonomy from temporal detachment is somewhat arbitrary in itself.

This apparent dependence on the authorial intent is further indicated when Gadamer appears to endorse Plato's observation about the weakness of the written text, which is that once the author's discourse exists as written text it can be subject to misconception. Therefore, by implication, in this concession is recognition that, in the presence of the author, the act of speaking means the oral text of the speaking is not autonomous. For Gadamer and Ricoeur, it is once the text is written and the author becomes a reader that the text becomes autonomous.

(b) Authorial Intent and the Written Text

Gadamer shows what would appear to be his primary reason for his assertion that a change in relationship occurs in written text. He states that:

> [In] contrast to the spoken word there is no other aid in the interpretation of the written word. Thus the important thing here is, in a special sense, the "art" of writing. [*This is the reason for the enormous difference that exists between what is spoken and what is written, between the style of spoken material and the*

> *far higher demands of style that a literary work has to satisfy.*] The spoken word interprets itself to an astonishing degree, by the way of speaking, the tone of voice, the tempo etc., but also by the circumstances in which it is spoken.[61]

However, this distinction is exactly what the author must allow for in the creation of a monologue, as opposed to the dialogical situation. The author must intentionally include within the text that which will direct the reader despite that which is absent due to the nature of monologue, as opposed to dialogue. This intentional endeavor is composition.

Ricoeur, in his discussion of "Message and Reference," shows that his thinking is similar in that referencing is grounded in the dialogical situation; referencing surrounds the dialogue, which is shattered by writing.[62] What is significant is that his assertion is that what is shattered is the event of dialogue as the means of communication; hence, creating the implication that, in the thought of Ricoeur, dialogue becomes the base model for understanding communication.

However, what is being suggested in this work is that on the one hand speech and literary text are different modes of communication, yet on the other hand both essentially take the format of monologue. A monologue is created directly as a monologue, and meaning is both anterior and has a unitary source, or single authorship. Conversely, meaning in dialogue unfolds in a situation of duality, or dual authorship. Whilst both parties in a dialogue may anticipate the meaning they intend, and even seek to control the unfolding of the dialogue to reach that intention, the reality is that meaning of a dialogue is posterior not anterior. Both monologue and dialogue are forms of communication, but each involves very different dynamics at the point of origin. However, in yet another sense a dialogue is itself a series of monologues, with each party responding to the monologue of the other, and each then modifying or clarifying his or her responsive monologue. Yet in each monologue, constituting the dialogue, meaning is anterior and each participant responds to an intended meaning of the other. Meaning is always both anterior (as that of the author) and posterior (as that of the reader/hearer). The opportunity that the dialogical situation presents is that of modification of meaning due to direct input and feedback. However, where an author of a literary text is still extant, dialogue is possible.

Ricoeur recognizes that in the event of speaking, meaning is the speaker's. Thus in each monologue, constituting the dialogue, authorial intent is anterior and determinate in meaning. In each instance of speaking in a dialogue it is conceivable that each party to the dialogue can use writing as the means of communication, with the

---

61. Gadamer, *Truth and Method*, 355. The italicized section in brackets is inserted as the text of a footnote at the conclusion of the phrase "the 'art' of writing." The italics are added to distinguish the footnote from the text. This is quoted in its context as it emphasizes his perception of the importance of what he is saying to the viewpoint he has, which extinguishes the voice of the author.

62. Ricoeur, *Interpretation Theory*, 34–35.

result that the whole dialogue can be a series of written monologues. It is the temporal nature of the respondents, the being-there of each, that is the difference.

Yet, it is also conceivable that a dialogue can be achieved without proximity of the participants, for example, by mail, email, instant messaging via the Internet, and so on. Further, as mentioned previously, a reader can dialogue with an author. It is also conceivable that at the conclusion of the dialogue that the posterior meaning of each participant is different, with each therefore as the "author" of a different meaning. The problem of written text is that of the issues raised by Gadamer, and these problems will still exist in any dialogue conducted as written text. In the written text the author has to deliberately (i.e., intentionally) include in the text that which will communicate what would have been communicated in the event of saying.

Writing does not shatter the situation of dialogue, but what can and usually does change, when an author releases a written text into the world of readers, is the opportunity for dialogue. Nevertheless, as has been observed, an author can receive feedback (i.e., experience dialogue) and as a result rethink, revise, and release a new written text. Nevertheless, the anterior meaning of the author in each of his or her texts is unique to each written text, despite any similarities. In the absence of dialogue the opportunity for modification of meaning is what changes. Because meaning is an act of persons, it is unique to each person; and to speak of a reader understanding authorial meaning is illusory and speculative at best, whether in the situation of dialogue or written text. Clearly, at this stage of the discussion, in the absence of any modification of reader meaning through dialogue with the author, the possibilities of reader meaning would become endless. Thus, for Ricoeur the only avenue of authorial meaning impacting interpretation is the ideality of the semantics of the sentence, which relates to the use of language. Hence, in this fashion the autonomous text is freed from the constraints of the authorial intent, therefore meaning, of the author.

Yet retention of the term *authorial meaning* recognizes a critically important aspect of the text, that is, that the text exists intentionally. Although its being is as text, the text itself exists due to intentional composition by a person in whom meaning resides. The real issue is not the communicability of the author's meaning but that of the author's intention. If authorial intent were equivalent to authorial meaning, then Ricoeur's argument would represent an insurmountable problem to dealing with authorial intent. If, alternatively, authorial intent undergoes an *Aufhebung* in the act of *parole*, the issue becomes not detectability and sameness of meaning but detectability and understanding of intention as an attribute of the text.

It is the event of writing that leads to that appearance of the text, and the nature of this created text must be considered. Ricoeur examines the presumption that all literary text occurs as something anterior to speech itself.[63] If the concept taken of speech is that of an individual act of *parole*, then speech and text have a similar status

---

63. Ricoeur, *From Text to Action*, 102.

with respect to language.[64] Whilst it is historically demonstrable that speaking precedes writing in time, in the contemporary situation, where writing may be chosen over speaking as the format of communication, writing then "takes the very place of speech, occurring at the site where speech could have emerged."[65] Consequently, the literary text as a direct creation exists as a literary text only when it is not transcription of speech.[66] It is the direct inscription "in written letters what the discourse means."[67] Ricoeur subsequently acknowledges that in the act of writing there is a "direct inscription of intention."[68] Ricoeur's analysis is consistent with the assertion in this work that this inscription has, as its referent, an authorial intention; and without that authorial intent this inscription becomes at best a stretch of linguistic components, *langue*. Ricoeur asserts that the system of language, *langue*, is not itself a message, having only "virtual existence." Only the act of *parole* gives actuality to language.[69] The message (i.e., the literary text) is the result of *parole*.

Ricoeur's reasoning is sound, and it shows that the literary situation is not an instance of dialogue.[70] The creation of the composition separates the act of writing and that of reading with no line of communication between them.[71] Ricoeur subsequently considers the possibility of discussing an author's work with the author, so his implication cannot be that communication cannot occur between the writer and reader. A situation can even be envisaged where the author can be temporally present in the reading. However the two acts themselves (i.e., writing and reading) still occur separately and do not involve dialogue. Dialogue is subsequent to the act of *parole* that gave rise to the text. The text becomes the subject of any ensuing dialogue. Yet, as noted previously, when a dialogue is recognized to be a series of monologues, then this is true of each instance of monologue that is a part of the dialogue; monologue is obscured in the situation of speaking dialogue. Nevertheless, the creation of literary text is not itself an act of dialogue. As Ricoeur states, the composition "produces a double eclipse of the writer and reader" and "thereby replaces the relation of dialogue."[72] Hence, dialogue cannot be the base model for the text.

Ricoeur's own work reveals that his analysis of the situation of speech betrays his own basic understanding of the dialogical situation as the basic model.[73] It is on this

---

64. Ibid.
65. Ibid.
66. Ibid.
67. Ibid.
68. Ibid., 103.
69. Ricoeur, *Interpretation Theory* 9.
70. Ricoeur, *From Text to Action*, 102.
71. Ibid., 103.
72. Ibid.

73. Ibid., 104. It was noted above that in *Interpretation Theory*, 34–35, Ricoeur describes the situation of writing-reading to be an explosion of the "dialogical situation."

basis that Ricoeur derives the concept of semantic autonomy. This situation creates what could almost be described as an *ontic fallacy*. At the very place of its being as communication, Ricoeur uses the paradigm of dialogue, which it is not: it is instead monologue. Consequently, his development from that situation has an epistemological weakness at its foundation that reverberates throughout his theory. If the idea of the author's intent is inherent in the text then the concept of autonomy of the text on the basis of detachment is flawed. A mandatory requirement to assert autonomy of the text is detachment from any active impact of authorial intent. The *Mona Lisa* can be detached from the artist Leonardo Da Vinci, but it is always the *Mona Lisa* due to authorial intent of the artist that continues to exert its impact.

A further observation can be made by considering a quote from each author (i.e., Gadamer and Ricoeur) that demonstrates each writer's own implication of direct presence and voice that are attributed to the very authors to whom they refer. In discussing an aspect of Plato's work, Gadamer states: "Plato's intention seems quite clear to me..."[74] Similarly, Ricoeur, in discussing Frege's text states: "This postulation of existence as the ground of identification is what Frege ultimately meant when he said that we are not satisfied by the sense alone..."[75] It is important to put these quotes in the text rather than in the footnotes because of what they show. The issue is not the matter the text relates to in the quote but rather the form of reference to other authors. Gadamer and Ricoeur both give the authors they refer to actual presence in the naming of them; that is, they are attributing their own conclusions to the thoughts of the authors in the saying of the text. Further, both Gadamer and Ricoeur attribute their own comments to the intent of the authors they are discussing, not the intention of the texts they are discussing. This is either a mistake in the writing or a recognition that to discuss an author's discourse is to discuss what they intended.

Ricoeur, as does Gadamer,[76] asserts that what is to be understood in a text is neither the authorial intent that is laying "hidden behind the text" nor the historical situation of an intended audience and issues related to this (in Ricoeur's work it is irrelevant as to whom a text is addressed, since it is read by whoever picks it up, e.g., Ricoeur himself).[77] What is to be appropriated is the meaning of the text itself, "nothing other than the power of disclosing a world that constitutes the reference of

---

74. Gadamer, *Truth and Method*, 368. This is an example of the sort of thing that occurs in relationship to the many other authors whose work he considers.

75. Ricoeur, *Interpretation Theory*, 21. As with Gadamer this is a sample of what does occur in the work of Ricoeur.

76. Gadamer, *Truth and Method*, 300. Gadamer makes a similar observation about the historical approach. The historian, in seeking to go into the hidden realm behind the text, is seeking something the text is not designed to give. The ultimate failure of this approach, for Gadamer, is that the historian has the same problem as any reader; they cannot detach themselves from reading in their own situatedness, 304. Ricoeur, in discussing his conclusions in *Interpretation Theory*, notes Gadamer's contribution to the understanding of moving beyond the authorial intent and the audience. Ricoeur, *Interpretation Theory*, 92.

77. Ricoeur, *Interpretation Theory*, 92.

the text."[78] As a result, Ricoeur's contention is that in this process his interpretation theory has moved as far as possible away from the ideal of Romanticist hermeneutics and the pursuit of understanding a "foreign psyche."[79] Whilst the need for the movement away from the concepts of Romanticist hermeneutics is not disputed, what is disputed is that the authorial intent is a matter of a "foreign psyche." There are sufficient grounds to assume the presence of the authorial intent remains in some manner associated with the text.

(c) Authorial Intent and the Referential Nature of the Text

In Ricoeur the text discloses by reference a world before the reader, yet somewhat arbitrarily the text is incapable of referencing the world behind the text, that is, that of the author and intended audience. This world behind the text is evidently a foreign world incapable of being understood, due to the "non-ostensive reference of the text," for its impact on the meaning of the text.[80] Perhaps the reasoning of his view of the text's inability to reference to the world of the author and audience is Ricoeur's own presupposition that hermeneutics must move away from the presuppositions of Romanticism.[81] Nicholas Wolterstorff, in evaluating Ricoeur's concept of text sense, notes that this tendency to limit reference means that what is ignored is what Wolterstorff has called "designative content."[82] The same noematic content can have differing designations depending on the speaker of the sentence, and this speaker is often missing in the linguistic unit.[83] Walhout has noted that often the desire to avoid the concept of reference, in the modern situation, is because the concept of reference has become tied up with metaphysical questions of reality.[84] His suggestion of the term *descriptive reference* to overcome this has been discussed previously.

This problematical debate may indeed be behind Ricoeur's reluctance to pursue what he seems to lean toward in the very idea of reference. The basic concept Ricoeur has accepted is that the verbal meaning, as an object of ideality, is distinct from and irreducible to the thoughts relating to the authorial intent, mentioned previously.[85] Vanhoozer acknowledges that the central insight he attributes to Ricoeur is his concept that interpreters situate themselves in front of the text, which in Ricoeur's concept

78. Ibid.

79. Ibid.

80. Ibid., 87. Ricoeur, returning to the issue of reference, notes: "The sense of a text is not behind the text, but in front of it . . . What has to be understood is not the initial situation of discourse, but what points towards a possible world thanks to the non-ostensive reference of the text."

81. Wolterstorff, *Divine Discourse*, 147. Wolterstorff also makes reference to this possibility in Ricoeur's reluctance to admit a reference his language seems to acknowledge.

82. Ibid., 138–39.

83. Ibid.

84. Walhout, "Narrative Hermeneutics," 73.

85. See also, Wolterstorff, *Divine Discourse*, 146–47.

of symbol gives rise to thought, opening up a new world in front of the text.[86] This is the only referential world Ricoeur allows.

However, if focusing excessively on the past without regard to the future (i.e., the present reader's unfolding situation hinders vision in the present for the future), then perhaps it can be equally stated that excessive focus on the future without regard to the past (i.e., the tradition that the writer has written from and the context in which the discourse occurred), as Ricoeur essentially proposes, is in danger of losing its roots. This loss will impact the determination of the validity of future directions. As an illustration, it can be conceded that, in order to use a map to get to where a person desires to go, what is primarily needed is knowledge of where a person is located in relation to where they want to go. However, knowledge of where that person has come from can act as a reference point, and can then supply information about whether the current location is the result of a mistaken understanding of the course to be followed. That person may need to retrace the path or make a course correction. Such an orientation also gives a context to allow that person to understand the journey as a whole. There is no reason that precludes an interpreter's ability to discern past understandings back as far as the author.[87]

Although Ricoeur's primary focus relating to meaning is the world that opens up in front of the reader, in fairness to the work of Ricoeur, it must be acknowledged that he does recognize the importance of tradition. However, its value is descriptive in his theory of texts, forming a backdrop in the determination of meaning.[88] It is not determinate in meaning. Although the issue of alienations and the impact on these issues of authorial intent and intended audience, raised in Gadamer, affect perception of the authorial intent, they do not address the issues of availability and desirability.

How is it, therefore, that these authors, holding the view just expressed (Gadamer approaches the situation differently but the view is the same), can give presence and authority to authors from a foreign world, as just noted? Ricoeur gives some insightful thoughts on the antihistoricist reaction, typified in Frege and Husserl. Historicism is based upon a presupposition that literary content, the writing of the author, receives its "intelligibility from its connection" to the intended audience and their context.[89] The alternate concept, suggested by Frege and Husserl, which Ricoeur takes as his

---

86. Vanhoozer, "Joy of Yes," 27. The concept of Ricoeur's use of symbol as illustrative in hermeneutics was discussed in the propositions of chapter 3 of this book.

87. Vanhoozer, "Discourse on Matter," 27.

88. Ricoeur, *Conflict of Interpretations*, 27. Ricoeur's analysis sets meaning to be a function of the synchronic aspect, which concerns linguistics and is the science of the system. Tradition is the diachronic aspect and is descriptive. Understanding is not the recovery of meaning, but understanding the system allows recovery of meaning, 33. Perhaps his understanding of the role of tradition, though the word is not used the idea of the word is within the discussion, is his discussion of *appropriation* (italics added), which has to do with the actualization in the life of those addressed by the discourse. He even notes that this concept could be seen, if misconceived, as a return to the Romanticist concept incorporating authorial intent, *Interpretation Theory*, 92.

89. Ricoeur, *Interpretation Theory*, 89.

launching position, is outlined previously. Ricoeur himself adopts the antihistoricist stand,[90] and takes the view that the concept of verbal meaning relates to sentences and an ideality referenced by the sentence, not what someone has in his or her mind,[91] thus rendering as irrelevant the intent of the author and the context and understanding of the intended audience.

The goal of interpretation is to "render contemporaneous, to assimilate in the sense of making similar" and this goal is realized in actualizing "the meaning of the text for the present reader."[92] The means of actualization is the concept of appropriation. In this total hermeneutical process, in Ricoeur's view, the problem of historicism is overcome and what occurs is in fact "faithful to the original intention of Schleiermacher's hermeneutics."[93] A true understanding of the authorial intent is achieved, not in understanding the authorial intent at the time of writing, but in "the power of disclosure implied in his discourse beyond the limited horizon of his own existential situation."[94] In other words, the author saw something in his or her subject matter that he or she committed to writing; what he or she saw has the power of transcending his or her own situatedness into the world of the reader. Ricoeur views appropriation as being similar to Gadamer's proposal of the fusion of horizons, in that the world-horizon of the reader is fused with that of the writer, and "the ideality of the text is the mediating link in this process of horizon fusing."[95] The text is no longer representing either the author or reader; it is mediating between them in the pursuit of applied meaning.

Ricoeur highlights that the text has a power of disclosure, the result of which is to see what the author presented to be seen; yet, for Ricoeur, seen in its potential for the present unfettered by the past. Yet to achieve this in Ricoeur, the author must first disappear in the past to reappear in the present. This language is very similar to what is proposed as happening in the act of *parole*, an *Aufhebung* in which the authorial intent is transformed from the consciousness of the author to become an agent of disclosure in the composition related to the text. The authorial intent is first negated to then be retained in the composition. What Ricoeur has recognized is that a text has within it the power of self-disclosure. What he has not pursued is how the facility of self-disclosure leading to understanding is inherently resident in the text. The ability of self-disclosure implies inherent intent. Therefore, Ricoeur's analysis perhaps also highlights the disappearance of the author's intent as consciousness to reappear in the guise of autonomy in his work.

90. Ibid., 91.
91. Ibid., 90.
92. Ibid., 92.
93. Ibid., 93.
94. Ibid.
95. Ibid.

"The Reports of the Author's Death Have Been Greatly Exaggerated"*

It must be agreed that there cannot be a contention of the reappearance, in the interpretive event, of the consciousness of the author; hence, any concept of authorial intent related to the text is indeed independent of the psyche of the author. However, nor can there be a contention of an authorless text. The argument for autonomy is driven by the presupposition of an opposition to interpreted meaning being tied to the consciousness of the author. The suggested transforming of the authorial intent from consciousness of the author into an aspect of the composition, in the act of *parole*, is the way forward for understanding the negation and retention of authorial intent in the interpretation of written texts. The inability to recognize this in the postmodern philosophical paradigm is related to the postmodernists' view of the text.

The argument advanced by Ricoeur, of the autonomous text, is simply one that allows the reader to proceed directly to the "what it means" of a text without any consideration of "what it meant." It is the argument asserting the autonomy of the text that effectively authorizes the reader to proceed directly to "what it means," that is, the assertion of the autonomy of the text is the presupposition, or prejudice, that the interpreter hermeneutically proceeds on. Ricoeur's belief is that the internal dialectic of the linguistic processes of the text will provide sufficient direction to guide the reader in fulfilling his concept of, what is essentially, a proposed interpretation of authorial intent.

Stendhal recognized that, with historical documents, the question of meaning splits into two senses: "What did it mean?" and "What does it mean?" Further, Stendhal recognized that these two senses must be kept apart so that the descriptive nature of the pursuit of the "what it meant" of a text can be examined in its own right.[96] However, in a real sense every written text once released by the author into the world of readers has already become a historical document. This is the inverse implication of what Gadamer noted about the concept of the contemporary addressee. He asserts that this concept is shaky and can have only restricted validity, as the problem is "what is contemporary?" Where is the line drawn, since yesterday and tomorrow are contemporary with the present?[97] Similarly, everyday prior to today is history, and the time at which the text is completed and released is already history at the time of release.

Consequently, the approach that distinguishes between "what it meant" and "what it means" has general validity and application in the handling of all texts. When the history of the text is recent, the two senses will effectively appear to merge; it is the passage of time that will lead to the distinction between the two senses, due to its changes in situatedness. The investigation of "what it meant," in effect what Ricoeur labels historicism, yields an understanding of the intent of the writer at a particular place and at a particular time that then provides the basis for an understanding, or

---

96. Stendhal, "Biblical Theology, Contemporary," 419. The work of Stendhal and the issues of "what it meant" and "what it means" have been considered previously.

97. Gadamer, *Truth and Method*, 357.

to use Ricoeur's phrase, a basis for an *actualization* of "what it means." Stendhal also recognized moving to "what it means" is neither a direct nor simple process; it involves translation not only of words but thought forms, and is a creative act.[98] This is the same place to which Ricoeur desired to arrive, but, unlike Ricoeur's contention, it is achieved without disregard of the author, his or her setting, and the setting of the intended audience.

Autonomy: The Disputable Theory, Not the Indisputable Fact

The real question is the validity of the proposition of the autonomous text, so fundamental and important to Ricoeur's hermeneutic.[99] What is proposed to happen in writing is the detachment of meaning from the event.[100] In this situation the semantic autonomy of the text "appears."[101] However, it must be noted that the "appearance" is proposed to be based on the unconditional acceptance of the first proposition, concerning detachment of authorial intent from verbal meaning with the event.[102] Yet even in this concept, Ricoeur shows that in one sense he has recognized the ongoing impact of intention of the author without himself recognizing this impact; that is, he describes it but doesn't see it. Ricoeur notes that the authorial meaning becomes a dimension of the text and becomes the dialectical counterpart of the verbal meaning.[103] Hence, in this way Ricoeur retains an impact of authorial intention without ever recognizing that it is intention that has now become an aspect of the text.

Meaning, as has been emphasized previously, is an act of persons not texts; hence acceptance of this first assertion, concerning detachment of authorial intent from verbal meaning of the text, is based on a faulty understanding of both the entity of the text and the issue of meaning. Meaning cannot be detached from a psyche and therefore meaning is never an aspect of a text, as observed by Ong. Due to the *Aufhebung* that occurs in the act of *parole*, what detaches is intent as an aspect of an author's psyche to become intent as a self-disclosing aspect of the text. Intent is initially an act of persons; however, the intentionally-done act contains within it the *intentioned*-ness that allows

---

98. Stendhal, "Biblical Theology, Contemporary," 427.

99. Ricoeur, *Interpretation Theory*, 30.

100. Ibid., 25. The adjectives he uses to describe the situation, "nascent and inchoate," in his context, suggest something just begun but with a sense of promise and potential.

101. Ibid.

102. Ibid., 29. Ricoeur makes the distinction between the mental intention of the author and the verbal meaning of the text. However, in the *Aufhebung*, of which he himself takes note as the disappearance of the event to be retained as meaning, he has ignored the transformation of authorial intent. As a he result he has missed that the verbal meaning of the text is directed by the intentioned-ness of the author, 12. This establishes the ability of self-disclosure of the matter of the text.

103. Ibid., 30. He also notes that the concepts of author and authorial meaning raise hermeneutical problems contemporaneous with the semantic autonomy.

its understanding. Meaning can never be an act of a text, but intention can become an aspect of the text. Meaning in interpretation is always the reader's meaning, never the text's or author's. The issue is the degree to which the reader has understood and has been impacted by the *otherness* inherent due to the intention that has become an aspect of the text.

Ricoeur gives what amounts to default recognition of this *intentioned*-ness of the message in declaring that the event of speech allows "the transition from the linguistics of the code to the linguistics of the message."[104] Because the proposition of autonomy is a proposition that is conditional on another proposition, it is more properly an implication, and as such must be regarded as conditional not unconditional.[105] The problem is that Ricoeur proceeds with the theory treating this as unconditional—it is no longer an implication. This is revealed only a few pages further where he states: "Inscription becomes synonymous with the semantic autonomy of the text, which results from the disconnection of the mental intention of the author from the verbal meaning of the text, of what the author meant and what the text means."[106] This implies that, for Ricoeur, the authorial intent belongs to the event, and in the disappearance of the event is disconnected from meaning in relationship to the written text. This leaves meaning as a function of the text.

However, there is also a further inherent presupposition in this statement that is revealed in his conclusions to *Interpretation Theory*. The concept of verbal meaning, being textual meaning, as opposed to the concept of authorial meaning, as thought in the mind of the author, is due to a prior acceptance by Ricoeur of the concept of verbal meaning of a sentence being an ideal object independent of the author.[107] The result of his acceptance of this is a presupposition that verbal meaning, which relates to the individual sentences in the discourse, and authorial meaning, which relates to the mind of the author, can and do exist as separate entities.

Wolterstorff, in his analysis of Ricoeur's hermeneutic, notes that it is reasonable to "assume that the well-formed sentences of a language *have meanings*—that they come with meanings."[108] Where used by people literally, the noematic content (Ricoeur's *sense* of the text[109]) of what the person says is just what the sentence means.[110] However, people often don't speak either literally or use literalness as an exact measure. Hence, the authorial intent, since the author is the user of the sentence, and its mean-

---

104. Ibid., 11. This is the distinction between semiotics, which investigates the code, and semantics as discourse meaning.

105. Newman, *Grammar of Assent*, 259.

106. Ricoeur, *Interpretation Theory*, 30.

107. Ibid., 90.

108. Wolterstorff, *Divine Discourse*, 140.

109. Ibid., 139. (Italics original.) Wolterstorff shows how the noematic content is Ricoeur's *sense* of the text.

110. Ibid., 140.

ing must become determinate.[111] The authorial intent is not what the author is thinking on a matter, but rather, in the written text, authorial intent is what the author has communicated in disclosing his or her thought on a matter. The object should not be, and in this there can be agreement with Ricoeur, to get somehow into the thinking of the author as a retrograde step to go backwards into the mind of the author, as Ricoeur highlights about Romanticism.

Authors are pointing forward to what they "mean"; hence, for them at the time of inscription, meaning is not a "meant." Consequently, understanding for a reader is what an author "means" in the situation of the reader. Yet, in order to establish this understanding authoritatively, the reader requires first an examination and understanding of the "meant" of the author when he or she wrote. The object is to understand the thought of the author on a matter, and in the expressing of that thought the author has used sentences in a composition. The composition is the context of the individual sentences, and composition is a creation of an author and not something created by language; language is the medium of communication of the composition.

The sentence, as has been previously noted, is the basic unit of meaning in discourse. However, the meaning of the discourse as composition is not just the sum total of the verbal meanings of the sentences, in the same way the meaning of a sentence is not just the sum total of the meaning of individual words that comprise the sentence. The authorial intent is that which is behind the usage of the meaning of sentences that then gives the sentences meaning in the discourse. Wolterstorff examines in detail Ricoeur's contention of text sense interpretation and concludes that "the *meaning* of the sentence used in some act of discourse, coupled with the *linguistic context* of the sentence on that occasion, is not enough to determine the noematic content of that act of discourse."[112]

Thiselton, in consideration of the issue of the study of the meaning of individual words, notes that an individual word separated from its context in a text is not a primary bearer of meaning, but "a stretch of language."[113] In extending this to the sentence as a unit of meaning, remembering that Ricoeur notes his theory relates to sentence meaning, consider the following example of the potential problem: "That was filthy." The usual verbal meaning would be that whatever "that" was, it was either disgustingly dirty or extremely offensive. However, if this sentence was found to be in the mouth of an early twenty-first century youth subculture in Australia, it would actually mean that whatever "that" was, it was really good. The person using the words

---

111. Vanhoozer, *Is There a Meaning*, 204. Vanhoozer notes that sentences are meaningful actions by a person, not simply the result of a language system. It follows that their employment in discourse is similarly meaningful.

112. Wolterstorff, *Divine Discourse*, 152. In a later discussion, where he returns to the this issue of text sense, he asserts that, after a discussion in which he illustrates his own thinking, the critical assumption of text sense interpretation is that every text has one sense and this assumption is false, 171–73.

113. Thiselton, *Two Horizons*, 129.

and phrases intends the meaning of them. Therefore, it is the authorial intent that would be decisive, or the primary context, for correct understanding and usage of verbal meaning, which is the secondary context.

Because the basic semantic unit of a composition is the sentence, it would not then seem unreasonable to suggest that, although a sentence can have a basic linguistic meaning, when separated from its context in the composition the sentence should not be considered to be only the primary bearer of meaning but also a stretch of language. Consider the following example, from the biblical text, of a sentence taken from a composition: "You see then that a man is justified by works, and not by faith only" (Jas 2:24). Peter Davids notes that, in this statement, James comes close to the appearance of a direct contradiction of Paul.[114] Davids examines the thinking behind a possible contradiction of Paul, done either deliberately or accidentally, and concludes that had this been James's intention he would have totally misunderstood Paul, and that James's "use of biblical citations and the meanings of the similar expressions are totally different."[115] In the context of the composition, James can just as easily be seen to be using his own independent ideas developed from the common Jewish tradition, in which both he and Paul stood.[116] Davids then offers an exegesis of the text, showing that in the context suggested, based on a review of Pauline texts, Paul would have endorsed the essence of what James was saying. Davids then concludes the discussion of this verse by saying, "The important point is that one must not read this verse with Pauline definitions in mind, but rather must allow James to speak out of his own background."[117] Basically this sentence in James's epistle could be subject to different interpretations.

This constitutes an example of what Wolterstorff concluded, that is, that the same noematic content can involve differing meanings depending on who the speaker is, as noted previously in the discussion of Ricoeur's concept of text sense. However, not only the speaker but also the audience is impacting on meaning. Returning to the example from James, if James had addressed the letter to either Rome or the region of Galatia, then the meaning would be, or would at least have the appearance of, a direct contradiction of Pauline thought. If the statement quoted from James were authored by one of the people Paul opposes in his letter to the Galatians, the intention would be direct contradiction. Paul says of these people that they must be totally rejected (Gal 1:6–9), that their motivation is suspect (Gal 4:17), and that their agenda is their own preservation (Gal 6:12–13). This is not Paul's view of James (Gal 2:9).

It has been previously noted that Ricoeur does acknowledge the importance of the tradition in which a text stands, although his discussion primarily concerned the

---

114. Davids, *Epistle of James*, 130. The statement by James appears to be a direct contradiction of Pauline passages such as Rom 4:2, 6 and Gal 2:16.

115. Ibid., 131.

116. Ibid.

117. Ibid., 132.

literary tradition. However, in this case, even a consideration of historical tradition could be misleading since James, Paul, and Paul's opponents in Galatia all share a common Jewish tradition. The identity (i.e., signatory) and intention of the author together with the identity of the intended audience are decisive in meaning, without which potential meanings could cancel one another out, or, in a worse case scenario, set in motion opposing views of justification that would be difficult to reconcile as inspired by the same Spirit. Although this passage from James is a single illustration and could be claimed to be a unique case, any example sets a precedent, since textual autonomy and verbal meaning precludes anterior impact of intention.

The authorial intent is, in the event of writing, the context of the linguistic meaning of the semantic unit, that is, of the sentence. The author in his or her discourse has also intentionally employed this semantic unit. Yet the contention of Frege and Husserl, which Ricoeur accepts, is that this verbal meaning is irreducible to the intent of the author, and this therefore presupposes dissociation or there is no connection even at the time of the event of writing. Therefore, the decision that there is dissociation of authorial intent and verbal meaning, in the detachment of the text from the author, is itself an inherent presupposition, unsubstantiated at its point of assertion.

The assertion of detachment has led to an implication of dissociation of what is itself only implied to be dissociable, that is, event (and by implication authorial intent) and verbal meaning. This is what has led to an implication of autonomy of the text in meaning. The preceding reasoning does not disprove what amounts to this assertion of Ricoeur, which assertion is the semantic autonomy of the text. What this reasoning does do is show that semantic autonomy is far from being an established assertion at this point; it is part of his theory of texts, not an assertion to be used as a basis for the theory. Moreover, not only is it a theory, it is a disputable theory.

The result is that it would seem that the assertions of the extinguishing of the authorial voice, and hence authorial intent, and that of the autonomy of the text, are premature and can be debated. These are implications that have become presuppositions in Ricoeur's theory of texts and, as such, open themselves to questioning. Consequently, there is no need to abandon the presupposition of authorial intent, the presence of the voice of the author, and the autonomy of the authorial-discourse, all of which also can equally be argued as implied, and therefore valid for consideration. The one thing that all the considered viewpoints agree on is the existence of the author, and that the author has intended a message. The issue concerns whether or not that authorial intent, which led to the written text, can be detected in relationship to the text; and if so is it determinate in a reader's meaning.

The Journey Back from Absent Presence

As regards to the authors and their intent, the movement in hermeneutics has seen the pendulum swing from the authors to the readers. In the classical approach of

"The Reports of the Author's Death Have Been Greatly Exaggerated"*

Schleiermacher to hermeneutics, the issue in interpretation was an understanding of a text from the perspective of the authors; that is, the pursuit of authorial intent was seen as definitive. The rise of interest in the situatedness of both the author and reader, and the perceived impact on interpretation shifted the pendulum. This situation also highlighted the detached nature of the text from the author. Questions began to be asked as to the accessibility of the authorial intent; and in the questioning the movement from a sense of certainty to uncertainty had ramifications for meaning, especially if the detached text was then considered as autonomous. The focus on linguistics amplified the difficulty in accessing the authorial intent, and so shifted the hermeneutical pendulum further away from the pursuit of authorial intent. Even if seen as existent, authorial intent was considered irrelevant. In deconstruction the pendulum has swung fully to the side of the readers; and now the authors, and hence authorial intent, are absent as presence and voice, in interpretation.

The concept of an autonomous text has failed to take account of the retention of the authorial intent in the act of *parole*. The argument that detachment results in autonomy is not compelling. The recognition of the transformation of authorial intent in the act of *parole* was not recognized, and sight of the author was lost. The primary reason for this is the failure to recognize the entity of the composition in its relationship to the entity of the text. The current theory on the entity of the text has resulted in the compositions concealment and therefore also the concealment of authorial intent; but despite this concealment the current theory has no way in which to contend and deal with the logic of its existence.

The current theory on the entity of the text also searches for some way to explain why this textual autonomy is suddenly constrained, and is not able to act with unrestrained abandonment. In both Ricoeur and Gadamer the recognition of restraint on meaning cannot be established without an indication of that constraint itself being an intention of the author. Therefore, the author intentionally develops a constraint, which is inherent within the text but detached from the author. In this inference Ricoeur and Gadamer, albeit unintentionally, infer the *Aufhebung* described in this work. Hence, for Ricoeur and Gadamer authorial intent is negated to reappear as almost the "spirit" of the text.

Deconstruction has recognized that autonomy means autonomous, not semi-autonomous, and has sought to cast off the restraint. Deconstruction has recognized that any idea of restraint related to an intention of the author allows the "ghost" of the author to "haunt" the process of interpretation. If the concept of autonomy is a term that reflects a philosophical inadequacy, as is argued in this work, then there needs to be recognition that something else is happening that needs to be disclosed. As the title of this chapter suggests, perhaps the announcement of the death of the author has occurred in the author's presence; hence, the reports of the author's death are indeed exaggerated. Consequently, the author and the presupposition of his or her authorial intent's impact on textual interpretation requires further consideration.

6 The Presupposition of Authorial Intent

Introduction

The previous chapter discussed the issue of textual autonomy with respect to the concept of authorial intent. The suggestion of authorial intent and its impact are evidenced, and the argument for autonomy is far from convincing. However, at the same time, what must be acknowledged is that the issue of authorial intent is fraught with difficulty in current methodological understanding. The question could be asked whether or not the retention and assertion of the importance of authorial intent is simply the attempt to legitimize an idea whose real purpose is some form of defense of the presence of the divine; that is, is it an attempt to protect the very idea of God? Consequently, the very presupposition of authorial intent must be considered as a general literary concept with hermeneutical significance.

The Possibility of Authorial Intent

The question of the accessibility of the authorial intent, with its associated difficulties, is really a secondary issue to the question of its existence. If authorial intent exists in relation to a text, then how it relates to a text must be pursued. If in connection with texts, as in deconstruction, authorial intent is a phantasm then there is nothing to pursue. Therefore, the question of the presupposition of authorial intent must start with a consideration of its very possibility, and hence with deconstruction's view related to this issue.[1]

Vanhoozer asks a question in the light of the claims of deconstruction that, in his view, has sought to undo the author, which question is asked on the basis of his assessment that deconstruction has sought to remove any semblance of authorial authority

---

1. This is the basic format of Vanhoozer's book *Is There a Meaning in This Text?* His starting point is the issues deconstruction has raised, from which point he pursues the issue of authorial intent.

impacting interpretation and controlling or influencing meaning.[2] He asks whether or not a voice is in a text and, if so, is it the author's.[3] Vanhoozer argues that the author is the first cause of the existence of the text and the controlling presence that gives unity to the textual composition.[4] Hence, in this scenario, the authorial intent represents access to the absolute meaning of any text; that is, if perfect communication between author and readers occurs, then the intent of the author would be the perception of the readers.

In the temporal absence of the author, as in the case of written text detached from the author, since it is the author's voice that gave rise to the text, the text itself is the only avenue to this absolute, should it exist. This is true whether meaning is considered by direct reference to an author's meaning, or as meaning itself in some way incarnated[5] in the text, as in Ricoeur and Gadamer, or alternately, some combination of these positions. Vanhoozer contends that the removal of the concept of the ultimate absolute lies at the heart of deconstructionism; that is, the God's-eye view of reality doesn't exist in deconstructionism.[6] The loss of the concept of the absolute leads ultimately to the loss of the author's voice, and the subsequent loss of authorial intent, which is replaced by the autonomous text freed from constraint.

In the thought of Derrida, considered a leading voice in deconstruction, "*There is nothing outside of the text* [there is no outside-text . . .]."[7] Concerning a literary text, "there has never been anything but writing" and "what opens meaning and language is writing as the disappearance of natural presence."[8] Derrida is not contesting the existence of an author who wrote but that a text has no ability, once written, to refer to any exterior world, including therefore, any authorial intent. Hence, there is no "natural presence" of the author either referenced in the text or related to the text.

If there is no "natural presence" related to the text, then there is no voice, authorial or otherwise, associated with the text.[9] Consequently, in the view of Derrida's deconstruction the only "natural presence" is that of the reader, who is therefore the only voice. Because meaning should not be considered a property of texts, but rather,

---

2. Vanhoozer, *Is There a Meaning*. This is the theme of chapter 2, 43.
3. Ibid.
4. Ibid., 104, 228.
5. Gadamer, *Truth and Method*, 378. Gadamer's view is that the Christian idea of incarnation does more justice to the nature of language. He does note that his reference is not to embodiment, as this would imply something that can be disembodied. He is contrasting the Greek concept, where embodiment simply means taking human form, whereas the Christian idea is God actually becoming human. This is conceded not to be the language of Ricoeur, but it does fit with his general concept of the semantic autonomy of the text. The text is meaning, and it is the concept of an absolute meaning that both authors would deny.
6. Vanhoozer, *Is There a Meaning*, 49.
7. Derrida, *Of Grammatology*, 158. Italics are original.
8. Ibid., 159.
9. Vanhoozer, *Is There a Meaning*, 60.

as a function of persons,[10] the reader, as the only person, is the only voice of meaning. Meaning then becomes a function of the reader not of the author or of the text.

Gadamer argues, on the basis of how horizons work in distanciation historically and on the nature of language, that there cannot be any one interpretation that is correct "in itself."[11] A changing audience was shown to lead to the situation where meaning can undergo relative change due to changed horizons.[12] Gadamer's concept, which is essentially the same idea as that of a changing audience expressed differently, is that the historical life of a tradition depends on constantly new assimilations and interpretations.[13] However, despite that fact that meaning undergoes apparent change with respect to differing audiences, Gadamer still asserts that "being bound by a situation" (i.e., the new hermeneutical situation) doesn't make validity of a meaning dissolve "into the subjective or occasional."[14] As Gadamer notes, "There can be no speech that does not bind the speaker and the person spoken to" in a communicative relationship.[15]

Therefore, readers cannot be considered as released from the obligations inherent in communication and relationship with authors and, most importantly, are not released to make of meaning what they will.[16] Stanley Fish, speaking from within the mindset[17] of deconstruction, sees the only constraint on a readers' meaning is the communities to which the readers belong.[18] This is similar to the recognition of the impact on meaning of the community in which interpretation occurs, discussed previously. Deconstruction has helped to bring into view the importance of this consideration in meaning. However, it is also important to realize that in deconstruction this impact of the readers' communities is the *only* real constraint recognized, and there is no recognition of a world outside the text and, hence, no voice of the author.[19] This would appear to be why there is an open disregard of any obligations inherent in

---

10. Ibid., 202. As Vanhoozer acknowledges, a text only has meaning (as a noun) when someone means (as a verb) something in its use.

11. Gadamer, *Truth and Method*, 358.

12. This is discussed in the first proposal in chapter 3.

13. Gadamer, *Truth and Method*, 358. He states "every interpretation has to adapt itself to the hermeneutical situation to which it belongs."

14. Ibid., 359.

15. Ibid.

16. Vanhoozer, *Is There a Meaning*, 202. Vanhoozer suggests that both author and reader are citizens of language, which as an environment is shared by both. There is a relationship in receiving an author's communication.

17. An important aspect of deconstruction is that it is a philosophy, or mindset, that has led to a view of textuality. It is not a discovery of a view of textuality that demanded a new mindset. It begins with a philosophical agenda, and this will be considered in this chapter.

18. Fish, *Is There a Text in this Class?*, 304.

19. Ibid., 303. (Italics added.)

communication, and relationship, between the readers and authors in deconstruction. The author as real presence is erased.[20]

Derrida asserts that his work has shown that the sign, so important in the work of Saussure, which is comprised of signifier and signified, and which exteriorizes, is something created in the logocentric system of writing and doesn't exist before writing.[21] His assertion is essentially that the concept of the sign is a contrivance created for the system of writing, and is not the recognition of how things function. If exteriority is lost then the sign falls into decay, but he also notes "our entire world and language would collapse with it"; so rather than suggest moving onto something else, the answer is to deconstruct the sign.[22] The sign refers to another sign rather than signifying that which is exterior.[23] Therefore, instead of a view of reality there is an endless interplay of signs.[24]

(a) A Philosophical not a Linguistic Decision

Thiselton exposes the real heart of the issue, concerning the debate on a text's ability to refer and exteriorize: "the path by which Derrida reaches this view of textuality is an explicitly philosophical one."[25] Wittgenstein observes that the primary responsibility of philosophy is description, not prescription; it "may in no way interfere with the actual use of language: it can in the end only describe it."[26] Thiselton also raises this issue concerning the nature of philosophy as a descriptive task, and notes further that this is an assertion by Bultmann and is accepted as axiomatic in Gadamer.[27] The function of philosophy is not the resolving of contradictions but the positioning of the reader to have a clearer view.[28]

---

20. Thiselton, *New Horizons*, 109. Thiselton discusses this concept of "erasure" in Derrida's work. He notes the comments by Gayatri Spivak, as Derrida's translator, that for Derrida erasure is the absence of presence (see Derrida, *Of Grammatology*, xvii). It is interesting to pick up the quote where Thiselton left off; ". . . of the lack at the origin that is the condition of thought and experience." The author, as originator of a text, is successfully erased.

21. Derrida, *Of Grammatology*, 14. Derrida considers logocentrism to be "the metaphysics of phonetic writing" that imposed itself on the world controlling writing, 3.

22. Ibid.

23. Ibid., 43.

24. Vanhoozer, *Is There a Meaning*, 111. This is Vanhoozers assessment of grammatology and what Derrida is seeking to do in suggesting it. Thiselton, *New Horizons*, 104. Thiselton, using Derrida's own words, shows this concept. Wolterstorff, *Discourse*, 159. Wolterstorff gives a lucid and detailed examination of Derrida's work. After examining what Derrida is saying on this issue, he tenders his "answer with apprehension," which shows he has reached the same conclusion as both Vanhoozer and Thiselton. Wolterstorff states as part of his assessment of what Derrida is asserting, "Everything is a 'trace' of other things. Everything points to other things . . ."

25. Thiselton, *New Horizons*, 104.

26. Wittgenstein, *Philosophical Investigations*, sect. 124.

27. Thiselton, *Two Horizons*, 28.

28. Wittgenstein, *Philosophical Investigations*, sect. 125. Admittedly, Wittgenstein is considering the subject of mathematics, but the context implies it is generally illustrative as implied in sect. 126.

However, this descriptive task of philosophy is, of necessity, interpretive; that is, it will involve developing an understanding of what is reality in what is described, and in performing this descriptive task it is conducted by a person having existing presuppositions about reality.[29] The description is conducted from within a viewpoint of an already established conception of reality; that is, the description itself is an interpretation, not pure objective description. Nevertheless, the view of what is seen (i.e., the description) can be examined without taking on the worldview of the one who is doing the describing.[30]

Philosophy is not the proposing of theory but an activity that is undertaken, in the sense that it involves clarification of thoughts.[31] Consequently, the result of philosophy (i.e., its completion) is not the proposing of propositions but the clarifying of them.[32] Therefore, it would seem wise to suggest that it is important to distinguish where description has moved to proposition and inference, and hence is no longer philosophy. If, as previously considered, composition is recognized as the imposing of a will on discourse (i.e., the author intends to write on a subject and subsequently composes the discourse), then it follows that when philosophy moves to proposition and inference it moves into a realm of composition. It is no longer description. The author now represents a worldview and is making an assertion concerning what *is*; that is, meaning is assigned to the description: it is no longer a description of what *is*.

An important aspect of philosophical inquiry is metaphysics, the field of study of being or reality.[33] As an aspect of philosophical endeavor, metaphysics concerns asking questions related to reality and being.[34] It is this philosophical aspect that, as Thiselton notes, constitutes Derrida's pathway to a view of textuality, that is, as a philosopher his view of what *is*. This is to say that Derrida's description in his discourse in *Of Grammatology* is in fact an interpretation viewed through the lens of his own metaphysics. It will be argued that the metaphysical position he argues from, but does not acknowledge as metaphysics, is *metaphysics of absence*.[35] Derrida's failure to acknowledge this shows that he views himself as describing the situation either from an unmetaphysical, or a nonmetaphysical, stance.

---

29. Gadamer, *Truth and Method*, 358. Gadamer notes; "To try to eliminate one's concepts in interpretation is not only impossible, but manifestly absurd."

30. Thiselton, *Two Horizons*, 10.

31. Wittgenstein, *Tractatus Logico-Philosophicus*, sect. 4.112.

32. Ibid. Thiselton notes this important aspect of Wittgenstein's work; see Thiselton, *Two Horizons*, 29.

33. Geisler, *Baker Encyclopedia of Christian Apologetics*, 446.

34. Ibid.

35. Derrida, *Of Grammatology*, 40. Derrida argues for the absence of a signatory, i.e., the meant of the author, and the absence of a referent, an absence of presence of "other," which results in anteriority of meaning impacting the text, i.e., gives "voice" to otherness. This view implies that meaning awaits creation by a reader, not understanding by a reader.

(b) The Metaphysics of Presence and Absence

Metaphysics, for Derrida, is the culprit that debased and repressed writing, and essentially hijacked what writing should have been.[36] The science of writing had been shaped, restricted, and ordered by "metaphor, metaphysics, and theology"; but now the science of *grammatology* has arrived as a liberating force from this repression.[37] In this new science, a glimpse is caught of the closure of the "historico-metaphysical epoch."[38] It is not the end of the epoch, seemingly because the new era arises as a dislocation from within it.[39]

It would seem logical to assume that Derrida would envisage the total escape from metaphysics. However, when Derrida is questioned on this subject he does not see the escape from metaphysics as possible.[40] In this is the recognition that metaphysics cannot be left behind. The problem is that any argument against metaphysics is of necessity a metaphysical argument.[41] The issue of metaphysics is part of the presuppositional world, or worldview, of a person and everyone has a worldview;[42] consequently, any argument against a particular worldview is an argument from within a worldview.

It is the metaphysics of the Western world, and the philosophy on which it developed, that seem to be the real target of Derrida's own discourse.[43] "Logocentric metaphysics" has impacted this development in Western philosophy since the days of the early Greek philosophers; that is, the impact has occurred over the span of three millennia in Derrida's view.[44] Wolterstorff states, "Derrida is metaphysics' relentless, indefatigable, fight-to-the-death opponent; his brief against discourse interpretation is that is it is metaphysical."[45] The concept of signification belongs to the history of metaphysics and "in a more explicit and more systematically articulated way to the narrower epoch of Christian creationism."[46] Derrida shows the inseparableness of this in his thinking: "The sign and divinity has the same place and time of birth. The age of the sign is essentially theological."[47]

---

36. Ibid., 3.

37. Ibid., 4. (Italics original.) It should be noted that in a note concerning the use of the word *theology* Derrida includes the metaphysics of atheism in that which has repressed writing.

38. Ibid.

39. Ibid.

40. Derrida, *Positions*, 17. This was an admission by Derrida in an interview with Julia Kristeva and is also noted by Wolterstorff in *Divine Discourse*, 162.

41. Wolterstorff, *Divine Discourse*, 162.

42. Vanhoozer, *Is There a Meaning*, 71.

43. Wolterstorff, *Divine Discourse*, 156.

44. Derrida, *Of Grammatology*, 8.

45. Wolterstorff, *Divine Discourse*, 156.

46. Derrida, *Of Grammatology*, 13.

47. Ibid., 14.

Derrida's view is that in this current emergence of grammatology, as representing writing as it always should have been, also seen is "the death of the civilization of the book."[48] Wolterstorff, referring to Derrida's *Writing and Difference*, notes that in Derrida's thinking the idea of the "Book" has controlled both thinking and writing; Derrida's tirade against it is because the book carries the assumption of meaning as anterior to writing, whereas for Derrida meaning awaits writing for meaning to come into existence.[49] Derrida considers that true writing "is also to be incapable of making meaning absolutely precede writing: it is thus to lower meaning while simultaneously elevating inscription."[50] Ricoeur moved meaning to the text away from the author; however, it was noted that meaning is an act of persons. Derrida is simply recognizing this, and frees meaning from either the author or the text; meaning awaits the reader to come into existence. In considering the views expressed by Derrida, Wolterstorff observes that if his line of thinking is followed, then "there is no divine Book on which we are to model our books, no divine thoughts after which to think our thoughts. The God of Leibniz—indeed, the Jewish God—will have to go."[51]

It may be that it is a coincidence, yet the implication of "the death of the civilization of the book" stated in *Of Grammatology*, in the light of these other works by Derrida, is one that carries theological overtones, that is, the death of metaphysical society in general, but especially that of all belief in a divine being as the ground of all being. It seems the divine being must to be cleared from the scene so that authorial intent, as giving meaning to writing, can at last be expelled so that meaning can pass into the hands of the reader and hence find its true place as the result of writing, not as writing's cause. Therefore, writing now becomes the antecedent of meaning, not the reverse, that is, there is no consideration that meaning gave birth to writing. Clearly, Derrida's opposition to metaphysics drives his view of hermeneutics. Wolterstorff concludes his examination of Derrida's argument against discourse interpretation by noting it is an argument against its perceived metaphysical subjugation; yet on the subject of metaphysics Derrida doesn't offer any argument, just avowed rejection.[52]

Vanhoozer notes that the oft-quoted statement of Derrida: "There is nothing outside the text" (which is also noted previously) is often misinterpreted.[53] He observes that this phrase has been trivialized to imply that Derrida is stating that things don't actually exist until writing occurs.[54] What Derrida denies is exteriorization of the text as providing any basis of meaning that is "stable" and "determinate."[55] This concept

---

48. Ibid., 8.

49. Wolterstorff, *Divine Discourse*, 161. Wolterstorff gives an extended quote from *Writing and Difference*, 11, showing the force of Derrida's feelings on this issue.

50. Derrida, *Writing*, 10.

51. Wolterstorff, *Divine Discourse*, 161.

52. Ibid., 171.

53. Vanhoozer, *Is There a Meaning*, 63.

54. Ibid.

55. Ibid.

was discussed in the preceding paragraph. Yet, there may be a deeper significance to Derrida's reasoning. What Vanhoozer seems to imply is that Derrida is simply trying to push meaning into a relativistic state wherein no definitive a priori meaning exists. This may indeed prove the eventual outcome for those who follow Derrida's supposedly nonmetaphysical metaphysics.

However, in his discourse, Derrida, in one section, follows a line of thought in his consideration of writing that implies a different agenda. He begins by noting the general usage of the word "language" in referring to a number of activities, and he then observes that all these activities become included under the term *writing*, presumably because language soon defaults to writing in his view of the impact of metaphysics (his use of the term *writing* here is directed at the notion of writing impacted by logocentrism and hence not true writing).[56] Writing moves into many spheres, controlling what these spheres are and become.[57] His discussion arrives at the example of a contemporary biologist who refers to writing as describing the "the most elementary processes of information within the living cell."[58] From this place, of having arrived at a basic concept of information, "the entire field covered by the cybernetic *program* will be the field of writing."[59] Derrida then makes a statement showing that the direction of his thinking is indeed the overthrowing of not only the idea of the metaphysical as a sphere of philosophy but the entirety of that which lies behind the metaphysical, the concept of any theological conception of humanity. He states that the theory of cybernetics will by itself "oust all metaphysical concepts—including the concepts of soul, of life, of value, of choice, of memory—which until recently served to separate the machine from man."[60] Even the very idea of humanity is metaphysical, and evidently, to find humanity the very idea of humanity must first be dehumanized so as to remove the metaphysical.[61]

If this is to be successfully achieved, then cybernetics must first retain the current notion of writing "until its own historico-metaphysical character is also exposed" (in other words, until every last vestige of the metaphysical is exposed, even from within itself, and at last expunged). Then it is envisaged that at last what is achieved is "the origin of *meaning* in general."[62] What will this brave new world look like? He has no idea; as yet there is no indication, just that it is not "meaning" as currently employed.[63]

56. Derrida, *Of Grammatology*, 9.

57. Ibid.

58. Ibid.

59. Ibid.

60. Ibid.

61. Lawlor, "Jacques Derrida," section 3, "Basic Argumentation and its Implications: Time, Hearing-Oneself-Speak, the Secret, and Sovereignty." Lawlor observes this to be a basic principle of Derrida's thought, i.e., that there is no clear separation of human and thing into two distinct substances, nor are they reducible one to the other. Thus there can be no ontological impasse in need of traversing.

62. Derrida, *Of Grammatology*, 9.

63. Ibid., 5.

Clearly the destruction of the metaphysical is Derrida's agenda, as Wolterstorff, Vanhoozer, and Thiselton, among others, have noted. It is not just the destabilizing and relativization of meaning that is his aim; it is the overthrowing of meaning as it itself is understood. Atheistic humanism, which is Derrida's effective position,[64] understands all life as evolving, not coming to being by direct creation or even by a theistic understanding of evolution. The code is writing itself, as it goes, and therefore gives itself meaning. This is the pattern that nature follows in this line of thought. This is essentially what he is proposing; that is, there is no design or anterior meaning directing the process, and meaning develops, or unfolds, from the process. However, evidently even the expression of meaning it seeks to give itself ends up interpreted by the metaphysical concept of meaning at this time, and so it becomes stuck within metaphysical language it would rather avoid.[65] Derrida's cherished hope seems to be that eventually cybernetics will expose and overthrow the whole superimposed system.

What is interesting is the tacit admission by Derrida that even appeal to language and linguistics, as in Ricoeur and Gadamer, does not overcome the fact that, for writing as understood and practiced, the author is determinate in meaning. Everything else is really only language games, seemingly deferring but not overriding this situation; authorial-discourse interpretation will always rear its head, provided that this head is not cut off and is completely overthrown. Only the total overthrow of meaning as it stands will ultimately change the current situation for Derrida. Therefore, unless Derrida is right in his understanding, authorial-discourse is what must be interpreted. The deconstructionist's only hope of breaking free of this tyranny is to attempt to bury the author. However, to achieve this they must first bury God and all that goes with belief. Hence Vanhoozer states, "The fates of the author of traditional literary criticism and of the God of traditional theism stand or fall together."[66]

It is almost as if Derrida desires to return to the time three millennia ago when, in his view, the problem that hijacked writing and interpretation started and changed the direction of what writing should have become in the first place, that is, what Derrida develops in grammatology. Vanhoozer calls the approach of deconstruction essentially an attempt to remove "the ghost in the machine"; that is, the very concept of the author is a ploy to exteriorize language so that meaning is seen to give rise to language, and hence discourse and the text.[67] This is not the position of nonacceptance of the reality of the author but rather the proposition that authorial intention is not

---

64. This is a description from within metaphysics; but as Derrida has acknowledged, at this time that particular language is the language that must be used. That which seeks the erasure of God is atheistic, and humanism simply bases importance as beginning with humanity not the divine. Hence, the view proposed that this position is Derrida's effective expressed position without speaking to his own *pistological* mindset.

65. Wolterstorff, *Divine Discourse*, 165. Wolterstorff discusses this problem Derrida laments, that the one seeking to speak against metaphysics must use metaphysical language.

66. Vanhoozer, *Is There a Meaning*, 71.

67. Ibid., 62.

determinate and that authorial voice is really only a composite of the impact of the tradition in which it stands.[68] Vanhoozer seems to suggest that deconstruction's objective is to reduce the authorial voice to that of phantasm.

Yet, as Thiselton points out, no individual exists having formed himself or herself, nor has any individual pursued the quest for knowledge *de novo*; rather, an individual inherits a preexistent "shared public world" that forms the basis of the pursuit of knowledge.[69] An author is inescapably impacted by the tradition in which he or she stands, and his or her authorial voice will reflect that. Nevertheless, as an individual the author is not the composite of that tradition; the author's tradition has acted as a mentor, and as an individual the author's response to that mentoring is what he or she has become.

In the light of the preceding conversation, the ghost in the machine that Derrida would like to exorcise is that tradition itself, which is where the metaphysical impact is coming from; hence, the objective to liberate the individual from that impact, and the only way to do that is to first reduce humanity to machine so as to begin again. Through the tradition in which an individual stands, a corporate memory is transmitted.[70] This tradition and corporate memory includes belief, and so automatically introduces the language of metaphysics that the individual has "taken over" from the community.[71] A "shared public world" preexists the advent of the individual and impacts his or her thinking, shaping the terms on which knowledge shall be tested.[72] An individual is free to evaluate, and Derrida particularly seeks to free the individual from this metaphysical bondage, but despite this fact the shared public world will condition the appropriate criteria for the evaluation.[73] Thus what is implied is that tradition has a "voice" that cannot be muted, even if the author is denied direct impact in determination of meaning.

Although, in the religious sphere, the passed-on traditions become "underrated" in modern society; the "ghost in the machine" remains unexorcised, because the individual's quest for knowledge does not begin isolated from history and community.[74] Derrida has recognized that this "voice" speaks through the author and it cannot be silenced unless it is removed. In this recognition he has also recognized that any presence of the author will give "voice" to that tradition; that is, there is an impact of authorial intent even when it is linguistically erased. Perhaps in Derrida's desire to undo this impact of three millennia of tradition thereby releasing humanity from metaphysical bondage—which in his view reinforces logocentrism—he would echo John Dryden's words in *The Conquest of Granada*:

68. Ibid.
69. Thiselton, *Thiselton On Hermeneutics*, 703.
70. Ibid., 701.
71. Ibid.
72. Ibid., 703.
73. Ibid.
74. Ibid., 702–3.

> I am as free as nature first made man
> > Ere the base laws of servitude began
>
> When wild in woods the noble savage ran

Thiselton states, "Knowing, believing and especially understanding depend on some kind of sharing and on some kind of experiencing of continuity."[75] It is language that makes possible this pooling, sharing, and transmission; a transmission that is not only geographical but also within time, that is, from generation to generation.[76] Language provides the ability for continuity. Thiselton goes on to note that "Language shapes the frame of reference through which knowledge is *grasped*, and within which it is *criticized*."[77] Whilst this impact does not exclude ways of seeing the world, it does encourage ways of seeing the world; that is, language's impact cannot be denied in shaping an individual's mindset. At the very beginning of Derrida's discourse *Of Grammatology*, he addresses and attacks the issue of language as having become essentially perverted by this metaphysical inheritance.[78]

The discourse in *Of Grammatology* is primarily a discourse against the understanding of language that stands in the metaphysically impacted tradition of logocentrism. Wolterstorff states that Derrida, in his work, "argues that discourse interpretation rests on assumptions characteristic of what he calls 'metaphysics,' when it comes to metaphysics itself he doesn't argue but simply declares his rejection."[79] However, on examination, Derrida's attack on language is his argument against metaphysics. This appears to be the reasoning behind his attempt to deconstruct the language of logocentrism, that is, to remove any sense of ability of exterior reference and at least mute the "ghost (of metaphysics) in the machine" until it can be exorcised in the brave new world.

The moment a person asks a question concerning metaphysical issues, then that person has begun to use the language of metaphysics simply by addressing the question. Hence, as Derrida admits, metaphysics is unavoidable and any other view is idealistic, existing only at the end of the deconstructionist's rainbow. Metaphysics is inherent in language, and the moment writing occurs metaphysics is transmitted as memory with language, which in turn makes reference to it, unless the signifier points only to another sign and the signified is denied any exteriority, resulting in the "voice" of metaphysics being muted. This is the path Derrida follows.

Derrida observes that in his view the "epoch of the logos [i.e., logocentrism] thus debases writing . . . as a fall into the exteriority of meaning."[80] The concept developed, in this epoch, of the difference between signifier and signified is the basis of this fall

---

75. Ibid., 704.
76. Ibid., 706.
77. Ibid. (Italics original.)
78. Derrida, *Of Grammatology*, 6.
79. Wolterstorff, *Divine Discourse*, 171.
80. Derrida, *Of Grammatology*, 13. (Bracket comment added for clarity.)

into exteriority.[81] This "difference" is an "appurtenance," that is, an accessory of, or that which belongs to, the epoch, which is "organized and hierarchized in a history"; this "difference" belongs to the "great epoch covered by the history of metaphysics."[82] This "appurtenance" is fundamental to the integrity of the epoch and is "irreducible," by which he seems to mean that metaphysics cannot be eliminated by an attempt to reduce the issue to one of science.[83] The accessory always brings with it "all its metaphysico-theological roots," together with all the baggage that adheres to these roots; it is a total package.[84] The absolute logos, as baggage that still clings to the roots, "was an infinite creative subjectivity in medieval theology: the intelligible face of the sign remains turned toward the word and face of God."[85] The concept of "appurtenance" is carefully chosen, because the nature of an accessory is that it can be dispensed with and disposed of.

The system of language impacted by logocentrism can't help itself; it exteriorizes. And in exteriorizing it references the metaphysical nature inherent in language-use. The issue this system must eventually raise is that of God; therefore, God is now embedded in the tradition that stands behind and is transmitted with the language. In this scenario, meaning antedates text, and this meaning is the author's meaning.

The subject matter of Derrida's first chapter in *Of Grammatology* concerns the "End of the Book."[86] The end of the book is in fact the announcement of the death of the book, and at last, with this death, writing is rebirthed to become what it should have been.[87] Vanhoozer notes that the concept of the book "suggests totality." This concept automatically alludes to an author and a meaning; deconstruction includes the view that this tendency of the concept of the book is "inherently theological."[88] Derrida states that this concept of the book "is the encyclopedic protection of theology and of logocentrism against the disruption of writing."[89] Clearly, in his thinking, the concept of the book belongs to the system of logocentrism as an invention of this system, since in his understanding this system essentially commandeered writing three millennia ago. The concept of the book is simply an attempt to avoid the inspection and exposure by the incisive insight of writing (as it is becoming in Derrida's understanding), which will reveal the metaphysics that lies as a lurking presence that controls meaning.

81. Ibid.
82. Ibid.
83. Ibid.
84. Ibid.
85. Ibid.
86. Ibid., 6.
87. Ibid., 8.
88. Vanhoozer, *Is There a Meaning*, 104.
89. Derrida, *Of Grammatology*, 18.

It is no wonder that Vanhoozer's opinion is that the real target in this is not the author per se but "meaning itself."[90] Hence, Vanhoozer's assessment is that, for Derrida, "Books stabilize, control, and close down the play of meaning."[91] If the text is removed from the context of the book, hence destroying the book, a surface covering of the text is stripped away that removes the values, ideals, and meaning inherent in logocentrism.[92] This stripping frees the text from any imposed unity so that meaning is unrestricted. The issue of meaning now passes into the hands of the reader, who evidently now has the opportunity to find meaning free of metaphysics.

The author, it seems, is simply the Trojan horse of metaphysics that exteriorization allows into the text, thereby losing logocentrism to destroy the text by reforming it into a book. It is no wonder that deconstruction decided it needed to go beyond Gadamer and Ricoeur, for whom the author has at least an indirect presence, in that it is the authors' discourse that is continued by the reader. In both Gadamer and Ricoeur this subsequently has an influence on the readers' meaning, in the sense that the discourse is set up to dialectically bring the reader into some form of communication with the author's discourse.

In Ricoeur's thought the text acts as a linguistic mediator between the author and reader, and in Gadamer's thought the text is the foundation of a dialogical interaction concerning the *Sache* of the author. For both Gadamer and Ricoeur, meaning is with the reader. However, Gadamer proposes that the object of the reader, through a communication process, is to make one's own what is alien, that is, to make the text, or discourse of what the author said, one's own. However, for Gadamer it is still the author who said it, and in this is continued recognition of the author.[93] The meaning arrived at in this process is neither exclusively the reader's nor the author's: it is a common meaning.[94] Ricoeur takes event as the foundation. The event is comprised of the saying of the author (the writing) and the saying of the interpreter (the reading). Between these two events is the written text, which has semantic autonomy. The ideality of the text mediates the fusing of the horizons of author and reader, but it is still the author's horizon with which the reader is undergoing a fusion.[95]

The end result of both is similar in that what occurs is a reader who has been impacted in some way by an author in the hermeneutical process. In both these views the tradition in which the text stands, and hence the tradition that has impacted the author, has input and therefore impact on the reader. In deconstruction this must surely be seen as what is fundamentally a back door for the metaphysics that has informed the author. Therefore, it would seem that what is essential is to not only deny

---

90. Vanhoozer, *Is There a Meaning*, 99.
91. Ibid., 104.
92. Derrida, *Of Grammatology*, 18.
93. Gadamer, *Truth and Method*: 360.
94. Ibid., 350.
95. Ricoeur, *Interpretation Theory*: 91.

The Presupposition of Authorial Intent

the author's direct "voice" or "presence" but to also cut off any "voice" of the tradition in which the author has stood. The speaking subject is removed not just muted.

A key characteristic in postmodern thinking has been the removal of the "speaking subject."[96] Thiselton examines this proposition from the aspect of the nature of language. He observes that the nature of language involves a speaking person contrary to the proposition of removal.[97] The route Derrida takes in the expunging of the speaking voice is again decidedly metaphysical. The dominant idea of presence in the history of logocentrism, hence of a speaking voice, moved from a place of "objectivity" (i.e., the ideality of the image and the substantiality of the likeness, via Cartesian thought) to "representation" (i.e., "of the *idea* as the modification of a self-present substance, conscious and certain of itself at the moment of relationship to itself").[98] In the context of grammar, the word *modification* implies an addition. Thus, the concept of representation is that an *idea* becomes added and associated with the text due to a supposed perception of real presence associated with the text.

Ideality and substantiality interrelate in the "element of the *res cogitans*" (i.e., the mental substance or thought world of the person) by "a movement of pure auto-affection," which, in Derrida, is what consciousness is (i.e., "the experience of pure auto-affection").[99] It would seem the implication is that the mindset, affected by logocentrism, acts in giving-oneself-a-pleasure[100] by the conception of this presence, and itself gives to this presence a sense of being absolute. However, as auto-affection, it is a supplement, as is writing. Therefore, it is something added to speech, or oral discourse, and as such it exists in the mind of the reader; it is not a real presence.[101] The movement has undergone transformation from object, to mental substance, and then to an idea that rests in the imagination.

The concept of the supplement is developed from the writings of Rousseau, taken from his own understanding of himself as a writer.[102] The danger of writing, noting that languages are for speaking and writing is simply a supplement to speech, is that

---

96. Thiselton, *New Horizons*: 127.

97. Ibid., 128. He concludes this particular discussion, on the need for a speaking subject, by noting, "in the end some kind of operational purchase is needed between language and bio-socio-physical embodiment." 129.

98. Derrida, *Of Grammatology*, 97. With the use of the phrase "motif of presence" and the general tone of a discussion of the writings, Rousseau indicates that his discussion does concern written text, and is so taken in this context. Hence, *eidos* and *ousia* are taken to roughly mean "signifier" and "signified," since *eidos* is indicated as "ideality" and *ousia* as substantiality. (All use of italics original.)

99. Ibid., 98.

100. Ibid., 165. This is the essential form of expression he gives to the term auto-affection, giving-oneself-a-presence (or pleasure).

101. Ibid. See also, 98, on auto-affection being presence in the mind of the individual. Onanism is a physical expression of auto-affection, 167. An important motif in Rousseau is that, in oral address, presence is at the same time promised and refused. Derrida notes that in Rousseau the speech raised above writing is speech as it should have been, 141.

102. Ibid., 142.

representation, in writing, claims to be a presence.[103] The interplay of absence and presence, the motif, is taken from the self-torture Rousseau understands himself to have gone through in coming to the place of writing.[104] It is a desire for recognition that feeds the struggle, and the choice of absence is so that his true worth can be seen, which would not be seen if he was present (i.e., as in the oral situation), and writing is the visual manifestation of that struggle.[105] Hence, writing is a supplement, an addition, and a giving-oneself-pleasure to enjoy recognition; therefore, it is an auto-affection.

The representation appears to be a presence. But this presence is an absence, an addition that can be subtracted from the text; hence, it must be deconstructed to denude the text.[106] The concept of consciousness, the experience of presence, is therefore an auto-affection; that is, it exists primarily as a self indulgent addition. Hence, this would imply that such things as the importance of consciousness in Gadamer are simply auto-affections; that is, the metaphysical is really just auto-affection—something that is done as a giving-oneself-pleasure—its reality is its impact on the person not its existence as real presence.

The entirety of the concept of God, including proof of existence, morality, the absolute and the impact of divinity, is all part of this element of auto-affection, and for those impacted by logocentrism God is the name of this element.[107] The importance of Rousseau, for Derrida, is that in this age of metaphysics Rousseau is the philosopher that had a profound insight concerning writing.[108] Derrida sees that Rousseau's condemnation of the concept of a universal characteristic is not from a theological basis, as to its possibility, but that it "seemed to suspend the voice"; that is, it took over the auto-affection and essentially put it on hold.[109] What threatens in Rousseau, and by implication what is happening in the present, is the emergence of writing as it should be, free from metaphysics.[110] Derrida's assertion of this being a nontheological decision is really a subterfuge to deflect a realization that it is indeed theological. His assertion is based on the concept that there is no real presence at hand and the only version of the divine left, if it existed, would be some sort of Deism as deferred presence, since Theism concerns presence. Derrida's is indeed a theologically informed and impacted decision.

The concept of presence is related to the experience of writing in Derrida's understanding of Rousseau. It is the establishing of presence rather than absence that is achieved in the reappropriation of presence in auto-affection, which is not resisted

103. Ibid., 144.
104. Ibid., 142.
105. Ibid.
106. Ibid., 18.
107. Ibid., 98.
108. Ibid.
109. Ibid., 99.
110. Ibid.

by différence; that is, *it is not a going backwards into metaphysics, provided it is seen as supplementary*.[111] The imagination, where auto-affection operates, is able to treat presence as a singularity, or absolute, and defer the uncertainty—différence—between presence and absence that a person moves through in a machine like repeatability in experiencing life, which machine-like repeatability defies the idea of a singularity. This reality doesn't prevent the imagination from seeing a singularity to grant oneself the pleasure of a definitive meaning, which is not possible since the sign in reality points to other signs and is not referring to a definitive meaning. Such an auto-affection doesn't constitute a return to metaphysics and can be enjoyed provided its supplementary nature is recognized. Thus meaning as the idea of what a text refers to is not real but imaginary.

This is in contrast to Rousseau's theory of writing, which recognizes the danger of supplementation as addition.[112] The supplement, determining the representative image, becomes a surplus that is "art, *techné* image, representation, convention, etc., come as supplements to nature and are rich with this entire cumulating function."[113] The supplement creates a world in the imagination and this is where the presence resides. It is the supplement, not presence, which is exterior and as such is other than the text.[114] Although Derrida does not propose it, what is implied in his work is that this imagined presence is the "voice" with which one dialogues when they "believe" themselves to be in dialogue with real presence. Therefore, by default any supposed authorial or speaking voice is relegated into auto-affection.

This vehicle of the imagination is capable of providing an unending supply of supplements to gratify desire, that is, the drive of onanism or auto-affection.[115] This concept of onanism is eventually revealed as not just having analogy in language but is indistinguishable from its physical counterpart, sexual auto-affection.[116] It is only metaphysics that seeks to distinguish between them as an imposed sense of morality; admittedly Derrida doesn't mention the imposition of morality, but he certainly implies it. This conclusion of Derrida's, concerning the indistinguishable nature of language and physical auto-affection, is a more critical indicator of his thinking than it appears to be in his discourse. Derrida's use of this conclusion to assert the abolishment of metaphysics is similar to Ricoeur's assertion of the semantic autonomy of the text. In the same fashion as Ricoeur, Derrida's assertion is in reality an implication that requires first accepting Derrida's conclusion on which the assertion is based, which is that only metaphysics has caused the distinction between the imagination of presence and sexual self gratification. The imagination of presence is not an actual otherness

---

111. Ibid., 144. Difference doesn't oppose appropriation, 143. (Italics added.)
112. Ibid.
113. Ibid. (Italics original.)
114. Ibid., 145.
115. Ibid., 153.
116. Ibid., 167.

but in reality pure self-gratification. Derrida infers the lack of difference between them and then essentially on that basis asserts the abolishing of the metaphysical. What is occurring in reference in relation to meaning is simply auto-affection, the assumption of reality regarding presence can only occur because of the assumption of metaphysics. Derrida's view of metaphysics is of pure addition. Like his concept of auto-affection and onanism as indistinguishable he uses to consign metaphysics to phantasm, his view on presence is simply the result of an assumption of no real presence, not its proof.

The basis for elimination of the "speaking subject" occurs when the following concepts are accepted: first, the concept of the supplement (not just the concept of addition but that writing is a supplement of speech, which in itself bears closer scrutiny) and, second, the concept that auto-affection in language (consciousness as self-inspired imagination) and physical auto-affection are indistinguishable. Metaphysics has excluded nonpresence, and in so doing has established a concept of real presence by determining an exteriority that was in reality the supplement.[117] The concepts of exclusion and inclusion work within the supplement, not the text.

Derrida then presents his own paradox: "one annuls addition by considering it a pure addition. *What is added is nothing because it is added to a full presence to which it is exterior.*"[118] As a result the concept of "origin or nature is nothing but the myth of addition, of supplementarity annulled by being purely additive."[119] Contra to this, Ong, whose position on authorial intent is similar to Ricoeur's and Gadamer's, observes that writing should be seen as the complement of oral discourse.[120] Thus, he carries the idea of fulfillment rather than addition. The idea of supplement is usually that of completing or enhancing, as addition, and this would also be consistent with Ong's view. This area of supplement is an area of play of presence and absence, and metaphysics can occur in this supplement but cannot realize it as supplement, or addition.[121] There is nothing outside the text, but metaphyics occurring within the supplement doesn't realize that in reality it can't get out of the text and so assumes itself to be real and the projected presence to be real when it is a phantasm.

Therefore, the realm of presence, divine or otherwise, as understood in metaphysics, is imaginary; and the reality is the thinking individual. All that exists is self and auto-affection firing the imagination; this is the proposed reality. Essentially, this nonmetaphysics is the metaphysics of humanity replacing deity, and the vehicle of Derrida's proposition is language stripped of the metaphysics of logocentrism. Stripped of metaphysics, which belongs to the exterior supplement that as an addition is disposable, there is nothing outside the text because there is nothing outside the

117. Ibid.
118. Ibid. (Italics original.)
119. Ibid.
120. Ong, *Orality and Literacy*, 5.
121. Derrida, *Of Grammatology*, 167.

individual. Meaning is given by humanity; meaning is not discerned by humanity. That is, meaning is not anterior but posterior. Even communication, as conversation, is two individuals auto-affecting reciprocally, each echoing the auto-affection of the other. The universal is self-centered, in the true sense of that term.

Consequently, for the deconstructionist, the absence of the "speaking subject" occurs because it only ever exists in the imagination of the author when writing, or the reader when reading. The speaking subject is never a real presence and so must be deconstructed for interpretation to occur. If the danger of not removing the speaking subject is in leaving metaphysical roots and baggage attached, then the danger in using deconstruction to remove the speaking subject, as a methodology, is the implication of its roots the methodology will leave behind of proposing a metaphysics based on the absence of presence and its baggage that will attend the process of removing the speaking subject.

Wolterstorff is correct in observing, as noted previously, that Derrida's argument against discourse interpretation is due to its association with metaphysics.[122] However, Wolterstorff is incorrect in viewing that Derrida simply declares his rejection of metaphysics without offering any argument. Derrida uses language as a guise for a metaphysical argument and always remains within metaphysical language, despite his protestations of abhorrence. If, as in Derrida, logos is the metaphysics of presence, then deconstruction is the *metaphysics of absence*. This may also be Thiselton's implication: "Derrida's exclusion of Being might be said to betray more 'metaphysical confidence,' even if in the service of an anti-metaphysical philosophy."[123] As Derrida himself declares: "Only *pure absence*—not the absence of this or that, but the absence of everything in which all presence is announced—can *inspire*, in other words can *work*, and then make one work."[124]

The argument against the author is *pistological*. As such, this argument attempts to remove the author and the very idea of a divine being. This divine being includes the God of traditional theism; and as Vanhoozer observed, the concept of the divine and that of the author stand or fall together. This occurs because in the swing of the pendulum from the author to the reader is a corresponding swing from a divine-centered universe to a self-centered universe. The argument against the presupposition of authorial intent and against the need to consider it in the interpretive process is neither compelling nor convincing.

---

122. Wolterstorff, *Divine Discourse*, 171.
123. Thiselton, *New Horizons*, 108.
124. Derrida, *Writing*, 8. (Italics original.)

7 Metaphysics

Unrealistic Constraint or Realistic Context

INTRODUCTION

IT WAS SHOWN IN the preceding chapter that deconstruction is neither unmetaphysical nor nonmetaphysical in its approach. Rather, it is best considered as the *metaphysics of absence*. However, deconstruction does raise questions about how texts are viewed and how they are approached in their relationship to authors and readers. The view of a *metaphysics of presence* must also be considered as the only valid alternative to that of *absence*; to paraphrase the concept put forward by Blaise Pascal concerning the reality of the divine, previously considered,[1] *presence* is or it is not. Such issues as to how metaphysics is perceived and how a metaphysical subject perceives should be examined. Also, if a metaphysics of presence is asserted, how does an individual such as an interpreter/reader communicate with presence, and how does presence communicate with the individual? Dogmatic assertion of a metaphysics of presence may serve as an answer for those individuals who are committed to a metaphysics of presence, but that assertion does not address the aforementioned issues and questions. In addressing such issues and questions, the opportunity is presented for a better understanding of texts and their relationship to authors and readers. Also, for the Christian, a better understanding of how a metaphysics of presence functions from a philosophical consideration can aid in understanding how the Holy Spirit communicates, without having to resort immediately to a dogmatic assertion of a special hermeneutic.

---

1. See the reference to Pascal below and also in ch. 2, "An Introduction to Arational and Nonrational Knowledge, (b) Nonrational Knowledge."

The Idea of the Divine and the Absolute

The previous chapter began to highlight an important inference that can be drawn. The concept of the existence or nonexistence of the absolute is idealistic; it is a nonsolvable problem and it is nondemonstrable within the sphere of human empirical reasoning. The absolute can be inferred to exist through the process of reasoning, as in the thinking of Kant considered previously, but it cannot be unilaterally identified from a human perspective. However, it is not just the concept of the absolute, or presence, that is idealistic. The concept of nonabsolute, or absence, as the antithesis of the absolute, is equally idealistic; that is, the nonexistence of the absolute can itself only be inferred. It is a matter of a belief about reality that is beyond the capability, and it may be said warrant, of human empirical reason. Whatever position is held about the concept of the absolute, the discussion is one about the absolute; and the subsequent view of reality held is reasoned through *pistological* knowledge not reasoned through rational objective knowledge.

The decision by an author, or a reader, on the existence of the absolute, or divine, is consequently a *pistological* one with hermeneutical impact and not a hermeneutical one with *pistological* impact. *Pistology* is a view of reality that sets a context from which hermeneutics is conducted. Vanhoozer states, what is for him, a "general rule describing the relation between meaning and *metaphysics*: textual meaning will only be as determinate and decidable as the conception of reality that it ultimately presupposes."[2] It is a matter of the belief of the author or reader, which the author imparts in the writing or that impacts the presuppositions of the reader in his or her reading. The *pistology* precedes and informs the hermeneutics. It is not a reasoned decision that demands uncritical acceptance as rational reason. The *pistology* becomes the context in which the world is seen and described, and, it is in this way, it becomes the context in which hermeneutics is conducted. Vanhoozer has acknowledged, with many other theologians, that no theologian enjoys the God's-eye view of reality.[3] Such a view of reality is believed to exist or it is not. Although Christianity asserts that God has stood in our shoes, nevertheless, as Vanhoozer proposes we don't stand in his within our context of human frailty. The author or reader operates on the presupposition of his or her belief.

Pascal noted that a person assents to one of two propositions: God is or God is not.[4] Rational reason can neither decide for nor defend either proposition.[5] If, as Vanhoozer has noted previously, rejection of the absolute results in consequent rejection of the divine, then acceptance of the divine is acceptance of the absolute. Hence, Pascal's proposition could equally be rephrased as "The absolute is or it is

---

2. Vanhoozer, *Is There a Meaning*, 123. (Italics original.)
3. Vanhoozer, *First Theology*, 309.
4. Pascal, "Pensées," sect. 233.
5. Ibid.

not." Again, rational reason neither decides nor defends either proposition, and the postmodern rejection of the absolute is a belief, an assent to a proposition, which is based on inferences from its reasoning not a proposition secured within reason. The absolute is inferred by reasoning based on presuppositions held that are not demonstrably achieved by a process of rational objective reason.

Hegel asserted that the matter of philosophy is "the actual cognition of what truly is," but as a result it is first necessary to understand cognition.[6] Cognition could be either regarded as an instrument to lay hold of the absolute, or, the "medium through which to catch sight of it."[7] However, the application of an instrument reshapes what is being observed; that is, the instrument itself impacts what becomes known.[8] Alternately, if cognition is seen as a medium through which truth is received, the problem is that truth is not seen as it is but as it is through the medium.[9] What is inferred by Hegel's observations and can be acknowledged is that what is interpreted is drawn into the realm of the interpreter, that is, the very act of interpreting makes any conceptualization concerning the absolute a relative conceptualization. As Vanhoozer stated and is also inferred by Hegel's observations, this conceptualization can only be expressed from the realm of the interpreter and is never itself an absolute value, being always relative to the interpreter, which is also what Gadamer and Ricoeur have both observed as postmodern philosophers.

Consequently, any attempt at identification of an absolute, from within the process of reason, immediately becomes a relative perception of that absolute, and as such the relative meaning is no longer the absolute meaning itself. Yet the meaning is a perception of that which is absolute. Therefore, a decision about the existence or otherwise of the absolute is a *pistological* decision based on *nonrational* knowledge, not a decision from a process of reasoning based on *rational* knowledge. The person undertaking the search for the context of the "world," in which self and the concept of finite objects find their place, brings the enquirer to a place of needing to consider the absolute and hence the divine.[10] It is a decision, which once made, forms part of the presuppositional world of a person, subsequently impacting this person's worldview and acting as a prejudice in his or her thinking, which will be written into their texts as authors and can be imported into text as readers.

(a) A Pistological Decision

In chapter 3 of this book, an argument was put forward, and a *prima fascia* case established, proposing that *pistology*, or belief, is an inherent form of knowledge common

---

6. Hegel, "Phenomenology," 101.
7. Ibid.
8. Ibid., 102.
9. Ibid.
10. Pannenberg, *Metaphysics and the Idea of God*, 16.

to all people that is communicated in their literary texts. It was noted that, for any successful interpretation of the text, interpretation requires an interpreter to be open to the standpoint of the author's belief about the subject matter and his or her assumptions about the belief of the intended audience. If the beliefs of an author concerning the *Sache* are inherent in a text, then the belief of the interpreter should not be determinate, as the basis of understanding, in the act of interpretation of the text, if the text is to be understood in the light of any authorial intent.

The interpreter's own beliefs can only be injected into the process as comment and inference subsequent to the interpretative event, often designated as application or appropriation. The issue of interpretation, if the object is the author's meaning, is an understanding of the composition from the viewpoint of the authorial intent and not a critique of the composition from the reader's viewpoint; any analysis of that composition must be subsequent to interpretation; that is, interpretation should deal with what an author said.

Unbelief and belief, in relationship to a proposition, are both *pistological* positions that determine reality for a person and equally impact both the act of writing and the act of reading.[11] The only other *pistological* position seemingly possible is that of agnosticism, which is to profess to not know and be undecided, hence positioning a person as not assenting to either of the other possible *pistological* positions. On the surface this can seem an almost neutral position, as though there is such a *pistological* position as a belief of not knowing. However, to be undecided and not know is to question either position and, as John Henry Newman has pointed out, to question a proposition is the result of a mental act of doubt.[12] The usual concept of doubt is that of a "deliberate recognition" that a proposition is uncertain.[13] This situation is an assent to a proposition at variance with the initial proposition, and, as Newman has noted, this is the situation of disbelief.[14] Disbelief is another way of stating unbelief, and so the effect is the same as unbelief. Consequently, active disbelief in both propositions must lead to a double-minded approach; that is, at best agnosticism results in a vacillating presuppositional world.

The individuals possess a *pistological* stance to the world that has the effect of positioning them in their perception of the world. This is an inescapable conclusion that embraces all people. It has been suggested previously that the *pistological* framework of an individual determines the presuppositions through which he or she perceives reality that is, it provides a mechanism for determining what is true or false, and hence what is accepted, and consequently what meaning is assigned to what is perceived in a worldview. It is the context in which the facts an individual holds are positioned in

---

11. Gadamer, *Truth and Method*, 296. Gadamer notes that even unbelief is defined in terms of the faith demanded.

12. Newman, *Grammar of Assent*, 5.

13. Ibid., 7.

14. Ibid., 8.

viewing the world. The failure by an interpreter to recognize and acknowledge this creates prejudice in perception.

(b) The Pistological Position: Recognition and Nonrecognition

Gadamer's discussion of the problems facing the historian in dealing with history supplies a powerful analogy that demonstrates how a prejudice is created. The failure to recognize self as standing in a worldview that shapes the view of the subject matter is naive, and so results in the individual's inability to deal with the subject matter in a way it deserves.[15] This is analogous to holding a view of self that sees self as acting from an unmetaphysical stance, that is, to see self as able to perceive and evaluate free from metaphysical agenda. However, for Gadamer the "naïveté becomes truly abysmal" when the interpreter becomes aware of the difficulties, and then contends that his or her own concepts and ideas are laid aside for the purpose of investigation.[16] This would, by analogy, be the same as viewing self as being able to act from a nonmetaphysical stance. Here the individual recognizes his or her metaphysical stance but asserts the ability to perceive and evaluate without subjecting the matter to his or her own metaphysical stance. Either position therefore renders the investigation, in Gadamer's view, as not able to deal with the subject matter in a way that the subject matter deserves.

The problem is not being in possession of a metaphysical viewpoint, either compatible or incompatible with that of an author; it is the failure of the interpreter to recognize his or her own metaphysical viewpoint. The view of textuality arrived at by Derrida is distorted because of an unacknowledged presupposition of a metaphysics of absence. If someone considers himself or herself as not possessing a metaphysical position (i.e., sees self as unmetaphysical in his or her analysis and perception), then his or her view of textuality will be distorted. Hence it is a naïveté, which impacts the discourse and interpretation of that discourse. Derrida also asserts that those who deal with exteriority as reference (i.e., the supplement, finding meaning and "voice") have succumbed to metaphysics, which he sees himself to be avoiding. Hence, he views himself as nonmetaphysical. In the light of Gadamer's observations, this can be regarded as abysmal on the part of the interpreter, in this case Derrida; and these aspects, as a naïveté, impair and distort the handling of the subject matter, which must be taken into account.

The work of Wittgenstein assists in indicating why this naïveté is caused in a situation where it may not be able to be seen. He notes that to write a book on a subject that concerned the issue "The world as I found it," the writing subject would have to also, within it, report on his or her body and how it related to this world.[17] The

---

15. Gadamer, *Truth and Method*, 358.
16. Ibid.
17. Wittgenstein, *Tractatus*, sect. 5.631.

author has to report on him or herself within the world. However, this would have the effect of "isolating the subject or rather of showing that in an important sense there is no subject: that is to say, of it alone in this book mention could *not* be made."[18] The subject doing the description cannot be contained within the description: who then is doing the description? Consequently, the "subject does not belong to the world but it is a limit of the world."[19] This is the metaphysical subject[20] and Wittgenstein therefore asks where this metaphysical subject is to be found. His analogy to explain this is the eye and what it sees, because in looking you don't see the eye, it does the looking and doesn't see itself; therefore, it cannot take account of itself in the looking.[21]

Connected to this is the fact that an individual's experience, the encounter with the world he or she sees, does not occur because the dictates of rational reasoning meant it must occur, which would therefore be the same for all those seeing the world.[22] That is to say, an individual's experience is not predetermined by the logic of the system; rather the individual's experience is new and unique for the individual. Everything seen can be seen differently and everything described can be described differently.[23] To use Vanhoozer's terminology, the only one who can enjoy the God's-eye view of reality, which would take in the totality of views, is God.

In the metaphysics of absence, individuals become, in his or her own perception, divine in the sense of their own perspective of reality; and in such a situation everything does indeed become relative to the individual's perception. Hence, solipsism occurs as being the perceived state of reality, that is, that the world *is* the way "I" perceive it. Wittgenstein states that the "I in solipsism shrinks to an extensionless point and there remains the reality coordinated with it."[24] If the extensionless point is taken to be the center of a world, which the idea and presentation by Wittgenstein of extensionless certainly implies, then reality is only understood as it relates to the individual; that is, the perception is that self becomes the center of the world.

Pascal, as discussed previously, put forward that only one of two propositions is possible: God is or God is not. It is important to also recognize, at this point of the discussion, that the issue of Pascal's wager concerns the perception of the individual on the existence of God, not the existence of God. The act of believing neither makes God exist or not exist, but it changes the perspective of the individual on the world he or she sees. Interpretation is an issue of perception, and so this observation is important to the process and understanding of the concept of interpretation. In the terminology of the preceding discussion, this translates to acceptance of one of

18. Ibid.
19. Ibid., sect. 5.632.
20. Ibid., sect. 5.641.
21. Ibid., sect. 5.632.
22. Ibid., sect. 5.634.
23. Ibid.
24. Ibid., sect. 5.64.

two propositions: "presence is" or "absence is" (i.e., "presence is not"). Whichever is believed alters the perception of the individual. As Wittgenstein has observed, the seeing self is the metaphysical self (i.e., the one seeing already has asserted a belief in "presence" or "absence") and the resultant set of presuppositions of the person seeing is the lens of the eye that he or she doesn't see.

In the case of "presence," the individual sees the world as existing within "presence" and receiving meaning in this referential world of this "presence." The individual exists relative to the world. In the case of "absence," the situation is essentially solipsism. The individual sees the world as existing relative to his or her perspective, hence he or she gives meaning from his or her perspective at the center of the world, as he or she perceives it. The world exists relative to the individual. Consequently, hermeneutics does not disclose reality as it is in its state of being but allows a perception of reality by the seeing subject that is, reality is understood relative to the subject.

Wittgenstein makes a further observation about the metaphysical self that gives further understanding on the concept of perception. A result of the reasoning that establishes the metaphysical self is that this can be considered as a "non-psychological I."[25] The world that is seen is the individual's world and this is how the "I occurs in philosophy."[26] He then makes the following observation: "The philosophical I is not the man, not the human body or the human soul of which psychology treats, but the metaphysical subject, the limit—not a part of the world."[27] Wittgenstein indicates a realm of consciousness that exists beyond the human soul that, although interacting with the world of the individual, is not part of the world, that is, not arising within the world yet is in communication with the world. Wittgenstein's observations, or descriptions, are as a philosopher and he makes no further inferences about this realm. In the understanding of Derrida, this realm is an "exteriority," and as such it is the metaphysical realm that he wishes to expose as a phantasm. Evidently, for Wittgenstein, the indescribability of this realm does not make it a phantasm, just indescribable yet existing.

The Eternal Realm: Escaping from the Finite-Infinite Circle

The theologian would understand Wittgenstein's observation to be referring to the spirit realm, a realm of existence that is not physical and not the realm of the soul as that of the thinking individual, that is, Wittgenstein's observation suggests a realm that is set apart from these realms. Hegel is another philosopher who grappled with similar issues but did so from the viewpoint of religion and the concept of spirit. Hegel recognized that in the age of the enlightenment reason asserted itself, and as a result

25. Ibid., sect. 5.641.
26. Ibid.
27. Ibid.

under this influence envisaging religion, as faith, being in opposition to reason.[28] Reason became mere intellect, placing that which it viewed "better than it in a *faith outside and above* itself, as a *beyond*."[29] Hegel then notes that, for Kant, this domain of knowing is incapable of being known by reason.[30] As a result of this conception of things, "the highest idea does not at the same time have reality."[31]

Hegel notes that the important philosophers of his time (i.e., Kant, Fitche, and Jacobi) found themselves largely in agreement with Thomistic thinking, which Hegel states was that "the absolute is no more against reason than it is for it; it is beyond reason."[32] The problem was that the only positive knowledge that reason could acknowledge was therefore only from within its own frame of reference, that is, only that which is finite and empirical.[33] The eternal, as a realm beyond this, is mindless or empty for an acquisition of knowledge.[34]

The realm of knowledge that could be known, the finite and empirical, is all that is in the world, the realm of ordinary existence.[35] Yet this is the realm Wittgenstein noted that the metaphysical self sees, yet is at the same time itself separate from it since the metaphysical self is able to see it. Wittgenstein has essentially noted that the "I" that sees exists in a realm beyond the realm of the physical and the realm of rational objective reason, which realms it sees as separate from them, which is also Hegel's distinction.

Hegel observes that all that is left for religion is to build temples and altars in the heart of the individual, with the result that "in sighs and prayers the individual seeks for the God who he denies himself in intuition, because of the risk that the intellect will cognize what is intuited as a mere thing, reducing the sacred grove to mere timber."[36] However, the very thing that is being sought, the absolute and eternal, is not given since it is perceived as beyond reason with no ability to communicate with reason.[37] Therefore, for the individual there is a longing to communicate with the metaphysical that Wittgenstein noted as existing, yet the existence of which is not a "being" of the finite empirical realm.

The finite becomes the sole reality and therefore absolute, and as a result the finite and the infinite are both posited as absolute, with the finite and infinite standing each

---

28. Hegel, "Jena Writings," 73.
29. Ibid.
30. Ibid., 74.
31. Ibid.
32. Ibid.
33. Ibid.
34. Ibid.
35. Ibid.
36. Ibid.
37. Ibid., 75.

as the antithesis of the other.[38] The eternal remains beyond this antithesis, therefore effectively beyond the infinite, since the infinite receives its identity from that which it is opposite to, that is, the finite.[39] Hegel observes that in this reasoning (because both finite and infinite are absolute with the eternal beyond this realm) the eternal cannot be fathomed or grasped, with the result that God is beyond "the boundary stakes of reason."[40] Therefore, the metaphysical is that which is beyond the capabilities of a reasoning process based upon rational apprehension of knowledge. The philosophers' musings in Hegel's time of the eighteenth century were not new. Philosophy in Hegel's day arrived at the same place Paul noted Greek philosophy, based on Plato and Aristotle, had got in his time of the first century, as recorded in Acts 17:23. Paul notes that in Greek thought the God of worship is unknown and evidently unknowable. Hegel recognized philosophy in his day had arrived at the same place and faced the same problem. The eternal remained elusive.

This concept of thesis and antithesis in the relationship of finite and infinite means that the reasoning process can never escape a circular path that leaves it trapped within rational reason.[41] This can also be seen to imply that the process of dialectic, which as Gadamer noted seems designed by Plato to restrain misunderstanding and misuse, both intentional and unintentional,[42] is also a contributing factor in the entrapment of the process of reasoning. The nature of the dialectic is to redirect the reasoning of the individual back toward the pole he or she came from, that is, to stop the process getting off-track. Therefore, in Hegel's view, philosophy so trapped "cannot aim at the cognition of God [hence the metaphysical], but only at what is called the cognition of human being."[43] Thus philosophy, as understood on the basis of reason, presents a primarily abstract "concept of an empirical humanity all tangled up in limitations, and to stay immovably impaled on the stake of the absolute antithesis."[44] Hegel notes that in this situation the "soul as thing is transformed into the ego."[45]

This is the "extensionless point" that the "I" in solipsism shrinks to, and cannot go beyond, as noted by Wittgenstein. The metaphysical is denied communication from the side of rational reason, and so unless the metaphysical can communicate (i.e., find "voice" from processes other than rational reason), it is treated as though nonexistent. Therefore, eventually, as in Derrida's discourse, the metaphysical is erased as nonexistent. The metaphysical has simply collapsed into the realm of "I" and the solipsism is

38. Ibid., 77.

39. Ibid. See also, 79, where Hegel states, "The infinite has a being of its own only in its tie with the finite."

40. Ibid.

41. Ibid., 79.

42. Gadamer, *Dialogue and Dialectic*, 126.

43. Hegel, "Jena Writings," 81. The comments within the brackets are added as a natural implication in line with the subject matter under discussion.

44. Ibid.

45. Ibid., 83.

complete. In this situation the soul, as the source of rational reasoning and intellect, becomes absolute. However, there exists many "I's" within the world and, with each being absolute, the absolute becomes relative to each "I"; that is, the metaphysics of absence is the basis of relativism. In this situation, when metaphysics of absence is employed, it is indeed logical that authorial intent exists only in the solipsism of the author's world, and, as a result, cannot be determinate in the solipsism of the reader's world.

Hegel found in Christianity an answer to this problem. He proposed that which is not confined within reason yet is found through self-consciousness is able to relate to human reason. The true and absolute finds substance in the concept of the representation of the absolute as *spirit*.[46] However, Hegel's is not a theology in the sense of viewing the world from the divine perspective, it is rather viewing the divine from the world's perspective; hence, it is a spiritual metaphysics.[47] The scriptural text, Rom 1:19–20, reveals an understanding of how God is viewed from the human side, without the benefit of an understanding from God's own viewpoint. Though the context of this passage is within a Christian text, and hence perspective, its description is of the divine perspective that all humanity perceives. Paul notes that the knowledge humanity can have of God is "manifest within" the individual. Communication from the divine side is knowable *within* the human context of physical and reasoning limitations. Paul further notes that this knowability of the divine realm comes from the principle of "reference" (i.e., God's divine realm). Though invisible to the human eye and reason, this know-ability is referenced by what God made, which is a "universal" principle. This principle applies to the whole of existence and to all individuals. God's personality is hinted at: "His invisible . . ." and "His eternal power and Godhead . . ." But God is not personally identified, which is the province of a theology. God remains implicated in the reference, yet he is not identifiable. The sense that the universe references the divine is essentially an assertion that metaphysics is indeed an aspect of existence, not a theological development subsequently added to existence. Therefore, as a principle of the universe, metaphysics should be a foundation principle of all interpretation. Metaphysics, which is accessed and developed within the individual through reference, is how the individual breaks out of the circle of the finite-infinite.

Paul, though having been born a Diaspora Jew (i.e., born outside the land of Israel), was raised in Jerusalem from his youth and was involved in the Rabbinic school of Gamaliel (Acts 22:3; 26:4). His background and philosophy was not developed on the basis of Greek philosophy. Paul showed a capacity for understanding Greek philosophy and religion, (e.g., Acts 17). However, his usage of the concept of logos is in the same fashion as in the Johannine use. The Greek concept of logos is a vehicle to

---

46. Hegel, "Phenomenology," 96. Hegel's reference to spirit is an adoption of the concept he found articulated in John 4:24, stating, "God is Spirit." (Italics original.)

47. Gadamer, *Truth and Method*, 433. Gadamer describes Hegel's concepts as an "idealistic spiritualism of a metaphysics of infinity."

help in understanding what is occurring in the advent of Christ (John 1:1, "In the beginning was the Word"). However, John 1:14, "the Word became flesh and dwelt among us," revolutionizes the worldview of the world impacted by Greek philosophy in the embodiment of the Word, which is contrary to Greek thought.[48] Similarly, Paul makes reference to concepts held in the Greek world, but he uses them to communicate his understanding; that is, these concepts are used for the purposes of communication not formation. In Acts 17:23, for example, Paul writes that the unknown and unknowable God becomes known in the person of Christ.

Therefore, the background to Paul's assertion, mentioned in Rom 1:19–20, is not Hellenism but Judaism. His idea of reference may be inferred by such concepts as the creation, that is, that humanity is created in the image of God (Gen 1:26–27). And "therefore" in their being humanity references the divine. Passages, such as Psalm 19, express that the creation is a voice of reference to the divine. There is sufficient foundation within Judaism as the basis for Paul's thoughts in Rom 1:19–20 without the need to import ideas from Greek thought. Paul's own description of his upbringing, that he was "taught according to the strictness of our fathers' law, and was zealous toward God," would mitigate against importation of ideas. Paul indicates a metaphysical world, but developed on a totally different basis to that of Hegel. However, both see the metaphysical is a referent of the physical. Thus, the individual in the metaphysics of presence gets outside the circle.

The Referential Principle: Metaphysics of Presence and Absence

Because the principle of reference is universal it can be used universally; that is, it works within rational reason but has the ability to connect and understand that which is outside rational reason. In chapter 3 of this book, a case was set out to establish a basis of the existence of categories of knowledge other than rational. Because these categories are themselves knowledge (i.e., they involve what can be known), they are describable and communicable. It was further suggested that the knowledge acquired, as knowledge, could be a basis of reasoning processes.

Reference can access and allow communication with and through these other categories of the *arational* (i.e., the subjective) and the *nonrational* (i.e., the *pistological*, or metaphysical). The principle of reference is therefore, in the biblical understanding of the world, a basic principle of interpretation. The ability of reference is located on the human side of the communication, since, as it set out in Rom 1:19–20, reference uses what is known as its basis, having the ability to refer to what is not known. This is actually a basic principle of all inquiry; that is, the use of what is known to discover what, at that time, is not known. In deconstruction, Derrida has employed the

---

48. Ibid., 379. Gadamer discusses this very issue concerning these texts.

principle of reference so that the metaphysics of absence can prevent the metaphysics of presence from impacting the reader, that is, signs refer to other signs, keeping the reader within the text. This is not the discrediting of reference but seeking a discrediting of the ability to reference outside the text. Derrida creates a new circle to circumvent the tendency to reference that becomes automatic in metaphysics of presence; that is, Derrida uses reference to deny the form of reference he doesn't want.

Hegel seems to have taken note of the concept of reference, with its ability to get outside rational reason, and the ability of the metaphysical to manifest within the individual through reference.[49] Hegel's view of spirit is not developed from within theology. His is rather a theologically impacted concept, adapted into an understanding, which he developed from the Greek philosophy of Plato and Aristotle.[50] He views spirit as the direct opposite of matter, with an essence of freedom, so that all the qualities of spirit exist only through freedom.[51] His reasoning is that this freedom is operational when the existence of the individual depends on the individual; that is, the individual is not dependent for his or her existence on that which is external to the individual within this world.[52] He states in this situation that the "self-contained existence of Spirit is none other than self-consciousness—consciousness of one's own being."[53] This freedom that is the essence of spirit is his concept of what drives history to unfold; it is "none other than the progress of the consciousness of Freedom."[54]

These concepts from Hegel's understanding of history serve as a good paradigm through which to understand and highlight two aspects that are important in his understanding of spirit. Spirit works out from its domain into the domain of the individual and is then manifest as self-consciousness. The metaphysical world impacts and outworks in the physical world, which is subordinate to the metaphysical, and the metaphysical is *the final cause of the world at large*."[55] This is not to say that all that is in the world derives its source from faith, as though a version of fideism. But it is to say that the perception of reality that a person possesses will give context and understanding to the world he or she sees. The issue, then, is not the nature of reality but the nature of perception; that is, it is a hermeneutical issue.

---

49. Hegel, "Phenomenology," 125. In a discussion of representation and its purpose, he notes "*representation* constitutes the middle term between pure thought and consciousness as such." (Italics original.)

50. Gadamer, *Truth and Method*, 418. Gadamer notes that Hegel's development is from within Greek thought and he states, "whoever wants to learn from the Greeks has always first to learn from Hegel."

51. Hegel, *Philosophy of History*, 17.

52. Ibid.

53. Ibid.

54. Ibid., 19.

55. Ibid. (Italics original.) Hegel uses the word "spiritual" not "metaphysical," but this appears to be the concept behind his usage of the word.

Although he does not use the term "absence," Hegel discusses the situation of self-consciousness that "one-sidedly grasps only *its own* divestment."[56] This situation appears to be metaphysical—a movement of spirit—but spirit, as being, has not moved out into consciousness and "divested" itself to become self-consciousness, per his use of the term (to use Derrida's terminology, spirit is "absent.")[57] In this situation the individual will experience a perception of reality that is a phantasm, but since this perception is essentially only a facade of the metaphysical there will be no metaphysical impact from outside the person, that is, no real presence.[58] Yet the perception will have satisfied itself that it has fulfilled the metaphysical issue that Wittgenstein proposed; that is, the "I" who observes is separate from the world and is a metaphysical subject. Hegel notes that in this situation "Spirit is in this way only *imagined* into existence; this imagining is the *visionary dreaming . . .* that insinuates into both nature and history."[59] This situation impacts both the view of nature—the world, and history, the place in the world—and the view of tradition. Hegel's description describes clearly the situation of the metaphysics of absence in Derrida, including the operation of imagination in auto-affection. Hegel's discussion is of mythical representations that form part of religions in general that are other than true spirit, yet his description fits the understanding of deconstruction. This underlines the reality that deconstruction is indeed metaphysics, which has designated its own metaphysics as nonmetaphysics, or, as has been suggested in this work, it is in reality the *metaphysics of absence*.

If the situation is not to be a phantasm (i.e., not merely imagination of the individual, but genuine and having actual being), then it comes from reception of spirit.[60] In Hegel's understanding genuine reception of spirit comes as perception of "immediate consciousness" that in turn takes the shape of self-consciousness in the individual, the absolute spirit takes, for itself, this shape of self-consciousness.[61] Within the individual reception of spirit now appears as faith; that is, it becomes *pistological* knowledge not rational knowledge, and the person of the individual is involved in personal encounter with the divine.[62] What takes place is neither representation, which is the mode of contact, nor a trigger of the imagination creating a thought of contact, but is God beheld "immediately and sensuously as a self."[63] Furthermore, since the perception is occurring as self-consciousness within the human world, this perception of God is perceived as "an actual human individual."[64] Therefore, within Hegel's de-

---

56. Hegel, "Phenomenology," 119. (Italics original.)
57. Ibid.
58. Ibid.
59. Ibid. (Italics original.)
60. Ibid., 120.
61. Ibid.
62. Ibid.
63. Ibid., 121.
64. Ibid.

scription, not only "voice" of real presence is possible but real communication is also possible. This reception of spirit is not the possession of an individual, which would remove freedom, but interaction and communication with an individual. In Hegel's view this process is how revelation of true religion occurs.[65]

THE INTERACTION OF THE DIVINE AND THE HUMAN: THE METAPHYSICAL DIMENSION

Hegel's concept that spirit comes as an immediate consciousness has obvious affinity with the phenomenology of Husserl, whom he preceded. Hegel's concept is clearly one of an "intuitiveness" in immediate presentation. However, this is not inconsistent with the biblical record itself. The biblical record is a discourse of God, yet the hand of God is not the hand of direct authorship of this discourse within the world. In his consideration of the New Testament texts, Thomas E. Boomershine concluded the evidence suggests that Jesus was literate.[66] He therefore suggested the model of Socrates as an explanation of how Jesus can be the "seminal figure" of a movement that engages literacy, when Jesus himself wrote nothing.[67]

The Genesis record is a discourse of God that occurs in the same fashion, as Boomershine notes in the life and ministry of Jesus; it is God's discourse written by a disciple, that is, an inspired believer.[68] Therefore, the writing of the saying occurs within the world and is not represented as descending into the world; further, the writing is a creation within the world and is the immanent record of a transcendent discourse. Also by adopting this approach (i.e., the divine inspiring the writer rather than the divine being the direct author), the divine, like Socrates, can inhabit the text in real presence and dialogue. Thus, to describe himself and his action in the world, God moves himself from the metaphysical "I" of authorship to a place of having description and presence within the world the author describes.

The Genesis record opens with the divine fiat of the beginning, which is that God created the universe. As a proposition it can be accepted (i.e., as in the metaphysics of presence) or it can be rejected (i.e., as in the metaphysics of absence). It cannot be modified or renegotiated. Following this statement of divine fiat, in Gen 1:2 God is present as "being" before logos issues forth in the act of creation. The earth was, in its initial state, unordered; however, the "Spirit of God was hovering over the face of the waters." The communication, or logos, of God is not separated from his being but is contingent with it. However, this does not act as cause of his being. Spirit is already present prior to the issuing forth of logos in Gen 1:3. To use Wittgenstein's concept, God is the metaphysical subject, being transcendent with respect to the world and

---

65. Ibid.
66. Boomershine, "Jesus of Nazareth," 22.
67. Ibid., 23.
68. Ibid.

separate from the world, which having created, he is seeing. Hence, God's being is not contained within the world he created but can be identified from within it.

As Wittgenstein also observed, the form of the metaphysical subject can be described in its involvement with the world it sees. This form must of necessity refer back to the subject, which Hegel recognized must be linked to a discussion of Spirit in the case of the divine, that is, God is Spirit. The metaphysical subject "God" is transcendent, but the Spirit is predicated with respect to God; that is, the Spirit enters the world of the text, becoming the form that the speaking subject describes of himself within the world. The Spirit is the immanence of God and is able to refer back to the transcendent speaking subject because the Genesis record places Spirit in a predicated position with respect to the subject God. Hegel examined the concept of predication and noted that the subject becomes manifest in the predication of the subject (e.g., within the present discussion) in statements such as "God is creator of heaven and earth" and "God is Spirit." The predicate gives God presence within the world.[69] Predication refers back to the subject in the event of discourse.

The nature of the metaphysical subject's description is a discourse, and Ricoeur noted that in the discourse event (i.e., speech and/or the act of writing as inscription of speech), the inner structure of the nature of the sentence is to refer to the speaking subject. The utterance's meaning refers to the utterer's meaning due to the self-reference of discourse.[70] In Ricoeur this reference to the subject is only in the event of discourse, that is, dialogue, as his philosophy of interpretation is prefaced by the detachment of the written text from this event, which results in the semantic autonomy of the text, as previously discussed. Reference is a natural feature of event, and detachment changes this to muted (in the case of Ricoeur), or to erased (in the case of Derrida).

The Detachment of Presence

The critical question at this point for perception of the metaphysical is the issue of detachment. Does the metaphysical subject become detached from its logos in the case of written text, due to temporal detachment, irrespective of any perceived difficulty with handling reference, as in Gadamer and Ricoeur? Another way of phrasing this, in the light of the thinking of Derrida, is to posit the question: Does logos become text in its detachment? In the context of this examination of hermeneutics, the question becomes: Does composition simply become text in its detachment? The issue of semantic autonomy hangs on the concept of detachment. In the metaphysics of presence, meaning is a metaphysical issue, which is also no more than the simple recognition that the speaking subject, giving a description of the world, is the metaphysical

---

69. Hegel, "Phenomenology," 121.
70. Ricoeur, *Interpretation Theory*, 13.

subject. In the metaphysics of absence, meaning is an issue of imagination, nothing more than pure auto-affection. In this case it is the reader who is autonomous, not the text.

Therefore, the issue of the semantic autonomy of the text is a metaphysical issue; that is, it relates to metaphysical perception. The only other possibility for Ricoeur's concept is that the semantic autonomy of the text is pure happenstance.[71] However, this would suggest that temporality can break the connection with the metaphysical; in this case humanity's alienation from the divine (i.e., the world of reference that is accessed in a metaphysics of presence) becomes pure happenstance. If this is Ricoeur's position, then what is denied is the inherent ability of the text to reference backwards to the author, as the subject, which it would in the event of discourse. Ricoeur does not question the ability of texts to reference. Rather, his discussion of symbol and metaphor, and his concept of interpretation as projecting a world before the reader, testifies to his belief as to the ability of a text to reference. His view, if it were one of serendipity, would then have to imply a failure *of*, or breakdown *in*, metaphysical perception occurring in its detachment. Furthermore, if his view is one of happenstance, then it also faces the situation of the possibility of the reader entering into dialogue with the author, in which case semantic autonomy would be lost. Consequently, semantic autonomy cannot be considered as an inherent element of written text. Detachment is merely a temporal element associated with the text and as such does not negate authorial intent. Ricoeur does not discuss the nature of this rupture, just the fortuitousness of the breakdown.

Furthermore, his concept is one of autonomy not autocracy. Hence the text's self-rule relates to how the rules are established within which it has autonomy. Without this self-rule, the text is indeed autocratic. Ricoeur's theory of interpretation does set out his understanding of the "rules of engagement" in interpretation, and one of his *created rules* is the autonomy of the text. The rules he establishes, or recognizes as inherent, cause his theory to flow to the place he desired to go to when he began; that is, Ricoeur's theory itself reveals the very principle of authorial intention.

In the previous discussion of his concepts, it is the direct voice of the author (i.e., real presence), which is denied; but the author is granted a back door in a form of absent presence. This occurs in that the discourse is the author's, and meaning is established between author and reader as a fusion of their respective horizons via mediation of the ideality of the text. If this is a genuine fusion, then the issue of metaphysical perception operates and occurs without mention or consideration.

---

71. Ibid., 100. Ricoeur, in endnote 5, p. 79 of the 4th Essay, in discussing the concept that valid interpretation is founded on authorial intention, makes the following statement: "the intention of the author is lost as a physical event." This would seem to imply that happenstance might indeed be his reasoning. If so, this would in turn imply that his theory of interpretation fortuitously occurs due to random chance, i.e. primarily serendipity. This serendipity means, therefore, that authorial intent in writing "has no other [means of] expression than the verbal meaning of the text itself." (Ibid.). This is the sense of the text, discussed previously.

Metaphysics, as Derrida observed, is inescapable, not as a trap in which a person exists, but as the context of human existence. Ricoeur, like Gadamer, does recognize the metaphysical task. This is seen in his definitive statement on semantics, which he calls "the theory that relates the inner or immanent constitution of the sense to the outer or transcendent intention of the reference."[72]

A further problem, in Ricoeur's thought, is that the text is granted as having the faculty of meaning, being implied by the concept of semantic autonomy; that is, it has presence. Yet, as previously noted by Ong, discourse is discontinued in written text until continued in and by a reader, which militates against text as presence. Hence, the concept of metaphysical perception is not so easily avoided, which involves the speaking subject, or author of the text and his or her intention.

In the Judeo-Christian understanding of the origins of the universe, as mentioned previously, being and logos are contingent. This is also true for the description of humanity. In Gen 1:26–30, as part of the divine fiat of creation, God issues forth logos for the creation of humanity, male and female. However, in the account of Gen 2:7 the formation is described from a concept of immanence; God forms humanity from the dust of the earth, God is hands-on and no "logos" occurs. Yet, the human so formed is lifeless until God breathes life into the nostrils of the human. The implication of the text is that of a fully formed yet lifeless being that does not live until the breath, or spirit, enters and expresses life. Being is directly conferred by the "Being" of all being, and is a direct impartation not a creation by logos; thereby, it is transcendent with respect to this world. It has been previously observed that language and understanding are primordial; they are there at the beginning, in the biblical worldview. However, the text of Genesis 2 shows that as with the divine, being occurs before any logos issues forth. The scriptural view is that which becomes apparent in analysis; that is, metaphysics sets the context of logos, and this will impact the task of interpretation in making what is foreign one's own.

Some immediate observations can be made about the biblical concept of creation and its philosophical descriptions. In Gen 1:3–5, light, the energy source for all life, is first brought into the realm of this universe. In this process time is created, since the concept of the first day suggests the introduction of time. Everything that is created beyond this moment will have the horizon of time. Heidegger, in his philosophy, asserts that, in his thinking, time is the horizon of *Dasein*, the expression of individual being-within-the-world.[73] As noted previously in the Genesis account, because *Dasein* is in this world, *Dasein* is created within time.

However, the biblical account also shows that, in the case of the creation of human being, being is conferred and is not endemic to the creation; that is, the living being did not exist just from the formation of the elements within the creation, but instead required an act of God in conferring it. This is to say the human being has

---

72. Ibid., 21–22.
73. Heidegger, *Being and Time*, 39.

both dimensions, those of the finite-infinite circle and the eternal, resident within the one being. This would seem to be the thrust of Eccl 3:11: "He [i.e., God as creator] has made everything beautiful in its time. Also He has put eternity in their [i.e., human beings] hearts, except that no one can find out the work that God does from beginning to end." (Bracketed comments added for clarification). This text also points to the problematic that has been the discussion of this chapter; that is, one does not proceed from the finite-infinite to the eternal by a process of reasoning based on rational knowledge; rather another form of knowledge is required, the *nonrational* knowledge of the metaphysical.

The "logos" does not arise from within the creation, but arises externally and is expressed within the creation. This also indicates the why and how of the concept of reference to the external and metaphysical, noted in the Pauline text of Rom 1:19–20. Hence, also indicating why philosophers, in their descriptions, find themselves addressing such issues. The "logos of God" from exteriority enters the realm of this existence giving meaning, hence order and structure. The sense of purpose and destiny both within and for humanity arises through the external logos, as in Gen 1:26–30, that is, such things as the drive towards achievement, the drive towards survival, and in Gen 2:18–22 the drive to relationship and community. None of this is endemic or necessitated by the nature of the universe itself. Removal of the Supreme Being and external reference of the logos has the tragic consequence of reducing humanity to that of the machine, which Derrida announces with seeming delight.[74]

Finally, in the Genesis account, morality and ethics do not arise within the system but from exteriority of the logos. This is seen when the concept of right and wrong is established by God's declaration in the garden. Adam is commanded not to eat of the tree of the knowledge of good and evil in the midst of the garden, and is warned of the consequence of disobedience (Gen 2:15–17). Gadamer also observes that moral reasoning occurs on the basis of something already known.[75] Technical knowledge can be learned and forgotten, but moral knowledge is neither learned nor forgotten and has the appearance of being absolute.[76] Therefore, as a philosopher not holding the concept of the absolute, Gadamer acknowledges the appearance of absoluteness, and hence exteriority of morality. The Christian philosopher Francis Schaeffer points out that there "must be an absolute if there are to be *morals*, and there must be an absolute if there are to be real *values*."[77] He goes on to state that if "there is no absolute beyond man's ideas, then there is no final appeal to judge between individuals and groups whose moral judgments conflict."[78] The collapsing of the metaphysics of presence into metaphysics of absence removes these aspects, such as destiny and

---

74. Derrida, *Of Grammatology*, 9. This observation of Derrida's has been considered above.
75. Gadamer, *Truth and Method*, 283.
76. Ibid.
77. Schaeffer, *How Should We Then Live?* 145.
78. Ibid.

promise, together with morality and ethics. However, their spontaneous arisal within humanity despite the metaphysics of absence, which does occur, makes reference to the metaphysics of presence.

A Turn that U-Turns: From Metaphysics to Language in Postmodernism

Thiselton notes that in Heidegger's search for the understanding of being he experiences "an ambivalence" in his later life.[79] Thiselton observes that Heidegger in his later life saw being as somehow residing in language, but, at the same time, realized that this was an awkward concept and desired to retreat from it.[80] Thiselton takes note that the later Heidegger did not abandon the quest for the "Being of beings," but he no longer searched in the area of metaphysics.[81] In his initial search (i.e., in *Being and Time*) Heidegger notes that, in the search for the answer to the question of being, there is "*a priori* an enigma."[82] The enigma is that life is conducted with at least a rudimentary understanding of Being, and yet it is still "veiled in darkness."[83] So for Heidegger the question of Being not only lacks a clear answer but the question itself is obscure and lacking direction.[84] In essence Heidegger abandoned metaphysics because he could not escape the finite-infinite circle.

The biblical account suggests that being exists within time, as Heidegger observed, and so can to a degree be understood within time. It was noted previously that Heidegger saw time as the horizon of *Dasein*. However, the biblical account also implies that pursuit of the question of being is not successfully addressed without consideration of the fact that being is conferred from outside time and this universe; that is, it is a metaphysical, or transcendent, issue; and, further, it is conferred by a Supreme Being, as the "Being of beings." Without this concept of being as transcendent, no answer will be found to the question of the Being of beings. This observation agrees with Heidegger's later observation. Heidegger discovered what the biblical text predicted. But the difference is that Heidegger, rather than turning to what metaphysics pointed to (i.e., a Supreme Being) as an answer to the question, turned instead from metaphysics to a concept of language that he himself was ambivalent about.

Thiselton notes that Heidegger shares Derrida's belief that "metaphysics has reached the end of the road."[85] However, Derrida realized that the door on metaphys-

---

79. Thiselton, *New Horizons*, 108.
80. Ibid.
81. Ibid., 106.
82. Heidegger, *Being and Time*, 23. (Italics original.)
83. Ibid. Heidegger notes that every inquiry, as a seeking, "gets guided beforehand by what is sought," implying a form of *a priori* knowledge, 24.
84. Ibid., 24.
85. Thiselton, *New Horizons*, 106.

ics can't be shut until the absence of God is pronounced, that is, God is put under erasure, and hence the metaphysics proposed is one of absence. If the concept of the Supreme Being (i.e., God) is removed from the Genesis account, what is left is that "matter" exists, with the probable implication that it always has. This "matter" spontaneously converts to energy, or light, which without a divine guiding hand becomes an explosion. Structure appears inorganically, implying that disorder leads to order. And then, eventually, information arises and organic matter, some manner of life, develops spontaneously. There exists some internal driving mechanism, unidentified and unidentifiable, causing life, which through trial and error develops into ever-improving states of being in the direction of the eventual appearance of humanity.

Whilst such a description in a metaphysics of absence would have some identification with modern theories of evolution, even the most liberal interpretation of scriptural authorship could not suggest Genesis is an attempt to adapt the concept of modern evolution to a Supreme Being. The most extreme and liberal views of the authorship of Genesis still predate modern evolutionary concepts by millennia. Yet the same path is followed, except for the guiding hand of the Divine, and it is this exteriority that allows the unfolding of structure and order. Gadamer, who does not subscribe to a concept of spiritual metaphysics, cautions science in its terminology in this area. He notes that a concept such as adaptation presupposes that the natural situation is one of a lack of adaptation.[86] Being should, in this scenario, be endemic, which it is not, as is agreed by philosophers; and information must arise spontaneously, which it can't. So the only option in pursuing the concepts of hermeneutics, in the absence of a Supreme Being and the concept of metaphysical existence, is a concept of language as somehow preexisting so that being and information can come into existence. However, the end of the road for such a concept is that the logos precedes being, and being itself becomes derivative. The hermeneutical implications of such a view are enormous: in essence the only recourse to meaning would be epistemology, and ontology would be a derivative of epistemology.

What Heidegger implied and suggested with ambivalence, Gadamer also proposed but without the same ambivalence. Gadamer saw that classical metaphysics' concept of truth rested upon theological foundations, so that what is insoluble for the finite mind is resolved in the infinite mind of God.[87] Modern science developed a metaphysical idea of the "knowing subject being adequate to the object of knowledge," which Gadamer believes to be without justification.[88] His own view is that philosophy can no longer pursue a theological basis of metaphysics, as in Hegel; nor can the secularized versions of metaphysics, as found in science, engage in this pursuit due to the flaw of balancing the dialectic of finite and infinite, which Hegel also pointed out,

---

86. Gadamer, *Truth and Method*, 417.
87. Gadamer, *Philosophical Hermeneutics*, 74–75.
88. Gadamer, *Truth and Method*, 417.

as noted previously.[89] Yet, nor can philosophy dismiss the transcendental nature of metaphysical philosophy, the lack of which, as interpreted by Gadamer, resulted in a decline of philosophical knowledge following Hegel's death.[90] Therefore, for Gadamer, the task of metaphysics continues but it cannot be solved as classical metaphysics.[91] He asks if there is an answer "that does not venture to affirm the infinity of the divine mind and yet is able to do justice to the infinite correspondence of soul and being?"[92] His alternate proposition to metaphysics as metaphysics is the way of language as fulfilling the task of metaphysics.[93]

Thus, for Gadamer, neither the metaphysics of presence nor the metaphysics of absence, which denies transcendence as a dimension, is tenable. Rather, the metaphysical task is pursued in language. Then, for Gadamer, "language is the central point where 'I' and the world meet, or rather, manifest their original unity."[94] Consequently, Gadamer replaces the metaphysical subject of Wittgenstein with a metaphysical impact of language that relates "I" and the world viewed. Although Gadamer himself does not state it, his view is essentially to drop the term *logos* and replace it with *language*; that is, language is "logos" without the metaphysical baggage. Consequently, what happens in his concept of language is a nontheological, or nonspiritual, format of "logos" that retains its metaphysical potential. His proposal is essentially pseudo-metaphysics; that is, in his view language will perform the same task without the baggage inherent in metaphysics. This formulation will still retain the essence of metaphysics, and it effectively becomes the same thing in terms of perception. Gadamer suggests a metaphysics that eliminates the Supreme Being, yet seeks to retain the domain of the Supreme Being as a pseudo-presence; that is, Gadamer's metaphysical substitute will retain the domain of reference that is significant to hermeneutics. However, like the concept of absence, his is a statement about presence. As a result, what Gadamer highlights is that metaphysical perception cannot be dismissed or dispensed with, whether or not the view is presence or absence or even pseudo-presence.

It is acknowledged that neither Ricoeur nor Gadamer would be likely to perceive themselves as developing their hermeneutical theories in the metaphysics of presence. However, both acknowledge metaphysical aspects, Gadamer directly and Ricoeur in the admission of reference. Therefore, their theories fall within the domain of the metaphysics of presence, without any *pistological* implications being made on their understanding within that domain. In the metaphysics of absence, even pseudo-metaphysics of reference is denied, since transcendence itself is denied; hence all exterior reference is denied. Therefore, the argument for the autonomy of the text occurs

---

89. Gadamer, *Philosophical Hermeneutics*, 75.
90. Ibid., 74.
91. Ibid., 75.
92. Ibid.
93. Ibid.
94. Gadamer, *Truth and Method*, 431.

primarily within the province of the metaphysics of presence, in the metaphysics of absence there is no argument to resolve because the reader is the autonomous entity.

The argument for the autonomy of the text, within the metaphysics of presence, contains the issue of temporality that is, the author has metaphysical presence but is temporally absent. This disjunction, or detachment from the text, separates the metaphysical presence of the author from the text. The concern that arises relates to the availability and knowability of authorial intent in the hermeneutical task. Alternately, the argument for autonomy, within the metaphysics of absence, is based on the collapsing of the metaphysical as an empty domain, and, as a result, authorial intent is the same as authorial meaning, consequently relating only to the writing with no impact on the reading. Therefore, the author is not only absent temporally but also has no metaphysical presence, only absence. The fallacy of this view lies in the presupposition that the collapsing of the metaphysical domain somehow results in either an unmetaphysical or a nonmetaphysical approach to the task, the fallacy of which is considered previously.

The presupposition of either "God is present" or "God is absent," without any definition of what is meant by the term "God," is a metaphysical decision independent of rational objective reason and is a matter of *pistological* reasoning, that is, the domain of metaphysics. The term "God" is used here in almost a generic sense in recognition that what is being considered is a *pistological* viewpoint. A theological viewpoint is a particular defining, and thereby identifying, of the term, and is a decision within *pistology*. The inherent assumption, in the metaphysics of absence, is that the collapsing of the *nonrational* domain of knowledge leaves only the *rational* and *arational* domains as the real. However, the *pistology* of absence held by an author or reader impacts and shapes their view of the other domains of knowledge; that is, their pistology is acting metaphysically in determining reality impacting as an absence of presence. Ironically, ultimately the individual holding to a pistology of absence is in reality holding a view within the domain of presence; that is, absence only has meaning in the light of an understanding of presence, or, to use Derrida's term, erasure assumes the existence of something that was erased. An analogy can be seen in the issue of light and darkness. Darkness is a state of the absence of light, and is consequently a statement about light. Similarly absence is a statement about presence and inherently involves a discussion of presence, hence metaphysics.

A Biblical Excursus

The following section considers the concept of autonomy from within a *pistology* of presence, and within this domain, from a theology of the Judeo-Christian use of the term "God." As has been previously noted, the adoption of a worldview does not preclude an individual from engaging in descriptive task as a valid endeavor. Adopting a worldview also does not disqualify the individual, as previously noted, from making inferences based on his or her descriptions.

It has been noted previously that in the opening of the Gospel of John (John 1:1–3), there is a Johannine echoing of Gen 1:1. The use of brackets can help reveal what can be seen as a form of paraphrase, or clarification, in the Gospel of John of the Genesis text: "In the beginning [was the Word, and the Word was with God, and the Word was God. He was in the beginning with] God. All things were made [through Him, and without Him nothing was made that was made]." The first bracket paraphrases the word "God;" the second bracket is a clarification of "made"—showing the intimate involvement that connects "made" and "God" in the person of Jesus. This connection highlights God's immanence, or real presence. God is not disinterested transcendence, nor is God some form of deistic absence. If the brackets are collapsed, the statement takes the form: "In the beginning God, *by* whom all things were made *directly*." This statement is the essence of Gen 1:1.[95]

The identification of the possible authorial intent of the Gospel of John has been considered previously. The intent of the author relates to the revealing of the person of Jesus in his unique identification as the Messiah and Son of God (John 20:30–31). Consequently, the author's approach is not an attempt to write a paraphrase of Genesis. However, nor is his reasoning simply to use the Genesis account as an illustration for launching his gospel account. The manner of his phrasing actually starts the account of Jesus at the beginning; that is, the Johannine account locates itself and the person of Jesus in the Genesis account. The point of departure is John 1:4 when the author relates the life manifest in Jesus to the concept of light. In the Genesis account of Gen 1:3, having established that matter has been made and the being of God is present in the Spirit of God, the author of Genesis states the divine decree that brings into being the presence of light, so that the act of creation can proceed. This is the departure point for the writer of the Gospel, the light that for him is the basis of life, and is the object of his Gospel. The act of paraphrasing in the Gospel of John is not purely illustrative, and is intentionally located in the actual Genesis.

The resultant Johannine paraphrase of the word "God" brings an important aspect into sharp focus. The startling revelation of John 1:14–15 is that the logos became incarnate and was made manifest among humanity, who then beheld God as actual humanity in and through the person of Jesus. The Johannine use, in John 1:1, 14, of the term ὁ λογοσ indicates the transcendent and immanent identity of Jesus; since in the incarnation as immanence within the world, he remains ὁ λογοσ. Gadamer noted that this concept of the incarnation, with its mystical union, offered a distinct contribution of Christianity to the field of hermeneutics.[96]

Greek metaphysics, in its consideration of the Being-of-beings, saw fulfillment in thought, considering thought of *nous* as essentially the transcendent.[97] The

---

95. The words "by" and "directly" are added to indicate agency.
96. Gadamer, *Truth and Method*, 379.
97. Ibid., 414.

verbalization of the logos is the presence of being.[98] Whilst logos can appear in human form, it is only appearance, and is a facility of its ability to be embodied and disembodied, with disembodiment being the pure and therefore preferred form.[99] Gadamer viewed this concept in Christian thought, of the incarnation, as having the following contribution to hermeneutics: "If the Word became flesh and the reality of the spirit was perfected only in this incarnation, then the logos is freed from its spirituality, which means, at the same time, from its cosmic potential."[100] In this thought the phenomenon of language disengages from "its immersion in the ideality of meaning, and offers it to philosophical reflection."[101] In his continuing discussion it is the mystical union of logos and flesh that is important in hermeneutics.[102] His usage is as illustration to the connection between *langue* and language as spoken, which can take various finite forms. However, in this finitude is infinitude of meaning that can be developed and interpreted.[103]

Hence, Gadamer's view seems to be that language is at the same time transcendent and immanent, and he has developed this concept on the illustration of the Christian concept of the incarnation. Understanding as an event occurs through the application of what is universal to the particular individuals' situation, i.e. the union, or fusion, of what is transcendent and what is immanent, results in understanding.[104] Language has a universal nature in that it is not bound to a realm of the speakable as opposed to the realm of the unspeakable; there is nothing that is known that cannot be said.[105] He thus observes: "Our capacity for saying keeps pace untiringly with the universality of reason."[106] Therefore, language has an aspect that acts transcendently because it is always available for an individual to supply meaning.

This view maintains, for him, the concept that hermeneutics can retain the task of metaphysics, and can do so without the spiritual or logical reasoning associated with either the theological baggage of dependence on the divine mind or limitations of rational objective reasoning of the scientific streams of thought. His concern is to move on from theological concepts in metaphysics. Consequently, it is the illustration he desires to use not the theology. Therefore, as a philosopher Gadamer is employing the description without the worldview, which is a legitimate aim, that is, using a description within a differing worldview.

98. Ibid.
99. Ibid., 378.
100. Ibid., 379.
101. Ibid.
102. Gadamer, *Philosophical Hermeneutics*, 59. Gadamer notes that in Greek thought logos became rendered as reason or thought. However, the primary meaning of logos is language.
103. Gadamer, *Truth and Method*, 416.
104. Ibid., 278.
105. Gadamer, *Philosophical Hermeneutics*, 67. Gadamer also notes that knowledge that cannot be applied, therefore articulated, remains meaningless, *Truth and Method*, 279.
106. Ibid.

However, at times, Gadamer resorts to spiritual language in his description. He asserts that language has a spiritual reality, which is "*Pneuma*, the spirit, which unifies I and Thou."[107] He contends that in every occasion of dialogue "a spirit rules" that facilitates the event of communication.[108] This represents what appears to be an almost Hegelian approach to the subject of language. The introduction of the concept of transcendence brings the discussion into the realm of metaphysics. This shows that the language of metaphysics is inherent, and, as a result, the treatment required occurs within the domain of the metaphysics of presence.

The illustration Gadamer used from the Christian understanding of this domain had other implications for hermeneutics that he did not explore. These implications indicate that semantic autonomy may be an inference based on prior presuppositions, not a fact due to the circumstance of detachment. The Johannine treatment of Genesis, placing the person of Jesus as *the logos* at the beginning, shows that the logos that issues forth at the creation is never viewed as impersonal, or abstract, but always comes forth as meaning relating to the intent of a person. Ricoeur also agrees that in the case of the event of speaking, meaning is the author's meaning. In the Genesis account it was noted that being and logos are contingent, the Spirit is present before logos is articulated in creation. The Johannine account highlights not just contingency but that logos has its cause in being—i.e., logos can be viewed as thought or reason (as in Greek thought), or as simply meaning language (as Gadamer suggests)—but logos does not transcend being. Without being, logos does not itself find being; that is, logos has no inherent meaning until employed by being.

Gadamer observes that the naturalness of language (i.e., it is always there) makes inquiry about the origin of language an impossibility; thus, the conception of a situation where humanity was without language is *inconceivable*.[109] As a result the question of the origin of language, for humanity, is excluded because this question can only be addressed within language.[110] Therefore, Gadamer makes what is considered a fundamental assertion, which is that humanity is composed of individuals, who as beings possess language.[111] Consequently, as a philosopher who will not consider the metaphysical inference from what is a metaphysical observation, he does not follow the direction of the reasoning to that which is exterior, and consequently notes only the appearance of preexistence not its implications. The consideration of any implications of such an observation leads the inquiry outside the text, that is, outside the immanence of human finitude. To phrase it in Gadamer's thinking, language is the mark of human finitude, i.e. the evidence of human finitude, and is always itself beyond

---

107. Ibid., 65.
108. Ibid., 66.
109. Ibid., 60–61. (Italics added.)
110. Ibid., 61.
111. Ibid., 59.

humanity.[112] Again, it is notable that Gadamer wishes to stay within the benefits of the metaphysics of presence but not its implications.

It is interesting in the biblical account of the creation that the faculty of language appears as almost an aspect of being;[113] that is, God speaks to humanity as recorded in Gen 1:28–30 and Gen 2:16–17 and is evidently understood, which is the direction that Gadamer approaches. The Johannine account places logos with the being of the person of Jesus, which also suggests language is a faculty of being. Humanity inherently engaged in language at this point, and as Gadamer notes it is ludicrous to pursue the issue by, for example, isolating a child to discover the original language of creation.[114] The confounding of languages in Genesis 11 concerns the spoken language at that time. It is not the faculty of language that is confounded; people continue to communicate. The metaphysics of presence also suggests what Gadamer has offered as description, but with the added advantage of following the implications.

Scripture asserts that the incarnation of the logos and the advent of Christ were foreordained from the foundation of the world, that is, from the Genesis account under consideration (1 Pet 1:20). Paul declares that the incarnation occurred at precisely the right moment in history (Gal 4:4) and that the unfolding of the world, geographically and historically, since the creation was in accordance with the logos of God (Acts 17:24–28). Therefore, neither the text of the creation itself, referred to in the discussion of Rom 1:19–20, nor the historical record in historical documents (i.e., the historicity of humanity in the Scripture) has become autonomous from the author. The documents and the creation to a degree are detached from the author. Hence, they are available to any reader to make of them what they will, but they are not considered autonomous with respect to the authorial intent. This is further confirmed in the book of Hebrews. The opening verses proclaim that "God who at various times and in various ways spoke in time past to the fathers by the prophets, has in these last days spoken to us by *His* Son." (Italics original.) God's word is related to his being and he remains attached to all logos that issues forth from him. The logos was with God, in the creation; the logos retains identity and direction toward the incarnation, and the concept of eschatology itself suggests the authorial intent remains definitive, although the texts are detached.

It was noted previously that the Scripture is not handed to humanity from outside time. The source of Scripture is transcendent but the medium is mediated through human authors and is therefore immanent. The concept was also noted that, like Socrates, God is the one speaking, but he himself does not directly write, although it is his discourse. The act of writing not only relates a discourse into a world of readers but also establishes a context, or world, that the discourse occurs within, which is an

---

112. Ibid., 64.

113. Ibid., 67. Gadamer suggests language as a medium of being, which simply defers the question of preexistence in regard to *Dasein*.

114. Ibid., 63.

important aspect in the writing. The reader enters that world, that is, the world that is the creation of the author. The first verses of Genesis 1 establish the context for the saying of God. Composition not only relates discourse but also supplies the context that determines how the discourse is to be interpreted and understood; that is, composition vitally concerns the authorial intent.

Gadamer does not see the creation account as being a real process; his interest is "the processual element in the word."[115] In following this line of reasoning, he highlights the illustration used by Thomas Acquinas of the concept of a mirror, which Gadamer confirms as a brilliant illustration.[116] The mind searches for the word to express a thought, and when the word is chosen the object is present in it; the word then becomes a mirror in which this object is seen.[117] The concept is that the mirror nowhere extends beyond the image and only mirrors the one thing; that is, it reproduces only the image before it.[118] However, this concept is artificially narrow in that a mirror not only reproduces the image of an object but also the context of the object is mirrored. Hence, if the mirror is extended the context is revealed, and this relates the object to its world. As Hegel has observed, the subject is universal and in one sense is meaningless without predication, that is, without some context giving it immanence.[119]

The Return of the Author

The preceding discussion, as was noted at the outset of this chapter, is conducted from within the metaphysics of presence, although the departure points of the metaphysics of absence were noted. Furthermore, the discussion is conducted within a particular understanding of this domain (i.e., the presupposition of Christianity), and concerned a particular text (i.e., the scriptural text). The subject matter of the text is theological and the presence, or Supreme Being, is presupposed to be the God of Scripture. However, the question arises: is this view one which requires a special hermeneutic? Alternately, is the view simply the application of a special use of hermeneutics of what is true of all texts? It is suggested that the latter is the case.

In chapter five the issue of the announcement of the death of the author in modern hermeneutics was discussed. This announcement is premature and occurs in the presence of the author, although the author's presence is not recognized. The debate focused on the wrong issue. The author impacts due to an *Aufhebung* in the act of *parole* whereby the authorial intent is transformed to become an aspect of the text as the antecedent of the composition. This moves the debate away from the psyche, hence

115. Gadamer, *Truth and Method*, 384.
116. Ibid.
117. Ibid.
118. Ibid.
119. Hegel, "Phenomenology," 95.

person of the author, which had been the area of contention. This situation left us with the problem of identifying what is a referential aspect as the antecedent of the text. The investigation turned to the issue of metaphysics. In any discussion of metaphysics related to the interpretation of texts the issue of authorial intent is also raised. There is good reason for this, which will be explored in the next chapter.

8 Authorial Intent as the Metaphysical Subject and Presence

Introduction

THE LAST TWO CHAPTERS have addressed metaphysics in relation to texts and their interpretation. Metaphysics has often been assumed to deal primarily with religious issues and becomes a form of appendage that individuals consider if they wish to discuss religion. However, what became clear is that metaphysics allows description of how nonrational knowledge is handled by the individual. Human consciousness deals with and processes rational knowledge, arational knowledge, and nonrational knowledge. The issue of metaphysics therefore affects all individuals. Contra Derrida metaphysics is not the contrivance of human philosophy to justify the concept of reference. Rather, metaphysics is the philosophical endeavor to describe the functioning of reference within the domain of human consciousness. Gadamer also recognized the folly of abandoning the task of metaphysics. Gadamer considered this issue so important that he sought to propose seeing language itself as the means of dealing with this domain of consciousness that could avoid using the word metaphysics and the religious overtones it has been given. The antecedent of the text is that to which the text refers, hence it is an issue of reference, that is, metaphysics.

Wittgenstein identified the metaphysical subject as the "I" who writes in describing world. Hence, for any text, the author is that metaphysical subject who describes the world he or she sees by means of the text.[1] In the instance of the biblical text, the divine is assumed to be the speaking subject, hence sourced from transcendent meaning. But the divine is speaking through the human author, and it is the human who gives present meaning, hence immanence. As a result, even in the case of the biblical text, the view of the world, and hence reality, is that from the perspective of the

---

1. Wittgenstein, *Tractatus*, sect. 5.641.

human author. This understanding means that the subjective aspect, or element, of the message is developed in the context of a metaphysical understanding. Metaphysics thus brings the author into prominence and shows how the *Sache* is to be viewed in relation to reality. Wolfhart Pannenberg noted that in the previous two centuries the prevalent view has been that metaphysical discussion, as impacting philosophical endeavor, had come to an end.[2] It is interesting that over the same time frame there has been a corresponding loss of interest in the authorial intent and its impact on the meaning of the text.

The author, by means of composition, creates a world that is designed to present the *Sache* (or subject matter of the text), and hence to place it within a reality that is the author's perception. It is this understanding that is available for the reader of this *Sache*. This understanding is not reality as it is but reality as perceived by the author. Consequently, the author as the metaphysical subject becomes the point of origin for the view of reality related to the text. The author uses his or her creation of a written text, which is composed so as to communicate context as integral to the discourse, as a communication for the reader who is not present in the writing. As has been previously noted, the author communicates not just *rational* knowledge, or content, but also *arational* and *nonrational* knowledge. The authorial intent, in involving each domain of knowledge, gives being to that which the author wishes to communicate. Authorial intent is transcendent in that it is capable of interpretation into different languages, within the universal concept of language as the medium of communication.

In essence the author invites readers to place themselves in the position of the metaphysical subject to see what the author saw of the subject matter. The object is not to think the author's thoughts, therefore to stand in a foreign psyche, as Ricoeur correctly observes.[3] The referencing of the text does not coincide with "the inner life of another ego, but the disclosure of a possible way of looking at things, which is the genuine referential power of the text."[4] Ricoeur understood that the view of an author is forward, that is, he or she is creating a world through language. Therefore, to perceive the authorial intent correctly is to allow it to disclose this world in a way that can be understood. Authorial intent functions for the reader to look forward into the world created by the author.

The object is the making of the authorial intention the reader's own in terms of understanding. This objective of interpretation is not the understanding of the author's thinking but understanding the author's perception of the subject matter. Consideration of a wide variety of texts by an author will grant a reader some insight, and therefore understanding, into an author's thinking. However, this is still not the inner life of the author's ego. The issues of *context* and the *various categories of knowledge* highlighted in the text are sufficient basis for achieving this task; that is, the text is not

2. Pannenberg, *Metaphysics*, 3.
3. Ricoeur, *Interpretation Theory*, 92.
4. Ibid.

an impartation of the inner mind of the author but provides a relevant understanding of the author's mind, or his or her perceptions, on the *Sache*. The text, and hence authorial meaning, is an immanent expression of that transcendental authorial intent; that is, it is the meaning of the author to a particular audience (the *where* of the text) at a particular time (the *when* of the text). However, the referent of the text is that authorial intent that led to the authorial meaning, which is the transcendent meaning of the language of the author.

Transformation of Authorial Intent: A Radicalization from Psyche to Attribute

The concept that semantic autonomy of the text frees it from the authorial intent, thus leading to textual sense interpretation, is a presupposition of Ricoeur's. However, it was suggested that in this concept Ricoeur has ignored the *Aufhebung* that occurs of the authorial intent in the event of *parole*. In this event the authorial intent undergoes transformation from an aspect of the author's psyche into a form suitable for communication. The *Aufhebung* involving the authorial intent means that the author remains within the text as presence, yet not as the personality of the author, since the authorial intent has undergone transformation from the psyche of the author. As such authorial intent in theory remains detectable within the communication although having undergone aspects of both sublation and subsumption.

Ricoeur's basis for the dissociation is an inference based initially on his observation concerning the temporal detachment of the text from the author after the event of writing; such detachment being a reasonable observation. If, as in Ricoeur's thinking, the authorial intent is purely an aspect of the psyche of the author that remains within the psyche of the author, then there is some force to the observation of the resultant semantic autonomy of the text. Conversely, if the authorial intent has undergone an *Aufhebung* in the act of *parole*, transforming it into an aspect of the communication, then detachment from the psyche of the author does not result in an autonomous text.

The assumption of semantic autonomy of the text following this supposed dissociation is the essential authorizing principle that allows the reader to ignore the "what it meant" of a text and proceed directly to "what it means." The reader is authorized to ignore both authorial intent and intended meaning for a particular audience. Essentially, the concept of a particular audience remains linked to the authorial intent, which is now detached and hence nonfunctioning in Ricoeur's understanding. However, the validity of this assumption (i.e., that dissociation of the authorial intent from the verbal meaning is either equivalent to detachment or the necessary result of detachment) is questionable when the *Aufhebung* of authorial intent is recognized in the event of *parole*.

(a) Monologue Not Dialogue: Base Modeling for Written Text

Ricoeur's launching pad is the change that occurs both between and within the speaking-hearing and writing-reading dynamics of discourse.[5] Ricoeur does acknowledge that writing is not simply a degeneration or supplement of speech, as in Derrida,[6] but that it is a unique and different means of communication, taking his basis from what he views as the explosion of the dialogical situation.[7] As has been discussed previously, his resultant view appears to be a form of serendipity, an accident of the change in nature from dialogue that simply ended up being fortuitous. However, also as previously noted, this ignores the fact that writing is created directly as monologue in the format of a composition and is not developed from a dialogue. Dialogue by nature involves speaker and hearer in immediate direct relationship, whereas monologue involves speaker and hearer in a detached indirect relationship with different dynamics. Neither is present, nor is personal presence necessary in the event involving the other.

Whilst communicative discourse always involves the concept of a sender-receiver, the dialogical model is only one model, and is not the base model. Dialogue involves an active involvement, or presence, wherein both parties are actively engaged in transmitting information in an exchange of information. Yet, even in this situation each communication is, in one sense, separately a monologue, as has been previously observed. An important aspect in dialogue is that the exchange is two-way and meaning is under negotiation. This is not the situation in monologue wherein its discourse meaning is not under negotiation. Monologue is nevertheless also a form of communication, for example, this (or any) book, a journal article, or even a teaching session (live, recorded, or written). All of these forms can involve a "dialogical model" internally (such as commenting on other authors), or can be affected by dialogue (as in feedback) that can even lead to revision. However, these are monologues in format not dialogues. In a monological style, any dialogue occurs only in the imagination of the author; but the dialogical modeling in this case is a form of monologue wherein the author anticipates a potential dialogue.

---

5. Ibid., 29.

6. Derrida, *Positions*, 24–25. Ricoeur, *Interpretation Theory*, 26. Ricoeur suggests that in this view Derrida has missed the grounding of both modes of communication in the same nature of discourse.

7. Ricoeur, *Interpretation Theory*, 29. It has been previously suggested that contra Ricoeur's suggestion, writing other than transcription does not begin as a development of or from a dialogical event. However, as Ricoeur acknowledges, the common root of both is they concern the communication of a message, 26, which affords commonalities.

(b) A Dialogical Model Within Monologue

Malpas asserts that Gadamer is known for his use of the "'dialogical' character" in his method and writing.[8] The very use of grammatical highlighting shows that there is a distinction between this usage and dialogue itself, that is, it is used as model or illustration. He further notes that dialogue is Gadamer's style in his thinking and writing.[9] However, it has been well established previously that neither Ricoeur nor Gadamer hold to the concept of authorial intent as real presence within a text, yet it was also noted that both have seemed to assume presence in their style. Thus, it is important to recognize that a "dialogical model" is not dialogue (especially in Gadamer and Ricoeur, both of whom deny real presence of authorial intent in written text); it is simply a style of writing a monologue. Therefore, it has the model of dialogue in the format of monologue.

Even in the situation where real presence, and in particular authorial intent, is the metaphysical view of an author (e.g., in this book or in the works of Vanhoozer, Thiselton, and Fee), it is the "speaking voice" of another, not the person of the author, that is engaged concerning the *Sache*, or matter. It is not the personality, hence psyche, of another author that is engaged but the presence of his or her "speaking voice." Therefore, a "dialogical model" is employed in responding to the "speaking voice"; it is not an actual dialogue with the "speaking voice" or with the psyche of the referenced author. It is an engagement with an author's thinking on a subject by means of accessing his or her thinking via his or her "speaking voice" (hence authorial intent, related to their text) not an engagement with the author's thinking as personality.

A "dialogical model" does not imply a presence of interacting psyches within the text, so also the concept of a "speaking voice," or authorial intent within a text, does not imply a presence of a foreign psyche within the text. This is the implication that Ricoeur objected to. It has been pointed out in this book that both Ricoeur and Gadamer seek to engage the thinking of other authors, hence the "speaking voice" of other authors. However, it suits their theories to deny authorial intent, and so they don't call it that, they just access it.

The question that arises is this: how does the "dialogical model" work both within a text and in interpretation? The following is a suggested explanation of a modeling for the "dialogical model" of interpretation. Gadamer, as previously noted, in studying Plato, observed that apart from a deliberate application of dialectic by an author there is an almost hidden dialectic of the *One* and the *Many*. This also corresponds to Ricoeur's use of the two naïvetés in explanation and understanding. Essentially what happens is the one personality (i.e., the author/interpreter) moves between two poles and at each point takes on the view of that pole in the light of the "voice" to which he or she has just been listening. Thus, what occurs is the employment of a concept

---

8. Malpas, "Hans-Georg Gadamer."
9. Ibid.

similar to that of "performance interpretation" suggested by Wolterstorff,[10] which concept also fits the model of this concept of dialectic.

The "dialogical model," in the case of interpretation of another author, occurs when the individual "imagines" a performance by the other author of his or her "speaking voice." This is done in the light of what the interpreter has just been considering from his or her own view of reality, or point of origin, and the matter he or she is considering. Therefore, the interpreter creates an almost pseudo-dialogue by being the "voice" of the author who is not present in the reading. This is accomplished by moving between these poles of the interpreter's own "voice" and the "speaking voice" of the other author. As also noted previously, if a variety of material by the other author has "mentored" the interpreter's thinking, he or she will gain an appreciation of how the mindset of the other author views issues, from the other author's own point of origin.

The subsequent result will be an ability *not to think authors' thoughts after them* but rather to, in a manner of speaking, *think the authors' thoughts before them*, that is, to project forward into the world in front of the text, a concept which concept leads to the very aim Ricoeur expressed in dealing with the text of another author.[11] This use of the structure of dialectic as a basis for a "dialogical model" recognizes that each author represents a metaphysical "self" that observes the world from a particular point of origin.

(c) The Speaking Subject as a Metaphysical Construct

The very concept of the aim for a composition is to be self-sufficient in the author's communication. In essence Ricoeur's view on interpretation is along the same lines as Derrida's in the sense that their view of interpretation involves a degeneration of the dialogical situation. In Ricoeur this simply ended up as being fortuitous. However, the erasure of the presence of the author, as the speaking subject, erases the dimension of the text that is metaphysically described and impacted. Gadamer has recognized this, who as previously noted, argues for the reinclusion of the metaphysical task despite maintaining the absence of the authorial presence. However, the issue of the referential nature of the text again raises the issues of authorial discourse in the reaching out to metaphysical concepts. It is the work of Derrida that has highlighted this connection most forcefully.

In Derrida's thought the use of the principle of signifier and signified dominates language, encompassing the writer, who is taken by surprise.[12] His implication, as the discourse unfolds, is that the very act of writing becomes captive, despite any desire

---

10. Wolterstorff, *Divine Discourse*, 171. This concept suggested by Wolterstorff is considered in later sections for its applications.

11. Ricoeur, *Interpretation Theory*, 93.

12. Derrida, *Of Grammatology*, 159–60.

an author may have had to not be entrapped in metaphysics. It is an atmosphere that surrounds language due to the logocentrism of the epoch, considered previously, in which the language and the very concept of written text has arisen. This is indicated where he notes, "the person writing is inscribed in a determined textual system."[13] If this is an accurate translation, and not an editorial gloss by the translator, then the implication of not stating "each person writing inscribes in" or "each person writing has their inscription in," has an important implication. Stating that the writer is actually inscribed in a determined textual system, is to therefore postulate that the writer is caught in an atmosphere simply by using language, and exists trapped within metaphysics so that what the author writes will of necessity reflect that. The reader who desires to deconstruct the text needs to be aware of and compensate for this situation.[14] For Derrida the "entire history of texts, and within it the history of literary forms in the West, should be studied from this point of view."[15] No writer or text is exempted, including Derrida himself.

Derrida notes that the issue of the supplement is not "merely psychoanalytical" but also he himself, as reader, works within the same language system.[16] Derrida was critical of what he saw as Saussure's handing over of understanding of semiology to psychologists. However, Saussure was simply noting that language is a system of signs that expresses ideas, which must involve discussion of the psyche, and that linguistics of language is a branch of the general science of semiology.[17] Derrida, whilst recognizing that he himself lived within the history of psychoanalysis, was mindful of the fact that psychoanalysis itself developed under the history of metaphysics and needed itself to take account of this.[18] As always, the enemy that Derrida seeks to deny any foothold is metaphysics.

How should Derrida go about this task of reading to deal with this issue? Since this sort of question itself comes from within the system, there is no satisfactory response. As a result, Derrida gave himself the privilege of being *exorbitant*.[19] This is a beginning point toward his deconstruction of this completely pervasive problem of metaphysics. What then follows is a play on the word *orb*, or sphere. He moves to the word *orbit*, as the circular-like track inscribed by a planet, and notes that to "*exceed the metaphysical orb is an attempt get out of the orbit.*" Thus, he introduces the justification of the choice of ex-orbitant (i.e., to get out of orbit), which has commonly become used to mean extravagant and excessively overpriced.[20] The play on the word

13. Ibid., 160.
14. Ibid., 19, 160.
15. Ibid., 160.
16. Ibid. Derrida had previously criticized Saussure's deference to psychology, 40.
17. Saussure, *Course in General Linguistics*, 16.
18. Derrida, *Of Grammatology*, 161.
19. Ibid. (Italics original.)
20. Ibid., 162. (Italics original.)

exorbitant itself is self-evident, that is, between its derivation and usage. The aim is to exit this extravagant sphere of metaphysics and its domination of the text.

Derrida does not use the term *dialectic*, yet like Hegel, as noted previously, Derrida recognizes that the structure promotes circularity that traps the writer or reader. Gadamer suggests that this aspect of text, and therefore written language, is an authorial device, in the absence of an author's presence, to purposefully contain the reader within the limits of the author's discourse. Hence arises Derrida's need to insist firstly that the text cannot reference and secondly that there is no Book, or authorial presence. Derrida, like Gadamer, recognizes this aspect of written text within the history of metaphysics; however, for Derrida this is a negative situation from which one must escape. This is the orbit within the sphere of metaphysics he wishes to exit. Derrida notes that the nature of the movement of "supplementarity" is to behave dialectically, although he doesn't use the word *dialectic* in this context.[21]

Although his argument is wordy and convoluted, the basic thrust is to ignore the concept of the book when handling texts by an author. This produces a form of randomness in approach that defies the dictates of metaphysics, since metaphysics implies the idea of anterior meaning. The reader then moves from sign to sign in the textual chain and gives no place to representation (i.e., the signified), since the desire for presence inherent in the signified is born from the abyss of representation.[22]

Derrida's passion for exiting the metaphysical sphere, to remove its influence over the text, is reminiscent of Bultmann's desire, in theology, to demythologize the biblical text.[23] Bultmann's attack was not on the concept of the metaphysical, in contrast to Derrida, but upon the representation of supernatural events in Scripture, which he saw as incompatible with modern science and hence untenable.[24] Like Derrida on metaphysics, Bultmann asserted that the element of myth was introduced to speak of transcendent powers, and is not reality or a necessity in understanding the text.[25]

Thiselton notes that Bultmann saw that belief in myth (i.e., the supernatural realm of spirits, miracles, and so forth) was inconsistent with reality. Hence, to demythologize was not a rejection of Scripture but of its worldview.[26] However, the original concept of myth was not a fictional story to convey metaphysical truth but a true story that conveyed metaphysical truth.[27] Catalin Partenie points out that Plato constructed fictional myth as a teaching tool and therefore it is an author, not something demanded by the concept, who introduces the idea of the fictional nature into

21. Ibid., 268.
22. Ibid., 163.
23. Bultmann, "New Testament and Mythology," 3. As the name suggests this is the subject matter of the article.
24. Ibid.
25. Ibid., 10–11.
26. Thiselton, *Two Horizons*, 259.
27. Partenie, "Plato's Myths."

the idea of myth.[28] For Bultmann myth must be treated as fictional. In order for a text to be suitable for modern humanity, the mythical world of the text needed the myth collapsed and hence removed.

Consequently, Bultmann's inherent assumption is that the biblical writers constructed myth in order to explain metaphysical knowledge rather than employing what they had received and believed to be a "true story, a story that unveils the true origin of the world and human beings."[29] Hence, Bultmann has relegated to the imagination of the writer the representation of the metaphysical, which is a similar conclusion to Derrida's. In rejecting a worldview, Bultmann rejected the metaphysical lens of the eye through which an author views the world, as has Derrida. Both intentionally disregard a possible intention an author had in his writing.

The point of departure is a total disregard, or absence, of signatory and a refusal to allow any place to representation, that is, referent. Wolterstorff considers not the metaphysics of absence that underlies Derrida's description of method, but looks at the method itself. On the basis of his considerations, he proposes a form of interpretation that opens an understanding of what believers have done over the millennia. His suggestion is a concept of "performance interpretation," which is an innovative approach.[30] The believer can use the facility of the imagination to "hear" the text as spoken, hence performed, by God.

Derrida's metaphysics of absence has highlighted a very important aspect in understanding; metaphysics directly involves the speaking subject, that is, the author and authorial intent. In order to escape the metaphysical orbit, it is first necessary to erase the author, which effectively allows an assertion of denial of reference and anterior meaning. This becomes the starting point for "*pure absence*," which is the emptiness that is the starting point of true literature.[31] This absence is not an erasure of something that was present but the recognition that there never was any presence.[32] Consequently, there is nothing that can be referred to and any idea of reference is actually a projection forward through an auto-affection of the imagination of the author and reader. The projection is not an anterior meaning, simply a supplement one grants oneself. If there is a pure absence then any concept of meaning in the world, due to an "absolute subject" giving meaning as anterior, is "shattered."[33] Meaning comes into existence and finds its fulfillment in saying or writing; thus, for Derrida writing is

---

28. Ibid.

29. Ibid. Partenie is not discussing the biblical text or Bultmann but is simply observing the originary concept of myth.

30. Wolterstorff, *Divine Discourse*, 171.

31. Derrida, *Writing*, 8. (Italics original.)

32. Ibid.

33. Ibid., 10.

"inaugural" and launches forward not knowing fully where it is going, and meaning is its future.[34]

In the same way that the physical world is meaningless when it is viewed as developing in the absence of the divine (i.e., fortuitous random accidents that result in increased order and development with the resultant increase in the gene pool that then unfolds new meaning), each new text is meaningless in a transcendent sense. The text didn't arise from meaning, but is meaningful in an immanent sense in that it imparts, or projects, meaning. In such a situation reference can only point forward and cannot detect anterior meaning as a basis for understanding reality. At the point of origin there is nothing but a "black hole" that consumes anterior reference, and no light emanates forth from this origin in the metaphysics of absence. The idea that there ever was any "light" of meaning flowing from the point of origin is simply a prejudice induced by logocentrism for Derrida.[35]

The Possibility That God Speaks in Authorial Discourse

If the concept of a divine voice that is coexistent with the authorial voice is to be considered possible, without resorting to a special hermeneutic, the first issue that must be taken up is the opportunity within textuality for the occurrence of a divine voice, that is, the possibility of a voice other than the author's to be heard. Wolterstorff has presented well-reasoned and nontheological arguments indicating that this is in fact a quite natural feature of discourse, as used and practiced within the context of all humanity.[36] He considers the concept of "double agency discourse," wherein one person can compose a text for another person who then lends his or her authority to the text so that it becomes the second person's discourse.[37]

In developing this concept Wolterstorff considers such diverse things as a secretary composing a letter for an executive, who then signs the letter making it effectively the executive's discourse, and the concept of the employment by someone of a "ghostwriter" to write his or her story. This ghostwriter writes in his or her own words the ideas of another so that the ghostwriter discourses as the other person.[38] Wolterstorff also examines concepts such as "deputized discourse"[39] (e.g., the concept

---

34. Ibid., 11.

35. Ibid.

36. Wolterstorff, *Divine Discourse*, 37–57. This is a chapter entitled "Many Modes of Discourse" in which he begins by discussing common and extensively used modes of discourse that involve one person speaking through another to varying degrees. Whilst he does consider the extension into theological concepts of biblical text, it is an extension of the idea not the genesis of the idea.

37. Ibid., 38.

38. Ibid., 39.

39. Ibid., 42.

of an ambassador) and "appropriated discourse,"[40] wherein one person can take the discourse of another, either simply as text or even the whole intent of the discourse, and assert an agreement such that he or she have appropriated the text, or even the discourse, as his or her own. The concept of "appropriated discourse" would also apply to works such as this thesis, where the voice of other authors are used to address a given subject matter. All of these examples have obvious potential to allow that, in the texts of biblical authors, the "voice" of God can be heard without resorting to a special hermeneutic. Interpretation in this case is simply a special use of an operational hermeneutic, that is, it is a theologically applied hermeneutic.

A further example that can be suggested, having particular application to the concept of a divine voice within the text, is that of an authorized biographer. A person can employ a biographer, or a publisher can even require a biographer, to tell the story of another. The biographer is authorized to tell the story of another person. The object of biographers is not to inject themselves into the story but simply to tell the story, such that it is the narrative of the one about whom they write. The narrative is not released as discourse until the person written about agrees that the narrative is indeed his or her story, told how they recollect and understand it.

Consequently, the subject of the discourse (i.e., the view of reality or point of origin from which the discourse proceeds) is not that of the authorial voice. The discourse is the ideas and observations of one person expressed in the discourse of another, but the act of *parole* is one performed by the biographer as author, not the one who is the subject of the narrative. The act of *parole* may be monitored and influenced by the one who is the subject of the discourse in such a way that there is almost an intermingling of intentions. Nevertheless, it remains that the resultant act of *parole*, even if including an impact of another voice, is that of the author. The one about whom the text is written primarily authorizes that the ideas have been successfully transmitted in the text of the biographer according to the subject's own understanding. Therefore, within an authorized biography, two distinct voices can be heard, but the purpose of one of the voices is to essentially cause his or her own voice to undergo an *Aufhebung* so that the primary voice that is heard is that of the subject of the biography. Nevertheless, the biographer takes the place of author in telling the story, and the work is recognized as the biographer's discourse.

A biographer may write on the whole of a life or any part or event thereof (e.g., within the Christian world a minister may authorize a narrative of their ministry life) or, alternately, an event or series of events during that time. It is quite conceivable that a person may authorize a biography of his or her history before assuming a prominent position as a way of indicating his or her roots and the pathway to the time of moving into a position of prominence. A biographer may also have become part of the story and be selected specifically because he himself is part of the story.

---

40. Ibid., 51.

Authorial Intent as the Metaphysical Subject and Presence

The indications from the beginning of both Luke and Acts offer an illustration of this situation. The opening stanzas within each biblical book suggest common authorship (Luke 1:1–4 and Acts 1:1). In the case of Luke, the author is not himself part of the origins but has researched from witnesses an understanding of the story from its origin. In the book of Acts, it is noticeable that in the author's narrative, during the course of the period of time represented, that he himself has become part of the narrative. An example can be found in Acts 16:10–13: "concluding that the Lord had called *us* to preach the gospel . . . sailing from Troas, *we* ran a straight course . . . *we* were staying in that city . . . on the Sabbath day *we* went out of the city . . . *we* sat down and spoke . . ."[41] This inclusive form of reference (i.e., the movement to the first person) does not occur until chapter 16 of Acts, which leads to a reasonable inference that this is the time the author himself became part of the story. The indication is that where a biographer becomes part of the story he can at times make direct assertions in the discourse and yet maintain the overall perspective of narrator of the story of others.

At this point in the discussion, an important aspect is revealed in the model used that, although having a particular theological application, is a special use of what is a general principle. Within Christian thought, using the Genesis text, the element that is both transcendent and immanent is spirit (Gen 1:2), where the Spirit is present, hence immanent, yet is divine and transcendent. Therefore, in Christian metaphysics, the working of the Holy Spirit is seen as a special use of this principle. The Spirit is contemporary with the *logos*,[42] and the mention of Spirit is prior to that of the proceeding of logos, which essentially provides a context for articulation of logos, so that the logos is able to fulfill itself. It is the Spirit that allows the maintenance of the relationship between transcendent meaning and immanent meaning. Within the model used of the metaphysics of presence, and in particular in a Christian understanding, this relationship begun in Genesis moves to real presence of the Person of the Spirit in the New Testament texts.

Jesus, though being ὁ λογοσ incarnate, is led by the Spirit (Luke 4:1) and commands his disciples at the direction of the Spirit (Acts 1:3). All the gospel accounts agree that Jesus' articulation of logos, as message and proclamation, does not occur until the Spirit comes upon him (Matt 3:13–17), and then proclamation (Matt 4:17). See also Mark 1:9–11, 14–15; and Luke 3:21–22, with verse 23 marking the beginning of ministry; and then proclamation 4:16–20. The Johannine handling of the event is retrospective and his ministry has begun with it (John 1:29–34). The disciples will in turn be led by the Spirit and Spirit guided into "all truth" (i.e., through perception of reality as seen by the Spirit, through the Spirit's capacity to relate the transcendent to the immanent, John 16:13). Paul asserts that the believer led by the Spirit is capable

---

41. The emphasis is added to highlight the first person reference.

42. The Johannine text therefore carries a strong allusion to the trinity, i.e., the placing of the person of Jesus as the logos (being himself co-equal with God, Philip 2:6) into a contemporary setting with God and the Spirit of God in the beginning of the scriptural account of creation.

of applying transcendent truth into everyday application (Gal 5:16–25). The Spirit is able to position the believer to perceive the "God's-eye-viewpoint" in his or her own particularity, not as being, as it were, in God's shoes, but by perception of what God would see if he was in a person's shoes (1 Cor 2:6–16). The Spirit performs an interpretive function not only by direct speech, as exteriority, but also as a mentoring influence, implied in impact on perception of such concepts as guide and lead. The Spirit thereby works out into the life of the believer, incarnating itself in the life of the believer, for example, walking in the Spirit and producing the fruit of the Spirit (Gal 5:16–25). This sort of understanding may have been Hegel's inspiration for the development of his concept of Spirit.

Metaphysics: Authorial Intent as a Dimension of the Text

An important conclusion reachable in the previous discussion concerning absence or presence of the authorial intent is that it is inseparably linked to metaphysics; that is, the argument for or against authorial intent is a metaphysical argument. The purpose here is to specifically focus on the issue of authorial intent in any discussion of metaphysics, rather than to pursue an in-depth general discussion of metaphysics.

An argument has been put forward that authorial intent undergoes transformation from being an aspect of the psyche of the author to that of being an aspect of the communication; that is, the text is a composition of the author's message intended by the author. In the act of *parole*, being a willful act, the authorial intent (the concept of "intent" as purpose suggests "will" in action) undergoes *Aufhebung* through both semiotic and semantic application, leading to the authorial intent (the willfulness of the author relating to the subject matter) undergoing a transformation from the psyche of the author to becoming an aspect of the communication. It was further proposed that the resultant situation meant that, in relation to a text, the transformed authorial intent relates not to the personality, or psyche, of the author, but rather relates to the point of origin, or "being" of the text; that is, the view of reality taken by the author that forms both the basis of understanding and the point from which his or her text is to be viewed by the reader. The authorial intent is the metaphysical "I" that, as Wittgenstein noted, viewed the world when an author writes. This brings the central issue of authorial intent to be one of metaphysics, since it concerns the being of the text and its relationship to reality as perceived by the author.

The composition has "being" due to the authorial intent but without proposing attachment to the authorial psyche. The simplest illustration that can be used is that of a work of art. This illustration is often used when discussing the issue of interpretation, for example, in Gadamer's concept of "aesthetic consciousness." It is the work of art, especially poetry, which is used in Wimsatt and Beardsley's discussion of the Intentional Fallacy. In the discussion of the Intentional Fallacy in this book, it was noted that the appeal by the author in his or her work of art is probably primarily to the *arational* dimension, or aesthetic consciousness, of human being. A work of art either appeals to a person or it does not, hence the interestedness of the observer and any subsequent interpretive process is joined due to this dimension of disclosure of its "being," that is, this dimension of human being determines the direction of the interpretive process. In their discussion, Wimsatt and Beardsley contended that a poem should not mean, but simply "be"; further, they declare that this *being* can only "be" through its meaning (since the medium is words).[43] They go on to note, regarding the poem, that though the medium is words, "yet it *is*, simply *is*, in the sense that we have no excuse for inquiring what part is intended or meant."[44] In this they grant that the creation of the text does not occur by accident but is the result of an intention. It is just that, in their view, intention is not the standard by which the work should be judged.[45] Hence, they grant that authorial intent gives the work "being," and so they seek to distinguish the work from the psyche of the author (i.e., that which was in the author's thinking in the creation has "being"), thereby granting, as in Ricoeur, autonomy to the work.

"All cars live in a garage, if you live in a garage you must be a car." That is to say the fallacy is the phrasing of the proposition. The concept they work on can be understood by way of a few simple questions: If the poet did not succeed in his or her intention, then how do you find that out? Where do you go to find out what the poet intended to do to measure this against what the poet did do? If the poet succeeded, then the poem itself is evidence and no question needed; conversely if the poet did not succeed, then the poem is not sufficient evidence of authorial intent and, so the inquiry must go outside the poem for the evidence of an intention that did not succeed.[46] The proposition Wimsatt and Beardsley propose is considered from the perspective of the author, since only the author will know if he or she "succeeded" in his or her intention.

However, for the interpreter the work is the manifestation of the authorial intent, that is, the piece of work the interpreter has, which is agreed to be the result of authorial intent. The object is to understand the authorial intent associated with the work of art or text that discloses the composition that is presented, not the authorial intent as it was before they composed the work of art or text, which intent was an aspect of the author's psyche. The object of interpretation is to interpret, not critique authorial intent, which only the author can undertake. It seems likely that most authors of art works generally would be the severest critics of the works that they produce, and can see what they could have changed or done better, and so forth.

43. Wimsatt, *Verbal Icon*, 3. (Italics added for emphasis.)
44. Ibid. (Italics original.)
45. Ibid., 4.
46. Ibid., 2.

Nevertheless, the work of art is (as Wimsatt and Beardsley note) what it "is" and exists as a manifestation of an authorial intention that is absolute, in the sense that once the work has being it stands as extant. Even if an author was to revisit a work and redo it, this would become a second work of art, following the first work of art released into the world of receptors. A revision of a work does not replace the first one except in the mind of the author. The issue is not the authorial intent from the author's perspective but from the reception of that which is the result of authorial intent. That is, the authorial intent should be examined from the perspective that the work itself is the absolute of the author's intent. Such an examination should not be based on a supposed intent still resident within the author that may or may not differ from the expressed authorial intent.

This reasoning extends naturally to literary texts in general, since an author may revise and resubmit his or her work. Such activities do not change the existence of the original work, however, and interpreters often do comparisons by considering the merits of each version, that is, the original and the revision. Although revision presents a new and fresh perspective on the subject matter, the standing vision of a work may be considered by the observer to offer a better vision than the revision of the subject matter (e.g., authors will comment on issues such as the contrasts between the earlier and later Heidegger and Wittgenstein). A text, or work of art, once it is extant has being, and that being is a function of the authorial intent at the time of creation. Wimsatt and Beardsley also concede this.

The contention that the work of art has being other than the simple materials of which it is composed, whether they be words on a page, paint and canvas, or rock, plaster, or any material suitable for sculpting, is illustrated by consideration of the work as a created work. If a person was to change some aspect or part of a sculpture or painting, the result is considered defacement of the author's work. Imagine a scenario where a person decided that the *Mona Lisa* could be improved to more correctly exemplify the author's intent. If such a person tried to act upon that impulse with the extant *Mona Lisa* he or she would be arrested, not congratulated. If such a person succeeded, then the Louvre would immediately begin a restoration process to remove that which takes the work of art from being the original creation, and go on to restore it to the original authorial state of being. Conversely, such a person could decide to repaint the *Mona Lisa* as he or she believes da Vinci intended, but the result can never be da Vinci's work; that is, it is not the *Mona Lisa*. The authorial intent gives being to the work of art, and the being of the work of art is the application of an authorial intent to the materials. It is that authorial intent that makes the work a unique creation and no longer just materials that have been brought together. The subsequent value of the work of art is in the authorial intent not the materials.

In a work of art, uniqueness is due to the originary work of its creator. It is the creator of the work who gives the work being as a work of art; that is, it is the hand of the sculptor on the rock, or the brush in the hand of the painter, that transforms the materials into a work of art. The monetary value of the work of art resides in the original work of art itself created by the author. However, the aesthetic value of the authorial intent can be copied and reproduced in other formats and settings. A person can acquire a copy of a sculpture or painting (in the case of a painting this is the concept of a print or even the reprint, which itself is a copy of the print, hence twice removed from the original work of art). Although the copy is not composed of the original materials, that which the work of art represents, the authorial intent, can be appreciated and seen in a manner other than its original state.

The being of the authorial intent can be referenced, evaluated, and transformed into materials other than the original. This is true also of all literary texts, and as Gadamer and others have noted, as discussed previously, the issue of translation as opposed to transcription highlights the need to transfer thought forms into the second language, further indicating that the being, or authorial intent, is the antecedent of the text. The text as a message directly references the authorial intent. This reasoning also indicates that this is not an authorial intent residing within the psyche of the author, but rather that this being of the text or work of art is the communicated authorial intent. The authorial intent is a dimension of the created work, and not just the authorial meaning of the text. It is this reality, within the concept of presence, that highlights the nature of the authorial intent as one of being, and this is subsequently what makes authorial intent inseparable from metaphysical discussion.

(a) Abandoning Metaphysics Abandons the Authorial Intent

Pannenberg has observed that in the last two centuries there has been a movement in philosophical thinking, including theology, to consider philosophy as entering into a post-metaphysical era.[47] When metaphysics is removed from the agenda of discussion it is reasonably easy to predict that this will effectively lead to a decay and eventual disuse of the idea of authorial intent. This has in fact already occurred, and in postmodern philosophy, as in Ricoeur and Gadamer, authorial intent is considered to be irrelevant. Derrida went even further in this thinking and, in deconstruction, erased authorial intent altogether. However, in recent times there has also been a renewed call for the reinclusion of the discussion of metaphysics in philosophical thinking.[48] The recognition that authorial intent gives the dimension of being to the message of a text is recognition of its metaphysical nature and lends impetus to this call.

In the thinking of Kant, metaphysics was the science that revealed issues such as the concepts of God and the Absolute.[49] However, in attempting to deal with the identity of this Supreme Being and the absolute he concluded, "The argument has failed to give us the least concept of the properties of a necessary being, and indeed is utterly

---

47. Pannenberg, *Metaphysics*, 3.
48. Ibid., 4.
49. Kant, *Pure Reason*, 46.

ineffective."[50] This knowledge, for Kant, is not really knowable within the bounds of empirical knowledge, gained through the processes of rational objective reason, and the identity of the Supreme Being is consequently unknowable. It is not really a large step to infer, within this line of thinking, the arrival at the concept that metaphysics is effectively beyond discussion. As has been previously noted, Kant's observation is contrasted with the thinking of Pascal, for whom God is also unknowable by rational objective reason (i.e., empirical knowledge) but is knowable through the agency of belief, which is the metaphysical dimension of humanity.[51] Consequently, through the agency of the metaphysical dimension of humanity, knowledge can be acquired regarding the divine, the absolute, and therefore the concept of authorship can be known. The subject of authorship raises the issue of authorial intent with its impartation of being to a created work.

Derrida makes a similar observation to that of Pannenberg regarding the decline in consideration of metaphysics. Derrida views that an important moment of the "great rationalisms of the seventeenth century" was "the determination of absolute presence is constituted as self-presence, as subjectivity."[52] This is seen as a dawning, as it were, of the realization that the concept of absolute presence is a phantasm, something made up in the imagination of authors and interpreters and is not actual presence, or being. The work of Derrida, which speaks from the metaphysics of absence not presence, has highlighted the interconnectedness of all these issues, that is, the divine, the absolute, and the concept of authorial intent. Derrida views them as clinging to the "metaphysico-theological roots" of what he designates to be the "appurtenance" of the difference between signifier and signified.[53] The idea of an "appurtenance" is that of an accessory that attaches to a way of doing things, or lifestyle. In the thinking of Derrida, everything stems from this accessory belonging to the metaphysics of presence that implies an exteriority in the understanding of signifier and signified.[54] Consequently, the idea of reference as exteriority can be dispensed with as having been just an accessory of "logocentrism," which is the lifestyle, or "spirit" to use Hegel's idea, of the text. Dispensing with the appurtenance dispenses with the author. Hence, in deconstruction authorial intent is placed under erasure.

(b) Authorial Intent as Anterior to the Text

Derrida also highlights an astute and important observation, one that is not only important to his theories of deconstruction but also to all hermeneutics when dealing with a literary text. All exteriority of reference has its generation from within the

50. Ibid., 498.
51. Pascal, "Pensées," sect. 233.
52. Derrida, *Of Grammatology*, 16.
53. Ibid., 13.
54. Ibid., 18.

concept of the book, that is, the hermeneut must start within the text of the book and is referred from that text.[55] In the thinking of Derrida, this referencing is simply a phantasm, "The idea of the book is the idea of a totality, finite or infinite, of the signifier; this totality of the signifier cannot be a totality, unless a totality constituted by the signified preexists it, supervises its inscriptions and its signs, and is independent of it in its ideality."[56]

However, his reasoning indicates the hinge of his argument: that meaning is not anterior; that is, that which the signifier signifies cannot preexist it. It seems that Derrida's argument is that meaning doesn't exist without the text where the signifier is signified. Thereby he implies that meaning exists only in the mind of the author or interpreter, hence becoming an accessory. Nonetheless, if meaning does preexist then he has correctly identified why metaphysics is essential to understanding the anterior meaning, that is, the meant of the author that gives the book its totality. Derrida's quote above could be rephrased, from the perspective of the metaphysics of presence, in a way that evidences the nature of the anterior meaning that is predetermined by the authorial intent. *The book of the author is the totality (i.e., the view of reality and being), finite or infinite, of the signifier; this totality of the signifier must be a totality, because a totality constituted by the signified (as predetermined by the author) preexists it, supervises its inscriptions and its signs, and is independent of it in its ideality.*[57] The issue of anterior meaning is one of the referencing of the text, which is a hermeneutical issue. Anterior meaning then interacts with the metaphysics of the interpreter, which is not an epistemological hermeneutical issue of the text.

The work of Derrida has unintentionally highlighted an important aspect within the metaphysics of presence, which is that the hermeneut must begin with the text for an understanding of any meaning that is the referent of the text. Consequently, the being of the text as message is referenced by or from the text, but is exterior to the text. The hermeneut, working within the metaphysics of presence, cannot begin from the anterior reference; that is, the hermeneut cannot begin from the perspective of the authorial intent as something that is located within the personality or psyche of the author.

(c) Authorial Intent: Seeing What the Author Saw

Therefore, Derrida has brought into perspective that if the anterior meaning is believed to exist, which is pure auto-affection within the metaphysics of absence (i.e.,

---

55. Derrida, *Writing*, 76.
56. Derrida, *Of Grammatology*, 18.
57. This rephrasing is not an adaptation or use of the text of Derrida but it highlights that the same rationality can be viewed from different points of origin, i.e., presence or absence, so that meaning is based on the matter of perspective, not hermeneutics. Hermeneutics allows the matter to be viewed from the perspective of the one doing hermeneutics. The adaptation is of Derrida's insight.

Derrida's position) but perceived as an extant reality in the metaphysics of presence, then the psyche of the author represents the author's perspective, or authorial intent, as mindset of the author, from which the author views the *Sache*. Conversely, the transformation of the authorial intent into being as a referent of the text creates the potentiality of a mindset for an interpreter, from which perspective that interpreter can view the *Sache* and see what the author saw. It is this latter concept of the authorial intent that is the anterior meaning, which is the antecedent of the text. In the process of interpretation, this "being" undergoes a reverse transformation from that which was previously considered in the authorial act of *parole* to become an aspect of the psyche, or consciousness, of the interpreter. As a result of these two acts of transformation, that which transforms a stretch of language into a composition and message (i.e., the authorial intent) becomes available in the world of the interpreter in the same fashion as that which transforms materials into a work of art, giving it unique shape and perspective. Hence the same *Sache*, having been understood from the perspective of the author by the interpreter, is subsequently viewed from the world of the interpreter.

This fulfills the specified aim of Ricoeur, in that the world horizon of the reader is fused with the world horizon of the writer. An aspect of Ricoeur's conclusions is his suggestion that "the ideality of the text is the mediating link in this process of horizon fusing."[58] However, the true ideality of the text is the authorial intent as antecedent of the text, and this is the anterior meaning referenced as being of the text, not as Ricoeur suggests in his work as the "sense" of the text. Consequently, the concept of true hermeneutical reflective consciousness asserted by Gadamer is also fulfilled. Gadamer asserts that the truth of this hermeneutical consciousness is translation, for when hermeneutics is conducted in the fashion of an act of translation what is foreign "becomes one's own, not by destroying it critically or reproducing it uncritically, but by explicating it within one's own horizons with one's own concepts and thus giving it new validity."[59]

(d) Authorial Intent: Giving Being to Composition

The contention of both Ricoeur and Gadamer of the autonomy of the text, making the text a stretch of language (having no supervising anterior meaning conferring its "being" due to authorial intent) ignores the composition of the text, or that which makes it a message and not just a stretch of language. Both of these philosophers do consider the text to be a message and do consider the concept of exterior reference, unlike Derrida. Nevertheless, both of these philosophers deny any access or reference to authorial intent, which is that which confers the "being," or status, as composition and message. This is not a denial of the originary work of an author, but it is a denial

---

58. Ricoeur, *Interpretation Theory*, 93.
59. Gadamer, *Philosophical Hermeneutics*, 94.

of any reference to the authorial intent, which is what gives being to the work of that author. In both Ricoeur and Gadamer, the concept of the message and its ability to reference is now the province of language, not that of anterior meaning. Hence, both avoid metaphysics of presence impacting interpretation.

The recognition of these transformations of the authorial intent that retain its impact on the "being" of the text, and hence the text's ability to reference anterior meaning, is important. This suggests that the composition as the creation of an author is not disregarded in what is proposed during interpretation, so that what is interpreted is the message of the author in the world of the interpreter. It is the authorial intent that transforms a block of marble into a sculpture as a creative work, it is the authorial intent that transforms paints and canvas into a picture as a creative work, and it is similarly the authorial intent that transforms language into a composition as a creative work.

When this authorial intent is ignored then the receptor/interpreter becomes the de facto creator of the sculpture, painting, or literary text as a work of art. The suggestion that a text lacks meaning until given meaning by an interpreter is to suggest that a work of art is not a work of art until declared so by an interpreter. Though its monetary value, and hence prominence, as a work of art will be determined by the interpreter/receptor, its existence, or "being," as a work of art is due to the anterior work of a creator, who applied authorial intent to the materials that resulted in what is presented to the interpreter.

Ricoeur's treatment of his theory of interpretation bears out the observation of Pannenberg that philosophy has largely viewed itself in the postmodern era as being post-metaphysical. Ricoeur does not consider this aspect at all and it doesn't figure in his discussions, even his observation concerning the view of Derrida considers mechanism not philosophy.[60] Ricoeur's departure from metaphysical discussion is not avoidance as such, and consequently is not announced as a departure; but he departs specifically from the authorial intent and it is this that results in a departure from any consideration of metaphysics.

In the theory of Ricoeur, what happens in the instance of the written text is "the full manifestation of something that is in a virtual state, something nascent and inchoate, in living speech, namely the detachment of meaning from the event."[61] This detachment does not occur in the case of dialogue where "the subjective intention of the speaker and the discourse's meaning overlap each other in such a way that it is the same thing to understand what the speaker means and what his discourse means."[62] This possibility of detachment lies dormant but is filled with potential for expression when discourse becomes written. Essentially, his view is that the case of speaking-hearing circumvents the potential expression of the detached discourse, and it is the

60. Ricoeur, *Interpretation Theory*, 26.
61. Ibid., 25.
62. Ibid., 29.

subjective that limits the universality of the objective. Then with written discourse "the author's intention and the meaning of the text cease to coincide" and hence the semantic autonomy of the text is manifest.[63] At this point, despite any importance placed by Ricoeur on the composition as the work of art, the composition is lost as composition and what remains is *langue*.

(e) Dialogue to Monologue: Reinstituting Composition as Work of Art

It is important at this stage to take into account what Ricoeur is referring to in his view of both spoken and written discourse. As has been previously noted, Ricoeur does not consider written discourse to simply be a case of dialogue. In fact he specifically notes its individuality, as does the work of Ong previously mentioned.[64] However, Ricoeur shows how his thinking leans when declaring that with writing the "dialogical situation has been exploded"[65] and then later when he observes that "Hermeneutics begins where dialogue ends."[66] This indicates that a basic presupposition in the work of Ricoeur is that dialogue acts as the base model of the situation speaking-hearing.

However, as has also been noted previously, this is an incorrect assumption. Speaking-hearing can be a situation of either monologue or dialogue; but monologue is uniquely the model for the case of writing-hearing, since, as Ricoeur agrees, it cannot be viewed as a case of dialogue. Consequently, the base model that must be used for written text as communication is monologue. As has been noted previously, a dialogical model can be a means employed in the development of a monologue. However, this model is in reality a dialectical approach wherein the author or interpreter moves themselves between two poles: that is, in the case of the writing, the dialogical model involves an imagined interaction of the author with the reader; and, in the case of reading, the reader conducts an imagined interaction with the author. The same person undertakes both voices and moves between them, hence the reality is a form of dialectic but the concept is one of a dialogical model.

Ricoeur's views are consequently based on a model that contains an inherently flawed presupposition. This distinction is not a minor or insignificant distinction because a monologue is not constructed in the same way as dialogue. Aspects of the dialogical situation must consciously be included in a monologue that are inherent in the nature of dialogue, for example, issues such as the *arational* and *nonrational* dimensions of communication. Further, in monologue meaning is always anterior

---

63. Ibid.

64. Ibid. Other examples of this differentiation have been noted in his other works, e.g., *From Text to Action* (1991).

65. Ibid.

66. Ibid., 32.

to authorial intent. By contrast, in the case of dialogue meaning is contemporary to authorial intent.

Ricoeur's view of the detachment of anterior meaning, as authorial intent, only works if dialogue is the base model. This is because in dialogue anterior meaning—as authorial intent—and verbal meaning are contemporaneous. However, in the case of monologue as written discourse, authorial intent becomes anterior, as the supervising perspective of the development of the monologue, and it is subsequently the antecedent of the verbal meaning of the text, which references this anterior meaning. This is the situation in both instances of communication, that is, speaking-hearing and writing-reading. In the situation of dialogue, the impact of metaphysics in being and meaning occurs in the person of the speaker; the speaker is there "in the genuine sense of being-there, of *Da-sein*."[67] Hence, there is no need for the speaker to consciously address this metaphysical dimension because it happens in the course of the dialogue.

This is not the case with monologue; in the situation of monologue the impact of metaphysics, relating to being and meaning, is first transformed into a referential aspect of the language of the text. As has been shown previously, the authorial intent cannot function anteriorly, in the sense of relating to the psyche, hence consciousness, of the author to give meaning to the text. The authorial intent accessed is instead the authorial intent accessed from the text because anterior meaning is transformed in the act of *parole* as "being" referenced from the text. The consequence of this flawed assumption in Ricoeur, of indisoluble attachment of authorial intent to the psyche of the author, is that the assertion of the autonomy of the text is not sustainable on the basis of the argument provided. Therefore, the proposed disjunction between the authorial intent and the objective meaning, supposedly occurring in the temporal detachment of the text from the author, cannot be regarded as authoritatively conferring autonomy upon the semantic meaning of the text.

CAN THE AUTHOR RECOVER FROM APHONIA?

In the postmodern world even if the author's existence is recognized, the author is *aphonic*, or without voice, in the task of interpretation. The author has been denied any impact on meaning other than a possible condescension of the interpreter, at the interpreter's discretion, in acknowledging his or her existence. The author has been gagged by the trivialization of ontology, hence negating any concerns about the being of the text, and by the declaring of metaphysics as *out of bounds* on the basis of a metaphysical argument. Those arguing against metaphysics raise their argument to the level of absurdity in considering their position as either nonmetaphysical or unmetaphysical. However, despite Roland Barthes declaration of the death of the author, he and others, including Julia Kristeva who stands closer to Derrida, have discovered that text has a voice. The question is: Is it the author back from the dead?

---

67. Ibid., 29.

9

The "Who?" Question

Is There a Speaking Voice of the Text?

Introduction

THE PREVIOUS CHAPTER OF this book revealed that the argument *against* the existence of authorial intent in relationship to a text is a metaphysical argument. The view of metaphysics of absence, as developed in Derrida, argues for the exclusion of the author and authorial intent in hermeneutics. The written text has been reduced to a stretch of language where meaning is accessed through various semiotic and semantic analyses of the reader. This approach reduces the text to the ontology of an impersonal being whose meaning is at the mercy of the interpreter. However, the text refuses to lie in quiet submission to this interpretive autopsy. As the thought of Roland Barthes has recognized, readers find themselves addressed by a *speaking voice*.[1] The presence of this speaking voice indicates that the being of the text has been misjudged and misunderstood.

Previously, in consideration of the philosophical base of hermeneutics, note was taken of Thiselton's observation that Julia Kristeva, who is in many respects close to the thinking of Derrida, reinstated the speaking subject of the text.[2] Thiselton observes that this reinstatement is not a return to "traditional notions of the author behind a text," it is rather a recognition that texts have a writing or speaking subject.[3] For Thiselton this reflects concerns "about relations between language and the human body," in the discussion of textuality.[4] The concept of a *who*[5] of a text is not so easily

1. Barthes, "Death of the Author," 2.
2. Thiselton, *New Horizons*, 128.
3. Ibid., 129.
4. Ibid.
5. The questions Who? Why? What? When? and Where? are important in the unfolding of this chapter. Consequently, when reference to these questions is in view with regard to the hermeneutical task, italics will be used for emphasis.

dismissed. Once the issue of existence of a *voice*, in whatever form, is accepted, then its impact, if any, in interpretation must be evaluated. In the thinking of Ricoeur and Gadamer, philosophers who represent the postmodern situation considered previously, authorial intent is inaccessible and irrelevant, and hence has no impact. However, the author creeps back into focus, even in deconstruction, when the concept of voice appears. This concept should not be ignored and must be evaluated.

The realization that any argument about authorship enters the domain of metaphysical discussion infers an ontic nature to the concept of authorial intent. Therefore, the discussion of the authorial intent will sit more comfortably in the area of ontology rather than epistemology. Epistemology by nature involves a descriptive task and therefore cannot establish the "being" in the description, since description involves *what is* and does not establish the being of *what is*. Thiselton notes that the descriptive task does little more than refer to the events.[6] However, the recognition of speech-act theory has focused on the realization that there can be a doing in the saying.[7] This recognition also highlights that written text has being other than mere description.

It has been noted previously that the language of *nonrational* knowledge is that of assent, assertion, and inference; where inference is a conclusion drawn on the implicit premise of what is asserted. In the stating of the language of assent, assertion, and inference, one actually gives being (i.e., brings things into existence) rather than describes. The assertion, "I believe Jesus died, was buried, and rose again," gives the assertion operational being in the "I" of the statement as well as communicating *that* one believes. Such an assertion does not establish the "being" of the event within the horizon of temporal history, as other than the speaker, but establishes its "being" within the temporal life of the speaker. Hence, the Pauline declaration of what will make salvation operational in a life of a person is seen in Rom 10:9, "That if you confess with your mouth the Lord Jesus and believe in your heart that God has raised Him from the dead, you will be saved." The Pauline assertion, when the hearer assents to it, brings about an actual state of being in a person's life, that is, salvation. The assent involves internalization and externalization, resulting in a new state of being.

This also seems consistent with the Johannine recording of the assertion of Jesus regarding a new state of being, as in John 3:1–15 where Jesus' encounter with Nicodemus is recorded. Without being "born again" operational life within the Christian faith does not occur. It is important to consider the ontic nature and affect of *nonrational* knowledge. The ontic nature of authorial intent indicates that the language and effect that should be examined to reveal the authorial intent is that of *nonrational* knowledge, that is, described in assent, assertion, and inference. Though this concept does not exhaust the concept of authorial intent or represent the scope of ontology it does disclose a significant aspect.

---

6. Thiselton, *New Horizons*, 274.
7. Ibid. This concept is also significant in the work of Vanhoozer, as has been noted previously.

Authorial Intent and Being of the Text

In taking a broad view of the consideration of the hermeneutics of texts, the scope of the interpretive quest could be condensed to the following five questions: (1) *Who*? (2) *Why*? (3) *What*? (4) *When*? and (5) *Where*? These questions elicit disclosure in the primary categories that have been examined, to differing degrees, concerning issues of authorship (the *who*), motivation (the *why*), content (the *what*), historical context (the *when*), and cultural context of the intended audience, or specific locale within the general historical context (the *where*).[8] In the postmodern situation questions 1, 4, and 5 have been specifically discarded.[9] Yet it would seem logical that any interpreter involved in an examination of *why* when dealing with a text should raise the issue both of *who* and *where*. When the hearer/reader constitutes the intended audience[10] the questions *when* and *where* do not occur. The presence of an unintended audience, be that a more contemporary reader distanced in time or a different cultural setting within the same historical era, should result in the question of *why* capturing *when* and *where*.[11] The fact that these questions seemingly do not occur in semantics is not insignificant in the general consideration of the *who*, or the speaking subject, of a text. The specific aim of this chapter is to examine the *who* of a discourse, therefore of the text, which will involve reference to the *why* and *what* of the text.

(a) When and Where: Establishing the Semantic Range

The questions of *when* and *where* operate together to inform interpreters about the context in which the communication occurred. The issues of the historical situation and the intended audience have been considered in other sections of the work. It is important to note the significance of *when* and *where* in the pursuit of semantics,

---

8. Ricoeur, *Oneself*, 58. Ricoeur's journey into the hermeneutics of the self are referred to in the development of this chapter. He notes, in this work, a similar set of questions but does not use them in the first instance as referred to here. Ricoeur, having discussed speech-act theory in a section on a pragmatic approach, notes the relationship between the subject and the doing of the action, and puts forth a similar set of questions (he includes *how?* in his list) that could function together in elucidating an understanding of an action. His object is the integrated network of questions that disclose action. Consequently, he is dealing with the hermeneutics of an action and not the meaning of a text. Hence, Ricoeur's work is not relating these questions to the areas indicated in this work, yet it is of note that these are questions that disclose, and they do relate to and disclose these areas. Ricoeur does not use or intend these questions as set out here. Yet, the advent of a text is an action and the meaning of the text is integral to that action as an action, i.e., its reason for being, hence the overlap.

9. Ricoeur, *Hermeneutics and the Human Sciences*, 165. The position of Gadamer and Ricoeur on authorial intent and the original receptors has been considered in a previous section of this book. However, here Ricoeur, in his assertion of autonomy of the text, specifically shows the exclusion of these three areas.

10. The term *intended audience* is used as being more inclusive and less based in a moment of history than the term *original hearers*.

11. The rationale for this will be addressed in the unfolding situation.

remembering that the deliberate, or willful, act of *parole* is in many ways the semantic moment of the text. The text, as composition and a creation of the author, comes into being as an entity in the act of *parole*. Therefore, the instant of creation depends on the semantic range available to the author to express the *what*, or content, of the communication.

The phenomenal world[12] of the author as the experiential domain of temporal existence clearly has a significant impact on the semantic range available to the author. The phenomenal world is impacted by issues such as the situatedness within history, the nature and scope of language, the political and religious milieu, and so on. This should be evident enough as to be considered idiomatic. Certainly the tradition and community of an author, as entities within the phenomenal world in which an author stands, have a dramatic impact on the semantic range available for expression.[13]

However, the noumenal world has at least an equal impact on the semantic range available to the author. The very issue of the metaphysics of presence or absence impacts the semantic range of the author. Whether this world is seen in a purely Kantian way,[14] or as the spirit realm, also impacts this issue. Denis Lara notes in commenting on Kant's view of the noumenal world that not only is it outside time (hence offering a perception of the existence of the eternal, which itself greatly impacts the understanding of the author) it is also not available for cognition in the same sense as the phenomenal world. Objects, or entities, in the noumenal world may be postulated but not apprehended through rational means because entities of a metaphysical nature are apprehended as knowledge through *nonrational* means.[15] These objects are presented to a person through the agency of assent, assertion, or inference. They are accepted, and therefore become part of the noumenal world; or they are rejected and therefore are excluded from it. The acceptance or rejection of *nonrational* knowledge significantly impacts the semantic range available for use by the author. Finally, both the Kantian view and that of a spirit realm assert that the noumenal world is impacting and operating as a form of foundation to the phenomenal world, thereby providing a context for the knowledge obtained as *rational* knowledge. This must be regarded as significantly impacting the semantic range of an author in the creation of texts.

Consequently, ignoring the questions of *when* and *where*, purely from the point of view of the information supplied on the semantic range available to the author in the act of *parole*, disregards that which has a significant impact on interpretation and consequently meaning of a text. It would therefore seem that the postmodern view of

---

12. Lara, "Kant and Hume on Morality," See the 3rd feature in the "Brief Overview of Kant's Ethics."

13. Thiselton, *Thiselton On Hermeneutics*, 702. Thiselton discusses this issue at length in this chapter of his book concerning the concept of corporate memory.

14. Lara, "Kant and Hume on Morality." See the 3rd feature in the "Brief Overview of Kant's Ethics."

15. The concept of *nonrational* knowledge is discussed in chapter 2 of this book.

discarding these questions is itself questionable purely on this basis. If these questions are discarded in the pursuit of semantics, the only semantics available to the reader/interpreter are those of the interpreter, or, as in Fish, the interpretive community. Reader-response hermeneutics in this situation is implicit and the only avenue of recourse is to the interpreter.

Ricoeur's aversion to the romanticist notion of authorial intent as integral to his interpretation theory has been previously noted and discussed at length. His concern is the issue of the inclusion of a foreign psyche that is caught up in the issue of authorial intent.[16] However, as a philosopher who focuses on semantics, his aversion to authorial intent and any subsequent recognition of the intended audience, together with his relegation of history and tradition (of the author) to a secondary role, has dismissed a significant source of the semantics involved in the text. It is hardly surprising that his interpretive theory sees a far greater range of potential meaning associated with the text in the absence of the author, or to use his phrasing when the text "escapes the finite horizon lived by its author." His theory essentially escapes any semantic constraint and explanation inherent in the act of *parole*.[17] His focus on language must draw some of this back into the fold of his semantics, since it is impossible to translate a language and ideas without regard to their place in history. Nevertheless, his theory represents a significant loss in the message of the author and hence does not give due recognition to the "otherness" of the author.

(b) Constraint or Opportunity

Thiselton recognizes in the work of Ricoeur a "fundamental principle of hermeneutics including biblical interpretation" in the development of the hermeneutics of suspicion.[18] This suspicion is necessary to expose and remove any tendency to iconoclasm. Hence the disguises and masks are "stripped away."[19] Thiselton notes Ricoeur's investigation of Marx, Nietzsche, and Freud as the "masters of suspicion," noting also Ricoeur's positive direction taken in considering suspicion.[20] It creates openness to genuine interpretation.

However, Ricoeur also shows another side to the operation of suspicion, also associated with the "masters of suspicion." This is the problem of manipulation due to authoritarian influences such as the "magisterium as the rule of orthodoxy."[21] In other

16. Ricoeur, *Interpretation Theory*, 92.
17. Ibid., 30.
18. Thiselton, *New Horizons*, 347.
19. Ibid., 348.
20. Ibid.
21. Ricoeur, *Essays on Biblical Interpretation*, 74. Ricoeur's language is significant in displaying an intensity of feeling in this area by asserting that it is this tendency "that I deplore and am seeking to combat."

words the concept of constraining, such as by consideration of authorial intent and the semantic range available, becomes objectionable due to the possibility of constraint and manipulation. Thiselton also believes that this potential problem, highlighted by these authors and others, needs to be taken seriously.[22] However, not all Christian claims should be interpreted in this fashion as attempts to legitimize particular uses of power.[23] Misunderstanding doesn't constitute an attempt to manipulate or legitimize a power structure. In fact Scripture offers a safeguard in the attitude toward "the other" in the declaration of Rom 13:10 that "Love does no harm to a neighbor." A genuine person who is mindful of the impact on others in what he or she asserts may be misguided, but this genuine person will not do harm when remaining within the context of the faith.

In the case of the deliberate manipulation of texts, the issue is the user not the text. Wittgenstein noted that the world is neither good nor evil, and that evil enters through a person, the subject.[24] Good and evil are not properties in the world; they belong to the predication of the subject, that is, the person.[25] Nuclear power can be used to light up a city or blow up a city; the issue is the user not the nuclear power. The concern that something could be used to manipulate others can itself become manipulation of texts, if the meaning is stripped from texts in general to prevent meaning from being assigned incorrectly in particular texts, such as religious texts.

(c) Communication by Language

It has previously been observed that in the reflective thinking of Gadamer language ascends to fulfilling the role of metaphysics.[26] Language for Gadamer provides the opportunity for the mediation of the finite and infinite appropriate to humanity.[27] Wittgenstein makes the observation that humanity's ability to communicate does not exist because of language; communication is a means of influencing others and of furthering human achievement.[28] He notes, "Without the use of speech and writing people could not communicate."[29] Language is a tool used in communicating; language is not responsible for communication.

Ricoeur does not go so far as Gadamer. Indeed, Ricoeur notes that the view that language is everything leads to a closed mentality in interpretation.[30] Yet he does see

22. Thiselton, *Interpreting God*, ix.
23. Ibid.
24. Wittgenstein, *Notebooks*, 79e.
25. Ibid.
26. Gadamer, *Philosophical Hermeneutics*, 75.
27. Ibid., 80.
28. Wittgenstein, *Investigations*, 137e (491).
29. Ibid.
30. Ricoeur, *Oneself*, 301.

within language the ability to express being,[31] and consequently within language there exists the capability to express metaphysics without language assuming the status of metaphysics. Hence, language is the means of expression and communication of being from within the thinking of a person. An author uses language to express thoughts, although semantic choices are constrained by that which is available to an author, that is, within language and the *when* and *where* associated with the text. These choices limit the facility of communication, not the imagination of the author. Language does not the limit of the thought of an author, but does limit the expression of those thoughts. As discussed in the previous chapter, the text is a creation of an author expressed and communicated in language; the text is not a creation of language. Hence, the limitation is not to the meaning but the expression of that meaning.

The human imagination is capable of thinking in the impossible; for example, in reading a novel the human mind can enter the world of and cope with that which defies rationality, such as in fantasy and science fiction. Therefore, the human mind, in its musings, is capable of moving outside that which normally constrains. Further, the inflation of language and proliferation of languages indicates that language does not constrain the imagination but is adapted by the imagination for the human mind's continuing development to suit the need to communicate. This is readily seen in the development of subcultures and changes in community. Technological changes provide a ceaseless flow of examples, for example, the proliferation of computers and the Internet and the subsequent development of words specific to this environment such as *e-mail*. The constraint of language does not constrain the ability to imagine and think, just the ability to express the world. In expressing the world in a text language limits the world,[32] however, this should not be seen as a limit on the world imagined.

What is said in discourse can be restated using different words. A discource can even be translated into other languages, which indicates that langugae is a vehicle of a propositional content.[33] The very act of translation requires that the transference of thought forms and presuppositions expressed in the originating text are placed into the new situation.[34] Language is employed to express thought, not to contain or restrict thought. However, this expression of language is not simply a description of an entity or the relaying of information. It is a world that is literally set before the interpreter/reader. Kevin Vanhoozer, in a tribute to Paul Ricoeur, noted a central insight that Ricoeur had contributed, namely that an interpreter situates him or herself in front of the text, which then opens a new world in front of the text.[35] Ricoeur states that the text "speaks of a possible world and of a possible way of orienting oneself

---

31. Ibid.
32. Wittgenstein, *Tractatus*, sect.5.62.
33. Ricoeur, *Interpretation Theory*, 9.
34. Caird, *Language and Imagery of the Bible*, 2.
35. Vanhoozer, "Joy of Yes," 27.

within it."³⁶ The Pentecostal writer Randolph Tate similarly proposed the idea of the world of the text.³⁷ However, unlike Ricoeur, Tate noted the importance of the world of the author and that of the reader are of equal importance in the interpretation of texts. This world is a world conveyed in and through language but not constrained by it; it is the expression that is constrained. The purpose of language is to present the world for the perception of the reader; it is not the purpose of the world of the text to present language to the reader.

If the constraint is that of language, not that of thought, then it is conceivable to suggest that with a different *when* and *where* (i.e., a different semantic range made available) meaning can then undergo apparent change, that is, adaptation into a new semantic range. This would be simply due to a differing or perhaps even greater capacity to express the thought. The impact on meaning of the unintended audience was also examined earlier in this work, and the resultant grounds for proposing that the process of interpretation opens up into new worlds, that is, relevant meaning in the situation of the *when* and *where* of the receptor. It has been suggested that the unintended audience may be seen to result in what amounts to a revision of the author in the light of new understanding. Clearly this cannot refer to the person of the author. However, if authorial intent is detectable and evident as suggested in this work, then the interaction of the "world of the receptor" and the "world of the text" can indeed be seen to "fuse," as in Gadamer, Ricoeur, and Thiselton, resulting in what has the appearance of a revision of the authorial intent and its application.

This place would seem to be where Ricoeur suggests is the end point of his interpretation theory. Ricoeur views his theory as faithful to the original intention of Schleiermacher's hermeneutics. Ricoeur expresses it this way: "To understand an author better than he could understand himself is to display the power of disclosure implied in his discourse beyond the limited horizon of his own existential situation."³⁸ However, as has been noted on numerous occasions in this work, his theory entails the dismissal of the authorial intent and the situation of the intended audience.

Yet if the authorial intent should be considered more as an ontological entity than a description within the world of the text, then authorial intent relates to the being of the world of the text. The content of the message (i.e., the "*what*" of the text) is then set in the context of this world of the text, whose ontology, or "being," is disclosed by the authorial intent. More importantly, since it is a world set before the reader/interpreter to view or perceive, the reader/interpreter can bring entities from within his or her own world into the world of the text and so describe new entities in the world of the text, the being of which is set by the authorial intent. This has important implications for the interaction of the believer with the biblical text and the paradox

---

36. Ricoeur, *Interpretation Theory*, 88.
37. Tate, *Biblical Interpretation*, xv–xxi.
38. Ricoeur, *Interpretation Theory*, 93.

of the Scripture, that is, how a text can be a vehicle for both the human and divine author at the same time.

Consequently, if a speaking voice is associated with a text, this then raises questions that should be pursued. Why in the postmodern situation does this voice pass undetected? If there is a voice and it is not the person of the author, how is that voice to be understood in both its being and what it says? If a voice is associated with a text, how does the reader/interpreter interact with this voice? The *who* of the text as the speaking subject must be investigated.

Pursuing the "Who?" of the Text

The *who* of the text in Heidegger's thought is an ontological question.[39] Heidegger's work concerns the *who* of *Dasein*, hence selfhood. Ricoeur's work follows a similar line.[40] This is a question of being and draws attention to the fact that the search for *who*, as a hermeneutical endeavor, whether concerning self or the author, has an ontological basis. Ricoeur notes this in his work and further observes that in the pursuit of semantics the question of *who* moves to the periphery and the questions *why* and *what* become central.[41] Conversely, pragmatics[42] is not concerned with "empirical description of acts of communication," and so rather than focusing on the statement it looks at the "act of speaking itself."[43] In this investigation the "I" and the "you" of interlocution become central,[44] that is, the *who* of speaking comes into view.

Therefore, it seems reasonable to infer that in the semantic approach, with its resultant effect of moving the question of *who* to the periphery due to its epistemological understanding, a resultant movement away from interaction with the ontology of the speaking voice of the text takes place.[45] If this is indeed the case, this then indicates that within the pursuit of epistemology there can occur description of being but no actual encounter with existence and hence otherness of that being; that is, the *who* becomes a *what*. This inference would seem confirmed by Ricoeur's observation on the weakness of Speech-Act Theory with respect to the ontological question of

---

39. Heidegger, *Being and Time*, 64.

40. Ricoeur, *Conflict of Interpretations*, 225–35. Ricoeur devotes a section of the work to this issue of the subject in the thought of Heidegger. Ricoeur's work *Oneself as Another* is a study of the issue of identifying self, and he refers to Heidegger's concept of the question of "who," see 58–61.

41. Ricoeur, *Oneself*, 59.

42. Ibid., 40. Ricoeur sets out the sense of his use of the term "pragmatics" in relation to language: "a theory of language as it is used in specific contexts of interlocution," hence the link with Speech-Act Theory.

43. Ibid.

44. Ibid.

45. Ricoeur, *Conflict of Interpretations*, 16. Semantic analysis on its own creates an illusion of language as an absolute and so must be referred to existence. There is a need to integrate semantics with ontology. Hence, at this earlier time Ricoeur realized the potentially hazardous movement away from ontology, which could create the illusion of an absolute of language.

who. He points out that the focus of the theory is upon the act, not the agent.[46] He then observes: "At the price of this elision the transcendental conditions of communication can be entirely stripped of psychological import and held to be regulations of language (*langue*) and not of speech."[47] This he notes is a "despsychologizing" of language.[48] Hence, he devotes a chapter in *Oneself as Another* to a study that concerns "The Agentless Semantics of Action."[49]

Semantics is referential, in contrast to the reflexive nature of pragmatics, in which the interlocution of persons comes into view.[50] The semantic approach to the action discloses an agentless action. The semantics of an action essentially fails to "see" the agent of the action due to an opposing ontology to that of the person, which is the "ontology of autonomous events."[51] Consequently, the referential task, so important to the interpretive theory of Ricoeur, offers in its approach some understanding of Ricoeur's view of the autonomy of the text detached from the author. The movement from agent to event is a necessary conclusion of the nature of Ricoeur's view of semantics, thereby constituting a potential weakness in the semantic (or dare it be said epistemological) approach, that is, a failure to come to grips with the agent.

Ricoeur does note that although the referential approach fails to encounter the agent, in the ontological sense of the question of *who*, it can refer to the agent conceptually by the use of personal pronouns.[52] Ricoeur notes in passing that the arc of pronouns (e.g., I, you, he, she, and so on) moves the conceptual status of the person into the third person in grammatical status. This note in passing, within the context of the composition or narrative, tells the reader that he is moving to an answer, which is foreshadowed by a previous statement, that at "the end of this study [i.e., the current study, or chapter, concerning "The Agentless Semantics of Action"] our problem will be to turn this challenge to our advantage, by making the investigation into the 'what?-why?' of action the grand detour at the end of which the question 'who?' returns in force." That is, the *who* remains in the background and is brought forward.[53] Indeed, after following the "grand detour" the final chapter of Ricoeur's book proposes an ontology to address this question.[54]

---

46. Ricoeur, *Oneself*, 47.
47. Ibid.
48. Ibid.
49. Ibid., 56–87.
50. Ibid., 40.
51. Ibid., 89.
52. Ibid., 60.
53. Ibid., 59. See also 16–17, where Ricoeur discusses this concept of the detour via "why?-what?" as the basic plan of the book.
54. Ibid., 297–356. Titled "What Ontology in View."

From the perspective of language treated on an epistemological basis is a concealment of the question *who* in the treatment of hermeneutics.[55] This results in Ricoeur's proposed grand detour, so that the question that presents in the first instance (i.e., *who?*) becomes the final question addressed. Theory approached in such a way reverses the common sense concept of discourse, that is, that someone says something to someone, and instead becomes oneself who had something said (to them) by someone. Furthermore, if the author and audience are disregarded, then all that is left is something (that has been said), that is, the *what* or content. The question *why* can move in no other direction than that of agentless semantics, that is, to capture and disclose the *what*. The question of *what* is terminal, since the *who*, or someone, has become a something, despite any reference to personhood by the grammatical third person.

Further, in Ricoeur's theory the concept of any intended audience can have no impact on meaning (i.e., there is no traversing of "why?-what?" to *when* and *where*); hence, the referential approach alights upon and remains upon "why?-what?", that is, *the process has become terminal*. It is easy to foresee in this circumstance the movement to language as an absolute. Because the very nature of the question *why* results in explanation, hence descriptive reference, it does not naturally move in the direction of *who*, as Ricoeur has so convincingly argued. As has been discussed previously, Ricoeur does not deny the *fact* of the author. Indeed, the opposite is true; hence, he himself does not end in a postmodern deconstructionism. What he disregards is the impact of authorial intent. Deconstruction has simply terminated the process at *what* because it has disregarded both the agent, or *who*, and the historical questions of *when-where*. Because the process is terminal there is no deferred question of *who* to be considered. Any ontological evaluation of existence is lost at both ends of the process.

Ricoeur's "grand detour," when taken, has the effect of circumventing the termination of the process at the question *what*. Ricoeur does not disregard the author, just the issue of authorial intent. This position is probably best illustrated by his own comments in his conclusions of *Interpretation Theory*. His theory is faithful to the original intention of Schleiermacher in pursuit of the understanding of the author, further that his method results in the full disclosure of the potential within what an author said.[56] If, as seen previously, the process of Ricoeur's approach in *Oneself as Another* gives insight on his assertion of autonomy of the text, then this similarly shows how Ricoeur can consider that, in disregarding authorial intent, he has not ignored the author so as to end up with a semantic "agentless action" of an authorless text.

In the event of dialogue, Ricoeur acknowledges that meaning is the speaker's, hence the author's.[57] Understanding the discourse meaning is the same thing as

---

55. Ibid., 59. This concept is referred to often in his work.
56. Ricoeur, *Interpretation Theory*, 93. This is referred to previously and quoted.
57. Ibid., 29.

understanding the speaker's meaning.[58] Even the polysemic nature of words and phrases is screened, and is therefore limited by the event of the speaking author.[59] In other words, there is a constraint on meaning that is not applicable to the "autonomous text." It would seem that it is this potential of constraint that concerns Ricoeur, and by deferring the question of *who*, rather than beginning with it, he allows a full scope of potential meaning before coming back to an ontology of the *who*, that is, the author. Furthermore, this concept of deferral allows a continuous realization of new or developed meaning of the "why?-what?" The occasion of each event of interpretation results in this deferment and so allows the engagement of the world of the interpreter in exploring polysemy.

The concept that closure of the text should not necessarily result in closure of the interpretation of that text, hence meaning, is one that Marshall proposed in dealing with Scripture.[60] An authoritative meaning in one context may have a different authoritative meaning in a different context.[61] However, the closure of interpretation of that text assumes a static nature, not a dynamic nature, of the text. If the text is seen as a dynamic entity itself, there is then no need to close the relative meaning of the text nor is there a need to postulate ongoing attachment to the person of the author. The above addresses Ricoeur's concerns to allow the text to open a world before the reader, rather than to lock the interpreter into a situation from which he or she is inherently distanced. The above approach will also address the concern to retain that which seems the common sense approach, that is, that the text has an author.[62] Therefore, in a reevaluation of authorial intent in the question of *who*, considered as an ontological question, and a recognition of the impact of the fusion of horizons allowing the content to essentially be seen from two worldviews, there is scope to proceed.

The "Why" Question: Ontological Capture of "Who"

The question *why* would seem to naturally lead to explanation and therefore description; but the question *why* does not of necessity raise the question *who*.[63] In the question "Why did the accident happen?" the answer can indicate both a *who*, as in "The driver lost control of the car"; and it can indicate impersonal agency, as in "The brakes on the car failed." Consequently, it would seem reasonable to suggest that the question *why* has within it an implicit ability for capture of the question of agency. Consequently, it is the question *why* that should provide the link between ontology and epistemology, that is, between the agent and the action of that agent. Following the

---

58. Ibid.
59. Ibid., 17.
60. Marshall, *Beyond the Bible*, 54. This issue has been discussed at length in chapter 3.
61. Ibid., 56.
62. Cunningham, *Reading After Theory*, 54.
63. Ricoeur, *Oneself*, 63.

direction of the question *why* in its capture and disclosure of *what* assumes to some degree that the implicit question of agency has been captured.

Ricoeur notes that pragmatics and semantics, in relationship to language, are irreducible with respect to one another, that is, one cannot substitute for the other, and yet each draws from the other in its practice.[64] Hence, neither are they mutually exclusive in the interpretation of texts. The question *why*, as noted previously, discloses the *what* in a referential way in the investigation of semantics, that is, the content as a communication. However, the question of motivation also provides the link between authorial intent and the issues concerning the question of *when* and *where*; that is, the *why* should provide the link to be able to cover the scope of *who* said what and to whom. The question of *why* a text is written should automatically direct attention to the intended audience, since *why* discloses how the *what*, or the content, is to be related to reality, hence the world, as projected by the author. The question *why* has an implicit aspect that captures the ontological aspect of *who* is addressed; that is, *why* captures the ontological aspects of the interlocution in the author's relating of the *what* to reality, but not within its semantic task.

The term *Aufhebung* was referred to previously in the work of both Hegel and Ricoeur to indicate that which appears and yet disappears although seemingly retained. The question *why* has within it an implicit *Aufhebung* that instantaneously captures the ontology of the *who* of speaker/author and the *who* of the audience. Thus, the question *why* should lead from the question of *who* to the questions of *when* and *where*. The issues related to content concern *what* is said and *what* it is said about,[65] but it is understood in the context of by whom and to whom it is said. Therefore, the *what* of the saying can only be properly understood and given meaning by dealing with its context; that is, disclosure of meaning occurs in pursuing the question *who* and the questions *when* and *where* in the consideration of *what* is said.

Consequently, it would seem that the very concept of discourse (i.e., that someone says something to someone) also implies initially the order of questions that should be followed. In the case of dialogue, the first issue faced is ontological, a *who* addresses a someone. However, this is not the case in written text, because a text rather than a speaker confronts the interpreter. Ricoeur notes that the text has the effect of separating the acts of writing and reading so that there is no communicative connection between them.[66] Derrida raises the issue of entering a text with a disregard of the nature of the book (i.e., the connections proposed by the idea of anterior meaning), which is to disregard the *who* and authorial intention and hence, for Derrida, circumvent logocentrism.[67] Derrida is deliberately employing an idea of randomness, yet in reality, though reading is not always random; a reader does not always enter a text either

---

64. Ibid., 40.
65. Ricoeur, *Interpretation Theory*, 19.
66. Ricoeur, *From Text to Action*, 103.
67. Derrida, *Of Grammatology*: 162.

at the beginning or with advance understanding of the questions proposed for the task of interpretation. The motivation to engage a text by a reader can be an author, it can be an issue that the reader pursues, or it can even be casual interest, for example, filling in time or picking up a novel for the first time. A reader can enter a text in pursuit of particular content without any real regard to the world of the text or author. There is no compulsory mode or method by which reading *must* be undertaken, whatever the theoretical argument(s) for what *should* be done.

This need not be considered a problem. A work of art may be viewed as a whole or some aspect can catch the eye of the audience. In the same way that authorial intent transforms paints and canvas into a work of art or the chiseling of a sculptor upon some block of material transforms into a sculpture, so the authorial intent in the act of *parole* "paints" and "sculpts" a world in words. If the person perceiving is drawn into the world of the painting, the sculpture, or the text, this person will move within that world in an act of discovery, taking note of all the entities within that world. The text—the composition, or work of art—is cast in the particular language employed. The text may never be verbally declared. Yet, text is a spoken word, a *logos*, of a composition or a narrative that projects, by creating, a world into which the reader enters.

If an ideal process was undertaken, it would probably lead to a consideration of the questions in the order asked, with each disclosure contributing to the one that follows it. In this situation the question of the ontology is the primary question. The interpreter must consider the being of the text before pulling it apart in the investigation of *what* it is saying. The simplest illustration is that of anatomy and physiology: To perform anatomy, as a descriptive task, the body must first be dead. Physiology requires examination of the interaction of functions in a living situation. Both tasks are necessary, but each is an entirely different approach that informs one another in pursuit of understanding the living person.

It remains to be considered how the being of the person of the author (the *who*) and the being of the text are related, since it is the author who gives being to the text, even though the text is detached from the author, as highlighted by Ricoeur.

THE "WHO" QUESTION: TAKING A DIFFERENT ROUTE

Ricoeur anticipates the direct approach to the question of *who* as an ontological question. The introductory chapter of *Oneself as Another*, in the search for selfhood (i.e., how the subject posits self), first considers the Cartesian "I" by way of a brief review of Descartes *cogito*.[68] Ricoeur takes note that Descartes found that the addition of the question concerned with "knowing *what* I am" led to "a more developed expression of the cogito."[69] Hence, it would seem reasonable to suggest that this is the beginning for Ricoeur: he finds that the indication of the starting place to discover the *who* is to

68. Ricoeur, *Oneself*, 4–11.
69. Ibid., 7. (Italics original.)

begin with the *what*. Thus, at an early stage in his thinking Ricoeur indicates that the referential approach is the place to begin the search for *who*.

Although the questioning process begins with *who*, this investigation becomes immediately deferred. In many ways this would seem to present an understanding of his thinking in his theory. Ricoeur also takes note that in Descartes's recognition of the divine is a profound effect on the cogito. This effect occurs in the recognition of the "Other" that causes a representation of the divine self within the cogito.[70] Here is the other aspect that will determine the search: the true self is only found in otherness within the self.

Ricoeur then considers the thoughts of Nietzsche. This consideration results in what Ricoeur styles as the "shattered cogito" in contrast to Descartes's "exalted cogito."[71] Ricoeur then states, "Exalted subject, humiliated subject: it seems that it is always through a complete reversal of this sort that one approaches the subject; one could thus conclude that the 'I' of the philosophies of the subject is *atopos*, without any assured place in discourse."[72] Hence, in his reasoning the search for the subject can only proceed by following the line of reasoning that is open, that is, the referential approach; remembering that for Ricoeur reference here is not metaphysical but a matter of semantics concerning the verbal meaning of the text as an ideality.

What Ricoeur mentioned in passing will now be taken note of and examined. In the referential task of semantics, the speaker can use personal pronouns to represent, or portray, the concept of persons; but the portrayal is in the grammatical third person, including the first and second person pronouns. Consequently, although the grammatical first or second person is used (more amenable to the reflexive task), the concept of the person is thrown into a third person status grammatically (more amenable to the referential task).[73] It is here that the weakness of the epistemological approach, as a referential task, displays itself most forcefully. The referential task on its own can offer only a representation of person or psyche and cannot, as Ricoeur has so ably demonstrated in *Oneself as Another*, consider the being that animates an entity in being a person. There is no possibility of inferring consciousness from the semantic route. In this route taken by Ricoeur, if a person is indicated, and persons are known to have a consciousness, it is possible to state that the person indicated in the third person has a consciousness but no descriptive evaluation is possible of the "being" of that particular person is indicated. Ricoeur's approach also does not supply or reveal that which can reanimate, and consequently the text remains a thing to be

---

70. Ibid., 9.
71. Ibid., 11–16.
72. Ibid., 16. (Italics original.)
73. Ibid., 46. Ricoeur presents a thorough argument showing that the reflexive approach privileges the first and second person and essentially excludes the third person. The third person is only a thing spoken about. Conversely, since the third person can indeed be a nonperson it is more amenable to description as an entity within the text. Hence, semantics privileges the third person in its approach.

described.⁷⁴ If epistemology is to continue to be the route followed to eventually get to the agent as a person in the examination, then it is understandable why Ricoeur suggests it can only be done by a "grand detour." Before taking this observation as a point of departure, some comments of interest can be made.

(a) Appearance of the Author in the Text

As a result of this movement to the third person in the referential task, if the speaking subject wishes to come within the purview of the reader/interpreter as a describable entity within the world of the text, then he or she must move self to this concept of projection of a person in the third person. In the concept of constatives, an aspect of the speech act can be unsaid.⁷⁵ To use Ricoeur's analogy,⁷⁶ the statements "the cat is on the mat" and "I affirm that the cat is on the mat" both have the same truth value, but the former is purely referential and the latter has a reflexive element that draws attention to the maker of the statement.

However, apart from the semantic observations Ricoeur is making, this analogy brings into view another aspect. Hegel highlighted that it is predication that gives the subject meaning, which is to say that the subject is meaningless without predication.⁷⁷ Predication forms an important aspect of Ricoeur's interpretive theory, and it is the universal nature of the predicate that is one of the primary presuppositions of his discussion of discourse.⁷⁸ It is hardly surprising that his theory focuses on semantics and epistemology, since the predicate is the *what* of the saying and is that which is most amenable to the referential approach of semantics. In the concept of pursuing *what* is said and *what* it is said about, the subject has already moved to the third person, so as to be subjected to description of an entity of the same rank as a nonperson. Only the concept of personhood is retained.

Yet, a writer can use a device, as indeed a speaker can also use, to place himself or herself within the world of the writer's or speaker's "created" discourse. The statement "God is good" is such that the predicate available for referential analysis is "is good." The designation of God is nonspecific and almost generic. However, in the statement "I affirm that God is good" the complete statement "God is good" has moved into the predicate. Now, not only does referential analysis focus on a description of "is good"

---

74. This issue of the nature of the text has been considered in chapters 3 and 4. In the thinking of Ong the text is not even discourse unless engaged by a person. Ricoeur and Gadamer would not go so far, but certainly they treat the text as not having real entity until engaged by the interpreter. Its being is as language not message.

75. Ricoeur, *Oneself*, 43.

76. Ibid.

77. Hegel, "Phenomenology," 95.

78. Ricoeur, *Interpretation Theory*, 10. Hegel noted that without the subject the predicate takes on a universal nature, Hegel, "Phenomenology," 96.

but also focuses on the description that "God is good." In this case God is now a particular person that is identified as the God of "I," that is, the speaker.

Therefore, this device can also be available for placing oneself into the predicate, which allows a description of self. This interaction of subject and predicate is what results in the predicate becoming actual knowledge.[79] In the second statement "I" is the subject, but the actual knowledge of the predicate is that "God is good," and the statement "I affirm that God is good" gives this predicate actual being in the life of "I." More importantly, if God is the speaker, then in a declaration such as "I am the God who is good" the movement of himself into the predicate gives him place within the world of the text as a person, whose description is that he is good. The prefixing with "I" as the subject has moved God into the predicate. However, this device allows the speaker/author to appear within the world he creates by speaking with the prefixing of "I" in ascribing to self.

This device is used in Scripture. The prophet speaking in the first person on behalf of the divine can move to third person whilst still speaking in the first person. Consider Isa 43:1–18. In these verses the prophet proclaims in the first person the speaking of the divine. In verse 1 there is the assertion of Israel's existence as a people due to his (i.e., the Lord's, because the prophet speaks for God in using the first person "I") creative work. In this vein God then moves in succeeding verses to a discussion of his redemption of them in various situations. The exhortation is that people should trust him due to this powerfully demonstrated activity (e.g., verses 10–13). However, in verse 14 there is a perceptible change: "Thus says the Lord, your Redeemer, the Holy One of Israel, your King." In this situation "your Redeemer, the Holy One of Israel, your King" can now be substituted for "I," that is, the one speaking. These appellations have been made rich in descriptive language in the preceding verses. This description places the "I" within the story and part of the description of the text; the "I" is all these things and all these things are now gathered up into the subject, the "I." This could be stated as "Your Redeemer, the Holy One of Israel, your King says . . ." or "I say . . ." In this fashion God becomes a player within the drama of the world he created.

The concept of the prophet is that of the one who speaks for another as the other. This allows the divine influence upon the prophet to place God into the place where, in addition to being the speaking subject in the prophet, there is a movement to the concept of a person within the predicate through the prophet. Hence, God becomes describable as an agent within the world he creates, in inspiring the prophet. Before assuming that this requires some form of special dispensation, or hermeneutic, that allows the "person" of God, consider the concept of an authorized biography. In the biography, as opposed to the autobiography, the biographer (employed by the one who is spoken about) is able to portray that person within the world as part of the world. The speaking voice of the biographer can do what the one who is the true author

---

79. Ricoeur, "Phenomenology," 96.

cannot do, the one about whom the text is written. By using the biographer, the true subject appears within the predicate of the world, that is, becomes a describable entity.

The work of Wittgenstein, along the lines of this subject, has been considered in a previous chapter of this book. He notes that in the analogy of "seeing" an important aspect is disclosed; that is, the eye that sees does not see itself in the looking.[80] Essentially, in his contention, this explanation illustrates the problem of the metaphysical "I" who in describing the world as he or she sees it cannot see himself or herself within that world. Therefore, as an author who brings the world into existence through the creative medium of word, the author does not see himself within that world. The use of the biographer overcomes this problem. Not only is the true author now visible but also interacts with the world. Thus, to be seen as an agent *within* as well as an agent *of* this world he created, God employed biographers, people he inspired to write. Whatever one believes about Scripture, the existence of God, or the concept of inspiration, the concept of someone speaking through another is sound.

One other point that can be made before concluding this digression concerns the very concept of the eye/"I" that sees but does not see itself. If the author is interacting within the world, this interaction occurs within his or her world. In other words, as an autobiographer, an author cannot see himself or herself through the eyes of others. This, however, becomes possible by way of the biography; that is, the eye/"I" that sees a world and wishes to create it can become seen through the eyes of another, the biographer. In this way the eye/"I" thereby becomes describable within the world. Hence, even Jesus, who did not write, "employed" those to write so that he could be seen within the world through the eyes of others. These issues are not small issues. In consideration of the biblical text, developed in the area that semantics does open up, the result is that the being of God is seen in his interaction within the world and is describable, and therefore he subjects himself to epistemological investigation.

The following phrase is suggested as a maxim in returning to the concept of authorial intent: *the task of epistemology assumes a prior ontology, or, the thing to be known must have its being as it is to be known for it to be known*. Ontology is the first task and not just the last. As a result, it should be the activity that undergirds epistemology. However, it must also be noted that either one without the other leads to no actual knowledge. As Hegel has noted, actual knowledge is in the predicated subject, not just in the subject or predicate alone.

(b) The Problematic of the Person of "Who": The Priority of Ontology

The observation by Wittgenstein that the "I" that sees does not see itself should alert the interpreter to a realization that semantic analysis will not observe, within the

---

80. Wittgenstein, *Tractatus*, Sect.5.633.

description, the author other than via the sorts of devices available, as mentioned previously. As such observation of the author will not be as a person other than a character within the narrative, therefore any observation of the author will be simply the concept of a person stripped of being, and hence consciousness, as a person. Essentially, the result is a narrative description of a person, but that person is without being as a person. The rejection of authorial intent, because of its suspected ties to a foreign psyche (that of the author as foreign to the interpreter), would seem to begin here, that is, in the pursuit of *who* via semantics where the author is encountered within the *what* of the text, not as a person.

Ricoeur observes that he has considered the assessment just made regarding the referential approach. In considering the "concealment of the question 'who?'" he contends that it is insufficient to appeal to the nature of the semantic approach that *does*[81] tend to make the *who* a something.[82] Although there is a "capture" of the *who* by a something (i.e., in attempting to pursue the *who* the journey to agency is caught up as it were in impersonal discussion as a thing under consideration), there is nothing within the practice and principles of semantics that prevents an autonomy of the question of *who*, the someone, from *what*, the something.[83] The question *who* can be answered by use of proper names, demonstrative pronouns, and definite description; and also the agent has an ability, through the use of words such as personal pronouns, to designate themselves (noted previously).[84] Ricoeur contends therefore it is not the referential approach, as such, that is responsible for the concealment.[85]

Yet, as noted previously, Ricoeur also observes that the use of such devices by the agent does not supply an answer to the concealment, for Ricoeur observes (also noted previously) that this action by the agent results in the concept of a person, not the being of a person or the actuality of personhood. Therefore, although this approach can describe that which has being and is presented within the text, that being itself is not available to be evaluated. Consequently, the being is an inherent assumption in the description employing the concept of a person. Hence, even in this defense of semantics it would seem rather to confirm what is suggested as a maxim: *the task of epistemology assumes a prior ontology, or, the thing to be known must have its being as it is to be known for it to be known.*

(c) The Priority of Listening: Recognizing Authorial Being in Intent

Nonetheless, following the lead of Ricoeur, it is important to note that the tasks of semantics (epistemological description) and pragmatics (ontological description)

---

81. Italics are added for emphasis, not as indication of Ricoeur's work.
82. Ricoeur, *Oneself*, 59.
83. Ibid.
84. Ibid., 59–60.
85. Ibid., 60.

are irreducible but interdependent, that is, each avails itself of that acquired by the other.[86] It is further suggested that they are also not mutually exclusive; that is, to do one is not to exclude the other, since through the process of reasoning there is a free exchange of what is acquired. They have different agendas in the process of understanding, but as has been stated and bears repeating, both are essential in the process of hermeneutics for understanding to occur. What *is* suggested is that there is a distinction in priority, since epistemological description assumes what it requires as a presupposition, that is, ontological attribution of being as the starting point.

Both studies involve the discovery, acquisition, and assimilation of knowledge. In ontology, knowledge is posited to the self; that is, the person to whom it is posited assumes what is discovered, acquired, and assimilated as fact. Hence, in many ways this is a passive task, that is, a listening *to* "voice," although not in its initiation as a task, since all discovery, acquisition, and assimilation occurs through the question[87] (note the five questions that guide—or should guide—the hermeneutical process). Ontological investigation in hermeneutics is, or should be, based in otherness.

Conversely, in epistemology (involving acquisition of belief as justified and justifiable—hence working from the self) knowledge is posited by the self; that is, self establishes the belief in the knowledge to assume and present it as fact, without an awareness of the other as being, only in description. (Yet even here it should be noted that if the author has not used self-reference, as indicated by Ricoeur, then no description is possible.) Consequently, knowledge is established as fact from the perspective of self and justified to others, not just posited to others. Hence, epistemology is an active task, thas is, a speaking *of* "voice," and is based in projection of the self. Epistemological investigation seeks a description that facilitates the understanding of what is, and it seeks the understanding of being in its context.

Consequently, it is suggested that as a broad understanding, or big picture, ontology occurs within community and subsequently establishes self within community. Alternatively, epistemology occurs in the projection of self from community and subsequently establishes the individual within the world. This leads to a general observation that ontology results in perception of *otherness*, or understanding; and epistemology is the process whereby there is individualization or particularization of that which is "other" in its application to the self, or knowing. Since the individual operates from community, this projection should result in the broadening of the community, that is, expand the horizons of both. Philosophies at different times have operated at these extremes and at different points in between.

Scripture exalts both the community and the self, and humiliates neither.[88] Humility is displayed as an action that operates from the self or community in exalting

---

86. Ibid., 40.

87. Gadamer, *Truth and Method*, 326. This is how the hermeneutical task is engaged.

88. Ricoeur, *Oneself*, 318. Ricoeur also contends that the process he has traversed avoids the positions of exaltation and humiliation of the cogito. In the positing of the cogito the search for certainty

the one who is "other." This is well set out in Phil 2:1–11 where humility is extolled, with Jesus being the example to be *mimicked*. In the scriptural account it is sin (which focuses exclusively on the self, Isa 53:6) that causes the action of humiliation (of community or self) as opposed to the act of humility. Humility is an attitude toward others, and it is also an event one undertakes; it is not an event that happens to self, in the passive sense of being humiliated. Humility is not an attitude toward self but others in the scriptural idea.

Consequently, from the viewpoint of Scripture it can be seen that humility requires a willingness to perceive and listen to *being* (i.e., *other* than self), which is significant in the general hermeneutical task. In the same way that self should exalt that which is other (the community), the other (or community) should value and exalt the value of the individual within that community. Exaltation is an action undertaken by the one who is other than the self. The Philippians passage noted shows both humility and exaltation. Consequently, if this scriptural principle is carried into general hermeneutics, then both manipulation and self-determinism are equally avoided, with neither self nor community subsumed, either by the other. The pursuit of ontology involves perception of the being of that whose being is other than self, and hence inherently must involve willingness to listen, allowing disclosure to the self. The practice of epistemology (in the pursuit of belief that is justified and justifiable) involves the descriptive process, and hence by its nature of questioning involves speaking and projection from the self.

The concept of the question *who* at this point has strange properties, for it would appear logical that this involves first speaking, that is, to even ask the question *who*. Essentially, Ricoeur's journey in *Oneself as Another* follows this line of logical approach. The desire to ask the question *who* ends in a deferral of the question through the realization that questioning throws the process in a seemingly opposite direction, and in his book the very process of questioning is the "capture" (to use his phrase) and concealment of the *who* in the pair "why?-what?" The concept of an ontology of events plays a significant role in this, causing an opaqueness that denies the traversing of it to the *who*. As a result an ontology is sought that is "more consonant with the

---

moves through a process of elevation of the "I" of the "I think," 4. In the humiliation of the cogito, the cogito is "reduced to sheer illusion following the Neitzschean critique," 299. Ricoeur believes that in his proposal of the dialectic of selfhood and otherness there is a resolution that "keeps self from occupying the place of foundation" and this prohibition prevents exaltation or humiliation from occurring, 318. The aim is to avoid either humiliation or exaltation, but Ricoeur's view is removal of the ability of the self to do either, which is an attempt to reach the same place as the scriptural viewpoint. However, the scriptural "route," rather than being that of passivity (which Ricoeur acknowledges and extols, 318), involves an active participation of the self, so that humility as a substantive refers to that which has been achieved in the action of the self, rather than humiliation as a substantive referring to that which has happened to the self in the action of another. Both avoid humiliation. In contrast the scriptural route ends in exaltation of the self by the other without it being due to ambition and hence self-effort. This is exaltation of the self without the positing of the self as exalted.

search for the self, the genuine place of linkage between the action and its agent."[89] The journey ends in proposing an alternate ontology, which is presented in the final chapter of Ricoeur's book.[90]

It could be proposed that a simplification of Ricoeur's approach could be to state that at the end of speaking is listening. Although this comment would definitely be an oversimplification of what Thiselton calls a "crowning work" on the subject matter of understanding the hermeneutics of self and a "masterly" work by Ricoeur.[91] Nevertheless, this simple statement is suggested as a valid brief overview of the journey. The concept of listening, as a conclusion to the process of questioning, in fact is logical: the renewal of questioning implies listening has occurred, whether for clarification or for further exploration or for some other reasoning. The Scripture in Prov 18:13 also bears witness to this as a basic principle: "He who answers a matter before he hears *it*, It *is* folly and shame to him"; or in the pithy manner of Eugene Peterson, "Answering before listening is both stupid and rude" (The Message).

Consequently, an apparent paradox is introduced by this recognition. The concept of the *who* implies a questioning, yet the process of questioning only leads to the *who* when it is deferred through the initiation of a semantic then pragmatic approach to potentially reappear as a question at the conclusion. It is no wonder that the thinking of hermeneutics, and philosophy in general, has moved away from concepts such as God, the Absolute, the author, and indeed any concept of anterior meaning (as Derrida suggests), all of which involve some concept of consciousness, or person as other than self, at the initiation of the process. The descriptive referential, hence epistemological, route begins with speaking not listening; undoubtedly because, as Gadamer has astutely observed, the "hermeneutical task becomes automatically a questioning of things and is always in part determined by this . . . (thereby placing) . . . the hermeneutical work on a firm basis."[92] The pursuit of understanding occurs due to an attitude of questioning.

Yet, the nature of what has occurred should alert the inquirer who lingers at the consideration of where it started. *Someone* (a communicator or author) has said *something* (content) to *someone* (a receptor or reader); hence, the process of understanding should start with *someone* (the receptor) listening, with this then resulting in pursuit of understanding of the *something* that *someone* (the communicator), has said. Hermeneutical theory began at the beginning of the statement of the basic idea, with a consideration from the perspective of the communicator rather than the receptor, that is, the author-centered approach. Yet has now moved to an exclusion of the author in a reader-centered approach, having abandoned the first step in communication of

---

89. Ibid., 74. This concept of a different ontology is further explained to show its need to link the elements uncovered, 86.
90. Ibid., 297. This chapter is aptly titled "What Ontology in View."
91. Thiselton, *Interpreting God*, 73. 117.
92. Gadamer, *Truth and Method*, 238.

listening to the author. Whilst the event of discourse begins with the communicator, the event of understanding begins with the receptor. But the pursuit of understanding includes the inherent assumption that something has been listened to. The someone who speaks is acknowledged first in the basic idea, hence the author-centered approach has the appearance of being reasonable when it is considered that the reader/interpreter begins with what has already been said by the author who is no longer present and is to be listened to as a someone.

Consequently, some form of listening (or its equivalent in the process of reading) must occur *or* the reader/interpreter is not in receipt of a message of which to inquire.[93] It is interesting to note, as Thiselton has observed, that even in the field of deconstruction (the extreme side of reader approaches) there has been movement back to the realization that the hermeneutical process involves having listened to some form of voice.[94] Consequently, the hermeneutical process begins and ends with listening, or at least it should, which is reminiscent of the pithy saying that is used to emphasize the value of listening: "when God made us he gave us one mouth and two ears."

The first step in the process toward interpretation begins with an interestedness in the material, or text, as Bultmann so astutely recognized; interpretation begins with a presupposition of vital interest in the subject matter of the text and as a result the interpreter investigates in a purposive manner.[95] Hence, the interpreter comes to the task via an implicit question that has motivated his or her inquiry (i.e., one he or she has asked within the realm of self), and the hermeneutical process concerning a specific message has not yet begun. However, what has occurred is a decision to pursue a message and to then engage in hermeneutics. The reader/interpreter positions self to "listen" to the text, as composition or message, after which the process of hermeneutics will begin. Even where these two things seem almost coincidental, as in the entering of a text at a point of interest, they are logically different and both must occur. Hence, the hermeneutical quest for *who* does not begin with the question *who*; it begins with listening to a *who*. The ontological problem begins here in the concept of the act of listening, and the process by nature begins with otherness not self.

Hermeneutics: Posterior to What Is Listened To

In the study of *nonrational* knowledge, the issue of community knowledge was considered, in what Thiselton entitled "Corporate Memory."[96] He noted that knowledge was generally considered to be that which the individual had apprehended and tested for himself or herself.[97] Belief was considered to be that which the individual had

---

93. Thiselton, *New Horizons*, 315.
94. Ibid., 128.
95. Bultmann, "The Problem of Hermeneutics," 119.
96. Thiselton, *Thiselton On Hermeneutics*, 701.
97. Ibid.

"taken over" from the community or learned from others. Furthermore, since what is passed on may be correct or incorrect it is not considered knowledge until the individual tests it for himself or herself.[98] Consequently, following the model of Cartesian doubt, questioning beliefs and traditions becomes the beginning of knowledge.[99] The role of the community, hence tradition, becomes diminished and the role of the individual expands to subsume the community role.[100] The empiricist tradition develops where individuals receive input from outside as though they themselves were blank sheets of paper.[101] Consequently, the religious sphere and inherited traditions become "underrated."[102]

Pannenberg takes note of the approach in Heidegger to consider that God is drawn into philosophy, yet as Pannenberg observes this involves a prior assumption that the divine idea is not already part of the reality philosophy seeks to describe.[103] In the discussion of *nonrational* knowledge, the realization that the concept of belief is part of human beingness was explored. It was noted that belief is communicated by the language of assent, assertion, and inference and is activated as knowledge in the life of a person when accepted from others. Thus *nonrational* knowledge is as much knowledge as the *rational* knowledge that is acquired in the development of the cogito. This knowledge in beliefs, traditions, and the culture of a person contribute, if not supply, the presuppositions with which the individual begins the quest for understanding of his or her world.

Thiselton contends that it is important to realize that an individual doesn't begin his or her quest for knowledge *de novo* as isolated from history and community.[104] A "shared public world" preexists, and the individual and his or her thinking is done from this basis.[105] This world not only provides a presuppositional framework, it also shapes "terms" on which the knowledge will be tested, thus conditioning what will be accepted as appropriate criteria for the evaluation of that knowledge.[106] Thomas Kuhn in *The Structure of Scientific Revolutions* notes that the role of history in science parallels the concept of tradition, which then becomes the context for the analysis of new theory.[107] This history is developed in the practice of science and is a contributing factor of the basis of what becomes recounted in textbooks that expound the body of

---

98. Ibid.
99. Ibid., 702.
100. Ibid.
101. Ibid.
102. Ibid.
103. Pannenberg, *Metaphysics*, 12.
104. Thiselton, *Thiselton On Hermeneutics*, 703.
105. Ibid.
106. Ibid.
107. Kuhn, *Structure of Scientific Revolutions*, 7.

accepted theory.[108] The student joins "men who learned the basis of their field from some concrete models."[109] Therefore, the student as a novice reads the textbooks and comes under the influence and impact of the "elders" of the community. Presumably the student believes what he or she is taught, and this becomes the basis from which the student will launch to form his or her own self-identity.

It would seem reasonable to suggest that a baby learns by ontological means before epistemological means; for example, a baby doesn't learn the word *mother* to understand what a mother is, but rather a baby learns the word *mother* to describe the knowledge he or she has obtained by belief through experience of interaction, hence listening, to the mother. This seems to be the principle of the novice, as noted by Thiselton and Kuhn, from differing fields, that is, that knowledge is first acquired by belief in listening and accepting, and this provides the presuppositional framework for the launching of the self. Therefore, the hermeneutical journey should begin in similar fashion. The interpreter listens as a novice, but with presuppositions that will orient himself or herself in the process. However, the questioning and epistemological approach is secondary not primary and is based upon a received world, the world of the text.

Listening to the Text

The concept of "listening" to a text presents a picture that is hard to visualize, yet Ong notes that in the reading of a text a form of verbalization occurs even if it is just in the imagination of the reader.[110] This observation opens the way for the application of performance interpretation. Unlike the situation of the text, it seems reasonable to assume that a person would have no conceptual difficulty with "watching and listening" to a DVD or "listening" to a CD of a speaker, as an actual act of listening. Yet all three are monologues not dialogues, and all three also involve an author not present; it is just that the DVD and CD create an illusion of proximity of the person of the speaker, who in reality is detached and removed. All three involve the "speaking" of an author; the text simply suffers from greater difficulty in imagining or conceiving a speaker.

The DVD and CD are the result of forms of digitalized information that is converted into sight and/or sound to represent the actual event. This is not a re-creation nor a restoration of the original event, because there is no author present. It is equally, with the text, a representation of the event. Therefore, there is no real difference other than perceptual. The perceptual difference occurs because of the loss of domains of knowledge in a movement from the DVD to the CD and then to the text.

In the movement from the DVD to the CD there is a loss of information of a particular form that requires the receptor to exercise his or her imagination to replace the

---

108. Ibid., 10.
109. Ibid., 11.
110. Ong, *Orality and Literacy*, 8.

visual and nonverbal communication. Using only the medium available, the author of a CD must consciously include audio elements like tone of voice, words, and so forth to compensate for the fact that a CD is not a DVD, which can portray both audio and visual information. In the movement from the CD to the text there is a further loss of information, that is, the loss of tone of voice and resultant emphases and attitudes within the delivery of the message. Here in the case of the text there is the maximum stimulation of the imagination of the receptor. The author in this situation, beginning with the writing of a text, must consciously deal with both these limitations with the means he or she has (i.e., words formed into sentences) to compose or message. The author of the text is seeking to stimulate the imagination of the reader to "fill-in" these missing domains of knowledge.

As a result the transcript of the text of a CD or DVD is not a composition (although it is a text) for the reason it lacks these domains; that is, the author has not composed the text to fulfill the visual and/or hearing acuity lost in the concept of the text.[111] The transcript can and most probably will contain answers to each of the five questions used as a basis for a hermeneutical inquiry. The author can be designated, and usually is for copyright purposes; the *when* and *where* are usually included in a transcript; and the text of the transcript can offer answers to *why* and *what*. Yet despite ticking all the boxes, as it were, the transcript does not qualify as a complete message and hence will fail to represent the "speaking" author in the same way as the DVD or CD. However, as suggested previously, there is no real conceptual difference between the text (as composition), the CD, and the DVD. Consequently, if the DVD and the CD has a "speaking" author, so does the text. When the composition is composed, as opposed to the situation of transcription, it is conceptually the same as the DVD and CD, that is, the continuation of discourse by other means. Therefore, it is reasonable to infer that conceptually the text, as a composition, has a "speaking" voice to which the reader listens.

The presentation of a "speaking" voice carries with it the assumption of an ability to hear the "speaking" voice with understanding, that is, a communicator assumes that the receptor will be able to understand the message.[112] This concept raises the issue of the "intended audience" as one that the author believes will be in a position to "listen" to the message communicated. Ricoeur is quite dismissive of this concept of intended audience and argues that it is irrelevant for whom the text was intended because the text can be picked up and read by anyone; that is, the audience is universal.[113] On the surface Ricoeur's claim seems to have a certain validity and forcefulness.

---

111. This issue has been discussed at length previously in chapters 2 and 3 concerning the issue of *rational, arational,* and *nonrational* knowledge.

112. Schleiermacher, *Hermeneutics*, 58. Schleiermacher asserts, "No text is intended in such a way that its hearers could not possibly understand."

113. Ricoeur, *Interpretation Theory*, 92.

However, this view is from the viewpoint of the reader not the author, who it can be agreed has no means of controlling who reads the text.

Yet in respect to meaning in relationship to a text, Ricoeur's observation can be at least brought into question through some simple illustrations. It is admitted that all of these illustrations involve texts that are intentionally not released as universal, which can seem therefore to be a trivializing of Ricoeur's views, or even to be a ruse. However, the concept of detachment of the text from the author, so important in the work of Ricoeur, is not based on an intention of the author to have a universally intended audience. The truth is quite the opposite; Ricoeur is simply noting that the release of the text creates a happenstance of universal release, whatever the intention of the author.[114] The intention of the author in regard to audience is immaterial; universal audience is simply what occurred. Consequently, it is proposed that the following illustrations do highlight an important issue concerning intentionality.

In this modern age of the Internet, many people, if not most in some societies, have an e-mail address. This address ensures that an e-mail message can be uniquely sent to them as an intended audience. However, mistakes can and do happen which cause e-mails to arrive at the wrong e-mail address. As a result e-mail messages often contain a disclaimer that essentially states that if the recipient is not the intended recipient, then the mistaken recipient should delete the e-mail. This is not necessarily an attempt to forbid or even stop the recipient from reading the e-mail, particularly because the disclaimer is often at the conclusion of the e-mail message itself. This disclaimer is to alert the recipient to the fact that the message is not intended for him or her. In that circumstance either the e-mail message will have no relevance to the recipient, or the recipient may not be in a position to really understand the contents of the message.

Also, when postal mail is received into the household mailbox or into a post office box, if the mail is not addressed to the resident or renter of the post office box, then most likely it was placed there by mistake. That piece of mail is not intended for the person who received it. Generally, that piece of mail is returned to the postal service unopened, and indeed in most countries it is considered illegal to open a piece of mail when a person is not the intended audience. That piece of mail does not apply to that person, and he or she is an unintended recipient of that mail.

The same is true of the very concept of censorship, where there is an assumed responsibility to make sure that some things can only be placed in the hands of particular individuals and are not allowed to reach an unintended audience; that is, censored materials are only allowed to a specific audience who therefore become, by default, the intended audience. In this case the intended audience is determined not necessarily from the authorial side but the reader's side, yet the principle is exactly the same. Finally, government censorship is often undertaken with a stated basis of purely

---

114. This concept in Ricoeur has been previously referred to in ch. 7, sect: The Detachment of Presence.

being that the unintended recipient is not in command of sufficient information to understand the communication, especially in context. In the case of businesses and governments, the author of a text can feel that the contents are personal so as to only be properly understood by the intended recipient.

These examples illustrate that there can be an intended audience for whom an author anticipates his or her message will be relevant and understandable, and even conversely that an unintended audience may not be in a position to understand the message. Just because a text is generally released (i.e., able to be availed by a universal audience) does not inherently imply that the author cannot have an intended audience, nor does it negate or exclude the author having an intended audience. The universal release can be an author's means of reaching an unknown yet intended audience, that is, one that will identify with the world of the text. Therefore, universal release can simply be a means, and may have no sense of indication of intention. Whatever the reasons for its universal release, the universal availability of a text cannot negate any intentionality. The question of intentionality, as what is listened to, must be considered.

10 Intentionality and Authorial Intention

The "Speaking" Voice

Introduction

THISELTON NOTES THAT THE "very idea" of authorial intention has been the recipient of "a series of heavy attacks" that make its discussion complex.[1] He further observes that the "traditional view has not been helped by the insistence of Gadamer and Ricoeur that once a text has been committed to writing, it no longer 'belongs' to the horizon of the author."[2] Hence, to even discuss authorial intention in the era of postmodern thought is considered passé. However, as noted in previous chapters, the detachment emphasized in postmodern thought is conceded and recognized. Yet the subsequent assertion of the autonomous text, with respect to both author and intended audience, which is the critical distinction as highlighted in Ricoeur, is not conceded. In fact, the notion of automous text is tenuous and is unable to be successfully demonstrated. Such a position also assumes a particular view of authorial intent, which is that it is identified as an attribute indistinguishable from the psyche of the author. This approach has also only assessed authorial intent from an epistemological viewpoint, whereas our examination discloses authorial intent's ontological nature.

There are two inherent questions that present themselves in the very term "authorial intent." First, how is the term "authorial intent" to be taken? Authorial intent involves two substantives that have become one term, which itself is used as substantive, that is one speaks of *the* authorial intent in the discussion. Second, how is this term to be viewed with respect to the very idea of intentionality?

---

1. Thiselton, *New Horizons*, 38.
2. Ibid.

The Term "Authorial Intent"

It is important to point out what is not intended to be covered in this section, because in the modern-postmodern setting even the phrase "authorial intent" can conjure a variety of responses and hence assumptions on what is being discussed. An assertion of Thiselton's was referred to in an earlier chapter concerning the nature of authorial intent, that is, how it is to be perceived in the light of current (and past) theory. He observes that the term "intent" is best seen adverbially and "*to write with an intention is to write in a way that is directed towards a goal.*"[3] His reasoning is that unequivocally "for Wittgenstein and for Searle, and implicitly for Schleiermacher, 'to intend' a linguistic meaning is emphatically *not to perform some action or process separable from the linguistic act or process itself.*"[4] He then takes note that Wittgenstein's dismissiveness of the idea of "intend to" as an imperative is a far-fetched idea (i.e., one assumes as a directive to the hearer).[5] Hence, Thiselton and Vanhoozer,[6] as prominent evangelical writers and theologians, especially on this topic, are faced with the terminus of the pursuit of the authorial intent at the *what*; that is, as the work of Ricoeur has ably demonstrated, this pursuit of authorial intent terminates in the descriptive semantic task of linguistics. Therefore, evaluation of authorial intent as adverbial is a description of *what* the author has done in writing the text. This semantic task is a wrong direction.

Vanhoozer defines a text as "*a communicative act of a communicative agent fixed by writing.*"[7] A section of *Is There a Meaning in This Text?* concerns what Vanhoozer styles as "speech rehabilitation," which is that speech, or discourse, has the nature of action.[8] His object is to arrive at a place where he can pursue meaning, in relation to a text, as "a matter of communicative action," concerning both the "doing" of the act and the resultant text, or "deed," that is, by implication what is done in the act.[9] Hence, a text is "communicative action fixed by writing" wherein is inscribed "propositional content" and "energy," or "illocutionary force"; and there is a momentum about texts such that allows the impact of the author in interpretation of that text.[10] The implied parallel with the concepts developed in speech-act theory,

---

3. Ibid., 560. (Italics original.)

4. Ibid., 559. (Italics original.)

5. Ibid.

6. Vanhoozer, *Is There a Meaning*, 39. Vanhoozer states that language "is a kind of sacrament, a means of communicating meaning through verbal signs." He views both author and reader as citizens of language and both are bound to the observation and respect of the boundaries and operation of language, 204.

7. Ibid., 225. (Italics original.)

8. Ibid., 207–18.

9. Ibid., 218. The implication of the text as the "done" of the action is based on his continuing discussion, 220, where he is distinguishing between action and event. The concept of a deliberate action done itself implies intentionality.

10. Ibid., 229.

especially in the work of Austin and Searle (whom Vanhoozer likens as the Luther and Melanchthon of speech act philosophy), to those of the locutionary, illocutionary, and perlocutionary is evident.[11]

Ricoeur, in his theory, discusses the contribution of the recognition of these speech acts.[12] In his discussion he sets the basis for his assertion that the locutionary act is the most easily inscribable of these acts, as it "exteriorizes itself in the sentence." The illocutionary act, due to its ability to be misunderstood, presents more difficulties in inscription. The perlocutionary act is the "least inscribable."[13] The perlocutionary act, or what is achieved in the speaking (e.g., fear, persuasion, seduction, joy, and so on) is such that the nonlinguistic has priority over the linguistic, and it is less an intentional act on behalf of the author than it is a stimulus.[14] The other acts relate to intentionality, but it is in terms of what is achieved, that is, the adverbial sense of "intentionally," and not in terms of the psychological aspect of intention that remains with the author in the detachment of the text from the author.[15]

Vanhoozer does note that the perlocutionary act can have a sense of intentionality, as is evidenced in the Gospel of John.[16] However, largely one would have to agree with Ricoeur, for whatever perlocutionary act an author may intend, the perlocutionary act performed by the reader, that is, the impact of the speaking, is more problematic in linkage with the intention of the author. The important aspect of this discussion is that in Vanhoozer's work the problem identified by Ricoeur, and discussed previously, of the capture of the agent by the something that occurs, in emphasis upon the act, is not overcome. Certainly in Vanhoozer's work the consideration of speech as act does raise the issue of the agent of the action, the *who* of the text, but in the manner of the ontology of impersonal event. In this ontological paradigm, intentionality is adverbial and so authorial intent is that which is achieved in the appearance of the text and is not an aspect of reflection in the text identifying the agent. Furthermore, the discussion remains at the linguistic level, and in semantics the opaqueness of the referential approach prevents the perception of the agent as a *who*. However, in reflection, which does focus on the person, there is an opaqueness that obscures the *what* of the text, unless there is an ontological movement to that of impersonal event.

---

11. Ibid., 209. Vanhoozer discusses this in the lead up to his concepts. This emphasis on speech-acts is a strong feature of his analysis and proposals, and is referred to a number of times in this book and other works by Vanhoozer.

12. Ricoeur, *Interpretation Theory*, 14–19.

13. Ibid., 27–28. The possibility of misunderstanding with the illocutionary act is because one illocutionary act can be mistaken for another, yet it is inscribable by various "linguistic marks," 17. Further, in "spoken discourse the illocutionary force depends on mimicry and gesture, and upon the non-articulated aspects of discourse, which we call prosody," 27.

14. Ibid., 18.

15. Ibid. In this work Ricoeur does not refer to this concept of intentionality, i.e., as adverbial, but does discuss it at some length in *Oneself as Another*, which will be discussed concerning "Intention."

16. Vanhoozer, *Is There a Meaning*, 224. This concept in relationship to this text of John's Gospel is considered earlier in this thesis, 59–60.

The term "authorial intent," having become itself a substantive, hence a total concept, is composed of the substantives "author" and "intent." In this there is a recognition of agent, a *who*, and intent, a mental directedness of attention resulting in an action. Vanhoozer has sought to maintain that balance between person and action that results in the text. His discussion of the four concepts of agency of the author and conceptual ways of dealing with the idea of presence of the author are innovative and well presented.[17] Certainly his discussion of the possibility of being able to conceive of the presence of the author in relationship to the text offers ideas for understanding the "speaking voice" that is listened to, as discussed previously.[18] As far as the basic concept of the author and his or her intent is concerned, there can be large agreement and consent, subsequently this issue does not need recounting here.

Vanhoozer suggests, "Authorial intention is always located in a network of beliefs and practices that form the background for communicative action."[19] Hence, his suggestion is similar to that suggested in this work, where it has been suggested that the way to view the authorial intent is as a referent of the text. He indicates that largely his view is similar to "intent" in the work of Hirsch; that is, the authorial intent and resultant meaning is fixed in the text and remains the standard against which interpretation occurs.[20] However, in acknowledging this as a standard, he also acknowledges room for maneuverings concerning relevant meaning to readers and interpreters. This is similar to that which has been argued in this work; the authorial intent represents an absolute but the reader/interpreter is always dealing with a relative meaning of that absolute.

In this work the point of departure is not an issue with authorial intent, as discussed previously, but rather in taking note of the following issues in this discussion. The author remains a person only conceptually and undergoes the stripping of personhood to be discussed as a something. Also, note is taken that this concept weaves in and around speech act concepts of the locutionary, illocutionary, and perlocutionary acts, which are disclosed linguistically and remain in the domain of semantics, despite the inclusion of analogical note being taken of the linguistics, which nevertheless still remains descriptive. Consequently, although there is much to agree with, the

---

17. Ibid., 201–80. This chapter of his book "Resurrecting the Author: Meaning As Communicative Action" represents a very penetrating analysis and strong argument for the concept of authorial intent. As he states, "I believe in the reality of the author's intention, for without it I cannot explain the emergence of meaning, that is to say, how meaning supervenes on written marks," 249.

18. Ibid., 237–40. As he notes, his development uses literary and linguistic notions to mediate this presence, thus placing the ideas within the province of textual considerations, 238. However, his examples and argument are in particular using analogies from scriptural concepts and probably for this reason, and quite unjustly, would not be widely considered in general hermeneutics. Although as discussed in Gadamer's work, whose work is decidedly not from a religious perspective, Gadamer takes note of the importance of the contribution of the impact of the Christian concept of incarnation to the philosophical aspect of hermeneutics, see *Truth and Method*, 379.

19. Ibid., 249.

20. Ibid., 259–63.

problematic remains that the *what* is not traversed to arrive at the *who*. Hence, for all the desire of recognition of the agent, and the implication of the agent's presence as concept, the process terminates at the *what* of the text, which, as Ricoeur has explored, remains unsatisfactory in pursuit of answering the *who* question.

This situation leaves the interpreter with a passion for the agent, and his or her place in the meaning of the texts written, but also confronts the interpreter with an inability to get around the problematic of the something and the subsequent dismissal of the person of the author into simply an effect on the text. What is needed is a way to traverse the "why?-what?" without either transgressing it or transcending it.

Transgression of this semantic approach would lose all the powerful and valuable work done in the descriptive referential understanding revealed in the epistemological semantic approach. This embraces the full breadth of genre, historicity of both author and audience, and their importance to semantics and, subsequently, the meaning exposed in the epistemological approach. In the work of Vanhoozer, all the questions receive due attention and respect toward an understanding of what the author intentionally means, and the resultant impact on meaning of this in the fusion with the horizon of the interpreter in dealing with the text. The adverbial form "intentionally" is used purposefully to distinguish it from the concepts to be developed beyond the descriptive task.

Equally, transcending this issue would call into play a special hermeneutic and place the argument outside the concepts of general hermeneutics. This renders the answer as religious and irrelevant in general discussion, thereby excluding the writer, operating from a Christian perspective, having voice in so-called "secular" discussions, for example, those in science, sociology, and psychology. This is equally unsatisfactory, so what is needed is a traversing of this issue so that in the Christian setting one can propose a special use of a hermeneutical principle.

A possible illustration is that of aerodynamics. A plane flies not in a transgression of the law of gravity, nor in transcending it by some law/principle operating outside the temporal nature of gravity. Rather, the principles of aerodynamics allow the plane to traverse the problem, and so the plane flies. Hence, as Ricoeur notes, the way forward is ontological not epistemological, but in a way that traverses not transcends. Consequently, the answer must involve linguistic marks, so as not to transgress (in the illustration, aerodynamics actually makes use of gravity but also brings other factors into operation).

However, the answer does involve an alternate ontological view to that of impersonal event. The title given to this section is "The Term 'Authorial Intent,'" and it has been noted that the two substantives (i.e., author and intent) have ontological and epistemological implications respectively. Consequently, the place to begin, so as to traverse rather than transgress or transcend, is the term that can allow the discussion to "take off" and not be "earth bound" in the descriptive or epistemological task (i.e., intent), since to begin with the ontological aspect risks a seeming transcendence.

Intention: Intentionality and "Intention To"

Vanhoozer notes that, despite Ricoeur's apparent dismissal of authorial intention in interpretation, in his analysis he often makes reference to the author, which shows an awareness of the author.[21] Ricoeur is neither a denier nor despiser of the author, nor does he deny that there is an authorial intention, but for Ricoeur it is part of the fleeting event that perishes in the event of discourse.[22] All three of the primary authors considered in the work, Vanhoozer, Thiselton, and Ricoeur, firmly reject linking the concept of authorial intent to the Romanticist idea of authorial intent, that is, as in the superintending concept of a foreign psyche. Yet, both Vanhoozer and Thiselton hold positive, though differing, views on authorial intent and its importance to hermeneutics. Conversely, Ricoeur regards authorial intent not only as inaccessible but unnecessary to interpretation. In fact by escaping this horizon of the author the text enters a whole new field of possibilities and it is here that, for Ricoeur, hermeneutics in dealing with texts really begins, i.e. the "autonomous text."[23]

Certainly a significant factor in this view adopted by Ricoeur is that of the relationship of the authorial intent to the person of the author. Understanding this relationship, for Ricoeur, means looking for something hidden behind the text that exerts a controlling influence over meaning and restricting the reader, then trying to relate that to the consciousness of the author.[24] On this aspect Vanhoozer and Thiselton would be in agreement, so this reasoning doesn't offer a complete picture of Ricoeur's rejection of authorial intent. As noted previously, an important aspect of Ricoeur's study of the hermeneutics of the self in *Oneself as Another* was his realization that in pursuit of the hermeneutical task, the concept of the person of the author (i.e., *who*), the question becomes deferred, and the process of semantics leads to a capture of the person to a conceptual semantic reference.

Hence, in the descriptive task everything flows downhill to the *what*. And as suggested in this work, this becomes terminal. The person is never realized as being, but rather only as concept; that is, a possible description of *what* the being is with no understanding of the *who* of being is as an agent. The arrival at this point causes the analysis of Ricoeur's concept of "an agentless semantics of action," to arrive at an ontological category that by its very nature is exclusive of the category of selfhood. This is the ontology of the impersonal event.[25] Essentially, this precludes the concept of a consciousness impacting meaning in the descriptive task; it would need to transcend or transgress to impact meaning.

---

21. Ibid., 214, 16. Ricoeur's understanding on this has been dealt with at length in previous chapters.

22. Ibid., 215.

23. Ricoeur, *Interpretation Theory*, 29–30. One would almost imagine that had Ricoeur discovered that it was knowable and had impact, it would have been a source of disappointment to him.

24. Ibid., 92.

25. Ricoeur, *Oneself*, 60–61.

It is through the discussion of intention, which begins in a consciousness, that the adverbial nature of intention is disclosed, in a seeking of the relationship between agent and action. Ricoeur notes that one would expect that "a conceptual analysis of intention would lead from the pair "what?-why?" to the question *who*: "Is not intention, phenomenologically speaking, the aiming of a consciousness in the direction of something I am to do?"[26] The answer is that despite the seeming implied direction, it does not follow this course. If one is concerned with public meaning, not private, there is a turning from this seemingly logical direction phenomenologically speaking.[27] The public meaning, accessible in language, can only be related to accomplished intention, that is, an act done intentionally.[28] The concept of "intention-to" is what is private and without declaration remains that way, so that no one can know what undeclared intentions a person may or may not have.[29] The concept of "intention-to" is a statement of future conditions and the only temporal aspect that can be given occurs if there is a declaration of it, hence giving it temporal embodiment.[30]

Ricoeur shows that analysis of intention is possible if three basic understandings of intention are recognized: the action that has been done with intention, the action being undertaken with intention, and the declaration of "intention-to."[31] The first two situations are qualifications of an action that has or is being observed and therefore results in the adverbial sense of intention.[32] Thiselton's observation concerning his own assessment is that this sense is how authorial intent should be understood, that is, the adverbial sense, as noted previously, which may stem from this reasoning. He does not mention this aspect of Ricoeur's work in this analysis, so it seems an independent yet similar conclusion. As Ricoeur notes, this usage of intention is one "that exemplifies in the least explicit way the relation of interpretation to the agent." The concept "intention-to" closely relates to that of the agent, but qualifying the action as done intentionally can be examined independently to any consideration of the agent possessing the intention.[33] The consideration of intentional in this case, as a qualifier of the action, concerns the "what?" (as part of the "what?-why?") of the action, and is able to be disclosed by the question "why?" as an explanation of what was done, and as a result the analysis leads further away from the question of the agent.[34]

In Ricoeur's opinion the obliteration of the question *who* by the emphasis on "what?-why?" occurs because the "exclusive concern with the truth of the description"

26. Ibid., 67.
27. Ibid., 68.
28. Ibid.
29. Ibid.
30. Ibid.
31. Ibid.
32. Ibid.
33. Ibid.
34. Ibid., 68, 70.

Intentionality and Authorial Intention

tends to overshadow interest in assigning action to the agent.[35] Ricoeur observes that, in his view, it is due to the "style of analytical philosophy and to its almost exclusive preoccupation with description, as well as with truth claims appropriate to description, that it ignores problems pertaining to attestation."[36] The concept of attestation of the "intention-to" relates to truthfulness, rather than a description of truth as knowledge, relating therefore to the person and, hence in Ricoeur, to the phenomenological dimension rather than descriptive approach.[37] This discloses the form of the sense of intention that captures, or "privileges," the agent, which does not occur in the adverbial sense. This creates a form of frustration in the desire to pursue authorial intent, as the intention of a person, for the interpreter in the task of interpretation of the text, when it is pursued primarily as an action that intentionally results in the creation of the text.

The treatment of intention adverbially, therefore as qualifying the action, allows it to be subordinated to the descriptive task of the completed event.[38] Even with the use of the first person pronoun (e.g., "I intentionally struck the blow"), the past tense verb directs attention to the objective side of the intention, and hence the answer to the question *why* privileges the action side not the agent, since it will focus on the blow struck; that is, it requires an explanation that will focus on the descriptive side, which is that of the action.[39] The intention has occurred prior to the action but was not in the public arena. This also provides a natural division between the idea of action done intentionally and action done with the "intention-to," which is a forward looking.[40] It is this substantive use of the idea of intention that has direct reference to the agent, that is, "intention-to," or intent.

Ricoeur considers the verb tenses used, which in the case of intentionally done action is basically always the past tense, but in the case of "intention-to" in the substantive form the verb tense that is used is the future tense.[41] Therefore, the difference that is the cause of the two senses (i.e., adverbial and substantive) is primarily one of temporality.[42] Ricoeur therefore raises the issue that the concept of the adverbial usage, the intention with which something is done, is in reality a weak form of "intention-to," since the intention was logically formed before the action. It is purely a matter of temporal appearance of the event that is the difference between the two. He notes that where a null delay apparently occurs (i.e., between formation of intention and event), if a person is asked after the event whether or not something was done intentionally,

---

35. Ibid., 72.
36. Ibid.
37. Ibid., 72–73.
38. Ibid., 75.
39. Ibid., 70.
40. Ibid.
41. Ibid., 79.
42. Ibid. This is the basis of the discussion following in this paragraph.

the person's answer will be expressed in the form of an "intention-to." The reason for the action is "intention-to" in the sense that, had the person deliberated, this is the intention with which the action would have been done.

The issue becomes: what device can be used to highlight the agent in this recognition? The concept of motivation in its relationship to intention brings up the issue of judgment, especially the idea of unconditional judgment as that which engages action in relationship to intention.[43] In this situation the agent whose intention it is comes into view. When this view is taken, actions that take time unfold in a sense of anticipation, as in the example Ricoeur uses where the writer of a poem in writing each verse already intends the poem in its entirety. Ricoeur notes that "the anticipated future transiting through the present in the direction of a completed past."[44] The concept of "intention-to" is no longer a simple qualification of action, and so relates directly to the agent. The adverbial usage, privileged in the ontology of events, in this situation has called for an alternate ontological approach as a basis for moving beyond the adverbial usage of intention.[45] This ontology "would be that of being in the making, possessing de jure the problematic of selfhood."[46]

Authorial Intent: The Ontological Route

Two important observations can be made that are each significant in the discussion of authorial intent and its relationship to hermeneutics. First, in the case of the subject under discussion in this section, that is, that of authorial intent, the discussion of "intention" raises an important issue. Namely, the concept of authorial intent that is based on examining what the author intentionally did has focused on the weaker side of the concept of intent, having been focused on the adverbial sense. The reason this has occurred is the inherent assumption of the ontology of events imposed by the nature of the inquiry, that is, the descriptive semantic task. It is therefore argued in this work that an ontological approach to authorial intent will be far more fruitful in making the connection with intention as substantive, hence personal, and interpretation.

Each of the three main authors concerned has acknowledged that the interpretive process should not introduce the connection of the consciousness of the author

43. Ibid., 82.
44. Ibid.
45. Ibid., 85.

46. Ibid., 86. The concept of selfhood, in dealing with the subject of identity, is that of *ipse*-identity as opposed to *idem*-identity, which Ricoeur links to the ontology of events. These concepts of identity flow throughout the book as basic reference points. The initial distinction is that *idem* is sameness, the sense of permanence in time; this is contrasted with the idea of temporal *ipse* (selfhood), hence changing and variable, but still the same one, *idem*-identity. For example, at any stage in a life, e.g., youth, middle age, or old age, there is a difference in selfhood, the person in time, but it is the same person at each stage. Hence, the concept of selfhood portrays an unfolding ontology, a developing being, yet each point in time is unique. The treatment of actions tends to portray these selfhoods as the same entities descriptively.

as a direct implication. However, the author and the reader/interpreter both possess a consciousness, and whilst it is not reasonable to assume that the text connects the consciousness of one to the other, it is reasonable to believe that the author seeks some empathetic identification with the consciousness of the interpreter, and similarly for the interpreter with that of the author. As Vanhoozer notes, the interpreter can seek to recover thoughts of the author "not by psychological intuition but by historical inference—by an analysis of the author's *public* communicative action."[47] It is interesting to note that Vanhoozer recognizes the importance of the consciousness of the author, and seeks to use the only means seemingly available, which is the semantic descriptive basis. However, what is also inherent in his observation is that the consciousness that he seeks to connect with is that of rational objective knowledge, that is, what Gadamer recognized as historical consciousness. However, what should be recognized is that it is a basic aspect of being that humanity has an *ontic*-consciousness,[48] and it is with this consciousness that the connection should be sought for the purpose Vanhoozer seeks. Hence, if this is to be related to the communicative action of the author, what must be considered is the language of this consciousness.

The second inference that can be drawn, which is no less significant, especially in the Christian community in dealing with sacred text, if not any religious community, concerns the traversing of the *what* by moving to an alternate ontological framework. In examining the semantics of the text, note was taken of the three acts, that is, the locutionary, illocutionary, and perlocutionary acts. Ricoeur noted that there was a decreasing tendency to be inscribable, with the perlocutionary act being difficult to inscribe. Hence, the semantic route terminates in the *what* of the text at the perlocutionary act.

Vanhoozer proposes what he terms a "fourth dimension" of speech act, the interlocutionary act.[49] Ricoeur, who relates the interlocutionary act to the instance of dialogue, also covers this concept, that is, someone says something to someone.[50] It would seem in Vanhoozer's thinking that the interlocutionary act restores the concept of personhood to the process. However, with the written text there is no interlocutor, unless the text itself is considered the interlocutor, or middleman. Hence, despite Vanhoozer's attempt to restore personhood, the process still terminates in the *what*, that is, in the three acts noted previously.

---

47. Vanhoozer, *Is There a Meaning*, 230.

48. This term has been developed in this work as one that shows the nature of the aspect of consciousness involved.

49. Vanhoozer, *Is There a Meaning*, 219.

50. Ricoeur, *Interpretation Theory*, 14.

Is There An Author in this Text?

(a) Moving from What to Who

In consideration of the ontological nature of the authorial intent, the opportunity arises to traverse the *what* and connect with a *who*. In Ricoeur's final chapter of *Oneself as Another*, he develops the concept of the *self* being able to perceive itself as *other than self*.[51] Hence, the otherness in view is not another person; it is the same person who perceives self as other than self.[52] Ricoeur has his own agenda in this discussion in which his topic is the hermeneutics of the self. However, in the present discussion concerning the hermeneutics of texts, it is suggested that this *other* that is recognized as *other* is potentially the self having been impacted by the original author. This is not as fanciful as it may seem when Ricoeur's own analysis of the end point of his interpretive theory is considered.

Ricoeur's theory doesn't consider the concept of authorial intent as impacting meaning, yet he does claim that the end result is closer to original intention of Schleiermacher's desire. This has been noted before but bears repeating in this context: that to "understand an author better than he could understand himself is to display the power of disclosure implied in his discourse beyond the limited horizon of his own existential situation."[53] Ricoeur, without consideration of authorial intent, believes that the message he sees is what the author would have seen had he escaped his horizon. In other words, Ricoeur can see the *other*, that is, the original author, within himself, in the sense of what the author would have seen. Consequently, if the *what* is traversed through the ontological route, the self sees itself as *other* than self, that is, as a self impacted by the original author. This is a primary aim of the scriptural text. The authorial intent, as an ontological entity, can be in a position to impart the being necessary to empower the reader toward a changed view of self.

One other aspect of Ricoeur's analysis that is relevant to this discussion is his nonrecognition of the ontological beginning of the process. This is evidenced at the beginning of the fifth study, "Personal Identity and Narrative Identity."[54] The process begins as a descriptive task and it is through the application of narrative that there is a movement to the prescriptive task (i.e., assigning of action to an agent).[55] Narrative is the link that can affect the transition from the descriptive, the *what*, to the

---

51. Ricoeur, *Oneself*, 317–19. (Italics added.) Ricoeur's "engine room," as it were, that confers an ability to see self as other than self without some form of split personality is uncovered in a convoluted discussion in a section called "Selfhood and Ontology," 302–17. In essence what confers upon the individual this dialectic nature is what Ricoeur calls "*a ground at once actual and potentiality,*" 315 (italics original). The occurrence of these things at the same time is that which discloses a dialectic of self and otherness, yet being the same person who is also other, 317.

52. Ibid., 318.

53. Ricoeur, *Interpretation Theory*, 93.

54. Ricoeur, *Oneself*, 113–39.

55. Ibid., 114.

prescriptive, the *who*.⁵⁶ However, no consideration is given to the fact that a narrative is listened to so as to achieve the very ends Ricoeur seeks. Ricoeur's process in the search for the understanding of the self begins essentially on a Cartesian basis, that is, it begins with the being of "I" as a given that will be explored.

Roger Lundin points out that Descartes's approach first establishes his own certainty, which then becomes the basis from which, beginning from his own self-consciousness, he will prove the existence of God and the external world.⁵⁷ Lundin notes, including himself in the postmodern era, that the postmodern person has developed the habit of defining self "over against the history from which we have emerged and against which we contend," as is evidenced by the penchant for the prefixing of "post-" to terms.⁵⁸ The theme of Lundin's text is that of the fatherless state humanity finds itself in after Descartes, with the result that life is outworked from self, or as an orphan.⁵⁹ The effect of beginning from a Cartesian basis (i.e., a model that begins with self and ends in the hermeneutics of the self) means Ricoeur's hermeneutics are that of the orphan,⁶⁰ whatever his belief system, and in this there needs to be a caution in the understanding of his work. Consequently, there is a dimension that is missing in the beginning of the process, and this absence impacts by exerting a gravitational-like effect upon the work.

It should be axiomatic that being comes from being, since existence as a self begins with the conferral of being by another, that is, parents. Jesus, in explaining the concept of existence as a Christian, did not employ a special hermeneutic from outside the world, but made special use of the illustration of being born from within the world, John 3:1–15. It is noticeable that what Jesus told Nicodemus is not so much what he had to do as what had to happen to him; that is, being a Christian begins in the otherness of God. Hence, ontological understanding comes not from a descriptive process, nor a prescriptive process as ascription from self, it comes from that which is other. Ascription, in the sense of confession, is what allows the creation of being, or what brings being into reality in a life. Nonetheless, the act of ascription is based on what has been received from that which is other, not the ability of the Cartesian "I" to acquire the knowledge through descriptive means. Simply stating the situation one can experience the biblical dynamic of salvation, thus giving it being in the life, without a comprehensive understanding. This is not mystical, in the sense of outside this world, but is an appropriation within the world of otherness, from a special use (which is mystical or spiritual) of the ontic nature that is part of human being.

56. Ibid.

57. Lundin, "Interpreting Orphans," 12. It is interesting to note that Ricoeur's book, *Oneself as Another*, immediately moves to a discussion of the cogito from the introduction, setting out the basic direction of his study.

58. Ibid., 15.

59. Ibid., 3.

60. Ricoeur, *Conflict of Interpretations* 17. Ricoeur acknowledges the Cartesian cogito as a basis of his thought in the pursuit of the hermeneutics of self.

Ricoeur in one sense recognizes this in saying, "hermeneutics is thus, explicitly or implicitly, self-understanding by means of understanding others."[61] Consequently, he is seemingly recognizing that the basis of understanding self is indeed seeing both others in self and self in others. For instance, a basic tenet of Judeo-Christian thought is that humanity is made in the image of God (Gen 1:26–27). Yet Ricoeur, having said this, notes that his thinking begins with the "I" of Cartesian thought, which demonstrates that, although the resultant perception is of the other, that which is other is first object not person. This is critical as Ricoeur's approach begins not based upon the ontology of a person, but on the ontology of impersonal events, and has to make an ontological "switch" in the midst of the process to perceive the person.

In what should be the paradigm, the process begins with the ontology of the person and moves to that of impersonal events for the descriptive phase, to return to the ontology of the person in the assimilation into being. In this paradigm, although the perception of otherness at the end is seen within the concept of selfhood, it is expressly understanding of another person. Hence, in this paradigm of hermeneutics the impersonal nature of the author in the descriptive phase is rectified and reconciled in the final ontological phase. In this way the perception is not the author made in the image of self, but self perceived reflected in the image of the author.[62]

This statement requires some qualification since it does not involve "the self" becoming the author but rather the perception of the potential of self in the other, that is, the author. The decision to assimilate that likeness is that of appropriation. In hermeneutical conception this involves having seen what the author is saying, hence what the author meant, within the perspective of self and not as an absolute. This makes the meaning of the author understandable to the self, which is then given meaning within the world of self. God having made man in his image begins the process on the ontology of the person and not as object, that is, not in an impersonal ontology of events. However, this is not so that the interpreter is assimilated into God's world but rather so that God's world is assimilated into the world of the interpreter. It is this critical nuance that Ricoeur's work has highlighted.

(b) A Biblical Indicator in Traversing the What

The perception of the self in the divine first requires a divine condescension, whether that is the revelation of God through his speaking in the biblical text or the person of Jesus Christ (Heb 1:1–3). Extending this beyond Judeo-Christian understanding, the metaphysics of presence means otherness as anterior, whether or not this otherness is

---

61. Ibid.

62. It is the view of the author of this work that the former situation occurs in the paradigm suggested by Ricoeur, i.e. the author made in the image of self; not the latter suggested in this work, i.e. self seen in the image of the author. This is not meant in any way to be a pejorative remark, due to a tremendous respect for his work, merely an observational conclusion.

conceptually a person or not. In the metaphysics of absence, as set out in the work of Derrida, the only person one looks back and sees is self as one was before the game of linguistics began. Beyond self there is only "*pure absence*—not the absence of this or that, but the absence of everything in which all presence is announced."[63] Consequently, the first movement that should be made in the interpretative task is not that of assertion of a Cartesian "I" but that of openness to otherness, whether that otherness is presence or absence (where the otherness is simply a total absence of anything or anyone), for in Derrida it is the absence that "can *inspire*, in other words, can *work*, and make one work."[64]

Accordingly, although the text presents itself in an ontology of impersonal event, as highlighted in the work of Ricoeur, the Being of the being of this impersonal ontology, is an assumption of a *nonrational* knowableness, which will be the basis of what is essentially a process of *a priori* reasoning in the hermeneutical process. This is true for both the authors and the hermeneuts. However, concerning the composition of the text, the authors are the ones attributing being and the hermeneuts are dealing with being that is attributed and presented to themselves.

Interestingly enough, it is Ricoeur's thought that provides an initial understanding of how a person can be brought into an ontological event and how it is communicated. His proposal is the idea of the symbol.[65] Ricoeur uses narrative to act in this way between description and prescription in the preceding discussion; it operates between them allowing a form of communication that allows one to traverse to the other.[66] Ricoeur examines the concept of mimesis in the fictional narrative, using the word mimetic to demonstrate the conjunction "between fiction and the representation of the real."[67] He notes the use in Aristotle as mimesis of human action in poetics; however, Ricoeur observes that this should not be understood as simply imitation, in the sense of copying an existing model.[68] Ricoeur proposes that what is in view is a "creative imitation" so that what mimesis imitates is not "the effectivity of events but their logical structure, their meaning."[69] The idea is not reduplication of reality but the representation of humanity as better than in reality, and hence mimesis "is a kind of metaphor of reality."[70] It is a disclosure of potentiality for the self in the mimetic performance. Ricoeur does not allude to it, yet this seems to be the basic idea of the hero. This concept would seem to be often employed by authors who write fiction to

63. Derrida, *Writing*, 8.
64. Ibid.
65. Ricoeur, *Conflict of Interpretations*, 16. This concept of Ricoeur's and its development has been discussed in chapter 4 of this work on the nature of authorial intent in the interpretive process.
66. Ricoeur, *Oneself* 114. This is a theme of the chapter "Personal Identity and Narrative Identity," 113–39.
67. Ricoeur, *Hermeneutics* 291.
68. Ibid., 292.
69. Ibid.
70. Ibid.

sell books, but in the writing attempt to present life in a particular light, which may be intended to be reflected into the life of the reader by the author or, alternatively, can be intended by the reader in the light of what he or she has read.

There is a resonance with a scriptural principle in what Ricoeur articulates in the instance of fiction. In both Jas 1:22–25 and 2 Cor 3:17–18, the concept is presented of a person looking into a mirror, where the mirror is the biblical text, and who sees in the mirror a better reality of what he or she can be, and is then encouraged that the potential they see is not only realizable but it is achievable within the horizon of their life. Therefore, as Ricoeur indicates concerning mimesis, there is a creative imitation that results in an incorporation of a self as potential into a self as actual. The passage supports the view that there is a potentiality for a movement from the representation to the real that is, the world of the text is what is real and achievable, not an ideal beyond the person. The person is projected forward into the world of the text and understanding has moved from an epistemological basis to an ontological basis that is, what was represented has become being of the person.

This is Ricoeur's view on what true interpretation should be about. The epistemological concerns of the hermeneutical task, which are genuine and must be examined, must also in turn be subordinated to ontological preoccupations "whereby *understanding* ceases to appear as a simple *mode of knowing* in order to become a *way of being* and a way of relating to beings and to being."[71] Consequently, it could be suggested that for the reader/interpreter epistemology is a means of achieving, or moving toward, ontology. The text can be a creative presentation of what the real can be, which is capable of mimesis into the life of the person. Fictional narrative offers escape from reality; nonfictional narrative offers potentiality in achieving new reality, yet both operate in the same way. In both, the object is to draw the reader into the world of the text.[72] Fiction offers an alternate reality and nonfiction a new view and possible potential of the reality that is, that is, a new potential for being in the world.

The account in James presents the idea of an activity by the reader/hearer in effecting the change he or she perceives; that is, the text presents the possibility of the formation of an "intention-to" in deciding to be a doer not just a hearer. Hearing thereby traverses the *what* into a doing; in other words, that which was described has undergone assimilation into an ontology of self in the hearer. In James's presentation (i.e., the speaking voice of the text) what the person sees is the real person, and to be less than that person is discordant with reality. Hence, as Ricoeur suggested, within the self is an ability to deal with self as actual, yet see self as potential, hence other than self, as actual, and be activated toward achievement of that potential. Yet all this is achieved through the authorial intent of the author of James, that is, not only

---

71. Ricoeur, *From Text to Action*: 52. (Italics original) Thiselton also endorses this observation by Ricoeur in *New Horizons*, 358.

72. See a previous discussion of the work of Limburg on this subject, 93.

the semantic description as impacting the person's understanding but an ontological equipping to traverse this epistemological understanding into action.

The passage in 2 Corinthians is more remarkable, in that change happens to the person through looking, hence implying impartation of being through looking into the mirror. This implication is not an observation that should just be noticed in passing but is significant. In the James account there is an implication of understanding and volitional action on the part of the observer, that is, the one looking into the mirror. Here in the 2 Corinthians passage there is the implication that, in their texts, authors may not only bring things into being in the saying but also actually impart potentiality of being to the reader, that is, empower the traversing not just present its possibility.[73] Here the *what*, the speech acts of locution, illocution, and perlocution, as that which impacts the hearer in the saying, are traversed to that which empowers the hearer into the world as an active agent. The concept in Ricoeur, of the world of the text opening up before the reader, shows that this is a sound hermeneutical principle. There can be a temptation in this understanding to move to a special hermeneutic. However, if alternatively there is recognition of an *ontic-consciousness* (i.e., a consciousness that is capable of perception and assimilation of *nonrational* knowledge, and also a recognition of the language associated with that ontology), what can be suggested is special use made of that which is already operating within human being.

In this case the text is not fiction, yet there are some basic observations that can be made about fiction, as literature, that have parallel with the idea of the biblical text. The author of fiction assumes divine status. The world of the text is one of his or her creation. There is predetermination in terms of the plot and of the lives of the characters, yet the narrative unfolds in accord with the understanding of the characters and their potential within the story. The author employs a narrator, who is essentially their inspired prophet, who will tell the story without injection of the personality of the narrator replacing the author's personality (the narrator in the case of a text, as opposed to a DVD or CD, is generally perceived as genderless as well), yet the author will retain the right to direct and redirect at will; that is, the author remains sovereign in the whole process. Whilst Roland Barthes noted the *voice* of the narrator, as well as the genderless nature and neutrality of that *voice*,[74] he missed the creatively intentioned nature of the text as a composition and hence made no connection between the *voice* and the author. In the biblical concept of the writing prophet there is scope for understanding the relationship of the narrator's voice to the person of the author. Therefore, if Scripture is received as nonfiction, although employing the same concepts in con-

---

73. The Christian reader understands the activity of the Holy Spirit in this empowering, as indicated within the text, acting as the agent of this transformation. However, as a textual situation the aspect that is of interest is that there is a traversing of the *what* of the text, to establish actual being in the reader. Subsequently, the mimetic action of the person activates that being the author has intended in the text. The recognition of the Spirit in the life of the Christian is an employing, by the divine, of that which is at work in the being of a person, i.e. a special use of hermeneutics.

74. Barthes, "Death of the Author," 2.

sideration of divine authorship, then the concept of fiction concerns the intent of the author rather than the nature of the genre.[75] A failure to recognize this distinction may be why alternately there can be a relegation of Scripture to the status of fiction.

Hence, the concept of mimesis presents a useful device to traverse the *what* of epistemology to the ontology of the person. Mimesis neither transgresses nor transcends the *what* of epistemology, in that it appropriates what is described ontologically. Hence, in mimesis there is a genuine traversing of the *what* as the public expression is a vital component of the private appropriation.

Identifying the Ontological Nature of Authorial Intent

It should not be surprising that this ontological nature should be revealed within the concept of authorial intent. Previously it has been shown, and considered at length, that the argument against the concept of the author, and hence authorial intent, is essentially a metaphysical one. It was also noted previously that the first movement in interpretation should be of an ontological nature in the sense of listening, and logically this should be to the author, which is followed by an epistemological movement. Now, finally, in following the direction illuminated in the work of Ricoeur concerning "intention-to" associated with the agent, or author, the ontological nature of the authorial intent is directly disclosed. Furthermore, as was indicated in adopting this line of thought, the adverbial sense, following the semantic route, is the weaker sense. The substantive nature, following the ontological route, is the stronger sense and should therefore be the context in which the adverbial sense is itself understood. This implies that this sense should be the first considered by the interpreter, which is consistent with the discovery that the first movement in the hermeneutical task is ontological.

In the pursuit of "why?-what?" (as used by Ricoeur), which primarily concerns the content (although as noted at the time there is good reason to believe that this should be extended to allow *why* to associate with "when?-where?" to impact the process), this capture of *who* by something in following the descriptive route is not a hindrance. This is properly the province of semantics in dealing with what is within the text; however, what also should be noted is that which is within the text, that is, the composition, has being because it can be known. The issues are twofold. First, how did composition get its being; that is, what or who is the Being of its being? Second, how is that being disclosed in the textual situation of the composition? The author has being as a person and the composition associated with the text has being, and the issue is the relationship between these entities.

---

75. Wolterstorff, *Divine Discourse* 243. Wolterstorff develops the concept that fiction or nonfiction, as a status of the text, is determined by the "illocutionary stance taken toward that content," i.e., the stance toward the doing in the saying of the author (this is illustrated in the ensuing examples he cites).

Clearly, it can be initially asserted with some confidence that if a text has being, then the author is the Being of that being. As Vanhoozer has observed, the author is the reason "that it is" and the determiner of "what it is"; that is, with respect to the text, the author stands as its creator.[76] The very concept of "creator" inherently carries metaphysical implications, which in turn implies what has been observed; that is, the argument against the existence of an authorial intention, as opposed to its knowability, derives from a metaphysical base. Therefore, what is inferred is that *authorial intent is an ontological dimension of the text establishing the being of the text, which the author creates as the Being of being of the text*; which is to say the composition is accomplished in the creative act of the author.

This being is not simply an extension of the psyche of the author, nor is it a projection of the psyche of the author; it is the being the author gives to the world projected in the text, which then has its being in this attributed being. The being of the text is what the text exists as and its relationship to reality, thereby supplying a context in which the perception of "why?-what?" is understood. This could be restated as: the ontological nature of the text is the context in which epistemology is conducted. The purpose here is not the replacement or transcending of the descriptive approach; it is rather a discussion of the task that should be undertaken prior to the descriptive approach. It is the interaction of ontological-epistemological-ontological that results in understanding the meaning of the author, as meaning in the life and world of the reader/interpreter.

(a) Tradition: Impact as Pretextual

The concept of tradition and its impact have previously been dealt with at some length. It was noted that as in the case of a baby, so it is in the case of the novice in any field, that is, that the novice begins by listening with a resultant acceptance of the posited knowledge. This is the basis of the impact of a tradition upon an individual, but it also results in an interpretation of that tradition into the being, or life, of the individual, being both informative and formative. The individual appropriates tradition within his or her life as a presuppositional basis of understanding.

Ricoeur has noted that tradition is critical in interpretation; his observation is that, in interpretation of a text, if the tradition of the text is not integral to the task of interpretation, the tradition is dead.[77] If the tradition is dead, then this in turn greatly impacts the interpretation, which "does not spring from nowhere; rather, one interprets in order to make explicit, to extend, and so keep alive the tradition itself."[78] Consequently, it seems reasonable to suggest that interpretation without the impact of the tradition behind the text is not an interpretation of that text, since that which is

---

76. Vanhoozer, *Is There a Meaning*, 228.
77. Ricoeur, *Conflict of Interpretations*, 27.
78. Ibid.

vital to its very being as a text has been lost. The matter of the text is describable when the tradition is lost, but there is no being as context in which description occurs to make what is itself describable and understandable in its intention.

Although Ricoeur's discussion and comment concern not the author but the text,[79] it is suggested that since it is the author who gives being to the text, then the tradition in which the author stands *is* the tradition in which the text stands. The text is a creation of the author, in the same way a work of art is the creation of its author, and few would dispute the impact of tradition on the artist in the production of their work of art. The author, as a person within the world, has worked from an ontological base they have by "a *depositum*,"[80] engaging upon an epistemological search to understand the world in relation to their being, and it is from within this world that the author develops and communicates a message.

Hence, tradition impacts authors' texts. Consequently, the form of this impact and how it is communicated must be considered, or the tradition dies in that interpreter. If the text is intended by an author, then the textual tradition in which the text stands is therefore intentionally used by the author. To ignore, as Ricoeur does, the author's impact on interpretation and hence lose the impact of the tradition in which the author stands, is to isolate the text from the intention that has shaped its existence. The personal ontology in which the text began is effectively separated from the text. The result of which is that the interpretation loses access to the entity, hence being, of the composition and retains only the being of the text, which becomes an impersonal stretch of language. This is the postmodern situation.

Gadamer, whom Thiselton places at the inception of postmodern thought, sought to raise language to the level of metaphysics in his realization that the task of metaphysics is vital in interpretation. Gadamer agreed with abandoning a theologically impacted metaphysics but also recognized that, if metaphysics was abandoned altogether, there was a subsequent loss of an important dynamic in interpretation. Having recognized the text as distanced from the author, Gadamer wanted to avoid a personal ontology impacting meaning. This dynamic he felt could be fulfilled in what he saw as the universal nature of language. Thus, the text effectively becomes an impersonal stretch of language, with the restoration of a personal ontology in meaning being restored in the reader by the very nature of language. Because Gadamer avoids the issue of methodology, unlike Ricoeur who faced the issue and sought to propose a resolution, Gadamer doesn't have to deal with the mechanics of this restoration of a personal ontology.

---

79. This is not surprising given Ricoeur's views on authorial intent. However, in some ways this has the effect of making this point more forcefully; if authorial intent was valued in interpretation, the tradition of the author is vital.

80. Ricoeur, *Conflict of Interpretations*, 27. This is the term Ricoeur used, admittedly in a different context but with the same meaning descriptively; emphasis original.

Intentionality and Authorial Intention

Ricoeur, though impacted by Gadamer, saw the folly of raising language to this level and instead focused on the autonomy of the text and the ideality of language. The result is the same: the text becomes an impersonal stretch of language. Ricoeur recognized the hermeneutical problem of the resultant aporia in seeking to move from an impersonal ontology of event, which is the intentionally created text, to the personal ontology of the interpreter, since meaning is a function of a personal ontology. Ricoeur sought for a way to restore the personal ontology from this state of the ontology of the impersonal event, in which the text exists, by examining and expounding the hermeneutics of the self. Ricoeur provides a similar result to Gadamer, in that the final result is a personal ontology. But Ricoeur does it by traversing the aporia and not transcending it. What Gadamer does is effectively transcend the impersonal in what is essentially a universal metaphysics of language.

In the thought of Derrida, the text is simply composed of textual signs that signify other textual signs. Derrida, like Barthes, regards meaning as beginning with the reader not the writer; the text is simply a written text that awaits the reader for meaning. There is no ontological aporia in need of traversing or transcending, since discourse is reduced effectively to a *what* in that it is not a someone who said something to someone, it is simply a something that was said. Ricoeur recognized that Derrida detached writing from speech, therefore not grounding interpretation of texts in discourse; thereby Derrida avoids facing and hence dealing with the ontological aporia.[81] Ricoeur has astutely recognized the essentially presuppositional nature that this has on Derrida's thought. There is no being as discourse, let alone as authorial discourse, and consequently no ontological issue because the text simply has being as text. Subsequently, for Derrida meaning itself is always originary with advent of the reader. Derrida argues for the complete abandoning of metaphysics as he recognizes that this introduces the idea of author, the book, and therefore anterior meaning, that is, metaphysics will cause recognition that there is intended-ness regarding the text. Derrida also recognized the impact of metaphysics on language and so in his thought the text becomes simply that, a stretch of text. The last vestiges of any impact of intentionality on being of the text are stripped away. This represents an advance in deconstructive thought but a degeneration of the text in discourse interpretation.

It is this alteration in being of the text, when the impact of tradition is lost, that should catch the attention, because from one perspective the semantic route is still viable and can be undertaken. However, as it has been noted on several occasions, the author gives being to the text that discloses a world, referred to as the "world of the text." The loss of the tradition, in which both the author and text are standing, causes an impact on the being of the composition and hence of that world disclosed.

Ricoeur developed a concept of identity that recognized sameness and invariance: *idem* (identity as permanence of the self and unchanging) and *ipse* (identity as

---

81. Ricoeur, *Interpretation Theory*, 26. Ricoeur is not discussing the aporia here; however, it is the grounding of discourse in speech that leads to the aporia, which is discussed in *Oneself as Another*.

manifest selfhood in which is recognized temporality and the possibility of change).[82] Ricoeur develops the concepts of actuality and potentiality as operating within the realm of selfhood (i.e., *ipse*-identity) like dialectic poles.[83] This concept allowed the changing identity to undergo self-evaluation in terms of the actual situation and what potential there was for realization of the possibilities of *idem*-identity, representing that which is unchanging.[84] It is the tradition in which the self stands that gives the sense of being as unchanging, hence *idem*-identity.

Vanhoozer noted that culture (of which, tradition both in religion and community is a vital aspect) sets the ultimate in belief and values. Culture accomplishes the sharing of these things, and thus it is what confers historical particularity.[85] Consequently, culture, or tradition, is vital in the establishing of the mindset within which a person will understand self. If this is lost the community becomes cast adrift, as will a text in which the tradition that the author stood is disregarded. By way of illustration, one could imagine the planet Earth being plucked up from its current orbit and planted in some other foreign star system. It would be the same Earth (*idem*-identity), but its new orbit will cause selfhood (*ipse*-identity, speaking anthropomorphically) to be completely altered. All reference to its *idem*-identity, that makes it unchanging, would also be lost. In this situation identity collapses: it is the same Earth but no longer recognizes self. A new *idem*-identity must be first developed before any new *ipse*-identity is even possible. In the case of a text in which this occurs, the text does in fact become loosed from the horizon of the author to become whatever the reader wants, since it has lost identity. Therefore, disregard of tradition is a first step that leads to the chaos of unrestrained multiplicity of meaning, that is, disregard for authorial intent at a primal level.

This is exactly the analogy Derrida uses to describe what he termed the "metaphysical orb," which was the orbit he desired to escape from.[86] Derrida played on the word exorbitant (ex-*orbit*-ant) when describing his method of approach. This exorbitant state (extravagant in allowing self latitude) allowed him to jump into the text wherever he desired.[87] He could thus exit the orbit of the tradition of metaphysics himself, thereby essentially taking the text out of its orbit and placing it wherever he liked in the universe with total disregard for its anterior identity, which anterior identity he denied as real but is styled by Derrida as an identity that is the result of metaphysics. To coninue the analogy of a moved Earth, Derrida not only looses the text from its orbit, or *idem*-identity, he leaves it as a projectile constantly out of orbit,

---

82. Ricoeur, *Oneself*, 2–3, 115–19. Ricoeur alludes to this on a number of occasions, but these are the more descriptive passages.

83. Ibid., 315.

84. Ibid., 116–25.

85. Vanhoozer, *First Theology*, 310.

86. Derrida, *Of Grammatology*, 162. See also, 262, in this work.

87. Ibid.

and hence *ipse*-identity is not only changing but totally random, having no *idem*-identity as its reference point.

Essentially Derrida acknowledges that tradition has a gravitational effect on the text, as the sun does on the earth, which keeps it in orbit. The tradition is much larger and more extensive than deposited into any one member and therefore acts like the sun on a planet; it keeps it in an orbit that stabilizes its identity.[88] Tradition works in the same fashion upon those who are attached to it. This force is that which is unseen yet operational. This illustration of unseen yet operational indicates one other aspect of tradition that is important. Tradition is an unseen affect and should act as mentor not master, that is, in interpretation what should occur is the impact of tradition not the establishing of traditionalism.

Consequently, although an author may not either acknowledge or allude to this, tradition is affecting the author and his or her creation of the text, and therefore the interpretation of the world of the text is out of orbit without it. When no tradition is evident within the text, since the author was a person in history, his or her historical particularity can expose the tradition having the gravitational effect on the text. This is the weakest attestation to tradition and should be used with care. The author may have moved self into a different sphere (e.g., Saul/Paul's change from Judaism to Christianity), and hence the tradition operating the gravitational effect *is* a new star system, in that Paul gained both a new *idem*- and resultant *ipse*-identity. Paul is the apostle who expounds the concept of becoming a "new creation" in the event of salvation, where old things have passed away and *all* things have become new (2 Cor 5:17). Paul had not found a new God but God had created a new world in which life is to be conducted. The tradition of which he was now part had journeyed with the tradition of which he was formerly part, but was now translated into a new world. Paul remained within that same tradition, but it was now interpreted from an entirely different perspective. If an interpreter was unaware of this, then Paul's New Testament texts could be misunderstood, for example, if you read his New Testament texts as though he was a Jewish rabbi. If an interpreter is aware of this and yet disregards the tradition in which Paul stands, then the interpreter will not interpret Paul's texts according to the being Paul has given them.

It was previously noted that Thiselton considered the issue of reception history of a text.[89] Reception history can reveal the dual concept of how theology has shaped history and is shaped by history, that is, "effec*tive* history" and "effec*ted* history."[90] Scripture forms the foundation of Christian theology and, in looking at the history of the reception of a text, an interpreter can hear the "polyphonic" voices of past

---

88. Thiselton, *Thiselton On Hermeneutics*, 707. This is not the analogy used by Thiselton, but his point is the fact that tradition transcends the scope of immediate individual knowledge, providing the context for individual development.

89. Ibid., 39.

90. Ibid. (Emphasis original.)

interpretations.[91] In this way, even issues such as editorialization and apparent emendations to the text increase the amount of information available to the interpreter on the tradition's that impact the text. Thiselton observes that what is noticed, in reading the same passage in different situations, is that expectation is not uniform, as would be expected, but in this realization "openness to tradition" is promoted, which enhances the task of interpretation.[92] It was noted previously that tradition interprets and is itself interpreted. Tradition therefore must be considered not only diachronically, as impacting through history, but also synchronically, as how it is interpreted and impacting in the temporal moment. This is where reception history furthers the understanding of tradition. Hence, this can provide information on the tradition in which the text has stood and show the orbit in which it has moved.

In-text references to tradition by the author offer the securest means of understanding traditions impact. For here the author is directly linking the tradition in which they stand, that is, the *depositum* of which he or she is recipient, directly to the world of his or her creation in the text. The opening verse of Scripture itself establishes a tradition in which all that follows is to be understood, that is, "In the beginning God created..." (Gen 1:1). This is not just a general recognition of the idea of God, but it is a tradition of metaphysics of presence—and not only that, but within this metaphysics it is personal ontology, and is a particular person. Similarly, the opening verse of the New Testament first locates its revelation within a tradition, that is, "This is the book of the genealogy of Jesus Christ, the Son of David, the Son of Abraham" (Matt 1:1). Therefore, to correctly interpret the life of Jesus assumes his being in the tradition of David and Abraham, hence also remaining broadly through narrative connection within the tradition begun in Genesis. All the Pauline epistles are prefaced with an identification with a tradition located in the person of Jesus Christ, and hence located within the broader tradition indicated in Matt 1:1. This gives being to the writer's message and creates a context in which the descriptive task is to occur and therefore through which it is to be understood.

(b) Tradition: The Depositum

Ricoeur uses the word *depositum* in referring to textual tradition as a deposit, which the interpreter receives and subsequently impacts the interpretation, so that the tradition remains alive.[93] The principle is the same for the author as it is for the interpreter; that is, the author who writes that text must stand in that tradition in which it had been deposited. This knowledge is describable by the author, but is generally received by the author as ontological knowledge; that is, the knowledge is posited to the author, becoming "depositum." The highlighted similarities between the words *posit* and *de-*

---

91. Ibid., 40.
92. Ibid., 44.
93. Ricoeur, *Conflict of Interpretations*, 27.

posit-um is intentional to show the nature of the knowledge, that is, the knowledge is stated as reality. The concept of a deposit being passive, in the sense of received, as opposed to obtained as active, in the sense of achieved, highlights the different methods of acquisition of knowledge via the ontological route, which begins in otherness and results in understanding. In contrast, the epistemological route begins with the Cartesian "I," or similar, and is an active acquisition, which results in knowing.

Therefore, the ontic-language of tradition is that of assent, assertion, and inference, as covered previously in relationship to the work of Newman. The language of assent posits actuality of being and reality; it does not seek to prove it semantically. Such knowledge may be used semantically, but it is not established or transmitted in a descriptive process. Semantics in this case is simply description of the knowledge and not an analysis of its being as knowledge. Assent establishes the authoritative impact on the author. The tradition directly impacting the being of the author, who gives being to the text, is displayed in the declaration of assent; for example, in Rom 1:1–5, the authority to speak, as the "speaking voice," is based upon a commission that is underpinned by a tradition, to which the author gives assent. Whilst this passage may have theological implications in terms of the descriptive task, ontologically this passage establishes the being of the message, and this seems to be the more important issue to the speaker.

The assent identified directly impacts the material; for example, in many ways Paul's introduction in Romans chapter 1 proceeds to verse 15 before launching into full disclosure of content, verse 16, which is to expound the gospel. The substance of the verses initially considered, that is, Rom 1:1–5, is the tradition from which the gospel develops. The interpreter may not accept and assent to that which the author does, this is not the object of the author in the author's assent; that is, the issue is not a polemic one. Where polemic is based in that which is assented to, as in Galatians, there is a close association with what is assented to through the use of the first person by the author. That to which the author assents becomes the tradition in which his or her message is to be understood, regardless of agreement. Disregard of this is to not "listen" to the author, and hence to not only have prejudices but to impose them upon the text.

This also offers insight into the communication of knowledge; ontological knowledge is posited to become deposit, but epistemological knowledge (that which is justified and justifiable) is described so as to be available for analysis and assimilation (as opposed to the idea of passive reception as deposit). Epistemological knowledge moves from that which is public to that which is private. Ontological knowledge goes from that which is private to that which is private, and only the positing is public. In the positing of ontological knowledge, only the surface grammar is available publically. The referential nature of posited knowledge (i.e., how it is interpreted to become and remain understandable within a person) is private and therefore not semantically available.

In the case of texts such as the book of Esther, the gravitational effect of tradition is seen in the text. Unlike the texts just considered, the narrator adopts a seemingly neutral stand and does not identify a position to assent to. The first indication of the impact of tradition is in Esther 2:5 with the identification of a key character Mordecai as culturally a Jew, giving his national heritage and genealogy. Esther, after whom the book is named, becomes linked to the same cultural tradition, 2:7. In 2:20 the concept of a tradition lying behind the story is given in that Esther is identified not only individually as a Jew but also as part of a cohesive community, noting that she had not revealed "her family and her people." At the end of the conflict that begins with the destruction of Haman, it is the people who are victorious, that is, the Jews, 8:16–17. The story then becomes caught up in the tradition, and a feast is established linking the story to religion, 9:26–32.

In this story it is not the divine intervention of God that is highlighted; it lays below the surface, implied as working in the tradition. An active God is rather a presupposition, that is, to have the tradition is to have God active. If the tradition is lost, the activity of God is lost; but more importantly, if the tradition is lost the story loses its reason for being and the critical element to its identity as story. Whilst this example is but one book of Scripture, this one text within Scripture highlights what is at work in those books wherein the impact of tradition is understated. Tradition acts as mentor, behind the scenes as it were, not to be the story, as though it were the master, but exerting influence on shaping the story, so that it is a story of characters impacted by tradition. Hence, without the tradition the story can still be told, but its meaning and being (i.e., where it belongs in the universe of the human story) would be lost. The narrative becomes random and meaningless. Within the metaphysics of presence that is the Judeo-Christian sphere, one could speculate that this could be the divine reason for inclusion.

(c) Tradition: Ontological Language

The discussion of tradition, which is the beginnings of the author's ontology, hence the gravitational force impacting the text, highlights the nature of the language of ontology. Being is posited and, if accepted, becomes *depositum* in the recipient. If rejected, there is no *depositum* and being is different. Ricoeur's definitions of identity are useful here; there is *idem*-identity as sameness, in the sense that both the acceptor and rejecter are human beings, but there is a significantly different *ipse*-identity, that is, how one sees oneself within the orbit and world of human being. Acceptance or rejection then also changes how "self" sees the world. The situation is not as though the accepter has an ontology and the rejecter doesn't; each develops a different selfhood in acceptance or rejection.

As noted previously, this deposit is not realized by rational but instead by *non-rational* means. It is posited and assented to, that is, it is not discovered in the normal progress of rationalization within temporal existence, it is only realized in discourse through its disclosure by the agency of another person. The concept of that which is posited begins in otherness; its center of gravity is outside the self. The scriptural passage concerning the beginnings of human being in Gen 1:27-28 grounds self-identity in the otherness of God; humanity is made in the image of God. However, in this account this being arrives on the scene as a package that is, before this statement there isn't a person and after it there is. The account of the creation of the human being in the account in Gen 2:7 provides an important insight. God forms humanity from the dust of the ground, but the body so formed has existence as an entity but does not have living being. It is the breath of God into humanity that leads to the declaration "and man became a living being." Consequently, without the deposit from that which is other there is no living being; human being-ness is gratuitous, in the sense it is given and not earned, and is not a human achievement.

This view is anecdotally supported in the concept of how human life begins as a baby, as also has been noted previously. Life begins with a breath in, and without the breath in there is no breath out, that is, no respiration, and hence no temporal being. Furthermore, the baby is totally dependent on otherness. Further still, an important aspect to formation of the relationship with that which is other, is human need. It seems reasonable to suggest that self-identity comes initially not as an act of self, but as impartation from that which is other. This is really the way of the novice in any field. The growth of the person, or individuality (i.e., selfhood) is established in the exploration of self-identity by the Cartesian "I." The *depositum*'s assimilation into selfhood will occur by questioning, testing, and even challenging that which was deposited. Consequently, individuality is achieved by the assertion of the "I" into the world. In this way the tradition, or that which is assented to, becomes assimilated in the development of selfhood, as Ricoeur argues concerning the changeability of the *ipse*-identity. Yet what Ricoeur has not noted is that of which Thiselton takes note, that is, human life does not unfold as though selfhood was a blank sheet of paper; there is a deposited identity with which one begins.[94]

The deposit is assented to in being received, so tradition becomes the deposit the individual receives. However, as also noted previously, that tradition is always far broader than the individual, and the individual develops within the tradition. Consequently, although the tradition is accepted and assented to, it is untested and not personalized or individualized. This individualization process is that of assertion by the self of what was assented to, which process shapes, hence adapts, what has been assented to into the selfhood of the individual.[95]

---

94. Thiselton, *Thiselton On Hermeneutics*, 701-2. This is the theme of the chapter.

95. This discussion to this point of tradition and its outworking is largely based on Thiselton's observations in *Thiselton on Hermeneutics*, 701-25, on corporate memory, and Vanhoozer's observations in *First Theology*, 309-18, in conjunction with the development of the concept of *nonrational* knowledge in this work. The impact of Ricoeur's work has been referenced throughout the discussion.

This consideration of assent and assertion develops here along a line having a nuance of difference with the work of Newman, which was considered in the discussion of *nonrational* knowledge. In the work of Newman, assent is the mental process of holding the proposition and assertion is the annunciation.[96] Hence, assent is equivalent to assertion. However, as recognized here, assent, though not a conditional term in the sense that one accepts at first the tradition that is *depositum*, is nevertheless a more general term. It is the testing of the tradition of the individual that interprets tradition into the life of a person. This is manifest in the assertion. The assertion marks the posited being as becoming an active part of individual being, as has been examined in the annunciation of ontological language, for example, in the examples in James and 2 Corinthians. When it is recognized that assertion[97] carries the idea of belief and not simply repetition, there is the creation of being.

This offers an insight that has profound hermeneutical implications. That which comes as ontological *depositum* has the potential within its positing for mimetic performance by the receptor of that deposit. In the assertion that occurs in the mimetic performance, *being* of the deposit becomes individualized and actualized as *being* of the receptor. Consequently, within the ontological understanding of authorial intent, it is that of not only intention-to on the part of the author, but the presentation, or positing, of that which, in its mimetic performance, brings *being* in the doing for the reader. Therefore, it can be suggested that the descriptive epistemological task investigates what the author did intentionally, making it available *for* viewing. However, it can also be suggested that the reflexive ontological task creates and makes available a deposit to the reader/interpreter, making the deposit available *in* the doing. This is not a perlocutionary act, as in speech-act theory, since this is not an effect of the text upon the reader; it is an affect within the reader.

The form of knowledge that is acquired, in its being posited, is that of belief, that is, pistological knowledge is initially acquired through belief in the knowledge received as *depositum* from that which is other. The ontological task discloses this form of knowledge, and human ontic-consciousness is able subsequently to perceive it. Not only is pistological knowledge able to be perceived, but in its positing to the person acceptance results in actuality of *being* in the life of the person. The Scripture indicates this in passages such as Heb 11:1 (in this passage in Hebrews the author asserts that faith, i.e., expressed belief held by a person, constitutes an attribution of *being* by that person of that which is believed), and Rom 10:9 (in this Romans passage salvation becomes *being* with the acceptance and application to self of posited knowledge).

Pannenberg noted that in Heidegger's thought God is drawn into philosophy. However, Pannenberg suggests that responding to this involves a presupposition that the idea of the divine is not part of consciousness within the self.[98] The concept that

---

96. Newman, *Grammar of Assent*, 5.
97. Ibid., 5, 13.
98. Pannenberg, *Metaphysics*, 12.

an aspect of human consciousness is able to recognize and understand ontological statements, not just descriptively, but in terms of the being disclosed, must be explored. This has been previously alluded to and identified as the *ontic*-consciousness. It is this aspect that is able to "hear" the speaking voice and "understand" authorial intent. It is this aspect that "sees" the work of art and understands the composition, as an entity related to the text. If it is an aspect of consciousness, then it is not learned, but is primordial in human beings, and, as a result, operates hermeneutically even if not recognized. However, when it is not recognized the task of hermeneutics is misrepresented and malformed.

(d) Tradition: An Important Distinction on Absolute and Relative

In the preceding discussion of tradition, some inferences should be examined more closely. The first encounter that an individual has with tradition is as depositum, which seems to be an absolute. The tradition is then assimilated by the assertion of the Cartesian "I" as the tradition is drawn into the life of the person; that is, the tradition moves from being external to the person to becoming internalized and individualized within the life of the person. Consequently, this process is an interpretive process. Therefore, philosophically, as in all interpretive processes that result in meaning for the individual, this must lead to a relative value of the absolute of the tradition in which one stands.

Furthermore, the tradition in which an individual, or community, stands is itself a tradition that stands apart from other traditions, even where there may be common origins as in Judaism and Christianity. Anecdotally, this concept is well supported in the tendency to subculturation that occurs within a culture. In the metaphysics of absence each tradition exists as independent of all other traditions. However, for hermeneutic purposes each tradition functions itself as an absolute reference point, whether based on metaphysics of presence or absence. As a result the individual develops a relative meaning with respect to that tradition perceived as an absolute. Hence, tradition cannot be ignored even in the metaphysics of absence when it comes to hermeneutical implications.

The metaphysics of presence assumes a common origin for tradition. The biblical account, within the metaphysics of presence, recognizes the development of differing traditions stemming from the original human situation, through the narrative of the account of the Tower of Babel to the New Testament times, indicated in the sermon of Paul in Athens, recorded in Acts 17:22–31. Paul asserts that, based on his understanding from the tradition in which he stands, humanity has a common heritage that links all humanity, and further, these cultural differences are not only developed from the common source but the traditions so formed are intentioned by God; that is, they are capable of forming "intention to" in the life of the individual. It is interesting that for Paul the same absolute tradition has been interpreted in two distinct individual traditions within his own life, that is, Judaism and Christianity; their individual adherents see both of these traditions as themselves absolute.

Hegel's observations, considered previously, essentially noted the problem of the eternal was that although it is encounterable, the dialectic of finite-infinite traps the individual in such a way that the perception of the eternal is always relative. Similarly, here in tradition the same problem is encountered; that is, the dialectic of the *ipse*-identity of the self, encountering the *idem*-identity of the external tradition, always results in a relative value of that which is absolute. The "I" of selfhood, as *ipse*-identity and hence changeable, is the reason that meaning undergoes apparent change in the process of interpretation, when encountering the absolute, or unchangeable. Tradition functions in the same fashion as a text and the *idem*-identity of the text, that is, as unchangeable, encounters the *ipse*-identity of the self, as changeable. The resultant identity when developed from the dialectic action of the modes of identity is personalized in the individual.

The important issue is that the otherness of the text, that is, tradition, must be considered. The author uses the language of ontology as a primary source of the tradition impacting the text, and this is the author's individualization of the tradition in which he or she stands. Both of these aspects, that is, the language of the author and historical understanding of his or her tradition, can be known and evaluated by the interpreter in the dealing with the text of an author. Consequently, the absolute is not absolutely known from the human perspective; as Vanhoozer has noted no theologian enjoys the divine perspective of reality. The viewpoint perceived by the interpreter is always a relative view of the absolute, and that relative view impacts hermeneutically and consequently must be evaluated.

11 Disclosing the Being of the Text

Reanimation of the Objectified Text

Introduction

THE WORK OF RICOEUR has shown that when the interpreter begins with the written text, as opposed to seeking to interpret the discourse of a speaker who is present and with whom one is engaged in a dialogue, the text presents not with the ontology of a *who*, as personal, but rather with the ontology of an impersonal event.[1] The conceptualization of the *who* of the written text, in Ricoeur's approach, is undertaken in what amounts to a self-projection, where "otherness" is in essence a dimension of self.[2]

First, this highlights the impersonal nature of the text, which in Heidegger means that it equates with a "worldless" entity.[3] Second, since the text is impersonal it is therefore without the consciousness that belongs to a being like *Dasein*.[4] This in

---

1. Ricoeur, *Oneself*, 56–87. This is the theme of the chapter entitled "An Agentless Semantics of Action" and has been under discussion in the preceding two chapters of this book.

2. Ibid., 112. Ricoeur identifies an understanding of the "ontology of the self" to be his goal at the conclusion of the chapter "From Action to Agent," which then finds its fullest description in the final chapter "What Ontology in View?" where he develops the theme of otherness as what amounts to a projection of self. This concept has been considered in the previous chapter.

3. Heidegger, *Being and Time*, 81.

4. Ibid., 81–82. This is the theme developed. Heidegger points out that "worldless" entities cannot touch each other even if the space between them is reduced to zero. This occurs because for one entity to "touch" another entity assumes that entities that are "present-at-hand" are also "encounterable" by the entity "present-at-hand" that is touched. Although *Dasein* can be just "present-at-hand," it is never "worldless." The implication is that an entity such as *Dasein* is conscious of being "touched." This concept in Heidegger allows the concept developed by Ricoeur where the use of the third person has the concept of being personal but is treated as impersonal, i.e., a *what* and not a *who*. Consequently, within a text the reference to persons is conceptual as "person" but with an ontology of impersonal event.

turn highlights that the process of interpretation, that is, "I interpret," begins with "I" and, as the only consciousness involved, "I" is the basis of the postmodern emphasis on the reader/interpreter: the "I" who interprets. However, this implies that all interpretation occurs in the absence of "otherness," which "otherness" is always simply self-projection, or as Derrida concludes, mentioned previously, is auto-affection. If this is the case then Ricoeur's observation, concerning the implications of Nietzsche's work that there are only interpretations and in essence no reality just interpretations of it, would seem to be valid not only as an assessment of Nietzsche, but also that Nietzsche was seeing things as they are in reality.[5] Hence, the nature of the text is critical. It is objectification with a subjective impact and the *how* of this impact must be considered, or the objective and subjective remain at an impasse.

Traversing the Impasse: Epistemology to Ontology

Ricoeur notes what for him is the central problem in hermeneutics, which is the "opposition, disastrous in my [i.e., Ricoeur's] view, between explanation and understanding."[6] This is the opposition of epistemological concerns (dealing with "explanation") to ontological concerns (dealing with "understanding"), which in his view develops from the Romanticist hermeneutical tendency to "dissociate" these issues.[7] His object is to "search for a complementality between these two attitudes."[8] The pursuit of this task does lead to an apparent aporia, and Ricoeur states that it is this "very aporia that has instigated my own research."[9] The aporia occurs in pursuing the movement from epistemology to ontology where an apparent paradoxical impasse occurs, so that the movement proceeds neither naturally nor easily, and yet is critical to the task of hermeneutics.[10]

Schleiermacher noted that the task of hermeneutics deals with the art of understanding, not with the presentation of what is understood.[11] The issue of hermeneutics is "understanding" for the individual related to the self; that is, the disclosure in understanding makes possible the connection between the self and the said of the

---

5. Ricoeur, *Oneself*, 15. This would seem to be the true foundations of the impasse that Ricoeur seeks to address in his concept of the hermeneutic problem, see *From Text to Action*, 51, which is further discussed in this work. This concept specifically precludes an ontology of that which is "other" and in *Oneself as Another* Ricoeur seeks to pass the impasse in the hermeneutics of the self.

6. Ricoeur, *From Text to Action*: 51. Brackets added for clarification.

7. Ibid.

8. Ibid.

9. Ibid. The impasse that occurs in seeking to develop "understanding" and "explanation" as modes of knowing is not resolved by the recognition of a subordination of epistemology to ontology; "the aporia is not resolved but merely displaced elsewhere and thereby aggravated. It is no longer between two modalities of knowing within epistemology but between ontology and epistemology taken as a whole," 67.

10. Ibid. This is a problem that must be traversed rather than transcended or dismissed.

11. Schleiermacher, *Hermeneutic*, 96.

text. However, meaning is not just understanding but follows understanding as the application of what is understood to the self. Therefore, for understanding to become meaning within selfhood requires the movement from epistemology to ontology, and the very movement that must occur has reached a philosophical impasse. This is the aporia to which Ricoeur referred that makes the issue of meaning problematical when considered philosophically.

In the interpretation theory of Ricoeur, the issues of explanation and understanding, rather than being opposing poles, should be regarded as the two poles of a dialectic, the aim of which is meaning.[12] Hence the concept of understanding is to act dialectically in a way that results in meaning, therefore, representing the necessary movement from epistemology to ontology.[13] The problematic occurs due to the recognition that the pursuit of epistemology not only fails to raise the ontological question but it actually directs the hermeneut in an opposite direction.[14] In approaching this aporia, Ricoeur places himself within the philosophical conceptions and presuppositions of phenomenology,[15] and as such has been influenced not only by Husserl but also significantly by Heidegger and Gadamer.[16] Consequently, the background to Ricoeur's conceptualization of "understanding" as opening up the ontological question occurs within phenomenology; that is, the text is handled within a particular understanding and the presuppositional implications must be evaluated.

Consequently, not only the nature of the text but also how it is handled are equally important. The nature of the text is pursued in this chapter. It is misleading to assume that an author is communicating his or her consciousness. It is equally misleading to assume that the consciousness of the author is irrelevant to the text produced. What the author desires to communicate is a meaning that is developed in his or her consciousness and is subsequently transformed by an act of *parole* into a composition, which therefore constitutes the being of the text. The composition is the communication concerning a matter, as Ricoeur and others have highlighted, and not the communication of a consciousness. However, the consciousness of the author remains the composition's referent and despite any difficulties or impasse this must be considered in the process.

---

12. Ricoeur, *Interpretation Theory*, 71. This is a central theme of *Interpretation Theory*.

13. Heidegger, *Being and Time*, 193. The recognition that *meaning* is an act of persons not texts has been discussed at some length previously in this work. Consequently, this recognition moves *meaning* conceptually into the realm of ontology not epistemology. In this way *meaning* represents the impact on the being of a person of epistemology, i.e., epistemology particularized for the self.

14. This issue has been dealt with in the previous chapter.

15. Ricoeur, *From Text to Action*, 1.

16. Ibid., 23.

Traversing the Impasse: The Nature of the Text

In chapter 3 of this work, the concept of the nature of the text was considered in general terms. That examination was brief and primarily dealt with epistemological concerns, such as the concept of the text as a vehicle of communication, and issues such as the worlds of the author, text, and reader. However, note was taken in that discussion that the concept of the text as handled in modernism had overlooked the ontology of the situation. Ricoeur especially noted that in dealing with a text the issue had become a mode of knowing, that is, acquisition of knowledge. But Ricoeur's challenge was that knowledge is experienced in understanding and the correct concept is a mode of being. Certainly, Heidegger's development of the concept of ontological interpretation shows that the epistemological concerns should be properly developed in the light of the being of the text.[17] It is strange that Ricoeur fastened upon the implications of the ontological issue but did not explore the ontology of the text. The purpose here is to dig beneath epistemological concerns to uncover this ontology.

There are some preliminary observations that can be made, which have passed unnoticed in the development of this issues discussed so far. The counterpart to the "I interpret" of the interpreter is the "I explain" of the author, that is, someone says something to someone. In the composition an author seeks to make explicit, or public, a meaning that was private, that is, the author explicates in written form an explanation, which is the public presentation of that which was private and developed in the consciousness of the author. Consequently, the "explanation," or written text, sits between "I explain" of the author and "I interpret" of the interpreter as the public face that represents an understanding relevant to the self of the interpreter. It is the authorial intention to disclose this, and it is composed in such a way that it can be reanimated in encounter with the consciousness of an interpreter to result in a meaning, that is, understanding applied to self. This should be the "explanation" to which reference is made, that is, the explanation that is the author's.

In the hermeneutics of Ricoeur, the dialectic of "explanation" and "understanding" is not that of dealing with the explanation of the author, it is that of the interpreter, that is, the explanation that the interpreter gives to the text.[18] Therefore, it is in reality an interpreter's explanation of the explanation received, which is the author's written text. It is a dialectic of reading as opposed to a dialectic of writing, not one that considers the text as an explanation of the author.[19] Yet as noted previously, the text is first and foremost an explication, hence explanation, of the author. On the basis of Ricoeur's concept of the autonomous text, this becomes passed over without comment, because understanding and intent as related to the author are abolished in the

---

17. Heidegger's concept of ontological interpretation is discussed in section (a) below, "Ontology of the Impersonal Event."
18. Ricoeur, *Interpretation Theory*, 71–72.
19. Ibid., 72.

text.[20] Consequently, this may be Ricoeur's reasoning in not pursuing the issue of the ontology, or the being and relationship to reality, of the text.

Ricoeur's reasoning that highlights the ontology of the impersonal event that is the text is a sound reasoning, since to recognize any personal ontology of the text would tie it to the personality, hence psyche, of the author, as in Romanticism. Meaning is personal and private, belonging to the person, for both the author and interpreter, but the text is public. Meaning is only made public in the explanation, and any ontology present-at-hand is that of the explanation. However, this ontology, or being, lays not in "explanation" by the interpreter, but that of the author, that is, the text as present-at-hand for the interpreter is the author's explanation.

(a) Ontology of the Impersonal Event

Following the above reasoning, that which begins as a personal ontology of the self within the consciousness of the author is transformed into the ontology of the impersonal event, which is then reconverted to a personal ontology of the self within the interpreter. The intermediate stage of the ontology of the impersonal event (i.e., the text) is where all hermeneutics must begin, and it is the work of Ricoeur that has recognized and brought into focus the impersonal nature of this ontology and its implications. However, what Ricoeur has not done is to consider the being disclosed in this ontology of the impersonal event. Heidegger noted that ontological investigation "is a possible kind of interpreting," which he describes as "the working-out and appropriation of an understanding."[21] The following extended quote sets out how this "ontological interpretation" functions:

> In Ontological Interpretation an entity is to be laid bare with regard to its own state of Being; such an Interpretation obliges us first to give a phenomenal characterization of the entity we have taken as our theme, and thus bring it into the scope of our fore-having, with which all subsequent steps of our analysis are to conform.[22]

This should be the first step in dealing with the text so that the epistemological endeavor is developed within its proper ontological conditions and horizons.

What is proposed in this book is that although the composition does not have the ontology of a person, it does have being and its being is both disclosed in the text and can be perceived by the interpreter. Furthermore, its being is able to interact with the consciousness of the interpreter. If not, then the extreme of postmodernism is correct and meaning is not only a function of the reader in "I interpret," but also understanding from which meaning is developed is also reader dependent. This would

20. Ibid., 75.
21. Heidegger, *Being and Time*, 275.
22. Ibid.

occur because there is *only* relativism in understanding, and there is therefore no such thing as misunderstanding in dealing with the text. Hence, although the composition does have attributes of the ontology of the impersonal event in its being as a text, this is an inadequate qualification of its being as a composition. This is important if any otherness that is not simply a projection of the self, as in theories of Ricoeur, is to be encountered in interpretation.

As mentioned previously, the text, as composition, is the explication of an explanation concerning the subject matter that the author seeks to communicate. If the act of *parole* were simply one of transcription from the consciousness of the author to that of written text, then the interest of the act of *parole* to the task of hermeneutics would simply be as an event within this process. However, what is concealed is the traversing of an impasse that corresponds directly to that investigated by Ricoeur. If the movement from epistemology to ontology represents an aporia, then the movement from ontology to epistemology represents an equal and equally important aporia. This aporia precedes that which is discussed by Ricoeur. This is the route the author must traverse. In this process the author is the creator of the being of the *something said* of discourse in the form of a literary text, which is considered as having the impersonal ontology of an event in current hermeneutical theory. It is this literary text that the interpreter will use as the basis to develop a personal ontology of understanding related to "self." This "being" of the literary text so created by the author is critical in the interpreter's reanimation, resulting in a personal ontology.

Ricoeur's suggestion to traverse the route from epistemology to a personal ontology is a hermeneutics of the self. It seems reasonable to suggest that the author traverses the route from personal ontology to that of impersonal event, the public face epistemologically available, also within the domain of a hermeneutics of self. If the interpreter engages in an appropriation of an understanding of that which is "other" applied *to* "self," then the author must engage in an appropriation of an understanding belonging to "self" applied to that which is "other" than self. In considering traversing the aporia from epistemology to ontology, disclosed in Ricoeur, a number of issues and devices were considered, which are also available to the author in their traversing of the corresponding aporia. The use of tradition by assent, assertion, and inference establishes an orbit for the world of the being of the text. An author also uses genre, and he or she may also employ metaphor and even intend mimesis in this process in creating the text. The synthesis of this into a composition is the act of composing (i.e., the "I explain" of the author becomes "I compose in order to explain") and this results in the explanation that is the text. The creative nature of the act of *parole* in composing the text is the reason for the similarities, noted by most authors considered in this work, between the work of art and the text.

The object of the composition is to make evident, or to bring within the perceptibility of an interpreter, that which is concealed, that is, an understanding of the meaning of the author. It is here that an important observation must be made concerning the work of Ricoeur. In Ricoeur's thought experience is nontransferable that is, the transference from "one stream of consciousness" to "another stream of consciousness" cannot occur.[23] However, for Ricoeur the meaning of that experience is transferable by becoming public in the text.[24] It is Ricoeur's concept of sense interpretation and the concept of Husserlian ideology that allows meaning to appear in the impersonal ontology of event.[25] Nevertheless, as has been previously established, meaning is an act of persons; that is, meaning relates to a personal ontology, not an impersonal ontology. Meaning is essentially a cognitive act (i.e., a function of the *cogito*) and is therefore unique to each person, regardless of any similarity of meaning possible. Consequently, Ricoeur's concept ironically directly translates into the idea of transference from one stream of consciousness to another, which given his antithesis to Romanticist Hermeneutics he would strenuously oppose. It would seem that what Ricoeur is, or should be, suggesting is that understanding of the experience is transferable. It is possible to "see" the same thing as another (i.e., understand something) and yet develop difference, even if only as a nuance, of meaning.

Although Gadamer avoided the issue of the ontology of the impersonal event by avoiding method,[26] Ricoeur faced the question head-on and in so doing uncovered the issue of the nature of the impersonal ontology of the event as that of the text. Yet, since the author and audience are excluded from impacting meaning in his theory, Ricoeur is then left with no recourse except to propose that meaning must in some way be available in the ontology of the impersonal event. Presupposition has decided the issue, and again it brings to the fore the impact and determining influence of phenomenology in Ricoeur's work. In Heidegger, Gadamer, and Ricoeur,[27] as indeed with Derrida,[28] phenomenology is primordial and the basic state of existence. As such, phenomenology is never really considered as a presupposition by these authors.

---

23. Ricoeur, *Interpretation Theory*, 16.

24. Ibid.

25. Ricoeur, *From Text to Action*, 23. This is developed throughout the chapter titled "Phenomenology and Hermeneutics."

26. Ibid., 69. Ricoeur asks the question considering Gadamer's work *Truth AND Method*, whether or not it would be better titled *Truth OR Method*. (Capitalization of "and" as well as "or" is original in Ricoeur for emphasis). Thiselton observes in *New Horizons* what has been noted by others, that when it comes to implementation of Gadamer's principles into interpretation "Gadamer is painfully silent," 314.

27. Ibid., 23. Ricoeur notes the commonality of Gadamer and Heidegger in this position. Although Ricoeur uses the word presupposition in stating, "*phenomenology remains the unsurpassable presupposition of hermeneutics*" (italics original), his argument betters suits the idea of prerequisite rather than presupposition, if one wishes to engage in deregionalized hermeneutics.

28. Derrida, *Writing*, 155. Derrida makes it clear that he regards this position as an essentially presuppositionless one, freed from all metaphysical implication; "The phenomenologist . . . is the 'true positivist' who returns to the things themselves, and who is self-effacing before the originality and primordiality of meanings."

Heidegger notes that the term "meaning" is used when entities "within-the-world" are disclosed to *Dasein*, "that is, when they have come to be understood."[29] However, in reality that understanding is not the meaning but the entity, that is, its *being*.[30] The articulation of this we call "meaning," but meaning "is an existentiale of Dasein" and not "a property of entities."[31] *Dasein* only has meaning and *Dasein* only "can be meaningful or meaningless."[32] When "meaning" is interpreted in this way "then all entities whose kind of Being is of a character other than *Dasein*'s must be conceived as unmeaning, essentially devoid of any meaning at all."[33] This is not a value judgment concerning such entities but recognition of ontological properties.[34] It was noted previously that Heidegger considers such entities also as "worldless," hence incapable of "feeling," and as a result of these two recognitions it is therefore impossible for the text to either have meaning or impart something existential in communicating. Yet for any encounter with *otherness*, the text must indeed "touch" the interpreter, hence there is an issue of the being of the entity of the text that is yet concealed. The classification as an entity "within-the-world" is inadequate.

Therefore, despite the line of reasoning in Ricoeur's paradigm, the interpreter and not the text supplies "meaning," but this goes unnoticed. Ricoeur seeks to solve the problem by suggesting subjective and objective meaning. Ricoeur sees meaning as a property of the sentence, whilst admitting that meaning is something the speaker does as the subjective side of meaning.[35] The sentence's meaning is the "objective" side of meaning on which Ricoeur develops his concept of sense and reference.[36] The objective side is that which is public; that is, it is the universal predication. Nevertheless, if Heidegger's thought is followed, this concept of meaning is that which has the appearance of meaning in its articulation, but in itself is devoid of meaning in the existential sense of the word. Consequently, ontological interpretation suggests that in the articulation of the composition is a disclosure of the being of the text, but the issue of meaning is not resident within the text. Further, any association with meaning is due to a reference understood by the interpreter that results in meaning in its proper locus, that is, related to a personal ontology.

Within postmodern thought Derrida alone has realized the key nature of this issue of meaning and textuality, and, in his view, the idea of any anterior meaning preceding writing, and therefore acting in fashion as an absolute point of reference,

---

29. Heidegger, *Being and Time*, 192.
30. Ibid.
31. Ibid., 193.
32. Ibid.
33. Ibid.
34. Ibid.
35. Ricoeur, *Interpretation Theory*, 19.
36. Ibid., 19–23.

must be discarded.[37] Whilst Ricoeur simply regards anterior meaning as inaccessible, Derrida recognizes that its existence must be denied or it will haunt the process.[38] Whilst Ricoeur proposes a dialectic of the event of writing and the resultant meaning, which at least by his use of the word "writing" implies the author, it seems in essence that Derrida proposes a dialectic of the event of reading and auto-affection, the result of which is meaning. This removes the need to recognize the author, the text simply arrives and meaning is developed in the encounter. This would seem consistent with Derrida's position.

By limiting the issue to the impersonal ontology of the text, what follows is the Heideggerian view, which results in a text devoid of meaning, with no recourse to a personal ontology. In Derrida any attempt to resort to exteriority is to drag up from the "abyss of reference" the idea of the signified.[39] Yet as has been examined and highlighted, Derrida's view comes from the presupposition of metaphysics of absence. Also, as noted previously, his view of phenomenology as unprejudiced has caused opaqueness for him, resulting in unrecognized prejudice as a formative part of his presuppositional world. He has fallen victim to the very concept of prejudice he lays at the feet of those advocating the metaphysics of presence.[40] In the final analysis his arguments against presence and reference are rooted and developed in his presuppositional world, and are consequently not the result of some insight into textuality.

The concept of reference in the sense used by Ricoeur is inadequate in its inability to deal with meaning as defined in his own phenomenological viewpoint, as indicated previously. The concept of the absence of reference in Derrida is a presuppositional prejudice. It is here the true nature of the aporia is unveiled, for if one is able to show how reference can be used in moving from ontology to epistemology, then this opens the door to understanding of the corresponding aporia of moving from epistemology to ontology; that is, it is achieved by retracing the steps, as it were, of the line of reasoning whereby reference is used by the author in creation—in other words, composition, of the text.

However, this process of interpretation cannot be the re-creation of the personal ontology of the author, which is related to the consciousness of the author, and which, as Gadamer, Ricoeur, Thiselton, Vanhoozer and others have noted, relates to a foreign psyche not accessible to the interpreter. Furthermore, not only is the personal ontology of the author related to that consciousness, it is also related to it at a particular point in time that has passed into history, that is, a feature of the personal ontology of that which becomes text is that it exists temporally and therefore is historical. The author has moved on from that point and may well have an altered view; nevertheless,

---

37. Derrida, *Writing*, 10. In Derrida's view; "Meaning must await being said or written in order to inhabit itself," i.e., its existence is neither anterior nor posterior, 11.

38. Ibid.

39. Derrida, *Of Grammatology*, 163.

40. Derrida, *Writing*, 11.

any alteration, such as revision, doesn't change what was meant at the point in time of writing. Revision may supersede and replace, modify or clarify, but none of this changes the *meant* of the author, from which the original text receives its being. The hermeneutical task related to a text is unaffected by changes in the author's thinking subsequent to the time of the text's creation. As Gadamer has shown, the issue of distanciation, so prominent in Ricoeur's thinking, precludes such a leap to the consciousness of the author. To address this issue the ontological interpretation of the being of the text, which has been overlooked, must be considered.

The indicators to a solution of the problem of this aporia lie in taking note of something highlighted in Heidegger and Ricoeur. In considering *Being and Time*, previously, note was taken that although the text, as a worldless entity, cannot have meaning it does have the *appearance* of meaning in its articulation. Ricoeur took note that the impersonal ontology of events can make reference to the *concept* of persons. As part of the text such references lack actual personality but can be understood to possess personality; Heidegger notes that even when *Dasein* is treated as present-at-hand due to the situation in which it is considered *Dasein* is never worldless.[41] Consequently, the concept of a person can be conceived as *Dasein* within the imagination, not simply something present-at-hand. Within the consciousness of the author it seems reasonable to suggest that an author can imagine a person as a person, which the author can in turn convey textually as the concept of a person. Similarly, it seems equally reasonable to suggest that the interpreter is capable of taking the concept of a person that is conveyed in the text and subsequently "imagine" an actual person that represents the concept of the author.

Clearly such devices as metaphor and mimesis, which have been considered from the perspective of the reader, can have application. When included in the text such devices can make reference to personal being, though within the text existing not as Being-in but as being-present-at-hand-in-the-world, that is, as a worldless entity. There is nothing to preclude intentional use by an author. However, the success of the referencing of these devices lies in the ability of another *Dasein*, as an interpreter, to reanimate the referencing in the interpreter's personal ontology of the self. This is not an insignificant observation and is to be pursued.

(b) The Being of the Text

The concept of fixation of discourse in writing is where the thinking concerning the "being" of the text has stopped. Ricoeur, in connection with the question "What is a Text?" makes a definitive statement in saying: "Let us say that a text is any discourse fixed by writing."[42] This concept of writing as fixation is in this "definition . . . consti-

---

41. Heidegger, *Being and Time*, 82.
42. Ricoeur, *From Text to Action*, 101.

tutive of the text itself."[43] This is a statement of "being," and, as a statement of what constitutes a text (since the "Preface" of *From Text to Action* is written by Ricoeur himself), it can only be assumed that the translator's choice of a word that refers to a state of "being" is deliberate and acceptable to Ricoeur.[44] The text is discourse by other means than speech.[45]

Vanhoozer's concept, referred to previously, is that what is fixed is a "*communicative act*" of an author.[46] He states: "I now wish to define the text as *a communicative act of a communicative agent fixed by writing*."[47] This is similar to Ricoeur's concept of the "being" of the text. Vanhoozer's proposal is that the "proper ground for textual meaning" is the "communicative activity, not the subjectivity of the author."[48] Vanhoozer's concept has the advantage of setting up his own argument for the consideration of speech-act theory he will employ in developing meaning. This has the added advantage of maintenance of an importance of authorial intent. In a sense Vanhoozer's position seems an interpretation of Ricoeur's view that maintains the recognition of detachment from the consciousness of the author. Consequently, meaning is an issue related to the text apart from the consciousness of the author, yet Vanhoozer's view retains authorial impact in meaning.[49] The use of this phrase "*communicative act*" for what is fixed appears to be so as to distinguish Vanhoozer's concept from the issue of consciousness in the psychologizing, hence subjectivism, of the Romanticist era, decried by Ricoeur.[50] By distancing this from consciousness, he can assert that, as with other completed human actions, there can be "determinate meaning"; that is, meaning of the author is fixed in this communicative act and can be determined, at least theoretically.[51]

Ricoeur does not dispute the idea of determinate meaning in relationship to speech as discourse.[52] The concept of speech involves that of a personal ontology, which is consistent with Ricoeur's own value of submitting epistemology to a correct

---

43. Ibid.
44. Ibid., xii.
45. Ibid., 102–4. Ricoeur develops the idea that the text takes the place of speech in discourse.
46. Vanhoozer, *Is There a Meaning*, 225. (Italics original.)
47. Ibid. (Italics original.)
48. Ibid.
49. Ibid., 106–8. Vanhoozer discusses Ricoeur's concept in his development of his work as prefatory to developing his "Resurrection of the Author," which is part of the title of the section of the book, 201–80.
50. Ibid., 225. Vanhoozer places emphasis on this expression as avoiding subjectivity by getting into a discussion about consciousness of the author, yet retaining direct link to the author. He does not mention either Ricoeur or Romanticism in this context but does discuss both extensively earlier in the work.
51. Ibid. He states that the text "is what it is independently of our theories about and interpretations of it."
52. Ricoeur, *Interpretation Theory*, 29. He notes, "It is the same thing to understand what the speaker means and what his discourse means."

ontology. However, as Ricoeur has demonstrated the text does not have a personal ontology but the ontology of an impersonal event. The restriction of consciousness, consequently of meaning, to the meaning of the speaker that is constitutive in personal ontology, is loosed. Vanhoozer's concept of an act does not escape the ontology of the impersonal event; it simply seeks to retain authorial meaning, through maintaining authorial relationship with the text, as integral to the act.

In order to develop the idea of relationship of an author to his or her text, Vanhoozer considers the work of art. He prefaces this with a comment about the issue of the terms begotten or made that the church fathers considered in regard to how the Son's relationship to the Father was to be considered. The concept of "begotten" connotes likeness and "made" connotes unlike; that is, that which is *begotten* is like the one who begets (and is treated as a person) and that which is *made* is unlike (and is not deserving of the same respect).[53] He then argues that a text, like a work of art, "eludes" the distinction between "begotten" or "made," since a work of art is not the same as its creator nor is it completely foreign; Vanhoozer asserts it partakes of both.[54] The text and the work of art can be considered as "done" by their creator, that is, "neither *me* nor *made* by me."[55]

Vanhoozer then goes on to develop the subsequent idea that the work of art or text, on the issue of identity (which initiates the development of an ontology), is best viewed in Ricoeur's concept of *ipse*-identity.[56] As a result there is not sameness with the author but there is a constancy of relationship, such that the work of art or text alludes to its creator. However, in doing this it would seem he has either not understood this concept as developed by Ricoeur or has simply decided to adapt it to his own use. Ricoeur does not see the concepts of *idem*-identity and *ipse*-identity as alternate ways of viewing identity in the form of a choice between them. In an examination of Heidegger's concept of conscience, Ricoeur notes that this Heideggerian concept "confirms my working hypothesis that the distinction between selfhood and sameness does not simply concern two constellations of meaning but involves two modes of being."[57] They are viewed as modes of being of the same being; that is, the identity of being has two modes that act dialectically in identity. One does not exist or operate in the absence of the other. Vanhoozer's use suggests contrast in that he separates *idem* as a person from *ipse* as the text.

There is a problem that is exposed in his view that is revealed when he notes: "Books are created in the image of their reasonable creators just as rational creatures are in the image of God."[58] This shows a compounding of the problem of the issue

53. Vanhoozer, *Is There a Meaning*, 225.
54. Ibid.
55. Ibid. (Italics original.)
56. Ibid., 225–26.
57. Ricoeur, *Oneself*, 309.
58. Vanhoozer, *Is There a Meaning*, 226.

of identity, as just noted. Here he equates person and thing in the concept of entity, which the preceding discussion of Heidegger has elucidated, is a failure to realize the nature of "being" of the entities. Equation allows meaning to be a function of entities in general, but meaning relates to human "being" not nonhuman "being." Yet if meaning is to be developed as a function of the text, which is what Vanhoozer seeks, this equation in some form must be implied or the primary aporia of moving from impersonal to personal ontology returns in force. Consequently, the impasse is not traversed. However, in seeking to discuss the nature of the text, he has recognized that the simple distinction between the being of *Dasein* and entities present-at-hand is inadequate. There is a link between creator and creation.

There is a further potential problem for Vanhoozer's concept if he wishes to maintain the idea of stability of meaning as the author's meaning. The very nature of *ipse*-identity, as developed by Ricoeur and considered in the previous two chapters of this work, is that of change and adaptability. Hence, to liken the text and work of art to this identity is to also admit changeability in selfhood and subsequently in interpretive meaning. The concept of identity that transcends time, hence being unchangeable, is *idem*-identity. It would seem reasonable to suggest that the concept of *ipse*-identity best equates with the postmodern concept of changeability of meaning associated with dealing with texts.

Vanhoozer introduces potential confusion, not only in the equation of entities but also in not establishing of which entity he speaks. Clearly in the sense of *idem* the author is not the same as the text and the text is not the same as its author. However, in selfhood this is also true; that is, the selfhood of the author is not the selfhood of the text. In Ricoeur *idem* and *ipse* are modes of the same being. Consideration of the very idea of fixity, prominent in both Vanhoozer and Ricoeur, carries the implication that in identity of the text, as text, *idem*-identity is more appropriate. The author's text does not change within time; it remains the same text, hence the concept of fixity.

The issue of change concerns the issue of meaning, and meaning is a function of persons, the author and interpreter individually, not a function of impersonal entities such as the text. The "I create" of the author and the "I interpret" of the interpreter are both unique in that both are prefaced with "I" and these entities cannot be substituted for one another. Translation does not change the original text although it introduces possible changes of meaning due to the nature of translation; hence translation is best undertaken with texts as close to the original text of the author's as possible, within critical disciplines. It is important to also realize the direction of the flow of thought that is, the "I interpret" of the interpreter is that of seeking an understanding of the "I create" of the author. The issue of changing meaning is a function of the audience not the author, since the "I create" of the author does not change, unlike that of the audience. The apparent change is due to differing "I"s engaging the text; that is, the author remains the same but the audience changes. The apparent change in meaning is simply a relative understanding of the meaning the author had; that is, it is an appropriation of the *idem*-identity of the text that occurs within the *ipse*-identity of the interpreter.

Vanhoozer's primary focus is that of speech acts, that is, locutionary, illocutionary, and perlocutionary. Hence, his primary focus is the ontology of the impersonal event. He attempts to project beyond this to impact on the interpreter by implying that the momentum of the "illocutionary force" carries it through to impact on the interpreter.[59] This is an attempt to traverse the impasse of epistemology to ontology by brute force of the illocutionary act, but in the end a square peg does not fit a round hole. It has been noted previously that the impersonal ontology of the *what* of the text is terminal in that it fails to pass to the ontology of the self of the interpreter. Hence, a focus on the act as the means of understanding meaning results in having to resort to things such as the suggestion of force, or transgressing, to pass the impasse. Ricoeur's modeling offers far more potential for understanding how otherness can be applied to the self. He has simply ignored, or been blinded to, the "I create" of the author and the resultant "being" of the text that is the work of creation. The work of Vanhoozer has re-recognized the importance of the "I create" and this must be pursued.

Ong challenges this concept of fixity of discourse calling it a "widespread and fundamental" error, which is that "to put an utterance in writing is to remove it from this state of oral discourse and thus to 'fix' it."[60] Ong asserts that there is no way to fix discourse by writing; text separates the utterance and utterer "who, once he has written down his text, may as well be dead."[61] The written text acts as an interruption of discourse, an effect that will "string it out indefinitely in time and space."[62] The text exists as "a visual design" and only becomes utterance, hence the resumption of discourse, in "a living person's mind."[63] Meaning is the result of the act of resumption of discourse in the reader.[64] In this situation meaning is posterior and, logically in this situation, the result is the conclusion of Derrida; the text is simply signs referring to other signs, the meaning of which is wholly the province of the reader.[65]

Ong has highlighted the logical conclusion that would arise in Heidegger's concept of ontology; that is, the text is not a *Dasein* and is an entity present-at-hand that is given meaning by a *Dasein*. The being of this entity is that of a visual design, words on a piece of paper. The issues of language and meaning belong to an entity with the kind of being *Dasein* has. The text is portrayed as having *idem*-identity but only achieves *ipse*-identity (i.e., selfhood and expression) in the interaction with an entity

---

59. Ibid., 229.
60. Ong, "Interpretation," 8.
61. Ibid., 9.
62. Ibid.
63. Ibid.
64. Ibid.
65. Ibid. The thinking of Ong results in the same conclusions of Derrida, as is revealed when Ong asserts meaning only emerges in an extra-textual situation, thus "All text is pretext."

such as *Dasein*. However, Vanhoozer has highlighted the inadequacy of such a view in dealing with the work of art, that is, that which is composed by a creator, either art or literature. It seems that Heidegger's concept of the ontology of entities is either deficient or there is some other aspect that should be evaluated. Consequently, there is either another category of entity or modification within a category. There is also a need to investigate what it is within the consciousness of human being that can result in attribution of a dimension of being, which is itself unique to the kind of being *Dasein* has.

Ricoeur highlights what he calls the "the thing of the text" or "world of the text."[66] He states: "I can say that it is the central category, both for philosophical hermeneutics and for biblical hermeneutics."[67] This is the object of hermeneutics,[68] not the written marks but this world, thing or matter, of the text. In Ricoeur's thought this world opens up before the interpreter. The problem is that in the Heideggerian ontology, which Ricoeur uses as his basis, the text, as an entity present-at-hand, is worldless, with the result that any "world" is the projection of the interpreter and not the text.[69] As noted previously the issue in this situation is one of self-projection, not understanding of that which is other than self. Like the work of Vanhoozer considered previously, Ricoeur has to move to what Ong has styled as the extra-textual to do justice to the work of art that is the text. This is in essence the topic that Thiselton surveys in his discussion of the philosophical background of the hermeneutics of metacriticism.[70] Whilst not highlighting it as such, all three writers converge on this issue of the being of the text and the assumption as fact that it is an entity present-at-hand; this is an inadequate concept of the being of the text. Consideration of the concept of the work of art shows the way forward.

(c) A Dilemma of Being: Neither Dasein nor Present-at-Hand

There is a sense in which the "work of art" that is a painting, as an entity present-at-hand, is simply paints on canvas. Similarly, the "work of art" that is a statue, as an entity present-at-hand, is simply a block of stone. Yet a "being" with the kind of "being" *Dasein* has, perceives and understands a mode of "being" not described in the present-at-hand description of paints on a canvas or a block of stone. The "being" as "work of art" has an opaqueness and the "being" of that which is present-at-hand a

---

66. Ricoeur, *From Text to Action*, 91.
67. Ibid.
68. Ibid., 92.
69. Ricoeur, *Oneself*, 317. Ricoeur places the concept of otherness ontologically within the realm of selfhood, not that which is added to the self. Hence, projection of "world" as otherness is a projection within selfhood.
70. Thiselton, *New Horizons*, 313–43.

transparency. One "sees" the work of art, and "seeing" the present-at-hand requires a deliberate reorientation, such as in critiquing, in order to be seen.

The same holds true for the text. One reads the text as discourse, neither as print on paper, nor even as language, but it is the discourse, or composition, that one reads. The matter of the text has an opaqueness that affects perception of the present-at-hand (i.e., the print on paper or language), and hermeneutics specifically deals with this opaqueness, as Ricoeur has observed, noted previously. This "being" is different from that of the present-at-hand, though having the appearance of being related to it, for one cannot be seen without the other. The entities are linked but are not identical. It would seem tempting to move to what appears as inferred, which is Ricoeur's concept, mentioned previously, of differing modes of being, which is in essence what Vanhoozer has seemingly unintentionally attempted to do.

Before exploring the nature of this being further, there is another important observation that can be made. The observer can look at the "work of art" without moving beyond observation and perception itself, that is, without raising any thought of interpretation. In the case of the text, one can read without interpreting, yet to interpret one must read; hence, reading is a prior requisite of interpretation. However, it is not necessary to move beyond that appreciation of reading by engaging in interpretation. It is the work of Ricoeur that gives insight into this phenomenon. Ricoeur observes that *ipse*-identity (i.e., selfhood) has within it the ability to see self as another. Therefore, as it were, within selfhood is the ability to distance oneself from self (yet remain oneself) and therefore, to extend this idea, to enter the world of the matter of the text, without making that which is other than self become that of self.

Therefore, the locutionary act, illocutionary act, and perlocutionary act can all be experienced, understood, and appreciated without traversing the epistemological ground into the ontology of self. There is nothing about the illocutionary act itself that possess the force to move the interpreter forward. The decision to interpret is a movement subsequent to these acts. Reading can quite happily terminate at the perlocutionary act, as is generally done with a novel. Even if one decides that a text will be interpreted before engaging the text, the interpreter will have to become a reader and listener before he or she can become an interpreter. It is a mistake to equate reading and interpretation, as reading remains within the ontology of the event but interpretation requires a shift in ontological emphasis.

The preceding observations raise two separate, yet related issues. First, what is the nature of the mode of being that is the composition, as "work of art" or as "text"? Second, how is it that an entity with the kind of "being" *Dasein* has can perceive this mode of "being," and yet, though it is available in that which is present-at-hand, an entity without this kind of "being" cannot perceive it, though it can be seen?

(d) The Being of the Composition

In essence the difference between paints on a canvas or a block of marble and the creation of a "work of art" is authorial intent. The creator imposes his or her will through the use of brushes and paints or sculpturing tools upon the canvas or block of stone in order to create the work of art. Similarly, the author of a text imposes his or her will upon *langue* in an act of *parole* to create the discourse that is portrayed in the written text. The printed page and the words on the page are vehicles for mediating the composition, that is, the matter of the text. What the observer sees is a representation due to an authorial intent. Without that authorial intent there is no "work of art"; that is, there is no entity of the composition, just that of the text.

The authorial intent in this case is not an aspect of the consciousness of the author, which was operational in production of the "work or art" or text. It is a reconstruction from an author's consciousness of what the author saw presented for viewing, so that the observer can see what the author saw. It is not only *what is*, but also *what the author saw in what is*; that is, in the case of the text, what is said and what is said about it, considered in the context in which it is to be understood. The authorial intent is not what the creator saw but the means of "seeing" what the author saw, and results in the vehicle of publication, that is, making public that which was private, or the communication of what they saw.

Consequently, Vanhoozer's focus on the *communicative act* is understandable and moves in the right direction. Indeed, epistemology should review the concept of the *communicative act* as one aspect of its task. However, the object of the authors, or creators, is not the *communicative act* itself, which is primarily a vehicle to *represent* what the creators saw so as to *present* what they saw; the object of the authors/creators is the *seeing* of what they saw. Hence, the authorial intent is ontic in nature, in that it relates to the disclosure of entities and a view of a world. Its purpose, within the text or "work of art," is to make the observer aware of being of the "work of art" or text. The Heideggerian concept of understanding, focused as it is on "seeing,"[71] is more to the thought of what the authors desire. The *communicative act* is the intentionally done of the authors in order to communicate what is seen. The authors desire, in this sense, that the observers understand what they understood. Heidegger clarifies the conception of sight so as to move beyond the physical act of seeing, so that sight "lets entities which are accessible to it be encountered unconcealedly in themselves."[72] In the process of understanding, "being" is perceived in its connectedness, hence its relationship to reality, and is given its value in the world of the one seeing.[73]

In this sense the authorial intent is that which positions observers for viewing and presents to them the world viewed from that origin. The authorial intent is not the

---

71. Heidegger, *Being and Time*, 186.
72. Ibid., 187.
73. Ibid.

act of viewing or what is seen, it is the positioning of observers so that they see what the author saw. An observer can see a world, but if that observer is not positioned where the author was positioned, he or she won't see what the author saw.

What the author seeks is sameness of sight, that is, *sameness of understanding* (in the Heideggerian sense), *not sameness of meaning*, which is personal and different. It is important to note that *sameness of understanding* is sameness of perception, or perception of the same thing, not sameness of description of that perception. The meaning that observers will give to what they "see" is impacted by the interconnections of their own unique consciousness. Thinking, and hence development of meaning, is a derivative of understanding; that is, it is subsequent to understanding.[74]

Interpretation is, as noted previously, a further derivative of thinking, as it is always "I interpret." Interpretation is always grounded in an understanding "I" already has, a *"fore-sight."*[75] Heidegger asserts that when something is understood it is still veiled (to self is implied), and it is the appropriation to and by the self in the act of interpretation, which is the unveiling.[76] This interaction of what is understood and its appropriation, or the rudiments of the hermeneutical "circle," is the essence of the structuring of meaning.[77] Consequently, "All interpretation is grounded on understanding."[78]

Schleiermacher states that for him it is a canon that "in order to understand the first part correctly, the whole must have already been understood."[79] This is the essence of what Heidegger asserts, but with the additional observation that this apprehension of the whole involves the presuppositions of the interpreter.[80] In the case of dealing with a text, one already speaks and has understanding of the language he or she is to interpret, or interpretation is impossible. However, possession of a language involves *fore-sight* in the sense of pre-understanding, even if only purely on a Saussurian basis, that is, the referential nature of signifier and signified. Culture and subsequent subculturation, as previously noted, impacts language beyond this basic level. Previous encounters with an author, or another author from the same era or tradition, will also impact this *"fore-sight."* All of which goes to emphasize that Heidegger's assertion is well attested to.

The concept of "distanciation," developed by Ricoeur based on Gadamer's work, has its origins here in Heidegger's work. This distancing is not just an element of time but the recognition that every interpreter, and author, has his or her own unique set of

---

74. Ibid.

75. Ibid., 191.

76. Ibid. Heidegger states that which is veiled in this way "becomes conceptualizable through interpretation."

77. Ibid., 195.

78. Ibid.

79. Schleiermacher, *Hermeneutics*, 217.

80. Heidegger, *Being and Time*, 192.

presuppositions, irrespective of the degree of similarity of presuppositions. As a result sameness of meaning is illusory. There is an appearance of the possibility of sameness of meaning, but it remains unachievable. If one accepts the reasoning of Pannenberg that the idea of God and the absolute is part of human being, then there is only one point at which sameness of understanding, as sight, and sameness of meaning become coincident, that is, from the divine perspective or the point of origin (i.e., to "see" from the same place with the same set of presuppositions). It has been noted before that Vanhoozer, Thiselton, and Ricoeur all agree on this point; that is, no theologian, or for that matter person, enjoys "the God's eye view" of reality.[81] Every human being only ever possesses a relative view of God's view, which is perception of reality as it is in the true sense of absolute.

Nevertheless, similarity of presuppositions (hence understanding) obviously can possibly result in similarity of meaning. In his epistle to the Philippians, Paul declared of Timothy, whom he had trained and traveled with, that in Paul's estimation Timothy was "like-minded"; that is, by implication he had sameness of understanding and saw things the same way Paul himself did and possessed the same essential presuppositions. Thus, Paul could be confident that the meaning Timothy would give or apply, and act upon, would have a large degree of similarity to that of himself. Therefore, within a community, for example, the Christian community, broad agreement of presuppositions will result in similarity of meaning, which theoretically can approach extremely closely to sameness, yet within human being-ness sameness of meaning remains illusory.

Although sameness of meaning is illusory, this is not the case for sameness of understanding. It is logical that two people can stand at exactly the same place and see the same world. As Heidegger noted, physical eyesight is a general concept that falls within the provenance of understanding. Consequently, it is reasonable to assert that what one understands can be explained and what is explained can be understood. In essence this simple concept is what Ricoeur develops in this dialectic of "explanation and understanding" in dealing with interpretation of texts. The very concept of understanding links epistemology and ontology; that is, it involves both description and the being of the entity. It does this without being solely the province of either epistemology or ontology. The relationship between them is that each seeks and needs the other in understanding. Consequently, it is not a matter of either/or, nor is it a matter of mutual exclusivity, but it is rather an interdependence in understanding.

Sameness of meaning implies both sameness of understanding and sameness of thinking. Ricoeur has recognized this is the error of Romanticism that leads to disjunction due to the aporia in the relationship of epistemology and ontology. Ricoeur's answer, to the "revelation" of "distanciation," is to remove the issue from that of meaning of the author to meaning of the text, that is, separated from the psyche of the author. His problem is that as much as he may desire to return to otherness to

---

81. Vanhoozer, *First Theology* 309.

circumvent a self-centered "world," the only otherness possible is a self-projection.[82] In separating and thereby losing the author in the process of interpretation, he has lost the very thing he seeks: the potential for sameness of understanding.[83] Hence, in Ricoeur's theory of interpretation, explanation is not the author's but the interpreter's. The reason is that although Ricoeur can view the same world the author viewed (i.e., the content or matter of the text) he has lost the point of origin, the place from which to view the world that gives sameness of understanding, that is, the authorial intent. In so doing he has also lost the ontology of the being of that which is other than self.

The nature of "understanding" links the public domains of both author and interpreter. The failure to recognize that "thinking" is a derivative of understanding, as outlined by Heidegger, leads to the epistemological approach that results in the understanding of *understanding* itself as essentially derivative of thinking. Ricoeur's work has brilliantly brought to light that epistemology should lead to ontology, but in the process an ontological shift is essential. This shift occurs in *understanding*. Ricoeur's observation, based on the work of Gadamer and Heidegger, that the proper concerns of epistemology should be submitted to ontology, together with what has just been discussed, point to the realization that ontology provides the context of the world of the content; that is, epistemology is conducted in the context of a recognized ontology. This reinforces what was proposed as a canon of interpretation: *that which is to be known must have being as it is to be known, in order to be known.*

Therefore, to engage in epistemological tasks, such as exegesis, without first considering the ontology of the text, moves the content, the world described in the text, out of orbit. The only *idem*-identity in this situation is that of the present-at-hand texts of language on some form of media, and the result is that the being of the "work of art," or composition, which is linked to but is not identical with the text, is lost. Consequently, both aspects of identity of being of the composition are lost, that is, both the *idem*- and *ipse*- identities. The apparent retention of *idem*-identity in the present-at-hand text is illusory. The *idem*-identity of the present-at-hand text is sufficiently broad, which Ricoeur labels as its "polysemy," so that the primary identity of the work of art is now determined by the *ipse*-identity, or selfhood, assigned by the interpreter. Otherness, as otherness, has been totally divested from the text. All that remain in the text will be the foundational remnants, highlighted in the epistemological description of ontological statements that relate to the "being" of the text. The ascription of

---

82. Ricoeur, *Oneself*, 329. Ricoeur notes that there "is not a single one of our analyses in which this specific passivity of the self affected by the other than self is not announced." Ricoeur regards the experience of otherness as a "passivity" related to phenomenological discourse, as the counterpart of ontological discourse, which is the experience of the attestation of otherness, 318. This implies the concept of otherness experienced from the "self" side of the experience. Therefore, his desire for otherness is evident, but the route to otherness is always self. It would seem that what transpires is a *self-consciousness* of otherness rather than being *self* conscious of others.

83. Ricoeur, *Interpretation Theory*: 93. Ricoeur believes that the end result of his interpretation theory is an understanding of the author more faithful to the concept advanced by Schleiermacher.

"being" is lost to interpretation. It is therefore asserted that the nature of "being" of the text is not equivalent to the nature of "being" of the composition, and "being" of the composition must be retained.

(e) Createdness and "Being"

This implication should not be passed over without further consideration; that is, the implication that the concept of "being" of the text and "being" of the composition are not simply modes of "being" of the same entity. A digitized copy, as in a photograph, of the paints on canvas retains the "being" of the "work of art," although the "being" of the paints on canvas is now severed from the work of art. An entity with the same kind of "being" that *Dasein* has can still "understand," or "see" with appreciation, the "being" of the entity that is the "work of art." In one sense the "being" of the "work of art" in each case is interchangeable, one with the other. However, those of the text on paper and the digitization are not.

Thiselton, in a discussion of illocutionary acts, alludes to the same issue. His object is to differentiate between the idea of informing in a text (which relates to a descriptive task) and the action a text performs, for example, in a text describing an act of worship an act of worship is actually performed.[84] Thiselton builds upon the work of Wolterstorff and Walhout et al to show that a number of illocutionary acts can be performed in, or by, a text.[85] Essentially what he is pointing out is that a text does not only act referentially but can also bring about a state of being. If this is the case, then these aspects, or actions, must be considered as the ontological context within which the *what* of the action can be examined epistemologically. This being is attributable to (hence an attribute of) the one performing the act, whether the author of the text or a character within the text.

Thiselton acknowledges the problematic nature of this movement from text to "states of affairs outside language" and turns to the work of Searle as a basis for promoting discussion.[86] Thiselton takes note that Searle differentiated between "institutional facts" and "brute facts"; for example, in a person's act of bequeathing by writing a will there is an institutional fact of actually bringing about a state of being, that is, transfer of property, and a brute fact of the text itself.[87] Perhaps the most illustrative example referred to is Searle's concept of currency, where the brute fact of the piece of paper is a separate issue to the institutional fact of being actual currency supported by a government.[88] A state of being is brought about, and an entity created, that is linked to another entity but is distinguishable from it, that is, the entities of currency and a

84. Thiselton, "Communicative Action and Promise," 144.
85. Ibid., 145.
86. Ibid., 147.
87. Ibid.
88. Ibid.

piece of paper. This even holds in relationship to the example of the work of art described previously; that is, although a digitized copy of currency is not currency, it is identifiable as an entity in the copy. It is suggested that rather than attempting to find accommodation within the epistemological task, the ontological task is primary, that is, identification of the being created, and hence the concept of the illocutionary act described is in reality ontological. Epistemology is then rightly employed to examine the *what* of the being, which can ultimately move to the selfhood of the interpreter, as highlighted in Ricoeur. The act of worship by an author of a text, once understood as an act and what was done in the act, can promote intention-to act in the interpreter. The "intentioned-ness" of the text, and not just its description, is critical to the "intention-to" of the interpreter.

A further important observation that can be made is that two independent "beings" can perceive the same "work of art" without the need of one consciousness revealing it to the other.[89] Consequently, the "being" of the "work of art," though seemingly "being" that is uniquely perceived by the entity with the kind of "being" *Dasein* has, and largely therefore viewed by a sight beyond physical sight in the imagination, nevertheless exists independent of any one particular imagination. It also *therefore exists independently* of the imagination of the author-creator that gave it existence. As a result, it is inferred as an entity that is neither purely *Dasein*, though only this kind of being understands it, nor is it purely "being" of the present-at-hand, although it is present-at-hand in being accessible to any *Dasein*. It is "being" that exists in a dimension that defies the classifications so far advanced. In Vanhoozer's discussion of seeking to consider the issue of "begotten and made," in considering the text as "work of art," he noted that the answer is elusive. He sought the differentiation in a mode of being by resorting to Ricoeur's concept of identity. However, the answer lies in a recognition of a separate "being" itself and not simply a mode of "being."

It is suggested that the term that allows the differentiation as a category of "being" is that of "to create." Other than when applied to the concept of the "divine fiat" of "*creare ex nihilo*"—to create from nothing—the word *create* carries the idea of the causing of existence, hence "being," of some new entity from what is present-at-hand. However, though the entity so created is composed from that which is present-at-hand, it is also, due to the imposition of authorial intent in the act of creation, or act of *parole* in the case of a text, an entity whose "being" is distinct from that of which it is composed. Therefore, following the Heideggerian understanding, what is created is similar to *Dasein* in the sense that it can be present-at-hand and yet, like *Dasein*; but unlike the purely present-at-hand entity, it is not "worldless," hence "unmeaning." This fulfills what Vanhoozer observed, concerning the "work of art," that it "is neither the same as nor wholly different from its creator."[90]

---

89. Gadamer, *Philosophical Hermeneutics*, 102.

90. Vanhoozer, *Is There a Meaning*, 225. It is interesting that Vanhoozer uses the term "create" but essentially passes over its significance, without recognizing that the term itself attracts the very

Disclosing the Being of the Text

Vanhoozer considers the issue of the recognition of a "work of art" being identifiable with a particular person in his explication of the need of differentiation due to recognition that, though the work is not the person, there is some continuity with the person in the work.[91] Thus, the created work can be seen to inherently make some reference back to its creator. This operational principle would seem to be what the author of the biblical text is alluding to in Rom 1:19–20. This recognition in the biblical text helps to further clarify the concept of reference to the creator of a work. The entity that is created, in the case of the biblical text of Rom 1:19–20 "the world," makes reference not to the personality, therefore psyche, of the creator, but does inherently reflect attributes, in the sense of qualities and characteristics, of its creator. In Ps 19:1–4 the psalmist views the world as itself a communicator; that is, it is implied that the world has "being" that is essentially similar to that of a text by an author.[92] Because in this sense of a communicator the world is a text, in understanding its content (i.e., the matter of the text) is recognition of attribution of qualities and characteristics attributable *to* the person of the author, not attribution *of* personality. It is suggested that this attribution is due to the similarity to presence, which ascription the author of "being" bestows, that is, this tendency to attribution is inherent and not just due to speculation by the interpreter.

This concept of identification with a creator is inherent within all created entities. It is well recognized that types of cars are associated with a particular automotive company. Not only are physical attributes recognized but also attributable characteristics, such as reliability, economy, and so forth. These attributes are not recognition of *idem* or *ipse* identities of the present-at-hand materials that do constitute a physical being; they belong to the created entity as linked to its creator. Similarly, anecdotally the biblical recognition of the created world as manifesting, or revealing to be seen and hence understood, attributes of the creator is not a religious interpretation but a religious application. What the world reveals is that the creation, as a created entity, reveals that its creator clearly has the attributes of immense power and a status of divinity. The only presupposition is that of metaphysics of presence. Interpreters, holding a presupposition of metaphysics of absence, recognize this in their understanding, and subsequently distance themselves from it in meaning. Nevertheless, sameness of understanding is possible despite metaphysical presuppositions that prevent sameness of meaning.

---

differentiation he sought. In using its noun form he passed over its verbal significance as a transitive verb. As suggested his answer lay in mode of "being" and therefore did not consider the imparting of "being" inherent in the verbal form of "create."

91. Ibid., 226.

92. Gadamer, *Philosophical Hermeneutics*, 96, 101. Gadamer develops a similar principle in the "speaking" work of art. In consideration of the natural world, although he considers its aesthetics he does not recognize it as a work of art in the sense of what a person does, 97. If he did then Ps19 would be seen in this same light. In this his presupposition of a disregard of the world as created is revealed. This aspect of the "speaking" of the work of art in Gadamer's work will be considered again.

Is There An Author in this Text?

The preceding discussion began on an issue of understanding texts and was extended to works of art in general, with the inclusion of texts as a form of a work of art. However, in the course of the discussion an important implication suggests itself, which is that the work of art and text are themselves particular cases of the "being" of the created entity as the general category. There is sufficient reason to suggest this being is a distinct "being" that is neither *Dasein* nor purely that of the present-at-hand. The rudimentary proposal of a definition of "created being," as a result of these observations, is that "created being" is the imposition of authorial intention, or creative will of the creator, upon the present-at-hand so that the identity of the entity so "created" is not "understood," or "seen," as either that of the creator or the present-at-hand, but a different entity whose identity is only understood by, or visible to, an entity whose "being" is the same kind of "being" as *Dasein*.

During a discussion of aesthetics and hermeneutics, Gadamer, in consideration of the communicability of the work of art, notes that whatever directly addresses a person takes on person-like appearance.[93] This should be distinguished from anthropomorphism where person-like characteristics are attributed to the present-at-hand by the observer to aid understanding.[94] The work of art directly communicates in a direct engagement of the observer.[95] Thus, it seems a distinction should be made between an appearance of person-likeness and behaving with person-likeness, that is, the entity actually taking person-likeness. The present-at-hand, being worldless and unmeaning, however, can only have the appearance of person-likeness as that which is attributed to it, and as a result is only an object of understanding. Gadamer's reasoning presents the work of art as acting as subject in understanding, not just being conferred with subject-likeness by the observer. Whilst the concept of "distanciation" can be argued as leading to detachment of the authorial intention, as related to the psyche of the author, from a text, it is this concept of the work of art acting as subject that is in essence what allows, or presents, the appearance of the possibility of autonomy. It is no wonder that Gadamer saw importance in art and aesthetics in relationship to hermeneutics.

Yet, in recognizing this aspect of the work of art, Gadamer has inadvertently demonstrated that the being of the work of art cannot be that of the present-at-hand. Also, as Gadamer and Ricoeur, as well as many others, have argued, the text, or work of art, also cannot have the attribution of personality or psyche. This would open the door to a return of Romanticist theories of interpretation and place the issue back on Dilthey's ground. Consequently, it must be directly inferred that there is an entity whose being is not that of the present-at-hand, although it is present-at-hand, and

---

93. Ibid., 101.

94. Note that when *Dasein* is treated as present-at-hand, as discussed in Heidegger, it still retains the concept of a person, as in a text. Thus, it becomes essentially a self-attribution, unlike that entity whose being is present-at-hand, which requires attribution by an observer.

95. Gadamer, *Philosophical Hermeneutics*, 95.

not that of *Dasein*, although it does have inherent characteristics of *Dasein* ascribed to it, allowing this entity to act with person-likeness. The source and hence image of this person-likeness must be the creator, since it is other than the observer. This is implied in the work of art's ability to confront the observer, as Gadamer has pointed out. Further, as Gadamer has observed, the work of art continues to act as a work of art in the absence of its creator.[96] Therefore, this person-likeness is not that which is an extension of the "being" of the creator, but it is an intentional presence of the creator that confers the being. The "being" of this entity is "created being."

Before further examination of this being is conducted, it is important to ask if this "being" is simply a result of imagination, and therefore only an appearance of "being" and not "being" of an entity. That is, is it that the arguments for its identity are illusory in themselves? Gadamer endorses the concept of phenomenology's criticism in proposing as an error the conceiving of "aesthetic being" as a mode of "being."[97] Does this constitute a challenge to proposing "created being"? The aesthetic has an appearance of being, but in fact is an aspect of consciousness.[98] In essence the work of art only has "being" in the consciousness of an individual.[99] Certainly it must be conceded that the idea of beauty and aesthetics are a judgment of the individual and are unique to that individual.

However, this simply implies that aesthetic consciousness is that aspect of consciousness by which one apprehends the work of art; it does not imply that this is what creates the work of art. Aesthetics is to do with making relative to self that which is understood. Therefore, it may make the judgment on a work of art relative to self but it does not determine the "being" of the created entity. Consequently, the judgment that a work of art is beautiful or otherwise, or that it is masterful or ineffective, or that it even raises to the level of work of art, is indeed the observer's response to the "communicating" work of art. None of this changes the intentionality that makes it a work of art. Aesthetics offers no grounds for dismissal of the concept of "created being," but it does highlight that this "being" is perceptible only to a "being" whose "being" is the same kind of "being" as *Dasein*.

This entity of "created being" is able to speak, in the sense of communicate, after the fashion of a person. As noted in the previous chapter, there are reasonable grounds to suggest the idea of a "speaking voice," as associated with a text, which is not the person of the author, but when understood within metaphysics of presence does act as a representative of the author. The nature of "created being" confirms and gives identity to that voice. It is the observations by Gadamer on the work of art that offer great insight into the "speaking voice." The work of art not only communicates itself

---

96. Ibid., 96.
97. Gadamer, *Truth and Method*, 75.
98. Ibid.
99. Ibid., 76.

but also in doing this "occupies a timeless present."[100] The addressing of the observer also occurs such that "absolute contemporaneousness exists between the work and its present beholder that persists unhampered despite every intensification of the historical consciousness."[101] Barthes makes similar observations about the *speaking voice* of the literary text; time is not the same as the author who is past, but the *voice* is contemporaneous with the reader.[102] Gadamer observes, "The reality of the work of art and its expressive power cannot be restricted to its original historical horizon, in which the beholder was actually the contemporary of the creator."[103] If this is true, then the work of art's "reality," or "being," and "expressive power," or ability to relate itself to the reality of the observer, stands effectively outside time. In this sense the work of art takes on essentially a characteristic of transcendence, which Gadamer does see in language, as has previously been considered in relationship to his thinking.

Yet here a true conundrum exists in the sense in that, what stands effectively outside time[104] does not undergo change. However, Gadamer and Ricoeur are both adamant that meaning is not fixed as unchangeable but undergoes change in interpretation by an interpreter. As has been agreed to and noted in this work, there is not only room, but, considering the personal ontology of meaning that links it to the self, it is inevitable that meaning will undergo at least nuance of change due to differing interpreters. The real issue should be sameness of understanding, or perception, prior to appropriation to the world of self in meaning. The concept of sameness of understanding certainly is consistent with the unchanging, due to a timeless nature of the composition. The question must be pursued as to why sameness of understanding, and not undergoing change, can result in difference of meaning, therefore undergoing change, and yet be the same composition? In other words, how is the absolute made relative without being absolutely known?

Ricoeur, in what is agreed by Thiselton to be a brilliant insight and employed by Vanhoozer, as noted previously, has opened up the means of understanding this conundrum. As covered in the previous two chapters, Ricoeur identified two modes of "being" concerning identity, which were that of *idem*-identity and *ipse*-identity, which act dialectically in identity. The concept of permanence in time is a highly significant feature of *idem*-identity.[105] The opposing pole of the dialectic in *ipse*-identity features the sense of change and variability.[106] Ricoeur notes, "Identity in the sense of *ipse*

---

100. Gadamer, *Philosophical Hermeneutics*, 96.
101. Ibid., 95.
102. Barthes, "The Death of the Author," 4.
103. Gadamer, *Philosophical Hermeneutics*, 95.
104. To be timeless, as Gadamer asserts, is an equivalent idea.
105. Ricoeur, *Oneself*, 2.
106. Ibid.

implies no assertion concerning some unchanging core of personality."[107] Selfhood is the identity explored in that of *ipse* identity.

Consequently, the identity inherent in the text relates to the mode of *idem*-identity, not *ipse*-identity as suggested by Vanhoozer. Selfhood, in relation to the text, occurs when engaged by an interpreter; that is, the *ipse*-identity is a function of the interpreter in encounter with the text. Hence, the concept of sameness of understanding is not mutually exclusive with that of difference of meaning. It is the dialectic of the two poles of the differing modes of "being" that result in the interpreted understanding, that is, a relative understanding of an absolute. One pole of the identity of created-being is within the text and the other within the interpreter, thus interrelating both.

This nature extends to all created, or made, entities. The previous example of a motor vehicle is seen in that the created state gives it functional *idem*-identity. However, the passage of time can render it a classic, so that the *ipse*-identity established in encounter with *Dasein* can cause its selfhood to almost rise to the status of work of art. Yet it remains in its *idem*-identity a car. Although Heidegger was not using this terminology, he noted the same nature of the created, or made, entity. Heidegger noted that antiquities in a museum belong to past time and yet are still present-at-hand as contemporary.[108] Therefore, they remain items of use, as what they were, but are now out of use.[109] Consequently, their *idem*-identity is manifest as what they were, but their *ipse*-identity is related to the present understanding; that is, they have a conferred selfhood that alters their meaning, but the understanding remains the same. Their present value is not related to their *idem*-identity, but is now related to their place in time and therefore their *ipse*-identity. The text as composition and the work of art are simply particular examples of the entity of "created being."

The recognition that the work of art and the composition are both particular examples of the entity of "created being," not modes of the same being, also requires that they be considered separately, as individual entities, as well as together as examples of "created being." An important distinction suggests itself in a consideration of the understanding of each, that is, what is being viewed. The work of art is suggested by something the authors perceive in consideration of their worlds. This can be landscapes, people, tragedies, and so forth, or even characteristics such as pathos, pain, love, and the like. Regardless, the important thing is that the authors see something or someone they will represent in the work of art. The direction of perception (i.e., the thing to be viewed) is not what the authors saw but the representation of what they saw (i.e., the work of art). The referent of the work of art is not what is to be viewed but it is the position from which the work of art itself is to be viewed. For example, in Michelangelo's statue of *David*, the observer does not look at the statue to see a man; rather, from the place of the "being" of a man the observer considers the being of the

---

107. Ibid. (Italics original.)
108. Heidegger, *Being and Time*, 431.
109. Ibid., 432.

work of art that is the statue. The situation with the text as composition is the reverse of this situation. The thing to be viewed is the referent of the text not the text itself as in the work of art; this referent is the matter of the composition. In this instance the text is the place from which the referent is viewed. Gadamer's use of the work of art as a basis for severing any ties to the place in history of the work of art is misleading,[110] since in the case of the text as composition, to view the text itself as the work of art is not to understand, or "see," the composition; that is, it is to *not* see what the author saw.

The preceding observations disclose the concept of identity related to the nature of the being of the text as composition. Gadamer's consideration of the aesthetic would suggest that he would regard the implication of "created being" as an order of error comparable to that of the concept of "aesthetic being." However, it is Gadamer's observations that actually point to the actuality of this "being," hence indicating existence as an entity and not just as an experience of consciousness. As mentioned previously, Gadamer stressed the ability of the work of art, not only to directly communicate but also to do so in a confronting way.[111] Therefore, like the kind of "being" *Dasein* possesses, a work of art is capable of "touching" the person. However, Heidegger explained that this phenomenon of "touching" was unique to *Dasein*.[112] The text as composition therefore possesses this person-likeness that is an attribute of *Dasein*, that of "touching."

Nevertheless, though the entity of created being is capable of being touched by *Dasein*, it is incapable of experiencing that touch, which is consistent with its present-at-hand "being" and lack of personality as an entity, and as such it remains unchanged by that touch. As suggested previously, the nature of created being is disclosed as neither *Dasein* nor yet wholly that which is present-at-hand and worldless. Therefore, it is sound to suggest that this "being," at this point described as "created being," is indeed an entity. The "world" of the text, which is so important to Ricoeur's thinking, belongs to the *idem*-identity of the text and cannot be interpreted with an *ipse*-identity in its encounter as self-projection without first considering its ontology, which Ricoeur does not do. The otherness of the text relates to its possession of *idem* not *ipse* identity.

(f) Intentioned-ness and "Being"

The concept of the "speaking voice" and that of "touching" both imply the complementary concept of "intention." Intention is a directed act of a consciousness, and

---

110. Gadamer, *Philosophical Hermeneutics*, 101–3. This is a constant theme of this article in the book; however, these pages specifically address the issue and the perceived relationship to texts. It is interesting that although he uses the concept of art as an analogy for the textual situation, he does recognize the difference of focus, 101.

111. Ibid., 101.

112. Heidegger, *Being and Time*, 81.

therefore it is that of a person.¹¹³ Intention-to leads to an intentional act. However, this not only relates to the making of that which is made, it also relates to the thing made itself. Created being has directedness, often related to functionality (i.e., its existence) from the perspective of the creator, which relates to what it is intended to do, or achieve. Whether ones speaks concerning the car or computer, or entities such as the work of art and text, they have a directedness, which is the result of an intention-to of the author that must be cooperated with in order to function in accordance with purpose.

The concept of communication implies itself the concept of engaging someone in an act of communication. In the case of the work of art, the work of art has within it intention-to confront, to use Gadamer's word of what it does, and present itself to an observer. The object of the creator is for the observer to go to the work of art itself. A work of art uses its referent as the place of viewing, in order to draw attention to itself, by engaging the *ipse*-identity, that is, the selfhood, of the observer. In the case of the text of a composition, the intention-to is to refer the reader to its referent (i.e., its world) so that the world of the text is viewed from the text. This is the sense to which Ricoeur attracts in the idea of opening a world before the reader/interpreter. However, Ricoeur gives no place to the author, although he recognizes the directedness; that is, the text has inherent structure that directs the seeing of the interpreter.¹¹⁴ The object of the author is for the reader to go to the world projected. In Ricoeur this simply becomes the object of the text; the author is lost, having been drowned in a sea of subjectivity.

The *idem*-identity of the text as the creation of the author—which must be the locus of any concept of "intention" since this presents the person-likeness—seeks to engage the *ipse*-identity of the observer to enter the world of the text in an engagement of the imagination of the observer. The object of the author is not only to identify the place of viewing but to actually position the observer at this place, and this is therefore the intention of the author. In Ricoeur's thinking this is the basis of a twofold

---

113. Ricoeur, *Oneself*, 67. This is the essence of the phenomenological description. This issue is discussed by Ricoeur, 67–87, covering both the idea of the act and that of the idea of "intention to," in relating intention to the agent. This has been discussed at more length in the previous chapter.

114. Ricoeur, *From Text to Action*, 18. Ricoeur states his concept of the purpose of hermeneutics, "The task of hermeneutics . . . is twofold: to reconstruct the internal dynamic of the text, and to restore to the work its ability to project itself outside itself in the representation of a world that I could inhabit." For Ricoeur, to think of the author in this context seems to move to subjectivity, which he abhors, and yet he notes that to fully allow the text to disclose itself the interpreter must pay attention to this twofold work, which features the directedness, 17. He gives a more detailed view of the second of the twofold aspect, 17, as "the power that the work possesses to project itself outside itself and give birth to a world that would truly be the 'thing' referred to by the text." Thus Ricoeur takes note of the fact that an "intention-to" has conferred a directive function in the seeing of the interpreter. This dramatically sets out the significance of the appearance of intention inherent in a composition, but this intention is unrelated to a person. There is simply no reference to the Being-of-the-being, i.e., the author, just the "intentioned-ness" that is now an authorless attribute of the text.

task of hermeneutics, that is, the structure and the seeing.[115] However, in the task of hermeneutics, this twofold task is in reality two aspects of the same task. The purpose of the directedness is the seeing; the two things can be examined independently but cannot be understood independently. It was noted previously that "created being" has inherent within it person-likeness. As a result, "created being" is not worldless, as in the case of the entity present-at-hand, and hence is an entity whose "being," though not that of *Dasein*, nevertheless acts with intentionality, unlike the present-at-hand.

This intentionality is significant in understanding the nature of "created being." In the work of Ricoeur, previously discussed in his work *Oneself as Another*, note was taken of his argumentation concerning the substantive use of the concept of *intention* as the stronger sense and the adverbial usage of *intentionally*, the sense usually taken in arguing authorial intent, as the weaker sense.[116] However, the concept of intention can also be considered from its adjectival purpose, that is, the descriptive form of *intentioned*. This form can be used essentially as a suffix to "describe" an act, for example, an act can be considered to be well-intentioned, wrongly-intentioned, and so forth. The substantive aspect of *intention* attracts directly to the agent; while the adverbial form, as qualifying action by modifying the verb, is predication but is still primarily attracting to the agent, but in a weaker sense. However, the adjectival form has moved to the objective aspect and has much weaker reference to the agent. The adjectival focus is on the performance of and a description of the action. The adjectival form can act as a modifier of a noun, and thus with the adjectival form connection can be reestablished with the stronger form of *intention*, the substantive form. The adverbial form modifies the verb but the adjectival form, in its ability to modify a substantive, can relate what was done to the subject who did the action.

It is the "intentioned-ness" that directs the seeing of the interpreter; hence, it is the aspect of the structure of the text to which Ricoeur refers in his concept of the twofold task of hermeneutics. In Heidegger's development of understanding, his point of reference and analogy is that of "seeing" or "sight."[117] Therefore, in this conception of understanding, to see what the author saw is to understand what the author understood. Consequently, the "intentioned-ness," as structure of the text, seeks to firstly position the observer where the author stood in order to see, and then secondly to direct the gaze of the observer to the world the author saw. This "intentioned-ness" is therefore ontological in the truest sense of Heideggerian thought, since it fulfills the very concept of "*da sein*," that is, "be there."

This becomes important in the issue of handling the text, because the authorial intent is therefore disclosed in the ontological language employed by the author, that is, in assent, assertion, and inference that discloses the being of the composition.

---

115. Ibid., 17, 18.

116. Ricoeur, *Oneself*, 79–80. This is where Ricoeur discusses the issue of the stronger and weaker sense of intention.

117. Heidegger, *Being and Time*, 186–87.

Hence, the authorial intent is in a real sense the point of origin, or place of viewing, of the world the author wishes to disclose in his or her projection. It is the perspective of the "I" who sees the world. The content of the world that is seen is descriptive, hence is disclosed in its being as impersonal event in the task of epistemology. However, the context of the epistemological task is the ontology of intentioned-being.[118]

The entity of "created being," has person-likeness but not personality. Therefore, it cannot substitute for a person, and so to speak of intention-to in relationship to a text would be misleading. However, by adopting what is from one perspective the weakest sense, the adjectival sense, interest has moved from the person doing the action to performance and description of the action. Consequently, the adjectival form would seem to be the more appropriate form to consider the appearance of an apparent intention-to in "created being." This avoids the inference of personality that would become almost anthropomorphism, which would be only avoided on the technicality of the "being" as person-like. The entity whose being is that of "created being" is directed, and therefore behaves as intentioned-being.

This phrase intentioned-being is more general and is therefore a more appropriate phrase to that of "created being." The term "created" implies the *a priori* existence of a creator as personal, and hence this word is one that primarily attracts to metaphysics of presence. The term intentioned-being allows for both the presupposition of metaphysics of presence and the presupposition of metaphysics of absence. It is also a suitable term if a position like that of Ricoeur is adopted, that is, where meaning is seen to be inherent within the text in his concepts of sense-meaning. In intentioned-being, the being that *is*, as directed being, is within itself intentioned; genesis of this intentioned-ness in relationship to the text is a matter of presuppositions.

A Brief Excursus: Phenomenological Presuppositions

The prime movers in the development of postmodern thought in the field of hermeneutics have approached the subject of interpretation on a phenomenological basis. As a result postmodern thought has regained interest in ontology, especially that of the reader/interpreter. However, in the reawakening of this interest in ontology, a concurrent reawakening of the interest in the ontology of the author as the complement to that of the interpreter has not occured. The philosophical excursion back into ontology has only related to the reader/interpreter's side of hermeneutics. Epistemologically and ontologically authorial intent has been excluded or ignored. As has been previously noted in relationship to the work of Ricoeur, this is probably due in part to the psychological identity associated with the idea of authorial intent inherited from Romanticism. As agreed previously, following both Gadamer and Ricoeur's analysis, the only person, hence psyche, involved is the "I" of the interpreter; consequently,

---

118. The hyphenated form *intentioned-being* is developed as a phrase to act as a substantive for the being of an entity developed below.

understanding and meaning is the interpreter's. However, this in itself does not exclude the understanding being that of *otherness*, that is, in the case of a text *otherness* is due to authorial intent.

The exclusion also seems due, in part, to the fact that "I interpret" begins with epistemology, since interpretation is a reflective task initiated by an interpreter thinking about his or her understanding of the text. As Ricoeur has demonstrated, the movement to ontology is difficult in the light of the descriptive power of epistemology. Ricoeur recognized the necessity to submit epistemology to ontology, in the interpretive process. However, the ontology he focused upon is the ontology of the selfhood of the interpreter, not that of the author, due to the detachment of the person, hence psyche of the author, from the text. With the Heideggarian perspective of the text as an entity present-at-hand, therefore worldless, the ability to be touched by genuine otherness was lost. As previously argued, Ricoeur's concept fails to acknowledge that the task begins with listening to that which is other than self, and therefore the proper ontological context should be that of understanding *otherness* related to the text. This can only occur with the recognition of intentioned-being as an entity having an ontology that is neither wholly *Dasein* nor present-at-hand.

Whether or not it is acknowledged or intended, the composition as text has been assumed to be, and hence treated as, an entity that is purely present-at-hand. This is a deficient categorization. Therefore, within the presupposition of phenomenology, there is an unavoidable tendency to treat the text as impersonal and "unmeaning," which only regains these attributes in the interpreter.[119] The failure to perceive the entity of the text having the ontology of intentioned-being is a critical issue.

Certainly this exclusion and disregard of authorial intent is also due, to some degree, to the failure to recognize the *ontic* nature of authorial intent, as distinct from the personal ontology of the author. The authorial intention related to the psyche of the author is that which gives intentioned-being to the text and is that which also establishes its relationship to reality as a composition; that is, it is the Being of its being in its identity within the world. Consequently, the authorial intent in the act of *parole* is transformed into the *intentioned-ness* of the text. Therefore, in relationship to a composition, the substantive "authorial intention," to be evaluated in interpretation, is not that which is related to an author's psyche but the *intentioned-ness* of the text.

Yet, the question still remains as to why this ontic nature has been overlooked in postmodern thought. Is it as simple as the reasons just advanced, or is there a more complex issue at the very presuppositional basis of postmodern thought? Thiselton conceptually places Gadamer on the "boundary-line between modern and post-modern thought" and notes his work has facilitated the movement to a new paradigm in hermeneutics.[120] Consequently, phenomenology, an approach that Ricoeur shares with

---

119. Gadamer, *Truth and Method*, 349. Although Gadamer grants the status of partner to the text, it is clear that he regards it as "unmeaning" without the interpreter, or in the discussion, translator.

120. Thiselton, *New Horizons*, 314.

Gadamer (and with Derrida, who is another important contributor to postmodern thought), is at least the background in the conception of the postmodern thought. It is here, stemming from Heidegger, who impacted both Gadamer and Ricoeur, that a presupposition begins that will in essence exclude authorial intent, even though ironically it is its ontological roots, though not recognized, that have led to this exclusion.

Heidegger's Ontological Presupposition

Frederiek Depoortere in his book *The Death of God*, which examines the image of the death of God presented in Nietzsche, notes that in the thinking of Nietzsche "nature no longer points to a transcendent source beyond itself."[121] Some philosophers have rendered the understanding of this to be the end of, or death of, ontotheology.[122] Depoortere seeks to pursue the issue of whether or not the "critique of the metaphysical God also hits the Christian God," and his thought in the book is that they are too linked for this not to occur.[123] Depoortere observes that if philosophers in general are trying to distinguish between the metaphysical God and the Christian God, in Heidegger as a philosopher "the critique of the metaphysical God also hits the Christian God," with the result that in Heidegger this becomes the pronouncement of the death of the Christian God.[124]

Whether or not this is a fair assessment of Heidegger's thought probably can only be taken up with Heidegger himself. However, there can be no doubt that in Heidegger's vigorous attempt to distance himself from ontological tradition that he sees has developed from the time of Aristotle, there is an automatic distancing of himself from ontotheology as part of this tradition, which has developed from that time.[125] Heidegger specifically rules out any reference to the ontology developed in tradition as impacting a "true" understanding of ontology.[126] In so doing he creates an important presupposition in his work, one which will blind "understanding" of any impact of the Christian God, and one that opens the door to metaphysics of absence, developed to its ultimate statement in Derrida. The God of Scripture, not just the Christian God, is excluded from the development of ontology for Heidegger. For Heidegger only phenomenology, which begins with what presents itself as opposed

---

121. Depoortere, *Death of God*, vii.

122. Ibid., 3.

123. Ibid., 4. He observes that no clear-cut distinction is possible between a God of philosophers and a Christian God, 5. The concept of the metaphysical God is a result of reflection on the Christian God so that "the God of the Christian tradition *is* the metaphysical God of the philosophers," 12.

124. Ibid.

125. Heidegger, *Being and Time*, 42–49. Heidegger seeks "the destruction" of the traditional ontology that has enveloped the idea of being. He indicates his desire to begin to consider the question afresh, beginning with the ancient Greek philosophers and in particular Aristotle, 49. Hence, Depoortere's observation that the God Heidegger sought was that of the poets, *Death of God*, 5.

126. Ibid., 49.

to conceptions of its origins, represents a philosophical viewpoint that allows an unprejudiced investigation.[127]

Vanhoozer observed that, in his view, the "fates of the author of traditional literary criticism and of the God of traditional theism stand or fall together."[128] Vanhoozer's comments relate to a discussion about the unitary concept of the book; however, they also relate to the general concept of authorization of "intentioned-ness" present in an entity. The words *creator* and *author* can be used interchangeably without distortion of the concept of either. In the case of a text, one speaks of the author; in the case of the work of art, one speaks of the artist. However, one could alternately speak of the creator in both cases without any alteration of meaning to the concept of author and artist. The problem is that phenomenology does not consider the origins of existence, hence authorization of existence, just that existence is.[129]

For Heidegger a central thesis of his work is that, regarding the reality and substantiality of man, "the substance of man is existence."[130] His view of this substance is the specific exclusion of the idea of spirit, declaring "man's *substance* is not spirit as a synthesis of soul and body; it is rather *existence*."[131] Heidegger's view of the traditional concepts of body, soul, and spirit allows these designations to cover phenomenal domains that can be examined as themes.[132] They are ways of looking at being as opposed to actuality of being. The concept of the Being of *Dasein* does not come as a derivative of their consideration.[133]

It is interesting to note that had Heidegger based his search for being on the idea of the identity of the creator, as revealed in the LXX, he would have found support for the development of his ontology, but on the basis of the Being of the Creator. The translators of the LXX, in Exod 3:14, translated God's declaration of his name that discloses his identity as "εγω ειμι ὁ ῏Ων" ("Myself I am the one being," or, "I myself am the being").[134] In a proper understanding of ontotheology this is a presentation of the Being of being. It is an ontological statement that as an assertion is itself a statement that posits being, not a description of being. Heidegger argued for time as the horizon of *Dasein*, and hence being is locked into this temporal world and what transcends is specifically excluded.

---

127. Ibid., 50.

128. Vanhoozer, *Is There a Meaning*, 71.

129. Heidegger, *Being and Time*, 432. In discussion of the concept of *Dasein* in time, Heidegger notes *Dasein* can never be past, because it can never be present-at-hand (although as discussed previously Heidegger notes it can be treated as present-at-hand without implication on its being). Heidegger notes concerning *Dasein*, "if it is, it *exists*." (Italics original.)

130. Ibid., 255.

131. Ibid., 153.

132. Ibid., 73.

133. Ibid., 74.

134. Benton, *Septuagint with Apocrypha*, 73.

As a result Heidegger has not considered this, as it is excluded by his own presuppositions. Neither has he considered the biblical description of the created state of human being as an incorporation of both this temporal existence, in the creation of the body, and eternal existence, in the living human being-ness itself due directly to the inspiration (i.e., breath) of the divine into the body. In the biblical context Heidegger has placed humanity as having being, hence existence, of the same kind of being as the creation of all other living beings, Gen 1:20–25, which does have the horizon of time related to its being. Humanity has temporality as a mode of its being, as is observed by Heidegger and confirmed in the biblical text, Gen 2:7. But the same verse of Scripture indicates an eternal mode to human being in the breath of God as the source of its living-being, contrary to the accounts of the creation of all other living things. If the Being of being is lost then being simply presents itself as unattributable existence; that is, the substantiality of human being is existence as Heidegger proposed when considered without the transcending eternal mode of being.

It is also interesting to note that if Heidegger had taken his lead on being from the biblical concept, especially as disclosed in the LXX, he would also have found the answer to his problematic question. Heidegger took note that *Dasein* already has being, therefore a *foresight* or *fore-understanding*, when the investigation of its own *being* begins. He wondered at the origin of this being, which is disclosed in the scriptural account of human being. Consequently, in Heidegger's thought the creator and the concept of the author as a creator are lost. In developing the origins of his basic ontological concepts, he asserts specifically "we have nothing to do with a vicious relativizing of ontological standpoints."[135]

It is admitted that the preceding discussion is examined from within ontotheology. However, it does show that there are alternate presuppositions and ways of understanding being. How human being is understood is a matter of presuppositions, and the observer decides which presuppositions he or she will hold. Consequently, the observer will then evaluate the proposed being and his or her experience in the light of the proposed being. Subsequently, the observer will decide which meaning is given to the same understanding (i.e., that humanity is existent as living being), but noting that the point of origin taken will dramatically impact the meaning given in the life of the observer. This will subsequently impact their interpretation of texts at a primal level, since it will decide for the observer the possibility of real presence in otherness, as opposed to an understanding of otherness that is simply self-projection. Any subsequent argument on the meaning of a composition due to intention of that which is other than self will be decided on the basis of the presupposition, not the text.

Therefore, here in Heidegger's presuppositional basis is that which will initiate the disappearance of the author, and hence the ontology of the author manifest in authorial intent. Consequently, in Heidegger's understanding of human being, there is only that which is temporal; the eternal is not only excluded as outside comprehension, as

---

135. Heidegger, *Being and Time*, 44.

in Kant, but is excluded from being. It must be reemphasized that this is a matter of presupposition dictated by the constraints Heidegger placed on his search. It is not something whose reality demands that any concept of the impact of the eternal hermeneutically is simply "special hermeneutics," as distinct from "general hermeneutics." The relegation of the eternal to special hermeneutics and thereby excluded from general hermeneutics is itself an unfounded prejudice, which when applied causes alienation of those who refuse to be conformed by the prejudice. This alienation effectively seeks to exclude from general debate, concerning the understanding of a composition, those who hold that proper ontological interpretation recognizes the impact of genuine otherness due to authorship. This otherness is not a self projection but recognition of genuine otherness that is able to transcend the selfhood of a person and touch the person. The refusal to recognize that this is hermeneutically valid is a prejudice the aim of which is not hermeneutics but exclusion. The Christian God is not dead, just excluded.

12 Interpretation Theory

Discovering the Otherness *of the Text*

The Issue of Understanding

Introduction

THE ISSUE THAT BEGAN our journey in this book is that of the questions raised due to the conundrum and paradox apparently created by the Christian belief that through the text of Scripture, God both spoke in history and speaks today. The aim of the book is not theological as though either proving that God exists and speaks or prescribing what one should do because they hold this belief about Scripture. The reality of the person of God and that God speaks are matters of belief not hermeneutics. The aim of this book is to consider the issues and their implications as involved in the hermeneutical task. The conundrum and paradox both occur due to the issues of *spoke* and *speaking* when considered in relationship to literary texts and in their subsequent interpretation. Hence the conundrum and paradox concern communication in relationship to literary texts, which falls within the purview of the hermeneutical task.

If Scripture as a literary text is held to be a communication inspired by God, and the literary text is not simply viewed as dictation and transcription of God's speaking, this leads to the conundrum of how Scripture is at the same time both a human voice and a divine voice. If the conundrum can be answered in the affirmative this subsequently produces the paradox that the same text is therefore both a human and divine message. However, the true source of the apparent conundrum is revealed to be; can any author intentionally communicate by means of a literary text? The concept of one person speaking for or through another was dealt with and seen to a plausible aspect of hermeneutics. What has been discovered in the journey is that authors can and do intentionally speak in literary texts they compose. Furthermore, interpretation of an author's composition must be undertaken in the context of the authorial intent or it is not the composition that is interpreted but the text as a stretch of language. Hence the conundrum of Scripture is answered in the affirmative within philosophical hermeneutics. The author does speak and can speak for another and another can speak through the author. The issue of belief in the reality of the divine person as the voice that speaks through the author is theological not hermeneutical.

The issue of the paradox relates to the message of the composition, and hence in the first instance relies on the affirmative answer to the conundrum. If an author cannot intentionally speak and be understood in their composition then there is no authorial message and hence no paradox to be resolved. The paradox concerns the message of the human and divine authors being resident in the same composition. Therefore, the concept of the divine message assumes the reality of the human message of the author. Hence, the focus must now move to understanding and meaning in relationship to author's message in the interpretation of literary texts.

This issue of understanding and meaning is the third of the main issues that were identified in the beginning of the book, which were those of authorial intent, the nature of the text, and finally the issue of understanding and meaning. It is in the paradox that the concepts of the metaphysical dimension and referencing become highly significant. Resolution of the paradox will assume both can be referenced from the same composition. In this chapter concerning understanding, hence perception of otherness, the concept of the metaphysical and referencing is explored in more detail, as is the nature of the text from which the referencing occurs. Also explored is the concept of performance interpretation, which was mentioned previously but will be explored further in this chapter as it clearly can have potential application to the idea of meaning related to differing messages in the same composition.

What was proposed and argued through out this book is that authorial intent is an aspect of all texts. However, what was uncovered in the process of dealing with this issue is that authorial intent has mistakenly been considered within the domain of epistemology, thus linking authorial intent to knowing, as knowledge, rather than ontological and therefore determinative in the being of the text. Intent is an aspect of a person's psyche, and a text doesn't have a psyche. It is this mistaken understanding of authorial intent that has led to its marginalization and relegation to that of a belief as external to the text, since authorial intent is an aspect of a psyche and cannot be within the text. When authorial intent is properly recognized as an ontological aspect of the text and not that of a person, the issue then becomes the *intentioned-being* of the text, which is the entity that is the composition intended by the author.

In all texts the pre-understanding and presuppositional world of an author allows the impact of that which is other than the author to speak in and through the author. Even the concept of prophetic speech, as that inspired by another so that the author of the text speaks for another, has analogy in the concept of biography; and the *speaking voice* of any composition is related to the text, because any speaking voice or narrator at least must be seen to speak on behalf of the author. The concept of the entity of the composition as *intentioned-being* plus the ability of self to see self-as-other-than-self[1] in understanding provides opportunity for reevaluation in a rediscovery of the author's impact. Authors are able to make their composition a vehicle not only *of* their understanding but also to provide within their explanation, that is, the text as composition, a message that is contemporary *with* their own understanding. In this way the author directs the *"gaze"* of the interpreter to the message of another so that the interpreter sees what the author saw.

Understanding and Explanation: Disclosing the Entity of the Composition

In Ricoeur's modeling the key dialectic of explanation and understanding, from which meaning is developed, has both poles of the dialectic based in the *self* of the interpreter. Further, the interpreter is not dealing with an explanation the author presented, but instead the interpreter is constructing an explanation. *Self*-explanation is what will become the other pole of the dialectic for his or her interpretive task in Ricoeur's model. Ricoeur's concept appears to be based on Heidegger's concept of meaning. Heidegger asserts that in interpretation "understanding appropriates understandingly that which is understood by it."[2] Hence, it is the pursuit of a disclosure of the potential of what is understood.[3] The understanding of what is understood, as disclosed in this process, is then articulated, having been understood or brought close in interpretation.[4] It is this articulation that is defined as *meaning*.[5]

However, this articulation is not itself a communication to another. Rather, it is an articulation within the realm of the self, or self in communication with the self-as-other-than-self. Yet, if one is speaking to oneself, then just as for Roland Barthes in finding himself addressed by a text, the question arises: *who is speaking?* If one listens to oneself, then to whom does one listen? Ricoeur directs the attention to the solution to this conundrum. In Ricoeur's examination of the hermeneutics of the self, he took note of Heidegger's treatment of the conscience, which Ricoeur drew upon in his development of selfhood having two modes of being.[6] This concept of conscience provides the mechanics for understanding the function of the conscience where one is able to be one's own witness; that is, one is able to see self from a mode of being that

---

1. The use of hyphenation is deliberate and is used merely to draw attention to the grouping of the words to distinguish each as a term as distinct from the word *self*.
2. Heidegger, *Being and Time*, 188.
3. Ibid., 189.
4. Ibid., 190.
5. Ibid., 193.
6. Ricoeur, *Oneself*, 309. This has been considered in the previous chapter.

is self-as-another. This is Ricoeur's mechanics of the dialectic of understanding and explanation, that is, one explains to oneself in articulation of meaning.

Hence, the explanation proposed by Ricoeur is the *result* of understanding not the *cause*, or *precursor*, of understanding. It is an explanation that follows understanding of the interpreter; it does not precede it. If instead the text were viewed as an explanation of the author—as will be subsequently considered—then the explanation pole of the dialectic would precede understanding of the interpreter. In Ricoeur's modeling it is therefore essentially an explanation to the self that results in understanding for the self of that which is the text.

Since the being of the text as entity, in Ricoeur's model, is that of an impersonal ontology (i.e., a *what*), the text cannot touch the interpreter, as outlined by Heidegger. Consequently, although an otherness is encountered, in that the interpreter can *touch* the text, the text however cannot experience that *touch* nor can it *touch* the interpreter in Ricoeur's modeling. Therefore, the text is unresponsive and cannot be credited with the possession of voice. Any voice associated with the text then becomes purely an invention of the interpreter. This is what Derrida would define as an auto-affection of the interpreter. Because the text is nonresponsive in this postmodern understanding of it as an entity, and because the text does not *touch* the interpreter, there is no *otherness* that confronts and addresses the interpreter in the encounter with the text. This is the impasse that Ricoeur seeks to traverse in his theory, that is, the movement from an impersonal ontology of the text to a personal ontology of the text as the discourse of *someone*. In the case of dialogue, this occurs as an *otherness* that confronts and addresses the interpreter in a movement of the message directly to a personal ontology.

The dialectic that results in the meaning of the text for Ricoeur is one between understanding and explanation resulting in the personalization of that which is understood, but the whole process remains within the domain of self. Consequently, the dialectic Ricoeur is proposing features only one voice that speaks, which both invents and explicates the explanation; and it is this same voice that is listened to in providing understanding of the explanation, which is in all cases the self of the interpreter. This voice is neither a voice of the author nor of the text; it is purely a self-projection.

Ricoeur does recognize the potential problem of the subjectivism of the author, prevalent in Romanticist hermeneutics, being simply replaced by the subjectivism of the interpreter in postmodern hermeneutics, if it is conceded that "all hermeneutics terminates in self-understanding."[7] His answer to the problem is based in the idea of self being able to see self-as-other-than-self, and it is in this way, Ricoeur states, that the "matter of the text becomes my own . . . only if I disappropriate myself, in order to let the matter of the text be" and thereby "exchange the *me, master* of itself, for the *self, disciple* of the text."[8] Ricoeur assumes the ability of the text to act as other, yet the text is without the ability to in fact act as otherness capable of touching the observer, since

---

7. Rocoeur, *From Text to Action*, 35.
8. Ibid. (Hyphenation added as previously indicated; italics original.)

within phenomenology, as determined in Heidegger, the text is an entity present-at-hand and worldless, unlike *Dasein*. Any *otherness* is purely self-projection (i.e., that of a self-based creation of otherness), hence almost approaching anthropomorphism (i.e., a projection and attribution of personhood upon the impersonal being of the text).

(a) Otherness as Self-Creation: The Interpreter's Explanation

Ricoeur's argument seems largely an abstract one rather than a substantial one, having distinct similarity with the mechanics of that of both Barthes and Derrida. The *otherness* conceived in Ricoeur's model is in reality an indulgence one gives oneself after the fashion of either finding pleasure in the text (Barthes) or as an auto-affection by the interpreter (Derrida). Ricoeur's model is in essence a *creation of presence* by the interpreter based on an encounter with an impersonal text. This self generated, or created, presence is the understanding, hence perception, in the movement of the *Sache*, or matter of the text, from the impersonal ontology of the text to a personal ontology of the interpreter. The result for Ricoeur is that the text then has an ontological context consistent the interpretation of discourse as being that of a person.

It is this understanding of this so-called *otherness* that becomes the basis of the explanation that acts as counterpart for the interpreter in development of meaning. It is not an encounter with an actual presence but the imagined phantasm of Derrida. This self-generated encounter, resulting in understanding, is then interpreted in the domain of the hermeneutics of the self in the development of meaning. The experience is a presence, and hence encounter, that exists only in the imagination of the interpreter not in reality, hence its similarity to the thought of Barthes and Derrida on this aspect. Ricoeur's solution to the problem of subjectivism of the interpreter is therefore one that relies heavily on the integrity of the interpreter and has no way of monitoring the real achievement of the aim.

Consequently, the only real conclusion is that Ricoeur has recognized the potential problem but has no definitive answer, since the authorial intent, and as a result the *intentioned-ness* of the text, is excluded as *otherness*. Ricoeur's approach remains self-projection with no real reference to a concept of *effective* otherness. It is very difficult to see in this modeling how any effective otherness can in fact come into view, let alone impact the concept of the self. The only otherness is that which self will predetermine and allow. It is no wonder that the only measure of whether or not there is genuine relationship to the discourse as that of *someone* who wrote is the interpreter's integrity.

The question that seems most obvious is this: Why is it that Ricoeur must find this circuitous route to achieve a personal ontology if the discourse is to be considered from the aspect of being what *someone said to someone*? The important issue is that the written text presents itself in the impersonal ontology of the event and therefore as a thing, an object of investigation. The existence of the discourse is no longer of the form of a personal ontology, as in a dialogical situation; and to consider the text from the aspect of the personal ontology of the author is to impose an identity and deny the text's existence as a thing. Phenomenology has correctly exposed this flaw in the Romanticist approach. The subsequent ongoing misdirection of the task of hermeneutics, in the postmodern development of the argument concerning the text, is this one-dimensional view of the nature of the text as impersonal being. It is the recognition of the entity of the composition in the written text, as the second dimension of discourse, which, due to the two aspects of its nature as impersonal and personal, itself presents the possibility of connection with the impersonal ontology of a written text and a personal ontology of the person. This entity of the composition also prevents the issue of meaning being dealt with by means of objectification, the importance of which is discussed in the final chapter of this work.

Modernism recognized that the text is what presents to the reader, but sought to use the text by epistemological methodology as an access to the thinking of the author, or as existent as that which is to be structurally dismantled and examined as language having been detached from intention and now existing as message. Modernism thereby treats the text as something to be related to thinking and knowing, hence with an emphasis on epistemology as disclosing understanding and meaning, which treatment in fact subverts its identity, that is, its being and ontology. This problem was also recognized and made evident in the phenomenological approach, and philosophical hermeneutics must deal with the being of the text that confronts the reader/interpreter.

However, phenomenology's focus on being as either personal or impersonal has limited its vision so that it does not perceive the being of the composition. This being of the composition is neither personal nor impersonal though has aspects of both, and though related to the text it is not synonymous with the impersonal being of the written text. The postmodern approach has focused on the impersonal being of the written text and missed the being of the composition. This opaqueness due to the phenomenological approach bears examination.

The issue of phenomenology and its impact on the thinking and theory of Ricoeur has been examined previously. Phenomenology is not a pseudonym for postmodernism; however, as was noted previously, it has had a large impact on the presuppositional basis of the development of postmodern thought. The impact of phenomenology on the hermeneutics of Ricoeur and Gadamer, as leading philosophers in postmodern thought, is clear and has been referred to previously. Derrida's relationship to phenomenology is marked with ambivalence. Derrida developed his thinking under the influence of phenomenology in France and closely examined the works of Husserl and Heidegger.[9] Based on a work published by Derrida in 1973, Reynolds, in an examination of Derrida's thought for the *Internet Encyclopedia of Philosophy*,

---

9. Lawlor, "Jacques Derrida," section 1, "Life and Works."

notes Derrida's conclusion that phenomenology, despite its best intentions, is in the end a metaphysical approach.[10] However, in *Writing and Difference*, a major work of Derrida's published in 1978, Derrida states, "The phenomenologist . . . is the 'true positivist' who returns to the things themselves, and who is self-effacing before the originality and primordiality of meanings."[11] Thus, it would seem reasonable to suggest that phenomenology is important in the development of Derrida's thought. But Derrida eventually moved away from phenomenology defining his thought, due to its perceived problem of being in the end a metaphysical approach.

The aforementioned statement in *Writing and Difference* offers an indication of phenomenology's positive impact on Derrida despite its failing as metaphysics. This impact is the recognition of the importance of the *things* themselves, and this is germane to this current discussion concerning the idea of genuine presence. It is this idea of presence, hence authorial discourse interpretation, which Derrida so strongly opposed as being the result of the metaphysics of presence, as has been discussed at length in previous chapters. In many ways this seems to be what shaped his approach to literature and consequently hermeneutics. Both Ricoeur and Gadamer take note that in Husserl the *thing* that presents itself is where understanding begins, not in the mind of the person who is the author. Further, the being of the *thing* is an ideality that must be considered; both Ricoeur and Gadamer note Husserl's emphasis *to the things themselves*. It is Gadamer's 1960 essay "The Nature of Things and the Language of Things," included in *Philosophical Hermeneutics* published in 1976, which sheds light on this subject.[12]

Gadamer notes that in the expressions "*it is the nature of things*" and "*things speak for themselves*" there is an assertion of truth and not a reason given for the holding of these assertions as truth.[13] In the assertion is rejection of the way a person deals with *things* according to one's own personal purposes, and rather there is recognition that there is existence of *the thing* in these expressions that denies manipulation of it for human ends.[14] In this assertion the concept of the *thing*—the German *Sache*, which as a term is broader than just *thing* and encompasses the idea of the matter or issue of the text—stands as a concept distinct from that of the person.[15] In classical thinking the priority of the person over the thing was assumed: the being of the person is held in value in its being, whereas the thing is something to be used by the person.[16] Thus,

---

10. Reynolds, "Jacques Derrida," section 4, "Time and Phenomenology."

11. Derrida, *Writing*, 155. This assertion by Derrida was taken note of in a previous discussion examining the role of phenomenology as a presupposition of postmodern hermeneutics.

12. Gadamer, *Philosophical Hermeneutics*, 69–81.

13. Ibid., 69. Italics added for emphasis.

14. Ibid. Italics added for emphasis.

15. Ibid., 70.

16. Ibid. This also shows the echoes of Heidegger's categorization of being into personal and impersonal.

the result was a disregard of its being as a thing. However, in the assertion *it is the nature of things* is recognition that although a person may adapt the *thing* for usage, it has being of itself, which as Gadamer notes, "allows it to resist our efforts to use it in unsuitable ways."[17] In this recognition the priority of the person over the thing is reversed, and, although persons have the capacity of adaptation to each other, the thing is without this capacity, and so possesses an unalterable nature that the person must accommodate.[18] Hence, in this overturning Gadamer shows that effectively the person is called upon to abandon emphasis on a personal ontology.

In the common phrase that *things speak for themselves*, Gadamer is highlighting the demand to let the *thing* be heard as its own being; the *thing* is not something used as a consumable but as something that itself has existence.[19] This seems to be essentially the distinction that Ricoeur, from the phenomenological perspective, seeks to maintain. The text as a *thing* cannot just be subjected to use by an interpreter to impose upon it the mind of the author in total disregard for its being as a text. Hence, Ricoeur's first step is to deal with the *thing* he has encountered and understand it in its own ontological context. However, Ricoeur, although a postmodern thinker, has not abandoned interpretation to an impersonal ontology. Instead, Ricoeur emphasizes that the nature of discourse is *someone said something* and as a result in his theory seeks to traverse the aporia from the impersonal ontology to the personal ontology in the development of meaning; that is, Ricoeur seeks to relate the person and the *thing*.

The problem is that in the appearance of the written text as the *Sache*, the person of the author is detached following the event of writing. Further, it is the very nature of the *thing* to assert its priority over the person, thus making it not only detached but also therefore autonomous with respect to the author. The assertion of the autonomy of the text is critical in Ricoeur's theory. The only possible return to a personal ontology must take place in the hermeneutics of the self of the interpreter. This is the path followed by Ricoeur. Hence, it is the ontological categorizing of the text in phenomenology and the resultant presuppositions of phenomenology that preclude any impact of authorial intent.

Nevertheless, Ricoeur recognizes that in order for epistemology to be submitted to a correct ontology, and hence be the message of a person, means that the situation cannot be left in the hands of the impersonal being of the text. Consequently, Ricoeur observes the need to raise the hope of what amounts to a pseudo-authorial presence of the *someone* who said the *Sache*, which he pursues via the creation of a *presence* in a mode of being of the self. For Ricoeur, only in this way is justice done for discourse as being the discourse of *someone*, and thus not remain an impersonal ontology of

---

17. Ibid.

18. Ibid. This capacity of adaptation allows *changeability* within the entity unlike the impersonal, hence Ricoeur can note identity as having two modes of being, i.e. *idem*-identity, hence an unchangeableness, and *ipse*-identity, hence changeableness.

19. Ibid., 71.

the *something* that was said. In the route followed in the thinking of those holding similar positions to Barthes and Derrida, the text remains a *thing*. Yet, despite valiant attempts to make this a more palatable concept, the text retains an impersonal ontology. Ricoeur has recognized that this terminal nature of the impersonal ontology of the text fails to do justice to the nature of discourse.

This being of the *Sache* of the text, however, only has being because of an authorial intention. The nature of the text as composition is that it wishes to speak as discourse due to its genesis as discourse, which is at the intent of the author. Hence, true justice to this nature of discourse can only be achieved in recognition of the need to replace the defective ontology developed in phenomenological presuppositions with the ontology of the composition. The entity of the composition is contiguous with but not continuous with the being of the text as a *thing*. The being of the composition is neither personal nor impersonal. Having aspects of both ontologies creates an entity that is capable of speaking of itself and also is able to confront and demand a hearing.

The composition is an entity that has the ontology of *intentioned-being*[20] due to its *intentioned-ness*. As an entity it is unlike entities that have an impersonal ontology, which as entities don't have the ability to *touch* and *confront*, thereby address, entities having a personal ontology. Nevertheless, the composition's ontology of *intentioned-being* is such that it cannot itself experience that touching, which is due to its lack of a consciousness, unlike entities with a personal ontology. The composition is therefore not capable of forming *intention-to*, and is thereby not able to respond to being addressed and thus enter into dialogue, unlike entities with a personal ontology. The *intentioned-ness*, though an attribute of the text, is itself attributable to the author and is not self-generated; hence, as an entity the composition does not possess inherent changeability. Also, the composition, due to the nature of *intentioned-ness*, is not autonomous with respect to the author because it directly relates to the *intention-to* of the author.

Consequently, as an entity the composition does possess *presence* that is not the creation of the interpreter, and it is, or should be, this *presence* that the interpreter encounters in dealing with the text. It is this *presence* that is to be understood. Movement of the *Sache*[21] to a personal ontology in developing meaning is indeed a movement that occurs within the personal ontology of the interpreter. Therefore, any perception of presence being that of the person of the author must be, as Ricoeur has recognized, a presence that is self-generated by the interpreter, not an encounter with that of the author. However, any self-generation of *presence*, hence projection of *presence*, self-generated as a part of the interpretive process so as to move to a personal ontology should be based upon an understanding of the *presence* of the entity of the composition. This is critical because it is the possession of *intentioned-ness* that is the

20. This argument has been developed in chapter 11.
21. This word in its continued use is as the matter of the text: the what and about what of the text.

common attribute allowing movement from the ontology of *intentioned-being* to the ontology of *personal-being*, that is, the possession of *intentinoned-being* is what allows a transcendence of being that resolves the hermeneutical aporia.[22]

(b) The Issue of Presence: Self-Perception or Self-Projection?

The concern of this book is philosophical hermeneutics, which properly concerns elucidation and description of what is happening in interpretation. The event examined and described is that of discourse in which *someone said something to someone*. This event involves a movement of a communication from personal being—a *some-one* or author, hence personal ontology—communicating through the *said* as impersonal being—a *some-thing* or written text, hence impersonal ontology—to be understood by and have meaning for a personal being—a *some-one* or interpreter, hence returning to a personal ontology. In this undertaking, note has been taken that what the author supplies is a *something* and what the interpreter receives is this same *something* and this is where the task of hermeneutics begins. In other words, the task of hermeneutics in dealing with literary texts begins not with the *someone* who said, as it would in the situation of dialogue, but the *something* that was said.

The use of hyphenation in *some-thing* and *some-one* is deliberate so as to emphasize that, despite any conception of the identity and being of the composition, its being is nevertheless contiguous with the written text, whose being is marked by *thing*-ness, hence is impersonal. This stands in contrast to the realization that it is communicated by a person and interpreted by a person. However, the being of the composition, in distinction to the text with which it is associated, has attributes of both personal and impersonal being, being itself wholly neither as an entity. Hence, it is a category of being distinct from both personal and impersonal, and therefore has a distinct ontology that must be considered in interpretation.

Consequently, the composition's *presence*, once its existence as an entity in the process of interpretation is recognized, concerns in the truest sense τα μετα τα φυσικα—the things (or issues) after the things natural, which is the metaphysical—since it is an entity that is itself after the physical, after the *thing*-ness of the text. The entity of the composition is brought into view by the entity of the written text. If the genetive conception of the Greek phrase were taken instead of the accusative, it then concerns the things *with*—as associated with—the natural. The accusative case used in Aristotle, stated μετα φυσικα, carries the suggestion of being after the natural. The composition is an entity that is contiguous *with* the natural but is disclosed as an entity *after* the natural. It is an entity that, in its ontological interpretation disclosing it as an entity, is disclosed as a metaphysical entity.

---

22. Personal-being, having the capability of forming *intention-to*, not only possesses *intentioned-ness* but also due to this capability is itself capable of perception and understanding of *intentioned-ness*.

Interpretation Theory

The central issue thus becomes such: is this entity not only contiguous but also continuous with the being of the written text? This question itself poses a larger question of continuity: is there continuity or discontinuity between the person and the thing, hence by inference between man and machine? If on the one hand there is continuity between man and machine, as argued by Derrida,[23] then there is no aporia in this transition from personal to impersonal or *vice versa*, nor is there any presence of being with or after the natural. Also, if there is continuity then one cannot have privilege of presence, which privilege of presence is the essence of metaphysics for Derrida. Hence, the concept of the entity of the composition, where the author has privilege of presence over that which is composed, cannot exist for Derrida as an entity in its own right but becomes at best a mode of an entity. Also, with continuity, because it cannot be asserted with certainty where one entity ceases and another begins, interpretation then drifts into the uncertainty that marks the work of Derrida.

However, if on the other hand there is discontinuity, then there is singularity of being, which singularity of being Derrida strongly denies as an affectation of the husk of metaphyics that must be deconstructed.[24] With singularity of being and differences of ontology in that being of the personal and impersonal, the aporia appears in force. It is the recognition of the composition in its ontological nature of having aspects of both the personal and impersonal ontologies that can facilitate the traversing of this aporia. It is this entity of *intentioned-being* having aspects of both ontologies that is so significant in its recognition; but conversely it is this nature of its being that creates confusion when it is not recognized. This can be exemplified in a consideration of Derrida's assertion of continuity of man and machine.

This assertion has been briefly considered previously in Derrida's grand dream for grammatology, where eventually cybernetics, studying the code of communication and control in machine and living systems, will, as Derrida asserts, "oust all metaphysical concepts—including the concepts of soul, of life, of value, of choice, of memory—which until recently served to separate the machine from man."[25] Leonard Lawlor notes that Derrida projects that occurrences or events imprint on the organic—i.e. the living—in much the same way as in the inscribing of the machine is its repeatability.[26] Despite the seeming paradoxes in this similarity, Derrida proposes that this is evidence that there is no singularity of being between man and machine.[27] There is no separation of an irreplaceable singularity and machine-like repeatability.[28] However, in our journey what has been illuminated is the entity of *intentioned-being*,

---

23. Derrida's argument for this continuity and its inference has been considered previously in chapter 6, sect. (b) "The Metaphysics of Presence and Absence."

24. Lawlor, "Jacques Derrida".

25. Derrida, *Of Grammatology*, 9.

26. Lawlor, "Jacques Derrida," section 2, "The Incorruptibles."

27. Ibid., section 3, "Basic Argumentation and its Implications."

28. Ibid.

such as the work of art, the composition, and the designed machine. This entity, which is the result of *intention-to* of a creator, author, or designer, has an *intentioned-ness* imposed upon its *thing-ness* that is the making of the entity of *intentioned-being*. It is Derrida's metaphysics of absence that make this entity transparent to his philosophy; that is, it is his presupposition that privilege of presence is a phantasm.

Lawlor notes Derrida's internal wrestling with the apparent discord between the singularity of personal ontology and the "iterability" of the machine, which he is treating as impersonal. However, it is the entity of *intentioned-being* having aspects of *thing-ness* and *person*, which when it is unrecognized simply becomes at best a mode of being between the two as themselves modes of being, but when recognized is the entity that relates the two singularities. When this entity is unrecognized as an entity, there is the appearance of continuity of soul and thing—to use Gadamer's categorization—through the agency of the machine, which refuses either classification. This is due to the entity of the composition's ambivalent nature, which can cause it to submerge into either *thing-ness* or *person*.

The presence of the organic *machine* discovered within living systems, especially in recent times, emphasizes this ability philosophically to attempt to forge a commensurateness of soul and thing. The *thing-ness* of humanity, despite the seemingly innate *machine* of humanity, seen in the nature of the human body, does not prevent the recognition of singularity of being of the personal ontology. The scriptural record in Gen 2:7 clearly asserts that living-being as human-being is not in the body as some form of self starting mechanism in its *manufacture* as *machine* but is rather in the endowment of consciousness due to the expiration of God—of the breath of God—that becomes the inspiration of human-being, that is, God breathed life into humanity. Consciousness is truly metaphysical in that it is contiguous with the body but not continuous and is instead a direct endowment, in Christian thought. However, even anecdotally this appears consistent with what is, because the maintenance of life requires the residence of consciousness. The departure of conscious being is death. Even though machines—which are developed from *intention-to* of a person as *intentioned-ness* that can function due to this *intentioned-ness* with repeatability—can maintain the machine of the body, this is not equivalent to life, and without consciousness the *machine* of the body will cease to function independently.

When there is recognition of the singularity of soul and thing together with the recognition of the entity of the composition, then the being of the composition is privileged[29] in its existence with the written text by intent of the author. This entity therefore, although it is contiguous with the written text is not continuous with the

---

29. This concept of *opaqueness* has been discussed in detail in chapter 11, particularly in "Traversing the Impasse: The Nature of the Text," and directly about this particular issue in part (c) "A Dilemma of Being: Neither *Dasein* nor Present-at-Hand." In this previous discussion, note was taken that the opaqueness of the composition renders transparent the impersonal nature of the written text so that what is seen is the composition as the "work of art." Thus, the author privileges it in its existence so that the entity of the written text exists purely for the disclosure of the entity of the composition.

written text. This entity now exists having both a physical and a metaphysical aspect to its nature that has its own reality of presence, not just as a presence that is an auto-affection of the interpreter. This metaphysical aspect is critical to the ability of the entity to disclose itself in ontological interpretation. Removal in *deconstruction* of this so-called husk is in fact the destruction of the composition with the subsequent loss of its *intenioned-ness*, which was itself due to the *intention-to*, or authorial intent, of the author. It is in reality the defacing of the artist's work.

In both Ricoeur and Gadamer there is retention of singularity of identity of the entities, although in the phenomenological presuppositions of both there is the preclusion of any implication related to the *substantia* of entities. The issue of the view of *substantia* developed in Heidegger, which is seemingly continued in Ricoeur and Gadamer, is considered further below, 338–40. In essence Heidegger views that *existence* is the substance of *Dasein*, and as an entity *Dasein* cannot be conceived of in terms of *substantia* as within time; *Dasein* simply exists. However, if, as noted in the previous chapter, Heidegger had considered *substantia* of *Dasein* in terms of spirit he would have recognized *substantia* that, although impinging within time stood itself outside of time, thus giving this *substantia* the appearance of simply existing. As a result, in Heidegger, *Dasein* is not to be thought of as a subject and therefore definable. *Dasein* is an entity in action that is concerned with and asks questions about Being and is defined in its temporality within time.[30]

Nevertheless, Heidegger maintains the distinction between the personal (i.e., *Dasein*, which as an entity has world and can only have meaning or be meaningful) and the impersonal (i.e., the *thing* or essentially non-*Dasein*, which cannot have world and hence cannot have meaning or be meaningful). This is the singularity of identity retained in both Gadamer and Ricoeur. In this singularity of identity there is irreducibility so that there is no interchangeability of entities. Even though *Dasein* can appear *thing*-like, (e.g., in a text), *Dasein* is never thing-like. It is therefore this retention of singular identity that results in the aporia that Ricoeur pursues so ardently in order to traverse it, not transgress it, and thus retain a faithfulness to the nature of discourse in the task of hermeneutics.

However, it is this discussion in Gadamer's 1960 essay "The Nature of Things and the Language of Things" that is enlightening in the current discussion of presence and its relationship to a perception of metaphysics. Gadamer believed that the "dismissal of transcendental philosophical reflection involves a massive misunderstanding of its meaning."[31] He felt that the superiority of classical metaphysics was in transcending the dualism of subjectivity and object, that is, in Heideggerian terms *Dasein* and non-*Dasein* as considered previously.[32] The strength of classical metaphysics consisted of a harmony of soul and thing, but its weakness was that the resolution was found in the

---

30. Heidegger, *Being and Time*, 27–28.
31. Gadamer, *Philosophical Hermeneutics*, 74.
32. Ibid.

"infinite mind" of God, which for Gadamer is equally as unacceptable as the secular alternatives.[33] Consequently, the task of metaphysics could not be ignored, but also it could not be pursued as had been traditionally done.

Gadamer sought to propose an alternative to either of the positions, which for him was the way of language;[34] hence, his comparison and contrasting of the statements "the nature of things" and "the language of things." Gadamer pursues the relationship of the correspondence of word and thing, which finds resolution in language as the language of things. For Gadamer the mediation of finite and infinite that fulfills the task of metaphysics is language. In this way in language both the subjective and object find expression. Gadamer proposes that humanity's finite experience of the correspondence of words and things points to the very end proposed by traditional metaphysics. In language is the facility of harmonizing what was for traditional metaphysics the commensurateness of created-soul to created-things.[35]

The concept of *created* used in hyphenation moves the emphasis to *creator*, hence an emphasis on the person. But the argument for the way of language in fulfilling the metaphysical task allows the removal of the word *created*. Hegel (before Heidegger and Heidegger's student Gadamer) noted that the eternal—being beyond the finite-infinite circle—is considered beyond reason, which places the metaphysical beyond reason.[36] Hence, the metaphysical becomes indescribable abstraction, which therefore only has recourse back into reason as myth.

However, to describe the transcendence of the eternal as being that of escaping the horizon of time would be misleading, as a way of approaching the subject. This way of approach assumes that one begins with the Cartesian "I" and works out, the folly of which Heidegger alluded to in showing that the thinking being already has being. The folly becomes absurdity in the realization that such an approach makes the eternal a derivative of the horizon of time. Nevertheless, essentially this is what Gadamer has sought to do, although not beginning with the Cartesian "I" but with *Dasein*, whose being is existence. In seeking to understand the eternal, which he either in essence or by default assigns to the way of language, from the perspective of existence, Gadamer has fallen into what Hegel recognized as the trap of the finite-infinite cycle. The alternative to this is to begin with the eternal—which in theism is suggested to be a personal ontology—and then work into the finite-infinite, but this leaves the resolution within the infinite mind of God.

Nonetheless, irrespective of any theological aspects, what Gadamer has shown is that essentially language is the means of disclosure or revelation of the being of an entity. In the issue of disclosure or revelation in language, and also that of not only attribution of being but also genesis of being in and through language, Christianity

33. Ibid., 75.
34. Ibid.
35. Ibid., 81.
36. See chapter 7, "The Eternal Realm: Escaping from the Finite-Infinite Circle."

does not really demur. The scriptural text, as has been discussed in other sections of this book, does confirm both these things. The time-space continuum comes into being at the *word* of God, as does soul and created-thing as part of that universe; both are preceded by language. However, the divergence for Christian thought is clear in the opening texts of Scripture—Gen 1:1–3—the person of God and the actual *presence* of Spirit precede language; that is, language is derivative and dependent on *presence*, or a personal ontology, which thus privileges personal ontology over the impersonal ontology.

In Christian thought the age old conundrum of "what comes first, the chicken or the egg?" is solved in this ontological understanding of privilege of the personal ontology. The chicken is first, and then the egg. For Gadamer the point of perception of the interpretive task is that of *Dasein*—remembering that Gadamer is Heidegger's student—and *Dasein*'s being is defined within the horizon of time; hence, the conundrum remains a paradox, that is, both the chicken and the egg exist within time and there is no recourse to reason that can relate them, other than a transcendent ontology. It is quite fantastic that Ricoeur sees in the work of Gadamer a movement back from ontological problems to epistemological problems,[37] given Gadamer's apparent antithesis to methodology for solving interpretive issues. What Ricoeur recognizes is that Gadamer is not satisfied with an answer that ignores this issue of resorting to transcendence in the thinking of Heidegger. But essentially, at the same time, Gadamer recognizes that the ontology as its stands is at an impasse; hence Gadamer's view that hermeneutics has lost something in the turn from classical metaphysics. Gadamer instead does seek to face the issue head on.[38] Consequently, in Gadamer's thought the solution is that the commensurateness of personal ontology and impersonal ontology is the way of language. In this way language fulfills the metaphysical task. Both the personal and impersonal exist within time, and both speak as to their being within time; this is the broad category of the language of things. Language is the universal within which both personal and impersonal have their being.

The theist's point of divergence, from Gadamer's view, is Gadamer's exclusion of belief that the infinite mind of God resolves the impasse, which acts as a way of avoiding acknowledgement of the priority of a personal presence of the divine. This priority of personal presence, if adopted, in turn makes language derivative of personal ontology. Hence, in this way Gadamer avoids privilege of personal ontology over impersonal because, in recognition of the divine person, language has a source and is not itself the source. Therefore, it is the phenomenological presuppositions of Gadamer that decide the issue (i.e., what is believed about reality), as it is for any theist or atheist. Essentially, for Gadamer language is the true metaphysics of *presence*. The question of "what comes first the chicken or the egg?" would become a non-question,

---

37. Ricoeur, *From Text to Action*, 69.
38. Ibid.

or ruse, which has the purpose of establishing the privilege of the metaphysics of *presence*.

At the beginning of this section on presence, the distinction was made that philosophy should be about description of what *is*; that is, its major concern is indeed the idea of disclosure and revealing. Philosophy is about the bringing of reality within the understanding of humanity. However, describing reality draws within its scope categories of knowledge, hence knowing, which transcend rational objective knowledge, as has been noted throughout this book. Metaphysics, as science, in its ability to transcend singularity, hence categories of knowledge, without transgressing them, is therefore the domain where the categories of knowledge become disclosable, hence knowable, both intra- and inter- each category. Metaphysics operates with and after the natural to render that being beyond the natural visible within the natural.

Nevertheless, if metaphysics is not to be pure abstraction, then it must relate these categories of knowledge to the time-space continuum that is this world; that is, it must make them encounterable for *Dasein*. These categories of knowledge beyond human sight must be brought within human sight, and Gadamer has well described the means of achieving this goal, which is language. Language is able to give *presence*, hence voice, to metaphysics and render encounterable within the time-space continuum nonrational and arational knowledge. Language can therefore present these forms of knowledge in the same format as rational objective knowledge so that all forms of knowledge are available for the conscious reasoning process. It is ontic-consciousness that can differentiate between them in the reasoning process. These categories of knowledge are not accessible to the rational objective reason of the Cartesian "I," beginning with itself. Descartes and Kant have both shown that, in terms of reasoning, the Cartesian "I" deals in that which is knowable and discoverable within the horizon of time. The nonrational and arational whilst impacting within time arise as *givens* of human-being. These categories of *arational* or *nonrational* knowledge, apart from metaphysics, have the appearance of being *irrational*. However, without all these categories of knowledge, reality is not truly understandable; that is, without these categories of knowledge our vision of reality is severely distorted and skewed.

Hence, there can be broad agreement with Gadamer's observation that without this metaphysical task the overall task of interpretation suffers loss. Here in Gadamer's thought is recognition of at least the task of metaphysics as describing a dimension of being that is integral and vital in interpretation. This dimension is dismissed or destroyed in the concept of continuity of subject and object. It is a dimension that is not theological in its conception but is agreed to have been used by theology to provide an understanding of the infinite mind of the being of God. It is the source of knowledge that lies outside the self-generation capabilities of the Cartesian "I," thus, in this way enabling the Cartesian "I" to gain a comprehensive understanding of the reality it inhabits. Consequently, metaphysics is essential in making what is not of itself understandable to rational objective knowledge be understood.

However, conception of this issue of metaphysics—even as a task—is difficult and can appear to be an abstraction to the point that metaphysics and mythology can appear to be almost synonymous. The very nature of its scope and field of operation make the metaphysical task susceptible to this accusation. This is, in essence, the claim of Derrida; metaphysics is a supplement, that is, in the thought of Derrida metaphysics is an auto-affection the imagination grants oneself. It is perhaps for this reason that Ricoeur does not pursue this task as a metaphysical issue overtly but instead pursues the ontological task as the counterpart to the epistemological task, for if the task is pursued as a metaphysical task rather than an ontological task then the issue of *presence* will arise. Yet it is this very nature of the task of metaphysics that reveals an important hermeneutical principle: in recognition of this task of metaphysics is also disclosure of the means by which consciousness is able to make itself other-than-self in its understanding, which is via the medium of language.

Hegel observed that without predication the subject is universal and only has substance in predication.[39] Similarly, the thoughts of the consciousness without predication remain universal and without substance related to the time-space continuum. These only exist in the time-space continuum, and hence become knowable as otherness to another person, when consciousness gives the thoughts of the consciousness substance in language. This is the language of things as Gadamer described. The purpose of the language is not manipulation of the *thing* to serve the ends of the subject but to disclose consciousness in the creation of entities within the time-space continuum; the purpose of the language is to actually give being as well as to describe. Without the advent and the subsequent event of language, these aspects of consciousness can never be other-than-self; that is, without the expression in language they remain transcendent with respect to time and space. It is the expression in language that causes that which is both with and after the natural (i.e., the thoughts of a consciousness) to be disclosed as entities.

However, as metaphysical entities, nonrational and arational knowledge occupy time not space as spoken language, and can only occupy space as that which is with or after the natural, the *thing-ness* of the written text. These forms of knowledge are known in the fixation of language in the written text. This would explain Ong's recognition that only literary cultures are able to study, because "abstractly sequential, classificatory, explanatory examination of phenomena or of stated truths is impossible without writing and reading."[40] The concept of study requires an otherness of consciousness that is made available in written text, as only then is space occupied so that otherness is available in time and space.

Although it is not Ricoeur's purpose, his observations in *The Conflict of Interpretations* are illuminating. Ricoeur, in seeking to deal with the idea of interpretation of texts, infers what is proposed here: time is the point of attachment of these entities of

39. Hegel, "Phenomenology," 121.
40. Ong, *Orality and Literacy*, 8.

the consciousness that are given being without occupation of space. This occurs via an impersonal ontology with which these entities are contiguous but not continuous, for example, a written text. Ricoeur, rather than considering the concept of the horizons of the interpreter and the text for their historical situatedness, as in Thiselton, instead considers the horizons as horizons relating specifically to time, designating them the "time of transmission" and the "time of interpretation."[41]

Although the written text, in its *thing*-ness, occupies space it does not occupy time. Its existence is timeless. The written text is unchanged by time and has no interest as an entity in either the "time of transmission" or the "time of interpretation." It is *Dasein* whose concern is its being within time, as pointed out in Heidegger's thought. Thus, written text, as impersonal being, appears essentially transcendent with respect to time. However, alternatively, the composition occupies time and is transcendent with respect to space. The composition can be translated into different languages at whatever time is occupied by the interpreter, hence the composition occupies time, but as a metaphysical entity it does not occupy space. The purpose of the written text is to make the composition available in time so that the entity of the composition can subsequently be disclosed in space through the agency of language. However, the disclosure happens only with the advent of interpreters at points in time.

It is here that a further difference can be observed between the "work of art" as *intentioned-being* and the composition as *intentioned-being*. Gadamer also observed that the work of art occupies a timeless present.[42] He is not denying that the work of art stands in a tradition, and hence does have a *time of transmission* that can have impact on the interpreter's evaluation of the work of art.[43] However, the aesthetic consciousness of an observer directly engages with the work of art so that the work of art is experienced and speaks to the observer directly.[44] This can occur, and usually does initially, in the absence of consideration of the *time of transmission*. The observer then interprets this *saying* of the work of art in terms of his or her own tradition.[45] Thus, the work of art effectively occupies a "timeless present" and, as work of art, is unchanged by time. Any change in time, for instance any deterioration, is in its *thing-ness* as an impersonal entity not in its *intentioned-being* as work of art.

Gadamer's object is to highlight his own view of the realization of the "language of things" from a previous essay (a chapter of *Philosophical Hermeneutics*) and therefore highlight the linguistic nature of the existence of human being. His agenda is to reinforce the fulfillment of the metaphysical task in hermeneutics by the way of language.

---

41. Ricoeur, *Conflict of Interpretations*, 27.

42. Gadamer, *Philosophical Hermeneutics*, 96. This concept by Gadamer is discussed above in chapter 11, 2(e) "'Createdness' and Being."

43. Ibid. The phrase "time of transmission" is Ricoeur's; Gadamer talks of tradition, which is concerned with the time of transmission.

44. Ibid., 97.

45. Ibid.

However, his observation also highlights that the work of art is drawn directly into the time of the interpreter. The observation that the *time of transmission* can impact the *time of interpretation* even with the work of art doesn't change the concept of timelessness. Interpreters may modify this impact from within their own present, even to the point of potentially ignoring the *time of transmission*; the interpretation is not of time but occurs within the time of the interpreter.

Time in the case of the work of art is acting referentially to the artist and not hermeneutically for the work of art; that is, the *intentioned-ness* of the work of art by its nature references the *intention-to* of the artist, not as psyche but as attribute. This referencing may modify the interpreter's understanding of the work of art, nevertheless it is an accommodation the interpreter allows; it is not an understanding of otherness that makes demands on the task of interpretation. The work of art can be and is primarily directly interpreted into the time of the interpreter without reference to the element of time. This element of time relates to the interpreter's appreciation of the artist as highlighted from a previous discussion in this book.

The recognition of *intentioned-being* as an entity has been dealt with at length in this work. The defining attribute of *intentioned-being* is the attribute of *intentioned-ness* that is the result of the *intention-to* of the maker, that is, author, artist, designer, and so on. This attribute belonging to *intentioned-being* is ascribable to the maker and itself makes reference therefore to the maker; this can be stated as *intentioned-ness* of the entity reflects *intention-to* of the maker.[46] Previously, note was taken of the application of this in Scripture concerning the created universe referencing its maker (Rom 1:20), and that this *intentioned-ness* communicates, hence speaks, that is, addresses humanity (Ps 19:1–2, which is what Gadamer notes about the work of art). The text in Romans makes direct reference to the qualities of the maker, not an understanding of the message of the maker. It is the refusal to recognize the reality of the maker and act accordingly, not a failure to heed a message that is in view. Similarly, the text of the Psalm concerns not the message of the heavens and earth but rather in speaking the heavens and earth show the glory of God in that they display *intentioned-ness*. The rest of the Psalm likens their message to the commandments of God and the resultant impact on humanity to assist human life; the glorifying of God is a result of their grandeur. The interaction with *the time of transmission* is not related to message but is an appreciation of the author or artist.

Therefore, the work of art to which Gadamer refers occupies space by means of the *thing*-ness of its materials, but is drawn, or interpreted, into time due to the operation of a metaphysical task that can transcend the problem of time in its relationship to space. This is distinct from the composition as a work of art, which occupies time

---

46. This observation is based on the grammatical nature of the text, since *intention-to*, or intent, as a noun acts as a subject, which when pursued adverbially in the transition to the predicate is manifest as *intentionality*. Finally, it is transitioned to the predicate in the adjectival state of *intentioned-ness*, which as a description is therefore a reflection of the *intention-to* of the author.

but not space and can only be given present space—hence *presence*—in the interpreter. Hence the composition's appearance of being an auto-affection, as in Derrida, when it is a reality disclosed to the self, but its expression as reality is due to the task of metaphysics. In this way the metaphysical task though abstract is not myth. It is the written text, which does occupy space, that makes the contiguous entity of the composition available outside *the time of transmission*. The failure to *see* the composition leaves it with the appearance of auto-affection, the apparition of Derrida.

The singularity of the work of art exists in space but is only perceived by a being that possess an *ontic-consciousness* in *the time of interpretation*. The work of art may be reproduced but the reproduction is mimetic of the work of art; the value is that it can be seen and appreciated as work of art due to *ontic-consciousness*. However, this is only because of what occupies space, that is, the original, which is where the true value of the work of art resides. As has been considered previously, any attempt at changing the space, that is, seeking to alter the work of art, defaces the work of art as an entity *intentioned* by an artist.

The importance of the preceding discussion, concerning the differences of the work of art and the composition as entities of *intentioned-being*, is in the recognition of the singularity of the composition. The composition can undergo change of space and yet it itself is unchanged. This is evidenced in that hermeneutically it is recognized that the text can be stated in other words and even different languages and yet be the same composition. The singularity is the composition, and it is not a particular written text, unlike the work of art that is directly related to its original materials in its occupation of space. Hence, corruption of the text doesn't of necessity deface the composition as *intentioned-being*. What corruption of the text impacts is perception of the composition. In the science of textual criticism, concerning the biblical text, the object should not be reconstruction of the original text but should be perception of the original composition, which is contiguous with written text *but not* continuous with written text. The reconstruction of the text is valuable, not as though the original were re-created but because of what is contiguous with it. The genius of the function of *ontic-consciousness* is such that a certain degree of corruption of written text can occur without obscuring the view of the composition. Therefore, an exact duplication of the text is not critical. What is interpreted is the composition not the written text.

If this previous recognition was not the case, then translation would be technically impossible and fanciful at best, for without the entity of the composition what is translated is just words not message. Mention has been made previously of Caird's observation that translation involves not only words but also thoughts and ideas. Thoughts and ideas achieve otherness in language. Gadamer has well shown that translation is the basis of developing the concepts of interpretation. Thus, interpretation without recognition of the composition also becomes meaningless other than to the interpreter. The basis of relativism in interpretation is the nonrecognition of *intentioned-being*; conversely, relativity is the recognition of the existence of a singular *intentioned-being* to which a particular value of *intentioned-being* is referred.

It has been established that the nature of *intentioned-being* is being that is neither personal nor impersonal but has aspects of both. The personal aspect is due to the imposition of will, which is an aspect of personal ontology, for example, in the case of discourse due to the act of *parole* upon *thing-ness* that is the written text, which is an aspect of impersonal ontology. The imposition of will results in an *intentioned-ness* that now exists outside the psyche and hence outside the realm of a personal ontology but cannot itself be an aspect of impersonal ontology because the concept of intention has implications of meaning. As Heidegger has well outlined, impersonal ontology can neither have meaning nor be meaningful. As a result it is the recognition of the unique entity of *intentioned-being* that therefore, by its own nature as being, facilitates the traversing between personal and impersonal ontology.

However, whilst *intentioned-being's presence* as impersonal being can be accommodated its *presence* as personal being cannot be accommodated within the physical domain, as Kant also recognized. This creates a dilemma of perception that is insoluble without the task of metaphysics. Gadamer recognized the need for this metaphysical task or interpretation is inadequate, though he unfortunately did not recognize the nature of *intentioned-being*, for if he had he would have recognized *how* language fulfills the metaphysical task. Metaphysics allows language to give being to *intentioned-ness* and this is the *presence* that, working together with the *presence* of the impersonal being of the language as written text, allows disclosure of *intentioned-being*. This is the being the interpreter encounters and that should be the basis of understanding.

Nevertheless, as has been recognized this *intentioned-ness* is given space both by and in the interpreter, but it is a matter of *self-perception* of *presence* within the hermeneutics of the self not *self-projection* as creation of *presence* within the hermeneutics of the self. The locus of this *presence* for the interpreter is the imagination for perception but not for existence; and further, *intentioned-ness's* true nature excludes auto-affection, for then the *intentioned-ness* would be a function of the interpreter not the author, hence the composition could not then be in possession of *intentioned-ness*.

A Brief Excursus: Language

Gadamer has brought to the fore the important recognition that language itself is the means of giving *otherness* of being to the metaphysical, therefore enabling to become public that which belongs to the domain of the psyche. Without the means of language the pysche remains private and unavailabe within time-space. The use of language is the means of predication of the subjective. However, for Gadamer language is not the means of metaphysical expression; instead, essentially the way of language replaces metaphysics. In his thought the idea of interpretation in terms of the subjectivity of consciousness is a wrong conclusion. Rather there exists a "hermeneutical universe" characterized by a "mode of operation and the reality of language that transcends all individual consciousness."[47]

However, despite Gadamer's assertion, the issue of interest is this: if both person and thing speak, why is it that both are only *heard* by that being which possesses a personal ontology? The act of interpretation is only occurring in the subjectivity of a consciousness. Essentially, Gadamer has recognized that all interpretation is relative to the person as interpreter, but he has removed the idea of the author, that is, that interpretation is conducted relative to an intention an author had. More importantly it seems Gadamer believes that both person and thing inherently possess *intentioned-ness* due to this universal nature of language in which both derive being. If not, they could not be meaningful and hence speak or disclose their being. The source of *intention-to* resulting in *intentioned-ness* is implied to be language itself in its innate state; the person or thing is simply the vehicle not the source. For Gadamer the right word, not the subjectivity of the act of meaning, is that which gives expression to meaning.[48]

What Gadamer has done is to arrive at metaphysics of absence via a different route to that of Derrida. But for Gadamer it is an absence of personal presence not nothingness, as in Derrida. In making language the universal, Gadamer therefore seems to see this as the explanation why theism, especially ontotheology, sees the idea of the universe as *spoken* into being. Gadamer has assumed that the scriptural text on the nature of the universe is as it appears to a person, that is, it appears as if spoken into being by a person, because language appears to belong to persons. As was previously noted that, for Wittgenstein, it is the metaphysical "I" that sees the world, and the world therefore has the appearance of being determined from the perspective of a personal ontology. Because every individual "I" sees the world as relative to himself or herself, then the only resolution to unify the universe is to make the task of metaphysics resolvable in the infinite mind of God. This is what Gadamer seems to assume has happened.

In Gadamer's understanding of the universe the Scriptural accounts are effectively vehicles that convey the metaphysical truth: it is language that gives being to the universe. Hence, the accounts are myths, because they were developed on the basis of prejudice of the privilege of personal ontology, that is, the privilege of *presence* in the *metaphysics of presence*. Hence, it is God who is effectively relegated to the category of myth not the explanation of the universe. The universe is simply existential in that it *exists*, as in the thought of Heidegger, which *is its substance*, so it does not come into being. In an odd twist, the concept of creator is itself created for an explanation that evidently would not be comprehensible without some form of theism, that is, personal ontology, to the personal mind. It seems for Gadamer that at last truth is hitting the

---

47. Gadamer, *Philosophical Hermeneutics*, 80.
48. Ibid.

Interpretation Theory

light of day, and when the curtain is rolled back it is language that is revealed as the infinite universal.

Whether or not the German background in the Reformation contributed to Gadamer's views, and to what degree, is debatable. What is interesting is the correlation between his views and Scripture, but with the centrality of the creator removed. His thoughts on the importance of the concept of incarnation and its implications for hermeneutics have been previously considered. The Genesis account of creation features the concept of the personal God speaking, that is, issuing logos, which also has been dealt with previously. However, a brief examination of its flow of thought is quite revealing regarding Gadamer's thought.

In Gen 1:1 is the record of the creation of the heavens and the earth. Then in Gen 1:2 it is noted that the created world was "without form, and void"—"invisible [perhaps not recognizable in the form it now exists in?] and not properly prepared" in the LXX—and the Spirit of God is God present and at hand. It is of interest that, as far as the text is concerned, the initial formation results in a not-ordered world and does not specifically involve the speaking of God. The subsequent verses show that this initial statement is not simply an overview, that is, that the creation simply proceeds to be explained from this point. The speaking of God is the imposition of *intentioned-ness* upon what is. It cannot be stated that God did not speak as the means of creation of the *thing-ness* of the world, but what can be stated is that the writer of the text does not indicate God speaking at this moment in time. The *thing-ness* of the world is present in a disordered state. It is in verse 3 that the majesty unfolds of the creative act of the speaking God, so that what follows the speaking is the creation of that which has life, that is, including both plant and animal, and the creation of the *thing-ness* of the world in a specifically ordered state. Thus, if the person of the creator were considered as an added concept, as Gadamer appears to do, then the commensurateness of soul (as animate being) and thing would appear suggested as to be found in language. The speaking of God, the revelation in language, concerns the *intentioned* state of creation, that is, the creation in ordered form.

In the creation of *being* that has life, found in verses 11–12, 20–22, 24–25, and 26–28, an important aspect is the *intention-to* of the creator to endow the *intentioned-ness* of created being to transmit that *intentioned-ness* in reproduction of its own kind. Consequently, from a scientific viewpoint one would assume that this is what has come to be known as genetics, that is, the ability of *intentioned-ness* to be passed and imposed upon *thing-ness*. Although it may be a generalization and highly simplified, one might state that each being exists through the speaking of a language of things—to use Gadamer's term—and this speaking is the source of its *intentioned-ness*. However, unlike Gadamer's conception, this language of things, from the Judeo-Christian perspective, is in reality a translation of the divine language into the language of things. It is the removal of the person of the creator that produces the appearance that there is an innate language of things.

The creation of human life, Gen 1:26–28, as part of animate life, contains highly significant differences to the nonhuman animate life. This has been in part discussed previously in consideration of Gen 2:7, in the recognition of the endowment of the eternal dimension within human being created within the horizon of time. However, here note can also be taken of the statement in these verses that humanity is created in the image of God as a distinction to all other animate life. God is Spirit, which admittedly in Gen 1:2 in the Hebrew context may simply refer to being existent outside the time-space continuum. However, in John 4:23–24 Spirit is identified with a person as is the Father, and specifically not flesh and blood, especially at the time of the saying in Genesis. Consequently, this infers that the image of God in which man is made concerns the spirit and soul of humanity. The image of God is not innate in the *thing-ness* but is conferred as innate in the subjective being.

The immediate consequence of the conferral of this image is the endowment with dominion, or ability to rule over, verse 26, which is reinforced, verse 28, with the added endowment of an ability to establish order or rule. Hence, the image of God is related to the ability not only to pass on *intentioned-ness* but also to form *intention-to* and thereby through language create *intentioned-ness* and impose it upon animate life and *thing-ness*. This is realized in the transmission of things through tradition such as belief in the positing of assertion, assent, and inference. It is further realized in production of design and manufacture of machines, works of art, music, and also composition. It is the ability, as God did, to speak and use language creatively, and in the speaking to impose an *intentioned-ness* upon *thing-ness* that results in the entity of *intentioned-being*. The *ontic-consciousness*, which has been identified as part of subjective consciousness, allows the recognition and use of the facility of language in this divine endowment. Hence, it is *ontic-consciousness* that provides understanding and projection of *intentioned-ness* in the production of *intentioned-being*.

When the scriptural record is believed, as in Judeo-Christian thought, this is the reality of how things are. This biblical record also provides an understanding of the situation. In Gadamer's thought this is how things appear because of the imposition of a personal ontology and the privilege of presence in the metaphysics of *presence* on *what is*, by means of ontotheology. In Gadamer's view language is universal; but the language used by humanity, like Hegel's concept of the spirit of history, works out from that universal, therefore it is not equivalent to it. Language is not derivative of being for Gadamer, that is, the concept discussed of the person of the creator, but language has that appearance to humanity of being derivative of human-being because humanity has it as a given.

Nevertheless, language is the means both of formation and transmission of *intentioned-ness*, and interpretation should be about dealing with and understanding that *intentioned-ness*, which is formed and transmitted in language. This Gadamer has not recognized despite its logical flow from his own argument. Only then that which is foreign (i.e., that *intentioned-ness* that is understood) is made one's own,

Interpretation Theory

hence becomes an understanding from the perspective of the Cartesian "I," of what is understood; that is, this is how it becomes known.

Constructing Language to Disclose Intention

It is the interrelationship of understanding and knowing that results in meaning. This relationship and the concept of meaning will be pursued in the next chapter of this book. The nature of language is where the theorists such as Gadamer, Ricoeur, Barthes, and Derrida all arrive in their philosophy. Due to the scriptural account, it is also where Christian theorists and hermeneuts should also arrive. It is in language that *intentioned-being*, which does have an abstract aspect to its nature, is given being to this abstract aspect, which therefore should be the basis on which it is interpreted. Without the interpretation of *intentioned-being* humanity loses a critical aspect of its own humanity. This occurs in a reductionism that results in loss of the singularity that distinguishes humanity from the machine and also the machine from *thing-ness*. Gadamer has correctly asserted that in the dismissal of transcendental philosophical reflection there is a decline in philosophical knowledge.

(A) THE NATURE OF LANGUAGE

Philosophically, for all the theorists considered, humanity is a user of language. In Gadamer humanity is a user of the language that is the universal of all being. In Judeo-Christian thought humanity is the user of language of which the person of God is source, and who himself is the source of the divergent individual languages used by humanity, Gen 11:1–9. Ricoeur, in distinction from Gadamer, Derrida, and Barthes in postmodern thought, has recognized that the *intention-to* of the author is the inception of the text, and the text exists as a record of discourse due to this intentionality. Ricoeur has recognized that the tendency to structuralism in approaching language, for example even in post-structuralism as seen in Barthes and Derrida, has not taken account of the fact that discourse is not just language but the intentional use of language concerning a matter. This intentional usage of language places the employment of *langue* in a specific context, thereby making discourse meaning a function of the sentence, not a function of *langue*. The issue that Ricoeur demurs from is the recognition and interpretation of that intention in relationship to the *intention-to* of the author in dealing with written text. Ricoeur's attempt to do justice to the intentionality that is discourse is the hermeneutics of the self of the interpreter.

Gadamer notes that the conception of language in its symbolic form, hence also as code, detracts from the nature of language. In the direction of attention to the form of language, language becomes isolated "from what is spoken in and mediated through it."[49] In other words the treatment of language this way simply causes language to

---

49. Ibid., 76.

direct our attention to language, not the *Sache*, or matter, of what is said. It is small wonder that Derrida concludes that signs simply point to other signs. The purpose of the use of language is not the furtherance or promotion of language, nor is it just the designation of other language, but it is the creation of *intentioned-being*, whether this is as communication or alternately to give being to that which is abstract.

Consider the following illustration. If one is following signs to a particular destination, as when travelling in a car, and when one arrives there is no place in existence that is indicated by the signs, then truly the signs simply point to other signs. However, in this case the signs would be considered at the very least deceptive if not false and misleading. If, alternately, in following the signs one arrives at the destination, then the purpose of each sign is purely in its signification; that is, the wood and/or metal and paint of which a sign is composed as the signifier only have significance themselves in what is signified. In arrival at the signified, one has left behind the signifier.

The arbitrariness of the sign, as noted by Saussure, concerns the signifier not the signified. In the example just considered, one could have signifiers other than the traditional signpost that are known, for example, landmarks with known proximity to the destination. One begins with the signified, and the purpose of the lexical approach is a signifier that will be considered to denote the signified. To remain within the sign system, as proposed by Derrida, is to never reach the destination, which is essentially what he proposes. As Ricoeur notes concerning language, it is only within the system of language—i.e., *langue*—that signs point to other signs.[50]

It is the intentioned use of language that has meaning in discourse, not language. As noted previously, language as language has innate signification, but this is not meaning because meaning is an act of persons. The innate signification is what gives language the potential of meaning that is so important in Ricoeur's thinking, what he calls the sense of the sentence, for which the counterpart is its reference, that is, what is said, sense; and what is said about it, reference.[51] The sense is retained in that it is composed of *langue*, but the reference only becomes effective in the intentioned use of language.[52] In Ricoeur this reference is realized in the interpreter; however, its true place of realization is as the intention of the author. What Ricoeur has not considered is the transformation of authorial intent to *intentioned-ness* of the composition in the act of *parole*. Thus, the sense of language in the sentence relates to the conveyance of its reference in its *intentioned-ness*.

(B) Illustrations of Intentioned-ness Disclosed in Language

This book is written from within the Christian community and, as a result, the examples used are from Scripture. However, this is a special use of a hermeneutic principle

---

50. Ricoeur, *Interpretation Theory*, 20.
51. Ibid., 19.
52. Ibid.

Interpretation Theory

not special hermeneutics and therefore the principles are the same for any text. An example of *intentioned-ness* that allows disclosure of the composition is seen in the Gospel of John, which has been referred to previously for its disclosure of its marked directedness of *intention-to* of the author. Consider the following text taken from the Gospel of John 20:30–31:

> And truly Jesus did many other signs in the presence of His disciples, which are not written in this book; but these are written that you may believe that Jesus is the Christ, the Son of God, and that believing you may have life in His name.

The sense of what is said is that Jesus did many other signs in the presence of the disciples, such as what had just been dealt with by the writer in Jesus' post-resurrection encounter with Thomas (John 20:24–29). However, the reference, hence relationship to *intentioned-ness*, in the sentence concerns the intentional selectivity applied by the author; that is, he deliberately did not write, or include, some accounts of Jesus sign events. The writer then reveals his *intention-to* in his selectivity of those he did write; that is, those sign events experienced and selected create an *intentioned-being* that is the composition, hence an *intentioned-ness* in the composition. The reference of the sentence is the author's selectivity of that which will result in the intentioned disclosure of the recognition and belief that the Son of God, the Christ, is Jesus. The sign events and their incorporation into a narrative and teaching are composed with the *intentioned-ness* of revealing and promoting belief in this assertion. In the narration of one of the sign events within the composition, the assertion of belief appears in the mouth of one of the disciples who is not the writer (see Peter's declaration recorded in John 6:69). Peter makes other than self the belief, thus setting the pattern for the reader. The writer notes that Peter connected this belief with life to be experienced, verse 68, which is also part of the writer's *intentioned-ness*, disclosed when he notes in John 20:31, cited previously, that in believing the interpreter/reader might experience "life in His name." Consequently, it is clearly seen that recognition and identification of the *intentioned-ness* that is the being of the composition is vital in interpretation, and without it the reader cannot understand the otherness of what the writer has said, that is, *the what* of the matter of the text in the context of *what is said about it*.

Whether or not the interpreter himself or herself decides to accept and believe is irrelevant to the understanding of the *intentioned-ness* of the composition. However, the issue of meaning for the interpreter is the interpreter's knowing in relationship to the understanding of the otherness of the text. Nevertheless, this follows understanding. Vanhoozer sought to relate authorial intent to the illocutionary act of speech, the doing in the saying, which the writer of John reveals is that the interpreter will believe the assertion. Vanhoozer's emphasis stranded his thinking in the impersonal ontology of the event. Nevertheless, the aspect of the event on which he laid his focus is that act of speech that directly references the *intentioned-ness* of the text. The authorial intent undergoes transformation to become ontological, as part of the *intentioned-being*, which is an entity that is contiguous with the impersonal entity of the text but is not continuous with it. The authorial intent is disclosed in recognition of the *intentioned* use of language, not epistemologically in the description of the event.

The locutionary act references the sense of the text, that is, what is said, but it is the illocutionary act that references what it is said about. Disclosure of the perlocutionary act, which Ricoeur notes is the least inscribable aspect of the event of the text, is from an ontological disclosure in consideration of language. The perlocutionary act concerns the state of being of the interpreter that results from interpretation; that is, it directly communicates concerning a personal ontology. In the case of the current example, the writer of John does disclose his intended effect of interpretation of his text, which is that the interpreter will experience ongoing life in Jesus' name, that is, life in Christ.

This *intentioned* use of language, disclosing the entity of the composition, is often not as clearly asserted as in the example from John. In the example of the Gospel of John, the disclosure of the *intentioned-ness* functions in the fashion of a thesis statement, which also helps illustrate that a thesis statement itself, when present, directly asserts *intentioned-ness* of the text. Nevertheless, the *intentioned-being*, that is, being of the composition, is always present and detectable. It can be explored in the concept of inference where it is not asserted. However, when examining disclosure by inference, there is an element of speculation such that other factors, for example, tradition, need to be considered. As a result, when the being of the composition is disclosed primarily through inference the impact on the interpreter is more open ended, which can itself be deliberate on the part of the author. Where there is an intended audience, such as in the occasional nature of the epistles in Scripture, there can be, and usually is, an overall sense of *intentioned-ness*, which is directly related to the perception of the intended audience, such as a thesis statement type of approach. In a more general approach, such as a novel or narrative, the object is to draw the reader into the story so that *intentioned-ness* is experienced, thus disclosed, by inference. There is also often a sense of compartmentalization that is used by the author to intentionally address differing issues, or matters, either in a successive fashion or individual fashion.

The following example is of compartmentalization and inference regarding overall *intentioned-ness*. Matthew's Gospel presents an example where, in following the narrative, one experiences of the *intentioned-ness* as compartmentalization, revealed in language, in the writer's conclusion of each section. The writer uses a phrase that is the same in each case in the Greek text but varies slightly in the English translation, so that the *intentioned-ness* evident in the language can be missed in the English translation. The phrase is of the form—in English—"Now it came to pass when Jesus had finished—brought to conclusion or fulfillment—these . . ."[53] The differing closing

---

53. Matt 7:28, 11:1, 13:53, 19:1 and 26:1. The parenthetical comment is added to emphasize the nature of the Greek verb τελέω to complete or fulfill, hence end, therefore indicating closure of section.

statement makes reference to what has been discussed in each section. The final use of this format in Matt 26:1 has in the language used a sense of finality or almost closure of the Gospel in noting; "Now it came to pass when Jesus had finished *all* these sayings . . ." The italics are added to the word *all* to indicate the apparent finality of the statement. What follows this statement is a section that is common to all the Gospels, which is the account of the passion.

In this the writer indicates his *intention-to* in the *intentioned-ness* of the text he writes, which is his *intention-to* of writing his own unique account with his own agenda in the written text. The result of this intentionality of structure is the division of his Gospel into five sections, that is, compartmentalized narratives each composed with an individual agenda to contribute to a complete picture, or *intentioned-ness*, the writer intends the interpreter to see. This has echoes of the Pentateuch particularly, if as is commonly agreed, Matthew is specifically seeking to impact Diaspora Jews. An overview of Matt 13:54—19:1 provides an example of this *intentioned-ness*.

Jesus has just concluded a period of ministry, which Matthew contains in a section of his account, and has arrived in the regions of his own country (13:54). The nature of his teaching and the evidence of his miracles cause those of this region, who know him as a man, to ask the question of the form, "Who is this man?" or "Who does he think he is?" (13:54–56). They become offended with Jesus, and this causes a failure to recognize and hence honor him as a prophet, that is, to see that which is with the natural realm, or that which is located in the realm of humanity and phenomenal world. Note that the concluding discourse of this section in Matt 18 will specifically deal with the issues of offence and forgiveness and their impact on perception and hence life. In the center of this narrative section occurs an event in the region of Caesarea Philippi (Matt 16:13–20), where Jesus asks the disciples to tell him who do the people think he is? The answers of the disciples are in terms of human ministries, who each had significant impact. However, Jesus then asks who do they, the disciples, think he is? Peter's dialogue is well known and often referred to in his disclosure of what the disciples had come to believe: that Jesus is the Christ, the Son of God (Matt 16:16). Perception of Jesus' true nature is by disclosure of the Father and part of the theme of this section is that offense can therefore block perception of disclosure by the Father. The issue of the section, which the writer *intends* to confront the reader with, is the question that is asked at the beginning of the section: "Who is this man?"

Looking at the *intentioned-ness* of the language of each section allows the reader to conduct a similar treatment of each section. The overall *intentioned-ness* can be inferred in what is essentially a prologue of Matthew's text (Matt 1:1–17). The first verse essentially asserts the Gospel to be the book of the genealogy of Jesus Christ as son of Abraham and son of David. The narrative of the life and ministry of Jesus begins from verse 18. In a previous consideration of the Gospel of John, note was taken that John locates his gospel in the very beginning, indicating for the writer the eternal nature of Jesus (i.e., Gen 1:1–3). However, in the Gospel of Matthew, its writer, to find its point of continuity with the history of humanity, and therefore God's people in the Genesis narrative of Adam, infers it. This inference is seen in the similarity of Matt 1:1 and Gen 5:1 in the LXX, which as a Greek text can assist in highlighting similarities with the gospel.

In Matthew's account the story of Jesus is from a disclosure of that which is with or after the natural realm, hence the metaphysical and noumenal world; that is, Jesus is located in the story of humanity but with this story is the disclosure of Jesus as the Christ, bringing the eternal dimension into the human situation. This is a feature that is inferred throughout the Gospel of Matthew. The use of the phrase "kingdom of heaven" and the use of parables, especially in the section on kingdom parables in Matt 11:2—13:53, display spiritual truth that is with or after the natural.

One other aspect that can be inferred concerns the use of the phrase that creates sections of the Genesis narrative: "this is the—genealogy of, history of, account of . . ." various individuals. Mostly, the argument is made for this phrase to be a form of prologue. But the anecdotal evidence suggests its function as an epilogue or closing phrase, particularly in the early narratives. The first use of the phrase is Gen 2:4, "This is the history of the heavens and the earth when they were created . . ." However, the text that follows does not disclose this creative event, the preceding text does. The second occasion occurs, as mentioned, in relationship to the Matthew's Gospel, in Gen 5:1: "This is the book of the genealogy of Adam . . ." Yet, the account of Adam is again in the preceding text in the Genesis narrative, the following text is generations *from* Adam. Perhaps what can be inferred is that Matthew is linking his narrative with the line of promise in humanity, through Abraham and David; but his text is intended to disclose the Christ, that which comes after the natural. Thus, Matthew's Gospel begins with a conclusion that establishes Jesus' continuity with the story of humanity and the line of promise; but the fulfillment is in the Christ as the eternal, or to use Pauline language, Jesus is "the last Adam," (1 Cor 15:45).

Space does not permit pursuit of other examples of the use of language to give the composition it's *intentioned-being*. Issues such as person of address can direct attention, for example, the Pauline use of the first person throughout Galatians. This creates an *intentioned-ness* that draws readers' attention from the speaking voice of the text as a narrator disclosing an issue to that of direct engagement with the author specifically addressing an issue directly with the reader. The use of imperatives and other devices can create emotive *intentioned-ness* in engaging the reader, for example, in 2 Corinthians as has been noted by a number of commentators. The important concept is that the composition has *intentioned-being* that is critical to the ontological interpretation. And the ontological interpretation gives a context for the epistemological interpretation (i.e., the knowability), so that the interpreter's knowing is of an understanding of the otherness of the text. This otherness is the *intentioned-ness* due to the *intention-to* of the author. This *intentioned-ness* is due to the act of *parole* in which authorial intent is transformed from being an aspect of the author's psyche to becoming an aspect of the *intentioned-being* of the discourse.

Otherness as Self-perception: The Author's Explanation

When explanation is seen as the author's, then the encountered being of the text is a being that is attributable to the author, so that subsequent reference to genuine otherness is possible. Whilst it is the self of the interpreter that evaluates this being, the interpreter is not the one who is the "author" of it. Consequently, it brings genuine otherness into ontological encounter with the self. This *otherness* becomes possible in the identification of the *intentioned-being* of the text, which is able to touch the interpreter, thus there is genuine encounter with otherness. The interpreter's original understanding is of the explanation of the author.

Subsequently, drawing upon both Heidegger and Ricoeur, it can be asserted that in interpretation the interpreter appropriates understanding that has been understood of the author's explanation. Ricoeur's model offers an understanding of this process in which appropriation occurs. Self-as-another is the vehicle to explain to self what has been understood of the author's message. Therefore, the interpreter's successive understanding(s)—which are the interpreter's appropriated understanding(s) of that which was understood of the author's explanation—result from the fusion of the world horizon of the text with the world horizon of the interpreter. This "world of the text" is the creation of the author and therefore exists as an entity within the world due to the authorial *intentioned-ness* with which it is imbued and with which it touches. Due to the presence of *intentioned-ness*, which confers upon the text the ability of a composition to touch the reader, this world of the text cannot be termed worldless as an entity purely present-at-hand. The resultant interpreter's meaning in this modeling is a meaning relative to the understanding of the author, hence a perception of otherness.

In Ricoeur's model the ideality of the text mediates the world horizon of the writer and that of the reader to achieve for him an interpretation close to the intention of Schleiermacher's hermeneutics.[54] However, in the aforementioned modeling it is the *intentioned-ness* of the text that mediates between these worlds. It was noted previously that *intentioned-ness* references the author in such a way that the author's attributes are manifested (the example cited is Rom 1:20 where the world as *intentioned-being* makes reference to its author attributes not psyche). In other words *intentioned-ness* inherently references a person. Therefore, just beyond the horizon of *intentioned-ness* of a creation (i.e., the composition in the case of the written text) is the world of the author. As a result it is suggested that this modeling is actually closer to the intention of Schleiermacher's hermeneutics.

54. Ricoeur, *Interpretation Theory*, 93.

Nevertheless, what Ricoeur's modeling and argument has clearly highlighted is that hermeneutics is a task undertaken by a Cartesian "I" and involves making one's own what is the subject matter of the text. Hermeneutics is therefore always a relative task, even when undertaken within a community, and as a result meaning is always personal, although it may be submitted to a community. In dealing with a text, any statement of meaning is in reality not a statement of the author's meaning, but it is always an interpreted meaning belonging to the interpreter. The meaning understood is never indisputably the author's meaning.[55] Hermeneutical argument thus favors change of meaning in interpretation as a relativization, even if only as a nuance, as being unavoidable, since meaning is always relative to an "I" in "I interpret."

Consequently, as has been suggested in the previous two chapters of this work, sameness of meaning in dealing with authorial intent is an unrealistic aim. The more fruitful pursuit is the issue of sameness of what is understood, that is, the composition, which is an issue of perception of the self-disclosure of the entity of the composition as *intentioned-being*, the Being-of-being of which is the authorial intent of the author. It has been noted earlier in this work that there is an audience impact on interpreted meaning when dealing with texts. It is not the text changing but the audience. This recognition of the Cartesian "I," which is that interpretation is undertaken as "I interpret," is the reason for this relativization of meaning. Provided the explanation that is pursued is the author's, the relativity is not relativism; the interpretation is relative to that which is independent of the interpreter.

Otherness is referenced in understanding the entity of the composition, which is not an understanding of the meaning an author has, as a current possession. The composition is an understanding that relates to a meaning the author had, which he or she sought to disclose to any prospective interpreter, and which therefore becomes a "meant" that the author has communicated. Therefore, the first movement involving otherness, which is understanding, deals with what the author "meant," which is the authorial intent of the author available as *intentioned-ness*. It is the second movement of interpretation that results in "contemporary meaning," which is the relative meaning of the interpreter. The act of *parole* gives being to the communication so that author's meaning is no longer a private meaning, as a personal ontology, but it is the disclosure of an understanding that is now publicly available in the ontology of *intentioned-being*.

This act of *parole* by an author is what gives being to the true "explanation pole" of the dialectic. This concept of explanation as belonging to the author is thus shown to be the only way to proceed that can disclose any otherness. The other pole of the dialectic, being that of understanding, is operational within the interpreter. Thus, in this model there is genuine encounter with otherness in the task of interpretation.

---

55. Hirsch, *Validity in Interpretation*, 236. Even Hirsch, perhaps the most strident advocate of authorial meaning, hence intent, as acknowledged in Vanhoozer's work, notes, "However, no one can establish another's meaning with certainty."

Interpretation Theory

Consequently, that which is to be interpreted is encountered as otherness, and the meaning in the understanding is the interpreter's. Understanding, as related to the being of the interpreter, must be considered as the counterpart to the being of the text as a composition, which is the author's explanation. The understanding is by a self-disclosure of the text through an interpretive event of all the forms of knowledge involved, that is, *rational, arational,* and *nonrational*.

UNDERSTANDING: THE HEIDEGGERIAN PERSPECTIVE

Schleiermacher saw *understanding*, developed from an interplay of grammatical and psychological interpretation, as representing an interplay of universal and particular aspects.[56] Ricoeur discusses how this concept was picked up and extended in the work of Dilthey, with a focus on psychology and the human sciences in which was sought methodological conceptualization of *understanding*.[57] It is in this situation that understanding becomes simply a development or extension of thinking, hence knowing, which is analyzed by epistemological methodology. The presupposition of a methodological basis of understanding as a form of knowing is what leads to the construal of hermeneutics as essentially, and therefore primarily, epistemology. It is this presupposition that is strongly challenged in the work of Heidegger and Gadamer.[58] In Heidegger, and then further developed in Gadamer, understanding is seen not as a mode of knowing but one of being.

Heidegger contends that in developing the *cogito sum* Descartes focused on the *res cogitans* (thinking thing) without first considering the "being" of the thinking person; or as Heidegger puts it, *"the meaning of the Being of the 'sum.'"*[59] In other words, for Heidegger, Descartes focused on the thinking of *I think*, leaving *I am* as undetermined in *cogito sum*, and hence the "I" in *I think* becomes a presupposition with its ontology unable to be explored.[60] Subsequently, the concept of understanding in modernism that develops from Descartes's work has the appearance of largely being an issue of epistemology; that is, understanding is a task of the thinking "I" and is not regarded as integral to the being of the "I" who thinks. In this situation understanding becomes a derivative of thinking.

Whilst it is possible to understand without reflective thought, it is not possible to interpret without reflective thought. The issue of translation helps to illustrate this issue. Gadamer notes that all translation involves interpretation.[61] He also notes that where understanding occurs there is speech not translation; furthermore, to under-

---

56. Schleiermacher, *Hermeneutics*, 5.
57. Ricoeur, *From Text to Action*, 56–61.
58. Ibid., 61.
59. Heidegger, *Being and Time*, 46. (Italics original.)
60. Ibid., 126–27. Italics added.
61. Gadamer, *Truth and Method*, 346.

stand a foreign language means not having the need to translate it into your own.[62] In the act of translation there is a gap between the spirit of the original words and their reproduction in another language, and this gap can never be "completely closed."[63] This indicates that interpretation always involves reflective thinking, whereas understanding does not of necessity involve reflective thinking.

In Heidegger, interpretation is derivative of understanding,[64] and in this situation "thinking" must also be considered derivative of understanding.[65] This occurs because the articulation of interpretation is "the meaning,"[66] which is reflective in its origin as a process that results in intelligibility.[67] Heidegger's view, noted previously, is that interpretation is an "appropriation of understanding."[68] This sheds light on what Ricoeur observed, which is that the Heideggerian modeling of the process of interpretation begins with an impersonal ontology of the event. In Heidegger's thought, interpretation is an *action* within understanding. Therefore, it immediately attracts to this ontology, being itself an event.

Heidegger's thought is the basis on which Ricoeur can regard this recognition of interpretation as an action within understanding as a diversion from the agent, or a concealment of the agent. What Heidegger points out is that interpretation is not acquisition of information but is rather disclosure of possibilities "projected in understanding."[69] The nature of interpretation as event, therefore naturally attracting to epistemology, gives the impression of acquisition of knowledge as its primary goal. Such a direction subverts as misdirection the real idea of interpretation, which is to disclose possibilities for being, which in turn is to do with persons. It is this powerful insight Ricoeur brings into hermeneutical focus.

In the movement to postmodernism, note was taken of modernism's failure to recognize and deal with ontology, and also with its subsequent failure to develop and therefore produce the epistemological methodology of the human sciences that would allow access to the mind of the author. If the absolute meaning of a text existed as authorial intent, and involved the thinking author with its resultant authorial meaning, it was not demonstrated within methodology. Consequently, in this situation it is also easy to see why the concept of authorial intent becomes abandoned within

---

62. Ibid.

63. Ibid.

64. Heidegger, *Being and Time*, 195. Heidegger asserts that "interpretation is grounded on understanding."

65. Ibid., 385. Explanation and conceiving are species of cognition, which is rooted in *Dasein's* "fundamental *existentiale*." (Italics original.)

66. Ibid., 195. This issue of "meaning," which leads to the concept of the hermeneutical circle, is important and is pursued in the issue of the explanation pole of the dialectic.

67. Ibid. Heidegger develops the concept of "meaning" as the interaction of "disclosedness" that is reflected upon so that something becomes intelligible as something and maintains its intelligibility.

68. Ibid., 188.

69. Ibid., 189.

epistemology. However, the recovery of ontological categories in dealing with the text, in postmodernism, has focused on the interpreter, leaving the author abandoned and "out in the cold."

The concept of *Dasein* (being-there) in Heidegger's *Being and Time* concerns a seeking to analyze and explicate the nature of the "being" and the "there" of that being that is *Dasein*. Understanding is a phenomenon (hence having existential structure) that is "equiprimordial" with "state-of-mind" in constituting that "being."[70] Understanding works with "state-of-mind" in a way that discloses the "there," and it is not just a development from thinking; it is an attribute of "being."[71] Heidegger's thought is that state-of-mind "*implies a disclosive submission to the world, out of which we can encounter something that matters to us.*"[72] Understanding, working with "state-of-mind," brings that which matters within the domain of the being of self; hence, it presents the possibility of the particularizing of what is known to *Dasein*. Heidegger shows the concept of a disclosive nature of understanding, which particularizes what is known, by his observation that understanding presents potentiality for *Dasein*, a potentiality that projects possibilities.[73] This projection is a self-understanding that is unique to each *Dasein*. Heidegger's recognition of this nature of understanding is clearly what has impacted Ricoeur's concept of understanding texts as opening up a world before the interpreter.[74]

Understanding and Knowing

As noted previously, in Heidegger the task of interpretation develops within understanding. One can know that one understands, in which case interpretation is not necessary. Conversely, one can know that he or she does not understand, in which case interpretation becomes the vehicle to make one's own what is foreign. The interesting thing is that at this point one cannot know that one misunderstands. Misunderstanding can only be known reflectively; that is, misunderstanding is a realization that what one perceived self as understanding was indeed not understood. Rather the understanding on which the person proceeded was incorrect. The assumption of understanding is immediate as an *existentiale* of *Dasein*.

---

70. Ibid., 182. In a translator's note care is taken to help avoid focusing on the word *mind* in this phrase, hence confusing the concept with just a thinking process in the English translation "state-of-mind." The German word so translated speaks of a condition or "state in which one may be found" and consequently indicates a total package including general attitude at a point in time. Therefore, ordinary usage of the English phrase "state of mind," which is far broader than a state of thinking, corresponds to the basic idea; see note 2, 172.

71. Ricoeur, *Conflict of Interpretations*, 7.
72. Heidegger, *Being and Time*, 177.
73. Ibid., 184–85.
74. Ricoeur, *From Text to Action*, 64.

Misunderstanding is often disclosed in a process of interpretation of something else that is initially perceived as not understood, wherein during the process that which was previously seen as understood is exposed as misunderstood. Therefore, misunderstanding cannot itself be seen as the prerequisite of the interpretative task. Instead, misunderstanding is disclosed by experience that causes the person to directly revisit prior understanding, and what occurs in this revisiting of understanding is primarily ontological interpretation not epistemological interpretation. This results in a "perception" of having not understood initially, because the person originally understood incorrectly. It is the "not understanding" discovered in the revisiting of understanding that initiates the task of interpretation. The misunderstanding is exposed in the reflection upon the revisiting of understanding; that is, recognition of misunderstanding is still a reflective process.

Consequently, if cognition is seen as a derivative of understanding, misunderstanding is a further derivative once removed from understanding, being itself derivative of states of reflective cognition. It is always a reflective process that discloses misunderstanding. The result of this is the realization that misunderstanding can be disclosed epistemologically but, in requiring a revisiting of understanding, misunderstanding is not directly resolvable epistemologically. Previously, note has been taken that, unlike Heidegger and Gadamer, Ricoeur recognizes the importance of the methodological task of epistemology. However, Ricoeur noted that epistemology must be submitted to a correct ontology. Hence, in resolution of misunderstanding the first movement is ontological and is achieved in first revisiting the being of the composition. Therefore, it is in effect a revisiting of the authorial intent, as the being of the *intentioned-being* of the composition, which thereby establishes a context prior to any epistemological task. The ontological interpretation of authorial intent (i.e., understanding) should in all cases be the first step prior to the reflective task of epistemology (i.e., interpretation making what is foreign one's own).

An important aspect of this reasoning is what it discloses about understanding. Misunderstanding, in its very terminology, is within the province and hence provenance of understanding. Yet its existence is shown in a reflective disclosure, having therefore the appearance of being itself cognitively derived, in the same fashion as meaning. However, although misunderstanding is cognitively disclosed it is not cognitive in its inception; it is a direct application of misunderstanding as understanding, but it is not recognized as misunderstanding at its inception. If it were, it would no longer be misunderstanding but instead be a species of "not understanding." As such, misunderstanding is a concealed species of "not understanding," as belonging to understanding. The concept of a deliberate misunderstanding is not relevant, because deliberate misunderstanding implies understanding has occurred and is subverted by the interpreter.

Although specifying understanding as a "fundamental *existentiale*" and therefore not a "species of cognition" of *Dasein*,[75] Heidegger nevertheless noted understanding's ability to take on cognitive likeness, as in issues such as explanation and conceiving.[76] It is for this reason cognitive expression must be seen as derivative of understanding, as constituent of *Dasein*.[77] Heidegger notes that "knowing" is considered to be due to relationship between subject and object. As such its reality appears to exist exteriorly as in nature; however, for Heidegger, "knowing" is unique to the kind of beings who "know," that is, those having the kind of being that *Dasein* has.[78] Knowing belongs to the essential constitution of "Dasein's Being."[79] Heidegger acknowledges that this concept potentially raises a problem in the concept of knowledge, which thereby would need to transcend the subject, to exist as exterior.[80] Heidegger presents a discussion to show that his concept of knowing, that is, cognizing, doesn't have to raise the idea of moving from interior to exterior; the answer is in how "knowing" exists "outside" in the first place as "Being-already-alongside-the-world."[81] His consideration of "knowing," with its developed link to understanding, itself makes constant reference to the link between "knowing" and looking, which presupposes his development of the *existentiale* of understanding being an issue of disclosure.

Therefore, in Heidegger's development, concerning all the preceding discussion and issues, these all occur themselves within the existential of understanding. However, the discussion of misunderstanding has also revealed that the concept of "understanding" offers some powerful insights that can assist the task of hermeneutics. The task of understanding itself presents a way forward in finding a solution to the seeming aporia, or impasse, in the movement from epistemology to ontology. Understanding, in possessing what almost amounts to ambivalence in that it is ontological yet can appear as cognitive, must be able, in the one person, to relate epistemology and ontology, by allowing passage from one to the other.

Therefore, like Ricoeur's previous observations about the symbol, the concept of understanding, in the two sides to its nature, is able to relate to both ontology and epistemology. In dealing with Ricoeur's concept of the "symbol," it was suggested in this work that the concept of authorial intent has the features of the symbol in interpretation of texts. This discussion shows that this is so because authorial intent possesses ontological properties, which result in disclosure, or understanding. However, authorial intent also relates to content, or the *what* of the text, that is, what is viewed in the disclosure; and therefore on the basis of this disclosure in understanding, there

75. Heidegger, *Being and Time*, 385.
76. Ibid., 182.
77. Ibid.
78. Ibid., 87.
79. Ibid., 88.
80. Ibid.
81. Ibid., 88–89.

can be a movement to epistemology. Heidegger also noted in "knowing" the appearance of what seems to be transcendence of self, which he explains within his thought above. Yet this appearance transcendence is itself a clue indicating further possibilities within the understanding of understanding.

A Holistic Approach to Understanding

The presuppositions of the person doing the describing contribute to the creation of the *intentioned-ness*, which therefore manifests itself in the impact of authorial intent on the composition. This intent in turn directs what the reader sees and doesn't see from the viewpoint of the *intentioned-ness* of the composition. This section examines, in a brief excursus, these issues in Heidegger's work.

Numerous references have been made in the preceding sections to Heidegger pointing out the role of pre-understanding. Heidegger observes that the person investigating being already lives in an understanding of being, yet investigation shows that being remains veiled.[82] Ricoeur points out that the writer of poetry, as he or she writes each verse, already anticipates the completed work.[83] The *intention-to* of the writer is already acting to give the work *intentioned-ness* because of the anticipated direction, and reaches the ends where the writer intends. This is not just true of poetry but all writing; that is, even though a writer makes discoveries during the journey of writing, which can result in new *intention-to*, the course of the journey is set and the beginning of the work already anticipates its conclusion. What the author is explicating as understanding already carries within in it that which is already understood. That is to simply say that the writer has presuppositions that will direct his or her presentation consistent with his or her pre-understanding.

Heidegger's critique of Descartes's understanding of being focuses on what is Descartes's central problem, as perceived by Heidegger. This occurs with Descartes's definition of *res cogitans* (thinking thing) as *ens* (being) in his understanding of it as *ens creatum* (created being).[84] In this, for Heidegger, Descartes succumbed to medieval ontology, and in doing so caused the "implantation of a baleful prejudice" at the very inception of the consideration of being.[85] As was previously observed, Heidegger launches a virulent attack on traditional ontology, and hence ontotheology. This conceptualization in Descartes will lead Descartes to define being in terms of substantiality.[86] Heidegger's central thesis is that entities of the kind of being that *Dasein* possesses

---

82. Ibid., 23.
83. Ricoeur, *Oneself*, 82.
84. Heidegger, *Being and Time*, 46.
85. Ibid.
86. Ibid., 122. Heidegger saw that what Descartes was "trying to grasp ontologically" is in fact Nature, 128.

can't be conceived of in terms such as reality and substantiality; for Heidegger, "the substance of man is existence."[87]

Yet, the very concept of created being itself does raise the issue of *substantia*, since what is created has substance as an entity. Again, it is important to note that had Heidegger not confined his understanding of entities to *who* and *what* but also recognized the entity whose being is *intentioned-being*, he would have had an entity having being that transcends time, yet whose *substantia* giving it presence in this world in its link to the present-at-hand, that is, the *what*. However, the entity, though linked, is not equated with the present-at-hand because, as previously discussed, the work of art can be disclosed as an entity in different present-at-hand media, for example, digitized copy. The composition as an entity can be rewritten in different languages, yet remain the same composition; it can be converted to a form of digitization presented as a speaking voice on a CD or even DVD. The composition remains the same entity that is linked to differing present-at-hand entities. Therefore, the issue of *intentioned-being* and being of entities "present-at-hand" is not one of modes of being of the same entity. Consequently, there is within human beingness a precedent for being that is manifest in the world, yet whose being is only perceptible to human being but is itself distinct from the *substantia* of this world.

Hence, the idea that an entity can have being that is perceptible in this world, yet have *substantia* that is spirit, which is not itself perceptible as *substantia* within the world, has analogy. As noted previously, the biblical concept is that life, other than human being, is indeed defined within this world, having been directly created as living being within the confines of this creation (see Gen 1:20–25). The *substantia* of its being as within this world, that is, the realm of nature, is describable within the province of physical sciences. In this Descartes was correct. Yet so was Heidegger who recognized that this is inadequate as a description of human being, that is, the kind of being that is *Dasein*. In this, Descartes's view of being became limited in a way that led to modernism. Although Gen 1:26–28 gives an initial impression of human-being having similar being to that of other animate beings, the true nature of human-being is disclosed in Gen 2:7–25. The corporeal existence of man, as body, is indeed within the domain of this created world and has the horizon of time, but the *substantia* of the being of human being is not from within this created world. It is the breath of the Divine, who himself is Spirit (see John 4:24), that inspires the being of humanity as spirit, hence of having being of the same kind of being, and hence *substantia*, as that of the divine and therefore transcendent with respect to the horizon of time. This, Heidegger did not investigate, nor acknowledge. Yet the biblical account agrees in essence with his observations; the only real point of difference is recognition of the

87. Ibid., 255. Heidegger considered the idea that this proposal risks presenting the core of *Dasein* as a vapor that can disappear. His answer was that this very question assumes the concept of being to be related to the present-at-hand, even when not considering substance as corporeal, i.e., even if considering the idea of spirit, 153. He notes, "Yet man's "*substance*" is not spirit as a synthesis of soul and body; it is rather *existence*," 153. (Italics original.)

creator and that of "being" that is *ens creatum* as human-being with the horizon of time and at the same time *substantia* of spirit, hence outside time.

Consequently, at the very outset of Heidegger's investigation is the exclusion of any createdness of humanity. This concept means that at best any concept of God can only be deistic. What takes place, and indeed the very nature of being, occurs in the absence of God's involvement. This is taken to its logical conclusion in Derrida. Heidegger's rejection of "spirit," considered previously, is tied to his presupposition of his view that *substantia* is not the proper domain for the discussion of being. It is this that leads to his subsequent developing and defining *Dasein* within the domain of phenomenology. Heidegger desired to move away from the idea of *substantia* and took his lead from Husserl's thought that the constitution of a person is different from the things of nature.[88] Yet, this is in fact the biblical position, as outlined previously, even to the point, previously discussed, that in the LXX the disclosure to Moses of the identity of God, recorded in Exod 3:14, was interpreted to be an identification of God as ultimate being. He is ὁ Ὤν, *the One being*. The failure to acknowledge even the idea of God in his discussion, which idea Pannenberg notes is not excluded inherently from philosophical discussion, is what results in the ontology that is developed in Heidegger.

Ricoeur, like Heidegger and Gadamer, places himself within the presupposition of phenomenology, yet he himself does not discount the impact of the divine. Ricoeur finds in phenomenology the opportunity to move from what he terms regional hermeneutics, for example, biblical hermeneutics, to general hermeneutics, freed from the prejudice of regional concerns.[89] Consequently, it seems for Ricoeur phenomenology is almost prejudice free and therefore primarily looks at the task without itself having an agenda. This is similar to Heidegger's approach regarding ontology. However, because every interpreter has presuppositions that result in pre-understanding, this is then essentially an abstraction, because no one interpreter is free of presuppositions and can therefore do "general hermeneutics." Consequently, it may be said that phenomenology simply looks at the task as an abstraction, which can be useful. Nevertheless, to regard it as the "*unsurpassable presupposition of hermeneutics*," and therefore imply its importance as an essential prerequisite of hermeneutics, is itself a prejudice in the truest sense.[90] Therefore, the works of Ricoeur, Gadamer, and Heidegger are indeed useful tools in developing the hermeneutical task of the interpreter, but should not be used themselves uncritically and offer no reason to abandon the biblical viewpoint as a presupposition. It is not as if one viewpoint has disrobed itself of its presuppositions and therefore stands as the reference point par excellence.

---

88. Ibid., 73.

89. Ricoeur, *From Text to Action*, 51–71. This chapter titled "The Task of Hermeneutics" has this concept as its central theme, though not expressed in as many words; it is the thrust of the chapter.

90. Ibid., 23. (Italics original.)

Heidegger noted that in Descartes's conceptualization of being, substances become accessible in their attributes.[91] It is this strident insistence of Heidegger concerning "being" as existence and not *substantia* that appears to stop him considering "understanding" as an attribute of *Dasein*, that is, a characteristic of "spirit" as *substantia* of human being. However, recognition as an attribute would automatically imply the existence of the creator of that attribute, that is, the one to whom the attribute is attributable to, to whom Heidegger has denied impact. As an attribute it discloses something about the human being, and in the case of understanding as an attribute, this provides the possibility of encountering otherness.

If understanding is seen as an attribute of "spirit," the implication is that something foreign to the self is to be understood. Knowing, as active reflective thinking, then becomes an attribute of the human consciousness, having been instigated by the will, that is, the formation of *intention-to* within the self. Hence, understanding looks outward at the world but knowing is the orientation of self within the world perceived. Knowing is the internalization, or inward looking, and the resultant appropriating and application to self. Consequently, knowing directly derives meaning as relative to self. This biblical modeling achieves similar ends to the modeling of Heidegger; however, it places the initial importance not on self but on otherness.

The interpreter chooses which set of presuppositions he or she will allow to position him or her in the seeing. Presuppositions, as the basis of understanding, are the "eye" that doesn't see itself in the looking. This is the metaphysical "I" of the author, and these presuppositions function in the formation of *intended-ness* by the author, which are subsequently able to position the interpreter at the point of origin of viewing that the author had. These presuppositions consist of the *nonrational* knowledge that is posited, and once accepted becomes the basis of understanding. Because knowing is a willful personalization, this also allows interpreters, once they understand what the author saw, to then decide meaning for themselves in a reflective re-viewing of the content, or matter of the text, which occurs within their own presuppositions; having first understood the composition. If the interpreter accepts the presuppositional basis of the author, then interpreted meaning is a contemporary relative understanding of the author, that is, it approximates authorial meaning in the contemporary setting, as relative to the meaning the author had and explicated as understanding.

Understanding:
The Dialectic Pole of the Interpreter

In seeking to relate "knowing" and "knowledge," Heidegger developed the concept within the being of *Dasein*. *Dasein* directs itself toward something and in "knowing" grasps it, not by getting out of itself but in a primary form of being that is "always

---

91. Heidegger, *Being and Time*, 123.

'outside' alongside entities which it encounters and which belong to a world already discovered."[92] However, there can be an alternate way of viewing this issue. In Heidegger, "knowing" is derivative of understanding within the being of *Dasein*, and he noted that "knowing" is something only a being with *Dasein*'s kind of being does; that is, only *Dasein* knows in this sense of knowing. Thus, knowledge can be known by another *Dasein*, hence appearing exterior; yet this exteriority is only perceptible by the same kind of being as that of *Dasein*.

This has echoes of the issues of the concept of *intentioned-being*, discussed previously, which, as being, is only disclosed to a being with the kind of being *Dasein* has, including such things as the work of art and composition. Consequently, knowledge in all its forms, though being exteriorly understandable and communicable, does not really exist as exterior to the being of *Dasein*, other than in its link with the present-at-hand entity, which is consistent with Heidegger's concepts. It is being that is associated with the present-at-hand, but as an issue of meaning it is not the same being as the entity to which it is linked. It can be known by different *Dasein*s independently and individually, but is not something, which, as exteriority, is disclosed other than to *Dasein*.

Had Heidegger noted, or anticipated, this entity and its being as *intentioned-being*, it would have supplied the answers to the issue of knowing.[93] Only *Dasein* has consciousness of these entities, and this consciousness is primordial in the being of *Dasein*—it is not developed or constructed. This observation is seen as consistent with the biblical presentation by the author of Genesis, previously considered. It was noted that in the Genesis account understanding is indeed primordial—it is immediate and not learned or constructed. Knowing is an immediate counterpart, which is exemplified in the immediate directive and commands given to the created human being. Therefore, it is suggested that *Dasein* possesses not only aesthetic and historical consciousness, but also a third dimension of consciousness, titled in this work *ontic-consciousness*. This is a consciousness that perceives knowledge of being itself and is able to "see" the entities to which it relates. The imagination would therefore be suggested to be an attribute of this consciousness. It is this consciousness that allows a person to watch a two-dimensional world presented in visual media (e.g., a TV) and to "imagine," and therefore see, a three-dimensional world represented. It is this consciousness that allows a person to view a photo presentation of an event (e.g., a wedding album) and in the imagination reconstruct a representation of the event as event.

Knowledge can be both developed by an individual *Dasein* or it can be communicated from one person to another. Ong's observation, concerning literary culture, bears repeating: "abstractly sequential, classificatory, explanatory examination

---

92. Ibid., 89.

93. Ibid., 71. In Heidegger's ontology every entity is either a *who* (existence) or a *what* (present-at-hand).

of phenomena or of stated truths is impossible without writing and reading."[94] Consequently, literature, as both the composition and as transcription of data, provides a repository of knowledge for communication between people. However, this is only accessible to a being of the kind of being *Dasein* has, and is available in understanding to disclose both knowledge and being of entities. Hence, effective knowledge remains at all times within *Dasein*, yet is able to transcend the situatedness of each *Dasein* to be known by each *Dasein*.

Understanding as Sameness of Sight

Heidegger noted the tendency in common usage to use the word *meaning* as related to what is understood; that is, the disclosure of entities is perceived by the interpreter as the meaning of the entities.[95] However, this is not really meaning but the disclosure of the entity in its being.[96] This perception as meaning is in reality a self-disclosure as understanding. "Meaning" itself is essentially a step beyond this disclosure. It is this common usage of the word *meaning* that leads to the confusion of authorial meaning, which belongs to the author, and authorial understanding as the author's explanation, which is the communication of that meaning. The authorial intent provides the composition with *intentioned-being* that is the presentation of what the author understood, which is then presented by explication in an explanation. This is the being of the composition that exists as a result of the act of *parole*, which is a willful hence intentional act.

An author communicates the disclosure of what he or she saw. Understanding is not the author's meaning; understanding is the composition communicated by the author to position readers/interpreters and direct their vision so that they see what the author saw. There is no conceptual difficulty with the concept of one person taking another person to look at a view by standing where he or she stood and directing another's gaze to see what he or she saw. It is proposed in this work that this is the purpose of the composition, that is, sameness of understanding, or sameness of perception. Two people can view the same object yet develop differences of meaning in appropriation of what is understood.

Heidegger has argued that meaning is not something possessed by an entity but something only possessed by a person. Vanhoozer agrees, not with Heidegger per se, but with the concept that meaning is a function of persons.[97] In his discussion the person whose meaning is referred to in the text is the meaning of the author. However, if meaning is a function of persons, then the meaning of the text in interpretation is the interpreter's meaning, as discussed previously. Even Hirsch agrees, also noted pre-

94. Ong, *Orality and Literacy*, 8.
95. Heidegger, *Being and Time*, 192. (Italics added.)
96. Ibid.
97. Vanhoozer, *Is There a Meaning*, 202.

viously, that this meaning can never be equivalent to the author's meaning. The object of communication is an understanding of the composition as public, not a meaning as personal and private. The desire of an author is probably and reasonably seen to be one of provoking the interpreter to develop as close as possible similarity of meaning, but the vehicle to fulfill this desire is the communication of an understanding. Sameness of sight is at the discretion of the author, but similarity of meaning is that of the interpreter.

In noting that understanding is at the discretion of the author, this should not be seen to equal compulsion by the author. The interpreter can choose to not be led to the point of observation; following the direction is at the discretion of the interpreter. However, if direction is not followed, then he or she won't see what the author saw. One can see a view from another vantage point, in which case there is sameness of content but not sameness of understanding, because the interpreter has not stood where the author stood to see the content in the context from which the author saw it. Disregard of authorial intent can result in viewing the same content, but it cannot result in the understanding of the author. Hence, if the desire of the interpreter is understanding of the author, he or she will allow himself or herself to be positioned, which is respect for otherness represented in the text; that is, the interpreter will listen to the speaking voice of the text as other than self, which represents the author.

(a) Positioning for Understanding

The author seeks to first position the reader, or place the reader at the point from which observation will enable the reader to see what the author saw. In terms of the composition that which positions the reader is that which positioned the author, that is, where the author placed himself or herself in viewing the content. The authorial intent, reflecting the *intention-to* of the author, places before the interpreter the point of origin from which to see what the author saw. This directly involves the idea of presuppositions. These presuppositions are inherent in the tradition in which the author stands. This can be attributed to an author who is known to stand in a tradition, which as noted previously is the weakest form of attestation. It is that aspect of a tradition to which the author directly refers by assent, assertion, and inference that is the primary positioning of the interpreter. This positing by the author gives being to the composition. Generally speaking, therefore, authors should ideally provide these attestations to tradition in a prefatory manner, that is, as part of introductions or prefaces to books as a whole or an individual chapter. These attestations are recognized in language by the nature of positing being; and as such they are not descriptions of being but the imputation of being. Using them as descriptions that give exteriority to being is a secondary or subordinate task. Scriptural examples have been noted in this work. The important realization is that as disclosure of being, the knowledge posited is *nonrational*, and only *ontic-consciousness* of human being sees the disclosure.

(b) Directing Vision

Clearly, linguistic devices such as the imperative can be used to capture attention and direct the view in an intended direction. An author can also intentionally employ, or desire to elicit, perlocutionary responses that also have the effect of directing vision by capturing attention. This aspect of intentional use of perlocutionary effects has been discussed, and examples have been considered in this work. Narrative, by capturing the interpreter in the story, automatically directs vision by ordering the disclosure in front of the interpreter. Generally, genre is a device an author can use in this aspect of directing vision.

(c) Viewing the Content

This aspect concerns both the being of entities and their interconnectedness or relationship to reality, as perceived by the author. This is the world that the author saw from his or her point of origin. In seeing this world from the same position, sameness of understanding is achieved. Clearly, statements of being by characters within a narrative give being to entities within the content. Statements of being employing the third person, as discussed previously, also provide understanding of the content and are a device that authors can use to make themselves visible, though being the eye that sees. It is in this area of the viewing of the content that epistemology can be conducted as subordinate to a correct ontology.

Explanation: The Dialectic Pole of the Authorial Intent

The explanation is primarily explicated and thereby determined in the epistemological task, as a description of, and also being itself a direct representation of, the understanding of the author. This issue has been discussed in this work and is extensively discussed in each of the primary authors considered. The observations and methodology employed are not new and have been indicated as widely accepted. There are nonetheless some observations that can be made on the basis of this book.

(a) The Transcending of Self in Understanding

The idea of transcendence taken as an aspect of faith concerns transcending time within the concept of eternal as opposed to the finite-infinite conception. This has been discussed previously in this book. However, in the interpretive task as presented in the modeling developed, there is the opportunity to perceive the idea of transcendence. This can then be employed beyond interpretation in the realm of faith, that is, to make special use of an aspect hermeneutically operational in the understanding of any author's text.

The concept of *intentioned-being* developed in this work relates to knowledge in the following ways. The ability to grasp the work as a complete and unique entity relates to aesthetic consciousness, as has been outlined as related to the work of Gadamer. This is perceived as *arational knowledge*. The ability to perceive the work in its link and relationship to the present-at-hand entity is related to historical consciousness, that is, its place in time, or temporality. This relates to *rational knowledge*. The ability to perceive the work in its *intentioned-ness* as a functioning dynamic within the world as an entity is related to the *ontic-consciousness*. This relates to *nonrational knowledge*. Human imagination and consciousness have the ability to use these dimensions of knowledge to achieve a three-dimensional understanding of the author's work, that is, to understand the disclosure of the scope of entities and their connectedness, which is the content and hence "matter" or *Sache* of the text. Only in this complete picture is the explanation of the author properly understood.

However, for this understanding to be an understanding of the author requires the transcending of self by the interpreter in placing self at the point of origin of the author. Only then does the interpreter see what the author saw. The work of Ricoeur, together with the discussion of understanding previously described, provides the insight into achieving this state that is effectively a transcendence of self without ever becoming other than self. It is a hermeneutic principle that can have special use in the theological setting, not a special hermeneutic.

The work of Heidegger, developed further in Gadamer then Ricoeur, places emphasis on the concept of distanciation. It was noted that both Thiselton and Vanhoozer acknowledge and agree with the basic concept. It is this that Ricoeur sees as the primary reasoning for his concept of the autonomy of the text. However, the concepts of understanding set out previously, plus Ricoeur's concept of the ability within selfhood to see self as other-than-self, together with the three dimensional concept of consciousness, offer a way of dealing effectively with distanciation whilst not ignoring its reality.

All the forms of knowledge to be used must be available in the relationship to the text; the sentence is the semantic unit available to the authors. Another aspect available to the authors is the realization that they are communicating with another *Dasein*, within whom consciousness is the same as for the authors. The authors intend the explanations based on these two basic principles in communicating their understandings. The authors can reasonably (i.e., within the concept of reasoning in all forms of knowledge) expect the interpreters/readers to understand what they understand, and the explanation is endowed with *intentioned-being* to the end of this disclosure.

The ability of selfhood to "see" or "understand" self as other-than-self becomes significant when the interpreter assumes the presuppositions of the author. As set out previously, these are available in relationship to the text and include the historical context within the concept of tradition. The operation of the three dimensional aspect of consciousness allows the imagination of the interpreter to transcend his or her situatedness in a direct relativization to that of the author. A person can imagine himself or herself in another historical setting; this aspect was considered in the concept of the medium of narrative. This imagination can be that of an author in the setting of a novel, hence for entertainment, or that of an author for the purpose of interpretation. The interpreter does not become the author, so the sameness is not sameness of meaning and is not related to the psyche of the author. However, the interpreter transcends his or her situatedness to see what the author saw, and so sameness of understanding is achieved. Meaning will relate to the articulation, or self-explanation, that is undertaken by the interpreter in the integration of otherness into self. This, of necessity, provides the opportunity to impact the *intention-to* of the interpreter and can form part of the authorial intent, as has been discussed in this work. It is perhaps a defining feature of the concept of sacred text that it is presupposed as endowed with *intentioned-ness* that seeks to develop *intention-to* in the interpreter.

The positioning of self in the presuppositions of another, together with the three-dimensional aspect of consciousness that accesses within the communication the differing forms of knowledge available in the explanation, effectively cause a transcending of self. In this situation selfhood involves an ability to see self as impacted by the understanding of another, and in the seeing "imagine" self as that person seen. Thus, the text can confront self with "otherness" and within self *intention-to*, as a consequence of this encounter with otherness, can be formed within the domain of self so as to traverse from the epistemological description to the ontology of self resulting in change of self, that is, impacting the *ipse*-identity of a person. This is a process of conformation by an impact of *otherness*. Where new presuppositions are "believed" and adsorbed to form part of the *idem*-identity (i.e., the unchanging identity), transformation subsequently occurs.

This is a hermeneutical principle of which special use is made in Christianity. The text of Rom 10:9 asserts that if a person confesses the Lordship of Christ, hence undergo a change in *ipse*-identity due to adapting lifestyle to this recognition, and if that person believes in his or her heart that God raised Jesus from the dead (i.e., at the core of being or spirit), then a change of *idem*-identity is effected in making the presupposition one's own. This, in turn, effects salvation of the person. Salvation comes into actual being in this process and is not a description of being; and although salvation can be used epistemologically, it is in reality the attribution of being. The text of Romans chapters 6–8 and chapters 12–15 involve many exhortations for the person who has this personalized belief to form *intention-to*, with the result of giving meaning to what has been understood due to what has been believed. All of this is special use of hermeneutical principles operating in texts; it is not a suggestion of a special hermeneutic for the purpose of effecting salvation.

(b) The Transcending of Self in Performance Interpretation

In a previous section of this work, passing reference was made to Wolterstorff's proposal of "performance interpretation."[98] He prefaces the concept with a discussion of Ricoeur's concept of "sense of the text," concluding that consistent meaning is impossible, and in his view Ricoeur's concept is unworkable.[99] However, his implication is that people appearing to engage in text sense can actually be seen to be engaging in a form of authorial-discourse interpretation, hence the discussion of performance interpretation.[100] Wolterstorff notes that Ricoeur, in a discussion of "text sense interpretation," alludes to the concept he wishes to discuss, which is in Ricoeur's mention of the concept of a conductor being led by the musical score in a performance.[101] Wolterstorff's argument is that the conductor, or for that matter any instrumentalist, works from an author's composition and interprets it in each performance of the score.[102]

The purpose here is to pick up on the idea, rather than to discuss Wolterstorff's proposal. It is this principle that is relevant to the preceding discussions of understanding and consciousness. Ong noted that the act of reading itself results in listening, because the reader converts reading into sound, even if only in the imagination.[103] In other words a reader/interpreter almost inherently performs the composition. When the ability to transcend self in seeing self-as-other-than-self is put together with the three-dimensional concept of consciousness, then there is ample evidence to suggest that one can imagine the composer of the score, or text, performing the text for the observer.

The Christian can imagine Paul as a person performing his text for the sake of the contemporary reader; however, the performance takes place within the "situatedness" of the interpreter, hence understanding can be immediate to the interpreter's life. The Pauline usage of Hosea in Rom 9:25–26 would seem to be such a performance interpretation, because Paul in his text is discussing the bringing in of the Gentiles to salvation following the advent of Christ. But Hosea in his text is discussing the restoration of the Northern Kingdom at some time prior to the advent of Christ (Hos 2:23 and 1:10). Paul used the same "score" but gives it a different interpretation. Furthermore, Paul clearly felt that because the text is viewed as inspired, then the Holy Spirit, knowing the presuppositions of Hosea, could transcend the "situatedness" of Hosea for an understanding that is relevant to Paul's presuppositions. Nothing that has occurred

---

98. Wolterstorff, *Divine Discourse*, 171–82. "Performance Interpretation" is a chapter title.
99. Ibid., 173.
100. Ibid.
101. Ibid., 175.
102. Ibid., 176.
103. Ong, *Orality and Literacy*, 8. See also Ong, "Interpretation," 9.

here is outside viable hermeneutical concepts. It is the belief of the interpreter in the person of the Holy Spirit as a divine author that can make special use of the principle.

What is sometimes referred to as devotional interpretation is primarily performance interpretation. In the previous example Paul stood in a tradition that reached back prior to the cross, in fact reaching back to the tradition that precedes Hosea. Hence, although it is a performance of the text, it is based on presuppositions that have included up to Hosea's time and further developed since his time. Paul can subsequently believe his understanding is consistent with that of Hosea, however, the meaning is not the same. Hosea saw a Northern Kingdom out of covenant relationship restored to covenant relationship. In the tradition of humanity since Genesis, Paul sees the Gentiles as representing a people out of covenant relationship who are brought into covenant relationship in Christ. Paul would believe his understanding was consistent with Hosea's.

The Holy Spirit remains in relationship with believers as a presupposition of the believer. For the believer it is not a cognitive concept but a state of being, given actual being in statements of assent, assertion, and inference by the believer. This belief is the context of what is to be understood. However, what then takes place applies operational hermeneutics in making special use in relationship with the person of the Holy Spirit. Another person may accept or reject the presupposition; this is a matter of his or her own presuppositions. However, due to the incredible nature of understanding and consciousness, as an interpreter he or she is able to assume, or imagine, the presuppositions of the author and thereby understand what the author understood. It is the interpreter's meaning that will change due to his or her own presuppositions. Both the Holy Spirit and the believer are able to avail themselves of the principles of transcending self and consciousness in dealing with the scriptural text, as principles are operational in all beings that have the same kind of being as *Dasein*.

The realization that understanding is an attribute, not a cognitive development at the will of the person, allows the transcending of self. The transcending of self opens up the field of performance interpretation as a legitimate approach to authorial-discourse interpretation. The concept of God speaking in and through the text, whilst presupposing a belief about the Holy Spirit, simply employs operational hermeneutic principles. The believer should not be marginalized or considered mystical about his or her understanding. All people bring their own presuppositions to the task; hence the performance interpretation of a person who has an active disbelief can result in the same understanding, within performance interpretation, but will result with a different interpretation of the "score" that has been performed.

The ability to transcend self within the horizon of time as in performance interpretation offers an analogy for, and even sets a precedent for, the transcending of time itself. The issue is not the concept of transcending but the presuppositions of the interpreter. Scripture supports the idea that the holding of presuppositions positions the person for understanding that transcends his or her previous "situatedness," as indicated in Heb 11:3. "By faith we understand that the worlds were framed by the Word of God, so that the things which are seen were not made of things which are visible." It is the assent and assertion of belief that positions a person to understand and see what he or she previously did not understand and see. As has been referred to previously, when Paul "performed" texts he had previously understood as an orthodox Jew in the context of the faith he had assented to in his encounter with the otherness of Christ, he saw what he had not seen previously—a whole new world came within the range of his understanding. This is exemplified in numerous texts attributed to Pauline origin; however, it is most prevalent in the composition of Romans. Paul's communication (e.g., Romans) is presented on the basis that any person assenting to the same presuppositions will understand the same thing, thereby transcending his or her current "situatedness" as Paul did his.

13 Interpretation Theory

Discovering the Otherness *of the Text*

The Issue of Meaning: The Instantaneous Differential Perception of Understanding

Introduction

The point now arrived at is the business end of interpretation for the individual interpreter, who, as the reader, becomes effectively the *someone* to whom *something* is said, irrespective of any intended audience. This is the issue of meaning. Meaning is the in-life value the interpreter gives to what has been understood, which in the current discussion is the discourse conveyed by the written text. In the course of this discussion the following concepts have been examined. The issues of authorial intent and its impact, which in turn highlighted an important issue concerning a duality of being in the nature of the text, firstly in its *being* as an entity of written text having impersonal-being, and secondly in its *being* as an entity of *intentioned-being* that is the composition. This unique entity of the composition has aspects of the nature of both personal and impersonal being. Finally, in the previous chapter, a discussion on the issue of understanding was considered. This final chapter deals with this important issue of meaning. The place to start is its precursor, understanding.

Understanding, as noted in the last chapter, is seen either as an *existentiale* of human-being, if the view taken is one of recognition of *existence* as being, or, alternately, as an attribute of human-being if the view taken is *spirit* as being. What this means is that understanding is regarded as a function of being human not something cognitively derived, or developed, by assertion or positing of the *thinking* "I."

Therefore, regardless of the view of *substantia* of being, understanding is held as a given of that being. In Heidegger's work, *knowing* is a derivative of understanding, being itself a reflective activity of what is understood in applying what is understood to the self. However, in making *knowing* a derivative, a potential for objectification is exposed, because what is derived can be treated as object in inquiry. This in turn infers that meaning itself can be obtained methodologically as the result of objectification, as has happened in modernism.

Heidegger seemed to recognize this potential in this conceptualization of *knowing* and sought to deal with it by considering the implications of *knowing*. Heidegger noted that *knowing* appears to relate subject and object, hence implying an exteriority from the person in nature.[1] In this situation modernism's turn to epistemology to solve the problem of meaning would be the correct direction. However, Heidegger argued that *knowing* is related to being and is unique to the kind of being that is the being of *Dasein*.[2] This in turn, however, creates a problem with the concept of knowledge, which then needs to transcend the subject to become object and exist exterior.[3] Heidegger sought to resolve this in an explanation that made *knowing* exist already outside in a concept that he called *Being-already-alongside-the-world*.[4] Hence, in considering *knowing* as a derivative of understanding, although as a derivative it has a natural move toward an exteriority, it does so as essentially anticipated in the being of *Dasein* and *Dasein*'s relationships with the world.

In this way Heidegger solves the problem of a suggestion of the need of transcendence of the subject to deal with the concept of knowledge. It is interesting that Heidegger's student Gadamer, contra Heidegger, saw the need to return to the concept of transcendence hermeneutically and for this turned to language, rather than traditional concepts. The traditional concepts, although showing appreciation of the problem, in Gadamer's view had come up with the wrong answer. For Heidegger *knowing* was clearly a function of being, but he also recognized that if it is a derivative of understanding it moves to an exteriority that leads outside being. It is perhaps this implication that leads Gadamer to suggest the concept of the universal of language as fulfilling a role of transcendence without spiritual implications in relating soul and thing. This is certainly suggested by Gadamer's analysis in his essay "The Nature of Things and the Language of Things," referred to in the last chapter of this book on understanding. Heidegger's answer was to give knowing an exteriority that wasn't in reality an exteriority, as other than *Dasein*, but an aspect of *Dasein* that is in essence an exteriority. This seems more of an attempt by Heidegger to accommodate his theory than be effective in addressing the issue.

---

1. Heidegger, *Being and Time*, 87.
2. Ibid., 87–88.
3. Ibid., 88.
4. Ibid. Italics added for emphasis. The use of hyphenation in creating the term is original.

In addressing the problem of *meaning*, Heidegger circumvents the potential problem related to *knowing* by declaring *meaning* an *existentiale*, or function, of *Dasein*.[5] Meaning is not to be considered as essentially a second derivative of understanding, due to appearing derived from knowing, which would unavoidably indeed make meaning an exteriority. Removing meaning from a derivative status related to *knowing* solves this problem, instead placing meaning with understanding as *existentiale*, of which in Heidegger *knowing* is derivative. Ontologically, Heidegger argued soundly that meaning is something only a being with the kind of being that is *Dasein* does; meaning is not something that happens to *Dasein*, unlike understanding. Meaning is then something *Dasein* does with knowing as the derivative of understanding. This line of reasoning clearly shows that meaning is related to a personal ontology not *thing*-ness, including texts. The interpreter does not extract meaning out of the text, as though it were resident in the text. In interpretation the interpreter understands and derives knowing; because meaning is an existentiale of Dasein as is understanding—hence an aspect of being—it cannot be derived from knowing but meaning appropriates knowing. For Heidegger meaning is something a person does as a state of being not a state of knowing as cognitive, which was picked up in Ricoeur. Hence, meaning cannot be found or derived by epistemology

The problem is that meaning does have a derivative aspect, and this needs to be understood in its hermeneutical implications. There is almost a genuine concurrence of understanding, knowing and meaning, due to which concurrence important inferences can be drawn. The processes of understanding and knowing certainly show concurrence as processes that lead to *understood* and *known* as concurrent endpoints. However, the concurrence of meaning appears only at the endpoint, not prior; one can articulate a meaning during the processes, but at all points meaning can only be articulated by essentially considering the endpoint as having been reached. Hence, meaning has the appearance of operating as a derivative of understanding and knowing. This infers that, contra Heidegger, understanding and knowing are both functions of which the derivative is meaning.

The result of such a consideration is the implication that, in effect, *knowing* stands as counterpart to *understanding* and as such would itself be an attribute of being, or *existentiale* in Heidegger's terms. Certainly in terms of the biblical text of Genesis this is not a contrary conclusion. The human being in the immediate created state is depicted as capable of both understanding and knowing. In terms of Heidegger's development it is not inconsistent with his ontology, since this implication retains *knowing* within the domain of the being of *Dasein*. Consequently, rather than meaning as *existentiale*, because it is more suited to the concept of derivative, the counterparts understanding and knowing function together in the derivation of meaning. This seems a less tortuous approach than Heidegger's and also fits better with observation.

5. Ibid., 193.

However, the problem that suggests itself concerns the issue of *knowing* in its relationship to *understanding*. Heidegger's concept of knowing as derivative of understanding is essential to his own development of the concept of interpretation and the resultant concept of meaning. The act of *knowing* clearly involves cognition to a large degree, because it must ultimately be expressed as *I know*. Yet it is clearly related to understanding, for knowing assumes understanding. Heidegger's concept of *knowing* as derivative avoids contradiction in his development. It appears that in order to avoid a potentially derivative aspect from subsequently becoming determinative, meaning is removed by Heidegger to *existentiale*. Consequently, *knowing* is derivative in the functioning of understanding. This *knowing* is then used by the function of meaning. Hence, Heidegger's proposal that meaning is something *Dasein* does and not something that happens to *Dasein*.

The difficulty with this reasoning is that although it sounds consistent as a theory it presents problems in practice. The nature of meaning becomes static rather than dynamic. If a person is asked what did he or she mean in what he or she did or said, it certainly requires reflection to explain meaning; however, in the time of occurrence no reflection is needed to have meaning or to function with meaning. Meaning seems to operate instantaneously even if it is understood reflectively. Experience and encountering of ideas interact with meaning already operational, and in dialogue meaning happens in the moment of dialogue. Meaning, when pre-considered, results in an *intention-to* prior to expression; but it is in its expression that meaning is achieved. It is in articulation that *Dasein* has meaning and can be meaningful. This includes the concept of articulation within the domain of self before expression; it is an instantaneous expression to self. Hence, the suggestion here is that meaning is the derivative, or instantaneous value, of two functions. These functions are understanding and knowing. The issue is the relationship of understanding and knowing, if knowing is not considered a derivative of understanding. As a result the interrelationship of understanding and knowing must be examined so as to articulate how they function together with meaning as derivative.

The examination of this topic of meaning will proceed in two parts; Part A: Discovering the Instantaneous Nature of Meaning and Part B: Equivalence of Understanding Confers Relativity of Meaning. The understanding of an author can, due to the intention of the author as part of the author's psyche being transformed into the *intentioned-ness* of the composition, traverse ontological impasses and impact the understanding of the interpreter. Equivalence of understanding between author and interpreter results in relativity of meaning. Consequently, interpersonal communication happens despite detachment of the discourse from the author and displacement of the interpreter in time. The importance of this principle in its special use in biblical interpretation is evident in that the interpreter interprets in a way resulting in relativity of meaning with divine intention occurring within the life setting of the interpreter. However, this is a special use of hermeneutics not special hermeneutics, and as a result it is true of all written text as the discourse of a person and should be evaluated in all literary texts, that is, texts that are compositions.

Part A: Discovering the Instantaneous Nature of Meaning

This issue of understanding and knowing would seem solved for Gadamer because both of these functions are expressed in language. In a consideration of his essay on *The Nature of Things and the Language of Things*, he noted that language relates soul and thing such that each retains its entity and is interpreted on this basis. Therefore, the important issue is that in dealing with the *thing*, the person appreciates the thing's status as *otherness* rather than interpreting the thing in terms of its use to the person. Hence, before some *thing* can be applied to the self it must be understood in its *otherness* before being applied. Consequently, what we call understanding is in essence a knowing of *otherness*; and what we call knowing is an understanding of *otherness* in relationship to *self*. These functions are both functions within understanding, and *meaning is therefore the instantaneous value of understanding*.

These functions can be described individually as *I understand*, which is a perception of *otherness*, and *I know*, which is a perception of that *otherness* in relationship to self, that is, as applied to self. Consequently, although two terms will be used in the discussion, which are *I understand* and *I know*, it is with the realization that they are both functions within understanding. This further indicates why both understanding and knowing, when discussed above, appear best suited to being equally regarded as existentiale or attribute of being with meaning as the derivative value rather than as existentiale. In this way the complete concept of understanding brings *otherness* within the domain of self. This is the true aim of all interpretation.

An Introduction to Discourse Meaning

The nature of discourse, being of the format *someone said something to someone*, begins with the *someone* whose discourse it is. This immediately raises the issue of the communicability, or otherwise, of the author's intention as the *someone* who wrote. If the discourse is *someone's* at its inception to become *something said* that the interpreter interprets, then the following question arises: is the *intention-to* of the author and the resultant authorial intent simply an aspect of an author's psyche, which psyche is no longer present? If so, for the author's *intention-to* to impact meaning there would be an inference that the text can be considered an extension of that psyche, and this psyche therefore would have some form of continuity with the text. In this scenario the authorial intent would become the subject of the discourse with the implication that there is the existence of a connection allowing inter-subjectivity of author and reader. This, however, is not the case and the authorial intent perceived as an aspect of the author's psyche, impacting meaning, is no longer considered tenable, as it was in Romanticism, because the author's psyche does not have any demonstrable or inferred connection with the text or interpreter.

The impact of considering the existence of an attachment of the author's psyche through the text would involve not only the metaphysical but also the paranormal, because it would imply some form of mind reading between author and interpreter occurring. However, in the detachment of the text from the author there is an ontological issue that renders *any suggestion* of connection untenable. This occurs because in becoming a *something said* there is a major movement from a personal ontology, involving a psyche, to an impersonal ontology, where there is an absence of psyche. Consequently, authorial intent, when considered as an aspect of an author's psyche, cannot be asserted to be determinative in interpretation and hence meaning. Hence, there is not and cannot be a psychic continuity between text and author. The only direct connection to authorial intent in the interpretation of discourse, which can be considered as impacting the reader, is that of authorial intentionality, or the adverbial sense of intent. This is where consideration of authorial intent has progressed to, and which has been shown to be effectively terminal to interpretation of discourse as that of a person.

Ricoeur highlighted the problem with the adverbial sense, as discussed previously, which is that intentionality then belongs to the impersonal ontology of the text, because what is intentionally done directs attention to *what was done* and not to the doer of the action. Consequently, there is a further movement away from the personal ontology of the author. Considered from an ontological perspective, therefore, this presents an aporia, or impasse, recognized by Ricoeur. It would seem the authorial intent, as an aspect of the psyche of the author, cannot traverse to impact meaning for the reader. The impasse is the movement from an impersonal ontology, as the text, to a personal ontology, as the discourse of a person, because meaning is something only a person does and there is no personal connection between author and interpreter with the text.

This in turn presents a problematic for the idea, or belief, that God speaks in and through the author. This belief is a concept of discourse as dialogue that precedes the discourse that is represented by the written text. In dialogue, discourse meaning can be considered to be the author's or speaker's. The problem is however that only the human author, who in order to write has been involved in dialogue with God, would have direct access to authorial intent that is determinative of meaning as the meaning of God. The only solution seemingly available to a person desiring to retain the belief that God is speaking as determinative in and through the Scripture, where in written text the authorial intent is no longer determinative in meaning, is the assertion of a special hermeneutic to reestablish the connection with the meaning of God as determinative.

Such a solution would traverse the impasse, but would introduce a mystical domain of interpretation that is only available to someone who already believes. Further, as a method of interpretation the only issues where determinative meaning could be asserted would be those pertinent to other believers. This leaves the believer isolated from that part of humanity that does not believe, therefore subsequently unable to communicate authoritatively outside the faith on any issue where the believer's faith is impacted and at times determinative. It also assumes by default that interpretation is properly conducted in an absence of faith, which has been shown to be a simplistic and untenable idea. The concept of a special hermeneutic, whilst appealing as a means of traversing the impasse, is unsatisfactory as a means for communication beyond its own borders, whatever version of belief is proposed.

The Author's Movement to Explicate an Explanation

In the consideration of authorial intent what has been exposed in this book, but missed and therefore unexamined generally, is that in the inception of discourse as written text there is an *Aufhebung*. This German word is Hegel's term, also used by Derrida and Ricoeur, to portray a transformation that includes the idea of both submergence and subsumption, which are applied equally in a paradox where there is both loss and retention of identity. Unfortunately, there is not really an equivalent English word, so as a result the German term is retained with the same significance. In the act of *parole* a transformation of this nature is undergone by the authorial intent, which is transformed from being an aspect of the psyche as authorial intent, to reappear as an aspect of the text, which is the *intentioned*-ness of the text. In this form authorial intent is now considered from an adjectival usage of the noun form *intent*, hence also retaining the nominative sense.

Therefore, authorial intent is no longer restricted to describing the doing as in the adverbial usage, but it is now an objective description of the being of the content, having become an attribute of the predicate of the sentence. The act of *parole* is the intentional use of *langue*, resulting in the appearance of language; however, the act of *parole* disappears as event with the appearance of the written text, to reappear as the discourse represented in the written text.[6]

This intentionality of usage of *langue* is the context of the discourse as language and therefore is, or should be, ontologically important in its interpretation, or if not, as Barthes contends, language is simply an extension of *langue*. Meaning would therefore be reduced to the science of semiology found in words, codes, and symbolic messages independent of both author and interpreter. The appeal of the structuralist or poststructuralist view to the concept of interpretation is that there is no ontological aporia in need of traversing. Because meaning is an act of persons, and all of the philosophers

---

6. Ricoeur, *Interpretation Theory*, 7.

and theologians considered in this work effectively accept that meaning relates to persons, meaning in a structuralist approach to interpretation is a function of the two persons involved, that is, the author and interpreter, individually and independently. Therefore, in such a view, meaning of each is not relative to anything and thus relativism is unavoidable. Discourse has lost its nature as discourse being that of *someone*. Discourse is merely the extension of *langue* into impersonal language; it is *something said* and is no longer the discourse of *someone* to or for *someone*. Meaning is only a matter of what *someone* will make of the *langue* of the language, and thereby, in this view of textuality, creates not only a self-based but also a self-centered understanding of the universe.

The idea of code inherent in this view of textuality, as in Barthes and Derrida, carries within it a couple of implications. First, in a strict sense of *code* the concept would be that code is itself the system, that is, *langue* as a systematic arrangement of principles and laws would itself be determinative in the development of meaning. The imprecision of the system that is *langue* introduces a significant degree of uncertainty. This uncertainty greatly impacts any concept of successful transmission of *intention* in any message decoded. The text, with the loss of any impact of intention, therefore has a writer but not an author, because the idea of both origination and authorization inherent in the word *author* cannot be determinative. The writer or scribe can have no impact on any interpretive meaning, and is simply a vehicle. This is the essence of Barthes's argument and also the position of Derrida. There can be no anterior impact due to a meaning an author had, which is strongly argued by Derrida.

Second, a code is a set of words and symbols, in the case of a text, which itself has the purpose of referencing another set of words and symbols. The sign is a sign of other signs, with the result that one cannot escape from within the interplay of signs to any exterior concept of meaning; that is, there can be no referencing. The moment that one has a meaning, one is folded back into the sign system and new meaning is apparent that is different. Any concept of an absolute is untenable. Also, the uncertainty of the sign itself negates any idea of the decoding of a precise message. The idea of understanding discourse as that of *someone* other than self is a phantasm, to use Derrida's word. This is the position of Derrida and the inference in Barthes.

Ricoeur has highlighted that it is the extension of the concept of the code and the system of *langue* to being determinative in discourse meaning that is itself flawed. Also, true interpretation of discourse requires that epistemology be submitted to a correct ontology. The movement, *someone to something to someone*, inherent in the nature of discourse, presents ontological issues that are ignored in the aforementioned concept of textuality, probably due to the concept of continuity rather than singularity in the idea of personal and impersonal ontologies. It is the recognition of the first of these issues that exposes the second.

Ricoeur has effectively argued, as previously considered, that language is composed of two irreducible entities not just one: the sign, as in *langue*, and the sentence.

Whereas in *langue* meaning is a function of the signification of the sign, the problem is that the sentence as language, though composed of signs, is not itself a sign. As Ricoeur asserts, also noted previously, the sentence is not just a more complex word. Another way of saying this is the realization that sentence meaning is not just the sum total of the signs used in its formation. The concept of semantics is the ability to deal with meaning at the sentence level not the sign level, which is semiotics. Although the sense of a sentence can be projected on the basis of the semiological approach, the importance to language of the sentence as discourse is its reference, that is, not just what it says but what it says about the matter of the text. This reference of the discourse is the result of an intentional use of language and is therefore directly related to the *intention-to* of the author.

Consequently, this reference represents an *otherness* that only finds expression in an ontology that has a personal nature. As such the presence of *otherness* is unknown and unknowable to the impersonal ontology of the written text, therefore semiology does not detect it nor can it deal with it. This presence to Barthes is the pleasure that the reader develops for himself or herself in interaction with the text; whereas for Derrida it is a phantasm, a projection of the imagination, a supplement one grants oneself. It is Derrida's and Barthes's presuppositions, their view of the nature of the text and their approach to written text, however, that is the cause of the failure to recognize this reference and also creates opaqueness so that this reference is transparent and not seen, though present. Without *otherness* an interpreter's meaning is not a meaning related to discourse but instead related to *langue*, and it is therefore related to the system of language but unrelated to language in its semantic sense as the discourse of a person.

The interpreter begins with the written text representing *otherness* he or she wishes to make his or her own. This *otherness* has its genesis in another person, and understanding of the *otherness* should thus reflect some sense of relationship to understanding of the person. The other person, that is, the author, had a meaning that resulted in an *intention-to*, which in turn led to the written text the interpreter seeks to interpret. If a person has a meaning that he or she wishes to communicate, then that meaning is understandable to oneself, as such it is also explainable to oneself. Therefore, in the ability to see oneself as other-than-self and expain it to self is also the ability to explain it to others.

Consequently, within the hermeneutics of the self of the author there is the movement from that which is the province of a personal ontology, which is meaning, to that which acts between self and self-other-than-self, which is the explanation. It is the explanation that has an aspect of the nature of an impersonal ontology, because it can exist other than self and therefore as external to self, and can subsequently become available publically for communication. Whilst meaning is not transferable, being itself an act of persons not texts, meaning is understandable due to the given of understanding as *existentiale* or attribute. This understandable-*ness* is the communicable explanation made available in time and space in its association with the written text. Consequently, it is possible for an interpreter to experience the meaning of another person, the author, due to this *existentiale* or attribute of understanding, but the meaning understood by the interpreter is from the perspective of the self, or Cartesian "I" of the interpreter. This results not in sameness of meaning but meaning that results from the sameness of what is understood, that is, the explanation.

The verbal concept of meaning cannot be pursued without encountering the concept of significance, when considered from a lexical viewpoint. Hence, in order to arrive at personal meaning of the discourse, the pursuit is that of the significance of the discourse, the unit of meaning of which is the sentence. Therefore, prior to the task of interpretation, the interpreter needs to first gain an appreciation of the language as used intentionally by an author, not just as a system of *langue*. If an interpter begins with the sign system then, as has been noted, each signifier has a potential list of possible alternate signifiers, and each can create anything from nuances of difference to large differences in potential meaning assigned by the interpreter. In the sentence if each sign is capable of this ambivalence, then the interaction of signs gives almost unlimited possibilities for meaning, especially when there is interaction among sentences.

This is the direction Derrida has taken with no thought to the relationship of an impersonal and personal ontology as singularities that create an aporia that must be traversed. His view of continuity, in the relationship thing-machine-person, is either his attempt to dismiss ontological issues or a genuine belief that consciousness is no more than an extension of *thing-ness*. Ricoeur has considered this same aspect created by the system of signs, and in his work *Interpretation Theory: Discourse and the Surplus of Meaning* he values the potential of what he has designated to be the generation of a surplus of meaning by this means. Ricoeur, however, retains the nature of discourse as that of a person and also recognizes the singularity of identity of the ontologies of soul and thing in line with Heidegger and Heidegger's student Gadamer, with whom Ricoeur was a contemporary. Therefore, although a contemporary of the other French postmodern thinkers Barthes and Derrida, Ricoeur diverges dramatically from their approach. Ricoeur's theory requires that he traverse the ontological aporia so that interpretation and the resultant meaning are maintained in relationship to a personal ontology as that of the discourse of another person.

The Concept of Reference and Discourse Meaning

The development of discourse meaning is the result of an analysis in consideration of the signification related to the discourse.[7] Saussure noted that, in the relationship of signifier and signified in the sign, the signified draws in aspects of psyche due to

---

7. The basic understanding of the concept of meaning lexically immediately directs attention to that of significance.

its relationship to thought.[8] In other words, one cannot talk of significance without drawing attention to a referencing that occurs in the consciousness, hence psyche, of the personal ontology. In Derrida this very point is its negative in the whole concept of the sign, which he alights on in addressing Saussure's work.[9] Yet Derrida's assessment is based on the presupposition of his having correctly established that the metaphysics of presence, wherein is reference, is a phantasm that is beyond dispute and consequently is no longer to be regarded as just a presupposition of his work. However, this form of reference is no less real than the *seeing* of a work of art nor less real than the realm of *thought*, which exists for the psyche, yet does not occupy space. What concepts such as this point to is that meaning is related to consciousness and is indeed an act of persons and not an act of texts; texts cannot have meaning in their impersonal ontology, or *thing-ness*, as texts, which Heidegger has well explained. Therefore, meaning is not communicable as meaning, because meaning is related to consciousness as an aspect of the psyche. Nevertheless, what is communicable is an explanation that references meaning. This explanation is language in which thoughts are *given being* so as to become capable of existence independent of the consciousness, thus capable of traversing the ontology of the person of the author and suitable to be made public in the impersonal ontology of the text.

This is the tremendous difference, highlighted in Heidegger, that both Gadamer and Ricoeur after him have drawn attention to, that is, the importance of a singularity of identity of both soul and thing and the resultant impact of their difference of ontologies to the very process of interpretation, which Derrida and Barthes either do not see or intentionally ignore. Interpretation requires the traversing of the complementary impasse from the impersonal ontology of the text to the personal ontology of the interpreter. Consequently, without traversing the impasse from the impersonal nature of the text to the personal ontology of the interpreter, meaning, as meaning of the discourse of another person, is not possible to project.

The work of Walter Ong lays emphasis to this in his recognition that in written text words appear similar to things, since we can see and touch them.[10] As a result he notes that written words are the residue of discourse, which require reanimating in the interpreter to again be the discourse of a person.[11] Ong further noted that spoken language has no such residue.[12] Therefore, spoken language ceases to be retained as an entity within time-space, existing only in the domain of the memory, which as unique to each individual is not available publically. The discourse thus remains unavailable

---

8. Saussure, *Course in General Linguistics*, 16.

9. Derrida, *Of Grammatology*, 40, 160.

10. Ong, *Orality and Literacy*, 11.

11. Ibid. See also chapter 5 of this book, "Autonomous Text or Authorial Intent," where the discussion concerns this concept, the extinguishing of the voice of the author thus preventing what is essential for interpretation, i.e., the need of this reanimation in a person.

12. Ibid.

unless again appearing as spoken language reproduced from the individual memory. It is through the inanimate residue of written language that discourse retains being within the time-space continuum as an entity that is available publically. As Gadamer has stated, "Writing is the abstract ideality of language."[13]

It is the composition's personal aspect of its nature as *intentioned-being* that facilitates in this *re*-animation, or restoration to consciousness, of written text as discourse. This reanimation can only occur within the province of personal ontology. In order for *intention* to become communicable it must become public; that is, it must occupy time and space for both parties, with the result that there is the possibility of communing at the interpersonal level. For *intention* to become meaning the *intentionedness* must return to the private and internal of a personal ontology for *re*-animation, so that it is meaningful to the interpreter. Consequently, in the act of *parole*, which is the composing of the composition, what was *thought* in the psyche of the author, and hence abstract, is given concrete being through language, which thus becomes public and external to the psyche.

The situation of spoken language, for example, in the case of dialogue, results in a transient appearance in the time-space continuum of the being of the discourse that occurs and disappears in the event, which is noted in the work of Ricoeur.[14] This situation requires personal presence of both author and interpreter for perception and interaction with the entity that is the discourse, due to dialogue's transient nature in time-space.[15] Any other format based on the occasion of dialogue such as transcription, CD, or DVD is no longer the event but is a *re*-presentation of the event in the absence of the presence of speaker, hearer, or both.[16] In the situation of discourse as language, the impersonal entity, which endows the *intentioned-being* of the composition with its impersonal aspect that allows it to occupy time-space for its communicability, is *langue* as system.

Perhaps the best way to give clarity to this concept is to consider the critique of Ricoeur by Wolterstorff in *Divine Discourse*.[17] Wolterstorff begins his critique of Ricoeur by addressing the issue of the ontology of language. He shows his own understanding of Ricoeur by placing with the word "language" the word *langue* in parenthesis. This understanding is the basis of Wolterstorff's discussion.[18] In his view Wolterstorff suggests that for Ricoeur there is almost a sense of synonymy of the terms. It would seem in the ensuing discussion that Wolterstorff's own ontology of language

---

13. Gadamer, *Truth and Method*, 354.

14. Ricoeur, *Interpretation Theory*, 9, 27. The written text fixes the "said" of discourse as the event of speaking appears then disappears.

15. Ricoeur, *From Text to Action*, 104.

16. These different formats and the implications of each have been considered in earlier sections of this book; see ch. 2.

17. Wolterstorff, *Divine Discourse*, 130–52. The chapter is titled "In defense of authorial-discourse interpretation: Contra Ricoeur."

18. Ibid., 134.

is also based on this assumption, which assumption is essentially Saussurian. In Wolterstorff's analysis of Ricoeur, he shows his own entry level into the investigation of meaning is the code level. Ricoeur, however, unlike Barthes, does not equate language with the system, as has been highlighted often. Ricoeur emphasizes that the sentence though composed of signs is not itself a sign, and meaning of discourse relates to the sentence level not the semiotic, or code level. Language is the result of the act of *parole*, not its source.

Wolterstorff's quote of Ricoeur's work, taken from *Interpretation Theory* (p. 3), perhaps gives a wrong understanding of Ricoeur, as in that section Ricoeur is presenting an analysis of Saussure's work. Ricoeur does state, as is quoted by Wolterstorff, that *langue*—Ricoeur does not use the word language here—"is the code—or set of codes—on the basis of which a particular speaker produces *parole* as a particular message."[19] However, as is stressed, Ricoeur is examining Saussure's work and the implication the speaker produces *parole* is either a result of this, or misleading, because Ricoeur's concept is that the speaker in an act of *parole* produces the message, or discourse. Hence, *parole* is not produced but it is the act whereby the *intention-to* of the author produces the discourse; that is, the act of *parole* produces the discourse as that which exists beyond the event.

Ricoeur's view of language stands closer to that of Gadamer, although Ricoeur does not go as far as Gadamer in making language *the* universal. Ricoeur does take great effort to make a distinction between *langue* as system and language as used in discourse, hence Ricoeur's emphasis on the system as a "mere virtuality." His emphasis is actually simply a take on Saussure's own view[20] and is not an implication of nonexistence but a reference to *langue*'s impersonal nature, and that in the case of spoken language it does not appear as system due to its impersonal nature in what is a personal exchange; that is, it is not perceptible although present. Hence, Ricoeur's emphasis, although he does not highlight it as his emphasis, is effectively on the impersonal nature of the system that is, the system is not itself a function of a personal ontology but rather a thing that a personal ontology makes use of in the production of discourse. The system's importance is indeed its *thing*-ness since this is what allows *thought*, as an aspect of the psyche of the speaker, to become an independent entity within the time-space continuum. This entity as discourse is now public and available for communication. The system of *langue* is the source of the impersonal nature of the text that is contiguous with the *intentioned-being* that is the entity of the composition.

The problem with discourse as spoken language, in its transient nature, is its entropy, both from the aspect of information theory and as discourse; that is, there is a potential loss of information and discourse integrity in the mode of transmission. As public information, the discourse is immediately once removed from its accessibility

---

19. Ricoeur, *Interpretation Theory*, 3. (Italics original.)

20. Saussure, *Course in General Linguistics*, 13–16. Saussure is distinguishing between the executive side of language in *parole* and the system acting as a form of storehouse.

for communication, because it only exists for the public domain in accessing the memory of speaker and hearer. The discourse must be re-created to be re-presented, which introduces numbers of variables into any possible interpretation. These include such things as memory retention, deterioration and distortion over time, the sequence within time in the saying, the exactness in the saying, the perception of emphases by speaker and hearer, and so forth. All the numerous possible variables contribute to changes of meaning that can go from merely a nuance to dramatic differences, which then are further impacted by the subsequent changing audience, which has a similar impact on meaning. The discourse once spoken exists but may even become completely lost; that is, unusable discourse though having existed is no longer extant. Hence, the issue of entropy in spoken discourse is not insignificant.

This at least in part could be seen to be a factor that has affected Ong's assessment of the importance of written text. Ong's assertion and its significance bear repeating again in this particular context. He noted, "abstractly sequential, classificatory, explanatory examination of phenomena or of stated truths is impossible without writing and reading."[21] This occurs because of the accessibility within time-space that only becomes possible with the written text as discourse as opposed to spoken language as discourse. As with the paints on canvas or the block of stone in the concept of the work of art that is the painting and the statue, it is the writing of text that makes possible the presentation of the composition in the public domain and hence the possible accessibility to any reader/interpreter for study. In the writing is the fixing of impersonal being, with which the composition is contiguous but not continuous; and yet without this impersonal being the composition is neither available nor accessible.

It is Ong's observation about the written text and the culture of writing that opens up the issue that highlights the significant difference between spoken language and that of the written text, as expressions of discourse. This difference is in its impersonal being. The written text marks the loss of transparency of the *thing*-ness, as noted previously in spoken language. This *thing*-ness is what makes *thought* available, independent of the psyche as an entity in its being as language. This is the *thing*-ness that gives thought being within time-space as in the spoken situation but no longer remains virtual, to use Ricoeur's term, or unseen. Ong observes that in the case of written text words appear similar to things, with "visible marks" signaling words to decoders.[22] The person can now see and touch the words, hence Ong's observation that written text is the residue of discourse.[23]

The *thing*-ness that has become visible and now what intrudes itself into the discussion is the system, that is, *langue*. This impersonal entity provides access to the *being* of the composition. This entity of the composition is contiguous as an entity with and after the physical impersonal entity of the written text—thus having a

21. Ong, *Orality and Literacy*, 8.
22. Ibid., 11.
23. Ibid.

metaphysical aspect—and which entity of the composition is now available within the time-space continuum due to its relationship to the *thing*-ness of the system.

(a) Language and Communication

If the sentence, as the unit of discourse, is an expression of a thought, then the thought exists before its expression. Therefore, inferring the observation by Gadamer that language is innate,[24] however, it also infers that its expression is learned. A child has and uses language before he or she learns to speak a language, and the learning of a language is for communication purposes not for the individual to learn to think.[25] The event of communication between a child and parent occurs before a language is learned, and the learning of a language primarily facilitates that communication. In speaking language a person makes thought visible,[26] and hence, as is asserted in this work, language gives being to thought in the public domain.

Once a language is learned one thinks in that language, which is what gives the appearance that spoken language equals language. Spoken language limits the expression of thought, not thought itself; and essentially the capacity for expression expands with the expansion of reasoning, that is, thinking.[27] Hence, the sentence is not a code but the public being of *thought* for the purpose of communication; the sentence does not stand for the thought but is itself *the entity of thought detached from the psyche*. The sentence is thought in an inanimate state, no longer animate due to its detachment from consciousness; hence, an aspect of impersonal ontology or *thing*-ness appears. An animated state is only regained by the sentence as the discourse of a person. Ricoeur's assertion that the sentence though composed of signs is not itself a sign is important to remember, especially when dealing with written text.

Ricoeur recognized that the development of speech and writing as having different roots, as in the thought of Derrida, ignored the fact that both are modes and means of expression of discourse.[28] The primary difference, as the preceding observations revealed, is the visible expression of the system that occurs in written text. Gadamer's recognition that speech makes thought visible highlights the fact that the receptor doesn't see words but in a real sense perceives, or sees, the thought. This is not the case, however, in written text, because the receptor, now reader, first sees the words, hence the system, as physical, in order to then see the thought, as metaphysical.

---

24. Gadamer, *Philosophical Hermeneutics*, 60. Gadamer asserts, "Man is a being who possesses language."

25. Ibid., 60–63. In Gadamer's essay he discusses this concept of the appearance of language in the child, although his discussion is not about communication but concerns the desire of philosophers to deal with the origin of language. He notes that no such origin can be identified; yet language exists.

26. Ibid., 60.

27. Ibid., 67.

28. Ricoeur, *Interpretation Theory*, 26.

The problem, however, is that seeing the words of the text is not equal to seeing the thought the author had, or as Ricoeur has asserted, this could be stated as semiotics is not the same as semantics.

The concept of language makes direct reference to a concept of communication, even in Gadamer's universal approach, because in the language of things asserted by Gadamer is the assumption of the desire of language to express itself, or communicate. The desire to communicate raises the issue of intention and directs attention to the animate state; it is the person who communicates. Hence, although the written text is the being of thought in an inanimate state, as it were, its recognition as language indicates the need for *re*-animation in order to communicate. Heidegger's development of the concept of impersonal ontology would seem to preclude the idea of *thing*-ness having the facility of communicating, because *thing*-ness cannot touch though it can be touched; that is, *thing*-ness can be described and its being be disclosed by *Dasein*.

The failure of an interpreter in recognizing only the impersonal aspect of the entity of *intentioned-being*, which in reality has both the impersonal and personal aspects in its being, is critical. This limits vision as it is the personal aspect that can confer to ability to touch, in the Heideggarian concept of touch, and thereby facilitate reanimation of the entity of *intentioned-being* in a personal ontology. This entity when fully recognized thereby creates the opportunity to traverse the impasse that Ricoeur noted. The entity of *intentioned-being* makes communication between persons possible, despite the discourse needing to exist in an impersonal state external to personal ontology. Language, therefore, really only achieves the status of language in being communicated; consequently, language is only truly manifested in its being as the entity of language in the animate state, not the inanimate state.

Animation requires the presence of consciousness, and written text therefore only really regains the status of language when returned to personal ontology as the discourse of a person, as Ricoeur has recognized. Therefore, to speak of the structure and function of language has a direct parallel to that of anatomy and physiology in dealing with the living organism. It has been observed and stated many times that meaning is a function of persons not texts; hence, meaning is related to the functioning or animate state, not the inanimate state, that is, not the written text as text. Consequently, meaning relates to the physiology of language not the anatomy, that is, function of language not its structure. The purpose of understanding structure in relation to meaning is so as to understand its function.

Dissection and dismembering into parts has a primary requirement: that what is examined is no longer living, that is, no longer functioning. The purpose is to study the structure and inter-relationship of the parts as they relate to the functioning whole; that is, the purpose should be holistic. Jesus highlighted the problem of considering the animate situation as to its animate nature in John 3:8, where the animate state is compared to the wind. The wind cannot be seen; what is seen is the effect of the wind. Hence, the wind is understood in observing its functioning. Similarly, thought is only understood in its functioning as thought. The consciousness cannot be seen but its effects can, and only when restored to a consciousness is thought seen in its function; hence, only in this state is meaning possible. However, written text being inanimate, as opposed to spoken word being animate, does supply *thought* in a form suitable for structural study. Nevertheless, the study of the anatomy of thought in the inanimate state is undertaken in order to relate that structure to its function, that is, its physiology. Semiotics and semantics are both important but different disciplines applied to the same entity.

As with the consideration of the innate faculty of language in the child, so also what must be realized is that the living state of language occurs prior to the inanimate state of written text; and the animate state is not developed from the inanimate state.[29] Therefore, the inanimate state should be studied in the light of the animate. The school of thought that relates discourse meaning to structure, so that the sign points to other signs as its purpose, is thus to search for the living among the dead. The conclusion of such a search is that there are no living among the dead; in relationship to the current discussion it is the conclusion that there is no meaning in the text and *the observer must invent meaning in order for it to exist*. This inter-relationship of the animate and inanimate state is really the essence of what Heidegger recognized in his development of the hermeneutical circle; that is, one must understand the whole in order to understand the parts, and the understanding of the parts in turn impacts the understanding of the whole. It begins with the whole, or language, not with the parts, or linguistics, and the purpose is an understanding of the language in understanding the linguistics.

(b) The Importance of Reference in Relationship to Intention

In semiotics one understands the structure of the thought as inanimate. Hence it is the thought's relationship to the sentence as *langue*, or system, not the thinking of the thought as animate. The semiotic concept of meaning is that of meaning of the part, or sign, in its relationship to whole, or its meaning for the semantics of the sentence. Semiotics does not determine the meaning of the sentence, but in being understood it aids in the understanding of the sentence from which the sign gained its context. The sign is chosen with a signification already in mind, the meaning of the sentence preexists the structure of the sentence, and the signs and structure are chosen on the basis of suitability for this predetermined meaning of the sentence. Hence, the importance of Ricoeur's recognition is underlined, which is that though a sentence is composed of signs it is not itself a sign. The important consequence of this realization is that the structuring of signs is the result of meaning, not its cause. Hence, semiotics cannot supply the meaning of the sentence as it functions in the composition.

---

29. Ong, *Orality and Literacy*, 8. Ong's arguments from his research are very sound on this conceptualization of the nature and development of language.

In the event of interpretation, *intentioned-being* regains expression again as *thought*, being reanimated in the psyche of the interpreter. It is in this reanimation that thought regains the status of living language and the facility of referencing. The sense of *intention* linguistically in reference to the semiological concept of meaning, that is, in *langue* as system, is simply that the signifier *intends* the signified, but *that intention* doesn't go beyond that sign to other signs, other than lexically. The sense of *intention* in relationship to discourse meaning, however, is beyond the level of semiological meaning, relating instead to the sentence level, or semantic meaning. The *intention* in the use of signs during the act of *parole*, in composing the sentence, is the structuring of the signs in language for use in discourse. It is this *intention* concerning language and its semantic analysis that relates to the composition as *intentioned-being*, which is the concept of referencing being considered in this discussion of discourse meaning, its relationship is not to the referencing involved in that of *langue*.

The use of the sign to point to other signs, as a way of dealing with meaning of the written text as discourse, is thus in fact a misuse of the concept of the sign. The *intentioned-being* of the composition is not only impersonal as written text but is also personal, and it is in the personal aspect of its ontology that *intentioned-ness* is resident that relates to language meaning. The failure to recognize this results in the loss to the interpreter of the *intentioned-ness* that is imparted in the act of *parole*. An author can use grammar, tense, syntax, adjectives, moods, phrases including superlatives, statements of emotion that connect directly as aesthetic, pistological statements positing belief about something or someone, statements of being, the nature of verbs, and so on, to communicate *intentioned-ness*. All of this is beyond the concept of meaning in relationship to the semiological sign.

The work of Ong has shown that, other than as a trivialization of the concept of the semiological sign, the concept of writing and its system, or *langue*, is a much later development than the spoken language.[30] For Ong the system is a designed technology that was invented by human being for use in writing.[31] In other words this system is similar to the work of art and the machine in having associated with its impersonal ontology the ontology of *intentioned-being* in which *intention* is imposed on, and associated with, *thing*-ness.[32] Certainly an aspect of both invention and intention is seen in the sign. The arbitrariness of the sign is noted by Saussure and others commenting on his work, and this notion indicates deliberate choice in relating sign and signified not a mandatory relating of sign and signified. Hence, both invention and intention are employed in the creation of the system. This arbitrariness relates especially to the choice of signifier to be related to the signified. As noted previously, the signified is the purpose of existence of the signifier. Consequently, the *intentioned-being* of the system relates to the issue of the sign, and as is also mentioned previously, this is the limit of

---

30. Ibid., 83.
31. Ibid.
32. The concept of invention by humanity carries with it the idea of intention in inception.

the ability to reference. The concept of meaning related to intention in the system is the sign, and not beyond it.

However, in that it is *intentioned* the sign can touch the person and give the appearance of communicating. Hence, when the limit of the sign's reference is not recognized, there is a tendency to extend the code of the system to sentence meaning, that is, to make semantics simply an extension of semiotics. This, as has been stated, is a misuse of the sign that has been taken outside its intended sphere, that is, beyond its *intentioned-ness*. Consequently, within its *intentioned-ness*, meaning determined by having been touched by *intention* in encounter with the system, as the response of consciousness belonging to personal ontology, operates intra-sentence not inter-sentence, in reference to discourse meaning. An author can deliberately, that is, with intention, misuse and even alter the system in his or her communication of discourse. However, unless there is agreement regarding the system, for example, in some form of subcultural change or local colloquial expression, communication itself will become distorted and consequently be subject to misunderstanding.

The system exists to give being to the entity of the sentence as the inanimate entity of thought, detached from the psyche, having been given being in language. The system is also therefore the means by which the sentence can be dismembered and examined in its parts. However, the system places the sentence within time and space so that the *intentioned-being* of the composition, whose simplest unit is the sentence, can be given being as that existing with the physical. Discourse meaning relates to the semantics of the sentence. This has some affinity with Ricoeur's development of sense and reference, where the sense, the *what* of the thought, is dealt with in dealing with the sentence. The reference concerns the *about what*, or what the sentence says about the *Sache*, or matter, and how it says it, plus its contribution to the discourse as a whole. This moves toward understanding of the reference in discourse meaning.

The personal nature of meaning precludes the possibility of directly communicating meaning, because meaning is the province of the psyche of the personal ontology. Nevertheless, it is possible to communicate the *intentioned-ness* that signified the meaning in its referencing. This is the basis of the *intention-to* of the author, and which is therefore also the *intentioned-ness* that can direct attention of the interpreter in referencing. In the concept of intention itself are the concepts of aim and pursuit of objectives—the sense of purpose and deliberateness—all of which immediately direct attention away to a referencing. Hence, *intentioned-ness* is critical in interpretation of discourse meaning as being the discourse of *someone who said something*, because it is in the reanimation that the facility of referencing in discourse meaning is regained.

The regained facility of referencing has, due to the communication of *intentioned-ness*, a directedness of gaze in the referencing, which is to see what the author saw; thus, it is to understand what the author understood, which is the matter of the discourse. It is, however, understood from the perspective of self and then related as understanding to the world of self, the result of which is discourse meaning for the interpreter. As Heidegger states about interpretation, "understanding appropriates understandingly that which is understood by it."[33]

(c) Seeing the Intentioned-ness

Ricoeur's development of the hermeneutics of the self, discussed in detail in previous sections, has illuminated the mechanism whereby something can be understood by self and yet be an understanding that can be from a perspective of other-than-self. Ricoeur recognized that the identity of self has two modes of being: selfhood, or *ipse*-identity (which has within its capabilities the ability to undergo change, hence allowing recognition of self in a moment of time), and the unchangeableness of *idem*-identity (which is recognition of self independent of time). The concept that the self can see self undergo change with regard to the aspects of time and nature is anecdotally suggested in the concept of conscience, which confers the ability to *see* self undergo change with respect to these aspects. Thus seeing self as potentially other-than-self in the same moment of time. It is proposed that it is the possession within consciousness of *ontic-consciousness* that confers the ability to virtually triangulate this ability to see self in the moment of time and yet also see self as potentially other-than-self in the same moment of time. The triangulate nature of the situation occurs as it is self who sees self in both the moment and the potential of self as other-than-self.

This is similar to the concept of human sight in stereoscopic vision. The effect of depth perception, hence to see three-dimensionally and not two-dimensionally, is achieved by two forward facing eyes that have a slight separation, so that each eye sees the same thing but from a slightly different perspective. Animals such as birds, which do not have stereoscopic vision, have to move their head from side to side to get the same effect. The human consciousness has the ability to simultaneously interpret these two different perspectives to give, in effect, a single three-dimensional vision of self. Hence, both interpretations of self can be held at the same time, be assessed and compared and then brought relationally together in a single vision of what is seen. The brain effectively triangulates so that what is seen is not two visions but a single vision, which is already the synthesis and interpretation of the two visions.

As previously mentioned Ricoeur in his interpretation theory did not take note of the *Aufhebung* undergone by the authorial intent in the act of *parole*. Hence, he did not evaluate the aporia in the movement from the personal ontology of the author to the impersonal ontology of the written text. This aporia is traversed in that the author uses language intentionally so as to impart *intentioned-ness* thus creating the *intentioned-being* that is the composition. It is the composition, in the composing and in the understanding by the interpreter that allows the traversing of both aporias in the concept of interpretation of discourse meaning, that is, *someone said something to*

---

33. Heidegger, *Being and Time*, 188.

someone. The composition is with and after the physical; that is, it is truly metaphysical but not mythical as a creation of imagination. Like all metaphysical realities, the composition is simply recognized and seen in the imagination. As noted previously, there is a virtual *de-abstraction* of thought occurring with the composition in the being-of-its-being in language that renders it inanimate, and it is in the regaining of the state of being as *thought* that the composition is essentially again *abstracted*. Only then can discourse meaning be considered as its reference, that is, in the person of the interpreter.

Ricoeur took note of the Heideggerian concept that understanding of discourse is not initially understood as that of a person but as a projection of potentiality of world.[34] Hence, his perception was that interpretation begins with the ontology of impersonal being. However, this was done without considering the *intentioned-being* that is the composition, which is what the author desires seen, not the written text with which the composition is contiguous. This is the actual projection of world that Ricoeur sought, but which became excluded from his thought by his presuppositions and the asserted importance to his theory of the autonomous text. The written text, as impersonal being, can neither be seen to contain meaning nor have meaning. Hence, as impersonal being it is freed from all sense of intention, which recognition is perhaps behind Ricoeur's observation that the referencing that occurs in the dialogical situation is shattered by writing.[35] Therefore, although Ricoeur does recognize the need for the movement to a personal ontology to do justice to the personal nature of discourse, for Ricoeur it is only possible as a creation within the realm of the hermeneutics of self, not a perception of *otherness* in the hermeneutics of self.

The search for the significance, hence meaning, of a discourse that is a discourse of a person other-than-self, for self, requires firstly an understanding of its *otherness* as that which is other-than-self. The ability of self to see self as other-than-self, as outlined in Ricoeur, presents the potential for the interpreter to take on the presuppositions of the author, to avail self of the semantic range available to the author, to stand in one moment of time and yet see self in another moment of time, and finally relate these two *visions* in the *ontic-consciousness*.[36] This allows what Wolterstorff noted in his concept of performance-interpretation;[37] that is, self is able and positioned to perform the discourse, not the written text, but to perform the composition while seeing self as other-than-self (as the author), and hence from that perspective see what the author

---

34. Ricoeur, *Interpretation Theory*, 37.

35. Ibid., 35. His detailed explanation of his concept concerns the loss of various indicators and forms of reference that occur in the written text as opposed to the dialogical situation, hence the projected loss of any impact due to authorial intention.

36. In the concept of depth perception is the potential to see a potential place one could be in another moment of time, different from the position of the moment of time presently occupied, i.e., one can see a place that one could occupy if one was to move, which must of necessity refer to another moment of time.

37. Wolterstorff, *Divine Discourse*, 171.

saw. The relating of this to self in appropriating understandingly what is understood is the discourse meaning now within the domain of self, that is, what was foreign has become one's own, which is the completion and purpose of the task of hermeneutics.

Meaning as the Instantaneous Perception of Understanding

The first of five proposals used to launch this investigation of the hermeneutical task and to be examined for its hermeneutical impact was that of a changing audience. What was noted was that a changing audience results in changes of meaning. If the aim of hermeneutics is perceived to be sameness of meaning with an author, this presents a major impasse to achieving this aim. A fundamental reason for this changeableness, highlighted in examining the hermeneutical task, is because interpretation is always *I interpret*, and meaning is therefore always relative to the "I" who interprets. This can be understood to some degree by way of a brief review of Heidegger's concept of interpretation.

Heidegger argued that understanding has within itself a potential for projection of being, which Ricoeur describes as the projection of a world before the interpreter.[38] This projection of possibilities and their development is *interpretation*; hence Heidegger's view that in interpretation "understanding appropriates understandingly that which is understood by it."[39] In this way interpretation is seen to be derivative of understanding and not the reverse.[40] The implication of this is that interpretation is the means by which understanding reaches its projected potential world. The articulation of this interpretation is meaning.[41] Hence, interpretation is *understanding*, but it is particularly from the perspective of the "I" who interprets. It is the relating of understanding to the self that results in meaning, which fulfills the interpretive aim identified by Gadamer of making one's own that which is foreign.

Consequently, what is suggested by this in the hermeneutical task is that there is a movement *from* a perception of *otherness* and the resultant understanding of the entity of that *otherness*, due to ontological interpretation of that *otherness* in its being. This movement is *to* an understanding of that *otherness* in relationship to the self. Postmodern thought has correctly brought the focus concerning this issue of meaning to be in its relationship to the interpreter, *who* is the person undertaking the task of interpreting and *who* will be the one developing an interpretation of this potential in understanding, hence meaning. Therefore, meaning is always unique to the "I" who interprets.

---

38. Heidegger, *Being and Time*, 184.
39. Ibid., 188.
40. Ibid.
41. Ibid., 193.

(a) The Intentioned-ness of the Composition and Meaning

The issue of concern, however, is the perception of the *otherness*, which when understood and interpreted is the articulation that is meaning for the interpreter. The understanding that the interpreter should first experience is the understanding of the *otherness* that is the author's composition, or discourse. The postmodern severing of the composition from the author, so that there is no longer an author but a writer, has focused the ontological understanding of the nature of the text on its *thing*-ness as the *otherness* encountered. There is no personal aspect of *otherness* in the encounter with *thing*-ness other than that which is *imagined* by the interpreter. Hence, there will be no understanding of the discourse as that of a person, other than at the discretion of the interpreter in a hermeneutics of the self, as in Ricoeur's development of this concept.

Thing-ness is not a bearer of intention and can only be a vehicle of intentionality, that is, in that it is intentionally done. For example, a person can use a rock to build a house or smash a window. The person whose window is smashed does not ask if the rock intended to break the window but rather inquires if the person who threw the rock intended to break the window. The rock is not in possession of *intention*-to, either to build or to destroy. However, if the rock is thrown with intent, then the rock becomes a bearer of *intentioned*-ness related to its *thing*-ness. Nevertheless, it is a person in relationship to the rock who forms intention; the rock does not form any intention.

Any concept of intent, hence impact on meaning, related to the *thing* as *thing*-ness can only exist in the fashion of anthropomorphism. Such a conception would indeed make any implication of authorial intent, with the possibility of a *presence* other than *thing*-ness impacting meaning, the auto-affection Derrida proclaims it is. The view of anthropomorphism, however, is not ontological, that is, not part of the being of *thing*-ness but the imputation of personality that is virtual and non-existent within its *thing*-ness, being given *imagined* existence by the person in relationship to the thing. Anthropomorphism is no more than the projection and imposition of the interpreter's personal aspect, not a personal aspect within the ontology of the thing. Understanding and therefore meaning of the event relates to intent, and as such concerns the person not the thing, since only a being with a personal ontology can impart or perceive the *intentioned-ness* that will reference understanding.

In the example used, intention is related to the person who threw the rock, not the rock in its *thing*-ness. It was noted previously that in the Genesis account of the creation any *intentioned-ness* within the universe is due to the speaking of God imposing and imputing *intentioned-ness* in relationship to *thing*-ness. *Intentioned-ness* is not inherent in the *thing*-ness. If, however, the text is recognized as giving public being to an entity—which in its nature is related by being contiguous with the *thing*-ness of the text, and yet, as an entity, having an ontology that allows it to be the bearer of *intentioned*-ness—then the meaning of the interpreter can be related to an understanding due to the *intentioned*-ness of this entity. This entity associated with the *thing*-ness of the text is disclosed as the composition. This *intentioned-ness* of the composition is due to the speaking of the author imposing it upon the *thing*-ness of *langue* and thereby imputing to the composition the attribute of *intentioned-ness*.

The failure to recognize the entity of *intentioned-being*, which has aspects of both the impersonal and personal ontologies in its nature, is due to a mistaken ontological interpretation of discourse, as disclosed in an ontology of written text existing only in the recognition of the impersonal aspect. This results in the placing of the text, in its ontological interpretation, within the domain of an impersonal ontology. The only possible result, since the text is related to an impersonal ontology in respect to an articulation of meaning, is a meaning posited by the "I" of the interpreter. But this meaning is unrelated to any *otherness* having an attribute of reference, which can touch the interpreter and therefore can impact meaning.

The correct ontological interpretation, recognizing this entity of the composition relating written words to that of discourse of a person, discloses an *intentioned*-ness, which when understood by the person of the interpreter in its referencing can impact meaning. Therefore, the discourse can be examined in regard to intent, not as the intent of the psyche of the author but as an *intentioned-ness* that is an attribute of the discourse. The antecedent and direct referent of this *intentioned-ness* is the intent of the author. This *intentioned-being* can touch the interpreter so as to present its *intentioned-ness* to the interpreter. However, *intentioned-being* cannot respond to, or experience, the touch of the interpreter, since its ontology is not a personal ontology and it does not therefore possess a consciousness in order to behave responsively as subject. As a result the entity of *intentioned-being* cannot explain its *intentioned-ness*, it can only merely present it. The nature of intent in the subjective sense is to reference meaning, whereas in the adjectival form of *intentioned* its objective nature is to reference an understanding of that intent, thereby making reference to that authorial intent. In this situation, the entity of *intentioned-being* has an *otherness* that is not just *thing*-ness, and this *otherness* presents itself to the interpreter. Consequently, although meaning is the interpreter's, it is, or should be, developed relative to an understanding of the *intentioned-ness* of the discourse.

(b) The Derivative Instantaneous Nature of Meaning

Thiselton acknowledged that the concept of a comprehensive theory of meaning is unrealistic,[42] which simply follows from the uniqueness of each person as an individual, being in each case the unique "I" who interprets. The concept of the uncertainty of singularity of meaning, related to a text in the hands of an interpreter, is perhaps the hallmark of postmodern hermeneutics, as exemplified in Gadamer, Ricoeur,

---

42. Thiselton, *Thiselton On Hermeneutics*, 530.

Derrida, and Barthes, despite their individual differences in philosophical concepts. Postmodern thought stresses the multiplicity of possible readings, hence meanings, because its ontology is of the personal ontology of the interpreter in an encounter with the impersonal ontology of the text. Meaning, as something persons do, therefore, is always the interpreter's meaning. However, since the only personal ontological aspect in the hermeneutical event for postmodernism is that of the interpreter, this concept of meaning results in relativism. Conversely, the recognition of the *otherness* of the text that touches the interpreter with an *intentioned-ness*, which *intentioned-ness* is the effect of an authorial intent, results in an interpreter's meaning that is relative to this *otherness*, that is, relativity of meaning not relativism in meaning. This is the concept of meaning suggested here.

Heidegger recognized that the implication of how meaning occurred, that is, as the articulation of interpretation, meant that meaning itself is something *Dasein* does and not something that happens to *Dasein*.[43] He recognized that meaning is not a property of entities and only the person has meaning or is meaningful; and as a result, for Heidegger, meaning is identified as an *existentiale* of *Dasein*.[44] Consequently for Heidegger, like understanding itself, meaning is grounded in being. However, his view is developed in an ontological framework related to his own approach, which has been to consider the being of the *sum*, in Descartes's *cogito sum*, from the perspective of the "I" who thinks, rather than the "thinking I." Yet, interpretation *is* due to the assertion of the "thinking I" upon an understanding of that which is other-than-self. The concept of meaning as articulation of interpretation suggests this, since to articulate something for self is to put it together in the realm of thought, hence be positioned to express this articulation.

The concept that interpretation involves making one's own that which is foreign—making one's own that which is other-than-self—infers the assertion of the "I" of the interpreter. The concept of articulation by nature always having a present tense state suggests that thought is in a state of flux. Also, in being the articulation of interpretation, meaning therefore directly relates to understanding. Consequently, to use Heidegger's terminology but to redefine the concept, meaning is not an *existentiale* of *Dasein* but a direct derivative of understanding. Meaning, rather than being an *existentiale* of *Dasein*, is therefore suggested to be the instantaneous value of understanding, where understanding involves thought in motion. When it is recognized that the concept of *I know* (which understanding is of *self* in relationship to a perception of *otherness*) is a function of *understanding*, and *I understand* (which understanding is the perception of *otherness*) is also a function of *understanding*, then the derivative nature of meaning is therefore indicated. Understanding is not just a perception of knowledge but its connectedness and the potential projected in it;

---

43. Heidegger, *Being and Time*, 193.
44. Ibid. Italics of *existentiale* are original.

hence, interpretation is not just the acquisition of information.[45] Therefore, *I know* is not just to be in possession of knowledge but it is also to understand it.

It is clear a person can possess knowledge that he or she does not understand, but such knowledge has no meaning for this individual and cannot be used in a meaningful way. A person can know the Schrödinger time-dependent equation without understanding it (e.g., the writer of this book). However, as a result, this knowedge is not meaningful and cannot be used in a meaningful way by the person; that is, it is not understood and so is not related to the self except as a piece of information. Hence, although this knowledge can be known as information, the "I" of the self does not know it. A person can have knowledge about the hardware and software of a computer without understanding all of the knowledge and still use the computer meaningfully. However, that usage depends on the individual using the knowledge he or she posseses understandingly, and not on the knowledge not understood. A person can follow a set of instructions he or she does not understand to fix a problem, for example, a software problem in a computer. But a person who does understand it will fix the problem, and this allows that individual to proceed in the fashion of *I know*. The assertion of knowing something already assumes it is understood to the degree to which it is known. As in the case of the Schrödinger equation just mentioned, a person can understand that he or she knows it as information without understanding its meaning other than as information.

Heidegger's recognition of meaning in its relationship to interpretation uncovers the general concept of meaning's nature. Meaning is primarily the articulation of understanding from the perspective of the "I" of the person, hence indicating that meaning is the articulation of *I know* in its direct relationship to *I understand*. As Heidegger noted meaning is something that "I" do, not something that happens to me. Thus, only the person can have meaning or be meaningful. However, as an action of the "I" of the person, meaning is not related to reflectivity in description and retrieval of information but rather to the instantaneous observation of the relationship of *I know* and *I understand*. The concept of the word *articulate*, other than in its zoological usage, relates to present expression of an idea or thought in such a way that what is expressed indicates clear understanding. This word is often directly related to speech, again focusing the idea of meaning on the present nature of what is signified.

However, asking the question "What did you mean?" requires the person addressed to enter a reflectivity so that what is examined is a *meant* not a *meaning*, that is, to answer the question throws the examination into the past. Even a speculative question of the form "What will you mean?" would require the person asked to project himself or herself into the future beyond the event and explain a *meant* from that perspective, as being prior to the event. What is supplied in answer to questions about meaning is an explanation; hence discourse, which when understood leads to meaning for the inquirer. If meaning is the interpretation of the potential of understanding,

---

45. Ibid., 188.

as Heidegger proposes, then what has occurred in response to a question about meaning is essentially a reversal of the process. There has been a movement from meaning, to articulation to oneself of the potential projected in understanding that resulted in meaning and hence a dealing with that understanding, which understanding is then, in the act of *parole*, expressed in language as the explanation in order to communicate.

Gadamer notes that in communication where understanding occurs one has speech—articulation—not translation, hence not interpretation, which is a reflective task.[46] Hence, to understand a foreign language means not having to translate, or interpret, it.[47] Where a translator is translating to provide translation to others, Gadamer notes that the "translator must translate the meaning to be understood into a context in which the other speaker lives."[48] Essentially, this describes the undertaking of an author, which is to produce a discourse, which is the meaning he or she possesses that is the projection of an understanding of a matter, and this understanding is developed as an explanation to be understood in the life setting of a potential reader. Therefore, articulation of understanding is a speaking of meaning. Conversely, explanation of understanding, being reflective, is a spoken of meaning; that is, it is a *meant* of the author. Both author and interpreter deal with meaning, but the communication between them involves understanding manifest as explanation, so that in the understanding is the perception each of the other. The public aspect between them is the explanation.

The reflective nature of this process by the author, together with its being articulated in the consciousness, makes possible an explanation of the matter that is to be understood. The very concept of explanation is already beginning a movement to the external of the psyche, since in the concept of *I explain*, within the hermeneutics of self, is, or has become, a "conversation" between self and self-as-another, as Ricoeur has highlighted. The explanation projected by the person is of the understanding he or she has that is related to the meaning he or she had. Consequently, explanation is a projection of an understanding a person has, and for the reader/interpreter in interpreting that potential of that projection of understanding is meaning.

The written text of discourse is an explanation of the understanding an author has explicated so that the interpreter, as a person, can develop a meaning as the instantaneous value related to that understanding. It is the reader/interpreter's meaning, but it is developed, as application of *I know* relative to an understanding projected by the author. The discourse is an author intentionally making *thinking* become other-than-self, thereby making it external to the psyche that thought it, which discourse represents an understanding the author experienced as meaning related to self. As noted previously, once the understanding is made external it exists as an entity in the public domain as an explanation. Hence, interpretation of *otherness* only occurs

---

46. Gadamer, *Truth and Method*, 346. The parenthesis is added to emphasize the relationship.
47. Ibid.
48. Ibid.

when the explanation interpreted is that of a person other-than-self, which when put together with the interpreter's own understanding developed as *I know* functions in the derivation of meaning, which is similar to the approach of Ricoeur's suggested dialectic.

When people are reviewing matters for themselves while seeking to understand, this basic concept also holds. Essentially, in this situation one explains to oneself; that is, the self listens to an explanation that has the appearance of being by someone other than self, because if one listens to oneself to whom does one listen? This is the tremendous importance of the work of Ricoeur in illuminating the hermeneutics of the self, of which Thiselton also took note. Hence, it was noted previously that in this way *I explain*, even to oneself, immediately begins to detach understanding from the self. Understanding is therefore the attribute or *existentiale* that allows communication between self and others, hence it is that which allows a person to perceive the world of *otherness*. An explanation is firstly understood in its *otherness*, and then secondly brought near in *I interpret*. In this situation meaning *is* the interpreter's, as postmodernism has highlighted. However, in meaning's production by the interpreter, it is meaning relative to an understanding that is of the *otherness* of the matter, or *Sache*, of the text. Because the resultant composition is the explanation of the author's understanding, it bears direct relationship to the meaning the author had; and effectively without having to equal the author's meaning, the interpreter's meaning can then be developed as a value relative to that of the author's meaning.

The discussion of hermeneutics by nature turns to the issue of meaning, that is, the articulation of the interpretation of the potential projected in understanding, as is well explained in Heidegger. Meaning is thus the end-game of hermeneutics, and in the process of the hermeneutical task meaning has gone from being an issue of the consciousness of an author to that of the consciousness of an interpreter. Heidegger recognized that the nature of meaning was such that it is always personal, because only *Dasein* can have meaning and be meaningful. Consequently, it can be proposed that, in the light of the preceding discussion, meaning does not actually exist outside consciousness, hence outside personal ontology. The confusion arises in discussing meaning because of the impact of *intentioned-ness*, which can exist outside the psyche in association with that which is impersonal, as has also been discussed previously. This *intentioned-ness* has an appearance of referencing meaning, which can confuse the situation so that there can be the seeming inference that the referenced meaning is the author's, as in Romanticism.

Part B: Equivalence of Understanding Confers Relativity of Meaning

The preceding section of this chapter focused on the possibility of meaning and the description of how meaning could occur. At the conclusion of the section, note was taken of the instantaneous nature of meaning in relationship to understanding. The importance of this will be explored in more depth in this section of the chapter. Previous chapters of the book have dealt with the folly of interpretation to be the search for sameness of meaning. What has been indicated is that the search for relativity of meaning is best pursued in the study of understanding. These issues are now to be more fully explored. It is important in our discussion that we also cover the issues of technique and methodology, since although what has been suggested is that ontological interpretation is vital what must not be forgotten is the importance of epistemological interpretation. Therefore, how these approaches to interpretation interrelate will be discussed in this section.

INTRODUCTION: THE PRESENCE OF INTENTIONED-NESS IN THE DISCOURSE

The *intentioned-ness* of the discourse is an attribute of the entity of the composition, which entity has the ontology of *intentioned-being*. This *intentioned-ness* of the discourse references understanding not meaning. It is the interpreter's subsequent articulation of the interpretation of this understanding, in the domain of a personal ontology, which is meaning of the discourse. The ontology of *intentioned-being* is such that it is the means of communicating *intentioned-ness* and is therefore capable of touching, confronting, and challenging the interpreter. However, although it itself can be touched by the interpreter, it is not capable of experiencing or responding to the touch of the interpreter. As a result *intentioned-being* as an entity is not capable of formation of *intention-to*, therefore of originating the *intentioned-ness* it bears. Further to this, *intentioned-being* also cannot explain its *intentioned-ness* or defend it, merely present it to the interpreter, and therefore give it *presence* for the interpreter. The meaning of the interpreter should be developed in the light of the impact of this *presence* in order for the meaning to be discourse meaning.

Hermeneutics has generally focused on the appearance of the discourse, not on the appearing of the discourse. It has been noted that the task begins with the *something said by someone*. In order for the discourse to appear, *the someone* who said it becomes engaged in an act of *parole*, which is where the investigation of its appearing, as impacting discourse meaning, has largely terminated, being regarded as related to an inaccessible psyche beyond this point. However, the act of *parole* itself is the result of formation of an *intention-to* by the author. This formation is intended then designed so that the act of *parole* results in the communication of the discourse being not only what is said but also what it is said about. Ricoeur has rightly observed that this *intention-to* of the author is private as the subjective form of intent. This form of intent relates discourse to the person. Yet the purpose of the formation of the discourse from the author's perspective *is* the disclosure of this intent, that is, to move intent from the private to the public domain. Hence, the *Aufhebung* in relation to intent that has passed unnoticed in the appearing and expression of the discourse.

A generalized observation would be that for the meaning of one person to relate to the meaning of another person, it is the intent of the person communicating, which will impact meaning, that must become known to the other person. Therefore, for the receptor, whose meaning will be impacted, the intent of the communicator must become public. If not, then no such impact on meaning can occur on what is exclusively a subjective aspect of human being. As Hegel noted, the subject remains universal and is only known and knowable within the horizon of time by predication. Accordingly, the situation is similar for intent, which to become public and knowable as subject requires its predication. In this predication intent undergoes transition from subjectivity to objectivity. This predication by the author, that is, the discourse, involves both adverbial and adjectival aspects of intent.

The doing, as the adverbial aspect, or *intentionality*, is the indication of the transformation of intent from the private being in consciousness as thought, to a public being in language. This resultant public being in language is the adjectival aspect in both its descriptive and nominative senses, or in its *intentioned-ness*. It is the adjectival facility of both the descriptive and nominative senses that allow language to render thought public. The adjectival form facilitates description of entities and their interrelationship, together with the declaration and disclosure of being of an entity, in the expressing of an understanding perceived by the author. This interrelationship of the adverbial and adjectival forms of intent facilitate the thought that comprises this understanding to detach from the person who thought it. This thought is then subsequently made public and visible in its association with *langue*—the system to which the adverbial and adjectival forms belong—to be perceived, or "seen," by another. In this act of *parole* the discourse, which was private becomes public.

It is discourse in the mode of written text that allows the discourse to occupy space as well as time, which is then able to take the discourse beyond the time of transmission and make it available for a time of interpretation that is independent of the personal presence of the author. The resultant detachment from the author makes the discourse independent in regard to the time of interpretation, with respect to time and space. Nevertheless, the discourse is not autonomous because the time of transmission remains fixed and the understanding that is associated with the explanation, which is the author's written text, is an understanding related to meaning at a particular point in time. The discourse is an understanding that is the result of a *meant* of the author and cannot be considered as autonomous due to its direct dependence for its existence on the time of transmission.

An interpreter who enters the time of interpretation without regard to the time of transmission is not dealing with the discourse of the author, that is, with the discourse of *the someone who said the something*. The result is that the interpreter is not then dealing with the *Sache* or matter of the discourse that is due to the act of *parole* of the author. Such an interpreter can be seen to be dealing with the *what* of discourse, but he or she cannot be seen to be dealing with *what it is about*, that is, its reference, which to exist must now be invented.

The epistemological interpretation of a text, which discloses description, naturally relates to the adjectival aspect of *intentioned-ness*, and as such describes the appearance and interrelationship of entities in the interpreter's dealing with the text. However, by its nature the adjectival form, due to its substantival aspect, is also directly related to its ontological interpretation, which discloses being and therefore naturally relates to the nominative aspect of *intentioned-ness*. In this substantival usage ontological interpretation by the interpreter is able to both impute being and perceive being, since in ontological interpretation the nature of entities is to be self-disclosing. Both modes of interpretation are critical if the interpreter is to understand the composition and develop discourse meaning. As Ong noted, referred to a number of times in this work, for the study of the abstractly sequential nature of discourse, that is, thought in its relationship to other thoughts, and for the ability to classify and methodologically study the thoughts, what is required is the production of the written text. Written discourse remains available for study due to its continuing occupation of time and space.

An Illustrative Paradigm to Display Relativity of Meaning: Setting the Scene

Einstein's concept of relativity required a constant to relate the aspects of *energy* and *mass* within the physical universe. Similarly, in interpretation the written text supplies a constant in order to relate *understanding* and *explanation* in the abstract metaphysical universe. Here the word abstract is employed in the positive sense of referring to the realm of thought, as occupying time not space, hence real but not concrete. When that *explanation* is given the ability to occupy space in the expression of the written discourse, the explanation is then made available independent of author and reader. It is the employment of *langue*, as physical, by an author that allows the abstract, as metaphysical, to appear in the time and space universe. Equally, it is reference, as metaphysical, that allows the physical universe to *see* entities in the abstract universe.

The following use of Einstein's concept is not a formal treatment or formal proposal but is suggested as a paradigm to enable perception of the relationship of understanding, explanation, and meaning. Einstein recognized that the inter-conversion of mass and energy was directly related so that there is conservation, that is, there is a relativity of each to the other that maintains constancy. *Understanding*, like energy, confers potential and involves thought in a state of motion, and the articulation of the instantaneous value of understanding is meaning. *Explanation*, like mass, relates referentially to understanding by a specific relationship and can regain a status of understanding.

When discourse becomes written text it no longer just occupies time but also occupies space as *explanation*, thereby gaining substance within time-space. What occurs, in the fixing of the discourse in time, is that the author takes note of meanings he or she perceives, possesses, or intends (i.e., instantaneous values of understanding) for or about which he or she develops *intention-to* communicate. In communication this becomes explicated as an explanation. This instantaneous evaluation occurs at a point in time, being the time of transmission. In performing an act of observation of *thinking* at that point, which is no longer thought in motion, this observation becomes effectively a value of understanding, or meaning, at a fixed point in time; hence, this value is a *meant* of the understanding, no longer a meaning. The issue of concern is the relative relationship of these aspects of *thought* in their inter-conversion in communication.

(a) The Horizon of Time and Discourse

Although it was not his agenda, Heidegger highlighted the common horizon for the physical and the metaphysical, that is, the abstract that is with and after the physical, which is the horizon of time. Despite the tendency to use the concept of the metaphysical and the eternal as interchangeable, due to some confusion of terms, it is important to realize that the metaphysical is limited by the horizon of time, unlike the eternal.[49] What relates these aspects of understanding and explanation within the horizon of time is disclosed as the *time of transmission* and the *time of interpretation*. These time elements both explore and increase the potential of the explanation in relationship to projection of understanding.

All discourse, in order to be given being as discourse, must occupy time. This time is the time of transmission, and thus has the horizon of time. However, spoken discourse, although having an initial time of transmission, due to the problem of entropy mentioned previously and the need of re-creation in each presentation, which is due to its residence in the personal ontology of a memory, becomes effectively a revision of the time of transmission in each re-presentation. What is transpiring is that changes occur due to the new apparent time of transmission. Hence, Ong's important observation about the connection between written text and study, because the unique aspect of written text is the occupation of time and space, thereby causing a fixation of the time of transmission that is not changeable. This fixation in time and space in *the*

---

49. The concept of the eternal includes but extends beyond both the physical and the metaphysical. The contiguous nature of the relationship of the metaphysical to the physical, even by definition of the terms themselves, relates them both within the same time. The problematic is the non-occupation of space of the metaphysical, which therefore can only become visible by use of language to reference and create world. It is the non-occupation of space that infers the eternal in the metaphysical, which inference is misleading. In denial of reference, as in Derrida, is the attempt to collapse the metaphysical to non-realm. However, its reality is manifest in thought and art—where art is what is *referenced* by the materials used, not *in* the materials used—both of which occupy time as realities but not space.

time of transmission gives an important constant, and hence reference point, in regard to the task of hermeneutics in relationship to the discourse.

(b) Relativity of Understanding and the Problem of Time

It is also important to remember that, in the concept of understanding itself, what must be kept in mind is that language at the time of transmission limits the *expression* of thought, not the thinking of the thought. This realization therefore provides a natural opportunity for the potential of expansion in relationship to understanding with the expansion of the ability to express the thought. Finite time always has the opportunity to expand into infinite time, which due to the nature of the expansion means that no logical or natural end to this process is foreseeable other than the deliberate creation of a discontinuity. Therefore, similarly, due to the expansion of a thought, no end of an expansion of understanding is foreseeable within the horizon of time, because, as Gadamer has observed, language always expands to accommodate the thought, hence the expression of understanding. This perhaps gives insight into Gadamer's assertion of his view of the universality of language, since there is no foreseeable end to the expansion. This expansion is therefore in reality an expansion of the same understanding into a more developed form.

An analogy that can be suggested is an author's expansion of an idea into a discourse. Thought produces an idea; however, for semantic expression as language the idea is expressed as a sentence. Reflection leads to the expansion of the idea from a sentence into sentences in an expansion of the idea, thereby becoming a paragraph. Additional paragraphs can then associate and interrelate thoughts sequentially. Linguistically, the expansion from the sentence to sentences is what creates the nontraversable impasse for semiology in discourse meaning. It is not an expansion of signs and symbols into other sentences but a direct expansion of the semantic unit of the sentence into other sentences. Hence, the linguistics of semantics is required beyond the sentence in discourse meaning. Semiology can deal with each sentence individually but does not venture beyond the individual sentence. Chapters can be used to develop themes that unite the sequence of thoughts and volumes can supply sequence of discourses in series. The sequence of discourses can become effectively a unity of discourse, with a specialized use of this hermeneutical concept being applied in scriptural hermeneutics. This expansion of understanding of the discourse occurs within the context of an authorial intention. Therefore, the potential for expansion continues within an understanding that is not random but *intentioned*.

If the object is discourse meaning, then what interpreters do is continue with the expansion of the same understanding of the author into any new time of interpretation, being the time at which the interpreter engages in hermeneutics. Hence, although sameness of meaning is untenable, sameness of understanding appears to be tenable, at least as a basic concept. The problem is the apparent implication that in observing the instantaneous value of understanding, which is meaning, what has occurred is the stopping of the motion of thought involved in understanding in order to gain observation of its value, that is, its meaning, at that fixed point in time, which is the time of transmission. When understanding is thought of in these terms, then there is an inference of the existence of a knowable and precise, hence, absolute value, of understanding, which can exist in its exactness and precision in both author and interpreter. In this situation sameness of understanding would suggest an exactness that is non-demonstrable in reality. It also suggests that understanding is something the person does. But as Heidegger has pointed out, understanding happens to a person; it is not something done by a person.

The reality is that the nature of the instantaneous value is such that, as the tangent of a curve, the point at which the tangent touches the curve, as the point of observation, is like stopping to observe at that point, but it is not the stopping of the motion at that point. First, as a result, there is a problem created for the author in expressing that value exactly due to the time of reflection, turning observation at a point in time into a period of time, during which time thought remains in motion. The time of reflection occurs between the time of intention, the point at which the decision to communicate meaning was made, and the time of transmission. Consequently, meaning has moved past the *meant*, as it were, so that the observed value of understanding is being impacted by new understanding in such a way that what was a point now becomes a region on the curve; hence, the tangential point sought initially to disclose meaning is seemingly changing.

Therefore, by the time the text is released into the world of readers as fixed, there is a degree of uncertainty about the exactness of the point with a resultant uncertainty regarding any exactness of value. When authors detach from their text, (i.e., the written text is released into the world of readers), they often immediately begin to see some things differently and wish some things had been done differently. However, the text is now released and the only way to address this would be revision, which can and often does happen. Revision is the result of expansion of thought on the *Sache*. The released text is no longer meaning at a point in time but meaning over a period of time, hence no longer a *meant* as singular but a sequential series of points.

The problem is that meaning is an act of persons that is noncommunicable and can only be addressed outside, or external, to a personal ontology as a *meant* of discourse not a *meaning* of discourse, which is the province of the author and interpreter as persons individually and separately. The fixed point for the author occurs before the fixed discourse and this gap creates uncertainty with regard to any concept of an absolute value of the *meant* of the author as *the* point of observation. Hence, sameness in understanding, though conceptually possible, cannot be expressed in terms of exactness and precision of that understanding in both author and interpreter.

Second, there is a problem related to the interpreter who becomes effectively, from his or her own perspective, an observer of a point not a curve, which as noted previously is made uncertain because he or she is actually observing a curve not a point. If the time of reflection for the author is from the particular to the whole in developing discourse for the time of transmission, the time of reflection for the interpreter is from the whole, or point, to an understanding of the particular in interpreting the discourse. The time of reflection for the interpreter occurs between the time of intention to interpret and the time of interpretation. During this time the *I understand* of the interpreter, as the perception of *otherness*, will undergo change due to the process of revision inherent in reflection. Hence, meaning will appear to be like *shifting sands* during this time. Thus, the point of observation becomes uncertain for the interpreter, which further precludes the possibility of sameness of understanding being reached having exactness and precision of value.

(c) The Movement to Understanding of the Interpreter

It is appropriate to note at this time an observation related to linguistics that occurs due to the realization of the differences of viewing of the discourse since the author begins with the particular and the interpreter with the whole. The author begins with the idea and employs semiology in producing the sentence in the act of *parole*, hence Ricoeur's observation that the sentence is composed of signs, though it is not itself a sign. Semiology does not create the idea of the sentence but is employed in formation of the idea into the sentence. The author then moves to semantics in relating sentences to the thought being developed. The interpreter begins with the completed discourse and moves back through the parts, that is, chapters, sections, and paragraphs to arrive at the sentence. The interpreter can then engage in semiology, as after semantics, in dealing with the sentence. Hence, semiology is often the first step for the author but should be the last for the interpreter.

Meaning for both author and interpreter is a function of the relationship between *I understand* and *I know*. However, a primary difference is that the author is a possessor of meaning and the interpreter is a seeker of meaning. The author seeks to explicate the *I understand* that corresponds to this meaning, as the *otherness* that can be perceived. Yet, meaning requires both variables for its expression, thus it also requires *I know*, which is not explainable by the author, being unique to the individual. As a consequence it is not possible to explicate the *I know* of the author in the explanation that is the discourse. *I know* will now be a function of the interpreter. Hence, for the interpreter to gain appreciation of *I know* during the time of reflection, the *I understand* of the interpreter, as the perception of the *otherness* or supposed point that is the explanation, is undergoing constant revision, hence change, if the pursuit is of discourse meaning as the discourse of *someone*, that is, the author. Yet, discourse meaning relates to a stable perception of *otherness* but involves working with an unstable perception. Ricoeur addresses this concept in dealing with the concept of an initial grasp of understanding as involving a concept of a guess.[50] Hence, the point is shifting but for differing reasons than that of the author. This further exacerbates the problem of a concept of exaction and precision.

In Ricoeur, and postmodernism generally, this concept of dealing with the *I know* of the author is not addressed or pursued. It is reasonable to assume that this primarily occurs due to the immediate recognition of this concept's relationship to the psyche of the author, which is therefore moved into the realm of being "out of bounds" for any consideration. In the postmodern situation the only *I know* impacting meaning, as the derivative of the function of *I understand* and *I know*, is that of the interpreter. Within postmodern thought only Ricoeur has sought to pursue a consideration of the *I know* of the author, though not as directly being that of the author but instead as function within the hermeneutics of self of the interpreter. This development in Ricoeur is due to his concern to retain the concept of discourse as that of a person.

However, the *I know* of a person is not an entity but a function within the attribute or *existentiale* of understanding, and as such is an aspect of human being. The uniqueness of the *I know* of a person is due to its unique development within each person, and this formation is the result of the view of reality, hence presuppositions and beliefs. It is also the result of worldview and issues such as cultural impact. All of which to a large degree can be known, investigated, and even adopted by the self in perception of self-as-another. In this way the interpreter is positioned to be able to use performance interpretation in pursuing discourse meaning, and thereby perform the text for self as a performance of the author, but now relative to the time of interpretation. Consequently, although exactness is not possible, the relativity that is possible itself indicates that a concept of sameness of understanding can be pursued.

The recognition that there is a possibility of a relativity of understanding is an important recognition, despite the fact that a prescription of exactness of that understanding is not possible as objectively identifiable for both author and interpreter. This concept of relativity opens the door on a solution to the problem of a concept of sameness of understanding being a viable and usable concept in hermeneutics. Sameness of meaning has been shown to be an untenable concept; yet whilst sameness of understanding is conceptually tenable, it is also shown to have inherent problems in practice. Meaning has been shown to be a derivative of the variables involved in understanding; hence, sameness of understanding would result in relativity of meaning between author and interpreter. Therefore, if sameness of understanding were shown to be practically as well as conceptually tenable, then the issue of discourse meaning of the interpreter, as relative to the discourse meaning of the author, is viable. Nevertheless, without some point of contact, hence sameness for both author and interpreter,

---

50. Ricoeur, *Interpretation Theory*, 74. The discussion of the movement toward validation, or what is designated here as stability of perception of *otherness*, is dealt with in a subsequent discussion, 75–79.

even a concept of relativity of understanding, therefore meaning, between author and interpreter must be admitted to be highly speculative.

The concept of meaning, because the interpreter is agreed to begin with the *something said* of the discourse and not *the someone who said it*, must indeed be a function of the hermeneutics of the self of the interpreter. This places any relationship of meaning between author and interpreter, disclosed within the concept of the hermeneutics of self, as either due to a genuine and demonstrable relativity of perception or as an invention of the interpreter that is dependent on the integrity of the interpreter. Hence, this relationship is speculative at best. The concept of invention, although Ricoeur does not call it that, is primarily his view, and the proposed integrity of the interpreter is critical to his treatment of this issue. When perceived as an invention of the interpreter, this concept of relating discourse to the person of the author occurs wholly independent of any actual authorial impact. This is Ricoeur's autonomous text.

The concept that began this section of the discussion was an examination of the nature of the relationship between understanding and explanation. Explanation is the externalizing of understanding, so that *thought* is given external being in language, and in this way detaches from the psyche of an author to become available by becoming *visible* to an interpreter. This is the time of transmission. The explanation is that which is to be understood by the interpreter, and interpretation is a process whereby self, in understanding, appropriates understandingly that which is understood by it, which is the interpretation of the explanation of the author.[51] This is the time of interpretation. As the discussion has unfolded, the problematic introduced by considering the impact of the act of observation, by both author and interpreter, was disclosed. The result was the recognition of the introduction of degrees of uncertainty. This uncertainty makes sameness of understanding as an evaluation of meaning, taken at the points of time that form the horizon of time relating understanding and explanation, although conceptually tenable an inexact value on which to proceed. This creates a problem as a criterion for relativity of meaning.

(d) The Reference Point Effecting Relativity of Understanding

The course of the discussion has tended to convey the idea that the concept of the time of transmission and the time of interpretation are points in time. This treatment is convenient for the purposes of discussion. However, the reality is that although there is both a sense of a point in time of transmission when the discourse becomes written text detached from the author and a sense of a point in time when an interpreter's understanding is complete (i.e., something can be regarded as understood, hence a

---

51. This is Heidegger's concept of interpretation, as has been referred to previously.

point in time of interpretation), this is an incomplete picture. Realistically, both of these times are more properly periods of time in which these things occur.

In a sense the author, in the process of writing, is interpreting his or her own understanding. Interpretation is the development of the potential and projection of understanding, and the articulation of this interpretation is meaning. Furthermore, it is this articulation, or meaning, that is both *the what* and *the about what* of the discourse that is communicated as the explanation. The explanation therefore has correspondence directly to the author's meaning, without the need to suggest or imply any form of inter-subjective connection with the interpreter. This is occurring in the period of reflectivity that occurs between the point of intention to write and the point of transmission.

Similarly, the interpreter engages the explanation, and in a period of reflectivity moves toward the time of interpretation. Heidegger notes that understanding does not arise from interpretation; that is, understanding is not interpretation's cause.[52] Thus, the interpreter does not interpret to understand; but because understanding occurs the interpreter interprets, and the articulation of this interpretation is the interpreter's meaning. Therefore, in the case of understanding of the discourse, this meaning that results from the process is the discourse meaning from the perspective of the interpreter. The perception of a point at which the time of interpretation has occurred is this arrival at discourse meaning. However, our discussion has again further exacerbated the problem of sameness of understanding. The concept of exactness is problematic not only on the basis of the concept of the participants who are undertaking observation to deal with issues of time but also from the perspective of consideration of the time within which each of these events occur themselves.

The paradigm suggested previously is Einstein's concept of relativity in relating energy and mass, which is one dealing with the physical universe. But in using the paradigm the universe under discussion is the metaphysical universe. In this work, passing reference was taken of Einstein's formulation that established a relationship between energy and mass that resulted in conservation, or constancy of value. In the ensuing discussion it has been shown that understanding, rather than being suggested to have a constancy of value, undergoes expansion with respect to time. However, what has also been noted is that the idea of sameness of understanding, as a concept of constancy, relates to identity, or qualitative value, rather than a quantitative value; consequently, relativity of meaning is possible if it is a relative understanding that undergoes expansion in the time of interpretation.

The recognition that psychic connection, hence some form of intersubjectivity, between author and interpreter is not credible therefore means that only the author possesses the author's understanding and similarly the interpreter the interpreter's understanding. Understanding is always understood from the perspective of self; therefore, though common to persons understanding is individual and unique within

52. Heidegger, *Being and Time*. 188.

each person. Nonetheless, because understanding is well demonstrated to be innate within human being, it is reasonable to suggest that there can be evaluation and appreciation within the demonstrable hermeneutics of the self so that each is able to reasonably approximate the other's understanding. Yet, as a criterion of sameness this would also be inadequate due to the uncertainty created due to inexactness.

It is these two observations that lead to an important implication in this discussion: conceptually, sameness of understanding, hence relativity of meaning, is tenable but not practical; and understanding for each person is unique but is nevertheless at the same time common as attribute to all. What is implied is that understanding refuses to be objectified for the purposes of investigation. This should not be surprising in the light of Heidegger's concept of understanding as *existentiale* of the being of *Dasein*. Understanding is irreducible to something done by a person, although having the appearance of being something done. As Heidegger observed, as mentioned previously, understanding does not itself arise from interpretation.[53]

Hence, interpretation acts, in regard to understanding, in much the same way as a light switch or power switch on an appliance. The switch allows the potential to become manifest for the self, but it does not create the potential. Yet, interpretation has the appearance of invention of the potential, since it is what causes the disclosure of the potential. Hence, interpretation is not the doing of understanding but functions in allowing disclosure of understanding. Therefore, as would be indicated from Heidegger's observations, sameness of understanding, so as to establish a viable constancy of relationship between understanding and explanation, cannot be achieved through its being objectified and reproduced as a some*thing*. This highlights the problem in trying to find the possibility of identifying the point at which relativity becomes possible with any degree of certainty, if the search for this place or point is within the domain of the ontology of the person.

Gadamer observed, in considering language as the medium of hermeneutical experience, that to understand is to agree about the object; to understand is not to get inside the other person.[54] The issue of understanding and meaning becomes a matter of linguistics, and language becomes the middle ground where agreement can take place between two people.[55] The consequence of this realization is that relativity of understanding is not found in the domain of the personal ontology, as is confirmed in the preceding discussion, which reveals the problematic of taking the view of sameness of understanding as sameness of disclosure of understanding to both author and interpreter. The uniqueness of each person's personal ontology, within the general concept of personal ontology, and the problems of observation, in respect to treating the times of transmission and interpretation as points in time, render this approach to the problem unsuitable as a means for a concept of sameness. *Sameness of understand-*

---

53. Ibid.
54. Gadamer, *Truth and Method*, 346.
55. Ibid.

ing relates to sameness of what is to be understood, not the personal perception of that understanding.

The written text is the vehicle of language in written discourse, as opposed to speech as a vehicle in spoken discourse. As a result the written discourse provides a *something* that is independent of a personal ontology, yet due to *intentioned-ness* of the entity of the composition that is integral with the written text of the discourse, written discourse has a personal aspect that can therefore interact with a personal ontology. Also, since within space-time the discourse is fixed as written text, it has constancy independent of different interpreters, yet for each interpreter the written discourse is from the one author from whom it is also detached and independent within time and space. Consequently, each hermeneutical event as a hermeneutical task involves the same object, which, due to the nature of the text, makes reference to the person of the author in its referencing of the object to be understood, which is the *Sache* or matter of the text. The hermeneutical event therefore is an event that involves two persons who are separated in time but who each has the perception of involvement with the discourse of a person, which perception though imagined within the domain of a personal ontology is real not imaginary. It is not simply that of a person apprehending *thing*-ness, in the sense of ontological disclosure, nor simply making use of *thing*-ness. If so, meaning would become invention, as in Derrida's thinking.

The discussion began with the recognition that the factor relating understanding and explanation is that of time. This factor has two elements of time, the time of transmission and the time of interpretation. The time of transmission produces an unchangeable form of the discourse that provides constancy, and the time of interpretation allows the expansion of understanding to fulfill potential of the thought within the increased potential of expression in the time of interpretation. Yet in this expansion into understanding's fulfillment, it is effectively the same understanding if kept in relationship to the time of transmission. What is effectively occurring is simply the expansion of the same understanding. The nature of spoken and written discourse is the same; the difference between them is the state of being in their temporal displacement between the times of transmission and interpretation. It is the state of being of written discourse in this temporal displacement that confers the potential for expansion of understanding as relative to that of the author.

The hermeneutical issues are therefore the same for speech and writing, although due to the immediate situation of spoken discourse involving the presence of the persons, the situation of the written discourse requires a different approach to the hermeneutical task. As Ricoeur has pointed out, to separate speech and writing as having different roots, which would imply differing hermeneutical tasks for each, is an ontological misconception. This fixation of written text does render opaque what had been transparent, although present, in the spoken situation, which is the system of *langue*. The need to make this opaque, or visible, is the very issue of the situation of temporal separation, because the system is what provides the ability to give thought an identity as an entity detached from the *thinking I*, which is part of the psyche. The system is what allows the appearance of the object, hence matter of the text, to which Gadamer refers, and which must be supplied where there is temporal separation, either as re-creation from memory being re-spoken by a person, or as written text.

The aspect of constancy involving the written text is the result of this system, which has the ontology of *thing*-ness allowing it to become object and provides the opportunity for being contiguous with the entity of the composition. The entity of the composition having two aspects to its identity in its ontology, which are an impersonal and a personal aspect, allows the composition to be physical and yet possess the ability of referencing, hence also be metaphysical as an entity. Gadamer lamented the loss of a dimension in forsaking the transcendent aspect of philosophy, which he saw language restoring. It is this entity of the composition, which is expressed as language, not language itself, that fulfills the ends Gadamer sought. In spoken discourse the person deals directly with the composition and is unaware of the system; however, for study, as Ong has noted, and for sameness of understanding to be practical as well as conceptual, what is required is the written text. It is the written text that makes possible relativity of understanding between author and interpreter. It is the written text that provides the constant of the time of transmission. The critical importance of this hermeneutical principle for biblical hermeneutics is unmissable.

An Illustrative Paradigm to Display Relativity of Meaning: The Illustration

Einstein's relationship between energy and mass in his theory of relativity can now be used to illuminate and illustrate the relationship, that is, the relative nature, of understanding and explanation in which discourse meaning appears. The written text, as the explanation, is related to discourse understanding by time, which is specifically the time of transmission, and this time of transmission relates understanding and explanation directly to the discourse of the author. Consequently, in this way discourse understanding allows the conceptual possibility of an impact of the author's meaning without suggesting inter-subjectivity with the author's psyche. It is the element of the time of interpretation in encounter with the time of transmission that allows expansion of the explanation to be an understanding in the time of interpretation, which is however maintained in relationship to sameness of understanding. In this way discourse understanding results in discourse meaning for the interpreter that is relative to that of the author, hence establishing relativity of meaning not relativism in meaning.

The statement of this relationship must first be qualified by recognition of aspects of language and the human sciences. First, as has been developed in this work, language has a flexibility that allows it to operate in the presence of uncertainty or incompleteness. However, this nature of language, although advantageous in discourse, also gives language degrees of uncertainty if exactness and precision is required. Hence, physical scientific language is built around careful definition to minimize and even avoid this advantage that has become a disadvantage in communicating within physical sciences. Second, human sciences, in dealing with study of persons has the problem that, although there is a level at which all persons have a personal ontology, there is a uniqueness of the personal ontology in each person. Therefore, scientific study is conceptually possible as a discipline but is not exact and contains uncertainties, which must be both valued and considered in the approach of the human sciences due to that very individualism. The result is that statements made using Einstein's theorem, as a paradigm, cannot be considered as statements equivalent to those of the physical sciences, for example, statements of equality are not mathematical, and they are qualitative not quantitative, yet they are real statements of equality within the limitations of language and the human sciences.

(a) "Drawing" the Illustration of Equivalence

The paradigm suggested relates to Einstein's theorem of the relative nature of energy (E) and matter (m), expressed mathematically as $E=mc^2$, where the constant relating them is the speed of light (c) squared (i.e., c × c). As a linguistic statement this can be stated: Energy is equal to the mass multiplied by the speed of light squared.[56] This produces a problem in applying Einstein's work as a paradigm to the topic under discussion, that is, as a paradigm using the relationship between energy and mass for the relationship between explanation and understanding. Nevertheless, as a basic conceptualization it is abstractly (i.e., as an idea) suitable for use.

However, a problem arises in relating individual understandings as opposed to the concept of understanding, that is, those of the author and interpreter as persons. The problem is that whilst what is to be understood, the explanation, can exist as external to personal ontology, the event of understanding, that is, the understanding of the person, cannot exist outside personal ontology. As noted previously, the issue of understanding refuses to be objectified. The event of understanding is unique to the individual person. The interpreter never has exact equality of understanding, hence exact equality of meaning, with that of the author, even when the time of transmission is equal or similar to the time of interpretation and each person possesses the same or similar presuppositions. Hence, sameness of understanding is in relationship to what is understood, not in the event of understanding. No matter how close they may appear or even approach, individuality of personal ontology precludes exactness, as there is no way of knowing other than to actually become the other person.

It is here Christianity makes use of this hermeneutical principle of the preclusion of exactness, unless one was to become the other person. The advent of Jesus as

---

56. This statement is made as a general statement without scientifically defining the terms used, such as reference to the speed of light in a vacuum and so forth.

Christ and Son of God is believed within Christianity to be the incarnation of divine person within human being, as declared in John 1:14–18 and 20:30–31.[57] Even Gadamer took note, from purely a hermeneutical perspective, of the significance of the Christian concept of the incarnation as the most effective way to deal with the issue of understanding. The residence of the divine person in the personal ontology of Jesus as human allowed God, who made humanity in his image, to imagine from within being human. Therefore, with this belief for the Christian, in the divine actually becoming human an exactness of divine understanding from the human perspective became acheivable. God is able to affect relativity of understanding with humanity. Subsequently, in the Christian concept of redemption, resulting in the one believing being in Christ, it becomes acheivable for the human to become like the divine in this perception from within the human personal ontology. Through this agency humanity is able to affect relativity of understanding with the divine, manifest in the person of Jesus. The hermeneutical impact is due to belief, but the hermeneutical principle is simply the special use of principles already operational within the hermeneutical task.

Consequently, in the light of this problem of exactness, what should be considered is equivalence of understanding rather than equality of understanding of author and interpreter. The equality portrayed in using the paradigm, which does imply equal entities, when considered in the illustration, which doesn't imply equal entities, is better illustrated by using the word *equivalence* not sameness. Equivalence can imply equal but is better suited to refer to qualitative equality rather than quantitative equality. Equivalence is used, for example, in interpretation of Scripture into languages differing from the original language, where the aim is to say the same or similar thing but in a different language. This is effectively true of all translation from one language to another. Because both understandings, that is, that of the author and interpreter, belong to the same set of understandings related to the same explanation, the concept of equivalence of understandings seems more appropriate logically and therefore more appropriate as the basis of a paradigm rather than the mathematical implications of equality of understandings in using Einstein's concept.

Equivalency here logically possesses reflexivity, in that both the author's and the interpreter's understandings are equivalent to themselves. Also, logically there is symmetry, in that to say that the author's understanding is equivalent to the interpreter's is also to say that the interpreter's understanding is equivalent to the author's. The concept of expansion does not change the equivalency because the removal from the mathematical concept of equality removes the issue of quantitative value. The issue of sameness of understanding is sought in the qualitative issue, and this is the idea of equivalence. There is transitivity, as interpreters in a different time of interpretation, using the same explanation, can have equivalency of understanding with each other and the author. In all these situations equivalency can theoretically include the idea

---

57. The declaration of the author of the Gospel of John to this effect has been closely examined and referred to previously, being shown as directly related to the author's intention.

of equality; the problematic is the unknowability of equality outside the individual. In the situation of equivalency, when moving away from the abstract concept of understanding (U), the relationship between the author's understanding (Ua) and the interpreter's understanding (Ui) would be indicated as Ua~Ui, rather than the implication of quantitative equality in Ua=Ui when using Einstein's concept as a paradigm. Therefore, once the discussion moves to relationship of the understanding of the individuals, the symbol ~ indicating equivalent to, will be used rather than the symbol = indicating equal to, as the relationship between the understandings. The statement of sameness of understanding can now be stated in a more suitable form of equivalence of understanding.

(b) Formation of the Paradigm

The statement relating understanding (U) with explanation (e) is the following: understanding, as discourse understanding, is the result of the explanation explicated by the elements, hence factors, of the time of transmission (t_1) and the exponential[58] expansion in time due to the time of interpretation (t_2). In order to highlight the relationship, in regard to the use of the paradigm, the statement can be reformatted to resemble the mathematical version, remembering the proviso recognizing that it is *not* a mathematical statement but a qualitative one, as $U \sim e t_1 t_2$. This equating of understanding and explanation is within the recognition of the differences between the physical and human sciences, which human sciences, as well as the innate inexactness due to the nature of individuals, also draw within their scope the domain of the abstract, as with or after the physical, which is the metaphysical.

However, a further problem is that, as has been noted, the *thought* expands into the time of interpretation and as a result *understanding* expands into the time of interpretation. The idea of constancy does not relate to a value of understanding remaining constant. The metaphysical universe allows expansion in relationship to constancy and yet retains the quality of equivalence. Furthermore, the thought expands in a complex fashion, indicated by the use of the term *exponential*, not in a simple fashion, as would be the case in contrasting exponentially with linearly in a mathematical situation. This occurs because the change in time is impacted by a complexity of factors such as expansion of language, changes in culture, changes in science and technology, and so forth. The impacts and interactions of these effects compound the situation, and the situation cannot be evaluated as if illustrated by use in a linear fashion.

Therefore, in the development of the interpreter's understanding there is an exponential expansion of what is understood that is unique to each interpreter, yet, due

---

58. The term exponential is used as more descriptive of what takes place rather than that indicated if any of the ideas of simple multiplication or addition had been employed as illustrations. There are so many factors involved that if the effect could be mathematically depicted, such depiction would take the form of being exponential.

to the *intentioned-ness* of the explanation, it is an expansion that has direct relativity with the understanding of the author. The concept of exponential expansion brings a focus on the idea of the instantaneous nature of any evaluation, which correlates well with understanding as thought in motion in a personal ontology, in which functioning meaning is derived as the instantaneous evaluation. If the interpreter does not consider the entity of the composition, hence its *intentioned-ness*, then there is no expansion but simply invention, and meaning is unrelated to discourse meaning as the discourse of the author.

In the statement $U\sim et_1 t_2$, time (t) is the same, and it is the exponent of time relating these issues of transmission and interpretation that becomes a consideration. It is an impact that is added but acts exponentially. Hence, the statement could be rewritten as $U\sim et^{(w+i)}$ where w is the impact of the time at which the text is transmitted as *w*ritten text and i is the time of *i*nterpretation.[59] However, the effect is due to the displacement of the two times, not the intervening time. The time of interpretation, i, does not relate to a displacement with respect to the beginning of time but to the time of writing, w. Hence, if the time of interpretation, as the point in time that is a particular expression of the time of interpretation, is expressed as i_1, then i as the time of interpretation is indicated in the concept of $i\sim i_1 - w$. The exponential effect showing the expansion becomes $U\sim et^{(w+[i_1-w])}$, which when the time of interpretation is the same as the time of transmission then i is 0—since $i_1 \geq w$—and t in the relationship becomes t^w, that is, the time of transmission, and the concept holds. It is important to note that for the interpreter, even in the same time as the time of transmission of the author, the effect of the time element is still exponential in that understanding involves that which was inanimate becoming animate. In the case of the author, the author already knows his or her understanding of the issue, for him or her, is its explication as explanation. If there are differences in culture or presuppositions for the interpreter then the times are different, despite proximity of time itself, and the concept still holds.

Hence, the concept $U\sim et^{(w+i)}$ constitutes a reasonable paradigm with which to work. As an expression it displays the relationship between understanding and explanation showing the direct impact of the issue of time, as each develops his or her individual understanding, that is, the author in the writing and the interpreter in the interpretation. The differences in understanding in the interpreter are due to impact of the element of time, not change in the explanation. Further, this relationship also portrays the breadth of exponential impact of this element of time on the concept of understanding. The understanding of a person is related to time and that which makes this understanding relate to the discourse of another person, as *the someone who said something*, is the constant of the explanation. Explanation is a function of the composition, because the *intentioned-ness* relates to the composition and not the system of *langue* used in writing the text, which due its impersonal ontology cannot be the

---

59. The use of italics on a single letter is used within the words written and interpretation to highlight the use of the letters w and i as used in the paradigm.

bearer of intention. The next section will consider the problem of a misconception and it is there that the issues of the exponential expansion together with the uniqueness of individual understanding—with the result that they can only be related on the basis of equivalency not equality— reveal their importance.

It is the written text that makes possible the study and expression of this relativity. It is the written text, due its exactness as written text at the time of transmission, not as discourse, that makes possible the consideration of this equating in the task of hermeneutics, so that equivalence of understanding can result in relativity of discourse meaning. As a result the interpreter can interpret the written text as the discourse of another person and develop equivalence of understanding to find individual meaning in his or her own time relative to the meaning the author possessed in his or her own time. In this way the true aim of hermeneutics, as in Gadamer's concept of making one's own that which is foreign, or as in Ricoeur's concept of opening up a world of potential before the interpreter, is fulfilled in discourse meaning of the interpreter. Once the time of interpretation is fulfilled, this discourse meaning will interact with the understanding of the interpreter beyond the interpretation of the original discourse. This will produce for the interpreter new horizons and potential, which will be opened for expansion and expounding of new discourse by the interpreter. However, this will require the interpreter to become an author and communicate an explanation, resulting in new understanding in a new discourse with its own time of transmission.

Disclosure of the Relative Interaction of Epistemology and Ontology

Before addressing an indication of the approach to the hermeneutical task of discourse meaning, what should be addressed is a potential misconception, which can be exemplified by considering the work of Krister Stendhal. This misconception helps to expose the issue of this section. This is not intended as a critique of Stendhal's work but an observation based on the general approach used. In the modern period, meaning has been pursued on epistemological grounds as the primary approach. This is exemplified in Stendhal's approach where he focuses on the concept of this being a descriptive task.[60] Therefore, the pursuit of meaning has been as something to be cognitively obtained, which, despite the best of intentions, tends to objectify the concept of meaning as meaning. This has made epistemology the primary task, yet in an epistemological approach *meaning* can only be disclosed as a *meant*.

As a result, as revealed previously, this disclosure of the *meant* is no longer disclosure of meaning, which involves thought in motion. It is rather a reflection that, by the nature of reflection, treats thought in relationship to the past. This thought has undergone detachment from the person for expression as an entity that can exist

---

60. Stendhal, "Biblical Theology, Contemporary," 418–19. There are a number of references to this concept. See also his analysis of the Hermeneutic Question, 427.

outside the person; it is in a sense the storage form of thought as the explication of a meant of the discourse. Hence, in the storage form it is static and no longer thought in motion and no longer relates to disclosure of meaning. Examination of the meant of discourse, as in epistemology, is an anatomical approach to discourse not a physiological approach to discourse; the text is examined as inanimate, or dead, in order to gain insight into the functioning state of meaning already understood and explicated as a meant. Epistemology can never result in meaning, which is the animate state. Epistemological interpretation, when submitted to a correct ontology, deals with the explication of the *understood* of discourse, not the understanding of discourse, which is an ontological interpretation.

The postmodern thought of Derrida and Barthes, whilst not specifying the concept of epistemology, pursued meaning on the basis of semiotics in its approach. In their approach, meaning is not obtained. Instead, meaning is an invention of the interpreter, not extant in the text as meaning of the author, as in modernism. This has had essentially the same effect, in that the method used is the dismembering of the text, which is the very nature of semiotics. Such an approach, as with epistemology, can never be considered as having relativity to meaning of the author, which is in fact what they conclude. Hence, for them meaning is an invention directly by the interpreter developed as unrelated to authorial intent or meaning. The problem is that the conclusion of invention of meaning is already determined in the method used.

(a) The Importance of Meaning as Derivative Not Attained

Whilst invention of meaning is not the case in Gadamer and Ricoeur, what they have done is to seemingly accept the Heideggerian concept of meaning as an *existentiale* of *Dasein* in their ontological approach. They have made meaning an issue that flows *from* understanding, rather than as derivative in the event *of* understanding. Such an approach does suit the concept of the detachment of the text from the author. This detachment is proposed by both, although in a more developed argument in Ricoeur, and which detachment results in autonomy in the sense of the impact of authorial intention on meaning. However, if meaning is not *existentiale* but derivative as a function of understanding, then the understanding one is immediately dealing with in interpretation is the author's. This is simply the implication of dealing with the author's explanation, that is, the written text. The movement of meaning to *existentiale* removes the imperative nature, which is what makes meaning of the interpreter directly relative to that of the author in the derivative situation. As a result they have not seen the instantaneous nature of the concept of meaning, which in this work is considered as derivative, being the instantaneous value of understanding.

Heidegger observed that interpretation is grounded in understanding, as has been previously considered, and not the reverse. This therefore means that understanding does not arise from interpretation and is effectively thus post-understanding in Heidegger's concept.[61] Because meaning is the articulation of that interpretation, the inference is that what is occurring is the disclosure to self of understanding as operational in thinking; that is, what is implied in his own thinking is that meaning is essentially an instantaneous value of understanding. Hence, inferring, based on Heidegger's own assessment, that meaning is best viewed as the consequence, or derivative, in interpretation rather than inferring an *existentiale*, or attribute, of *Dasein*. It is possible that in Heidegger's case the problem he wished to circumvent is that of objectification that becomes possible with the concept of the derivative, as was noted in the discussion of *knowing*. However, meaning can be objectified, as has been considered, and the objectification is the production of the *meant* of discourse. Nevertheless, the difference between *meaning* and *meant*, being that of the animate state versus the inanimate, is a highly significant difference, of the order of that between ontology and epistemology. It is a difference that requires an ontological approach to conceptually traverse due to the impasse between animate and inanimate. Whatever the reasoning, Heidegger's treatment obscured the true nature of meaning. This misconception is furthered in the treatment of Gadamer and Ricoeur, hence in postmodern thought.

Gadamer and Ricoeur, in a presupposition of *existentiale*, have not perceived the relationship between understanding and meaning in its proper context. Hence, whilst they have not objectified this relationship they have treated it as another issue beyond that of understanding, where understanding pursued is of the author's discourse. Heidegger proposed that the articulation of interpretation is meaning. Consequently, Heidegger did not examine this implication himself, which is that as the interpreter articulates this interpretation, the articulation is meaning; it is not another issue to be pursued, but is instead in that moment the instantaneous value of understanding, or meaning. This meaning is a function of personal ontology and is not the result of cognitive objectification of meaning in the impersonal ontology of event.

Ricoeur pursues meaning in a concept of guess and validation used in relationship to the operation of the dialectic of understanding and explanation.[62] Ricoeur acknowledges that the creation of the explanation exteriorizes the event, therefore detaching it from personal ontology, and he has also acknowledged that understanding is ontological and related to intention.[63] Here he is speaking of dialogue, but the principle relates to discourse. Ricoeur in this discussion specifically rejects the concept of objectification in the event of interpretation. However, his employment of the word *guess*, as related to the interpreter's grasp of meaning, appears to be an attempt to avoid an implication of the guess being a grasp of the author's meaning. This is indicated in his statement, "we have to guess the meaning of the text because the author's intention is beyond our reach."[64] If meaning cannot be pursued as a separate issue, that

---

61. Heidegger, *Being and Time*, 188.
62. Ricoeur, *Interpretation Theory*, 74.
63. Ibid.
64. Ibid., 75.

is, if it is not an *existentiale* but a derivative, then this guess is directly relative to the author's meaning. This is because of equivalence of understanding due to explanation being the author's not the interpreter's, which concept of explanation developed in Ricoeur's treatment is as being the interpreter's. This postmodern concept has had a similar effect to the modern, structuralist, and post-structuralist concepts in causing disjunction between author and interpreter in regard to understanding.

(b) A Basic Illustration of Meaning as Understanding in Motion

The following is used as an illustrative concept of meaning rather than as a proposal of an actual paradigm, although there may be good grounds for doing so in a more formal approach to the issue of meaning. The memory in a computer is basically, maybe even somewhat simplistically, seen as composed of RAM (random access memory) and storage memory. The basic concept of RAM, although in modern computers this concept has developed well past the original processes, is that of volatile memory. It is thus memory in a state of flux immediately accessible in random order for usage. Storage memory can be accessed for specific use and even become operational within RAM. Hence, *meaning* is similar to RAM, as it is volatile understanding, which is *understanding* in a state of flux or motion. This volatile meaning can be stored as a meant, as that which is reflectively and reflexively understood. This stored meant can also be accessed when dealing with issues that relate to that meant, when the meant thus becomes again meaning and operational at an immediate presuppositional level in thinking about immediate issues involved in the consciousness. What is revealed is not a different form of understanding, nor a different mode of understanding, nor even a different attribute that interacts with understanding; it is a different state of understanding. Meaning is the movement to a volatile immediately operational state within the domain of the *thinking I*.

Consequently, the treatment of meaning as other than instantaneous understanding, as outlined, is proposed to be a misconception of the nature of meaning in its relationship to understanding. In the epistemological approach to meaning of Stendhal, he identified two senses that he felt should be kept apart: "What it meant" and "What it means." These two senses form the basis of two questions to be used in the approach to dealing with historical texts, such as Scripture. These questions are "What did it mean?" and "What does it mean?"[65] His approach, being from the concept of epistemology, and thereby treating meaning as object, did not consider the ontological aspect of understanding. Further, what is also not considered is that which relates the written text to understanding, hence meaning, which is the horizon of time, with its two elements of the times of transmission and interpretation working in concert, not individually. Stendhal saw the same importance but took up the

---

65. Stendhal, "Biblical Theology, Contemporary," 419.

issue from the epistemological not the ontological perspective. The epistemological approach to meaning, being descriptive, infers that it is possible to articulate meaning, as some*thing* that is independent of author and interpreter, which when considered ontologically itself, is a misunderstanding of understanding.

(c) This Disassociation of What Should Be Indissoluble as One Understanding

The result of his approach is to keep the two senses, that is, meant and means, separate issues that are dealt with individually and separately.[66] Stendhal saw that the need for a clear statement of "what it meant" was essential as the basis to proceed to "what it means."[67] As a result his leaning seems to point toward seeing the best approach to the issue is basically as two disciplines done by different people with different skill sets. It is here where a major misconception occurs, because when considered as an ontological issue the approach does not involve the separation of the times but the recognition and valuing of each in the one task of understanding. The concept should not be that of two understandings, which would be the result of the approach Stendhal suggests, but rather one understanding as it relates to the explanation, or to the biblical text. These epistemological questions are valid but only when the epistemology is submitted to a correct ontology. They are individual questions that provide the description of the text in the light of the elements of time involved. It is essential for the interpreter to consider both elements of time in his or her ontological interpretation during the same period of reflection, because without each there is not equivalence of understanding or therefore a correct perception of the expansion of understanding into the time of interpretation.

The understanding of meaning, as being able to be articulated as both meant and means separately, directly infers that the interpreter can state the author's meaning in such a way that it is mathematically equivalent to what the author has stated or would state if the author was in the interpreter's *Sitz im Leben*, that is, in-life-setting. This conclusion is highly speculative. The interpreter cannot become the author nor can either author or interpreter think from within the *Sitz im Leben* each of the other. The inexactness of language precludes any certainty of the interpreter's use of semiotic linguistics, and the degree of uncertainty in any such speculation begins to rise exponentially.

This is the problem with the Evangelical approach, as in Vanhoozer's treatment of the issue of meaning. The approach is tied to description, as description of the author's action, which therefore locks the normative approach, to use Vanhoozer's own terminology, into an issue of epistemology. As such, meaning is terminal in the

---

66. Ibid., 420. Stendhal notes that the individual has no internal criteria for keeping the two senses apart.

67. Ibid., 422.

concept of an impersonal ontology of the event, from which it can only escape via the hermeneutics of the self, as in Ricoeur. However, in Ricoeur's treatment, meaning is the interpreter's and is only related to the author's via the integrity of the interpreter. This becomes even more speculative as to any proposed relationship to the author's intent, depending wholly on the veracity of the interpreter.

The problem of the Evangelical approach of Thiselton in pursuing authorial intent as adverbial is that, although philosophically he has attempted to allow the ontological arguments to impact his philosophy of interpretation, this conceptualization of authorial intent becomes terminal in the adverbial form of intent. The difference of Thiselton's approach to Vanhoozer's is his recognition that the interpreter's articulation of the author's meaning can never be known to be precisely the author's, especially in the absence of the author. However, in considering that the text has appeared due to intentionality, this implies that, for Thiselton, there is ongoing impact of authorial intent. But it is an impact that he unfortunately does not take further. This is primarily because the adverbial form terminates in the impersonal event, as Ricoeur has ably and clearly outlined. In Thiselton's philosophical recognition that the issues of understanding and meaning are too complex to be dealt with as yielding precise results independent of the observer, is also the implication it will be impossible to specify a relativity of author's and interpreter's meaning. Hence, it will be hard to avoid a reality of relativism in practice.

The conception of meaning within the Evangelical treatment of meaning pursued in an epistemological approach, if expressed in the concept of the paradigm suggested, is of the form that understanding, hence meaning, of the explanation, that is, the composition related to the written text—remembering again that this treatment does not imply mathematical equality but is within the concept of language and the human sciences—is disclosed as $U_1 \sim et_1$, where U_1 is the author's understanding and t_1 is the time of transmission. On one hand this seems reasonable, because if the time of interpretation, in order to move to the interpreter's understanding, is now introduced as a factor, the statement then becomes $U_2 \sim et_1 t_2$. This is the formulation determined to relate understanding and explanation previously, which was shown to be able to be written as $U \sim et^{(w+i)}$. However, the author's understanding is not knowable due to the problem of singularity of identity of a person's personal ontology. Further, epistemology is only operational on one side of the formulation because it is related to the inanimate situation and understanding is animate. There is not equivalence with a state of dynamic equilibrium between the animate and inanimate situation, as though one could slot values in and note the effect on understanding. Rather, the animate situation in interpretation is the personal ontology of the interpreter, and the inanimate evaluation is reviewed as animate in the interpreter. Consequently, epistemology can only deal with the author's understood, despite the appearance of being able to reference the author's understanding, which actually occurs in the person of the interpreter due to the facility of referencing of the composition when reanimated in the interpreter.

The epistemological treatment therefore has a conceptual inference of the objectification of the author's understanding, which is a misconception of the nature of understanding. Further, there is also the implication that the consideration of the interpreter's meaning is an appropriation of the author's meaning and hence is primarily an addition to the author's understanding and not an expansion of the author's understanding. Vanhoozer specifically limits the interpreter's meaning to an appropriation.[68] Vanhoozer states, "*The Spirit's role in bringing about understanding is to witness to what is other than himself (meaning accomplished) and to bring its significance to bear on the reader (meaning supplied).*"[69] If his implication is not that the Spirit captures a person in a single event of understanding that dynamically moves from text to meaning, then the implication is clearly that of distinct knowable entities in which the reader/interpreter has added his or her interpretation for his or her own time to that of the author, under the guidance of the Spirit. If his implication is meant to be the first instance, then this infers special hermeneutics. If not, then the second instance infers that the Spirit does something that people could do for themselves unaided by the Spirit. This must be what is meant, because to infer that the Spirit performs either task due to the inability of the interpreter introduces a special hermeneutic. Presumably, by involving the Spirit there is in his view some religious significance to the event.

Either implication is unsatisfactory as disclosing the working of the Spirit, if what should be in view is the working of the Spirit with the interpreter as the one who inspired the authors in their inscribing of the biblical text. It assigns a minor subsidiary role to God as author of the message of the discourse in the task of biblical interpretation. The issue and relevance of the working of the Spirit suits ontological interpretation in supplying the ontology to which epistemology should be submitted.

This primary assumption of epistemological interpretation will result in a situation where the interpreter's understanding (U_2) will be given as $U_2 \sim U_1 + et_2$, where t_2 is the time of interpretation. This formulation is therefore $U_2 \sim et_1 + et_2$. This formulation has very different implications to the formulation showing the qualitative relationships of understanding and explanation as developed previously, which understanding positions the person to develop meaning. The following are some examples of some of the possible implications that result from this misconception.

---

68. Vanhoozer, *Is There a Meaning*, 265. Vanhoozer discusses at length throughout the book the concept of a uniqueness of meaning of the author that is considered, in his treatment, as accessible, which in turn implies the possibility of objectification. In discussing the Spirit he notes that the Spirit's role in interpretation "is to serve as the Spirit of significance and thus to apply meaning, not to change it." In a footnote related to this discussion he observes that exegesis can give us knowledge of textual *meaning* (italics added for emphasis). Hence, his view is that what occurs is an appropriation of the meaning of the author, which is knowable as the author's meaning, hence implying the knowability of the author's understanding.

69. Ibid., 413. (Italics original.)

The time of interpretation no longer is a factor of expansion but a figure of addition such that the author's understanding is implied as apparently preserved and potentially precisely identifiable. This implication is an ontological contradiction because it is already established that neither author nor interpreter can know the understanding, hence meaning, one of the other as exactness. Equivalence of understanding is not related to the individual's understanding but that which is to be understood, that is, the explanation. The author has an understanding he or she explicates as the explanation, and the interpreter develops an understanding that is relative to the author's due to dealing with the author's explanation. No matter how close speculation may appear to allow the issue, the reality is that ontologically meaning is uniquely a function of each person. Also, without using the word *subtraction*, there is the implication that removal of the interpreter's appropriation will somehow expose the author's understanding, hence make available access to authorial meaning. This does seem to be implied in some treatments, but it is fanciful at best. How can an interpreter remove his or her understanding from that of the author when ontologically the interpreter cannot know that understanding of the author in the first place? What the interpreter can know is what an author understood and, in the reanimation, thereby gain an understanding that is therefore directly relative to the author's. Finally and most importantly there are not two understandings but one, a single understanding that the interpreter develops in interaction with the entity of the composition. This understanding is developed in an interaction with the time of transmission and the time of interpretation; interpreters do not end up with two interpretations.

The epistemological approach as the primary approach, though having the appearance of appropriateness in that one begins the hermeneutical task with the *something said* not the *someone who said it*, is one in which formulation of meaning can only be known through the objectification of meaning as meant. Whether Heidegger's view of *existentiale* is taken, or alternately it is seen as a derivative of understanding, as in this work, ontologically this epistemological approach infers meaning as something a person acquires; however, ontologically meaning is not an acquisition but something a person derives as a function of understanding. When treated as acquisition, meaning becomes a derivative of epistemology, a derivative of knowing not being. This is the misconception and it results in an ontological fallacy that is critical. If this approach were correct, then Ricoeur's interpretation theory is not only possible but also probable. He has shown conclusively how and why the epistemological approach is terminal in the ontology of the impersonal event. In this situation the only return to a personal ontology possible, thereby avoiding the inferences of relativism in meaning of Derrida and Barthes, is in Ricoeur's treatment of the hermeneutics of the self.

Thiselton's own strong endorsement of this work of Ricoeur's in *Oneself as Another* as recapturing an impact of a personal ontology would imply his own acceptance of this conclusion. However, in this postmodern theory of interpretation there is no personal *otherness* possible except as a self-projection by the interpreter that is dependent on the integrity of the interpreter, with no effective means of evaluation. Anecdotally, in an epistemological view, one would expect that every interpreter, before commentating in his or her commentaries, would be able to demonstrate this unique precise meant of the author. If they are not able to do this then relativism is unavoidable, since the pursuit of what it means is based on what it meant as Stendhal argued, hence any attempt at articulation and appreciation of authorial intent would indeed be quixotic. However, the anecdotal evidence is completely contrary, and it is difficult to get agreement on translations, let alone an interpreted meant of an author by an interpreter in engaging translations. The various religious denominations and sects are all due to the *correct understanding of the author's meaning*, which makes their differences awkward to explain to anyone outside the faith as being proof of consistency of the faith. It is impossible to justify one above the other on the basis of epistemology.

The end result is relativism of faith due to relativism of meaning. Relativity of faith would assume that someone somewhere has identified the true interpretation to which all the others are relative. Unfortunately, modernism could not find this absolute but found in the search that the absolute moved further away. This led to disjunction of the person of the believer with living faith, and instead provided a doctrinal faith that is a matter of knowing before believing. Postmodernism sought to return to a personal ontology but, as is well exemplified in Ricoeur's thought, this is only possible as an interpreter's meaning because of the proposed autonomy of the text from the author. In so doing differences of interpretive meaning would be purely a function of individual interpreters with no concept of genuine demonstrable relativity to the author's.

Epistemology can be considered from the aspect of the study of knowing itself, and can also be considered from the concept of knowledge, its nature, presuppositions, foundations, methodology, extent, and validity. Hence, epistemology has a natural ontological aspect in that it relates directly to knowing. This would certainly encourage the idea of the epistemological approach as the beginning point for the task of hermeneutics. However, even if this were so the ontology to which one would move would be the impersonal ontology of the event, as has been noted and which Ricoeur has well argued. Further, without Ricoeur's hermeneutics of the self, meaning is terminal in an impersonal ontology and the concept of discourse meaning fanciful at best. As Ricoeur has noted, epistemology is important in interpretation only when it is submitted first to a correct ontology. Without ontological interpretation, epistemological interpretation is description without context; and ontological interpretation without epistemological interpretation is being without context. It takes both aspects for both the *what* and the *about what* of the discourse to be fulfilled in discourse meaning.

Finally, it is perhaps important to distinguish between knowing, as an event in understanding, and knowledge. Knowledge can be variously expressed in a semiotic fashion as the state of knowing, the range of what has been perceived or specific understanding of, or as information about a subject gained by experience or study. Knowledge is the result of knowing; that is, it is what is known. This nature immediately gives knowledge the potential of being impersonal; it can exist as a *what*, which is borne out in reality because any individual person can know knowledge once it is brought within the scope of human consciousness. Knowledge, although it can be an aspect of a psyche, is thus implied to be able to exist outside human consciousness. Knowledge is therefore capable of being related to *langue* in order to become detached from the psyche and exist as an entity, like all thought itself, because knowledge can be a component of thought in the individual. In this form, knowledge can be stored for use by any individual. Consequently, knowledge is directly derivative of knowing, which is a function of understanding.

Approaching Discourse Meaning

An author begins with a meaning for which he or she forms the *intention-to* communicate, and the eventual result of this intent will be the explanation the author will release in the time of transmission. The explanation is created in what is essentially a processs of reverse engineering. This process involves the author effectively seeking to slow down the motion of thought that is meaning so as to identify the articulation of the interpretation that is the meaning. The very concept of articulation shows the seeking to identify and individualize thoughts that are in motion. Interpretation was identified by Heidegger as understandingly appropriating *what* is understood, hence the appearance of a *what*, as that which is understood. What is understood is directly relative to the understanding, which when interpreted and articulated is meaning. In this process an author positions himself or herself to explicate the explanation as an exteriority of what is understood. It is the exteriority, that is, the explanation, that the interpreter will engage in the time of interpretation to reanimate when resumed as discourse in a personal ontology, so that understanding occurs, resulting in articulation of the interpretation of what is understood, hence making discourse meaning operational in the person of the interpreter.

As has been noted previously the explanation presents its impersonal aspect to the interpreter, the *something said*, because the composition, having the personal aspect, is perceived in an ontological interpretation as an entity that is contiguous with but not continuous with the impersonal nature of the text. It is this presentation of the impersonal aspect that gives the appearance that the process can be begun on an epistemological basis. In speech the interpreter is not aware of the presentation of the discourse in its relationship to the system, and epistemology does not suggest itself as a beginning place. However, even in dialogue one may ask the speaker what he or she means in use of a word or phrase. The nature of such an inquiry is semiotic rather than semantic; therefore such an inquiry directly identifies and deals with the system, although the inquirer would not conceptually think of this investigation of the system as impersonal. Generally, in spoken discourse, one perceives self as dealing directly with semantic linguistics not semiotic linguistics, because the visible aspect is the personal ontology of the speaker. This is not the case with written discourse, where the system is the visible aspect of the discourse. Yet, if the hermeneutical task is the same, then this appearance causes misdirection of the process to a primacy of epistemology. The primary task is ontological in both and will determine the context of epistemology. The primary ontological interpretation, the beginning of the hermeneutical task, is in listening. Listening is the first step in the reanimation or resumption of discourse.

This presents a problem in the postmodern thought of Gadamer and Ricoeur. In Ricoeur's theory, with detachment of the written text from the author, the discourse no longer has a speaker but an author. Walter Ong noted that in reading the text the reader listens to the text, even if only in the realm of the imagination. However, the issue is not listening as vocalization of the text, whether real or imagined. The issue is listening to the discourse of the author, not the vocalization of the system. It is the thinking of Barthes that shows the nature of the listening in view. Barthes noted that in reading the reader finds himself or herself addressed by a voice, which Barthes examined and decided to be unrelated to that of the author. Essentially his proposal is some form of narrator.

However, in the course of the investigation of this book, the true nature of this voice has been uncovered. This voice is due to the personal aspect of the entity of the composition as *intentioned-being*, which has the ability to confront, inform, and even interrogate the reader. Yet, this voice cannot be dialogued with, which Barthes also noted and used to discount the idea of the person of the author. This voice is able to address the reader and disclose the *intentioned-ness*, which is itself the transformed *intention-to* of the author due to the *Aufhebung* undergone by the authorial intent in the act of *parole*. In being spoken to by a voice, an understanding of *otherness* begins for the reader/interpreter who then is able to gain an initial understanding of the discourse, which also results in an initial grasp of discourse meaning. Additionally, due to being addressed by a voice that communicates *intentioned-ness*, which *intentioned-ness* is directly the result of the *intention-to* of the author, understanding the *otherness* of the discourse is already developing on a basis of equivalence of understanding relative to the understanding of the author. In this way, the voice positions the reader/interpreter for discourse meaning relative to that of the author. The differing ways that an author can convey *intentioned-ness* in and through the system have been considered. Therefore, in the course of reading the reader is listening to the disclosure of *intentioned-ness*. The resultant ontological interpretation in listening sets up the context for the epistemological interpretation. The rudimentary concept of what is transpiring is seen in the aligning of ontological interpretation with the physiology of discourse and epistemological interpretation with the anatomy of discourse, as has been suggested and used previously. Discourse meaning is in the bringing of these two approaches together in the one understanding.

Interpretation Theory

(a) Ontological and Epistemological Interpretation: A Synopsis

Epistemological interpretation largely deals with individual thoughts. These thoughts have become detached from the personal ontology of the psyche to exist as entities independent of the psyche; and the unit of thought in this externalization is the sentence. All discourse may not be about thinking, but all discourse is the encapsulation of thought in language in order to exist as external to the psyche. Due to the system of *langue*, thought has temporal existence as inanimate, and as language used in the entity of the composition, thought can reference understanding when returned to the realm of a personal ontology. In the written text the impersonal ability of the system to allow thought to exist in relationship to *thing*-ness also allows thought as inanimate to occupy space as well as time. This is the situation of which Ong spoke on the uniqueness of written text in allowing study of discourse. Epistemology can study the composition as to the makeup of the individual signs expressed in the sentence as the basic semantic unit, and the connectedness of a thought to other thoughts, suggesting possible understanding of interrelationships in discourse meaning. The reviewing of the signs in individual sentences compared to analysis of other sentences can also offer understanding of their usage by an author in his or her intention as signifiers, that is, a broad understanding of the signified in their usage in individual sentences of the discourse.

Reanimation is not a concept in which the text, having been examined epistemologically, is then made alive in some form of resurrection to observe its functioning in ontological interpretation. There is no dynamic equilibrium possible between the personal ontology of the author and his or her written text, from which he or she is detached. The inanimate situation of epistemological interpretation relates to the written text, but ontological interpretation, the animate situation, relates to the personal ontology of the interpreter. These two things interrelate between text and person, between the anatomical and physiological, in movement toward discourse meaning, and because Ua~Ui relativity of meaning occurs.

In Ricoeur's treatment, although he notes that epistemology should be submitted to a correct ontology, this submission is a last step, not an initial one. He specifically begins on the basis of an impersonal ontology, not recognizing the different ontology of the composition in relationship to the *something said* of discourse. Consequently, he excludes any concept of a personal aspect until his conclusion, which occurs in a personal ontology based on the hermeneutics of self, as developed in *Oneself as Another*. Consequently, the ontological interpretation as primary, disclosed in listening to the text, is thus lost. Ontological interpretation is vital in traversing the first aporia in the movement from the personal ontology of the author to the impersonal ontology of the written text. Recognition of the traversing of the initial aporia results in maintenance of the perception of discourse, as discourse of someone other than self.

Ricoeur's treatment only results in *pseudo-otherness* due to self-projection, not self-encounter of *otherness* as self-perception. Recognition of the ontological beginning maintains the correct perspective. The impasse Ricoeur recognizes is from the impersonal to the personal, in dealing with the text; and the impasse he either doesn't see, or ignores, is the impasse from the personal to the impersonal in the origination of the written text by the author. In recognizing the equivalent impasse the author traverses, together with the recognition of the entity of the composition with its unique ontology having a personal aspect, presents a complete picture of the task of hermeneutics, so that the discourse of a person is interpreted as the discourse of a person. The approach to the task should reflect the complete picture.

As Ricoeur noted in *Oneself as Another*, discussed in previous chapters of this book, the cognitive reflective aspect, disclosed in the epistemological interpretation, does not relate discourse to that of a person. It is the reflexive aspect, due to ontological interpretation, that allows what is description to be given being and context to be considered in the form of the discourse of a person. Discourse meaning is the dynamic interrelationship of these functions—as factors that interrelate in interpretation—which occurs in the consciousness of the person. The person is equipped with imagination and *ontic-consciousness* by means of which animation of discourse in the interpreter, being animation of the discourse in written text, results in discourse meaning and hence communication between persons. However, discourse meaning can only occur after the animation. Therefore, epistemological interpretation in dealing with the inanimate situation cannot result in discourse meaning; rather, it acts to inform the personal ontology of the interpreter in formation of meaning.

(b) Illustrating the Difference between Epistemology and Ontology

Heidegger almost intuitively recognized the parallel between *I see* and *I understand*, which relationship he developed in examining the concept of conscience. However, *I see* has two aspects, which are the act of seeing and the seen. Similarly *I understand* has two aspects, which are the act of understanding and the understood. Nevertheless, returning to the parallel concept of sight, it is important to realize that the seen knows nothing of the seeing, whereas the seeing knows the seen. Consequently, the understood knows nothing of the understanding, but in understanding is perception of the understood. It is one-way traffic, not two-way traffic. Epistemology, though appearing to be related to understanding in its defining, is actually relating to the understood of understanding. Epistemology is related to understanding in that it deals with the understood of the author, but epistemology is not the understanding of the author, which as its antecedent is the referent of the understood.

Thus, epistemology deals with knowledge, which is derivative of knowing as ontic in giving being to knowledge. It was noted previously that knowledge to be knowable is formed as that which can exist external to the psyche, since like all thought it is possible to express knowledge in language to be communicated, thereby becoming external to the psyche. What is known in the knowing by one person becomes *visible* to another person. Knowledge therefore, unlike knowing, becomes capable of objectification, and epistemology involves examination of this objectification, or examination of the *what* of discourse.

Meaning is derivative of understanding, being derived from *I know* as a function of *I understand*, and despite epistemology appearing to relate directly to meaning as a task epistemology can no more determine meaning than what is seen can determine seeing. Objectification of meaning results in a meant, which objectification is therefore the subject for epistemology. This objectification is no longer meaning, in the sense that as a meant of the author it has been detached from the state of meaning to be externalized, and hence be rendered inanimate in language as communication. Meaning is the result of ontological interpretation in a personal ontology in which what is known of the author's explanation becomes knowing in the interpreter. Epistemology provides encounter with an objective *otherness* of the text that is perceived in *I understand*, thence related to the self in *I know* and from these functions is derived discourse meaning of the author.

(c) Broadening the Concept of Ontological Interpretation

Epistemological practice has been addressed in numerous books and has no need to be taken further here. However, ontological interpretation in its relationship to the epistemological task bears closer examination. In Heidegger's treatment, ontological interpretation is primarily related to a disclosure of the being of entities.[70] This is more a less the task of perceiving what Heidegger's student Gadamer asserted in his understanding of language as the universal, which is that *things speak for themselves*. This creates the impression of the individualization of entities in isolation from other entities. In the real world, entities do not exist in isolation but exist in a context that greatly impacts meaning. It is perception of entities as existing in isolation that suggests the concept that they must speak for themselves in order to be known. This observation is misleading in the sense that, as Heidegger himself recognized, meaning is something persons do, not things. Hence, to say *things speak for themselves* can carry the false implication that the thing communicates. If this is intended, it flies in the face of what Heidegger asserts, which is that things do not have meaning or are meaningful, therefore they don't communicate. Consequently, a proper conclusion would be that an entity has being that is not determined by the person, yet, meaning is a consideration of the entity in its context and setting as it relates to the person.

Hence, this concept of ontological interpretation is too narrow in consideration of the hermeneutical task. The context and interrelationship of entities is critical in the hermeneutical task. It has been noted often that epistemology, as descriptive analysis,

---

70. Heidegger, *Being and Time*, 275.

must be submitted to a correct ontology. In other words, epistemological investigation requires understanding of context in order to properly disclose objective *otherness*. The analysis of the seen, to return to the parallel of understanding, requires input from the seeing to give perspective, in order to relate position of viewing to what is seen, the provision of setting in mood and timing, and also an understanding of the context just outside the seeing of the seen, which has an important impact on interpretation of what is seen. Without this sort of input from the ontological perspective, interpretation becomes one-dimensional. Understanding is a holistic grasp from both epistemological and ontological interpretation in their interrelationship. One-dimensional meaning leads to wrong conclusions in a three-dimensional existence.

One important aspect of the tremendous contribution of Ricoeur to understanding the hermeneutical task is developed in his focus upon what is supplied for the task to be undertaken, that is, the written text. Ricoeur has been careful to always develop his treatment from the text and to show the connection with language. Hence, ontological interpretation is not an importation into the text, but must be discovered and developed from the text. Ontological interpretation will employ the concept of referencing; this is almost really a logical extension to the realization that ontological interpretation is the seeing not the seen. The concept of referencing, which Derrida decries as outside the text, is outside the system of langue, because it relates to that which is with and after the physical, yet ontological interpretation is seen from the origin of the physical, and therefore not outside the text as related to discourse. In this, Derrida's argument is misleading. The semantic unit supplied is the sentence, and what is developed, is developed in consideration from this perspective. Consequently, it is reasonable to infer that, as for epistemological interpretation, it is the system of *langue* that makes visible that which is pursued and interpreted in the referencing of ontological interpretation. The various means indicating recognition of *langue* that reference in ontological interpretation have been considered in other sections of this book and do not need repetition here.

The realization that epistemology deals with what is objectified in the written text alludes to another important realization. In this pursuit epistemology deals with knowledge expressed as rational objective knowledge. Knowledge other than rational objective knowledge, that is, pistological, or nonrational knowledge and arational knowledge, can be inferred from description. Hence, reference to their presence can be epistemologically identified but they cannot be evaluated in their being as knowledge in epistemological interpretation nor can their impact on meaning be investigated. These forms of knowledge are knowable only within the domain of the personal ontology, and as inanimate these forms exist only as a reference to the metaphysical. This is the reason that nonrational and arational knowledge can come to be considered as unknowable and irrational, which is essentially how Kant decided to treat the metaphysical. Real but unknowable in a derivative sense, it is knowledge that simply presents itself. Yet it is this knowledge that will decide relationship to reality; it will decide the context of what is known in epistemology; and it will decide understanding and its derivative of meaning. Discourse meaning is informed by both epistemology and ontology but is decided on ontological grounds.

The conceptualization of the metaphysical as spiritual and mystic has blurred the issue of that which is metaphysical, so that the mention of the word metaphysical causes a knee-jerk reaction, as in Derrida. Only when the spiritual and mystical come within the horizon of time are they identified as metaphysical. However, it is the realm of the abstract, hence metaphysical, that is seen in the referencing. It is not only the belief of the author in terms of spiritual issues that is shown in referencing but also the author's belief about the portrayal of events, the relationships intra-textually, and so forth.

Consider the following illustration, using the text of Gen 22:2, wherein the reader is informed in the first verse that the story concerns the testing, or a proving, of Abraham. Here the language, when epistemologically considered, does not expose how this narrative should be taken. Is God testing Abraham so that God can learn something about Abraham; is God making Abraham earn the reward, as it were; or alternately is God drawing something out of Abraham? It is the context that will cause a correct referencing toward understanding and meaning. The divine instruction to Abraham in verse 2 is to "Take now your son, your only *son* Isaac, whom you love . . ." In this instruction the narration shows in first person usage the appreciation God has of what he is asking in the phrasing "your son, your only *son* Isaac, whom you love . . ."; and in the context of the complete narrative of Abraham, showing the struggle of faith that led to the birth of Isaac, this statement by God reflects the divine appreciation the depth of struggle Abraham will experience in the testing. The important word in this is *love*, which is the key to the situation: Abraham's love for his son. Epistemology can discover the reference to love but has no connection with understanding of this arational knowledge. These things put together, in showing the divine appreciation, indicate the reference is to testing as what it draws out of Abraham rather than testing as what it proves about him.

Ontological interpretation does not deal just with the disclosure of entities but also with disclosure of the reference inherent in nonrational and arational knowledge. These forms of knowledge establish the context for epistemological interpretation and if epistemology is undertaken without this consideration, as noted previously, it can only result in one-dimensional meaning. This is how such things as the rule of the magisterium and faith defined by dogmatism arise. Heidegger's view of ontological interpretation is presuppositional and is determined in his conception of understanding and the issue of interpretation. Heidegger, in consideration of understanding, developed a concept called "state-of-mind,"[71] which he declared as "equiprimordial" with understanding. This concept, essentially of mood, is what positions *Dasein* so

---

71. Heidegger, *Being and* Time, 172–74. This concept and how the phrase *state-of-mind* should be considered is also discussed in ch. 12 of this book, "Understanding: The Heideggerian Perspective."

that things become encounterable and the issue of relationship to self is determined. Essentially, Heidegger is describing what has been recognized here; that is, he is recognizing the complementary function to *I understand* is *I know*. Except, rather than recognize state-of-mind as the function *I know*, Heidegger makes state-of-mind a different issue as being "equiprimordial" with understanding, hence understanding always works with state-of-mind. If Heidegger had recognized state-of-mind as function rather than essentially *existentiale*, he would have had a broader basis to develop ontological interpretation to include the bringing near of entities and causing to matter to a person, hence would have been able to develop a context and interrelationship of entities. This broader basis of ontological interpretation is the proper foundation in order for it to work together with epistemology. Discourse meaning is the result of the interrelationship of epistemological and ontological interpretation so that there is proper reference to equivalence of understanding, and therefore the meaning derived is relative to that of the author, that is, Ui~Ua.

Epistemology and ontology as tasks involving study are something people do with texts not something texts do with people. Epistemology is the study of knowledge, examining the known but not the *knowing* of the known. Consequently, epistemology is primarily focused on the descriptive aspect, and its interpretive power is disclosure of the *understood* of discourse. Ontology, as the study of the nature of being concerns the perception of reality and the attribution of being within reality. Therefore, ontology studies the *knowing* of the known. As reflexive, the interpretive power of ontology is the disclosure of *understanding* the discourse of a speaking subject, the derivative of which understanding is meaning. Consequently, ontology is evaluation of the *seeing*, and epistemology is that of the *seen* in perception of understanding related to the task of hermeneutics.

Ontology's defining as a branch of metaphysics has led to misunderstanding, due to its perceiving metaphysics as primarily dealing with the spiritual and mystical. Its scope is abstract being, which can only be seen by referencing in association with language, and which, due to its relationship with the physical, exists within the horizon of time. Where the spiritual and mystical relate to the physical they are subject to metaphysics, but as such constitute a narrow area of metaphysical investigation. The realm of the eternal is outside the horizon of time; hence the spiritual and mystical, in their being, are beyond the sphere of metaphysics. It is association of the spiritual and mystical with language that brings them within the sphere of metaphysics.

Ontology concerns the broader picture of *seeing*, *knowing*, and *meaning* as abstract concepts with concrete consequences. Epistemology deals with the concrete consequences, but ontological interpretation is essential in disclosing the conceptualization of the consequence or there is no context in which the concrete relates to reality. Without ontological interpretation there is no discourse meaning as discourse of the person whose written text is studied in these tasks.

Listening and Ontological Interpretation in a Biblical Narrative

The Joseph narrative covers Gen 37 to 50. Whether or not the author is recognized as of Judeo origin may be debatable, but that the author is a follower of Yahwism is not. This observation provides a context in the consideration of the text as an authorial discourse. For the author this is history and it is the context of a faith that underpins the narrative of this history. If the narrative is examined as to structure for clues in ontological interpretation, it can be noted that it begins in Gen 37 with Joseph's dreams of greatness and concludes with Joseph's recognition that the divine intention in what occurred is that which has directed events. Joseph recognizes that, despite the difficulties he faced because of what was essentially betrayal by his brothers, in what took place it is evident that God intended good in what others intended as evil (see Gen 50:20). The author creates a promise-fulfillment form of structure. However, lest the reader be quick to link the Joseph narrative to the idea that it was some form of fixation by Joseph on the dream that drew him through his ordeal, the writer is careful to make sure the reader understands that the time when Joseph's brothers first appear before him is the time that he himself remembers the dreams (Gen 42:9). This is some years and a lot of experience after the original dreams (see Gen 37:5–11). Hence, the promise-fulfillment motif is of divine providence in the story, not the human ability or even the power of vision. This approach has enabled a sense of understanding not only of the narrative but a sense of its intention. What has occurred is essentially ontological interpretation in detecting and following the author's directions on how to view the narrative. It is a story of the enveloping nature of divine providence in the human story.

An amazing aspect of the story is found in Gen 37:15 where a seemingly chance encounter with a stranger becomes the hinge that opens the story. Without this encounter it may be a matter of speculation as to whether or not Joseph would have found his brothers that day, hence been sold into slavery, and eventually whether or not he would have risen to the power he experienced in Egypt under Pharaoh. It is speculation as to how the story would have unfolded on another day, since it is the attitude of his brothers that day that is important to what took place. Yet, this positioning of Joseph ultimately appears to have been divine provision for the survival of his people, who are the ones who will become the people of God. The narrator speaks to the reader in a way that makes the issue seem to be an intervention by the stranger. Joseph is wandering and the man pointedly asks Joseph, "What are you seeking?" Joseph mentions his brothers, and the stranger tells him where they went. Is this encounter a serendipitous encounter? Is it the presentation of a divine providence that surrounds the events in bringing about the divine intention? The direction the author gives the reader is of providence in noting it is the stranger who approaches Joseph and not the other way around. One would expect if Joseph is wandering lost and trying to find his brothers, which is what seems implied, then he would seek out the stranger. It is the stranger who seeks him out in the narrator's story. As a result of the encounter Joseph finds his brothers, is sold into slavery, and from here he ends up in prison, which is the place of divine appointment to the position of power that would save his people. All of this is dependent on the intervention of an unknown stranger.

The reader can decide that this is myth created just to argue for divine providence, or the reader could decide that it is serendipity that ended up being treated as though divine providence was in view—a sense that the author took advantage of the situation. However, whatever a reader may do with the story, the reader cannot escape the sense of context that the author gives to the story, and discourse meaning relates to its relativity to that of the author. It is ontological interpretation that uncovers this because it is the referencing of divine providence that is the key to understanding. Epistemology is undertaken from being submitted to a correct ontology. One may examine the text and note that the LXX, in treating Gen 37:15, translates the term *wandering* from the Hebrew texts by using a word that carries the idea of deception in lost and wandering. In this examination of the signs, that is, words, one may begin to speculate about the inferences. But interpretation will require moving this knowledge into the sphere of thought in motion, that is, understanding, in order to interpret. The understanding is shaped by the ontological interpretation of context. The important issue here is that there is a lot to be gained in the listening before dismembering the text in its analysis.

Concluding Remarks

Philip Clayton remarks that the result of the revolutions in both the physical and human sciences in the modern period "was to move humans from a position of ontological primacy."[72] As a result of this loss of primacy of human "being" in modernity, a consequent shift to an emphasis of "knowing" was given priority over "being." As Clayton observes, this ontological primacy was "replaced by the frightening immensity of infinite words, by a universe without a center, and by a blind process of natural selection."[73] The postmodern period has brought a shift in emphasis back to personal ontology, but it is the ontology of the interpreter, that is, the one who is interpreting this world into their lives, not the ontology of the author, that is, the one who provides what is interpreted. Without the sense of the author the universe remains empty and life retains its randomness. The inherent concept of *intentioned-ness* is not reconsidered nor reinstated. Life remains authorless, not only in an understanding of texts that results in detachment of meaning from authorial impact but also in life at its core of "being," other than in theistic religion.

---

72. Clayton, "Boundaries Crossed and Uncrossable," 92.
73. Ibid.

Roger Lundin developed the argument that Cartesian thought had moved humanity to essentially an orphaned state of being.[74] If it is the thought of Descartes that detached the thinking agent, rendering humanity effectively parentless, it is the thinking of Heidegger that has rendered humanity authorless. The orphan knows he or she has parents; the orphan simply lacks relationship with a parent. In the thought of Heidegger, as discussed previously, not only is human being parentless in terms of relationship but authorless in terms of being. Heidegger's thought moved to the isolation of "I" in order to seek a primordial answer.[75] The answer is found not in the "I" that posits itself, as in Descartes, but "I" becomes authentically itself "in the primordial individualization of the reticent resoluteness which exacts anxiety of itself."[76] At the core level of existence this anxiety promotes care, and only in the outworking of this care is identity found.[77]

In essence, in the isolated state of existence, identity is found not in anterior authorship—hence Derrida attacks vehemently the idea of anterior meaning—but in an inherent motivating force of anxiety. Even if a positive spin is placed on anxiety it is still based on the idea that only in self-alone is an answer discoverable. Identity of selfhood unfolds, not in a disclosure of what is but a disclosure of what can be. The concept of projecting forward is biblical; faith gives reality to hope projected (see Heb 11:1). However, in biblical thought the foundation that is projected from is grounded in a presupposition, not of isolation but of belongingness and an identity transmitted and deposited as the basis of understanding self in the universe. In Heidegger's thought, human being is alone in the universe at its very core and has to discover itself. It is small wonder that in postmodern hermeneutics authorial intent is considered passé, and because the author is now simply a writer, any *intentioned-ness* of the text is attributable to the interpreter not the author.

The postmodern shift, or turn, hermeneutically is based upon a phenomenology that assumes itself to be "de-regionalized" hermeneutics, to use Ricoeur's term. Ricoeur claims that the result of de-regionalization is general hermeneutics, which essentially amounts to a claim that it is normative. This is confirmed by his assumption that phenomenology is the presupposition *par excellence* in the hermeneutical task. However, as explored in this book, it is just that; that is, it is a presupposition that is believed and as a result orients understanding.

Furthermore, it is a presupposition that excludes at its core the concept of the author, or creator. The basis for this exclusion is an appropriation of its *pistology*, the metaphysics in which it derives its being and relationship to reality. It is no more authoritative than the biblical viewpoint, and as a result persons who operate from

---

74. Lundin, "Promise," 3. Lundin observes that the *cogito* (italics original) of Descartes is "a parentless, autonomous thinking agent who is dependent upon nothing outside himself for the truth he has uncovered within himself." This is developed as the theme of the article.

75. Heidegger, *Being and Time*, 151.

76. Ibid., 369.

77. Ibid.

the biblical viewpoint have no need to feel that their presuppositions should exclude them from the task, nor should they feel that they must distance themselves from their presuppositions. All those individuals engaged in physical sciences, human sciences and theology, or theological sciences—because theology does indeed concern the structure and behavior of the physical world in the context of a creator—all have a presuppositional basis that determines their understanding. In placing self within the presuppositions of others, each person can understand what the other understood. However, meaning for self is indeed the impact of the Cartesian "I," and even the biblical understanding recognizes the importance and centrality of this precept. Salvation is always individual in meaning, but it is corporate in understanding.

Therefore, the reality is that, despite the assertions by the postmodern authors considered, no interpreter is in a position to do general hermeneutics—it is always regional, if one holds to that terminology. A person cannot isolate himself or herself from his or her presuppositions in the hermeneutical task, no matter how aware the interpreter is of his or her presuppositions. As has been noted, Gadamer observed that to assume that one can distance himself or herself from his or her own presuppositions in interpretation is naïve, but to assume one does not have presuppositions in the task raises this to the level of absurdity.

Therefore, the concept of general hermeneutics is an abstraction, and in this is its value; that is, it highlights how the task unfolds as a task. The interpreter can, in this light, examine a text using this model to facilitate understanding, not decide understanding. The division into regional and general is misleading in that it implies that some interpreters have an agenda (those engaging in regional hermeneutics) and other interpreters do not have an agenda (those engaging in general hermeneutics). However, hermeneutics has as its end game the movement from understanding to meaning, and meaning is always regional; that is, it is the appropriation, or regionalization, within the Cartesian "I" of what is understood. It may be more appropriate to speak of regional interpretation and performance interpretation.

An important aspect highlighted in the analysis of this book is that understanding occurs at the level of existence, in the metaphysics of absence; or at the level of spirit, in the metaphysics of presence. In the removal of the concept of the author-creator as an issue, it is revealed that understanding is, or appears, primordial. Consequently, regardless of the belief of presence or absence, understanding is a given. However, understanding, as the "I" that sees, is predetermined by presuppositions, or beliefs, held. Said another way, understanding is based upon the posited *nonrational* knowledge resident as operational within the person. Understanding is a given of human being but perception of reality within each individual is neither uniform nor neutral.

Since self does not develop this, perception of reality is inherent having been posited either in recognition of tradition or simply regarded as innate. It is nevertheless this universal aspect of understanding that opens the door to understanding as being able to be independent of the observer. Each observer/interpreter can imagine the self as holding other presuppositions and therefore understand what another has understood. This can be done without surrendering one's own beliefs, because within selfhood is the ability to see self holding beliefs as other-than-self, holding potentially differing beliefs. In this process one can revisit his or her own understanding and modify or even change it, but this is not automatic, because one can decide not to accept the alternate view of self.

Understanding presents the possibility for change, but it does not mandate it. This hermeneutical principle is important in its special use within Christianity, which is that acceptance of posited knowledge is a decision that remains with the self. Thus, the Christian concept of salvation is possible within the practice of hermeneutics. This concept of understanding is also the basis of interpersonal and media communication, that is, to see what another sees, and is the basis of both sympathy and empathy. In the primordial idea of understanding, as attribute or *existentiale*, is the anticipation of *otherness*.

The concept of absence and presence here is not an implication as to the individual belief a person may have about the existence of God. It has been noted that Ricoeur had a functioning belief in the God of Scripture. Nevertheless, adoption of phenomenological concepts in hermeneutics employs metaphysics of absence as operational hermeneutically, as considered previously stemming from Husserl, through Heidegger in the rejection of spirit as *substantia*, and Gadamer's metaphysics of language, down to the present time. Hence, in Ricoeur the absence of authorial intent as an aspect of written text is retained together with the belief in the divine as the author of life.

The fear of fideism has prompted a refusal to consider the link between belief and knowing. Belief is the context of knowing not the birthplace of *I know*, so that understanding becomes possible, and hence what is knowable can indeed be known. Understanding is the perception of *otherness* not the determination of *otherness*. What "I" do concerning *otherness* is within my provenance. What a person does in terms of meaning is the assertion of the "I" in what is understood, that is, the appropriation of what is understood within the domain of self. Therefore, showing that belief can be altered in the assertion of "I," which thus alters the context of knowing. Within Christianity if this were not so then it would not be possible to go from unbelief to belief in the gospel by activation of human will. The appearance of free will would simply be a hoax. Hence, belief does not need to be feared as the birthplace of knowing. Context doesn't decide reality it merely decides perception of it. It is somewhat ironic that an acceptance of belief as a context of knowing opens the person to the *otherness* of the universe, whereas rejection of this centralizes knowing to the "I" and closes the door on the *otherness* of the universe, which must now only exist as a creation of the self. The result of this is a shift of the universe from being other-centered to being self-centered. The psychological and sociological ramifications of such a shift are enormous. The only possible development of self-identity in identifying self within the context of the universe is through *angst* not *faith*, anxiety—from which is the genesis of fear—not belief. This itself is therefore the birthplace of the fear of having surrendered to fideism in the recognition of both the absolute and the inability to obtain it and yet be able to exist relative to it.

The issue of hermeneutics is a consideration of *intentioned-being*, which itself is given being by authorial intent, in order that the interpreter can understand, or see, what the author understood, or saw. What is understood can be assimilated inwardly deriving meaning, which determines selfhood as expressed in life. Meaning is therefore the impact of what is understood, and understanding is the encounter with *otherness*. Meaning should not begin with self, but with understanding in the encounter of *otherness*. The view of interpretation as sameness of meaning is incredible. True interpretation as equivalence of understanding is credible.

In the course of this book, the ontological nature of authorial intent has been demonstrated. Consequently, the proper domain of interpretation for the correct disclosure and evaluation of authorial intent, which allows it to fulfill its function in the literary text, is ontological interpretation. What has been demonstrated in this book is that authorial intent is what gives being to the entity of the composition in relationship to a text, so that an observer is positioned to understand what the author understood, that is, see what the author saw. The author is present in the text not as a person, hence not invoking the psyche of the author, but in the *intentioned-being* of the text, which due to referencing the *intention-to* of the author has a personal aspect allowing *presence*. In the case of literary texts as discourse, what has been disclosed is that the entity that is this intentioned-being is the composition. Discourse is due to someone's intentional use of language resulting in *intentioned-ness* of the text. Discourse meaning involves understanding of that *intentioned-ness*.

An interpreter's meaning that is not relative to this *otherness* of the text is not a meaning related to an interpretation of the language of the discourse, but in the end is simply the creation of meaning relative to the impersonal being of *langue*. When the interpreter's meaning is relative to this *otherness* of the text, then there is interpretation of the *intentioned-being* of an author's discourse. The interpreter, in gaining equivalence of understanding of an author's discourse, develops a meaning unique to the interpreter but relative to the *otherness* of the author. Hence, the Christian, by developing equivalence of understanding with the author in the author's time, can explicate a relative meaning for his or her own time. The presupposition of belief makes special use of this perception. Interpretation of an author's intentional discourse is not sameness of meaning but relativity of meaning due to equivalence of understanding.

The *intentioned-being* gives the author that *presence* disclosing understanding on the matter of the text. In highlighting and examining the ontological nature of the authorial intent, together with its implications, explication and resultant impact, also together with the recognition and disclosure of the entity of the composition, what has been established is the importance of the title of the book, which question is answered: there is indeed an author in this text.

Bibliography

Ahn, Yongnan Jeon. "Various Debates in the Contemporary Pentecostal Hermeneutics." *The Spirit and Church* 2, no. 1 (May 2000): 19–52.

Anderson, Gordon. "Pentecostal Scholarship and Learning in a Postmodern World." *Pneuma* 27, no. 1 (Spring 2005): 115–23.

Barthes, Roland. "The Death of the Author." (1967). Online: www.tbook.constantvzw.org/wp-content/death_authorbarthes, 1–6.

———. *Elements of Semiology*. Translated by Annette Lavers and Colin Smith. New York: Noonday, 1967.

———. *The Pleasure of the Text*. Translated by Richard Miller. New York: Hill and Wang, 1975.

———. *Writing Degree Zero and Elements of Semiology*. Translated by Jonathan Cape Ltd. Boston: Beacon, 1967.

Beardsley, Monroe C. *Thinking Straight*. 4th ed. Upper Saddle River, NJ: Prentice Hall, 1975.

Benton, Sir Lancelot C. L. *The Septuagint with Apocrypha: Greek and English*. Peabody, MA: Hendrickson, 1986.

Bluck, John. *Christian Communication Reconsidered*. Geneva, CH: WCC Publications, 1989.

Boomershine, Thomas E. "Jesus of Nazareth and the Watershed of Ancient Orality and Literacy." *Semeia* 65 (1994): 7–36.

Brueggemann, Walter. *The Bible and Postmodern Imaginations: Texts under Negotiation*. London: SCM, 1993.

Bultmann, Rudolf. "The New Testament and Mythology." In *Kerygma and Myth*, edited by Hans Werner Bartsch, 1–44. New York: Harper and Row, 1953.

———. "The Problem of Hermeneutics." In *Hermeneutical Inquiry: The Interpretation of Texts*. Edited by David E. Klemm, 113–33. Atlanta: Scholars Press, 1986.

Caird, G. B. *The Language and Imagery of the Bible*. London: Gerald Duckworth, 1980.

Cargal, Timothy. "Beyond the Fundamentalist-Modernist Controversy: Pentecostals and Hermeneutics in a Post-Modern Age." *Pneuma* 15, no. 2 (1993): 163–87.

Carson, D. A. *The Gospel According to John*. Grand Rapids, MI: Wm. B. Eerdmans, 1991.

Cassuto, Umberto. *A Commentary on the Book of Genesis*. 1st ed. 2 vols. Vol. 2. Translated by Israel Abrahams. Jerusalem: Magnes, 1964. Reprint, 1992.

Clayton, Philip. "Boundaries Crossed and Uncrossable: Physical Science, Social Science, Theology." In *Transcending Boundaries in Philosophy and Theology: Reason, Meaning and Experience*. Edited by Kevin J. Vanhoozer and Martin Warner, 91–103. Hampshire, UK: Ashgate, 2007.

Cranfield, C. E. B. *Romans: A Shorter Commentary*. Grand Rapids, MI: Wm. B. Eerdmans, 1985.

Cunningham, Valentine. *Reading After Theory*. Oxford, UK: Blackwell, 2002.

Bibliography

Davids, Peter H. *The Epistle of James: A Commentary on the Greek Text*. Edited by I. Howard Marshall and W. Ward Gasque. In the series *The New International Greek Testament Commentary*. Grand Rapids, MI: Wm. B. Eerdmans, 1982.

Dempster, Murray W. "Paradigm Shifts and Hermeneutics: Confronting Issues Old and New." *Pneuma* 15, no. 2 (Fall 1993): 129–35.

Depoortere, Frederiek. *The Death of God: An Investigation into the History of the Western Concept of God*. London: T. & T. Clark, 2008.

Derrida, Jacques. *Of Grammatology*. Translated by Gayatri Chakravorty Spivak. Corrected 1997 ed. Baltimore: The Johns Hopkins University Press, 1997.

———. *Positions*. Translated by Alan Bass. Chicago: Chicago University Press, 1981.

———. *Writing and Difference*. Translated by Alan Bass. Chicago: Chicago University Press, 1978.

Erickson, Millard J. *Christian Theology: One Volume Edition*. Grand Rapids, MI: Baker, 1985.

Esler, Philip F. *New Testament Theology: Communion and Community*. Minneapolis: Fortress, 2005.

Fee, Gordon D. *Gospel and Spirit: Issues in New Testament Hermeneutics*. Peabody, MA: Hendrickson, 1991.

———. *Listening to the Spirit in the Text*. Grand Rapids, MI: Wm. B. Eerdmans, 2000.

Fish, Stanley. *Is There a Text in This Class? The Authority of Interpretive Communities*. Cambridge, MA: Harvard University Press, 1980. Reprint, 2000.

Gadamer, Hans-Georg. *Dialogue and Dialectic*. Translated by P. Christopher Smith. New Haven, CT: Yale University Press, 1980.

———. *Philosophical Hermeneutics*. Translated and edited by David E. Linge. Berkeley, CA: University of California, 1976.

———. *Truth and Method*. 2nd ed. New York: Crossroad, 1975.

———. "The Universality of the Hermeneutical Problem." In *Hermeneutical Inquiry: The Interpretation of Texts*, edited by David E. Klemm. Atlanta: Scholars Press, 1986.

Geisler, Norman L. *Baker Encyclopedia of Christian Apologetics*. Grand Rapids, MI: Baker, 1999.

Grenz, Stanley J., and John R. Franke. *Beyond Foundationalism: Shaping Theology in a Postmodern Context*. Louisvillle, KY: Westminster John Knox Press, 2001.

Hamilton, Victor P. *The Book of Genesis: Chapters 1–17*. Edited by R. K. Harrison and Robert L. Hubbard Jr. 2 vols. Vol. 1, in the series *The New International Commentary on the Old Testament*. Grand Rapids. MI: Wm. B. Eerdmans, 1990.

Hegel, Georg W. F. "Early Theological Writings (1793–1800)." In *G. W. F. Hegel: Theologian of the Spirit*, edited by Peter C. Hodgson, 39–71. Edinburgh: T. & T. Clark, 1997.

———. "Jena Writings (1802–1803)." In *G. W. F. Hegel: Theologian of the Spirit*, edited by Peter C. Hodgson, 72–91. Edinburgh: T. & T. Clark, 1997.

———. "Phenomenology of Spirit (1807)." In *G. W. F. Hegel: Theologian of the Spirit*, edited by Peter C. Hodgson, 92–136. Edinburgh: T. & T. Clark, 1997.

———. *The Philosophy of History*. Translated by J. Sibree. New York: Dover, 1956.

Heidegger, Martin. *Being and Time*. Translated by John Macquarrie and Edward Robinson. Oxford, UK: Basil Blackwell, 1962. Reprint, 1967.

Hirsch, E. D. *Validity in Interpretation*. New Haven, CT: Yale University Press, 1967.

Hofweber, Thomas. "Logic and Ontology." *The Stanford Encyclopedia of Philosophy* (Spring 2013). Online: http://plato.stanford.edu/archives/spr2013/entries/logic-ontology.

Israel, Richard D., Daniel E. Albrecht, and Randall G. McNally. "Pentecostals and Hermeneutics: Texts, Rituals and Community." *Pneuma* 15, no. 2 (1993): 137–61.

Jeanrond, Werner G. *Theological Hermeneutics : Development and Significance.* Paperback ed. London: SCM, 1994. Reprint, 3rd 2002.

Kant, Immanuel. *Immanuel Kant's Critique of Pure Reason.* 2nd ed. Translated by Norman Kemp Smith New York: St. Martin's, 1933. Reprint, 5th.

Klemm, David E. "Introduction to Schleiermacher's Address to the Academy." In *Hermeneutical Inquiry: The Interpretation of Texts*, edited by David E. Klemm. Atlanta: Scholars Press, 1986.

Kraft, Charles. *Christianity in Culture.* New York: Orbis, 1979.

Kuhn, Thomas S. *The Structure of Scientific Revolutions.* 2nd ed. Chicago: University of Chicago Press, 1970.

Ladd, George Eldon. *The New Testament and Criticism.* Grand Rapids, MI: Wm. B. Eerdmans, 1967.

Lara, Denis. "Kant and Hume on Morality." *The Stanford Encyclopedia of Philosophy.* Online: http://plato.stanford.edu/archives/spr2011/entries/kant-hume-morality.

LaSor, William Sanford. "Interpretation of Prophecy." In *Hermeneutics*, edited by Bernard Ramm, 94–117. Grand Rapids, MI: Baker, 1981.

Lawlor, Leonard. "Jacques Derrida." *Stanford Encyclopedia of Philosophy* (Fall 2011). Online: http://plato.stanford.edu/archives/fall2011/entries/derrida.

Limburg, James. *Old Stories for a New Time.* Atlanta: John Knox, 1983.

Lundin, Roger. "Interpreting Orphans: Hermeneutics in the Cartesian Tradition." In *The Promise of Hermeneutics*, 1–64. Grand Rapid, MI: Wm. B. Eerdmans, 1999.

Malpas, Jeff. "Hans-Georg Gadamer." *The Stanford Encyclopedia of Philosophy.* Online: http://plato.stanford.edu/archives/sum2009/entries/gadamer.

Marshall, I. Howard. *Beyond the Bible: Moving from Scripture to Theology: With Essays by Kevin J. Vanhoozer and Stanley E. Porter.* Grand Rapids: Baker Academic, 2004.

———. "'Historical Criticism' in New Testament Interpretation." In *New Testament Interpretation: Essays on Principles and Methods*, edited by I. Howard Marshall, 126–37. Grand Rapids, MI: Wm. B. Eerdmans, 1985.

Martin, James. "Toward a Post-Critical Paradigm." *New Testament Studies* 33 (1987): 370–85.

Menzies, Robert P. "Jumping Off the Postmodern Bandwagon." *Pneuma* 16, no. 1 (Spring 1994): 115–20.

Morgenstern, Julian. *The Book of Genesis: A Jewish Interpretation.* 2nd ed. New York: Schocken, 1965.

Newman, John Henry. *Grammar of Assent.* London: Longmans, 1901.

Nida, Eugene A. *Message and Mission: The Communication of the Christian Faith.* New York: Harper Row, 1960.

Ong, Walter J. *Orality and Literacy.* 2nd ed. New York: Routledge, 2002.

———. "Text as Interpretation: Mark and After." *Semeia* 39 (1987): 7–26.

Pannenberg, Wolfhart. *Jesus—God and Man.* Translated by Lewis L. Wilkins and Duane A. Priebe. 2nd ed. Philadelphia: Westminster, 1968.

———. *Metaphysics and the Idea of God.* Translated by Philip Clayton. Grand Rapids, MI: Wm. B. Eerdmans, 1990.

Parker, David C. *The Living Text of the Gospels.* Cambridge: Cambridge University Press, 1997.

Bibliography

Partenie, Catalin. "Plato's Myths." *The Stanford Encyclopedia of Philosphy.* Online: http://plato.stanford.edu/archives/fall2011/entries/plato-myths.

Pascal, Blaise. "Pensées." In *The Modern Library.* New York: Random House, 1941.

Polanyi, Michael. *Personal Knowledge: Towards a Post-Critical Philosophy.* Revised ed. New York: Harper & Row, 1962.

Reynolds, Jack. "Jacques Derrida." *Internet Encyclopedia of Philosophy* (Originally published November 2002; update January 2010). Online: http://www.iep.utm.edu/derrida.

Ricoeur, Paul. *The Conflict of Interpretations: Essays in Hermeneutics.* Translated by Kathleen McLaughlin. Edited by Don Ihde. Evanston, IL: Northwestern University Press, 1974.

———. *Essays on Biblical Interpretation.* Edited by Lewis S. Mudge. Philadelphia: Fortress, 1980.

———. *From Text to Action: Essays in Hermeneutics.* Translated by Kathleen Blamey and John B. Thompson. London: Continuum, 2008.

———. *Hermeneutics and the Human Sciences: Essays on Language, Action and Interpretation.* Translated and edited by John B. Thompson. New York: Cambridge University Press, 1981.

———. *Interpretation Theory: Discourse and the Surplus of Meaning.* Fort Worth, TX: Texas Christian University Press, 1976.

———. *Oneself as Another.* Translated by Kathleen Blamey. Chicago: Chicago University Press, 1992.

Saussure, Ferdinand de. *Course in General Linguistics.* Translated by Wade Baskin. Edited by Charles Bally and Albert Sechehaye in collaboration with Albert Riedlinger. New York: McGraw Hill, 1959.

Schaeffer, Francis A. *How Should We Then Live? The Rise and Decline of Western Thought and Culture.* Westwood, NJ: Fleming H. Revell, 1976.

Schleiermacher, Friedrich. "The Academy Addresses of 1829: On the Concept of Hermeneutics, with Reference to F. A. Wolf's Instructions and Asts' Textbook." In *Hermeneutical Inquiry: The Interpretation of Texts,* edited by David E. Klemm. Atlanta: Scholars Press, 1986.

———. *Hermeneutics: The Handwritten Manuscripts.* Translated by James Duke and Jack Frostman. Edited by Heinz Kimmerle, American Academy of Religion. Missoula, MT: Scholars Press, 1977.

Stanton, Graham N. "Presuppositions in New Testament Criticism." In *New Testament Interpretation: Essays on Principles and Methods,* edited by I. Howard Marshall, 60–72. Exeter, UK: Paternoster, 1985.

Stein, Robert H. "The Benefits of an Author-Oriented Approach to Hermeneutics." *Journal of Evangelical Theological Society* 44, no. 3 (September 2001): 451–66.

Stendhal, Krister. "Biblical Theology, Contemporary." In *The Interpreter's Dictionary of the Bible,* edited by George Arthur Buttrick, 418–32. New York: Abingdon, 1962.

Tate, W. Randolph. *Biblical Interpretation.* Peabody, MA: Hendrickson, 1991.

Thiselton, Anthony C. "Communicative Action and Promise in Interdisciplinary, Biblical and Theological Hermeneutics." In *The Promise of Hermeneutics,* 133–239. Grand Rapids, MI: Wm. B. Eerdmans, 1999.

———. *Interpreting God and the Postmodern Self: On Meaning, Manipulation and Promise.* Edited by Alasdair Heron and Iain Torrance, *Current Issues in Theology.* Edinburgh, UK: T. & T. Clark, 1995.

———. *New Horizons in Hermeneutics: The Theory and Practice of Transforming Biblical Reading.* Grand Rapids, MI: Zondervan, 1992.

———. *Thiselton on Hermeneutics: Collected Works with New Essays.* Grand Rapids, MI: Wm. B. Eerdmans, 2006.

———. *The Two Horizons: New Testament Hermeneutics and Philosophical Description with Special Reference to Heidegger, Bultmann and Wittgenstein.* Grand Rapids, MI: Wm. B. Eerdmans, 1980.

Vanhoozer, Kevin J. "Discourse on Matter: Hermeneutics and the 'Miracle' of Understanding." *International Journal of Systematic Theology* 17, no. 1 (Jan 2005): 5–37.

———. *First Theology: God, Scripture and Hermeneutics.* Downers Grove, IL: InterVarsity, 2002.

———. *Is There a Meaning in This Text?* Grand Rapids, MI: Zondervan, 1998.

———. "The Joy of Yes, Ricoeur: Philosopher of Hope." *Christian Century* 122, no. 17 (August 2005): 27–28.

———. "The World Well Staged? Theology, Culture, on Hermeneutics." In *God and Culture: Essays in Honor of Carl F. H. Henry*, edited by D. A. Carson and John D. Woodbridge, 1–30. Grand Rapids, MI: Wm. B. Eerdmans, 1993.

Walhout, Clarence. "Narrative Hermeneutics." In *The Promise of Hermeneutics*, 65–131. Grand Rapids, MI: Wm. B. Eerdmans, 1999.

Wimsatt, W. K., Jr. *The Verbal Icon: Studies in the Meaning of Poetry.* Lexington: University of Kentucky Press, 1954.

Wittgenstein, Ludwig. *Notebooks, 1914–1916.* Translated by G. E. M. Anscombe. Edited by G. H. von Wright and G. E. M. Anscombe. New York: Harper & Row, 1961.

———. *Philosophical Investigations.* Translated by G. E. M. Anscombe. German and English ed. New York: MacMillan, 1953.

———. *Tractatus Logico-Philosophicus.* Translated by F. P. Ramsey. Edited by C. K. Ogden. German and English ed, *International Library of Psychology Philosophy and Scientific Method.* London: Routledge and Kegan Paul, 1922. Reprint, 1958.

Wolterstorff, Nicholas. *Divine Discourse: Philosophical Reflections on the Claim That God Speaks.* New York: Cambridge University Press, 1995.

Wright, N. T. *The New Testament and the People of God.* Vol. 1. Minneapolis: Fortress, 1992.

Name Index

The works of Anthony Thiselton, Paul Ricoeur and Kevin Vanhoozer have been interacted with throughout the body of the book. The following selected authors of those consulted have been interacted with on important philosophical concepts concerning major themes addressed.

Barthes, Roland, 59, 98–109, 112–15, 108, 109, 122, 207, 208, 251, 255, 290, 303, 308, 309, 325, 357, 358, 359, 360–63, 375, 397, 403, 406

Derrida, Jacques, 97–101, 104, 109, 110, 113, 118, 124, 141, 143–57, 162, 164, 168–70, 172, 174–76, 179, 186, 189, 191–95, 201–5, 207–8, 220, 229, 249, 255–57, 266, 271–73, 278, 297, 304–7, 309, 311–12, 317, 320, 322, 325–26, 340, 357–61, 365, 373, 375, 382, 390, 397, 403, 410, 411, 415

Gadamer, Hans-Georg, 11, 19, 20, 27, 30, 49, 51, 60, 64, 86–88, 92, 95–99, 110, 113–14, 116–27, 129, 131–33, 139, 141–44, 148, 152, 154, 156, 160–62, 166–69, 172, 174–75, 177–78, 180–86, 190–91, 193, 198, 201, 204–5, 209, 210, 213, 215, 223, 227, 229, 236, 239, 245, 254–55, 267, 271, 273, 274, 282, 284, 286–90, 292–93, 295–97, 306–8, 312–25, 333, 336, 340, 346, 352, 355, 360, 361–63, 365–66, 372, 374, 377, 383, 389, 391, 393, 396–98, 406, 409, 416–17

Hegel, Georg, 29–30, 33, 124, 160, 164–72, 177–78, 182, 184, 193, 198, 202, 220, 223, 225, 264, 314, 317, 324, 357, 380

Heidegger, Martin, 23–24, 26, 79, 88, 91–92, 94–96, 98, 100, 104–5, 174, 176–77, 200, 216, 231, 262, 265–69, 271–74, 276–79, 281–84, 286, 288, 291–92, 294, 297–300, 303–7, 313–15, 318, 321–22, 331, 333–43, 346, 352–54, 360–61, 366–67, 370–72, 375–78, 382, 384, 387–89, 397–98, 403, 405, 408, 409, 411–12, 415, 417

Stendhal, Krister, 7, 13, 27, 32, 39, 51–52, 62, 67, 91–92, 133–34, 134, 396, 399, 400, 404

Wittgenstein, Ludwig, 55–56, 143–44, 162–66, 170–72, 178, 186, 198, 200, 213–14, 225, 237, 322

Wolterstorff, Nicholas, 120, 130, 135–37, 143, 145–46, 148, 150, 157, 191, 194–95, 252, 285, 348, 362, 363, 371

Subject Index

absolute, concepts of, 2–3, 21, 24, 34, 47, 68–70, 91, 93, 118, 141, 159–60, 165–67, 175, 200, 201–2, 283, 343, 404; as metaphysical "I," 166–67; in deconstruction, 141, 93, 151, 153–55, 358; language, 216n45, 218; tradition, 263–64; relativization, 3, 18–19, 19, 76, 93–94, 239, 264, 290, 384

aporia, 104, 105, 255, 266, 270, 308, 310, 311, 360, 407. *See also* hermeneutical impasse

author, appearance within text, 223–25

authorial intent: relationship to composition, 14, 75, 84, 184, 267, 270, 281, 302, 336, 343; psyche or dimension of the text, 16–17, 110, 134, 198–201, 204, 236, 253, 281, 331, 356–57; antecedent of texts, 47, 50, 55, 60–63, 67, 70, 75, 79, 81, 113, 123, 201, 204, 207; authorial intent and meaning, 11, 47, 50–51, 52, 54–55, 246, 277; symbolic function, 59–60, 62, 67, 79–80, 337; adverbial view, 50–51, 77, 88, 107, 237–38, 242–44, 252, 294, 356–57, 401; ontological nature, 85, 209, 215, 244–48, 253, 281–82, 296, 302, 336, 418; proposed function, 84, 281, 295, 328, 344; intentional fallacy, 9–10, 12, 198–99; detachment in *parole*, 16, 107, 123–25, 127, 133, 139, 184, 188, 198, 207, 221, 296, 326, 330, 357, 370, 379: metaphysical subject, 186–88, 253; as the speaking voice, 115, 194, 251, 302, 344; dismissal, 215, 226, 241; as a term, 236–40; adjectival view, 294–95, 332

Aufhebung, 124, 125, 127, 132, 134, 139, 184, 188, 196, 198, 220, 357, 370, 380; explained, 124

belief: as community deposit, 28, 35, 36, 53, 83, 149, 231; transmission, 230–32. *See also under* language, of belief. *See also under* presuppositions, belief

communication, 21, 27, 58, 60, 63–68, 103, 119, 128, 136, 166, 167, 293, 344, 363: language as vehicle, 5, 41–45, 80, 168, 182, 213–15, 365–67, 377. *See also* Figure 1: The Circle Model, 64

composition, 22, 25, 27, 267, 269, 270, 273, 302, 339, 364; orality vs textuality, 47–49; the speaking voice, 302; the author's message, 198, 270, 302, 339; being, 198, 270, 281–85, 294, 303–21, 336, 343, 362, 373–74, 379, 391, 395; as work of art, 205, 221, 276, 279, 280–81, 342; metaphysical entity, 370–72

consciousness: historical, 245, 290, 342; aesthetic, 198–99, 288–89, 292, 318, 342, 346; ontic-, 94, 245, 251, 262–63, 316, 320, 324, 342, 344, 370–71, 408

conundrum and paradox of Scripture, 1, 4–8, 13, 14, 21, 111–12, 301–2

deconstruction, 98, 142, 150, 157, 218; denial of authorship, 97, 139, 140–41, 143n20, 202. *See also under* absolute, concepts of, in deconstruction

dialectic, 78, 99, 114, 120, 134, 152, 166, 206, 256, 264, 267–68, 276, 291, 332

dialogue, 48–49, 58–9, 78, 80, 113, 117, 126–27, 128, 171, 189, 190, 206–7, 220, 304, 356

discourse: defined, 103; problematic ontology, 103–7; oral discourse, 47–48, 75, 156, 278; written discourse, 206, 207, 381, 390: dual speaking voice,

Subject Index

discourse (*cont.*)
    171, 183–84, 195–97; speech acts, 238–39; use of mimesis, 249–52, 274

epistemology, 3, 24, 96, 104, 209, 227, 281, 286, 404, 410; weakness and limitation, 77, 89, 104, 216, 222, 284, 302, 306, 333, 353, 401, 406; relationship to ontology, 23, 104, 177, 209, 225–27, 250, 253, 266n9, 266–67, 267n13, 270, 274, 283–84, 337, 396–97, 407–9, 411, 412; interpretive event, 16, 223, 227, 334, 336, 411

eternal, the: contrast with finite-infinite, 165–66, 264, 314; dimension of human-being, 174–75, 176, 299; realm or dimension, 164–68, 314; interpretive exclusion as prejudice, 300; differentiation from metaphysical dimension, 382, 382n

hermeneutic: special vs specialized use, 2, 5–6, 7, 8, 13, 14, 19–21, 65, 72, 83–84, 158, 195–6, 251, 300, 326–7, 346–47, 354, 357; general vs regional, 2–4, 41, 228, 340, 415–16

hermeneutic problem, 23–26, 86, 266, 333

hermeneutical impasse: impersonal to personal, 92, 100, 103–7, 238, 241, 248–49, 269–74, 277, 296, 305–6, 308, 310, 311, 313, 315, 318, 321, 356, 358, 361, 364, 370, 374, 391, 407; transcending, 240, 241, 246, 252, 255, 278, 309–10; transgressing, 240, 241, 252, 313; traversing, 92, 101, 105, 240, 246, 250–51, 252, 255, 270, 277, 278, 308, 313, 347, 354, 356, 360, 366, 370, 398, 408; epistemology to ontology, 266–67, 270. *See also under* epistemology, relationship to ontology

hermeneutics, purpose, 279, 280; of suspicion, 212–13

horizon, 8, 27, 27n69, 55, 56, 73, 87, 92, 94, 99, 115, 120, 142, 204, 219, 250, 256, 269, 331; time as, 174, 176, 209, 298–99, 314, 315, 316, 318, 324, 339–40, 349, 380, 382, 383, 387, 399, 411, 412; as presupposition, 89–90. *See also* presuppositions

identity, as *idem* and *ipse*, 244n46, 255–57, 260, 264, 278, 283, 284, 287, 290–91, 293, 347

imagination, 35, 36, 58, 94, 121, 153, 189, 194, 214, 232–33, 274, 286, 289, 293, 321, 348, 371; in deconstruction, 98, 109, 110, 155, 156, 157, 170, 173, 202, 305, 317, 359; in *ontic*-consciousness, 342, 346–47, 408

impasse. *See* hermeneutical impasse

intent, 239, 241–44; adverbial, *intentionally*, 50–51, 77, 87–88, 237, 238, 242–44, 252, 294, 356, 357, 380, 401; adjectival, *intentioned*, 294–95, 319n, 357, 374, 380–81

interpretive event, 62, 63, 76, 83, 102, 104, 133, 333; times of transmission, interpretation, 256, 59, 61, 79, 81, 82, 318, 319–20, 380, 382–85, 387, 390–91, 392, 394–96, 401, 403, 405; symbol as agent, 56–57, 59, 62, 66, 67, 76, 79, 80, 131, 249, 337; impact of belief, 1, 4, 5–6, 7, 13, 14, 26, 29, 36, 37, 81, 84, 111, 149, 159, 161, 231, 324, 349, 393, 417

knowledge, forms of, 26–41; *rational*, *arational* and *nonrational* outlined, 28–29, 30; *arational* and *nonrational*, 28, 29, 31–39, 44, 74, 77, 79, 80, 81, 82, 168, 179, 186, 187, 199, 206, 249, 316, 317, 333, 346, 410, 411

language: *langue*-system, 56–58, 102–3, 106, 108, 124, 128, 181, 206, 217, 281, 325–26, 357–64, 367–68, 374, 380–81, 390, 395, 405, 407, 410, 418; *parole*-speech, 16n, 90, 102, 106–8, 115, 123–25, 127–28, 132–34, 139, 184, 188, 196, 198, 204, 207, 211–12, 221, 267, 270, 281, 286, 296, 321, 326, 330, 332, 343, 357, 362–63, 368, 370, 377, 379, 380, 385, 406; pseudo-metaphysics, 176–8, 181–84, 213–14, 218, 254, 313–16, 321–22; of belief, 30; within deconstruction, 192; reference, 205, 360–65; nonrational knowledge, 209; external being of *thought* as entity, 214–15, 317, 320, 361, 363, 364, 365–69, 371, 375–77,

Subject Index

language (*cont.*)
380–82, 383, 387, 390–91, 396–97, 405, 407, 408–9; as a universal, 99, 181, 216n45, 254–55, 315, 322–23, 324, 325, 352, 363, 366, 383, 409. *See also under* absolute, concepts of, language. *See also* communication
listening to the text, 226–30, 232–35

metaphysics: operational sphere, 144–45; disclosing reference, 62, 79, 150–51, 167–71, 173, 175, 178, 186, 207, 302, 391, 410–12; making the abstract visible, 310, 313, 316–21, 365, 381, 382n, 412; absence or presence, 144–57, 158, 164, 175, 178–79, 204, 263; of presence, 169, 197, 203, 263; of absence, 163, 169, 170, 176–77, 179, 194–95, 202, 249; metaphysical subject, 163–64, 186, 171–72; metaphysical universe, 381, 388, 394. *See also under* authorial intent, metaphysical subject
monologue, 117, 119, 126, 128, 129, 189, 206–7; dialogical model, 190–91, 206

ontology: as task, 25–26, 225, 412; impersonal event, 217–18, 248, 249, 265, 269–74, 248, 276–77, 278, 304, 305–6, 308–9, 310–11; personal, 90–92, 103, 104, 254–55, 270, 272, 273, 274, 275, 276, 290, 306, 308–9, 312, 322, 353, 362, 369, 373, 374–75, 378, 379, 382, 384, 389–90, 392, 395, 398, 401, 406–8, 409, 410, 414; created being, 286–92, 293. *See also under* hermeneutical impasse, impersonal to personal. *See also under* text, the nature of, intentioned being

parole, the event of, 124–25, 128, 204, 212, 270; transformation of intent, 133, 207. *See also under* authorial intent, detachment in *parole*. *See also under* language, *parole*-speech
phenomenology, as hermeneutical presupposition, 267, 295–300, 306–7, 308, 340, 415

pistology: outlined, 27n75, 28, 159, 262, 368; impact of, 73, 83, 157, 160–61, 162–64, 178–79
presupposition, 3, 4, 6, 13, 23, 24, 29, 38, 40, 41, 44, 48, 49, 52, 72, 73, 79–80, 89–90, 118, 119, 130, 131, 133, 135; horizons, 89–90; belief, 2–7. *See also* horizon

reference, the principle of, 122, 168–69, 173, 203, 205, 217, 273, 285–86. *See also under* language, reference

Sache, the matter of the text, 51n27, 55, 60, 61, 64, 70, 75, 79, 116, 121–23, 152, 161, 187, 188, 190, 204, 305, 307–9, 326, 346, 369, 378, 380, 384, 390. *See also* text, the nature of
semantics, 25, 58, 75, 78, 101, 101n134, 108, 112, 127, 135n104, 137, 138, 174, 198, 208, 210, 216–18, 220, 222, 223, 225, 226, 237, 238, 241, 245, 252, 359, 367, 369, 383, 385, 406, 410; of discourse, 135, 252; semantic range, 210–12, 214, 215, 371
semiotics, 101, 103, 108, 109, 122, 359, 366, 367, 397; limitations, 101, 107–10, 367. *See also* semantics

text, the nature of, 12, 13–14, 16, 21–26, 62, 90, 92, 95, 96, 101, 111, 115, 139, 191, 266, 267, 359; the speaking voice, 104, 106, 107, 114, 119, 208, 216, 251, 292; ontological impasse, 105, 107; the issue of *fixity*, 237, 274–75, 277, 278; intentionality, 127; reference, 130–31; composition, 139, 204, 221, 251, 303, 309, 318, 320, 330, 332, 336, 343, 405; as impersonal event, 265, 276; ontology, 253, 268–69, 272, 274–79, 284–85, 351; impersonal being, 105, 269–74, 273, 306, 351, 361, 363, 373, 405; intentioned being, 251, 292–96, 302, 309–10, 318, 321, 328, 331, 351, 363. *See also under* composition, as work of art. *See also under* composition, being

429

Subject Index

textual autonomy, 118–23, 236, 308, 346, 404; detached vs autonomous, 61–63; disputed, 134–38, 172–74, 178, 188, 397
tradition, 37–38, 82–83, 231–32, 253–64, 318, 324, 328, 344, 346, 416

"work of art," concept of, 279–80, 285, 286, 288–92, 293, 318–20, 339, 342, 361, 364, 368, 412

www.ingramcontent.com/pod-product-compliance
Lightning Source LLC
Chambersburg PA
CBHW081146290426
44108CB00018B/2450